Digital Banking and Finance

A Handbook

Transformations in Banking, Finance and Regulation

Print ISSN: 2752-5821
Online ISSN: 2752-583X

Series Editors: Sabri Boubaker
(*EM Normandie Business School, France*)
Duc Khuong Nguyen
(*EMLV Business School, France*)

Presently, the banking and finance sectors evolve within a globalized and highly uncertain environment. Each business and financial decision requires careful consideration of country-specific and international factors due to high levels of shock transmission and volatility spillovers. Furthermore, it would be remiss to omit the COVID-19 health crisis, which caused harmful effects to all areas of the real economy and made profound changes in the way our firms, economies, and markets used to function.

Many other already well-known aspects, including the repercussions of quantitative easing policies, disruptive technologies in finance (e.g., FinTech, Big Data, Data Analytics, Artificial Intelligence, and Blockchains), as well as innovative financing instruments for startups (e.g., ICOs and crowdfunding) are currently revolutionizing banking and finance and posing numerous challenges to regulatory bodies and policymakers. Climate change emergencies also put pressure on governments and firms worldwide to improve policy on governance, corporate social responsibility, and sustainability practices.

This book series "Transformations in Banking, Finance and Regulation" attempts to address these issues by focusing on transformative perspectives in banking and finance. Accordingly, it provides evidence-based guidance, recommendations, and pathways to assist businesses and policy decision-makers through an interdisciplinary and in-depth understanding of ongoing changes in the behavior of economic agents.

Published

Vol. 17 *Digital Banking and Finance: A Handbook*
edited by Christopher E. C. Gan, Nirosha Hewa-Wellalage and Ahmed Imran Hunjra

Vol. 16 *Handbook on Data Envelopment Analysis in Business, Finance, and Sustainability: Recent Trends and Developments*
edited by Sabri Boubaker and Thanh Ngo

Vol. 15 *Artificial Intelligence and Beyond for Finance*
edited by Marco Corazza, René Garcia, Faisal Shah Khan, Davide La Torre and Hatem Masri

For the complete list of volumes in this series, please visit
www.worldscientific.com/series/tbfr

Transformations in Banking, Finance and Regulation

Volume 17

Digital Banking and Finance

A Handbook

Editors

Christopher E. C. Gan

Lincoln University, New Zealand

Nirosha Hewa-Wellalage

University of South Australia, Australia

Ahmed Imran Hunjra

IPAG Business School, France

World Scientific

NEW JERSEY • LONDON • SINGAPORE • GENEVA • BEIJING • SHANGHAI • TAIPEI • CHENNAI

Published by

World Scientific Publishing Europe Ltd.
57 Shelton Street, Covent Garden, London WC2H 9HE
Head office: 5 Toh Tuck Link, Singapore 596224
USA office: 27 Warren Street, Suite 401-402, Hackensack, NJ 07601

Library of Congress Cataloging-in-Publication Data
Names: Gan, Christopher, editor. | Hewa-Wellalage, Nirosha, editor. |
Hunjra, Ahmed Imran, editor.
Title: Digital banking and finance : a handbook / editors, Christopher E. C. Gan,
Lincoln University, New Zealand, Nirosha Hewa-Wellalage, University of South Australia,
Australia, Ahmed Imran Hunjra, IPAG Business School, France.
Description: New Jersey : World Scientific, [2025] |
Series: Transformations in banking, finance and regulation, 2752-5821 ; vol. 17 |
Includes bibliographical references and index.
Identifiers: LCCN 2024029684 | ISBN 9781800616240 (hardcover) |
ISBN 9781800616257 (ebook) | ISBN 9781800616264 (ebook other)
Subjects: LCSH: Financial services industry--Technological innovations. |
Finance--Technological innovations. | Internet banking.
Classification: LCC HG173 .D538 2025 | DDC 332--dc23/eng/20240628
LC record available at https://lccn.loc.gov/2024029684

British Library Cataloguing-in-Publication Data
A catalogue record for this book is available from the British Library.

For any available supplementary material, please visit
https://www.worldscientific.com/worldscibooks/10.1142/Q0479#t=suppl

Desk Editors: Nambirajan Karuppiah/Gabriel Rawlinson/Shi Ying Koe

Typeset by Stallion Press
Email: enquiries@stallionpress.com

https://doi.org/10.1142/9781800616257_fmatter

About the Editors

Christopher E. C. Gan is the head of the Department of Financial and Business Systems, Faculty of Agribusiness and Commerce, at Lincoln University, Christchurch, New Zealand. He is recognized internationally for his research leadership in banking, microfinance, stock markets and Asian financial economics. His approach is quantitative in nature with an applied focus. He has an extensive publication record in well-ranked peer-reviewed journals and is regularly cited by other researchers. He serves on the editorial boards of several distinguished international journals and is the chief editor of the *Review of Applied Economics*. He has won several awards for excellence in teaching, including the National Teaching Excellence Award in 2003.

Nirosha Hewa-Wellalage is an associate professor in Business Analytics at the University of South Australia. Her main research centers on issues related to corporate finance practises and explores the ways marginalized firms, such as micro, small and medium firms (SMEs), firms owned by females and ethnic minorities, and refugees financing their firms, find ways to be sustainable in the long run while contributing to economic development. Her publications, research awards and research grants demonstrate her ability to develop and implement a viable and relevant research agenda. She has presented her research at major international finance conferences and has received several best paper awards. Dr. Nirosha was awarded the International Corporate Governance Network (ICGN) outstanding scholar award, Young Researcher Award at the Baku World Science Forum, and Early Career Research Excellence Award from the Modelling and Simulation Society of Australia and New Zealand (MSSANZ). Currently, she is a principal researcher for three research grants from the Accounting and Finance Association of Australia and New Zealand (AFAANZ).

Ahmed Imran Hunjra has over 15 years of teaching and research experience across various international universities. He is currently working in the domains of corporate finance, corporate governance, and sustainability. He has published in top ranked journals. He also sits on the editorial boards of several ABS- and ABDC-indexed journals, including *International Review of Financial Analysis*, *Journal of International Financial Markets, Institution & Money*, *Pacific Basin Finance Journal*, *Global Finance Journal*, *Finance Research Letters*, *International Review of Economics & Finance*, *Technological Forecasting & Social Change*, *Journal of Environmental Management*, *Economic Modelling*, *International Journal of Finance & Economics*, *Research in International Business & Finance*, and *Quarterly Review of Economics & Finance*, among others. He has won several research awards, including the Best Researcher Award in 2023 and 2020 from Rabat Business School, Morocco, and PMAS-Arid Agriculture University Rawalpindi, Pakistan, respectively; the Emerald Literati Outstanding Reviewer Award in 2021 and 2023; and the ICAI Best Paper Award in 2022 and 2023.

https://doi.org/10.1142/9781800616257_fmatter

About the Contributors

Asad Abbas is working as an assistant professor in the Department of Management Sciences at COMSATS University, Islamabad, Pakistan. He did his master's and PhD in finance at the same university. He has attended several national and international conferences and training programs and has published several papers. His areas of interest are earnings management, earnings quality, corporate governance and digital finance.

Gul Afshan is an assistant professor at the Sukkur IBA University in Pakistan. She has published numerous research articles and book chapters in well-reputed journals in the areas of leadership and knowledge management.

Wajid Shakeel Ahmed holds a PhD in business administration, majoring in finance, from IQRA University, Islamabad, Pakistan, and an MSc in international finance and economic policy from the University of Glasgow, Scotland, UK. Currently, he is serving as a finance cluster head in the Management Sciences Department at COMSATS University, Islamabad Campus. His interest areas are advanced tools, techniques and expertise development in Stata, E-views and Python (Jupyter Notebook and Spyder environment). He frequently conducts training programs in Python, focusing on data analysis and visualization as well as data analytics in business intelligence for audiences from varying backgrounds, including both academicians and professionals not limited to the finance and business world.

Hammad Ali is recognized as an insightful researcher and esteemed visiting lecturer at the University of Layyah in Pakistan. He is also a PhD scholar at Ghazi University, Pakistan. With a robust portfolio of research, Mr. Hammad Ali is known for his extensive work in Environmental Degradation and Renewable Energy. His research has significantly contributed to the understanding of debt swaps, as evidenced by his publications in well-regarded academic journals. His pedagogical approach in the classroom is both engaging and thought-provoking, encouraging students to explore complex concepts with a critical eye. His contributions to academic discourse for future professionals are well acknowledged.

Dao Le Trang Anh is a lecturer at the Business School of RMIT University, Hanoi, Vietnam, and a visiting lecturer at Lincoln University in New Zealand. She earned her MSc in financial forecasting and investment at the University of Glasgow, UK, and her PhD in accounting and finance at Lincoln University. She has published a number of journal articles and book chapters in top-ranked journals in corporate finance, financial economics and stock markets. She was one of the "Literati Award Winners 2022" selected for contributing an "Outstanding Paper" in the *Journal of Economic Studies*. Dr. Anh's research areas are corporate finance, stock market and Asian studies.

Muhammad Arslan is a lecturer at Foundation University, Islamabad, Pakistan. He has more than six years of experience in both corporate roles and academia. His areas of interest include time series analysis, machine learning and forecasting. He has authored many research publications in renowned international journals.

Muhammad Azam is an assistant professor at Ghazi University, Dera Ghazi Khan, Pakistan, with over eight years of expertise in teaching and research focused on sustainable development, governance and financial economics. Adept in advanced quantitative research methods, he has a strong commitment to collaborative scholarship and engaged learning. His academic contributions are substantial, with numerous publications in ABDC- and ABS-indexed journals, such as the *International Review of Financial Analysis and Energy Economics*, alongside chapters in books published by Springer and Taylor & Francis. His work has been published in journals such as *Finance Research Letter*, *Economic Modeling* and the *Journal of*

Environment Management. His active participation in international conferences and his ability to effectively mentor graduate students showcase his dedication to academia. His research contributions further bolster the academic distinction in the fields in which he has devotedly served.

Tanveer Bagh is currently pursuing a PhD program in finance at the Central University of Finance and Economics in China. He is also concurrently holding positions as a lecturer and research associate at ILMA University in Pakistan. He earned his MS degree in finance from Riphah International University, Pakistan, in 2020, and his MBA from UAJK Pakistan. A prolific researcher, Tanveer has contributed significantly to the academic landscape, with his research papers being published in reputed journals indexed in the Web of Science. His diverse research interests encompass sustainable finance, behavioral finance, risk management, green finance, climate change and corporate finance.

Bushra Bibi completed her MS in finance at the Department of Business Administration at Ghazi University, Dera Ghazi Khan, Pakistan. She is currently engaged in research activities in the field of finance. Her research interests include corporate governance, financial performance and financial policies.

Elie Bouri is a professor of finance at the School of Business of the Lebanese American University in Lebanon. He was named among Clarivate Analytics' 2021, 2022 and 2023 Highly Cited Researchers in the field "Economics and Business." He has been a prolific publisher in the fields of financial economics, empirical finance and energy finance and economics. Dr. Bouri has published over 275 SSCI and SCI research papers and was twice profiled in *CFA Digest* and *Forbes*, along with others. One of his recent studies was accepted in the *Journal of Finance*.

Irfan Channi is recognized as an insightful associate professor at the COMSAT Vehari campus in Pakistan. With a robust portfolio of research, Irfan Channi is known for his extensive work in ESG and Corporate Finance. His research has significantly contributed to the understanding of debt swap, as evidenced by his publications in well-regarded academic journals. His pedagogical approach in the classroom is both engaging and thought-provoking, encouraging students to explore complex concepts with a critical eye. His contributions to academic discourse and his role in shaping future professionals are well acknowledged by his peers and students alike, establishing him as a pillar in the academic community. He is currently working in the area of econometric modeling and design.

Muhammad A. Cheema is a senior lecturer in finance, above the bar (equivalent to a North American associate professor), at Otago Business School, University of Otago, New Zealand. His research interests are investments, empirical asset pricing and behavioral finance. He has published 21 refereed articles in leading international journals, of which 17 are ranked A or A* by the Australian Business Deans Council. He is the first author of 15 of those articles. Dr. Cheema has presented his research at major international conferences and has received several best paper awards. Two prominent awards are the 2022 Ministry of Business, Innovation and Employment New Zealand Best Paper Award for Capital Markets and the 2019 CFA Society's Best Paper Award. Dr. Cheema's work has been featured several times in the financial press, at economic think tanks and associations of investment professionals, including the CFA Society, VoxEU, the Centre for Economic Policy Research, Wirtschaftswoche and Morningstar.

Mahnoor Hanif is a PhD scholar and holds an MBA in finance from PMAS-Arid Agriculture University Rawalpindi in Pakistan. She worked on corporate finance and corporate governance domains for her master's thesis. She is an early-career researcher and has published in several international refereed journals, including the *Journal of Financial Reporting and Accounting* and *Risks*. She has also published book chapters in well-known books by various publishers, including Springer Nature, World Scientific and Taylor & Francis. Her areas of interest are corporate finance, corporate governance, Islamic finance, sustainable finance and investment management-related issues. She is providing her services as a reviewer for many journals, including the *Journal of Sustainable Finance and Investment*, the *International Journal of Emerging Markets* and the *Journal of Economics and Administrative Sciences*.

Muhammad Haroon is a distinguished researcher at Ghazi University in Pakistan. Renowned for his academic rigor and insightful research methodologies, Mr. Haroon specializes in the fields of environmental sustainability and sustainable development. His dedication to unearthing new knowledge is evident in his numerous scholarly articles, which have been published in reputed academic journals. His innovative teaching methods and commitment to fostering intellectual curiosity among students have made him a beloved figure in the classroom. With a track record of successful research projects, Mr. Haroon continues to contribute significantly to his field, inspiring a new generation of thinkers and practitioners. He is currently working in the area of econometric modeling and design.

Muhammad Hussain holds a degree in mechanical engineering and is currently doing a PhD in predictive analytics at the University of Wollongong in Australia. He is a reliability and asset management professional and has made significant contributions to the manufacturing, oil and gas sectors, with a focus on innovation strategy, technology and digital transformation. He is currently working in the manufacturing industry in New South Wales, Australia.

Kainat Iftikhar is a distinguished finance professional currently pursuing a PhD in finance at the Central University of Finance and Economics in China. Her expertise spans corporate risk management, digital finance, corporate reputation, corporate finance and green finance. With a track record of impactful research published in esteemed journals, Kainat is recognized for her comprehensive understanding of the financial landscape. Her work not only contributes to academic discourse but also holds practical implications for the industry. A forward-thinking researcher, Kainat is poised to make lasting contributions to the evolving field of finance.

Muhammad Shahzad Ijaz holds the position of assistant professor at Ilma University, Karachi, Pakistan. With a robust background spanning over a decade in the field of professional accounting, he has made significant contributions to academia/research. He earned his PhD in finance from the Capital University of Science & Technology, Islamabad, Pakistan. He was awarded a gold medal for his academic excellence during his MS (finance). He has worked as a visiting faculty member at a number of well-reputed universities, including Bahria University, STMU and Arid University. His scholarly endeavors have gained international recognition, as he has successfully published his research in leading international journals, such as *Economic Efficiency, Research Policy – JBE&M: Journal of Business – Economics & Management* and *Singapore Economic Review*. His primary research interest lies in the realm of banking, encompassing issues related to risk management, competition, financial literacy and bankruptcy prediction models. His current research mainly focuses on linkages between financial markets and financial stability.

Jatin Kumar Jaiswal is a doctoral research scholar in the Department of Commerce and Business Studies at the Central University of South Bihar, Gaya, Bihar, India. His research focuses on diverse areas such as self-help groups, microfinance, entrepreneurship, financial inclusion, women's empowerment, bibliometric analysis, scientometric analysis and altmetrics. Notably, he has adeptly formulated the research methodology and conducted comprehensive bibliometric analysis as part of his scholarly pursuits.

Shan Jin is a PhD candidate in the Department of Financial and Business Systems, Faculty of Agribusiness and Commerce, at Lincoln University, New Zealand. She obtained her master's in commerce and management (finance) in 2022. Her master's research focused on financial inclusion and household welfare in rural China. She received the Outstanding Investment Research Award in the CFA Institute Research Challenge in New Zealand. Her research focuses on carbon disclosure, corporate governance and financial markets.

Mushtaq Hussain Khan is a lecturer in banking and finance at the Cardiff School of Management of Cardiff Metropolitan University, Cardiff, Wales, UK. He received his PhD in management sciences (finance), from the Capital University of Science & Technology, Islamabad, Pakistan. Given his specialization in the development of Islamic economics, he has an enduring interest in issues related to corporate governance and corruption in dual banking systems, where both Islamic and conventional banks operate alongside each other. His existing research mainly focuses on using classical models in Islamic banking and finance; however, his research focus has shifted, and he intends to extend his current work to explore the use of FinTech in Islamic banking and finance for financial inclusion and climate change mitigation due to the tremendous growth in cryptocurrency ecosystems. The research in FinTech, where finance meets computing, is still in its infancy in the Islamic banking and finance sector.

Mansoor Ahmed Khuhro is an assistant professor at Shaheed Benazir Bhutto University, Sanghar Campus, Pakistan. He also holds the administrative position of director of the campus. He received his PhD from Putra Business School, Malaysia. He has published in the domains of psychological capital, leadership and justice.

Vikesh Kumar is a PhD student at the School of Financial Planning at Texas Tech University in the USA. His areas of interest are household finance, behavioral finance, portfolio management and household investments. Currently, he is working on a thesis "Consistencies and Inconsistencies of U.S. Households Investment Decisions." He has also received an award for "Outstanding Doctoral Research," recognizing his current project.

Imran Lohdi is a lecturer in economics at Ghazi University, Dera Ghazi Khan, Pakistan. His areas of research interest include behavior economics, the economics of happiness, economic growth and development, the behavioral aspects of environmental economics, the economics of education and labor economics. He has more than 15 years of teaching and research experience. He has published more than 20 research papers.

Adnan Manzoor is a vice president of the National Bank of Pakistan. He has carried out research as part of his master's program at IBA Karachi in Pakistan. His areas of research includes economic sustainability and sustainable entrepreneurship.

Rashid Mehmood is currently serving as an assistant professor in the UE Business School of the University of Education, Lahore, Pakistan, after completing his PhD in finance from PMAS-Arid Agriculture University, Rawalpindi, Pakistan. His areas of research interest include corporate diversification, corporate governance, corporate finance, financial risk management and financial policies. He has eight years of teaching and research experience and has supervised 20 MBA students in the field of finance. He has published more than 15 research papers in national and international journals.

Faten Moussa is an associate professor of finance at the Mediterranean Business School of South Mediterranean University in

Tunisia. Her research interests are corporate finance, financial markets, and digital finance; market efficiency and sustainable finance; and ESG. She has published in many journals.

Vusani Moyo is an associate professor and the head of finance at the University of Venda in South Africa. He holds a PhD in financial management sciences from the University of Pretoria, South Africa, an MSc in finance from the University of Leicester, UK, an MBA in finance from the University of Manchester, UK, and a BA (Hons) in accounting and finance (first class) from the University of Derby, UK. Vusani is an ICAEW-qualified chartered accountant (ACA), chartered management accountant (FCMA), chartered global management accountant (CGMA) and chartered certified accountant (FCCA). He has over 25 years of combined experience in academia and corporate environments. His current research interests are the capital structure of African financial and non-financial firms, the cash flow sensitivity of cash, investment cash flow sensitivities, banking regulations and capital structure, green banking and finance, the cost of capital, firm valuation and dividend policy.

Mirza Muhammad Naseer is a PhD scholar and special lecturer at Teesside University's International Business School in Middlesbrough, United Kingdom. He has authored scholarly articles in internationally recognized academic journals. His research focuses on corporate social responsibility, corporate finance, climate finance and sustainable finance.

Ayodeji Michael Obadire serves as a senior lecturer in finance and holds the position of portfolio manager for research and innovation at the Botswana Accountancy College in Botswana. He oversees the research and innovation activities and fosters a culture of research and innovation excellence within the institution. Dr. Obadire earned his PhD in finance and accounting, as well as an MCom in cost and management accounting, from the University of Venda, South Africa. He has also successfully completed training in the fundamentals of statistics at Stanford University, USA. Dr. Obadire is an ICAN-qualified chartered accountant (ACA), chartered management accountant (ACMA), chartered global management accountant (CGMA) and certified professional accountant (ACPA). With over a decade of cumulative experience in academia and corporate environments, he brings a wealth of expertise to his roles. His current research interests span various areas, including corporate finance, banking regulations and capital structure, green financing, firm valuation and corporate governance.

Dharen Kumar Pandey is an assistant professor of commerce at Magadh University, Bihar, India, and a postdoctoral researcher at the Faculty of Business, Economics and Social Development, University Malaysia Terengganu, Malaysia. He has 10 years of industry and teaching experience and holds a PhD in commerce from Banaras Hindu University. He has published three books and over 50 research papers in refereed journals indexed and listed in Scopus, the Web of Science, ABDC, ABS and other indexes, including the *International Review of Economics and Finance*, *Journal of Behavioral and Experimental Finance*, *Journal of Business Research* and *Finance Research Letters.* He holds the post of honorary secretary of the Indian Accounting Association, Patna Branch, and serves as the chief editor of the *International Journal of Accounting, Business and Finance* and an associate editor of *BIMTECH Business Perspectives* and *Business Perspectives and Research.*

Arslan Ali Raza is currently pursuing a PhD degree in computer science at Kohat University of Science and Technology, Kohat, in Pakistan. He is a lecturer in computer science at COMSATS University, Islamabad, Vehari Campus, Vehari, Pakistan. His research interests include natural language engineering, semantic orientation, data mining, machine learning and artificial intelligence.

Anum Shafique is a lecturer at Arid Agriculture University, Rawalpindi, Pakistan. She has over 10 years of experience in both the corporate world and academia. Her areas of interest include financial market volatility, forecasting and time series analysis. She has authored many research publications in national and international journals.

Akmal Shahzad is a postdoctoral fellow at Islamic International University Malaysia and has a PhD in business administration, majoring in finance, from IQRA University, Islamabad, Pakistan. He is an assistant professor and an HEC-approved supervisor at Preston University, Islamabad. He has more than 20 years of teaching and non-teaching experience. He has published research papers in several international journals and has participated in a number of international research conferences as a presenter and session chair.

Jamaltul Nizam Bin Shamsuddin is a PhD candidate in finance at Lincoln University in New Zealand. His research interests include FinTech, insurance, Islamic finance and banking, with his PhD research topic being insurance technology (InsurTech). He holds a master's in Islamic finance and banking and a degree in accounting (hons). He also served as a research associate for "Malaysia Islamic Finance Education Report (MIFER) Atlas 2021 & Beyond," funded by the International Council of Islamic Finance Educators (ICIFE). He is a registered member of the Malaysian Institute of Accountants (MIA) and an associated member of CPA Australia. He became an ASEAN chartered accountant in 2012 and is a member of ICIFE, AFAANZ and the American Risk and Insurance Association. He is currently working on a research paper pertaining to the topic of InsurTech and a book chapter on FinTech.

Ujala Siddique is a research assistant at the Centre for Aerospace & Security Studies (CASS), Islamabad, in Pakistan. She holds a PhD from the University of Malaysia and an MPhil in government and public policy from the National Defence University (NDU), Islamabad. Additionally, she possesses master's degrees in English literature and economics. In the past, she served as adjunct faculty at QAU, NUML, Bahria University, and NDU, Islamabad. She also has industry experience at various organizations, including Zion Tech, the Higher Education Commission (HEC) in Islamabad, the Centre of Policy and Management (CPM), NRPU and USAID's Skill Development Initiative. She has presented her work at four international conferences and has published 11 research papers in hyphenate journals. Her research interests encompass public policy, economics, security, employee behavior and the socioeconomic significance of CPEC.

Kenneth R. Szulczyk is an associate professor in economics at Al Akhawayn University in Morocco. He has taught economics, finance and quantitative courses in Bosnia & Herzegovina, Kazakhstan, Malaysia, Morocco and the United States. His research is focused on renewable energy and behavioral finance but has eclectic interests in applied econometrics, programming and political economy. Dr. Szulczyk has published 28 articles, with 14 as the first author.

Sixteen articles are defined as Q1 by Clarivate Web of Science journal rankings. Furthermore, he has presented at several conferences and was awarded three best paper awards. In addition, he has one registered copyright for software with the U.S. Patent Office.

Runguo Xu received his bachelor's degree from Dongguk University, South Korea. In 2021, he received a master's degree from Sogang University in South Korea. He is currently a PhD student at Yonsei University, also in South Korea. His main research interests are regional economy and international trade. He has carried out research related to the optimization and integration of financial performance of Chinese enterprises, optimization operations in urban areas and green investment. He has published in several top journals, such as *Resources Policy*.

Ghulam Hussain Khan Zaigham received his PhD in business administration from the University of Science and Technology of China (USTC) in 2020. He is currently an assistant professor at the Department of Management at COMSATS University, Islamabad, in Pakistan. His current focus of research is on corporate finance, behavioral finance, online behavior, adolescent psychology and information system research, including individuals' intentions toward different financial products. He has been involved in teaching and research at both the undergraduate and postgraduate levels. He has published a number of research papers in national and international journals and conferences of high repute.

Yi Zhou received his master's degree from Southeast University in China. Now, he works in the Internal Audit Department of the Bank of Jiangsu, China. His research interests include finance, accounting and auditing. His research has been published in several SCI- and SSCI-indexed journals.

Bushra Zulfiqar is currently working as an assistant professor of finance at the University Institute of Management Sciences, PMAS-Arid Agriculture University Rawalpindi, Pakistan. She has over two decades of teaching experience and, as an HEC-recognized supervisor, has guided many master's and PhD students. Her research interests are focused on broader aspects of corporate finance, corporate governance, financial risk management and portfolio management.

She has published several research papers in prestigious journals such as *Frontiers in Psychology*, the *Journal of Basic and Applied Scientific Research*, the *American Journal of Scientific Research*, *Cogent Business & Management*, the *International Journal of Management* and the *Journal of Business & Economics*.

https://doi.org/10.1142/9781800616257_fmatter

Contents

https://doi.org/10.1142/9781800616257_fmatter

List of Figures

https://doi.org/10.1142/9781800616257_fmatter

List of Tables

https://doi.org/10.1142/9781800616257_fmatter

Introduction

Welcome to *Digital Banking and Finance: A Handbook*, a comprehensive guide to navigating the dynamic and transformative landscape of financial services in the digital era. This handbook is the culmination of insights, expertise and perspectives from leading professionals and scholars within the realms of finance, technology and business.

The convergence of technological advancements and financial services has reshaped the way we perceive and engage with banking and finance. This handbook aims to serve as a definitive resource, offering a detailed exploration of the multifaceted dimensions, emerging trends and transformative innovations in digital banking and finance. Unlike chapters in a traditional textbook, you will find a curated collection of chapters covering a wide spectrum of topics, ranging from the fundamentals of digital banking to cutting-edge advancements in financial technology (FinTech), regulatory landscapes, cybersecurity challenges and the implications of digital currencies and decentralized finance (DeFi).

Chapter 1 provides an overview of FinTech, with a summary of FinTech definitions and the key drivers behind its evolutionary journey. The chapter discusses the major segments of FinTech based on its core business functions while shedding light on the dynamic challenges and inherent risks accompanying FinTech's rapid growth. The chapter also discusses potential economic implications, offering insights into future research directions in the evolving financial industry. Chapter 2 deals with the role of digital technology in the digital financial industry. Digital finance places significant emphasis on the advancement of cybersecurity and risk management. The chapter demonstrates the importance of digital technology as it has given rise to the establishment of FinTech (the transition from physical bank branches to online banking). Chapter 3 explores the impact of the trading activity of digital currencies (digital finance) on climate change. Chapter 4 provides an overview of how financial inclusion affects bank stability in emerging economies. The effects of financial inclusion on the safety of financial institutions are the focus of this chapter. The chapter demonstrates that financial inclusion is positively related to bank stability. Chapter 5 deals with navigating the digital finance landscape during COVID-19. This chapter uses bibliometric analysis to analyze digital finance literature and provides a comprehensive overview for future exploration. Chapter 6 offers a review on the digital finance revolution, trends and global impacts. The chapter focuses on the analysis of global advancements in digital finance, highlighting the significant impact of investments in the FinTech and mobile money sectors.

Chapter 7 reviews the history of digital innovation in insurance, also known as insurance technology (InsurTech), and how technology has underpinned the expansion of InsurTech in recent years. The chapter examines previous and current studies in InsurTech and how the implementation of digital transformation may impact the industry's long-term viability. Chapter 8 demonstrates big data applications in the banking sector. The chapter highlights the trends in banks in relation to big data applications and the value of utilizing digital technologies for client acquisition, retention and satisfaction. Chapter 9 provides an overview of digital assets in disarray: unraveling herd behavior during the COVID-19 pandemic and the Russia–Ukraine War. The chapter sets out to uncover patterns of herd behavior during distinct temporal segments, including the full sample and during periods of geopolitical tension and global crises, namely the Russia–Ukraine War and post-COVID-19 periods. Chapter 10 attempts to forecast Bitcoin with traditional as well as machine learning approaches to determine which methods are more robust. A hybrid approach of GARCH–LSTM has been empirically applied to the data. The findings of the chapter reveal that machine learning methods outperform traditional methods.

Chapter 11 explains how economic policy uncertainty predicts cryptocurrency returns. The chapter finds that economic policy uncertainty (EPU) positively predicts cryptocurrency returns in the short run for subsequent 1-month returns and in the long run for subsequent 6- and 12-month returns. It proves that the EPU predicts better in the long run than in the short run since mispricing takes time to correct. Chapter 12 examines the valuation of bank shares in the digital age. The chapter evaluates the suitability and equivalency of the variants of the dividend discount, market multiples, residual income and abnormal earnings growth equity asset valuation models in valuing bank shares in the digital age. Chapter 13 explores the intersection of corporate governance and digital finance (risks, rewards and policy ramifications). The chapter focuses on how technological advancements influence new approaches to money management. The chapter sheds light on anticipating trends that include decentralized governance models, enhanced cybersecurity measures, the integration of artificial intelligence and global standardization. Chapter 14 explains the prospects and challenges of asset tokenization. The chapter attempts to uncover some of the prospects and challenges of asset tokenization which the decentralized financial world of tokenization and its players may face, including the complexities associated with the codification and creation of digital tokens, regulatory challenges, fear of entering the universe of virtual reality, having no tangible holding of assets, the evolution and development of the digital market, overcoming trust deficits among counterparties, identifying appropriate assets and the discovery and integration of demand–supply mechanisms. Chapter 15 reviews central bank digital currencies (CBDCs), touted to be the future of money. The chapter explores the intricate aspects and consequences associated with CBDCs, an emerging subject of interest in both scholarly research and policy deliberations. The chapter emphasizes the importance of conducting country- and region-specific case studies to fully comprehend the complex ramifications of CBDC layout in various social and economic domains. Chapter 16 demonstrates how digital financial inclusion (DFI) influences bank innovation capability, focusing on the commercial banks in China, from a risk-taking perspective. The study identifies a positive and significant relationship between DFI and the banks' innovation capabilities.

We extend our heartfelt gratitude to the contributing authors, whose expertise and commitment shaped this handbook. Their contributions illuminate the complexities and nuances of the digital banking and finance ecosystem, making this handbook an indispensable reference for practitioners, educators, students and anyone seeking a deeper understanding of this rapidly evolving field. We would like to acknowledge, with thanks, the editorial team and all those involved in the production of this handbook for their dedication and diligence in ensuring the accuracy and coherence of the content presented herein.

Digital finance is a fascinating subject for us. We hope that this handbook serves as a compass, guiding readers through the intricacies of digital banking and finance while inspiring continued exploration and innovation in this ever-evolving domain.

We are thrilled to present this book, the result of our research and dedication. We hope that readers will provide us with critical comments to help us refine our work.

https://doi.org/10.1142/9781800616257_0001

Chapter 1

FinTech: The Digital Era of the Financial Industry

Shan Jin* and Christopher Gan†

Department of Financial and Business Systems,
Lincoln University, Christchurch, New Zealand
**shan.jin@lincolnuni.ac.nz*
†*christopher.gan@lincoln.ac.nz*

Abstract

The financial industry has undergone a digital transition over the past decades, with the emergence of FinTech, a portmanteau of "financial" and "technology." This rapidly growing concept has transformed how individuals, businesses and institutions access financial services. It has reshaped the financial landscape through internet connectivity, spearheaded by internet giants. FinTech has disrupted traditional financial industries with a wide array of business applications, ranging from mobile payments to online insurance, digital financing and wealth management. Technologies in finance continue to evolve, with the application of blockchain, artificial intelligence (AI) and the Internet of Things (IoT) continuing to transform the landscape of the financial industry. Against this backdrop, this chapter provides a comprehensive overview of FinTech, offering valuable insights for future research. It begins with a summary of the definitions of FinTech, providing historical context and exploring the key drivers behind its evolutionary journey. The chapter also delves into the major segments of FinTech based on its core business functions while shedding light on the dynamic challenges and inherent risks associated with its rapid growth. This chapter not only serves as a reference for understanding the FinTech phenomenon but also contributes to discussions on its potential economic implications and offers insights into potential research directions in the evolving financial industry.

Keywords: FinTech, digital finance, financial industry, digital transformation, cyber security.

1.1. Introduction

Financial technology, commonly referred to as "FinTech," is an emerging topic among governments, the financial industry and academia. The progress of globalization and the digital revolution have made digital transformation a necessity for the financial industry. This involves integrating new technologies into their operations to create added value and acquire a competitive advantage (Martinčević *et al.*, 2020). FinTech companies gained public attention after the 2008 global financial crisis and quickly became popular with consumers by differentiating themselves from traditional banks. FinTech has radically changed the fundamentals of the financial industry by providing an entirely digitized customer experience as well as cost-effective and user-friendly products and services (Capgemini, 2021a). The term "FinTech" was first coined in the 1990s by Citigroup, which initiated a project to promote technological collaboration among technology firms outside the financial industry (Kutler, 1993). To date, the term FinTech is not only confined to initiatives by financial industry outsiders or individual projects but also includes a wide range of companies offering financial solutions with cutting-edge technologies.

The growth in FinTech adoption has been faster than we had anticipated. In 2021, as reported by KPMG's "The Pulse of FinTech," the FinTech sector experienced exceptional growth despite the global COVID-19 pandemic. Global investments in FinTech reached US$210 billion across 5,684 deals, notably involving blockchain and cryptocurrencies (KPMG, 2022). Historically, the banking sector has been a technology leader among industries, with banks typically investing 4.7–9.4% of their total operating income in IT (Gopalan *et al.*, 2012). However, the uniqueness of today's FinTech lies outside the realm of traditional financial institutions. This has spawned a new breed of financial companies that offer various bank-like services, including digital financing, mobile payments, digital insurance and wealth management services.

The distinction between traditional financial firms and technology institutions has become blurred. In other words, traditional financial service providers are becoming tech-savvy, whereas technology giants are now expanding their products and services into the financial services sector (Hendershott *et al.*, 2021). Both FinTech start-ups and mature tech firms have gained ground in the finance industry worldwide. Companies such as Google, Apple, Facebook, Tencent and Alibaba have penetrated financial sectors, offering a wide variety of products and services, putting traditional financial companies, particularly incumbent banks, under great pressure (Hendershott *et al.*, 2021). Past studies have found that digital technology and automation enable financial intermediaries to better understand customer needs (Riemer *et al.*, 2017), improve operating efficiency (Chen, 2020; Leong & Sung, 2018) and reduce information asymmetry (Feyen *et al.*, 2021). However, whether the rise of FinTech acts as a disruptive technology (i.e. substitution effect) or serves as a complement to the traditional financial industry remains controversial. Moreover, the effect of FinTech varies under different contexts and economies.

Initiatives in FinTech rely on shifting macroeconomic conditions and triggers from both demand and supply perspectives. These include tighter banking regulations following the 2008 global financial crisis, advancements in information and communication technology (ICT), evolving customer preferences and perceptions toward technology and the emerging digitalization requirements in the post-pandemic era. The synergy of these factors has turned FinTech into a new paradigm (Alt *et al.*, 2018). However, there is no consensus on the definition, evolution and segments of FinTech in the literature. The meaning of FinTech is somewhat ambiguous and varies across different business contexts (Arner *et al.*, 2015). On the other hand, the rapid integration of finance and advanced technology creates challenges in the financial sector for balancing potential benefits and risks stemming from the evolution of FinTech. Frauds, cybersecurity, illegal fundraising and data privacy issues induced by technology are major concerns that have created regulatory challenges due to insufficient government oversight and law enforcement (Ng & Kwok, 2017; University of Cambridge, 2019). The concealment of disruptive technologies increases the frangibility of the financial system, posing systemic risks. Those uncertainties and potential risks cannot be neglected.

The enormous amount of interest and studies concerning FinTech developments highlight its impact on the global financial sector, including different industries and ecosystems. The primary objective of this chapter is to present an inclusive landscape of FinTech, encompassing its definitions and evolutionary context. This chapter aims to serve as a valuable resource for readers seeking a holistic understanding of the FinTech landscape. The chapter also delves into the foundational technologies underpinning FinTech and explores its applications within the financial industry. This provides a background on FinTech in various fields and offers a comprehensive review for future studies in FinTech. In addition to the categories of FinTech, four core segments (mobile payments, insurance technology, wealth management and digital financing) are examined with evidence from both developed and developing economies to demonstrate the global impact of these innovations. Additionally, the relationship between FinTech and incumbents as well as the risks associated with FinTech development are discussed to understand how it transforms and disrupts the financial services landscape and its potential costs and benefits.

The rest of the chapter is organized as follows. Section 1.2 summarizes the definition of FinTech according to different studies. Section 1.3 illustrates the background and drivers of FinTech. Section 1.4 covers the segments of FinTech centered on business functions. Section 1.5 discusses the relationship between FinTech and traditional financial institutions. Section 1.6 describes the potential risks and challenges in FinTech development. Section 1.7 concludes the chapter.

1.2. Definition of FinTech

FinTech, or "financial technology," is a catch-all term referring to the synthesis of financial solutions that leverage advanced digital technologies. This combination of two areas is difficult to define due to the complexity and diversity of its business contexts. Therefore, it is important to review the broad definitions of FinTech based on previous studies to establish a strong foundation for further discussion.

Some define FinTech as covering start-ups aimed at disrupting incumbent financial institutions. For instance, the World Economic Forum (2017) limits the definition of FinTech to small, technology-based newcomers in the financial industry, excluding large technology corporations foraying into the financial service market or established financial institutions seeking to strengthen their technological focus. Milian *et al.* (2019) describe FinTech as forward-thinking companies active in the financial industry that take advantage of communication technology, widespread access to the internet and automated information processing. On the other hand, Nicoletti (2017) describes FinTech as initiatives that utilize ICT in the financial services sector with disruptive and novel business models. Nevertheless, it is notable that although FinTech is often associated with start-ups since it is an emerging trend, traditional firms are adopting new business models by implementing advanced financial technology solutions, such as online and mobile services. Therefore, the scope of FinTech encompasses both start-ups and traditional financial institutions equipped with advanced technologies, as well as collaborations between the two. In the same vein, Puschmann (2017) characterizes FinTech as an umbrella term encompassing innovative financial solutions driven by information technology (IT). Likewise, the Basel Committee on Banking Supervision (BCBS) (2018) specifies that the term FinTech designates a wide array of innovations by both incumbent banks and start-ups.

Schueffel (2016) points out that although the FinTech phenomenon has been applied to a variety of business backgrounds, the definitions are inconsistent and ambiguous. Thus, no universal definition of FinTech has been derived. The author therefore defines FinTech as a new financial industry that utilizes technology to enhance financial activities. Zavolokina *et al.* (2016) propose a conceptual framework for FinTech with regard to its actual meaning and function. FinTech can be defined in terms of three dimensions: an input, a mechanism and an output. In a nutshell, FinTech is the combination of technology, organizations and money flow that transforms, disrupts or establishes new business models or processes through the application of IT, leading to increased market competition. Gomber *et al.* (2017) differentiate FinTech from digital finance and/or e-finance by defining digital finance as the digitalization of the entire financial industry. It covers all electronic-transactable products and services, such as automated teller machines (ATMs), credit cards, online banking, electronic exchange systems and mobile services. In contrast, FinTech describes the intersection of advanced internet technologies and established business activities in the financial sector.

The Financial Stability Board (FSB) (2017) defines FinTech based on the scope of services: FinTech is a technology-enabled innovation that has the potential to create new business models, processes and applications which materially influence the provision of financial services. Leong & Sung (2018) describe FinTech as a cross-disciplinary subject composed of finance, technology and innovation management. In other words, FinTech aims to optimize financial processes through the innovative use of technology-based solutions, with these new innovative ideas potentially contributing to new business models and/or businesses. On the other hand, Dorfleitner *et al.* (2017) assert that it is impossible to derive a restrictive definition of FinTech that applies to all the businesses associated with the term. Because FinTech firms are exposed to a variety of business models offering diverse products and services, it is inadequate to construct a general definition for the term. As a result, authors contextualize FinTech according to the segments of its business models, including finance, asset management and payment. In addition, according to a 2019 Global FinTech report by PwC, the boundaries between financial services companies and technology, media and telecommunication firms have become so blurred that they have become almost indistinguishable. Therefore, FinTech represents the combination of financial services and technology, reshaping how financial businesses operate and interact with customers, regulators and other industries. Table 1.1 summarizes the definitions of FinTech from previous studies.

Table 1.1. Summary of FinTech definitions.

Author(s)	**Definition**
World Economic Forum (2017)	FinTech includes small, technology-based, and new entrants to the financial industry, while it excludes large technology corporations who participate in the financial service market or established financial institutions who are strengthening their technological focuses.
Milian *et al.* (2019)	Forward-thinking companies active in the financial industry that take advantage of communication technology, the wide spread of the internet and automated information processes.
Nicoletti (2017)	Initiatives that utilize information and communication technology (ICT) in the financial service sector with disruptive and novel business models.
Puschmann (2017)	An umbrella term that includes innovative financial solutions driven by IT.
Schueffel (2016)	A new financial industry that utilizes technology to enhance financial activities.
Zavolokina *et al.* (2016)	The combination of technology, organizations and money flow that transform, disrupt, or establish new business models or processes through the application of information technology (IT) and lead to increased competition in the market.
Gomber *et al.* (2017)	The interlink between advanced internet technologies and established business activities in the financial sector.
Financial Stability Board (2017)	A technology-enabled innovation that has the potential to create new business models, processes and applications which materially influence the provision of financial services.
Leong & Sung (2018)	A cross-disciplinary subject that consists of finance, technology and innovation management.
PwC (2019)	The combination of financial services and technology that is reshaping the way in which financial businesses operate and interact with customers, regulators and others from different industries.

1.3. Background and Emergence of FinTech

1.3.1. *Evolution of FinTech*

Alt *et al.* (2018) point out that the emergence of FinTech has not occurred in a vacuum but is built on the long legacy of technological evolution. Even though FinTech is a relatively new concept, its history can be traced back to the 1800s. Arner *et al.* (2015) categorize the evolution of FinTech into three distinct stages (see Figure 1.1).

1.3.1.1. *FinTech 1.0 (1866–1967)*

The initial development began in 1866–1967, when the financial and technology industries interacted and influenced each other during this period. A landmark interlink between finance and technology was the first successful transatlantic telegraph cable laid in 1866. The invention of the electronic telegraph allowed the transmission of information across geographical barriers and laid the groundwork for financial globalization, which had profound implications for the financial industry. Examples include the first universal credit card introduced by Diners' Club Inc. in 1950 and the formation of the Interbank Card Association (now MasterCard) by a group of banks in America in 1966 (Arner *et al.*, 2015). In particular, the establishment of the fax machine by Xerox Corporation in 1964 and the introduction of email dramatically improved the effectiveness and efficiency of communication, fostering financial globalization (Nicoletti, 2017). Therefore, the financial industry was considered closely interlinked with technology from the public's point of view.

Figure 1.1. Evolution of FinTech.
Source: Arner *et al.* (2015).

1.3.1.2. *FinTech 2.0 (1967–2008)*

In the second phase of FinTech, traditional financial institutions began to heavily rely on technologies, adopting branch-focused business models to deliver financial products and services (Varga, 2017). It is undeniable that the most important and disruptive financial technology innovation was the launch of automated teller machines (ATMs) in 1967 by Barclays Bank in London. ATMs represent the first step toward widespread adoption of advanced technology in the financial sector, enabling basic transactions to be automated rather than involving human labor (Arner *et al.*, 2015). The introduction of ATMs demonstrated the potential for close interlinkage between technology and finance. Hence, many studies have marked the year of their introduction as the starting point of modern FinTech (Ashta & Biot-Paquerot, 2018; Nicoletti, 2017; Puschmann, 2017). Since then, various banking-related technologies have emerged, such as NASDAQ in 1971, the world's first electronic security trading system in the US; the Society of Worldwide Interbank Financial Telecommunications (SWIFT) in 1973; and the Trans-European Automated Real-time Gross Settlement Express Transfer System (TARGET) in 1999 (Alt *et al.*, 2018; Arner *et al.*, 2015).

The financial industry began to transition from analog to digital technologies in the 1990s. Lee & Shin (2018) state that the emergence of FinTech was influenced by the technological developments driven by the internet revolution in the early 1990s. The rise of the internet and e-commerce led to various digital business models in the financial industry, including internet banking, mobile payment and online brokerage services, which radically revolutionized how customers access banking services.

1.3.1.3. *FinTech 3.0 (2008–present)*

The current stage of FinTech is an ongoing process involving both technology-enabled companies and traditional financial institutions (Varga, 2017). According to Arner *et al.* (2015), in this era of FinTech 3.0, the whole financial service sector is undergoing full digitalization (known as digital finance or, interchangeably, e-finance), with financial transactions predominantly carried out by electronic means. Individual customers, businesses and market participants can access various financial services and products and obtain information without physical interaction with financial companies (Lee & Shin, 2018).

The enhanced computerization fostered by smartphone applications and Industry 4.0 has led to unprecedented levels of data collection, integration and analysis (Nicoletti, 2017). Emerging technologies in the financial industry, such as e-wallets, peer-to-peer business models and robo-advisors, allow financial services to be conveyed through multiple mediums outside traditional brick-and-mortar financial institutions (Ashta & Biot-Paquerot, 2018). For instance, the introduction of digital currency (i.e. Bitcoin) by Satoshi Nakamoto (2008), aiming to decentralize financial transactions without intervention from central banks, has dramatically changed the value chain of existing payment services (Nicoletti, 2017). As a result, the combination of IT, social media networking, artificial intelligence (AI) and big data analytics enables FinTech start-ups and technology giants to provide differentiated services compared to traditional financial institutions, allowing them to offer customized niche services with data-driven solutions (Lee & Shin, 2018).

1.3.2. *Common drivers of FinTech development*

The initiatives of FinTech depend on several triggers and synergistic effects from both supply and demand factors. The intensified banking regulation induced by the 2008 financial crisis, decreasing reluctance to access online services, the popularity of the internet-based economy and the emerging needs for digitization in the post-COVID-19 era are prominent examples that have promoted FinTech as a new paradigm. Understanding all these drivers is important to gain a better insight into the development of today's FinTech (FSB, 2017, 2019).

FSB (2017) identifies three inter-related drivers of financial innovation from both demand and supply perspectives: changing financial regulations, shifting client preferences and expectations and the evolution of technology. Precisely, changes in financial regulations are related to regulatory and legal requirements, as well as changing business incentives for incumbents and start-ups. Shifting customer preferences refers to altered customer expectations and needs due to the entry of new entrants who provide faster and more efficient services on a large scale compared to less technologically efficient financial institutions (Vučinić, 2020). Finally, advanced technologies, especially the application of programming interfaces (APIs), the popularity of mobile banking and smartphones and cloud computing, are major drivers of FinTech (FSB, 2019).

After the 2008 global financial crisis, the BCBS (2018) announced a Tier 2 capital reserve requirement to prevent contiguous bank failures which pose systemic risk to the entire financial system. Although FinTech companies face regulations, many of them are less stringent than those imposed on fully licensed banks. As a result, FinTech firms are able to offer new financial products with greater agility (Stulz, 2019). In the meantime, customers are becoming more tech-savvy. The younger generations, or "millennials," are digitally minded consumers who have gradually lost trust in incumbent banks after the 2008 global financial crisis and started embracing disruptive technologies. The Global Adoption Index report by EY (2019) shows that consumer adoption of FinTech significantly increased to 64% in 2019 compared to a 16% rate in 2015, when the first index was published. The changing consumer preferences for greater user friendliness, effectiveness and affordability without time and location restrictions are key structural drivers in the development of FinTech (Gomber *et al.*, 2017). Other factors from a demand perspective, including the forces that drive economic growth and development, are accelerating FinTech adoption in both economic frontiers and emerging countries. From the supply side, the development of advanced technologies, such as big data analytics, mobile technologies and high-capacity computation, is the primary catalyst for financial innovation since FinTech companies operate almost exclusively in a virtual environment (FSB, 2017). The following section describes three major technologies shaping the future of FinTech.

1.3.3. *Key technologies behind FinTech*

1.3.3.1. *Blockchain*

Blockchain is said to be the most disruptive innovation, with the potential to transform the global financial system and the nature of investment (Fanning & Centers, 2016). From a technological perspective, a blockchain is a list of continuous digitally timestamped blocks that are difficult to tamper with retroactively. The essence of blockchain is a multi-party consensus mechanism that employs decentralized peer-to-peer (P2P) networks and distributed cryptographic and mathematical algorithms (Hendershott *et al.*, 2021). The initial application of blockchain was the digital cryptocurrency Bitcoin by pseudonymous Satoshi Nakamoto (2008). However, the most important characteristic of blockchain is not the investment potential of Bitcoin or other cryptocurrencies but the underlying technology, called distributed ledger technology (DLT). The primary properties of DLT are security, traceability and immutability, which have profound implications for recording transactions and securing data (Ashta & Biot-Paquerot, 2018).

Globally, not only financial institutions but also other industries are endorsing blockchain technology to address the issues of complex credit verification, high costs, time-consuming processes and data transmission errors during financial transactions (Hendershott *et al.*, 2021). Blockchain has applications in P2P transactions, energy markets, supply chain verification, intellectual property management, etc. (International Finance Corporation, 2019). One of the top blockchain applications is smart contracts. A smart contract is a tiny computer protocol stored within a blockchain. It permits automatic transaction of trusted agreements among disparate and anonymous parties once predetermined conditions are satisfied (Koulu, 2016; Stulz, 2019). In simpler terms, a smart contract uses a distributed ledger to store contracts without the intervention of third-party intermediaries. Therefore, it has the potential to reduce the costs associated with trust. In addition, the speed and efficiency provided by DLT allow smart contracts to execute more complicated and sophisticated tasks among different parties (International Finance Corporation, 2019).

1.3.3.2. *Artificial intelligence*

Fong *et al.* (2021) define AI as one of the key technologies shaping the landscape of the financial industry. AI has gained a foothold in the financial service industry, where financial institutions employ AI technology or business models combined with FinTech apps to optimize business operations and increase revenue. AI enables more self-adaptive and effective business models through a high degree of automation. Cognitive intelligence enables machines to mimic human actions, interpret recognized information and learn from massive amounts of data to identify patterns, make decisions and self-improve (Deloitte, 2017).

Banks and other financial institutions are keen to embrace AI technology to fend off giant technology companies from encroaching into financial territory. AI applications can penetrate entire operation processes of the financial industry, from offering tailored customer products and services, intelligent robo-advisors and facial recognition authentication to fraud detection. As a result, companies can achieve greater operating efficiency through automation and machine learning. This allows companies to replace manual tasks with advanced diagnostics and real-time analysis of massive, complicated customer datasets (Fong *et al.*, 2021). Some significant applications of AI include enhancing cybersecurity through fraud detection and prevention applications, managing large-scale customer segmentation using machine learning, optical character recognition, natural language processing and improving customer service by offering tailored products and services (Despi, 2022).

1.3.3.3. *Internet of Things*

The Internet of Things (IoT) is another impressive technology that is reshaping the landscape of the financial industry. According to estimations by Chui *et al.* (2021), IoT could unleash a potential economic value of US$5.5–12.6 trillion globally by 2030. IoT is a network of interconnected computing devices that can gather and transfer data across wireless networks. It is therefore an essential foundation in conjunction with other advanced technologies used for collecting, interpreting and analyzing multi-source datasets (Nicoletti, 2017). From the FinTech perspective, interconnected devices and existing internet infrastructure allow for real-time remote monitoring, leading to more flexible pricing of financial services. For instance, the application of IoT helps insurers accurately assess clients' risks and streamline underwriting and claims processes. The accumulated data extracted by IoT through interaction with customers enable better customer relationship management by facilitating targeted customer engagement. Further, IoT in the banking industry reinforces risk management by ensuring that accounting records match actual transactions (Fong *et al.*, 2021).

1.4. Key Segments of FinTech

Due to the intricate nature of FinTech, it has often been categorized in prior studies based on its business models, operational procedures, offerings and organizational frameworks (Puschmann, 2017). FinTech encompasses a broad spectrum of financial services, including but not limited to digital payments, account management, crowdfunding and financing (Dorfleitner *et al.*, 2017; Gimpel *et al.*, 2018; Gomber *et al.*, 2017). In this chapter, we classify FinTech from a functional perspective based on EY Global Adoption Index Reports (2017, 2019). The categories are mobile transfer and payments, insurance technology, wealth management and digital financing. Figure 1.2 presents the top four most popular FinTech segments by consumer adoption rate from 2015 to 2019.

1.4.1. *Mobile transfer and payments*

Mobile payment services provide a streamlined payment experience in terms of convenience, ease of use and speed. According to the Global FinTech Adoption Index 2019, the mobile payment service

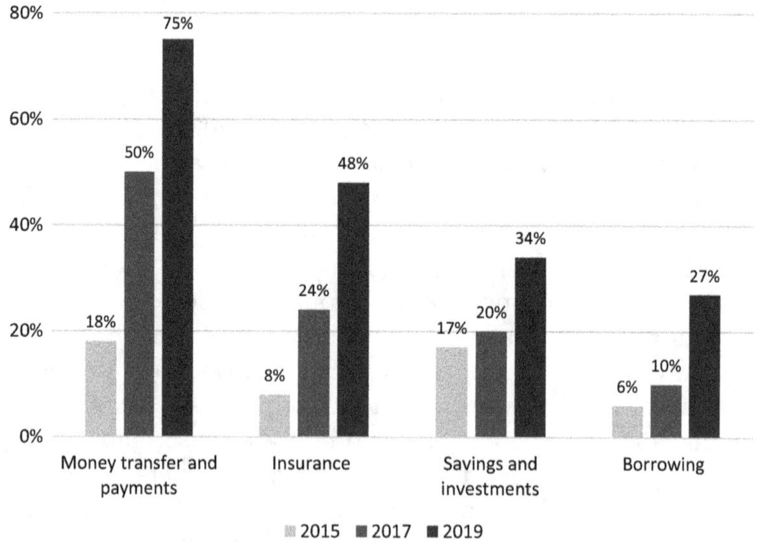

Figure 1.2. Comparison of FinTech categories ranked by adoption rate from 2015 to 2019.

Source: EY (2017, 2019).

segment is regarded as the simplest and most prevalent FinTech application, with 75% of customers reporting the use of at least one digital payment service in 2019. The initial development of mobile payments was fueled by online banking offered by established banks and the emerging demand for e-commerce, while it has shifted to a substitute for established payment functions (Gomber *et al.*, 2017). As a result, large technology firms, FinTech companies and social media giants such as Alibaba, Google and Apple have developed their own digital payment platforms and sought to provide payment-related value-added services. For example, Paypal, an online payment company, operates using a classic business model based on partnerships with existing companies and delivers additional services to its customers, resulting in mutual benefits for both businesses. In China, the two leading mobile payment service providers, Alipay and WeChat Pay, operated by Ant Group and Tencent, respectively, are shifting to a new paradigm, offering an "all-in-one" service to boost the customer experience. Specifically, Alipay has integrated its payment service with its parent company Ant Group to offer wealth management (Yu'e Bao), insurance services (ZhongAn), credit rating (Sesame Credit) and online lending services (MYBank). Correspondingly, WeChat Pay launched digital currency (QQ coin), wealth management (LiCaiTong) and online lending services (WeBank) for its customers (Zhang-Zhang *et al.*, 2020). These super apps are now attempting to disintermediate traditional financial institutions and change the ecosystem of current financial services.

The COVID-19 pandemic reinforced the shift toward cashless transactions and instant payment adoption. According to Bruno *et al.* (2021), cash payments on average declined by 16% in 2020. Although economic activities were halted because of the pandemic, the unprecedented demand for contactless payment, instant transaction settlements and new payment methods (e.g. cryptocurrency, buy now pay later and biometric and digital identity) orchestrated remarkable digital payment recovery and growth (Capgemini, 2021b). Under the acceleration of digital economies, cashless payment volumes are projected to rise by more than 80% from 2020 to 2025. The digital transformation is reshaping not only traditional payment services but also the entire payment infrastructure with new business models (PwC, 2021). Meanwhile, regulators globally have started piloting central bank digital currencies (CBDCs) to secure the availability of central bank currency and a resilient payment system. CBDCs and cryptocurrencies are expected to have the most disruptive effects in the next 20 years. China, for example, is a forerunner in developing a digital sovereign currency, with the digital RMB (e-yuan) being formally unveiled at the 2022 Beijing Winter Olympics (Bruno *et al.*, 2021). The development of CBDCs has extensive consequences for transforming monetary and payment systems, contributing to the establishment of a stable, secure and effective economic structure (Bhaskar *et al.*, 2022).

1.4.2. *Insurance technology*

The rise of FinTech, shifting customer behavior and disruptive technologies are driving a revolution in the insurance industry. Insurance technology (InsurTech) is considered an important subset of FinTech, having emerged as a standalone sector in the financial industry (Wilamowicz, 2019). According to the World InsurTech Report 2021 by Capgemini (2021b), customer intention to buy insurance rose approximately 7%, heightened by the COVID-19 pandemic conditions. Policyholders today seek insurance companies that prioritize the CARE (convenience, advice, reach) business model throughout the insurance process. This is in response to the increasing demand for constant connectivity and access to insurance policy details through multiple channels (convenience), personalized and adaptable insurance solutions that consider diverse risk profiles and individual preferences (advice) and a substantial level of digital interaction and engagement with insurance companies (reach).

Similar to their counterparts in FinTech, InsurTech companies can differentiate themselves from incumbents by their agile business models incorporating digital solutions. Although InsurTech is still in its infancy, it is beginning to change the ecosystem of the insurance industry by exploiting value through digital innovation across the entire insurance value chain. For instance, in Germany, Knip utilizes AI and robo-advisors to enhance customer engagement through digital distribution (Catlin *et al.*, 2017). The world's first automated life insurance platform, Anorak, in the UK, utilizes machine learning, data science and actuarial science technology to offer customized services and recommendations to a wide customer base (FinTech Global, 2019). The US-based insurance company Lemonade, Inc., has successfully digitized the entire insurance process through advanced in-house underwriting capabilities, a user-friendly mobile interface and the replacement of brokers and bureaucratic processes with AI and chatbots for claims processing. Consequently, Lemonade is able to better align the interests of insurers and policyholders by more accurately projecting returns and profits (Wilamowicz, 2019).

According to Chester *et al.* (2018), most InsurTech companies focus on facilitating or extending the insurance value chain rather than attempting to completely disrupt commercial lines. Although the rapid proliferation of InsurTech firms has posed challenges for incumbents, traditional insurers should consider them as potential partners rather than competitors because InsurTech companies lack the necessary scale and expertise. In addition, vast capital investments that enable new insurance propositions allow InsurTech companies to solidify their reputation as innovation frontrunners. Established insurers must evolve through mergers and acquisitions (M&A) or partnerships with InsurTech firms to strengthen their digital capabilities and maintain their market positions (Capgemini, 2021c). For instance, China's Ping An Insurance Group invested EUR41.5 million in the FinTech incubator Finleap to support its technological development and geographic expansion (Nicola, 2018). Lemonade, Inc., has entered into a quota share reinsurance agreement with seven reinsurers to enhance bottom-line stability and profitability predictability (Evans, 2020).

1.4.3. *Digital wealth management*

The emergence of FinTech is causing profound upheaval in the wealth management sector. Given the capacity to harness data for crafting highly individualized customer profiles to gain deeper insights into customer preferences in today's data-intensive society, the wealth management sector is shifting its business model from passive waiting to proactively meeting customer needs through data integration technology. Dorfleitner *et al.* (2017) divide wealth management into social trading, robo-advice, personal financial management and investment and banking. Social trading is a form of instrument that allows investors to observe and replicate their peers' trading strategies or expert traders' decisions based on information obtained in online communities (Doering *et al.*, 2015). The proliferation of the internet enables more individuals to make their own investments due to the sheer volume of data shared and viewed on social trading platforms such as eToro, Zulutrade and Collective2. As a result, retail investors can benefit from following the techniques and strategies of many traders without relying on professional investment experts (Pelster & Hofmann, 2018; Yang *et al.*, 2022).

The most common FinTech in savings and wealth management is robo-advisors. Robo-advisors are automated portfolio management systems that offer discretionary and algorithm-driven investment advice tailored to customer needs (Fein, 2015). A typical example is Wealthfront, a US FinTech company that provides investment services extensively based on complex algorithms. Wealthfront delivers diversified investment services using a simplified questionnaire to assess investors' risk preferences, investment objectives and financial capacity. The software then transforms the gathered data into individual investment portfolios, ensuring diversification, tax efficiency and the maintenance of the desired asset allocation (Wealthfront, 2022).

In addition, the personal financial management (PFM) segment of asset management includes FinTech institutions which provide private financial planning services. For this, FinTech companies primarily use software or mobile-based apps. Customers can visualize their aggregated bank account information, including financial summaries and transactions, through PFM applications (Haikel-Elsabeh *et al.*, 2016). There are also online-based asset management services classified under the investment and banking sub-category, including online wealth management involving both human advisors and robo-advisors, traditional banking services provided by FinTech companies with IT functionalities and others (Dorfleitner *et al.*, 2017).

1.4.4. *Digital financing*

Traditional financing channels include banks, stock markets, bonds, venture capital and personal networks. Digital financing through FinTech introduces alternative means for individuals and businesses to access the required funds via the internet (Gomber *et al.*, 2017). Crowdfunding and peer-to-peer lending represent the most prominent and disruptive business models in digital financing. They serve as effective tools for individuals, newcomers and entrepreneurs to raise funds, particularly for those with limited access to traditional bank loans (Lenz, 2016; Milne & Parboteeah, 2016).

1.4.4.1. *Crowdfunding*

Crowdfunding is a method of raising money collectively from a considerable number of individuals via the internet or social media, removing the need for financial intermediaries. It is considered an innovative approach for projects, start-ups and entrepreneurs seeking funds from multiple donors or investors (Albastaki, 2021). The crowdfunding process involves three key parties: the project initiator who requires funding, the investor who is interested in supporting the project and the moderating organization that provides a crowdfunding platform to facilitate information access and engagement between the two (Lee & Shin, 2018).

The World Bank Group (2013) categorized two main crowdfunding models: donation crowdfunding (i.e. donation- or reward-based) and crowdfund investing (i.e. equity-, lending- or royalty-based). The former serves as an appealing fund-raising choice for small businesses and initiatives. Donation crowdfunding raises capital from donations made by contributors who either do not expect monetary compensation or will receive non-financial compensation such as recognition or products based on their pledged amount. Kickstarter and Indiegogo stand out as examples of successful reward-based crowdfunding platforms. In the crowdfunding investment model, entrepreneurs raise capital by selling security instruments in the form of interest payments and/or expected returns linked to the company's financial performance. Examples of platforms for this approach include AngelList, MicroVentures and Fundable.

1.4.4.2. *Peer-to-peer lending*

The peer-to-peer (P2P) lending business model has emerged in recent years. Similar to crowdfunding, P2P lending provides an alternative means of financing for individuals and small enterprises that are unable to access formal credit through bank lending. The primary difference between traditional lending and P2P lending is that FinTech companies do not participate in the lending processes. Instead, they provide platforms to gather and match borrowers and lenders in the market while charging a fee for it (Lee & Shin, 2018).

According to Lenz (2016), the lending decisions made by banks rely on explicit information combined with non-codified information from potential borrowers, such as repayment capacity, income statements, credit history and customers' social and economic situations. In contrast, P2P platforms utilize big data analytics to evaluate extensive datasets about borrowers created from either the personal details given directly by customers or from information generated through their digital social footprint. In addition, unlike incumbent banks that accumulate risks by holding positions on their balance sheets, P2P platforms spread the risks across their users. As a result, the business model of P2P platforms allows them to deliver efficient and high-quality services with competitive interest rates compared to those offered by traditional financial institutions.

Lending Club is one of the largest P2P lending platforms in the US. It directly connects borrowers and lenders without the mediation of financial intermediaries. This approach makes financing more affordable and accessible for those in need while also increasing the profitability of money lenders (Schueffel, 2016). Although both P2P lending and crowdfunding are alternative financing channels and are often used synonymously, they serve different financing purposes. The primary focus of crowdfunding is raising funds for projects from a large group of people, whereas P2P lending involves loan agreements where lenders have credit claims to future interest and redemption payments (Lee & Shin, 2018).

1.5. Relationship between FinTech Companies and Traditional Financial Institutions

FinTech companies have radically transformed the landscape of the financial industry, sparking ongoing debates about whether they complement or substitute for conventional banks in the sector (Hunjra *et al.*, 2022). FinTech companies exploit competitive advantages by offering customized services at affordable prices and flexible products and services. These allow them to attract customers from underserved segments and fulfill different customer needs, thereby eroding the market shares and profits of traditional financial service providers (Harasim, 2021). On the other hand, banks are striving to maintain their financial standing and market power in the financial sector (Ha *et al.*, 2021). Although traditional incumbents initially perceived FinTech companies as competitive threats to their established models, there is now a shift toward collaboration to improve cost efficiency, capital allocation and client acquisition (Dietz *et al.*, 2016). Besides, FinTech has lowered the barriers for firms (from established financial institutions to start-ups to technology giants) to enter the financial market. It has created an intricate web of cooperative competition and conflict between FinTech companies and traditional financial institutions (PwC, 2019).

EY (2019) classified two types of FinTech propositions: disrupted and invented. Disrupted service means FinTech providers use innovative technologies to challenge traditional financial services provided by established incumbents, offering more compelling features such as cost reduction, enhanced convenience and advanced capabilities. As a result, this will change customer expectations toward financial service processes, thereby forcing incumbents to innovate in order to retain customers and market share. An innovative service in the FinTech sector refers to the creation of novel financial services or business models with the potential to redefine and revolutionize the operation of financial sectors. For example, the blockchain-based payment system and P2P transfers radically change the entire payment value chain, enabling a decentralized trading platform (Puschmann, 2017). Deloitte (2020) concludes that despite changing the delivery, structure and consumption of financial services, FinTech companies have not yet established themselves as market leaders or materially changed the competitive landscape. It is difficult for FinTech companies to establish a new ecosystem while improving the existing infrastructure and ecosystem of incumbents. Besides, customers' inclination to switch from traditional financial institutions to FinTech companies is overestimated.

Incumbents are catching up by offering an array of innovative products and services in response to the challenges posed by FinTech firms. PwC (2019) revealed that although financial service providers are leveraging cutting-edge technologies, they still lag behind digitally-bent technology firms in differentiating themselves. Firms should pursue cross-sector fusion, such as through M&A and joint ventures, to fill the skill gaps among themselves. In addition, the focus of FinTech companies is now shifting away from directly competing with incumbents and to increasingly forming partnerships with them, in which traditional financial institutions retain the relationship with end customers while FinTech companies assist in enhancing customer-centric approaches (Catlin *et al.*, 2017). For instance, the recent introduction of digital banking licenses in Hong Kong, Australia and Singapore is a striking example of the fusion and convergence between traditional financial services institutions and technology companies (PwC, 2019).

However, it is too early to conclude whether FinTech companies and traditional financial intermediaries compete, collaborate or coexist. The COVID-19 pandemic accelerated the second wave of FinTech, propelling the financial industry into a new phase. According to Deloitte (2020), collaboration between financial institutions and FinTech providers is necessary since their strengths and weaknesses are complementary. Specifically, incumbents have sufficient capital but are constrained by legacy systems, while FinTech companies possess innovative business models with fewer regulatory restrictions but may lack capital and industry expertise. However, they may encounter several hurdles. Traditional financial institutions, particularly banks, face heavy regulation and compliance considerations, which may hinder the collaboration process. A lack of industry experience will also reduce the credibility of the collaboration (Deloitte, 2020).

1.6. Challenges and Risks of FinTech

The current financial industry is undergoing unprecedented changes. The rapid integration of finance and advanced technology has opened up new opportunities and presented challenges within the financial sector, as it strives to balance the potential benefits and substantial risks arising from the evolution of FinTech. Frauds, cybersecurity threats, illegal fundraising and data privacy issues caused by technology are major regulatory challenges due to insufficient government oversight and law enforcement. The concealment of disruptive technologies increases the fragility of the financial system, thereby posing systematic risks (FSB, 2017). This sector focuses on cybersecurity and regulatory challenges as two primary risks during the evolution of FinTech.

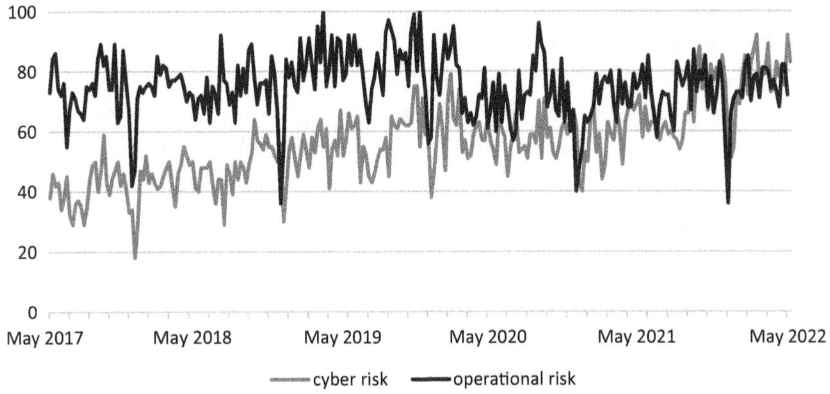

Figure 1.3. Global Google trend: Interest over time (2017–2022).
Note: Numbers represent global searches for "cyber risk" and "operational risk" relative to the highest point (100) from May 2017 to May 2022 (accessed on 31 May 2022).
Source: Google Trends.

1.6.1. *Cybersecurity*

The growing reliance on complex digital information technologies increases vulnerability to cyber risks. Research by IBM (2022) revealed that finance and insurance were the most attacked sectors from 2015 to 2020 across the globe. Aki Aldasoro *et al.* (2020) indicate that although cyber risk is a subcategory of firms' operational risk, search interest in cyber risk has been increasing worldwide and has become comparable to operational risk since 2020. We conducted the same trend analysis to track global search interest in "cyber risk" and "operational risk" (see Figure 1.3).

Buckley *et al.* (2019) consider cybersecurity to be one of the most significant sources of systemic risk and a national security challenge. The interfaces between digital financial systems are common sources of cybersecurity flaws, allowing simple cyberattacks and fraud to spread widely as a result of digitalization and globalization. Cyberattacks can exploit these security vulnerabilities to disrupt payment systems, compromise data security at custodian banks or central securities depositories and undermine the infrastructure on which the financial system relies. Although these are low-probability events, their occurrence could have catastrophic consequences for financial stability if not controlled effectively. To mitigate cyber risks, potential cyber vulnerabilities should be subjected to rigorous scrutiny.

Building a firewall is merely the first line of defense. In addition, proactive cyberattack risk management is essential, which includes creating contingency plans, implementing monitoring systems, integrating cybersecurity considerations in the early stages of system design and enhancing financial and technology literacy among individuals to reduce potential cybersecurity risks (FSB, 2017).

1.6.2. *Regulation*

Both traditional financial institutions and FinTech companies are subject to regulatory requirements. However, the scope and requirements of regulation vary depending on the type of services they provide and apply primarily to banks (Ho *et al.*, 2022). With the distinctions between services provided by traditional financial institutions and FinTech companies starting to blur, higher regulatory requirements and legal penalties for non-compliance have become critical (Deloitte, 2017).

Excessive but unregulated innovation may lead to significant risks, whereas stringent regulation and risk management can sometimes be perceived as obstacles to FinTech initiatives, stifling innovative and creative disruptive technologies. Therefore, greater coordination is expected among FinTech companies, traditional financial institutions and regulatory authorities to achieve a balance between innovation and regulation. Kane (1981) indicates a regulatory dialectic relationship between innovation and regulation. Innovation can be facilitated by deregulation and loophole mining. On the other hand, exogenous factors are accelerating uncertainties and environmental changes, thereby causing "re-regulation." However, innovative technologies may render traditional regulations obsolete.

The complexity and massive volume of data underscore the necessity of automating process monitoring and compliance for better outcomes. Therefore, it is essential to replace the traditional regulatory approach with regulatory technology (RegTech) to foster more effective supervision. Arner *et al.* (2015) argue that RegTech is more than just a subset of FinTech and represents a pivotal shift toward a new regulatory paradigm. It signifies a logical evolution of regulation within the financial industry, enabling regulators to proactively monitor and identify issues instead of reacting with actions and enforcements after the fact. The integration of information technology into the regulatory framework will facilitate more efficient risk prevention and regulatory compliance.

Many regulators have implemented proactive approaches such as regulatory sandboxes, allowing new innovative technologies to be experimented with within a well-defined regulatory environment and duration to balance the risks and benefits of FinTech innovation (Bromberg *et al.*, 2017). A significant evolution is open banking, which changes the landscape of the financial services industry. Open banking can be described as a regulatory regime where banks either voluntarily or mandatorily grant third-party service providers open access to customer financial data via application programming interfaces (APIs). This allows third-party providers to aggregate customer data from various sources to offer more personalized and customer-centric services (Nicholls, 2019). Many economies have launched initiatives to promote open banking, such as Consumer Data Rights (CDR) in Australia, the Open API Framework issued by the Hong Kong Monetary Authority and the API Playbook published by the Monetary Authority of Singapore (MAS), which facilitates competition in the financial services sector and leads to innovative products and effective credit and financing processes (Ziegler, 2021).

1.7. Summary

Although the financial industry is traditionally an early adopter and heavy user of new advancements in ICT, the rise of innovative business models and technology-enabled competitors substantially impacts current market dynamics. The emergence of financial technology has demonstrated remarkable influence in transforming the landscape of the current financial industry. Considering the need for contextualizing the rapid development of FinTech in business applications, this chapter provides a synopsis of the background, development, functionality and underlying challenges of FinTech.

We first review the definitions of FinTech, as summarized from prior studies, for a comprehensive understanding of its dynamic nature. We conclude that FinTech is a process that leverages cutting-edge technologies to improve, innovate or disrupt the delivery and use of financial services. The history of FinTech can be traced back to 1866, with its current phase emerging in the aftermath of the

2008 global financial crisis. The emergence of FinTech has been promoted by a confluence of factors, including regulatory changes, shifting customer preferences and technological advancements. Among them, the convergence of technologies such as blockchain, AI and the IoT is a major driving force contributing to the development of FinTech and will continue to reshape the landscape of the financial industry. Due to the multifaceted character of FinTech, this chapter provides additional insights into its various segments based on functionality, including mobile payments and transfers, insurance technology, digital financing and digital wealth management. Future research should focus on understanding how FinTech impacts traditional industries, the potential effects of digital currencies (CBDCs and cryptocurrencies) on the monetary system and the utilization of FinTech in response to evolving social, economic and political landscapes. FinTech has lowered the barriers for firms (from established financial institutions to start-ups to technology giants) to enter the financial market. As financial services transition to a digital platform, the boundary between them is blurring. Therefore, incumbents are increasingly acquiring or partnering with FinTech companies to cater to their tech-savvy clientele. Both FinTech companies and established financial institutions need to adopt a forward-looking approach to foster partnerships, as their strengths and weaknesses are complementary. Future research should investigate the evolving relationship between FinTech and traditional banks. Current FinTech is, however, characterized by both opportunities and risks that arise with its expansion. So, cybersecurity will become more critical than ever before. This serves as a wake-up call for policymakers and regulatory authorities to balance innovation with regulation, safeguarding customers' interests while ensuring financial stability.

References

Aki Aldasoro, I., Frost, J., Gambacorta, L., Leach, T., & Whyte, D. (2020). Operational and cyber risk in the financial sector. www.suerf.org/policynotes.

Albastaki, Y. A. (2021). When technology meets finance. In Albastaki, Y. A., Razzaque, A., & Sarea, A. M. (Eds.), *Innovative Strategies for Implementing FinTech in Banking* (pp. 1–21). Hershey, PA: IGI Global. https://doi.org/10.4018/978-1-7998-3257-7.ch001.

Alt, R., Beck, R., & Smits, M. T. (2018). FinTech and the transformation of the financial industry. *Electronic Markets*, 28(3), 235–243. Springer Verlag. https://doi.org/10.1007/s12525-018-0310-9.

Arner, D. W., Barberis, J. N., & Buckley, R. P. (2015). The evolution of FinTech: A new post-crisis paradigm? *SSRN Electronic Journal.* https://doi.org/10.2139/ssrn.2676553.

Ashta, A. & Biot-Paquerot, G. (2018). FinTech evolution: Strategic value management issues in a fast changing industry. *Strategic Change*, 27(4), 301–311. https://doi.org/10.1002/jsc.2203.

Basel Committee on Banking Supervision. (2018). Implications of fintech developments for banks and bank supervisors. https://www.bis.org/bcbs/publ/d431.html.

Bhaskar, R., Hunjra, A. I., Bansal, S., & Pandey, D. K. (2022). Central Bank digital currencies: Agendas for future research. *Research in International Business and Finance*, 62. https://doi.org/10.1016/j.ribaf.2022.101737.

Bromberg, L., Godwin, A., & Ramsay, I. (2017). Fintech sandboxes: Achieving a balance between regulation and innovation. *Journal of Banking and Finance Law and Practice*, 28(4). DOI: 10.33166/AETiC.2019.05.001.

Bruno, P., Denecker, O., & Niederkorn, M. (2021). Global payments 2021: Transformation amid turbulent undercurrents. https://www.mckinsey.com/industries/financial-services/our-insights/global-payments-2021-transformation-amid-turbulent-undercurrents.

Buckley, R. P., Arner, D. W., Zetzsche, D. A., & Selga, E. (2019). The dark side of digital financial transformation: The new risks of FinTech and the rise of TechRisk. *SSRN Electronic Journal.* https://doi.org/10.2139/ssrn.3478640.

Capgemini. (2021a). World FinTech Report 2021. https://fintechworldreport.com/.

Capgemini. (2021b). World Payments Report 2021. https://worldpaymentsreport.com/.

Catlin, T., Lorenz, J.-T., Münstermann, B., & Valentino, R. (2017). Insurtech — the threat that inspires. https://www.mckinsey.com/industries/financial-services/our-insights/insurtech-the-threat-that-inspires.

Chen, K.-C. (2020). Implications of Fintech developments for traditional banks. *International Journal of Economics and Financial Issues*, 10(5), 227–235. https://doi.org/10.32479/ijefi.10076.

Chester, A., Ham, S., Johansson, S., & Olesen, P. B. (2018). Commercial Lines Insurtech: A Pathway to Digital. https://www.mckinsey.com/~/media/McKinsey/Industries/Financial%20Services/Our%20Insights/Commercial%20lines%20insurtech%20A%20pathway%20to%20digital/Commercial-lines-insurtech-A-pathway-to-digital-final.pdf.

Chui, M., Collins, M., & Patel, M. (2021). IoT value set to accelerate through 2030: Where and how to capture it. https://www.mckinsey.com/business-functions/mckinsey-digital/our-insights/iot-value-set-to-accelerate-through-2030-where-and-how-to-capture-it.

Deloitte. (2017). The future of FinTechs: Risk and regulatory compliance. https://www2.deloitte.com/us/en/pages/regulatory/articles/future-of-fintechs-risk-and-regulatory-compliance.html.

Deloitte. (2020). Fintech — On the brink of further disruption. https://www2.deloitte.com/nl/nl/pages/financial-services/articles/fintech-on-the-brink-of-further-disruption.html.

Despi, J. B. P. (2022). Artificial intelligence: FinTech's innovation driver. https://www.philips.com/a-w/about/artificial-intelligence.html.

Dietz, M., Moon, J., & Radnai, M. (2016). FinTechs can help incumbents, not just disrupt them. https://www.mckinsey.com/industries/financial-services/our-insights/fintechs-can-help-incumbents-not-just-disrupt-them.

Doering, P., Neumann, S., & Paul, S. (2015). Remuneration and risk-taking — Empirical evidence for social trading. *SSRN Electronic Journal*. https://doi.org/10.2139/ssrn.2291421.

Dorfleitner, G., Hornuf, L., Schmitt, M., & Weber, M. (2017). Definition of FinTech and description of the FinTech industry. In Dorfleitner , G., Hornuf , L., Schmitt, M. & Weber, M. (Eds.), *FinTech in Germany* (pp. 5–10). Cham, Switzerland: Springer International Publishing. https://doi.org/10.1007/978-3-319-54666-7_2.

Evans, S. (2020). Lemonade files to go public and reveals Nephila as reinsurer. https://www.artemis.bm/news/lemonade-files-to-go-public-and-reveals-nephila-as-reinsurer/.

EY. (2017). Global fintech adoption index 2017. https://www.innovatefinance.com/reports/ey-fintech-adoption-index-2017/.

EY. (2019). Global fintech adoption index 2019. https://www.ey.com/en_gl/ey-global-fintech-adoption-index.

Fanning, K. & Centers, D. P. (2016). Blockchain and its coming impact on financial services. *Journal of Corporate Accounting and Finance*, 27(5), 53–57. https://doi.org/10.1002/jcaf.22179.

Fein, M. L. (2015). Robo-advisors: A closer look. *SSRN Electronic Journal*. https://doi.org/10.2139/ssrn.2658701.

Feyen, E., Frost, J., Gambacorta, L., Natarajan, H., & Saal, M. (2021). Fintech and the digital transformation of financial services: Implications for market structure and public policy. (No. 117).

Financial Stability Board (FSB). (2017). Financial Stability Implications from FinTech: Supervisory and Regulatory Issues that Merit Authorities' Attention. https://www.fsb.org/2017/06/financial-stability-implications-from-fintech/.

Financial Stability Board (FSB). (2019). FinTech and market structure in financial services: Market developments and potential financial stability implications. www.fsb.org/emailalert.

FinTech Global. (2019). Insurtech 100. https://fintech.global/insurtech100/.

Fong, D., Han, F., Liu, L., Qu, J., & Shek, A. (2021). Seven technologies shaping the future of fintech. https://www.mckinsey.com/cn/our-insights/our-insights/seven-technologies-shaping-the-future-of-fintech.

Gimpel, H., Rau, D., & Röglinger, M. (2018). Understanding FinTech start-ups – a taxonomy of consumer-oriented service offerings. *Electronic Markets*, 28(3), 245–264. https://doi.org/10.1007/s12525-017-0275-0.

Gomber, P., Koch, J.-A., & Siering, M. (2017). Digital finance and FinTech: Current research and future research directions. *Journal of Business Economics*, 87(5), 537–580. https://doi.org/10.1007/s11573-017-0852-x.

Gopalan, S., Jain, G., Kalani, G., & Tan, J. (2012). Breakthrough IT banking. https://www.mckinsey.com/capabilities/mckinsey-digital/our-insights/breakthrough-it-banking.

Ha, M., Gan, C., Nguyen, C., & Anthony, P. (2021). Self-organising (Kohonen) maps for the Vietnam banking industry. *Journal of Risk and Financial Management*, 14(10). https://doi.org/10.3390/jrfm14100485.

Haikel-Elsabeh, M., Nouet, S., & Nayaradou, M. (2016). How personal finance management influences consumers' motivations and behavior regarding online banking services. *Communications & Strategies*, 103(5), 15–34.

Harasim, J. (2021). FinTechs, BigTechs and banks—When cooperation and when competition? *Journal of Risk and Financial Management*, 14(12), 614. https://doi.org/10.3390/jrfm14120614.

Hendershott, T., Zhang, X. (Michael), Zhao, J. L., & Zheng, Z. (Eric). (2021). FinTech as a game changer: Overview of research frontiers. *Information Systems Research*, 32(1), 1–17. https://doi.org/10.1287/isre.2021.0997.

Ho, L. T., Gan, C., Jin, S., & Le, B. (2022). Does climate-related disclosures support sustainable finance in New Zealand? https://hdl.handle.net/10182/15409.

Hunjra, A. I., Islam, F., Verhoeven, P., & Hassan, M. K. (2022). The impact of a dual banking system on macroeconomic efficiency. *Research in International Business and Finance*, 61, 101647. https://doi.org/10.1016/j.ribaf.2022.101647.

IBM. (2022). X-Force Threat Intelligence Index 2022. https://www.ibm.com/security/data-breach/threat-intelligence/.

International Finance Corporation. (2019). Blockchain: Opportunities for Private Enterprises in Emerging Markets. 22/10/2023. https://www.ifc.org/wps/wcm/connect/publications_ext_content/ifc_external_publication_site/publications_listing_page/blockchain+report.

Kane, E. (1981). Accelerating inflation, technological innovation, and the decreasing effectiveness of banking regulation. *The Journal of Finance*, 36(2), 355–367. https://doi.org/10.3386/w0638.

Koulu, R. (2016). Blockchains and online dispute resolution: Smart contracts as an alternative to enforcement. *SCRIPTed*, 13(1), 40–69. https://doi.org/10.2966/scrip.130116.40.

KPMG. (2022). Pulse of Fintech H2' 21. https://assets.kpmg.com/content/dam/kpmg/xx/pdf/2022/02/pulse-of-fintech-h2-21.pdf

Kutler, J. (1993). Citibank is shedding individualistic image.

Lee, I. & Shin, Y. J. (2018). Fintech: Ecosystem, business models, investment decisions, and challenges. *Business Horizons*, 61(1), 35–46. https://doi.org/10.1016/j.bushor.2017.09.003.

Lenz, R. (2016). Peer-to-peer lending: Opportunities and risks. *European Journal of Risk Regulation*, 7(4), 688–700. https://doi.org/10.1017/S1867299X00010126.

Leong, K. & Sung, A. (2018). FinTech (financial technology): What is it and how to use technologies to create business value in FinTech way? *Management and Technology*, 9(2), 74–78.

Martinčević, I., Črnjević, S., & Klopotan, I. (2020). Fintech revolution in the financial industry. *ENTRENOVA-ENTerprise REsearch InNOVAtion* (pp. 563–571).

Milian, E. Z., Spinola, M. D. M., & Carvalho, M. M. D. (2019). Fintechs: A literature review and research agenda. *Electronic Commerce Research and Applications*, 34. https://doi.org/10.1016/j.elerap.2019.100833.

Milne, A. & Parboteeah, P. (2016). The business models and economics of peer-to-peer lending. *SSRN Electronic Journal*. https://doi.org/10.2139/ssrn.2763682.

Nakamoto, S. (2008). Bitcoin: A peer-to-peer electronic cash system. *Decentralized Business Review*, 21260. www.bitcoin.org.

Ng, A. W. & Kwok, B. K. B. (2017). Emergence of FinTech and cybersecurity in a global financial centre: Strategic approach by a regulator. *Journal of Financial Regulation and Compliance*, 25(4), 422–434. Emerald Group Publishing Ltd. https://doi.org/10.1108/JFRC-01-2017-0013.

Nicholls, C. C. (2019). Open banking and the rise of FinTech: Innovative finance and functional regulation. *Banking & Finance Law Review*, 35(1), 121–151. http://www.mas.gov.sg/Singapore-Financial-Centre/Smart-Financial-Centre/Fin-.

Nicola, S. (2018). China's Ping an buys stake in German fintech incubator finleap. https://www.bloomberg.com/news/articles/2018-11-19/china-s-ping-an-buys-stake-in-german-fintech-incubator-finleap.

Nicoletti, B. (2017). *The Future of FinTech.* Cham, Switzerland: Springer International Publishing. https://doi.org/10.1007/978-3-319-51415-4.

Pelster, M. & Hofmann, A. (2018). About the fear of reputational loss: Social trading and the disposition effect. *Journal of Banking & Finance*, 94, 75–88. https://doi.org/10.1016/j.jbankfin.2018.07.003.

Puschmann, T. (2017). Fintech. *Business & Information Systems Engineering*, 59(1), 69–76. https://doi.org/10.1007/s12599-017-0464-6.

PwC. (2019). Global FinTech Report 2019. https://www.pwc.com/gx/en/industries/financial-services/fintech-survey.html.

PwC. (2021). Payments 2025 & beyond. https://www.pwc.com/gx/en/industries/financial-services/publications/financial-services-in-2025/payments-in-2025.html.

Riemer, K., Hafermalz, E., Roosen, A., Boussand, N., El Aoufi, H., Mo, D., & Kosheliev, A. (2017). The fintech advantage: Harnessing digital technology, keeping the customer in focus. http://hdl.handle.net/2123/16259.

Schueffel, P. (2016). Taming the beast: A scientific definition of fintech. *Journal of Innovation Management Schueffel (JIM)*, 4, 32–54.

Stulz, R. M. (2019). FinTech, BigTech, and the future of banks. *Journal of Applied Corporate Finance*, 31(4), 86–97. https://doi.org/10.1111/jacf.12378.

University of Cambridge. (2019). Cyber Risk Outlook. https://www.jbs.cam.ac.uk/faculty-research/centres/risk/publications/technology-and-space/cyber-risk-outlook/cyber-risk-outlook-2019/.

Varga, D. (2017). Fintech, the new era of financial services. *Vezetéstudomány-Budapest Management Review*, 48(11), 22–32. https://doi.org/10.14267/VEZTUD.2017.11.03.

Vučinić, M. (2020). Fintech and financial stability potential influence of FinTech on financial stability, risks and benefits. *Journal of Central*

Banking Theory and Practice, 9(2), 43–66. https://doi.org/10.2478/jcbtp-2020-0013.

Wealthfront. (2022). Get your investing eggs in way more baskets. https://www.wealthfront.com/investing.

Wilamowicz, A. (2019). The great FinTech disruption: InsurTech. *Banking & Finance Law Review*, 34(2), 215–238. https://www.mckinsey.com/industries/financial-.

World Bank Group. (2013). Crowdfunding's Potential for the Developing World. https://openknowledge.worldbank.org/handle/10986/17626.

World Economic Forum. (2017). Beyond fintech: A pragmatic assessment of disruptive potential in financial services. https://www.weforum.org/reports/beyond-fintech-a-pragmatic-assessment-of-disruptive-potential-in-financial-services.

Yang, M., Zheng, Z. (Eric), & Mookerjee, V. (2022). How much is financial advice worth? The transparency-revenue tension in social trading. *Management Science*, 68(7), 5252–5268. https://doi.org/10.1287/mnsc.2021.4147.

Zavolokina, L., Dolata, M., & Schwabe, G. (2016). FinTech-what's in a name? *Thirty Seventh International Conference on Information Systems*. https://doi.org/10.5167/uzh-126806.

Zhang-Zhang, Y., Rohlfer, S., & Rajasekera, J. (2020). An eco-systematic view of cross-sector fintech: The case of Alibaba and Tencent. *Sustainability (Switzerland)*, 12(21), 1–25. https://doi.org/10.3390/su12218907.

Ziegler, T. (2021). Implementation of open banking protocols around the world. In Rau, R., Wardrop, R., & Zingales, L. (Eds.), *The Palgrave Handbook of Technological Finance* (pp. 751–782). Springer International Publishing. https://doi.org/10.1007/978-3-030-65117-6_27.

https://doi.org/10.1142/9781800616257_0002

Chapter 2

Role of Digital Technology in the Financial Industry

Muhammad Azam[*,‡], **Irfan Channi**[†,§], **and Muhammad Haroon**[*,¶]

**Department of Economics, Ghazi University, Dera Ghazi Khan, Pakistan*

[†]Department of Management Sciences, COMSAT Vehari, Vehari, Pakistan

[‡]muazam@gudgk.edu.pk

[§]irfanchani@cuivehari.edu.pk

[¶]haroonbaloch007.hb@gmail.com

Abstract

The management, investment and exchange of funds are being transformed by digital technology, driving a technological revolution in the financial sector. The proliferation of digital technology has given rise to the emergence of "financial technology," an umbrella term for cutting-edge digital finance solutions. Digital technology has enabled the transition from physical bank branches to online banking, granting clients convenient access to their financial transactions through mobile banking applications, electronic payment methods and digital wallets. Digital finance research and development (R&D) has yielded regulatory technology solutions that automate compliance processes, improve the accuracy of regulatory reporting and address concerns related to data privacy. Digital finance places significant emphasis on cybersecurity and risk management. Ongoing research endeavors aim to advance cybersecurity safeguards, threat detection systems and data protection procedures. Collaboration is of the utmost importance in the digital finance ecosystem, encompassing end users, banks, FinTech firms and programmers, in order to foster innovation and satisfy the financial needs of customers effectively. The increasing significance of international payments has prompted the digital banking industry to collaborate with neighboring countries, striving to streamline and reduce the expenses associated with cross-border transactions.

Keywords: Digital economy, financial industry, FinTech, cybersecurity, regulatory industry.

2.1. Introduction

The dynamic financial industry is experiencing a technological transformation that is altering the very nature of how money is handled, invested and transacted. "Financial technology," or "FinTech," refers to the rapidly developing and innovative sector of digital finance. In this chapter, we examine how the rise of digital technology is reshaping the financial services industry, from the challenges it is posing to traditional institutions to the innovations it is spawning in the form of consumer and business-facing products (Ofori *et al.*, 2023). Over the past several decades, there has been a major shift from traditional brick-and-mortar bank branches to internet banking. The growing use of digital technology has enabled convenient monetary transactions, previously requiring physical visits to a bank, now achievable through a few taps on a smartphone screen. Digital wallets, mobile banking apps and other forms of electronic payment have given customers unprecedented convenience and access to their financial resources. As a result of the COVID-19 pandemic's restrictions on face-to-face encounters, customers and financial institutions were encouraged to adopt digital alternatives in order to keep financial operations running smoothly (Deng *et al.*, 2019).

The widespread availability of smartphones and internet connectivity has contributed to this digital shift. Affordable cellphones and consistent internet access have helped close the financial inclusion gap by making financial services more accessible to people in previously unreachable locations. Because of this, formerly unbanked and underbanked individuals can now save, transfer and receive money, access credit and be a part of the formal financial ecosystem for the first time in their lives (Avelar-Sosa *et al.*, 2018). The digital finance sector has prompted a rethinking of the term "financial intermediation." Banks and other financial institutions face challenges from newer, more agile FinTech companies that use digital technology to offer a plethora of financial services and products. These upstarts are a threat to the established order because they provide new business models, simplified procedures and user-friendly interfaces. Traditional financial services have been disrupted by digital innovations such as peer-to-peer (P2P) lending platforms, robo-advisors and cryptocurrency exchanges (Lin *et al.*, 2022). Digital technology has greatly improved other aspects of finance. For example, blockchain technology has created secure and tamper-proof digital ledgers, which greatly simplify the process of recording and verifying (Han *et al.*, 2018) transactions.

In addition, data analytics and artificial intelligence (AI) have become critical components of the modern digital banking sector. Big data and machine learning (ML) algorithms are used by banks and FinTech firms to study client habits, calculate credit risks, detect fraud and customize financial offerings. These innovations allow businesses to make informed decisions based on consumer data, improve product offers based on individual preferences and provide a more satisfying experience for customers (Deng *et al.*, 2019). "Open banking" is another innovation born at the junction of finance and technology; it encourages financial institutions, FinTech firms and third-party developers to share and collaborate on data. Many nations have introduced laws for open banking that have made it possible for clients to safely disclose their financial information to vetted third parties (Peña-Martel *et al.*, 2018). On the other hand, governments are grappling with how to effectively manage these new technologies while striking a balance between innovation and consumer safety amidst the exponential growth of cryptocurrency and decentralized finance (DeFi) platforms (Michalik *et al.*, 2019).

This chapter further explores these questions, presenting an in-depth examination of digital technology's function in the online banking sector. We look at how digitalization has transformed the banking industry, the development of payment systems, the proliferation of FinTech companies, the use of blockchain and AI and the advent of open banking. In addition, we discuss the difficulties in regulating the sector. In order to demonstrate the relevance of these technical developments, we use real-world examples and case studies throughout this investigation (Sebestyén & Abonyi, 2021). This chapter examines the ramifications of digital technology on the financial industry, emphasizing its inception, theoretical underpinnings and effectiveness. It stresses the significance of acquainting oneself with pertinent theory and evidence in order to achieve success in this ever-evolving field. The chapter examines the expansion of the digital financial sector, which is propelled by technological advancements, regulatory reactions and the growing potential of digital infrastructure. The digital banking industry has focused on user experience and the development of intelligent mobile applications and user-friendly interfaces, which has contributed to the proliferation of digital financial services. The chapter recognizes the role of governmental policies and incentives in promoting the adoption of digital technology in this sector.

2.2. Literature Review and Theoretical Background

The digital financial industry has experienced a dramatic transition in recent years due to the widespread use of digital technologies. The goal of this chapter is to provide readers with a solid foundation for understanding how digital technology is altering the financial services landscape. A brief background on the origins of digitalization in finance is provided, followed by an examination of the theoretical underpinnings of the industry's forward momentum. Throughout the review, we refer to these theoretical roots to support our points (Shahzad *et al.*, 2022).

2.2.1. *The evolution of financial digitalization*

The gradual but steady use of digital technology in the financial sector was not an overnight phenomenon but rather emerged as a trend toward the end of the 20th century. The advent of the internet and widespread use of personal computers laid the groundwork for modern digital financial services. The 1990s marked the debut of one of the first avenues of digital finance – online banking; it allowed customers to remotely check account balances and execute basic transactions. Thus, the groundwork for the emerging digital finance industry had been built (Adam & Fazekas, 2021; Çelik *et al.*, 2022; Li *et al.*, 2019). In "Financial Technology and the Future of Banking," a classic work in this field, the author (Broby, 2021) looks at how digital technology has helped underrepresented people in developing nations get access to banking services. The author claim that digital financial services may help spread banking to those without access to banking because of the lower costs and fewer complications.

2.2.2. *Modeling digital financial systems*

The adoption of digital technology in finance may be analyzed through the lens of technology adoption theories. Perceived ease of use and perceived utility are major drivers of an individual's intentions to accept technology, according to the technology acceptance model (TAM) developed by Kallai *et al.* (2022), Asogwa (2012) and Mo *et al.* (2023). The TAM is useful for understanding why people utilize mobile banking applications and other types of digital payment processing in the realm of digital finance. Empirical evidence confirming the TAM's application to digital finance adoption is provided by studies such as "User Acceptance of Information Technology: Toward a Unified View" (Venkatesh *et al.*, 2003).

2.2.3. *Ideas about disruptive innovation*

The online banking sector may greatly benefit from the insights provided by disruptive innovation (Ayerbe *et al.*, 2022). Christensen contends that new technologies and business models may upend well-established industries. Disruptors in the financial industry include FinTech firms, which are challenging conventional banks by offering novel, customer-focused services (Ayerbe *et al.*, 2022; Kallai *et al.*, 2022; Khatun *et al.*, 2021). How FinTech is transforming financial services via the use of disruptive technologies is the subject of investigation in Miśkiewicz *et al.* (2022).

2.2.4. *Perspectives on financial inclusion*

Several theoretical frameworks support the objective of financial inclusion, which is important for many digital financial activities. According to Imran *et al.*'s (2023) dual financial system theory, two distinct financial systems may be operating in parallel in emerging nations. The goal of digital finance interventions is to close this gap by expanding access to mainstream financial services for previously underserved communities. The relevance of financial inclusion to economic growth is explored in "Access to Finance: An Unfinished Agenda" (Beck & Demirgüç-Kunt, 2008).

2.2.5. *The combination of blockchain and distributed ledger technology*

Because of their potential to change transactional procedures, blockchain and distributed ledger technology (DLT) have gained traction in the digital finance sector. The consensus mechanism model, proposed by Shahzad *et al.* (2022), is a theoretical framework that investigates the factors that make blockchain technology trustworthy. Additionally, Ricci *et al.*'s (2021) token economy framework investigates how blockchain tokens can represent multiple assets and possess economic value, opening the door for new financial models and ecosystems (Chen & Zhao, 2022; Khan *et al.*, 2022; Wang *et al.*, 2022b).

2.2.6. *Theories of regulation and policymaking*

There is a growing need for theoretical frameworks in the areas of regulation and policy in the digital financial sector (Zhang, 2023). The regulatory sandboxes concept proposes a regulatory framework that gives FinTech companies a safe place to experiment with new ideas without jeopardizing customer security or the stability of the market. This method addresses the problems of governing a dynamic sector by striking a balance between fostering innovation and maintaining regulatory oversight (Barykin *et al.*, 2020; Gadanidis, 2017; Salampasis & Mention, 2018). Figure 2.1 shows the relationships and flow between various concepts, such as the TAM.

2.3. Effects of New Technology on Banking and Finance

One of the most important developments in the history of the digital financial sector has been the complete digitalization of payment systems. Credit cards, mobile wallets and P2P payment systems have all revolutionized the way consumers and companies conduct financial transactions. Digital payment methods have become the standard,

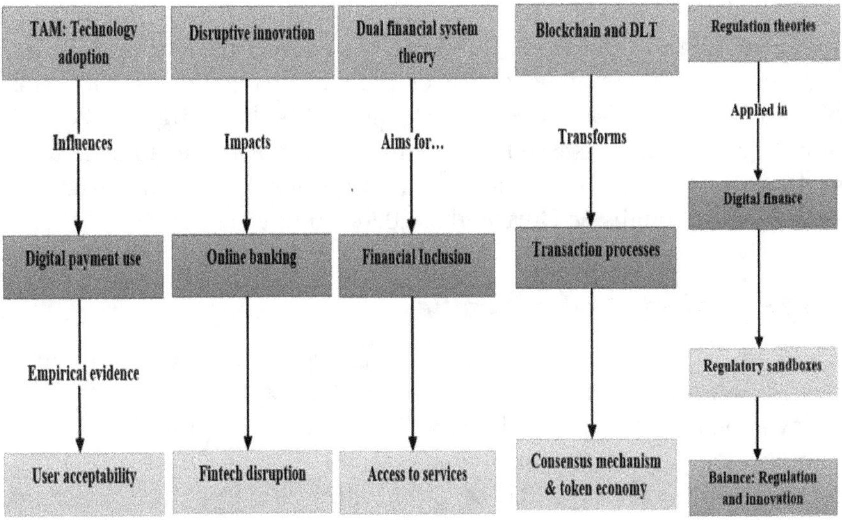

Figure 2.1. Relationships and flow between various concepts such as the technology adoption model.

replacing cash and check transactions. In the financial services industry, P2P lending platforms have emerged as a game-changer. Disintermediation, i.e. the elimination of middlemen, in financial transactions provides the theoretical basis for P2P lending. Platforms enabling this type of lending link borrowers and lenders directly, opening up new avenues for loan availability and investments, as studied by Khatun *et al.* (2021).

2.3.1. *DT and FI*

By lowering entry requirements, digital technology has been instrumental in expanding access to banking services and thus fostering financial inclusion. The World Bank promotes the use of digital channels and technology to increase access to financial services, particularly in underserved regions, via its Digital Financial Services (DFS) strategy. World Bank Group publications, such as *The Little Data Book on Financial Inclusion 2018*, emphasize the role of DFS in expanding access to financial services throughout the world (Chen *et al.*, 2021; Macchiavello & Siri, 2022).

The World Bank's 2016 *World Development Report* popularized the term "digital dividends" to describe the positive effects that digital technologies may have on development, particularly in the realm of financial inclusion. The report highlights how digital technology may allow underserved communities to join the formal banking system, potentially boosting economic development and mitigating poverty (Burroughs & Burroughs, 2020; Song *et al.*, 2022).

2.3.2. *Threats and difficulties*

There are hazards and difficulties associated with the digital finance sector. Several legislative, legal and technological hurdles need to be overcome in the transition to digital money. Cybersecurity risk management in the digital financial sector may be informed by theoretical frameworks (Matthess *et al.*, 2023; Xu *et al.*, 2023; Zhang *et al.*, 2022).

2.3.3. *Principles of digital technology's function in the finance sector*

Certain fundamental concepts explain the far-reaching effects of digital technology on financial services in the dynamic environment of the digital finance sector. Accessing, managing and interacting with monetary resources have all been profoundly altered by the advent of digitization, as discussed in other chapters. Here, we explore the underlying assumptions that characterize the impact of digital technology on this evolving industry (Ji *et al.*, 2021). This tenet aligns with the larger objective of "financial inclusion," ensuring all individuals, regardless of their location or economic standing, have access to a full range of financial products and services.

These online services have done away with the need for customers to physically visit banks, wait in queues or use paper documents. Faster processing of financial transactions is an extension of the notion of convenience that benefits both customers and banks (Wang *et al.*, 2021). The digital financial sector is characterized by upheaval and innovation. Disruptive technologies pose a threat to established industries and companies while opening the door for new, groundbreaking ventures like those in the FinTech sector. By highlighting how digital technology has altered the competitive environment, the idea of disruption encourages new developments in the financial services sector. To maintain their positions in the market, both new and established businesses must constantly experiment with new ideas (Song *et al.*, 2022).

The advent of digital technologies has ushered in a new age of data-driven decision-making in the financial sector. The basic idea is that with the help of data analytics and AI, banks can sift through mountains of data to learn more about their clients' habits, gauge the level of clients' risk tolerance and tailor their offerings to each individual. Using this data-driven strategy, businesses may better serve their customers and improve their services and internal processes (Chen *et al.*, 2021). In order to earn and retain their consumers' confidence, financial institutions and FinTech businesses must make safety a top priority. Blockchain, with its inherent security characteristics, has also emerged as a trusted technology backing cryptocurrencies and digital assets (Weili *et al.*, 2022).

The digital financial sector operates in a highly regulated and intricate market. Regulatory compliance is a notion that stresses the value of following all applicable rules and regulations. This is more important than ever, as governments and regulatory agencies seek a middle ground between encouraging innovation and protecting consumer interests. In order to promote innovation and provide regulatory oversight, compliance frameworks such as a regulatory sandbox have been implemented (Feng *et al.*, 2022). The importance of digital technology in the modern financial sector is summed up by these guiding concepts. They characterize how the advent of digital technology has made banking more widely accessible, productive and creative. To ensure that the development of digital financial services continues to benefit consumers, companies and society as a whole, these principles can serve as a navigational compass. Figure 2.2 shows the various functions of digital technology.

2.3.4. *Promotion of digital technology in the financial sector by government incentives and policies*

Governments throughout the world have launched initiatives to provide access to financial services for their citizens by implementing digital technologies. They attempt to alleviate poverty and boost

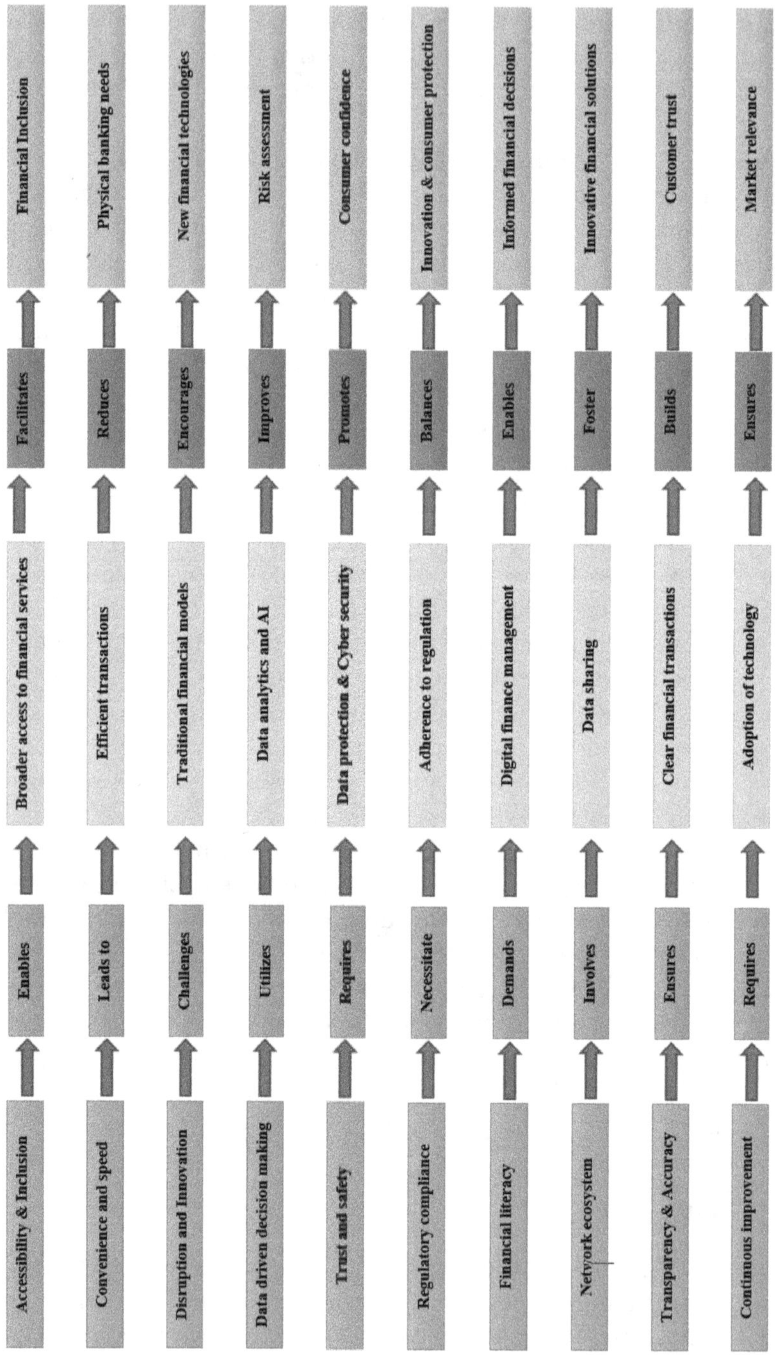

Figure 2.2. Digital technology's function.

economic growth by expanding access to financial services for disadvantaged groups. Financial institutions and FinTech firms are incentivized to create and expand digital financial services for the unbanked and underbanked by offering subsidies, grants and tax breaks. These programs frequently involve cooperation between governments, financial institutions and technology suppliers to offer low-cost, user-friendly digital financial solutions (Cao *et al.*, 2021; Ma & Zhu, 2022; Terho *et al.*, 2022).

New digital financial goods and services can be tested in "regulatory sandboxes" set up by governments to encourage innovation. These sandboxes provide a safe place for FinTech companies to try out new ideas while still adhering to all applicable financial rules and laws. Start-ups can improve their products in regulatory sandboxes without worrying about facing legal repercussions. These efforts have been critical in fostering FinTech innovation, increasing market competition and expanding consumer options in the digital financial sector.

Digital Identity and Know Your Customer (KYC) Initiatives: Digital identity solutions and improved KYC procedures are crucial components of the digital financial ecosystem. To provide citizens with safe and easy access to financial services, governments have realized the need for establishing a solid digital identification infrastructure. Numerous governments have introduced national digital identification projects to equip their citizens with online identifiers that are both reliable and foolproof. These efforts improve safety and make it easier for clients to begin using digital financial services by lowering the barriers they face throughout the onboarding process.

Governments have enacted data protection and privacy legislation to protect customer information as digital technologies in the financial sector grow increasingly important. Financial institutions and FinTech businesses are subject to stringent data security and privacy requirements, such as the EU's General Data Protection Regulation (GDPR) and data protection legislation in other nations. These policies are meant to safeguard customers' financial and personal information, and their enforcement falls within the purview of government agencies and regulatory groups (Kim *et al.*, 2021;

Lopez-Ercilla *et al.*, 2021; Zeng *et al.*, 2022; Zhang, 2021; Zhao *et al.*, 2023).

Governments recognize the significance of nurturing thriving FinTech ecosystems and strive to achieve them. They support FinTech businesses and innovation centers by providing a variety of resources, including regulatory sandboxes, financing, grants and incubator programs. These efforts foster an entrepreneurial spirit, attract top talent and make the local area more welcoming to FinTech companies.

E-Government and Digital Services Integration: To boost the efficiency of government services and promote digital financial inclusion, governments have incorporated digital financial services into their e-government platforms. Taxes, social benefits and other services provided by the government can now be accessed and paid for online. Because of this streamlining, citizens are more likely to use online banking and other digital financial services.

The promotion of digital technology in the digital finance sector has been greatly aided by government incentives and legislation. Governments have established an atmosphere conducive to the growth of digital financial services by encouraging innovation, guaranteeing consumer safety and eliminating regulatory hurdles. The sector as a whole benefits from these efforts, which ensure progress in attaining the larger societal objectives of financial inclusion, economic development and increased access to financial services. Governments will undoubtedly continue to play a crucial role in defining the future of the digital finance sector through deliberate regulations and incentives.

2.4. Participation of Stakeholders in the Digital Financial Sector

There are many different players in the digital finance industry, and they all have their own goals and responsibilities within the larger ecosystem. The prosperity and longevity of a sector depend on active participation by its stakeholders. Banks, FinTech companies, regulators, customers and technology firms are all vital to the success of the digital finance sector. The sector also relies heavily on the services of financial institutions, such as banks and credit unions. In an effort to expand their consumer base and provide better service, they are often the first to embrace innovative digital tools. To increase the use of digital financial solutions, it is crucial to communicate with these parties. So, it is no surprise that banks and FinTech firms have been more frequently working together to provide cutting-edge financial services and products.

2.4.1. *Problems facing the digital financial sector*

While the digital finance sector presents many exciting opportunities, it also confronts a number of critical difficulties that have an influence on stakeholders and the ecosystem as a whole. Cybersecurity threats are one of the biggest problems plaguing the online finance sector today. As more financial transactions and data transfers are performed online, the sector is becoming a prominent target for hackers and cybercriminals. Financial institutions and technology companies in particular need to make substantial investments in cybersecurity measures to ensure the safety of sensitive data and the continued confidence of their customers.

Digital technology holds the potential to improve financial inclusion for underserved and unbanked communities, but it also creates barriers to entry for these groups. Challenges to these populations' use of digital financial services include limited access, unaffordability and a lack of digital proficiency. For digital financial services to be successful, it is essential to first establish and then retain a high level of customer trust. Due to concerns about security and fraud, many customers are still hesitant to use digital financial services. To alleviate these fears and encourage widespread use, consumer education and awareness initiatives are crucial. Interoperability, which ensures that multiple digital financial systems work together effortlessly, is also a challenge. When several kinds of electronic currencies, such as digital wallets and financial applications, fail to work together smoothly, interoperability concerns arise.

2.4.2. *Implications of challenges*

Several parties and the industry as a whole are affected by the difficulties encountered in the digital financial sector. Financial institutions, FinTech businesses and technology suppliers need to invest heavily in cybersecurity measures to reduce the risk of cyberattacks. This involves adopting sophisticated encryption and threat detection systems, as well as performing regular security audits. Stakeholders should use adaptable regulatory techniques to meet the changing nature of regulations. This might include working closely with authorities, monitoring regulatory developments and making preemptive adjustments to operations as needed to guarantee compliance.

More stringent data protection procedures are required because of the significance of confidentiality when handling personal information. Encrypting data, obtaining consent for collecting personal information and ensuring transparency in data usage practices are all necessary steps. Designing digital financial solutions that are accessible to a wide audience is a top priority for stakeholders. This involves fixing accessibility issues and making interfaces easy to use for people with varied levels of computer literacy. Building consumer confidence calls for a strategy that focuses on the customer. All parties involved should emphasize open lines of communication, prompt responses from customer service representatives and intuitive interfaces that balance safety and use. Addressing interoperability issues requires collaboration among the concerned parties. Interoperability may be improved by adopting and adhering to industry standards and protocols, but this also requires cooperation between many parties.

2.4.3. *Recent challenges in the digital financial industry*

Rapid changes in the financial sector's regulatory environment create challenges related to compliance and regulatory ambiguity. FinTech developments such as cryptocurrencies, DeFi and digital assets pose challenges for governments and regulatory bodies, which are trying to figure out how to successfully regulate them. Cross-border businesses face difficulties due to a lack of uniformity in rules between countries, which may lead to legal issues for market players. It might be considered a waste of time and money for banks and FinTech companies to make the rapid adjustments necessary to keep up with regulatory changes and upgrades. The importance of environmental, social and governance (ESG) factors in the online banking sector

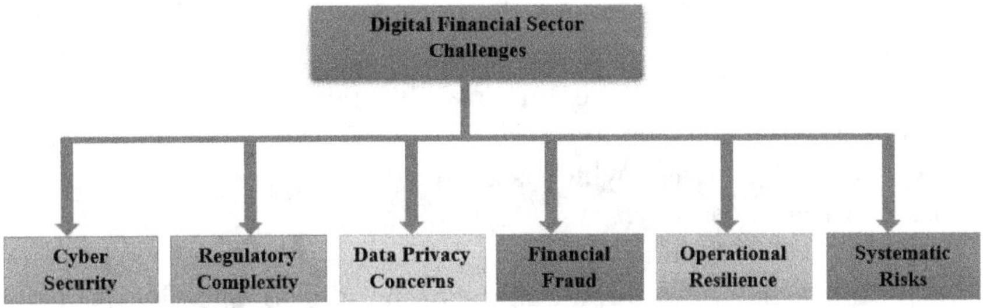

Figure 2.3. Digital finance: Challenges.

has grown in recent years. There is growing awareness of how economic actions affect environmental and social well-being. The need for banks and FinTech firms to address ESG concerns is increasing as digital financial services become more linked with these goals. The financial services business has both obstacles and opportunities in achieving ESG objectives while providing those services. Figure 2.3 illustrates the challenges faced in digital finance.

2.4.4. *The function of government policy in ensuring the long-term success of the digital financial sector*

The digital finance sector is at the crossroads of the banking and IT sectors, and it is revolutionizing the way we handle our finances. One of the many possibilities and problems that this expanding business presents is ensuring its long-term viability. The sector's rapid transition to digital technology may have far-reaching consequences for ecology, culture and the economy. In this section, we discuss the importance of public policy in fostering long-term success in the digital financial sector. We discuss what role governments and regulators may play in shaping the future of the digital financial sector, encouraging ethical practices and making sure it helps achieve broader sustainability objectives.

Sustainability in the digital financial sector is addressed through public policy on several fronts, including the ESG factors. Financial inclusion is prioritized by many governments because of its importance for social sustainability. Financial exclusion may be mitigated if digital technologies can enable underprivileged communities to gain more access to financial resources. To prevent marginalized groups from being left behind in the digital transition, regulators might require universal access to digital financial services. In addition, public policy should encourage financial literacy programs that help people make smarter and more farsighted decisions about their money in the digital age, which is good for everyone's financial health and the overall economy.

Regulation of digital payment systems is a prominent example of how public policy affects the long-term viability of the digital financial sector. Governments and regulatory agencies are responsible for protecting the safety, reliability and fairness of online payment systems as their use grows. Concerns such as preventing fraud, safeguarding consumers and ensuring a level playing field are all part of this. Trust in digital payment systems is bolstered by regulations that ensure financial transactions are conducted in a safe and secure environment, thus contributing to the long-term health of the economy.

Another key feature of sustainability in the digital financial sector is the promotion of responsible innovation. FinTech firms are driving innovation in the financial sector by releasing game-changing products and services. Public policy may achieve a balance between supporting innovation and defending against possible hazards. For instance, regulatory sandboxes provide a safe space for FinTech companies to experiment with new ideas under the watchful eye of regulators. This method permits exploration and education without jeopardizing customer security or market integrity.

Additionally, public policy may encourage openness and responsibility in the online banking industry. Regulations governing the ethical use of client data are necessary because of the proliferation of data analytics and AI. Financial institutions may better serve their customers by using data to their advantage if data privacy and security standards are in place to secure their customers' private information. Ethical guidelines for the use of algorithms and AI in financial decision-making can help avoid discriminatory practices and promote fairness, contributing to social sustainability.

Digital currencies and blockchain technology are not immune to the influence of public policies aimed at ensuring the long-term viability of the digital financial sector. Governments are struggling to figure out how to regulate cryptocurrencies as their popularity grows. Taxation policies, Anti-Money Laundering (AML) measures and KYC checks are critical for deterring criminal behavior and preserving economic security. Since cryptocurrency mining can be quite energy-intensive, it is important to identify mining techniques that do not harm the environment.

Blockchain technology, the basis of cryptocurrencies and applicable beyond the realm of digital currencies, necessitates regulatory frameworks of its own. Public policy may stimulate the development of blockchain solutions with positive environmental and social consequences. Sustainable items, such as minerals obtained in a socially responsible manner or organic foods, may have their origins tracked using blockchain-based supply chains. Regulations that encourage the use of such blockchain-based solutions have the potential to boost sustainability initiatives in many sectors.

2.5. Studying the Impact of Digital Technology on the Future of the Digital Financial Sector

The digital financial sector is reliant on R&D to remain at the cutting edge of technology. It's what keeps the industry moving forward, as it requires constant innovation and adaption of digital tools. Financial institutions, FinTech start-ups and technology suppliers cannot meet the ever-evolving demands of their clientele without investing heavily in R&D.

R&D in the digital finance industry is diverse and spans several disciplines. User experience (UX) and interface design are among the main focuses. As the sector becomes more digitalized, ensuring that digital platforms are user-friendly, intuitive and accessible is vital. R&D teams work relentlessly to enhance the designs of mobile banking applications, internet payment gateways and investment platforms. The objective is to design user interfaces that are more convenient and enjoyable to use than conventional methods of accessing financial services.

New financial products and services rely heavily on R&D efforts. Everything from DeFi platforms that allow P2P lending and borrowing without traditional intermediaries to personalized robo-advisors that use ML algorithms to craft investment portfolios tailored to individual preferences is included in this innovation. R&D is constantly improving and expanding the theoretical frameworks and models that support these breakthroughs.

R&D activities are also concentrated on blockchain technology and its use in digital banking. The distributed ledger features of blockchain are being investigated by researchers and developers for their potential to improve the safety, openness and efficacy of financial transactions. One way that blockchain R&D is influencing the financial sector is via the development of smart contracts, which enable the automatic execution of agreements between parties. These developments may well cause a paradigm shift in the financial services industry as a whole.

Cybersecurity and risk management are two areas where digital finance has made considerable investments in R&D. With the increased digitalization of financial services, the sector confronts heightened cybersecurity risks and data privacy issues. Advanced cybersecurity protections, threat detection systems and data protection processes are the constant focus of several research initiatives. Additionally, risk models and predictive analytics enabled by AI and ML are used to evaluate and lessen threats to digital transactions and investments.

The digital finance sector invests heavily in R&D, with a focus on cutting-edge technologies such as quantum computing. The development of quantum computing presents both risks and rewards since it has the potential to undermine current encryption systems and security mechanisms. The goal of this research is to use quantum computing for trustworthy financial transactions and data management while staying one step ahead of potential dangers.

R&D is essential in the area of regulatory compliance to guarantee that digital financial services remain aligned with the ever-changing regulatory environment. R&D efforts have resulted in regulatory technology (RegTech) solutions that help financial institutions automate compliance operations, monitor transactions for suspicious activity and maintain compliance with growing regulatory standards. In addition to saving money, these innovations make regulatory reporting more precise and efficient.

2.5.1. *How digital technology will change the future of the financial sector*

The impact of digital technology on the financial sector has been profoundly transformative. It has had far-reaching effects, from improving accessibility and convenience to stimulating innovation and increasing productivity. It is becoming clearer, as we look into the future of digital technology in this sector, that it will play a critical role in molding the financial ecosystem in the coming years.

There is no doubt that the widespread availability of digital technology has facilitated easy access to financial services for many. In the past, those who lived in rural or underserved regions found it much harder to access banking services since they had to physically visit a branch. However, the ubiquitous availability of cell phones and internet access, brought about by digital technology, has completely altered this scene. The widespread availability of banking services via mobile devices and laptops has made financial management a breeze for the average person. The rise of digital technology has greatly widened access to financial services, allowing formerly excluded groups to fully participate in modern economic life.

Digital technology has not only made financial transactions more accessible but has also made them more convenient than ever before. Long bank lines and paper checks are now a thing of the past. Today, users can quickly transfer money, pay bills and make purchases with a few clicks on their smartphones. The digital banking sector has produced user-friendly interfaces and smart mobile applications, prioritizing user experience. Individuals increasingly prefer the simplicity and speed of digital transactions, which has resulted in the widespread use of digital financial services.

In addition, advancements in digital technology have led to the development of cutting-edge financial services and products. In the FinTech sector in particular, the proliferation of new services is a direct result of the use of digital technologies. Traditional financial institutions have been disrupted, and the competitive environment has been transformed by new technologies, including P2P lending platforms, robo-advisors and DeFi apps. Incumbents have been forced to adapt and innovate with the emergence of these disruptors, which has resulted in better services and often more competitive pricing for customers. Customers of financial services are the ultimate beneficiaries of this dynamic competitive environment, which encourages constant development and new approaches.

In addition, digital technology has greatly improved the speed and openness of monetary dealings. Particularly, blockchain technology has been a game-changer in this respect. It provides immutable digital ledgers that cannot be altered, cutting out middlemen and lowering the risk of fraud. Automated smart contracts on a blockchain network streamline operations and leave less room for legal issues. Since this technology guarantees openness and immutability of documents, it also boosts confidence in financial transactions.

The success of digital technology in business has also been greatly aided by data analytics and AI. Financial institutions and FinTech firms can use these tools to study client patterns, evaluate credit risks and tailor their offerings to each individual. Big data and ML algorithms allow businesses to make evidence-based decisions, cater to customers' unique tastes and provide better service. Using AI-driven insights, banks could significantly improve their customer service by customizing their products and services according to an individual's financial situation and ambitions.

Several significant patterns and changes emerge when we consider the long-term future of digital technology in the finance sector. The constant development of new payment methods is a major change. There will likely be an even greater uptick in the use of digital wallets, contactless payments and the acceptance of cryptocurrencies, further diminishing the need for actual currency and conventional payment methods. The issuance and management of digital currencies by governments may also be revolutionized by the introduction of central bank digital currencies (CBDCs).

Decentralization, as shown by blockchain technology and DeFi, is also projected to grow in popularity. By eliminating the need for centralized institutions such as banks and payment processors, these technologies may usher in a new era of decentralized banking. This move might allow people to have more control over their financial assets and engage in P2P financial activities, eventually democratizing finance further.

The digital financial sector will continue to be a prime target for cybercriminals, making cybersecurity an essential area of concern. The industry will continue to invest in strong cybersecurity measures and research future technologies, such as quantum-resistant encryption, to preserve financial assets and data.

Governments will keep trying to find a middle ground between encouraging innovation and protecting consumers; therefore, the regulatory environment will continue to shift. There will be greater certainty and stability in the market once regulatory frameworks for cryptocurrencies, digital asset exchanges and FinTech businesses are well established.

2.6. Conclusions

The digital financial sector is a dynamic environment where digital technology plays a vital and revolutionary role, positioned at the crossroads of finance and technology. In this chapter, we explored the many facets of digital technology's impact on business, including its origins, theoretical foundations, impact on financial services and efficacy. As we wrap up our investigation, a few major conclusions stand out.

There has been a dramatic change in the accessibility, delivery and user experience of financial services because of digitization. This change did not happen quickly but rather was the culmination of decades of technical development. The development of the internet and the widespread availability of personal computers and mobile devices laid the groundwork for the modern digital financial services sector. Theoretical frameworks have provided valuable tools for studying the online banking sector, illuminating the dynamics of the market in relation to technology adoption, disruptive innovation, financial inclusion and regulatory and policy issues. These ideas have been crucial in explaining historical events and continue to shed light on current phenomena and open up exciting prospects for the future.

The widespread use of digital technology has revolutionized the financial services industry by increasing its availability, adaptability and efficacy. It has expanded access to financial services, hence democratizing the industry. Traditional financial services have been disrupted by digital innovations such as digital payment systems, P2P lending platforms, robo-advisors, cryptocurrencies and DeFi. FinTech firms have emerged as a disruptive force in the financial services sector of the digital economy. The creative business models, simplified procedures and user-friendly interfaces presented by these disruptors have forced the status quo to change or collapse. As a result of increased competition, customers now have access to more choices, many of which are available at lower prices.

The elimination of middlemen and the improvement of security are two major benefits of blockchain technology, which have led to its widespread adoption for recording and verifying financial transactions. "Smart contracts" – developed on blockchain platforms – automate contractual agreements, thereby eliminating the need for human intervention and reducing the likelihood of conflicts. AI and data analytics have also enabled more informed decision-making, customized financial offerings and enhanced user experiences.

Financial inclusion has been greatly aided by the spread of digital technologies. Millions of people and companies that were previously shut out of the financial system are now able to participate because digitization has lowered the barriers to entry for financial services. This is especially true in rural and underserved regions. The World Bank's notion of digital dividends highlights the potential for digital technology to have far-reaching positive effects on development. Despite the evident advantages of digital technology, there are also hazards and difficulties in the digital financial business. Constant worries about cyberattacks and data breaches call for strict safety precautions. Policymakers continue to seek a middle ground between fostering innovation and protecting consumer interests, which makes the framing of regulatory and compliance policies particularly challenging.

Looking forward, it is obvious that the digital financial sector will continue to develop due to a multitude of factors, including the emergence of new ideas, regulatory responses and the ever-growing potential of digital technology. The industry's digitalization journey is far from over, and we can expect significant, even revolutionary, changes in the years to come.

In conclusion, the persisting impact of digital technology on the financial sector is a testament to the strength of innovation and adaptability in the face of technological change. It has opened up access to financial services for more people, increased competition and boosted both the effectiveness and openness of financial markets. Although there are still obstacles to overcome, the banking sector has shown to be highly resilient and adept at capitalizing on digital technology, making it an essential part of the contemporary financial system. We must keep an eye on this rapidly evolving area, as digital technology remains a major factor in the ever-changing financial sector.

2.6.1. *Practical insights, future directions and implications*

The impact of digital technology on the finance sector has been revolutionary, with far-reaching repercussions for consumers, regulators and businesses alike. As we dive into these insightful findings and ramifications, we must also consider how this dynamic topic may evolve in terms of future research. One of the most useful takeaways is how much of a difference customer service can make. Financial institutions and FinTech businesses may now provide individualized services, simplify operations and prioritize customer satisfaction thanks to advancements in digital technology. This suggests that companies with a focus on efficiency and the needs of their customers would likely perform well in the emerging digital financial sector. More in-depth studies of client tastes and habits in the digital age might inform the design of even more individualized financial products in the future.

The regulatory framework is an important part of the digital finance sector. Regulators must balance the need to encourage innovation while protecting consumers and preserving the stability of the market as technology develops. A collaborative strategy, such as regulatory sandboxes, seems to strike the proper balance, according to practical observations. Innovative regulatory frameworks and their efficacy in a dynamic setting should be studied more in the future.

The use of digital technology has allowed previously disadvantaged individuals to gain access to financial services. Therefore, in practice, banks and governments should continue funding efforts to bring the unbanked into the financial mainstream. Future studies should focus on assessing the long-term effects of digital financial inclusion initiatives on GDP growth and equality. The advantages of digital technology are offset by concerns about security and privacy. The need for rigorous cybersecurity safeguards and constant monitoring is shown by real-world examples. Emerging cybersecurity dangers and possible remedies, as well as the ever-changing landscape of data protection rules, should be another focus of future studies. Innovative monetary ecosystems have been established thanks to blockchain technology and DeFi. Insights from the real world suggest that these technologies may threaten the status quo of financial intermediaries and give rise to entirely new financial models. Concerns about blockchain and DeFi's scalability, sustainability and regulatory compliance, as well as their potential effects on the financial sector, may be explored in future studies.

In conclusion, our literature study and theoretical backdrop have shed light on the essential significance of digital technology in the digital financial sector. We have examined the many facets of this dynamic business, including its origins and theoretical underpinnings, the growth of payment systems, the emergence of FinTech disruptors and the effects on financial inclusion (Guo *et al.*, 2023; Razzaq *et al.*, 2023; Yu *et al.*, 2020).

The rise of digital technology has altered the economic environment in exciting ways. Researchers, practitioners and policymakers who want to succeed in this dynamic field would do well to familiarize themselves with the relevant theory and evidence. As we proceed, the digital financial sector will likely continue to grow, driven by innovation, regulatory responses and the ever-expanding possibilities of digital technology (Wang *et al.*, 2022a).

References

Adam, I. & Fazekas, M. (2021). Are emerging technologies helping win the fight against corruption? A review of the state of evidence. *Information Economics and Policy*, 57, 100950. https://doi.org/10.1016/J.INFOECOPOL.2021.100950.

Asogwa, B. E. (2012). The challenge of managing electronic records in developing countries: Implications for records managers in sub Saharan Africa. *Records Management Journal*, 22(3), 198–211. https://doi.org/10.1108/09565691211283156.

Avelar-Sosa, L., García-Alcaraz, J. L., Mejía-Muñoz, J. M., Maldonado-Macías, A. A., & Hernández, G. A. (2018). Government support and market proximity: Exploring their relationship with supply chain agility and Financial performance. *Sustainability (Switzerland)*, 10(7). https://doi.org/10.3390/SU10072441.

Ayerbe, E., Berecibar, M., Clark, S., Franco, A. A., & Ruhland, J. (2022). Digitalization of battery manufacturing: Current status, challenges, and opportunities. *Advanced Energy Materials*, 12(17). https://doi.org/10.1002/aenm.202102696.

Barykin, S. Y., Kapustina, I. V., Sergeev, S. M., & Yadykin, V. K. (2020). Algorithmic foundations of economic and mathematical modeling of network logistics processes. *Journal of Open Innovation: Technology, Market, and Complexity*, 6(4), 1–16. https://doi.org/10.3390/joitmc6040189.

Beck, T. & Demirgüç-Kunt, A. (2008). Access to finance: An unfinished agenda. *The World Bank Economic Review*, 22(3), 383–396. https://doi.org/10.1093/wber/lhn021.

Broby, D. (2021). Financial technology and the future of banking. *Financial Innovation*, 7(1), 47.

Burroughs, B. & Burroughs, W. J. (2020). Digital logistics: Enchantment in distribution channels. *Technology in Society*, 62(April), 101277. https://doi.org/10.1016/j.techsoc.2020.101277.

Cao, S., Nie, L., Sun, H., Sun, W., & Taghizadeh-Hesary, F. (2021). Digital finance, green technological innovation and energy-environmental performance: Evidence from China's regional economies. *Journal of Cleaner Production*, 327. https://doi.org/10.1016/J.JCLEPRO.2021.129458.

Çelik, D., Meral, M. E., & Waseem, M. (2022). Investigation and analysis of effective approaches, opportunities, bottlenecks and future potential capabilities for digitalization of energy systems and sustainable development goals. *Electric Power Systems Research*, 211. https://doi.org/10.1016/j.epsr.2022.108251.

Chen, H. & Zhao, X. (2022). Green financial risk management based on intelligence service. *Journal of Cleaner Production*, 364. https://doi.org/10.1016/j.jclepro.2022.132617.

Chen, Y., Kumara, E. K., & Sivakumar, V. (2021). Investigation of finance industry on risk awareness model and digital economic growth. *Annals of Operations Research*. https://doi.org/10.1007/s10479-021-04287-7.

Deng, X., Huang, Z., & Cheng, X. (2019). FinTech and sustainable development: Evidence from China based on P2P data. *Sustainability (Switzerland)*, 11(22). https://doi.org/10.3390/SU11226434.

Feng, S., Zhang, R., & Li, G. (2022). Environmental decentralization, digital finance and green technology innovation. *Structural Change and Economic Dynamics*, 61, 70–83. https://doi.org/10.1016/J.STRUECO.2022.02.008.

Gadanidis, G. (2017). Artificial intelligence, computational thinking, and mathematics education. *International Journal of Information and Learning Technology*, 34(2), 133–139. https://doi.org/10.1108/IJILT-09-2016-0048.

Guo, B., Wang, Y., Zhang, H., Liang, C., Feng, Y., & Hu, F. (2023). Impact of the digital economy on high-quality urban economic development: Evidence from Chinese cities. *Economic Modelling*, 120. https://doi.org/10.1016/j.econmod.2023.106194.

Han, M., Li, Z., He, J., Wu, D., Xie, Y., & Baba, A. (2018, September). A novel blockchain-based education records verification solution. In

Proceedings of the 19th annual SIG conference on information technology education (pp. 178–183). https://doi.org/10.1145/3241815.3241870.

Ji, X., Wang, K., Xu, H., & Li, M. (2021). Has digital financial inclusion narrowed the urban-rural income gap: The role of entrepreneurship in China. *Sustainability (Switzerland)*, 13(15). https://doi.org/10.3390/SU13158292.

Kallai, T., Lendér, Z., & Lucz, G. (2022). What artificial intelligence and IoT (AIoT) can deliver to scale up the hydrogen economy? https://doi.org/10.13140/RG.2.2.32118.06726.

Khan, S. A. R., Ibrahim, R. L., Al-Amin, A. Q., & Yu, Z. (2022). An ideology of sustainability under technological revolution: Striving towards sustainable development. *Sustainability (Switzerland)*, 14(8). https://doi.org/10.3390/SU14084415.

Khatun, M. N., Mitra, S., & Sarker, M. N. I. (2021). Mobile banking during COVID-19 pandemic in Bangladesh: A novel mechanism to change and accelerate people's financial access. *Green Finance*, 3(3), 253–267. https://doi.org/10.3934/gf.2021013.

Kim, H. J., Yi, P., & Hong, J. I. (2021). Are schools digitally inclusive for all? Profiles of school digital inclusion using PISA 2018. *Computers & Education*, 170, 104226. https://doi.org/10.1016/j.compedu.2021.104226.

Li, J., Li, N., Peng, J., Cui, H., & Wu, Z. (2019). Energy consumption of cryptocurrency mining: A study of electricity consumption in mining cryptocurrencies. *Energy*, 168, 160–168. https://doi.org/10.1016/J.ENERGY.2018.11.046.

Lin, C.-Y., Chau, K. Y., Tran, T. K., Sadiq, M., Van, L., & Hien Phan, T. T. (2022). Development of renewable energy resources by green finance, volatility and risk: Empirical evidence from China. *Renewable Energy*, 201(P1), 821–831. https://doi.org/10.1016/j.renene.2022.10.086.

Ma, D. & Zhu, Q. (2022). Innovation in emerging economies: Research on the digital economy driving high-quality green development. *Journal of Business Research*, 145, 801–813. https://doi.org/10.1016/j.jbusres.2022.03.041.

Macchiavello, E. & Siri, M. (2022). Sustainable finance and fintech: Can technology contribute to achieving environmental goals? A preliminary assessment of "green fintech" and "sustainable digital finance." *European Company and Financial Law Review*, 19(1), 128–174. https://doi.org/10.1515/ECFR-2022-0005.

Matthess, M., Kunkel, S., Dachrodt, M. F., & Beier, G. (2023). The impact of digitalization on energy intensity in manufacturing sectors — A panel data analysis for Europe. *Journal of Cleaner Production*, 397. https://doi.org/10.1016/j.jclepro.2023.136598.

Michalik, A., Besenfelder, C., & Henke, M. (2019). Servitization of small- and medium-sized manufacturing enterprises: Facing barriers through the Dortmund management model. *IFAC-PapersOnLine*, 52(13), 2326–2331. https://doi.org/10.1016/j.ifacol.2019.11.553.

Miśkiewicz, R., Matan, K., & Karnowski, J. (2022). The role of crypto trading in the economy, renewable energy consumption and ecological degradation. *Energies*, 15(10). https://doi.org/10.3390/EN15103805.

Mo, Y., Sun, D., & Zhang, Y. (2023). Green finance assists agricultural sustainable development: Evidence from China. *Sustainability*, 15(3), 2056. https://doi.org/10.3390/SU15032056.

Ofori, E. K., Onifade, S. T., Ali, E. B., Alola, A. A., & Zhang, J. (2023). Achieving carbon neutrality in post COP26 in BRICS, MINT, and G7 economies: The role of financial development and governance indicators. *Journal of Cleaner Production*, 387(January), 135853. https://doi.org/10.1016/j.jclepro.2023.135853.

Peña-Martel, D., Pérez-Alemán, J., & Santana-Martín, D. J. (2018). The role of the media in creating earnings informativeness: Evidence from Spain. *BRQ Business Research Quarterly*, 21(3), 168–179. https://doi.org/10.1016/J.BRQ.2018.03.004.

Razzaq, A., Sharif, A., Ozturk, I., & Skare, M. (2023). Asymmetric influence of digital finance, and renewable energy technology innovation on green growth in China. *Renewable Energy*, 202, 310–319. https://doi.org/10.1016/j.renene.2022.11.082.

Ricci, R., Battaglia, D., & Neirotti, P. (2021). External knowledge search, opportunity recognition and industry 4.0 adoption in SMEs. *International Journal of Production Economics*, 240. https://doi.org/10.1016/j.ijpe.2021.108234.

Salampasis, D. & Mention, A. L. (2018). FinTech: Harnessing innovation for financial inclusion. In Chuen, D. K. L. & Deng, R. (Eds.), *Handbook of Blockchain, Digital Finance, and Inclusion* (Vol. 2, pp. 451–461). https://doi.org/10.1016/C2016-0-03679-3.

Sebestyén, V. & Abonyi, J. (2021). Data-driven comparative analysis of national adaptation pathways for Sustainable Development Goals. *Journal of Cleaner Production*, 319(December 2020), 128657. https://doi.org/10.1016/j.jclepro.2021.128657.

Shahzad, U., Ferraz, D., Nguyen, H. H., & Cui, L. (2022). Investigating the spill overs and connectedness between financial globalization, high-tech industries and environmental footprints: Fresh evidence in context of China. *Technological Forecasting and Social Change*, 174. https://doi.org/10.1016/J.TECHFORE.2021.121205.

Song, M., Peng, L., Shang, Y., & Zhao, X. (2022). Green technology progress and total factor productivity of resource-based enterprises:

A perspective of technical compensation of environmental regulation. *Technological Forecasting and Social Change*, 174. https://doi.org/10.1016/J.TECHFORE.2021.121276.

Terho, H., Mero, J., Siutla, L., & Jaakkola, E. (2022). Digital content marketing in business markets: Activities, consequences, and contingencies along the customer journey. *Industrial Marketing Management*, 105, 294–310. https://doi.org/10.1016/J.INDMARMAN.2022.06.006.

Venkatesh, V., Morris, M. G., Davis, G. B., & Davis, F. D. (2003). User acceptance of information technology: Toward a unified view. *MIS Quarterly*, 425–478. https://doi.org/10.2307/30036540.

Wang, J., Dong, K., Dong, X., & Taghizadeh-Hesary, F. (2022a). Assessing the digital economy and its carbon-mitigation effects: The case of China. *Energy Economics*, 113. https://doi.org/10.1016/j.eneco.2022.106198.

Wang, L., Chen, Y., Ramsey, T. S., & Hewings, G. J. D. (2021). Will researching digital technology really empower green development? *Technology in Society*, 66. https://doi.org/10.1016/j.techsoc.2021.101638.

Wang, Y., Lucey, B., Vigne, S. A., & Yarovaya, L. (2022b). An index of cryptocurrency environmental attention (ICEA). *China Finance Review International*, 12(3), 378–414. https://doi.org/10.1108/CFRI-09-2021-0191.

Weili, L., Khan, H., Khan, I., & Han, L. (2022). The impact of information and communication technology, financial development, and energy consumption on carbon dioxide emission: Evidence from the Belt and Road countries. *Environmental Science and Pollution Research*, 29(19), 27703–27718. https://doi.org/10.1007/S11356-021-18448-5/TABLES/6.

Xu, A., Qian, F., Ding, H., & Zhang, X. (2023). Digitalization of logistics for transition to a resource-efficient and circular economy. *Resources Policy*, 83. https://doi.org/10.1016/j.resourpol.2023.103616.

Yu, L., Zhao, D., Xue, Z., & Gao, Y. (2020). Research on the use of digital finance and the adoption of green control techniques by family farms in China. *Technology in Society*, 62. https://doi.org/10.1016/J.TECHSOC.2020.101323.

Zhang, D., Mohsin, M., & Taghizadeh-Hesary, F. (2022). Does green finance counteract the climate change mitigation: Asymmetric effect of renewable energy investment and R&D. *Energy Economics*, 113. https://doi.org/10.1016/j.eneco.2022.106183.

Zhang, H. (2021). Trade openness and green total factor productivity in China: The role of ICT-based digital trade. *Frontiers in Environmental Science*, 9. https://doi.org/10.3389/FENVS.2021.809339.

Zhang, Y. Q. (2023). Impact of green finance and environmental protection on green economic recovery in South Asian economies: mediating role of FinTech. *Economic Change and Restructuring.* https://doi.org/10.1007/S10644-023-09500-0.

Zeng, X., Li, S., & Yousaf, Z. (2022). Artificial intelligence adoption and digital innovation: How does digital resilience act as a mediator and training protocols as a moderator? *Sustainability (Switzerland)*, 14(14). https://doi.org/10.3390/SU14148286.

Zhao, S., Zhang, L., An, H., Peng, L., Zhou, H., & Hu, F. (2023). Has China's low-carbon strategy pushed forward the digital transformation of manufacturing enterprises? Evidence from the low-carbon city pilot policy. *Environmental Impact Assessment Review*, 102, 107184. https://doi.org/10.1016/j.eiar.2023.107184.

https://doi.org/10.1142/9781800616257_0003

Chapter 3

Impact of Digital Finance on Global Climate Change: Sectoral Evidence

Muhammad Shahzad Ijaz[*,§], **Mushtaq Hussain Khan**[†,¶], **and Ujala Siddique**[‡,‖]

**Ilma University, Karachi, Pakistan*
†Cardiff School of Management, Cardiff Metropolitan University, Cardiff, UK
‡Centre for Aerospace & Security Studies (CASS), Islamabad, Pakistan
§ms.ijaaz@gmail.com
¶mkhan3@cardiffmet.ac.uk
‖ujala.emails@gmail.com

Abstract

Concerning the issue of global climate change, an urgent response is required to decrease carbon emissions in alignment with the Paris Agreement (12 December 2015), particularly in achieving the Sustainable Development Goals (SDGs). Over the past few decades, the mining of cryptocurrencies has emerged as a significant contributor to carbon emissions due to the rapid growth of the cryptocurrency market, resulting in a substantial increase in the computational demands of mining machines and energy consumption associated with generating digital tokens. This chapter aims to investigate the impact of digital currency trading activities (digital finance) on climate change. To achieve this objective, this study employs the DCC-GARCH model using daily trading data of five major cryptocurrencies based on market capitalization (Bitcoin, Ethereum, Tether, BNB and Ripple) and global climate change (CO_2 emissions). Climate change data from five different sectors (power, ground transportation, residential, domestic aviation and international aviation) are used. The findings show that cryptocurrency mining (trading activity) leads to higher CO_2 emissions, particularly in the power sector, which, in turn, adversely impacts global climate change.

Keywords: Digital finance, cryptocurrency mining, CO_2 emissions, climate change.

3.1. Introduction

The role of digital finance in mitigating climate change issues is an emerging topic among academics and policymakers. On the one hand, the adverse impacts of climate change are widespread and can lead to more frequent extreme weather events, posing significant risks to public health (Zhang *et al.*, 2023). According to a 2018 report by the Intergovernmental Panel on Climate Change (IPCC), a global temperature increase of 1.5°C above pre-industrial levels due to the substantial rise in global carbon dioxide (CO_2) emissions may lead to irreversible environmental consequences, including the potential loss of Arctic ice and sea level rise. Taking swift and collective action is imperative to achieve a carbon-neutral transition, thereby mitigating the adverse impacts of climate change and addressing sustainability challenges, as emphasized by the IPCC in 2022. On the other hand, digital finance, in terms of technological advancements, not only brings new possibilities but also carries environmental implications. The cryptocurrency ecosystem, particularly blockchain technology, has seen a remarkable increase in market capitalization over the past decade. However, the growing energy consumption associated with blockchain-based crypto assets cannot be ignored (Corbet *et al.*, 2021; Huynh *et al.*, 2021). Moreover, Cambridge University's Bitcoin Electricity Consumption Index[1] estimated that Bitcoin mining accounts for 0.38% of global electricity consumption, surpassing the electricity consumption of individual countries such as Belgium and Finland. The rapid growth of blockchain technology and the cryptocurrency market poses a potential challenge to global climate change mitigation efforts (Jiang *et al.*, 2021; Truby, 2018). Therefore, it is imperative to understand the environmental implications of digital financial innovation in the context of climate change.

---

[1]https://ccaf.io/cbnsi/cbeci.

This chapter attempts to highlight the interconnectedness of digital finance and environmental sustainability; Table 3.1 provides a summary of recent work on the digital finance–climate change nexus. For this purpose, five major cryptocurrencies – Bitcoin,

Table 3.1. Recent work on digital finance and climate change.

Source	Objective of the study	Main findings
Li *et al.* (2023)	To explore the connectedness between digital finance and low-carbon energy transition using data from 283 cities in China.	Digital finance enhances carbon total factor productivity and the percentage of clean energy utilization in overall energy consumption, thereby exerting a substantial positive impact on the low-carbon energy transition.
Qin *et al.* (2022)	Examination of digital finance and carbon emissions from the household sector in China.	On average, they found that digital finance is positively linked with household carbon emissions due to an increase in the consumption of carbon-emitting products.
Yu *et al.* (2022a)	Examination of green digital finance and climate change mitigation in carbon neutrality using a sample of 60 economies.	They noted that promoting digitally accessible green finance contributes to the advancement of green and renewable energy sources while mitigating CO_2 emissions.
Zhang *et al.* (2023)	Examination of the environmental implications of cryptocurrency energy consumption on climate change. Particularly, this study linked Bitcoin mining with residential sector CO_2 emissions.	A significant directional causality between the energy usage of Bitcoin mining and CO_2 emissions was found.
Ren *et al.* (2023)	Investigation of digital finance and corporate Environment, Social and Governance (ESG) performance using panel data of Chinese A-share listed corporations.	They found a significant role of digital finance in improving a firm's ESG performance, especially the environmental and social components.

(*Continued*)

Table 3.1. (*Continued*)

Source	Objective of the study	Main findings
Zhang *et al.* (2022)	Investigation of digital finance and environmental protection.	A significant reduction in carbon emissions was found due to technological innovation in terms of sustainable digital products.
Guo & Tu (2023)	To explore the role of financial supervision in the link between digital finance and decarbonization using a panel dataset of 284 prefecture-level cities in China.	They found a nonlinear relationship between digital finance and carbon intensity. The results also revealed that ensuring effective financial supervision is a crucial prerequisite for digital finance to effectively contribute to decarbonization efforts.
Galanti & Özsoy (2022)	Examination of digital finance and climate change using a sample of Sub-Saharan African countries.	They noted that digital finance plays a mitigating role in CO_2 emissions.
Wu *et al.* (2022)	By employing Chinese provincial panel data from 2011 to 2019, this study explored the impact of digital finance on CO_2 emissions.	They found that with the evolution of digital finance, the effectiveness of CO_2 emission reduction is enhanced when accompanied by higher levels of financial regulation, green development and the green finance index.
Hou *et al.* (2023)	This study examined the impact of digital finance and green technology innovation on environmental quality in China.	Their findings indicated that the implementation of pilot zones for green finance reform and innovative policies has led to improved environmental quality. Furthermore, digital finance and green technology innovation play a significant intermediary role in the relationship between green financial policy and environmental quality.

Table 3.1. (*Continued*)

Source	Objective of the study	Main findings
Yang *et al.* (2023)	This research utilized panel data encompassing 280 cities in China from 2011 to 2019 to empirically investigate the effectiveness of digital finance in managing carbon emission reductions.	They noted that digital finance helps in the reduction of carbon emissions. Furthermore, it also contributes to the reduction of carbon emission intensity within regions.
Yu *et al.* (2022b)	This study examined the climate issue by considering the role of digital finance in renewable energy consumption.	The findings demonstrated that digital finance, including its extensive coverage and usage, has significantly enhanced renewable energy consumption in China, which, in turn, promotes environmental sustainability.
Zhao *et al.* (2021)	This study utilized balanced panel data at the provincial level in China, spanning the period from 2011 to 2018, as a sample to empirically examine the relationship between digital finance and carbon emissions.	They noted that digital finance plays a significant role in mitigating carbon emissions in China and improving environmental sustainability.
Xue *et al.* (2022)	Using panel data from 278 cities, spanning the period from 2011 to 2019, this study conducted an empirical analysis to examine the relationship between digital finance and carbon emissions.	They documented the evidence that digital finance effectively mitigates carbon emissions at the regional level.

Ethereum, Tether, BNB and XRP – are considered measures of digital finance. Additionally, CO_2 emissions from five different sectors, namely power, ground transportation, residential, domestic aviation and international aviation, are used to quantify climate change. For empirical evaluation, the DCC-GARCH model is employed using daily trading volumes data of cryptocurrencies and sectoral climate change activity data from 1 January 2019 to 31 December 2022.

Overall, the main findings of our chapter are as follows. First, the trading activity of cryptocurrencies significantly impacts sectoral carbon emissions. Second, evidence suggests that the persistence of past volatility predicts future volatility for crypto assets and sectoral emissions, with an exception for Ripple (XRP). Third, in the long run, spillover effects are observed between crypto assets and sectoral emissions across all 25 combinations of crypto–sector pairs. Nevertheless, in the short run, no significant link has been observed between: residential sector emissions and four crypto assets – BNB, Bitcoin, Ethereum and Ripple; ground transport emissions and two crypto assets – Bitcoin and USDT; and international aviation emissions and USDT.

Motivated by growing concerns regarding the environmental impacts of digital finance, this chapter contributes to the emerging literature. Specifically, this chapter complements the works of Hunjra & Hanif (2023), Li *et al.* (2023), Ho *et al.* (2022), Yu *et al.* (2022b), Zhang *et al.* (2022), Ha *et al.* (2021) and Cao *et al.* (2021).

3.2. Data and Empirical Evaluation

3.2.1. *Data*

This chapter attempts to unravel the dynamic linkages between digital finance and climate change. To measure climate change, we use the sectoral CO_2 emissions of five sectors, namely power, ground transport, residential, domestic aviation and international aviation, whereas digital finance is measured in terms of the trading activity of five major cryptocurrencies, namely Bitcoin, Ethereum, Tether, BNB and Ripple. Data regarding climate change are obtained from the website of Carbon Monitor.[2] Zhang *et al.* (2023) used the same data on CO_2 emissions as a measure of climate change. Additionally, the trading volumes of the cryptocurrencies are obtained from the

[2]https://carbonmonitor.org/.

Table 3.2. Details of variables used in the study.

Asset/index	Proxy	Abbreviation	Description
Crypto Assets	Bitcoin Ethereum Tether BNB XRP	BTC ETH USDT BNB XRP	The trading activity of five leading crypto assets selected based on market capitalization is considered a proxy for digital finance.
Climate Change	Power Ground Transport Residential Domestic Aviation International Aviation	Pow GTPT RSD DAVI IAVI	The primary reason for climate change lies in the emission of carbon dioxide (CO_2). Carbon Monitor is a global initiative that offers, for the first time, regularly updated, scientifically grounded approximations of daily CO_2 emissions.

CoinMarketCap[3] and Yahoo Finance websites. We use the daily trading volumes and sectoral CO_2 emissions data for the period spanning from 1 January 2019 to 31 December 2022. Table 3.2 presents the details of the variables used in the study for analysis.

3.2.2. *DCC-GARCH model*

For empirical investigation, the DCC-GARCH model (Engle, 2002) is used. Let the mean equation follow an AR(1) process for V_t:

$$V_t = \alpha + \varepsilon_t, \tag{3.1}$$

where V_t is the vector of volume data (level of activity data) of a given cryptocurrency (Bitcoin, Ethereum, Tether, BNB or XRP) and climate change (CO_2 emissions). Climate change data are used from five different sectors, namely power, ground transportation, residential, domestic aviation and international aviation. The residuals are

[3]https://coinmarketcap.com/.

modeled as

$$\epsilon_t = h_t^{1/2} z_t. \tag{3.2}$$

The variance equation of the DCC model takes the form

$$h_t = \Omega + \alpha\epsilon_{t-1}^2 + \beta h_{t-1}, \tag{3.3}$$

where h_t is a $n \times n$ conditional covariance matrix. α and β are the model parameters to capture the ARCH and GARCH effects.

The time-varying correlation estimator between the two types of assets is

$$\rho_{i,j,t} = \frac{q_{i,j,t}}{\sqrt{q_{i,i,t}q_{j,j,t}}}, \tag{3.4}$$

$$Q_t = (1 - \theta_1 - \theta_2)\bar{Q} + \theta_1 Z_{t-1}Z'_{t-1} + \theta_2 Q_{t-1}, \tag{3.5}$$

where Q_t and $\bar{Q}$ are the variance and covariance matrix of the standardized residuals z_t.

3.3. Empirical Analysis

3.3.1. *Preliminary analysis*

To investigate the spillover effect between digital finance and climate change, we apply the dynamic conditional correlation model. Table 3.3 presents the data description based on the natural logarithm of each series. Results show that the mean trading activity is positive for all crypto assets. The highest mean value is recorded for Tether (USDT), followed by Bitcoin (BTC), whereas the lowest mean trading activity is observed for BNB and Ripple (XRP). This shows the most and least traded crypto assets among the five cryptocurrencies. Further, average emissions are positive for all sectors except domestic aviation. The highest mean value is recorded for the power sector (POW), followed by the ground transport sector (GTPT), whereas the lowest mean emissions are observed for domestic aviation (DAVI) and international aviation (IAVI). This shows the highest and lowest carbon emissions among the five sectors. Overall, high standard deviations are observed for BNB, Ripple (XPR) and Tether (USDT), and low deviations are observed for the power (POW), ground transport (GTPT) and domestic aviation

Table 3.3. Descriptive statistics.

	Mean	SD	Kurt.	Skew.	Min.	Max.	JB	ARCH	ADF	Count
BNB	20.298	1.158	−0.566	−0.009	16.943	23.612	19.54*	0.139***	−4.617***	1461
BTC	24.031	0.565	1.007	−0.499	22.187	26.584	122.54*	0.178***	−8.656***	1461
ETH	23.297	0.641	−0.023	−0.252	21.517	25.159	15.58*	0.0634*	−7.209***	1461
USDT	24.418	0.785	0.866	−0.788	21.867	26.354	197.00*	0.056***	5.605***	1461
XRP	21.448	0.824	0.641	0.6823	19.233	24.333	138.37*	0.179***	−7.418***	1461
Pow	3.622	0.088	−0.283	−0.117	3.317	3.834	8.20*	0.150***	−7.308***	1461
GTPT	2.836	0.116	9.744	−2.512	2.039	2.989	7315.83*	0.756***	−16.686***	1461
RSD	2.150	0.490	−1.453	0.225	1.502	3.029	140.75*	0.077***	−1.461	1461
DAVI	−0.185	0.241	5.893	−2.256	−1.320	0.129	3353.56*	0.085***	5.011***	1461
IAVI	0.061	0.470	0.002	−0.838	−1.414	0.688	170.83*	0.288***	−2.126	1461

Note: * and *** denote the levels of significance at 10% and 1%.

(DAVI) sectors. For skewness, the data series are heavier to the right of the distribution except for Ripple (XRP) and the residential sector (RSD), whereas for kurtosis, all 10 series are platykurtic, showing that they differ from a normal distribution. The same findings are confirmed by the significant values of the Jarque–Bera statistic. On a final note, the augmented Dickey–Fuller (ADF) test indicates that all variables (except CO_2 emissions from the residential and international aviation sectors) are stationary at the 1% significance level. Moreover, the ARCH effect is also significant for all variables at the same level. ADF is the most widely used method for determining the stationarity of time-series data (Yadav *et al.*, 2023). Hence, dynamic conditional correlation (DCC) is applied in the next step to examine the dynamic linkages.

To visualize the pattern of each series, we present the graphical depiction of raw data in the form of time-series plots computed using log-transformed trading activity and sectoral carbon emissions in Figures 3.1 and 3.2, respectively. In Figure 3.1, trading activity is observed to vary over time, with an increasing trend in general. In addition, the trading activity of all crypto assets witnessed a significant shock at the onset of the COVID-19 crisis, which is clearly observable at the start of the year 2021. Moreover, Figure 3.2 presents the sectoral carbon emissions for the five sectors under study. A cyclical pattern is visible in almost all series, indicating a pattern in emissions over a specific period. International aviation experienced a significant decline due to COVID-19 restrictions. The remaining sectors, namely power, ground transportation and domestic aviation, also experienced a shock due to the pandemic, except for residential emissions. Lastly, we observe some degree of volatility clustering and spikes in all series.

3.3.2. *DCC-GARCH model results and discussion*

The study investigates the relationship between crypto assets and climate change by employing a generalized autoregressive conditional heteroskedasticity model using a dynamic conditional correlation model (DCC-GARCH). To conduct the statistical analysis, a bivariate DCC-GARCH approach is utilized, and the results are presented in Tables 3.4–3.8. These tables provide information about the spillover effects of crypto assets on sectoral climate change measured

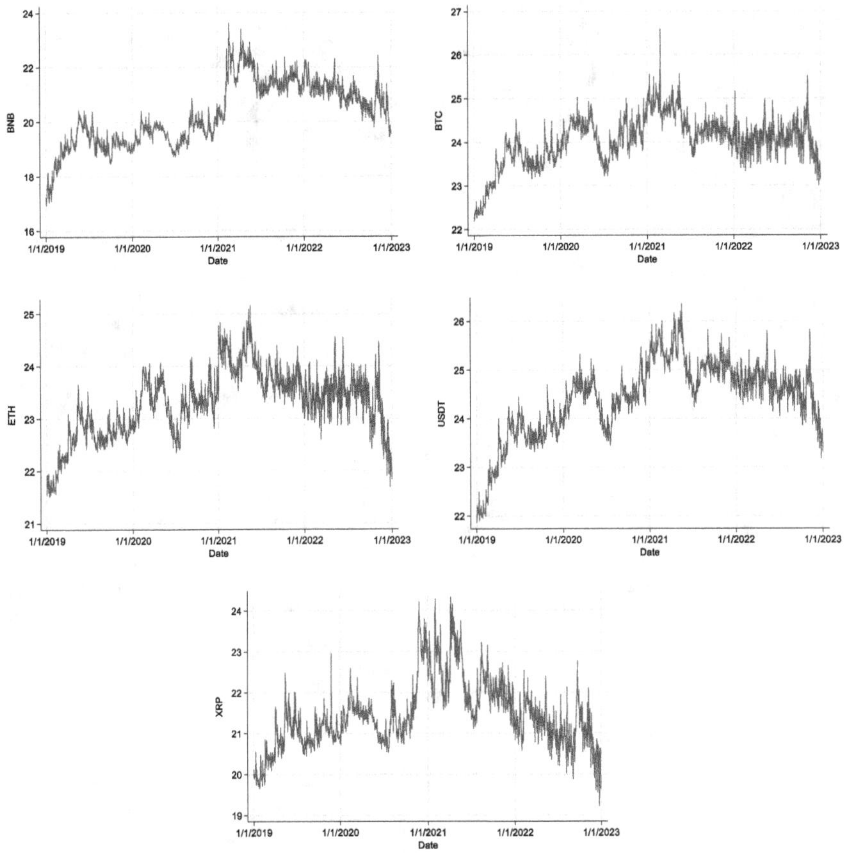

Figure 3.1. Graphical representation of crypto assets trading activity.

in terms of CO_2 emissions. The findings from the DCC model depict the dynamic connectedness between crypto assets and sectoral emissions, specifically in power, ground transport, residential, domestic aviation and international aviation (shown in Panels A–E, respectively).

In this analysis, the term "omega" represents the overall mean. Furthermore, alpha1 (ARCH) signifies the impact of the previous period's squared residuals or the error term derived from the mean equation, while beta1 (GARCH) indicates the impact of the previous period's forecasted variance. The sum of the ARCH and GARCH coefficients (alpha1 + beta1) is nearly equal to one, indicating a high

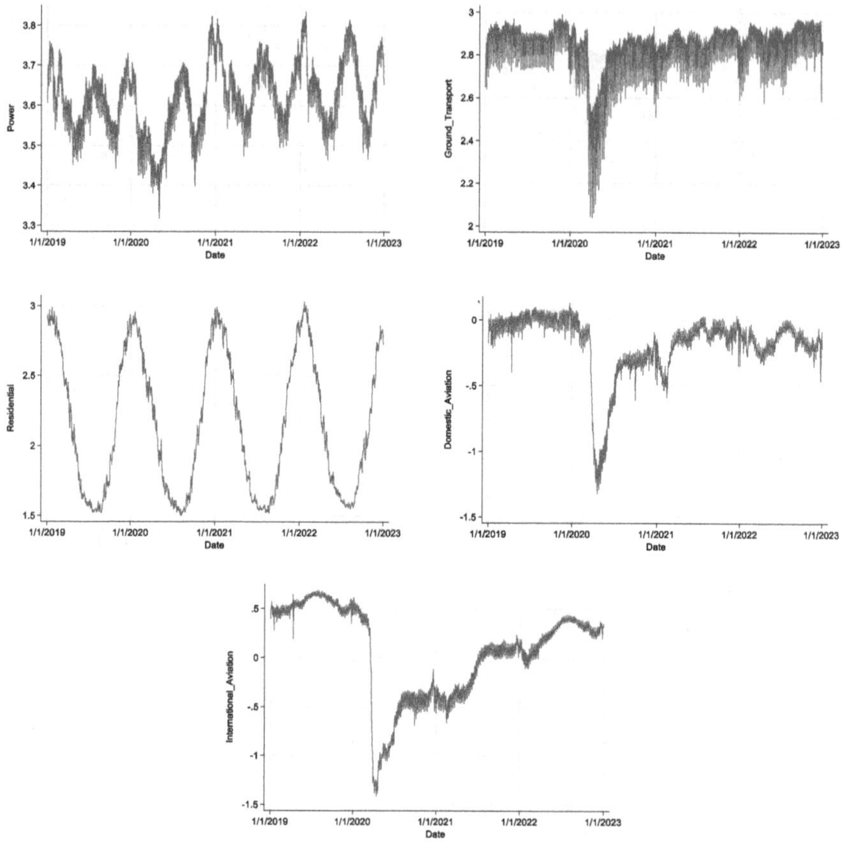

Figure 3.2. Graphical representation of CO_2 emissions.

level of persistence in volatility shocks. Moreover, the sum of alpha1 and beta1, which is a measure of volatility persistence, remains less than one, meeting the necessary condition for conditional variances to be finite. Notably, the higher values of beta1 compared to alpha1 suggest that past variances have a greater influence on the current variance.

In short, the DCC-GARCH model generates results in both univariate and bivariate GARCH settings. The univariate GARCH terms provide information about ARCH (volatility observed in the previous period) and GARCH (forecasted variance from the last period) (Sharma *et al.*, 2021). Additionally, the model produces the coefficients dcca1 and dccb1, which indicate the spillover or dynamic

Table 3.4. DCC-GARCH estimation results: Trading activity of crypto asset (BNB) and sectoral climate change (CO_2 emissions).

Panel A	Estimate	Std. error	P-value	Panel B	Estimate	Std. error	P-value
[BNB].omega	0.00030	0.00020	0.12128	[BNB].omega	0.00030	0.00020	0.12117
[BNB].alpha1	0.04194	0.00645	0.00000	[BNB].alpha1	0.04194	0.07643	0.00000
[BNB].beta1	0.95468	0.00521	0.00000	[BNB].beta1	0.95468	0.70521	0.00000
[Power].omega	0.00000	0.00000	0.00000	[GroundTransport].omega	0.00007	0.90003	0.00827
[Power].alpha1	0.00000	0.00010	0.99887	[GroundTransport].alpha1	0.03764	0.00587	0.00000
[Power].beta1	0.99900	0.00001	0.00000	[GroundTransport].beta1	0.95336	0.90398	0.00000
[Joint]dcca1	0.00770	0.00237	0.00115	[Joint]dcca1	0.01048	0.00501	0.03662
[Joint]dccb1	0.99118	0.00286	0.00000	[Joint]dccb1	0.98554	0.00764	0.00000
Panel C	**Estimate**	**Std. error**	**P-value**	**Panel D**	**Estimate**	**Std. error**	**P-value**
[BNB].omega	0.00030	0.00020	0.12099	[BNB].omega	0.00030	0.00020	0.12166
[BNB].alpha1	0.04194	0.00643	0.00000	[BNB].alpha1	0.04194	0.00648	0.00000
[BNB].beta1	0.95468	0.00521	0.00000	[BNB].beta1	0.95468	0.90521	0.00000
[Residential].omega	0.00001	0.00001	0.18556	[DomesticAviation].omega	0.00011	0.00005	0.04334
[Residential].alpha1	0.11044	0.01475	0.00000	[DomesticAviation].alpha1	0.03535	0.01283	0.00588
[Residential].beta1	0.88856	0.01301	0.00000	[DomesticAviation].beta1	0.93739	0.92029	0.00000
[Joint]dcca1	0.00000	0.00001	0.99941	[Joint]dcca1	0.01052	0.00419	0.01205
[Joint]dccb1	0.90931	0.06335	0.00000	[Joint]dccb1	0.98735	0.00551	0.00000
Panel E	**Estimate**	**Std. error**	**P-value**				
[BNB].omega	0.00030	0.00020	0.11966				
[BNB].alpha1	0.04194	0.00643	0.00000				
[BNB].beta1	0.95468	0.00521	0.00000				
[InternationalAviation].omega	0.00003	0.00001	0.04648				
[InternationalAviation].alpha1	0.12421	0.04295	0.00382				
[InternationalAviation].beta1	0.87459	0.03584	0.00000				
[Joint]dcca1	**0.00938**	**0.00412**	**0.02258**				
[Joint]dccb1	**0.98790**	**0.00583**	**0.00000**				

Table 3.5. DCC-GARCH estimation results: Trading activity of crypto asset (BTC) and sectoral climate change (CO_2 emissions).

Panel A	Estimate	Std. error	P-value	Panel B	Estimate	Std. error	P-value
[BTC].omega	0.00449	0.00201	0.02561	[BTC].omega	0.00449	0.00201	0.02531
[BTC].alpha1	0.14298	0.04382	0.00110	[BTC].alpha1	0.14298	0.04376	0.00108
[BTC].beta1	0.78734	0.06148	0.00000	[BTC].beta1	0.78734	0.06122	0.00000
[Power].omega	0.00000	0.00000	0.00000	[GroundTransport].omega	0.00007	0.00003	0.00829
[Power].alpha1	0.00000	0.00010	0.99887	[GroundTransport].alpha1	0.03764	0.00587	0.00000
[Power].beta1	0.99900	0.00001	0.00000	[GroundTransport].beta1	0.95336	0.00397	0.00000
[Joint]dcca1	0.00576	0.00189	0.00230	[Joint]dcca1	0.02743	0.03083	0.37359
[Joint]dccb1	0.99350	0.00239	0.00000	[Joint]dccb1	0.87016	0.20116	0.00002
Panel C	**Estimate**	**Std. error**	**P-value**	**Panel D**	**Estimate**	**Std. error**	**P-value**
[BTC].omega	0.00449	0.00201	0.02534	[BTC].omega	0.00449	0.00201	0.02576
[BTC].alpha1	0.14298	0.04377	0.00109	[BTC].alpha1	0.14298	0.04399	0.00115
[BTC].beta1	0.78734	0.06128	0.00000	[BTC].beta1	0.78734	0.06148	0.00000
[Residential].omega	0.00001	0.00001	0.18556	[DomesticAviation].omega	0.00011	0.00005	0.04348
[Residential].alpha1	0.11044	0.01475	0.00000	[DomesticAviation].alpha1	0.03535	0.01288	0.00607
[Residential].beta1	0.88856	0.01301	0.00000	[DomesticAviation].beta1	0.93739	0.02035	0.00000
[Joint]dcca1	0.00000	0.00000	0.97814	[Joint]dcca1	0.01405	0.00620	0.02347
[Joint]dccb1	0.90219	0.12284	0.00000	[Joint]dccb1	0.98204	0.00941	0.00000
Panel E	**Estimate**	**Std. error**	**P-value**				
[BTC].omega	0.00449	0.00201	0.02575				
[BTC].alpha1	0.14298	0.04529	0.00159				
[BTC].beta1	0.78734	0.06224	0.00000				
[InternationalAviation].omega	0.00003	0.00001	0.04575				
[InternationalAviation].alpha1	0.12421	0.04297	0.00384				
[InternationalAviation].beta1	0.87459	0.03587	0.00000				
[Joint]dcca1	0.02524	0.01606	0.11594				
[Joint]dccb1	0.96123	0.03096	0.00000				

Table 3.6. DCC-GARCH estimation results: Trading activity of crypto asset (ETH) and sectoral climate change (CO_2 emissions).

Panel A	Estimate	Std. error	P-value	Panel B	Estimate	Std. error	P-value
[ETH].omega	0.00010	0.00009	0.29351	[ETH].omega	0.00010	0.00009	0.29018
[ETH].alpha1	0.01734	0.00189	0.00000	[ETH].alpha1	0.01734	0.00187	0.00000
[ETH].beta1	0.98166	0.00020	0.00000	[ETH].beta1	0.98166	0.00020	0.00000
[Power].omega	0.00000	0.00000	0.00000	[GroundTransport].omega	0.00007	0.00003	0.00821
[Power].alpha1	0.00000	0.00010	0.99887	[GroundTransport].alpha1	0.03764	0.00587	0.00000
[Power].beta1	0.99900	0.00001	0.00000	[GroundTransport].beta1	0.95336	0.00397	0.00000
[Joint]dcca1	0.00567	0.00162	0.00046	[Joint]dcca1	0.00607	0.00271	0.02480
[Joint]dccb1	0.99368	0.00162	0.00000	[Joint]dccb1	0.99065	0.00395	0.00000

Panel C	Estimate	Std. error	P-value	Panel D	Estimate	Std. error	P-value
[ETH].omega	0.00010	0.00009	0.29015	[ETH].omega	0.00010	0.00009	0.29270
[ETH].alpha1	0.01734	0.00188	0.00000	[ETH].alpha1	0.01734	0.00189	0.00000
[ETH].beta1	0.98166	0.00020	0.00000	[ETH].beta1	0.98166	0.00020	0.00000
[Residential].omega	0.00001	0.00001	0.18564	[DomesticAviation].omega	0.00011	0.00005	0.04332
[Residential].alpha1	0.11044	0.01480	0.00000	[DomesticAviation].alpha1	0.03535	0.01285	0.00596
[Residential].beta1	0.88856	0.01305	0.00000	[DomesticAviation].beta1	0.93739	0.02031	0.00000
[Joint]dcca1	0.00356	0.01345	0.79121	[Joint]dcca1	0.00941	0.00331	0.00440
[Joint]dccb1	0.80624	0.06930	0.00000	[Joint]dccb1	0.98899	0.00406	0.00000

Panel E	Estimate	Std. error	P-value
[ETH].omega	0.00010	0.00009	0.29188
[ETH].alpha1	0.01734	0.00189	0.00000
[ETH].beta1	0.98166	0.00020	0.00000
[InternationalAviation].omega	0.00003	0.00001	0.04638
[InternationalAviation].alpha1	0.12421	0.04295	0.00383
[InternationalAviation].beta1	0.87459	0.03585	0.00000
[Joint]dcca1	0.00957	0.00357	0.00738
[Joint]dccb1	0.98907	0.00473	0.00000

Table 3.7. DCC-GARCH estimation results: Trading activity of crypto asset (USDT) and sectoral climate change (CO_2 emissions).

Panel A	**Estimate**	**Std. error**	**P-value**	**Panel B**	**Estimate**	**Std. error**	**P-value**
[USDT].omega	0.00007	0.00009	0.44264	[USDT].omega	0.00007	0.00009	0.44098
[USDT].alpha1	0.00918	0.00191	0.00000	[USDT].alpha1	0.00918	0.00191	0.00000
[USDT].beta1	0.98982	0.00017	0.00000	[USDT].beta1	0.98982	0.00017	0.00000
[Power].omega	0.00000	0.00000	0.00000	[GroundTransport].omega	0.00007	0.00003	0.00826
[Power].alpha1	0.00000	0.00010	0.99887	[GroundTransport].alpha1	0.03764	0.00587	0.00000
[Power].beta1	0.99900	0.00001	0.00000	[GroundTransport].beta1	0.95336	0.00397	0.00000
[Joint]dcca1	0.00487	0.00168	0.00365	[Joint]dcca1	0.01924	0.04441	0.66488
[Joint]dccb1	0.99461	0.00150	0.00000	[Joint]dccb1	0.87364	0.48342	0.07073
Panel C	**Estimate**	**Std. error**	**P-value**	**Panel D**	**Estimate**	**Std. error**	**P-value**
[USDT].omega	**0.00007**	**0.00009**	**0.44017**	**[USDT].omega**	**0.00007**	**0.00009**	**0.44300**
[USDT].alpha1	0.00918	0.00191	0.00000	[USDT].alpha1	0.00918	0.00192	0.00000
[USDT].beta1	0.98982	0.00017	0.00000	[USDT].beta1	0.98982	0.00017	0.00000
[Residential].omega	0.00001	0.00001	0.18556	[DomesticAviation].omega	0.00011	0.00005	0.04364
[Residential].alpha1	0.11044	0.01475	0.00000	[DomesticAviation].alpha1	0.03535	0.01287	0.00601
[Residential].beta1	0.88856	0.01300	0.00000	[DomesticAviation].beta1	0.93739	0.02034	0.00000
[Joint]dcca1	0.00000	0.00001	0.99705	[Joint]dcca1	0.01240	0.00437	0.00452
[Joint]dccb1	0.91067	0.13854	0.00000	[Joint]dccb1	0.98414	0.00592	0.00000
Panel E	**Estimate**	**Std. error**	**P-value**				
[USDT].omega	0.00007	0.00009	0.43974				
[USDT].alpha1	0.00918	0.00191	0.00000				
[USDT].beta1	0.98982	0.00017	0.00000				
[InternationalAviation].omega	0.00003	0.00001	0.04628				
[InternationalAviation].alpha1	0.12421	0.04296	0.00384				
[InternationalAviation].beta1	0.87459	0.03588	0.00000				
[Joint]dcca1	0.01767	0.01470	0.22948				
[Joint]dccb1	0.97598	0.02537	0.00000				

Table 3.8. DCC-GARCH estimation results: Trading activity of crypto asset (XRP) and sectoral climate change (CO_2 emissions).

Panel A	Estimate	Std. error	P-value	Panel B	Estimate	Std. error	P-value
[XRP].omega	0.02377	0.02925	0.41642	[XRP].omega	0.02377	0.02929	0.41699
[XRP].alpha1	0.18380	0.11562	0.11189	[XRP].alpha1	0.18380	0.11616	0.11357
[XRP].beta1	0.58732	0.39015	0.13223	[XRP].beta1	0.58732	0.39091	0.13298
[Power].omega	0.00000	0.00000	0.00000	[GroundTransport].omega	0.00007	0.00003	0.00818
[Power].alpha1	0.00000	0.00010	0.99887	[GroundTransport].alpha1	0.03764	0.00587	0.00000
[Power].beta1	0.99900	0.00001	0.00000	[GroundTransport].beta1	0.95336	0.00398	0.00000
[Joint]dcca1	0.00417	0.00220	0.05871	[Joint]dcca1	0.03552	0.01960	0.06995
[Joint]dccb1	0.99316	0.00397	0.00000	[Joint]dccb1	0.84267	0.10655	0.00000

Panel C	Estimate	Std. error	P-value	Panel D	Estimate	Std. error	P-value
[XRP].omega	0.02377	0.02919	0.41536	[XRP].omega	0.02377	0.02918	0.41522
[XRP].alpha1	0.18380	0.11542	0.11128	[XRP].alpha1	0.18380	0.11539	0.11117
[XRP].beta1	0.58732	0.38929	0.13137	[XRP].beta1	0.58732	0.38907	0.13116
[Residential].omega	0.00001	0.00001	0.18550	[DomesticAviation].omega	0.00011	0.00005	0.04349
[Residential].alpha1	0.11044	0.01475	0.00000	[DomesticAviation].alpha1	0.03535	0.01285	0.00593
[Residential].beta1	0.88856	0.01301	0.00000	[DomesticAviation].beta1	0.93739	0.02034	0.00000
[Joint]dcca1	0.00868	0.01015	0.39271	[Joint]dcca1	0.01440	0.00766	0.06029
[Joint]dccb1	0.93286	0.05855	0.00000	[Joint]dccb1	0.97992	0.01218	0.00000

Panel E	Estimate	Std. error	P-value
[XRP].omega	0.02377	0.02930	0.41709
[XRP].alpha1	0.18380	0.11620	0.11368
[XRP].beta1	0.58732	0.39105	0.13312
[InternationalAviation].omega	0.00003	0.00001	0.04704
[InternationalAviation].alpha1	0.12421	0.04294	0.00382
[InternationalAviation].beta1	0.87459	0.03584	0.00000
[Joint]dcca1	0.02861	0.01500	0.05657
[Joint]dccb1	0.81529	0.07117	0.00000

linkages between different assets and sectors in the short and long runs, respectively (Yadav *et al.*, 2020). Positive and significant values of dcca1 and dccb1 imply spillover effects in the short and long runs, respectively, while insignificant values indicate no spillover effects during the respective timeframes.

Table 3.4 reports the results of DCC-GARCH for the crypto asset BNB and sectoral CO_2 emissions. The results of the model depict the dynamic connections between BNB and sectoral emissions in power, ground transport, residential, domestic aviation and international aviation in Panels A–E, respectively. Most of the coefficient values are significant in capturing the volatility in this table. Here, alpha1 and beta1 of the crypto asset BNB are positive and significant for all sectoral emissions in Panels A–E. Only beta1 for power sector emissions is insignificant in Panel A. The significant alpha1 value indicates that the magnitude of the shock to the variance is significantly related to the future volatility of BNB and sectoral emissions. The insignificant value of power in Panel A shows that there is no persistence of past volatility. The signs of the terms are positive in all panels, indicating a positive relationship between past and current variance. This implies that the larger the magnitude of the shock to the variances of series, the higher the volatility in the market or sector. Further, beta1, the GARCH term, explains the persistence of previous volatility in predicting future volatility. The significant nature of the coefficients shows that past volatility has a persistent effect on future volatility and its predictions. Further, the sum of alpha1 and beta1 is closer to but less than one, highlighting the stability of the estimates. Additionally, the dcca1 and dccb1 coefficients generated by the model indicate the spillover or dynamic linkages between BNB crypto assets and sectoral emissions in the short and long runs, respectively (Yadav *et al.*, 2023). Positive and significant values of dcca1 and dccb1, except dcca1 in Panel C for residential, imply spillover effects in both the short and long runs; however, there are no spillover links between the trading activity of BNB and residential emissions in the short run.

Table 3.5 presents the findings from applying the DCC-GARCH model to analyze the relationship between the crypto asset Bitcoin (BTC) and sectoral CO_2 emissions. The results demonstrate the dynamic connections between BTC and sectoral emissions from power, ground transport, residential, domestic aviation and international aviation in Panels A–E, respectively. Most of the coefficient values in this table are statistically significant, indicating their effectiveness in capturing volatility. In Panels A–E, both alpha1 and beta1 coefficients for BTC are positive and significant in relation to all five sectoral emissions. The significant value of alpha1 suggests that the magnitude of shocks to the variance is significantly associated with the future volatility of both BTC and sectoral emissions. Across all panels, the signs of the coefficients are positive, indicating a positive relationship between past variance and current variance. This implies that larger shocks to the variances of the series result in higher volatilities in the market or sector. Additionally, the beta1 term, representing the GARCH component, explains the persistence of previous volatility in predicting future volatility. The significant coefficients highlight the enduring effect of past volatility on future volatility and its predictability. Furthermore, the sum of alpha1 and beta1 is close to but less than unity, indicating the stability of the estimates. Moreover, the dcca1 and dccb1 coefficients generated by the DCC-GARCH model reveal the spillover or dynamic linkages between BTC and sectoral emissions in the short and long runs, respectively (Hung, 2020). Positive and significant values of dcca1 and dccb1, except for dcca1 in Panels B and C for the transport and residential sectors, respectively, suggest spillover effects in both the short and long runs. However, there is no spillover link between the trading activity of BTC and emissions from the residential and transport sectors in the short run.

Table 3.6 presents the findings of the DCC-GARCH model concerning the relationship between the crypto asset Ethereum (ETH) and sectoral CO_2 emissions. The results demonstrate the dynamic connections between ETH and the five sectoral emissions in Panels A–E. The coefficient values in this table largely exhibit significance in capturing volatility. In Panels A–E, both the alpha1 and beta1 coefficients for ETH and sectoral emissions are positive and significant. The significant alpha1 coefficients indicate that the magnitude of shocks to the variance is significantly related to the future volatility of ETH and sectoral emissions. In all panels, the signs of the coefficients are positive, indicating a positive relationship between past and current variances. This implies that larger shocks to the variances of the series lead to higher volatility in the market or sector. Furthermore, beta1, the GARCH term, explains the persistence of previous volatility in predicting future volatility. The significant nature of these coefficients suggests that past volatility has a lasting impact on future volatility and its predictions. Moreover, the sum of alpha1 and beta1 is close to but less than unity, highlighting the stability of the estimates. Additionally, the dcca1 and dccb1 coefficients represent the spillover effects or dynamic linkages between ETH and sectoral emissions in the short and long runs, respectively (Kumar *et al.*, 2019). Positive and significant values of dcca1 and dccb1, except for dcca1 in Panel C for residential, indicate spillover effects in both the short and long runs. However, no spillover relationship exists between the trading activity of ETH and residential emissions in the short run.

Table 3.7 presents the findings of the DCC-GARCH analysis conducted on the crypto asset USDT and its relationship with sectoral CO_2 emissions. The results illustrate the dynamic connections between USDT and the sectoral emissions in power, ground transport, residential, domestic aviation and international aviation in Panels A–E, respectively. In this table, most of the coefficient values are statistically significant, indicating their ability to capture volatility. The alpha1 and beta1 coefficients for USDT and sectoral emissions in Panels A–E are positive and significant, except for alpha1 in the power sector emissions in Panel A, which is not statistically significant. The significant alpha1 coefficients suggest that the magnitude of the shock to the variance is significantly associated with the future volatility of both USDT and sectoral emissions. The insignificant value of the coefficient for power in Panel A indicates a lack of persistence in past volatility. Across all panels, the signs of the coefficients are positive, indicating a positive relationship between past variance and current variance. This implies that larger shocks to the series' variances result in higher market or sector volatility. Additionally, the beta1 term, representing the GARCH effect, explains the persistence of previous volatility in predicting future volatility. The significant coefficients highlight the persistent impact of past volatility on future volatility and its predictions. Furthermore, the sum of alpha1 and beta1 is close to but less than unity, indicating the stability of the estimates. Moreover, the dcca1 and dccb1 coefficients generated by the model depict the spillover or dynamic linkages between USDT and sectoral emissions in the short and long runs, respectively (Hung, 2020). The positive and significant values of dcca1 and dccb1, except for dcca1 in Panels B, C and E for transport, residential and international aviation sectoral emissions, respectively, suggest spillover effects in both the short and long runs. However, there is no spillover relationship between USDT trading activity and transport, residential or international aviation emissions in the short run.

Table 3.8 presents the findings of the DCC-GARCH model analyzing the relationship between the crypto asset Ripple (XRP) and sectoral CO_2 emissions. The results highlight the dynamic connections between XRP and the sectoral emissions in power, ground transport, residential, domestic aviation and international aviation in Panels A–E, respectively. Here, we find somewhat different outcomes. In Panels A–E, both alpha1 and beta1 coefficients for XRP are insignificant, whereas those for sectoral emissions are positive and significant. This suggests that the magnitude of shocks to the variance significantly influences the future volatility of sectoral emissions, but not for the crypto asset XRP. The significant coefficients highlight the enduring effect of past volatility on future volatility and its predictability. The sum of alpha1 and beta1 is close to but remains less than one, indicating stable estimates. Additionally, the model provides dcca1 and dccb1 coefficients, which indicate the spillover or dynamic linkages between XRP and sectoral emissions in the short and long runs, respectively. Positive and significant values of dcca1 and dccb1, except for dcca1 in Panel C concerning residential emissions, suggest spillover effects in both the short and long runs. However, there is no spillover link detected between the trading activity of XRP and residential emissions in the short run.

3.4. Conclusion

Sustainable economic development and climate change have become a focal point for global leaders in their efforts to combat environmental degradation. Despite other environmental consequences, it is believed that Bitcoin and other cryptocurrencies could contribute to global warming exceeding 2°C (Mora *et al.*, 2018). However, Baur & Oll (2022) emphasized the relative impact of Bitcoin and observed a decrease in portfolio carbon emissions with the inclusion of crypto assets. As a result, investors and other stakeholders are interested in further investigating the relationship between climate concerns and crypto assets. Our study aimed to explore the dynamic connections between the trading activity of crypto assets and sector-specific carbon emissions, as indicated by our research question.

To achieve our objective, we employed the dynamic conditional correlation (DCC) model to analyze the time-series data of crypto assets and their contribution to climate change in terms of carbon emissions within various sectors. We used five cryptocurrencies, namely Bitcoin (BTC), Ethereum (ETH), Tether (USDT), BNB (BNB) and Ripple (XRP), as proxies for digital finance. Additionally, we considered five sectoral measures of climate change based on carbon emissions in power, ground transportation, residential, domestic aviation and international aviation. The daily trading volumes and sectoral emissions data were obtained for the period spanning from 1 January 2019 to 31 December 2022.

The results indicate that USDT and Bitcoin exhibit the highest trading volumes, while Ripple and Tether have the lowest trading volumes among the sampled crypto assets. Furthermore, the power sector and ground transportation are the largest contributors to carbon emissions, whereas domestic and international aviation are the smallest contributors over the specified period. After confirming the presence of the ARCH effect, which indicates dynamic connections, the dynamic conditional correlation (DCC) model was applied to analyze the relationships between all five crypto assets and sectoral emissions.

The study reveals that the magnitude of a shock to the variance significantly affects the future volatility of both crypto assets and sectoral emissions. Moreover, the persistence of past volatility influences future volatility predictions for crypto assets and sectoral emissions, except for Ripple (XRP). Additionally, spillover effects are observed between crypto assets and sectoral emissions in the long run across all 25 crypto–sector pairs. However, in the short run, there is no significant link observed between residential sector emissions and BNB, Bitcoin, Ethereum and Ripple (RESID–BNB, RESID–BTC, RESID–ETH and RESID–XRP), ground transport emissions and Bitcoin and USDT (GTPT–BTC and GTPT–USDT), as well as international aviation emissions and USDT (IAVI–USDT).

Our findings provide important insights for policymakers and regulators, highlighting the necessity of crafting strategies to establish a sustainable cryptocurrency ecosystem by embracing environmentally friendly crypto mining practices. Our findings can be further refined through future research studies aimed at examining both conventional and sustainable cryptocurrencies to investigate whether the impact of sustainable cryptocurrencies on climate change differs from that of their conventional counterparts. We leave this issue for future studies.

References

Baur, D. G. & Oll, J. (2022). Bitcoin investments and climate change: A financial and carbon intensity perspective. *Finance Research Letters*, 47, 102575. https://doi.org/10.1016/j.frl.2021.102575.

Cao, S., Nie, L., Sun, H., Sun, W., & Taghizadeh-Hesary, F. (2021). Digital finance, green technological innovation and energy-environmental performance: Evidence from China's regional economies. *Journal of Cleaner Production*, 327, 129458. https://doi.org/10.1016/j.jclepro.2021.129458.

Corbet, S., Lucey, B., & Yarovaya, L. (2021). Bitcoin-energy markets interrelationships-New evidence. *Resources Policy*, 70, 101916. https://doi.org/10.1016/j.resourpol.2020.101916.

Engle, R. (2002). Dynamic conditional correlation: A simple class of multivariate generalized autoregressive conditional heteroskedasticity models. *Journal of Business & Economic Statistics*, 20(3), 339–350. https://doi.org/10.1198/073500102288618487.

Galanti, S. & Özsoy, Ç. Y. (2022). Digital finance, development, and climate change (No. 2920). Orleans Economics Laboratory/Laboratoire d'Economie d'Orleans (LEO), University of Orleans.

Guo, X. & Tu, Y. (2023). How digital finance affects carbon intensity–The moderating role of financial supervision. *Finance Research Letters*, 103862. https://doi.org/10.1016/j.frl.2023.103862.

Ha, M., Gan, C., Nguyen, C., & Anthony, P. (2021). Self-organising (Kohonen) maps for the Vietnam banking industry. *Journal of Risk and Financial Management*, 14(10), 485. https://doi.org/10.3390/jrfm14100485.

Ho, L., Gan, C., Jin, S., & Le, B. (2022). Does climate-related disclosures support sustainable finance in New Zealand? https://hdl.handle.net/10182/15409.

Hou, H., Zhu, Y., Wang, J., & Zhang, M. (2023). Will green financial policy help improve China's environmental quality? The role of digital finance and green technology innovation. *Environmental Science and Pollution Research*, 30(4), 10527–10539. https://doi.org/10.1007/s11356-022-22887-z.

Hung, N. T. (2020). An analysis of CEE equity market integration and their volatility spillover effects. *European Journal of Management and Business Economics*, 29(1), 23–40. https://doi.org/10.1108/EJMBE-01-2019-0007.

Hunjra, A. I. & Hanif, M. (2023). Central banking issues and challenges. *Reference Module in Social Sciences*. https://doi.org/10.1016/B978-0-44-313776-1.00113-6.

Huynh, T. L. D., Ahmed, R., Nasir, M. A., Shahbaz, M., & Huynh, N. Q. A. (2021). The nexus between black and digital gold: Evidence from US markets. *Annals of Operations Research*, 1–26. https://doi.org/10.1007/s10479-021-04192-z.

Intergovernmental Panel on Climate Change. (2018). *Global Warming of 1.5° C: An IPCC Special Report on the Impacts of Global Warming of 1.5° C above Pre-industrial Levels and Related Global Greenhouse Gas Emission Pathways, in the Context of Strengthening the Global Response to the Threat of Climate Change, Sustainable Development, and Efforts to Eradicate Poverty* (pp. 3–24). Intergovernmental Panel on Climate Change. Cambridge, UK: Cambridge University Press. https://doi.org/10.1017/9781009157940.

Jiang, S., Li, Y., Lu, Q., Hong, Y., Guan, D., Xiong, Y., & Wang, S. (2021). Policy assessments for the carbon emission flows and sustainability of bitcoin blockchain operation in China. *Nature Communications*, 12(1), 1–10. https://doi.org/10.1038/s41467-021-22256-3.

Kumar, S., Pradhan, A. K., Tiwari, A. K., & Kang, S. H. (2019). Correlations and volatility spillovers between oil, natural gas, and stock prices in India. *Resources Policy*, 62, 282–291. https://doi.org/10.1016/j.resourpol.2019.04.004.

Li, G., Wu, H., Jiang, J., & Zong, Q. (2023). Digital finance and the low-carbon energy transition (LCET) from the perspective of capital-biased technical progress. *Energy Economics*, 120, 106623. https://doi.org/10.1016/j.eneco.2023.106623.

Mora, C., Rollins, R. L., Taladay, K., Kantar, M. B., Chock, M. K., Shimada, M., & Franklin, E. C. (2018). Bitcoin emissions alone could push global warming above 2 C. *Nature Climate Change*, 8(11), 931–933. https://doi.org/10.1038/s41558-018-0321-8.

Qin, X., Wu, H., & Li, R. (2022). Digital finance and household carbon emissions in China. *China Economic Review*, 76, 101872. https://doi.org/10.1016/j.chieco.2022.101872.

Ren, X., Zeng, G., & Zhao, Y. (2023). Digital finance and corporate ESG performance: Empirical evidence from listed companies in China. *Pacific-Basin Finance Journal*, 79, 102019. https://doi.org/10.1016/j.pacfin.2023.102019.

Sharma, S., Aggarwal, V., & Yadav, M. P. (2021). Comparison of linear and non-linear GARCH models for forecasting volatility of select emerging countries. *Journal of Advances in Management Research*, 18(4), 526–547. https://doi.org/10.1108/JAMR-07-2020-0152.

Truby, J. (2018). Decarbonizing bitcoin: Law and policy choices for reducing the energy consumption of Blockchain technologies and digital currencies. *Energy Research & Social Science*, 44, 399–410. https://doi.org/10.1016/j.erss.2018.06.009.

Wu, M., Guo, J., Tian, H., & Hong, Y. (2022). Can digital finance promote peak carbon dioxide emissions? Evidence from China. *International Journal of Environmental Research and Public Health*, 19(21), 14276. https://doi.org/10.3390/ijerph192114276.

Xue, Q., Feng, S., Chen, K., & Li, M. (2022). Impact of digital finance on regional carbon emissions: An empirical study of sustainable development in China. *Sustainability*, 14(14), 8340. https://doi.org/10.3390/su14148340.

Yadav, M. P., Vasakarla, V., & Arora, M. (2020). Volatility spillover: Equity markets to commodity markets. *SCMS Journal of Indian Management*, 17(3), 103–113.

Yadav, N., Singh, A. B., & Tandon, P. (2023). Volatility spillover effects between Indian stock market and global stock markets: A DCC-GARCH model. *FIIB Business Review*, 23197145221141186. https://doi.org/10.1177/23197145221141.

Yang, G., Ding, Z., Wu, M., Gao, M., Yue, Z., & Wang, H. (2023). Can digital finance reduce carbon emission intensity? A perspective based on factor allocation distortions: Evidence from Chinese cities. *Environmental Science and Pollution Research*, 30(13), 38832–38852.

Yu, H., Wei, W., Li, J., & Li, Y. (2022). The impact of green digital finance on energy resources and climate change mitigation in carbon neutrality: Case of 60 economies. *Resources Policy*, 79, 103116. https://doi.org/10.1016/j.resourpol.2022.103116.

Yu, M., Tsai, F. S., Jin, H., & Zhang, H. (2022). Digital finance and renewable energy consumption: Evidence from China. *Financial Innovation*, 8(1), 58.

Zhang, D., Chen, X. H., Lau, C. K. M., & Xu, B. (2023). Implications of cryptocurrency energy usage on climate change. *Technological Forecasting and Social Change*, 187, 122219. https://doi.org/10.1016/j.techfore.2022.122219.

Zhang, D., Mohsin, M., & Taghizadeh-Hesary, F. (2022). Does green finance counteract the climate change mitigation: Asymmetric effect of renewable energy investment and R&D. *Energy Economics*, 113, 106183. https://doi.org/10.1016/j.eneco.2022.106183.

Zhao, H., Yang, Y., Li, N., Liu, D., & Li, H. (2021). How does digital finance affect carbon emissions? Evidence from an emerging market. *Sustainability*, 13(21), 12303. https://doi.org/10.3390/su132112303.

https://doi.org/10.1142/9781800616257_0004

Chapter 4

How Does Financial Inclusion Affect Bank Stability in Emerging Economies?

Runguo Xu

School of International Relations,
Yonsei University, Seoul, South Korea
xrg9606@126.com

Abstract

The effects of financial inclusion (FI) on the safety of financial institutions are the focus of this research. Statistical analysis is performed on data extracted from the annual reports of 116 listed banks in emerging Asian markets, covering the years 2012–2021. The data are analyzed by using the two-step dynamic panel system generalized estimating linear model (GMM). FI is measured using four proxies: the FI index, bank penetration, availability of financial services and usability. In addition, bank stability is assessed using the Z-score. The findings of the study show that FI is significantly and positively related to bank stability. Our results support the FI–stability correlation across all measures of FI. Policymakers should make appropriate decisions regarding risk-taking while considering factors such as FI. Adding market-based metrics of bank risk-taking and expanding the study's scope to include both established and emerging nations are two ways to achieve this goal.

Keywords: Financial inclusion, bank stability, dynamic panel approach, Asian emerging economies, banks.

4.1. Introduction

The concept of FI has evolved around the availability, use and accessibility of financial services for those who need them. FI is emerging as a key element in development strategies worldwide, offering substantial potential for reducing poverty (Wellalage *et al.*, 2021). Treviranus (2014) states that economic inclusion is no longer an alternative; it is now a necessity. FI is currently being examined as a coverage device to reap several macroeconomic benefits. Previous research defines the aim of basic economic services in the economic area as supplying low-cost, affordable financial options with minimal charges to the weaker sections of the populace without any discrimination (Varghese & Viswanathan, 2018). FI leads to stability in the operations of the financial sector. It is therefore important for the financial systems within firms to grow in order to avoid bankruptcy and achieve financial health. Therefore, executives of firms and financial institutions may require investors to allow more time for making progress in their financial systems (Ha *et al.*, 2021).

The process of achieving greater FI may have unintended negative consequences. Extending credit ratings to individuals without proper oversight leads to negative externalities. Expanding the pool of potential borrowers has the potential to lower lending criteria and dilute the quality of mortgage portfolios. In order to make banking services such as debit and deposit cards more accessible to a wider population at reasonable prices, FI must be supported by the necessary technological infrastructure. Better FI infrastructure boosts savings rates, alleviates poverty, raises living standards, creates more jobs, accelerates economic growth and fuels an economic boom (Park & Mecado, 2018). Most studies define FI as access to financial services for all members of society, especially the economically vulnerable, at reasonable costs and without bias (Chakravarty & Pal, 2013).

According to the literature and current theory of banking, when economic markets, borrower characteristics and depositor behaviors experience crisis or uncertainty, it can have a negative impact on the stability and performance of banks (Sarmiento & Galán, 2017). Bank risk-taking behavior refers to the propensity of some financial institutions to take risks during times of uncertainty. The health of the financial system is heavily dependent on the risk-taking habits of individual banks. Large portions of the population and businesses in low-income countries often lack access to adequate financial services due to factors such as a lack of convenient automated teller machines (ATMs), high fees associated with servicing small deposits and loans, difficulties establishing verifiable identities and restrictions on sharing financial data. When people are able to participate in the financial system, the economy as a whole benefits. In particular, FI effectively reduces poverty and inequality by making financial goods and services, such as savings, bank credit, insurance and payments, easily accessible in a secure environment (Jungo *et al.*, 2022). Banking is a powerful instrument for fostering economic growth and development. Having a strong banking system is essential for a country's economy to run smoothly.

Many governments have adopted and executed economic inclusion strategies as a result of the widespread attention the topic has garnered. A bank's capacity to diversify its risks and improve monetary stability may be aided, for example, by its ability to get access to financial offerings. Bank credits are the primary and least costly source of external financing for businesses; therefore, a more inclusive economy is good news for enterprises looking for funding outside their companies (Berger & DeYoung, 1997). FI has been shown to have positive social and economic effects, but its effect on financial stability, especially bank stability, is less well understood (Ahamed & Mallick, 2019). The banking system has proven to be a source of financial development and macroeconomic efficiency (Hunjra *et al.*, 2022). Banking institutions are crucial to economic growth because of the crucial role they play in the distribution of limited resources among borrowers and lenders. Scholarly interest in the factors that determine bank stability or risk-taking behaviors was already present prior to the subprime crisis and ensuing financial instability (Acharya & Naqvi, 2012). Because of the potential for systemic crises, it is crucial to consider the connection between financial inclusivity and financial soundness.

In this chapter, we conduct an empirical analysis of the relationship between FI and bank stability in emerging markets of Asia. Despite the fact that both developed and developing economies are suffering from a lack of FI, the latter are widely viewed as facing a more severe problem with financial exclusion. Although many developing nations have made great strides toward FI, there remain significant differences between developed and developing nations in areas such as account ownership, account use and savings and credit patterns, suggesting that FI is of greater importance to the latter. Furthermore, emerging countries are becoming increasingly reliant on banking institutions, even as they experience recurrent financial disruptions. Therefore, a stable financial system has a greater impact on the economies of these nations than on economies that rely less heavily on banks (Kroszner *et al.*, 2007). Second, we contribute to the research by investigating the impact of contextual diversity on the association between FI and bank stability.

In this research, we analyze how the expansion of banking services to underserved populations in emerging Asian markets has affected the security of the region's rising economies. Our dataset consists of 116 listed banks operating in 10 Asian emerging economies, spanning from 2012 to 2021. We apply the two-step dynamic panel system generalized estimating linear model (GMM) approach to examine the data. Our findings lend credence to the view that FI and stability are correlated, which implies that rising financial service penetration and access lead to a more secure banking sector and less risk-taking behavior on the part of financial institutions.

The remainder of the study is structured as follows. Section 4.2 presents the empirical literature related to this topic. Section 4.3 describes the data and methodology. Section 4.4 explains the empirical findings, followed by the discussion and conclusion in Sections 4.5 and 4.6, respectively.

4.2. Literature Review

Financial institutions play an important role in influencing economic growth and the allocation of financial resources (Telukdarie & Mungar, 2023). The development of physical branches by financial institutions in many places facilitated widespread FI and the smooth operation of various financial systems (Donou-Adonsou & Sylwester, 2016). Economic exclusion from official economic offerings diminishes social welfare, ultimately delaying the growth of a country's economic system (Naumenkova *et al.*, 2019).

Academics and policymakers alike have taken an avid interest in the link between economic inclusion and bank stability. A number of studies have attempted to elucidate the impact of FI on bank safety. However, the outcomes of most empirical investigations have been mixed. The debate over how FI affects the stability of financial institutions in practice continues. This research helps close the gap and makes a significant contribution to the existing body of knowledge. This research helps close the gap and makes a significant contribution to the existing body of knowledge which either use a disaggregated single indicator of FI or study the impact of FI on a variety of socioeconomic indicators.

4.2.1. *Financial inclusion and bank stability*

Inclusion in the financial system is crucial and cannot be stressed enough. Research shows that those in a community who don't use basic financial services can benefit from being included in the financial system. Moreover, Ghosh & Vinod (2017) suggest that women benefit just as much from financial services as men do. Access to banking services, such as savings accounts that form part of the framework of enterprise capital at a low fee (Ghosh & Vinod, 2017), is difficult for unbanked neighborhood groups to attain without FI. Bruhn & Love (2014) state that having access to financial services has a major effect on economic development by helping individuals stay employed and facilitating the establishment and growth of informal firms. Therefore, inclusive financial growth and sociopolitical stability rely on the positive effects of economic inclusion on a number of major socioeconomic indicators, which, in turn, might lead to more effective monetary intermediations and enhanced bank soundness. Further, in order to attract smaller borrowers, banks must be willing to take a greater reputational risk by outsourcing services such as credit score reviews.

The stability of a nation's economic machine is aided by a well-developed monetary system, which has a multiplicative effect on reducing poverty and inequality as well as enhancing banks' general performance (Margono *et al.*, 2010). Other banking instruments, such as financial institution assets and bank revenue, can also make contribution by encouraging inclusion and financial stability. Neaime &

Gaysset (2018) highlight the powerful impact of financial inclusivity on monetary stability benefits, such as reducing credit volatility, which is especially important during various phases of financial crises. Lee *et al.* (2020) demonstrate the mutually reinforcing nature of economic inclusion and economic stability. López & Winkler (2019) provide evidence that nations with high levels of economic participation are less likely to be harmed if borrowing and lending significantly reduce. More people having access to financial services is associated with greater financial institution stability (Ahamed & Mallick, 2019). The authors state that increasing FI and reducing the costs associated with opening new bank branches are key benefits of technological innovations such as mobile banking and ATMs. However, rapid credit expansion coupled with low loan portfolio quality has been found to negatively impact economic stability (López & Winkler, 2019). As a result of rising cyber threats, technical failures and recognition costs, striving for a high level of FI through expanded use of credit products might have a negative impact on economic security. The link between economic inclusion and financial stability has been widely studied in the empirical literature but is less explored in theoretical discussions.

Neaime & Gaysset (2018) point out that financial inclusivity has a direct impact on financial stability due to its role in lowering the volatility of deposits, which is crucial during times of economic turmoil. Lee *et al.* (2020) and López & Winkler (2019) support the notion of FI having a positive impact on bank stability. Aiming to better understand the relationship between FI and bank stability, Ahamed & Mallick (2019) find that greater public accessibility of financial institutions is correlated with increased stability of those institutions. They also find that the link is especially strong in banks that have a higher proportion of customer deposits and lower operating costs. Progress in FI stabilizes the banking system through digital payments and increased account ownership. This short summary of the relevant research on the FI–financial stability nexus highlights numerous difficulties that have been overlooked by previous studies. In order to examine the impact of FI on financial stability, previous research has largely focused on industrialized nations rather than emerging economies. Furthermore, the current research often comprises empirical studies on the broad link between the two, and few researchers have evaluated the heterogeneity of the aforementioned nexus, let alone its putative influencing mechanisms. For this reason, we suggest FI aspects as possible determinants of bank soundness by analyzing heterogeneity and channels in developing nations. After reviewing the literature, we suggest the following hypothesis:

HI: FI has a significant impact on bank stability.

4.2.2. *Control variables and bank stability*

The current study applies several important control variables for the analyses, including bank size, leverage, liquidity and growth. There has been a growing body of research investigating the correlation between these control variables and bank stability. Saunders *et al.* (1990) found that as bank size grew, risk-taking decreased and stability improved. Stiroh (2006) claims that the stability of banks increases as their size increases. According to the results of this research, there is a direct correlation between banks' leverage and their risk-taking behavior and stability, for the obvious reason that a speculator's leverage is a key driver of the motivation to take on excessive risk. Contrary to popular belief, additional equity capital is not required to prevent economic decline or to cushion the blow of unexpected adverse events. However, this notion was contested by Diamond & Rajan (2000), who found that equity requirements are mandated to incentivize prospective speculators and limit risk-taking. Regarding the influence of liquidity on credit risk, a negative relationship was discovered by Louati *et al.* (2015). Banks become more vulnerable to failure during periods of rapid expansion of credit in the economy as a whole. This problem affects all banks, including those whose loan growth rates are lower than those of their rivals. Amador *et al.* (2013) found that a prolonged excessive rise in loans led banks to take on more risk.

4.3. Methodology

With information gleaned from the annual reports of listed banks in emerging Asian economies from 2012 to 2021 (see Table 4.1), we examine the effect of FI on bank stability.

Table 4.1. Sample description.

Countries	Total no. of listed banks	Selected
China	19	7
India	38	20
Indonesia	43	17
Lebanon	6	6
Malaysia	10	8
Pakistan	37	20
The Philippines	18	18
Thailand	17	12
Turkey	16	8
Vietnam	11	3

Source: From the annual reports of each listed bank.

4.3.1. *Statistics*

Bank stability serves as the dependent variable, while FI is the independent variable in this study. Control variables used in the study are bank size, leverage, liquidity and growth. All these variables are described as follows. An indicator of the extent of people's access to financial services is the FI Index (IFI). The proportion of adults or households with access to banking institutions is one way of measuring FI, according to certain studies. Sarma & Pais (2011) construct an IFI based on the triad of banking service availability, customer convenience and banking service penetration.

4.3.1.1. *Banking penetration*

To be truly inclusive, monetary systems must be easily available to a large user base. The percentage of adults who have a bank account can be taken as a measure of banking access. The study's indicator of banking penetration is the ratio of individuals with bank accounts to the total population aged 15 years and above, as well as the proportion of small- and medium-sized enterprises (SMEs) with bank accounts.

4.3.1.2. *Availability of financial services*

Everyone should be able to access and use the financial system. Therefore, the number of outlets (branches, ATMs, etc.) is used as an availability indicator.

4.3.1.3. *Usability*

Despite having access to financial services, there may be sections of the population that are not yet able to fully utilize these opportunities. As a result, having a bank account alone is insufficient to demonstrate FI. Credits, deposits, payments, remittances and transfers are all indicators of FI. Sarma & Pais (2011) use indicators such as commercial bank loan balances and deposit balances as a percentage of GDP.

4.3.2. *Bank stability*

The Z-score has been extensively used as a measure of safety for financial institutions. The number of standard deviations a bank's returns must drop to become bankrupt is measured (Stiroh, 2006). It negatively correlates with the likelihood of bank failure.

The Z-score is calculated as follows:

$$Z = (\mathrm{ROA} + E/A)/\sigma\ \mathrm{ROA},$$

where ROA represents the return on assets, E/A represents the equity as a percentage of total assets and σ ROA represents the standard deviation of ROA. The Z-score values are quite skewed; therefore, we use their natural logarithms, which follow a normal distribution. For the remainder of the chapter, we consider only the natural logarithm of the Z-score. The control variables of our study are bank size, asset growth, leverage and liquidity. The details of each variable are provided in Table 4.2.

4.3.3. *Mathematical equation*

We apply the following regression model to analyze our data:

$$\begin{aligned}(\mathrm{BS})i,t = {}& \alpha + \beta 1(\mathrm{FII})i,t + \beta 2(\mathrm{BP})i,t + \beta 3(\mathrm{AFS})i,t \\ & + \beta 4(\mathrm{USA})i,t + \gamma 1(\mathrm{Lev})i,t + \gamma 2(\mathrm{Liq})i,t + \gamma 3(\mathrm{size})i,t \\ & + \gamma 4(\mathrm{Gw})i,t + \mu i,t. \end{aligned} \tag{4.1}$$

4.4. Results

In the following section, we explain the outcomes of our study. Descriptive analysis is performed on either the entire dataset or a

Table 4.2. Variables summary.

Name	Abbr.	Description	References
Bank Stability	BS	$Z = (\text{ROA} + \text{E/A})/\sigma$ ROA	Laeven & Levine (2009)
Financial Inclusion	FII	Index comprises BP, AFS and USA	Sarma & Pais (2011)
Banking Penetration	BP	Proportion of adult people that have an account at the bank	Sarma & Pais (2011)
Availability of Financial Services	AFS	Number of outlets (branches, ATMs)	Sarma & Pais (2011)
Usability	USA	Outstanding loans from commercial banks (% to GDP)	Sarma & Pais (2011)
Leverage	Lev	Equity to total assets ratio	Lepetit *et al.* (2008)
Liquidity	Liq	Deposits to total assets ratio	Wagner (2007)
Size	Size	Natural log of total assets	Lepetit *et al.* (2008)
Growth	Gw	Annual change in total assets	Abedifar *et al.* (2020)

subset of the dataset that has been summarized numerically. The average, median, standard deviation, highest and lowest values and total number of observations constitute the descriptive statistics. Summarizing and describing the features of a dataset is the function of descriptive statistics. This presents quantitative descriptions in an approachable format. Descriptive statistics help us make sense of complex data by reducing them to their most basic elements.

Table 4.3 displays the dataset's mean, median, maximum and minimum values and standard deviation for each variable, as well as the total number of observations. There is an uneven distribution of values throughout the years 2012–2021. Z-scores are used as the study's measure of stability. It is clear that there are no outliers in the data since the average values of stability of listed banks in emerging Asian economies follow a consistent pattern, with fewer variances in the values of bank risk-taking behavior. FI measures used in the study include the FI index and individual measures comprising the index, which show few variations in their values. Control variables in the

Table 4.3. Descriptive statistics.

	Mean	Median	Maximum	Minimum	Std. dev.	Obs.
BS	4.201	4.369	6.387	0.149	10.881	844
FII	0.056	0.031	0.882	0.001	0.075	844
BP	−0.491	−0.383	0.942	−1.999	0.641	844
AFS	0.567	0.576	0.792	0.165	0.170	844
USA	0.712	0.723	3.642	−0.698	1.239	844
Size	14.303	13.934	20.579	9.209	2.153	844
Lev	0.101	0.090	0.737	−0.113	0.093	844
Liq	0.757	0.750	2.780	0.034	0.278	844
Gw	0.163	0.123	3.866	−0.372	0.242	728

Note: BS is bank stability, FII is financial inclusion index, BP is bank penetration, AFS is availability of financial services, USA is usability, Size is bank size, Lev is leverage, Liq is liquidity and Gw is growth.

present study include Bank Size, Leverage, Liquidity and Growth. All these control variables show few variations in their values.

Multicollinearity refers to a situation in which the independent variables are highly correlated with one another. It's a type of data disruption that might make it difficult to trust the results of any inferences drawn from the data. Data multicollinearity can be identified in a number of ways. For example, we may use the straightforward correlation coefficient. The variance inflation factor (VIF) and its inverse, tolerance (1/VIF), are two more tools used for identifying multicollinearity. The VIF value should not be higher than 5 (Becker *et al.*, 2015). Multicollinearity becomes an issue when the VIF is 10 or above, or the tolerance is less than or equal to 0.2.

We use the VIF to verify multicollinearity in the analysis in Table 4.4. The values of VIF are not more than 5 (Becker *et al.*, 2015); therefore, we can confirm that there is no multicollinearity problem in this study. In statistics, correlation analysis is a tool for assessing the closeness of association between a set of numerical variables. When the correlation between two or more variables is high, the relationships between them are strong; conversely, when the correlation is low, the relationships between them are weak. Table 4.5 displays the estimated correlation matrix for all the studied explanatory factors using data from listed banks operating in emerging Asian economies. This is used to examine the problem of multicollinearity between the explanatory factors. Liquidity and

Table 4.4. Test of multicollinearity.

Variable	VIF	1/VIF
BP	4.24	0.2045
FII	3.87	0.2513
USA	3.16	0.3162
AFS	1.88	0.5330
Lev	1.87	0.5358
Liq	1.77	0.5636
Size	1.31	0.7609
Gw	1.08	0.9275

Note: VIF = Variance Inflation Factor.

Table 4.5. Correlation analysis.

	BS	FII	BP	AFS	USA	Size	Lev	Liq	Gw
BS	1.000								
FII	0.225	1.000							
BP	0.093	0.432	1.000						
AFS	0.204	0.193	0.252	1.000					
USA	0.019	0.434	0.454	0.334	1.000				
Size	0.242	0.024	0.204	0.037	0.394	1.000			
Lev	0.046	−0.160	0.332	0.024	−0.105	0.391	1.000		
Liq	0.200	−0.035	0.112	0.389	0.181	0.332	0.4831	1.000	
Gw	−0.091	−0.101	0.042	0.294	0.006	0.044	−0.021	−0.139	1.000

Note: BS is bank stability, FII is financial inclusion index, BP is bank penetration, AFS is availability of financial services, USA is usability, Size is bank size, Lev is leverage, Liq is liquidity and Gw is growth.

Leverage have the strongest connection at 0.4831, while growth and usability have the weakest at 0.006. Therefore, there is no problem with multicollinearity, as the findings of the correlation matrix indicate that there is little to no connection between the explanatory variables.

Relationships between a predictor variable and one or more independent variables can be investigated via regression analysis. For this investigation, we employed a two-stage system dynamic panel GMM estimate method, as suggested by Arellano & Bover (1995). It shines in situations where there are many periods but few cross-sections, (N) (T). Panel data, also known as longitudinal data, are a type of multi-dimensional data used in statistical and economic analysis. For the same companies or individuals, panel data collect information on a number of different occurrences, often over extended periods of time. Our adoption of the dynamic system GMM panel model was motivated by a few separate concerns. As a first step in correcting this misspecification, we must ensure that no important variables are left out. Second, in a dynamic panel model, when an explanatory factor and the error term are correlated, it is necessary to account for the endogeneity of the lagged dependent variable. Last but not least, the GMM estimator is superior when heteroskedasticity is present. It is employed to manage measurement errors and heterogeneity in panels that is not directly observable.

FI, as measured by the FI index, bank penetration, availability of financial services and usability, has a significant positive impact on bank stability. We find that the coefficients on the four financial indicators are significantly positive, suggesting that the Z-score moves in the same direction as the FI indicators. Because a higher Z-score means a more robust bank, bank steadiness increases with greater FI (see Table 4.6). Alternatively, banks' excessive risk-taking behavior can be mitigated with increased FI. This finding is in line with recent studies, such as the one by Lee *et al.* (2020).

Regarding the control variables, we also find consistent results with the existing literature. Bank size is positively correlated with bank soundness in the two estimations, supporting the view that larger banks are more stable. Our results also show that higher levels of capitalization and an abundance of liquid assets are good for bank soundness. Our results also corroborate the positive relationship between financial stability and economic growth. The coefficients of the growth rate are significantly positive, providing evidence that bank steadiness strengthens when the economy is booming.

We find that all four financial indicators have coefficients that are strongly positive, which suggests that the Z-score moves in the same direction as the FI indicators. Because a higher Z-score indicates a more stable bank, there is an increase in bank stability as a result of increased FI. Alternatively, the excessive risk-taking behavior of banks can be reduced by increasing access to financial services for more people. Recent research, such as that conducted by Lee *et al.* (2020), all points in the same direction regarding this conclusion.

Table 4.6. Two-step system dynamic panel estimation with Z-score.

	Model I		**Model II**		**Model III**		**Model IV**	
Variables	**Coef.**	**t-stat**	**Coef.**	**t-stat**	**Coef.**	**t-stat**	**Coef.**	**t-stat**
L1.	0.184^{***}	(3.13)	−0.150	(−0.82)	0.120	(0.60)	0.7587^{***}	(6.58)
L2.	-0.179^{***}	(−3.57)	-0.386^{***}	(−3.30)	-0.375^{***}	(−2.76)	0.1279^{**}	(2.39)
FII	$\mathbf{0.312^{**}}$	**(2.07)**	—	—	—	—	—	—
BP	—	—	$\mathbf{2.388^{***}}$	**(2.91)**	—	—	—	—
AFS	—	—	—	—	$\mathbf{0.756^{**}}$	**(1.97)**	—	—
USA	—	—	—	—	—	—	0.039^{**}	(2.25)
Size	−0.117	(−1.56)	0.259	(1.14)	0.234	(1.14)	0.012^{*}	(1.90)
Lev	−0.806	(−0.61)	5.478	(1.23)	4.419	(1.14)	0.033	(0.43)
Liq	1.228^{**}	(2.57)	−0.720	(−0.59)	0.593	(0.53)	0.025	(1.11)
Gw	−0.088	(−0.56)	-0.853^{**}	(−2.39)	−0.422	(−1.28)	−0.012	(−1.29)
C	5.635^{***}	(4.16)	1.144	(0.27)	1.336	(0.37)	−0.185	(−1.52)

Notes: L1. is first Lag of dependent variable, L2. is second Lag of dependent variable, BS is bank stability, FII is financial inclusion index, BP is bank penetration, AFS is availability of financial services, USA is usability, Size is bank size, Lev is leverage, Liq is liquidity and Gw is growth.***, ** and * denote significance levels at 1%, 5% and 10%, respectively.

4.5. Discussion

There is a strong correlation between the development of the banking sector and the expansion of economies, especially in developing countries. The financial and industrial security of this sector requires in-depth investigation to gain deep insights into the growth of this industry. Banks in developing nations have been compelled to diversify as a result of the increased competition and globalization brought about by the liberalization of the financial sector and the opening of financial markets. The stability of the banking sector is directly related to the extent to which its customers can access the financial services provided by this sector. This final part of the study attempts to determine how the different FI indexes stack up against one another. This section provides a concise overview of the study's aims and conclusions, including a general examination of the banking industry in emerging Asian economies. The section continues with a discussion of the study's results and suggestions before turning to the study's practical consequences. Across the board, the Z-score results corroborate the inclusion–stability relationship. Further, the conclusion implies that reducing financial exclusion can improve bank stability.

This research analyzes the banking industry in emerging Asian economies and provides ideas for improving financial stability through calculated risk-taking. Due to its importance to the economy, the banking sector in these nations must be strengthened. While making crucial financial decisions, bank managers, regulators and policymakers should take the recognized factors of financial stability into account. It is suggested that banks in developing Asian nations should profit from FI in the banking industry. However, effective risk management is essential for FI efforts. This research adds to the body of evidence recommending that FI aids banks in lowering risk and bolstering the financial system's stability.

4.6. Conclusion

The study set out to examine how FI affects banking stability using data from listed banks operating in 10 developing Asian nations. The Z-score is a measure of bank reliability. There are 215 listed banks in total, but we could only analyze 116 of them due to data limitations. We applied the dynamic panel technique to analyze the study data. Conclusions from this study imply that it will be useful for managers, regulators, policymakers and researchers. Insightful policy recommendations for developing economies can be derived from our research. Since FI has been shown to improve bank health in these nations, it is clear that achieving it is crucial for ensuring a stable and growing economy. FI promotion, however, must consider a number of potentially influential heterogeneity factors affecting the inclusion–stability nexus. The nexus is found to be weakened by policies such as expansionary monetary policies and a stronger investment climate, suggesting that a balance between the positive and negative effects of these and other measures should be considered during the process of enhancing FI.

Finally, this section discusses the limitations of the study and potential next steps for researchers. First, the scope of this research may be broadened by including both public and unregistered banks from the same pool of 10 Asian emerging economies. To expand upon this research further, we may also use market-based indicators of banks' risk-taking behavior. Third, comparing data from both established and emerging nations would be a welcome addition to the study's scope. Fourth, the study can be expanded by investigating how FI influences financial risk-taking in the banking sector. Finally, similar studies may be conducted focusing only on industrialized nations.

References

Abedifar, P., Bouslah, K., Hashem, S. Q., & Song, L. (2020). How informative are stock prices of Islamic Banks? *Journal of International Financial Markets, Institutions and Money,* 66, 101203. https://doi.org/10.1016/j.intfin.2020.101203.

Acharya, V. & Naqvi, H. (2012). The seeds of a crisis: A theory of bank liquidity and risk taking over the business cycle. *Journal of Financial Economics,* 106(2), 349–366. https://doi.org/10.1016/j.jfineco.2012.05.014.

Ahamed, M. M. & Mallick, S. K. (2019). Is financial inclusion good for bank stability? International evidence. *Journal of Economic Behavior & Organization,* 157, 403–427. https://doi.org/10.1016/j.jebo.2017.07.027.

Amador, J. S., Gómez-González, J. E., & Pabón, A. M. (2013). Loan growth and bank risk: New evidence. *Financial Markets and Portfolio Management,* 27(4), 365–379. DOI:10.1007/s11408-013-0217-6.

Arellano, M. & Bover, O. (1995). Another look at the instrumental variable estimation of error-components models. *Journal of Econometrics,* 68(1), 29–51. https://doi.org/10.1016/0304-4076(94)01642-D.

Becker, J. M., Ringle, C. M., Sarstedt, M., & Völckner, F. (2015). How collinearity affects mixture regression results. *Marketing Letters,* 26, 643–659. https://link.springer.com/article/10.1007/s11002-014-9299-9.

Berger, A. N. & DeYoung, R. (1997). Problem loans and cost efficiency in commercial banks. *Journal of Banking & Finance,* 21(6), 849–870. https://doi.org/10.1016/S0378-4266(97)00003-4.

Bruhn, M. & Love, I. (2014). The real impact of improved access to finance: Evidence from Mexico. *Journal of Finance,* 69, 1347–1376. https://doi.org/10.1111/jofi.12091.

Chakravarty, S. R. & Pal, R. (2013). Financial inclusion in India: An axiomatic approach. *Journal of Policy Modeling,* 35(5), 813–837. https://doi.org/10.1016/j.jpolmod.2012.12.007.

Diamond, D. W. & Rajan, R. G. (2000). A theory of bank capital. *The Journal of Finance,* 55(6), 2431–2465. https://doi.org/10.1111/0022-1082.00296.

Donou-Adonsou, F. & Sylwester, K. (2016). Financial development and poverty reduction in developing countries: New evidence from banks and microfinance institutions. *Review of Development Finance,* 6(1), 82–90. https://doi.org/10.1016/j.rdf.2016.06.002.

Ghosh, S. & Vinod, D. (2017). What constrains financial inclusion for women? Evidence from Indian micro data. *World Development,* 92, 60–81. https://doi.org/10.1016/j.worlddev.2016.11.011.

Ha, M., Gan, C., Nguyen, C., & Anthony, P. (2021). Self-organising (Kohonen) maps for the Vietnam banking industry. *Journal of Risk and Financial Management,* 14(10), 485. https://doi.org/10.3390/jrfm14100485.

Hunjra, A. I., Islam, F., Verhoeven, P., & Hassan, M. K. (2022). The impact of a dual banking system on macroeconomic efficiency. *Research in International Business and Finance,* 61, 101647. https://doi.org/10.1016/j.ribaf.2022.101647.

Jungo, J., Madaleno, M., & Botelho, A. (2022). The relationship between financial inclusion and monetary policy: A comparative study of countries' in Sub-Saharan Africa and Latin America and the Caribbean. *Journal of African Business*, 23(3), 794–815. https://doi.org/10.1080/15228916.2021.1930810.

Kroszner, R. S., Laeven, L., & Klingebiel, D. (2007). Banking crises, financial dependence, and growth. *Journal of Financial Economics,* 84(1), 187–228. https://doi.org/10.1016/j.jfineco.2006.05.001.

Laeven, L. & Levine, R. (2009). Bank governance, regulation and risk taking. *Journal of Financial Economics,* 93(2), 259–275. https://doi.org/10.1016/j.jfineco.2008.09.003.

Lee, C. C., Wang, C. W., & Ho, S. J. (2020). Financial inclusion, financial innovation, and firms' sales growth. *International Review of Economics & Finance,* 66, 189–205. https://doi.org/10.1016/j.iref.2019.11.021.

Lepetit, L., Nys, E., Rous, P., & Tarazi, A. (2008). Bank income structure and risk: An empirical analysis of European banks. *Journal of Banking & Finance,* 32(8), 1452–1467. https://doi.org/10.1016/j.jbankfin.2007.12.002.

López, T. & Winkler, A. (2019). Does financial inclusion mitigate credit boom-bust cycles? *Journal of Financial Stability,* 43, 116–129. https://doi.org/10.1016/j.jfs.2019.06.001.

Louati, S., Abida, I. G., & Boujelbene, Y. (2015). Capital adequacy implications on Islamic and non-Islamic bank's behavior: Does market power matter? *Borsa Istanbul Review,* 15(3), 192–204. https://doi.org/10.1016/j.bir.2015.04.001.

Margono, H., Sharma, S. C., & Melvin Ii, P. D. (2010). Cost efficiency, economies of scale, technological progress and productivity in Indonesian banks. *Journal of Asian Economics,* 21(1), 53–65. https://doi.org/10.1016/j.asieco.2009.06.001.

Naumenkova, S., Mishchenko, S., & Dorofeiev, D. (2019). Digital financial inclusion: Evidence from Ukraine. *Investment Management & Financial Innovations*, 16(3), 194. http://dx.doi.org/10.21511/imfi.16(3).2019.18.

Neaime, S. & Gaysset, I. (2018). Financial inclusion and stability in MENA: Evidence from poverty and inequality. *Finance Research Letters,* 24, 230–237. https://doi.org/10.1016/j.frl.2017.09.007.

Park, C. Y. & Mercado, R. V. (2021). Financial inclusion: New measurement and cross-country impact assessment 1. In *Financial Inclusion in Asia and Beyond* (pp. 98–128). London, UK: Routledge. http://dx.doi.org/10.22617/WPS189270-2.

Sarma, M. & Pais, J. (2011). Financial inclusion and development. *Journal of International Development,* 23(5), 613–628. https://doi.org/10.1002/jid.1698.

Sarmiento, M. & Galán, J. E. (2017). The influence of risk-taking on bank efficiency: Evidence from Colombia. *Emerging Markets Review,* 32, 52–73. https://doi.org/10.1016/j.ememar.2017.05.007.

Saunders, A., Strock, E., & Travlos, N. G. (1990). Ownership structure, deregulation, and bank risk taking. *The Journal of Finance*, 45(2), 643–654. https://doi.org/10.1111/j.15406261.1990.tb03709.x.

Stiroh, K. J. (2006). A portfolio view of banking with interest and noninterest activities. *Journal of Money, Credit and Banking*, 1351–1361. 10.1353/mcb.2006.0075.

Telukdarie, A. & Mungar, A. (2023). The impact of digital financial technology on accelerating financial inclusion in developing economies. *Procedia Computer Science*, 217, 670–678. https://doi.org/10.1016/j.procs.2022.12.263.

Treviranus, J. (2014). Leveraging the web as a platform for economic inclusion. *Behavioral Sciences & the Law*, 32(1), 94–103. https://doi.org/10.1002/bsl.2105.

Varghese, G. & Viswanathan, L. (2018). Financial inclusion: Opportunities, issues and challenges. *Theoretical Economics Letters*, 8(11), 1935–1942. DOI:10.4236/ojapps.2022.123024.

Wagner, W. (2007). The liquidity of bank assets and banking stability. *Journal of Banking & Finance*, 31(1), 121–139. https://doi.org/10.1016/j.jbankfin.2005.07.019.

Wellalage, N. H., Hunjra, A. I., Manita, R., & Locke, S. M. (2021). Information communication technology and financial inclusion of innovative entrepreneurs. *Technological Forecasting and Social Change*, 163, 120416. https://doi.org/10.1016/j.techfore.2020.120416.

https://doi.org/10.1142/9781800616257_0005

Chapter 5

Navigating the Digital Finance Landscape Amid COVID-19: A Bibliometric Analysis

Jatin Kumar Jaiswal[*,‡] **and Dharen Kumar Pandey**[†,§]

[*] *Department of Commerce and Business Studies, Central University of South Bihar, Gaya, India*

[†] *P. G. Department of Commerce, Magadh University, Bodhgaya, India*

[‡] *jatin@cusb.ac.in*

[§] *dharenp@gmail.com*

Abstract

This chapter uses bibliometric analysis to analyze the digital finance literature during COVID-19, extracting 240 articles from the Scopus database published between 2020 and 2024. The analysis of publication trends reveals a steady increase from 11 articles in 2020 to 90 in 2023. Notably, the *Journal of Open Innovation: Technology, Market, and Complexity* emerges as a top-contributing source, sharing the first rank with 10 documents. *Technological Forecasting and Social Change* leads in citations, while Akpan *et al.* (2022) is the most-cited document. Rabbani leads with five documents. China dominates in country contributions, and the Agricultural University of Athens ranks highest among affiliations. We unveil collaboration networks and identify 12 significant themes in digital finance research during COVID-19, providing a comprehensive overview for future exploration.

Keywords: Digital finance, bibliometric analysis, COVID-19, pandemic, FinTech.

5.1. Introduction

Digital finance uses digital technologies to conduct financial transactions and manage financial activities (Feng *et al.*, 2022; Ghosh & Hom Chaudhury, 2022; Thomas & Hedrick-Wong, 2019). It encompasses various services, including online banking, mobile payments, digital wallets and blockchain-based transactions (Khando *et al.*, 2022; Turi, 2023). Digital finance has revolutionized the traditional financial industry by providing individuals and businesses with convenient and efficient tools to access, transfer and manage their finances (Gomber *et al.*, 2017; Pazarbasioglu *et al.*, 2020). One of the key aspects of digital finance is its ability to break down geographical barriers, allowing people to conduct cross-border financial transactions seamlessly (Pazarbasioglu *et al.*, 2020; Shahrokhi, 2008). This has benefited individuals in remote or underserved areas with limited access to traditional banking services (Gupta & Kanungo, 2022; Ozili, 2018). The importance of digital finance lies in its ability to enhance financial inclusion, improve efficiency and foster economic growth (Alhammadi, 2023; Gabor & Brooks, 2020). By providing a platform for secure and accessible financial services, digital finance can bring millions of previously excluded individuals into the formal financial system (Arner *et al.*, 2020; Mhlanga, 2020). This inclusivity can empower individuals by providing them with the tools to save, invest and access credit, ultimately reducing poverty. Furthermore, digital finance streamlines processes, reduces costs and enhances transparency, making financial transactions faster and more reliable (Pazarbasioglu *et al.*, 2020; Shahrokhi, 2008). In a broader context, the growth of digital finance contributes to the overall development of a digital economy by fostering innovation and creating new opportunities for businesses and individuals alike.

The COVID-19 pandemic not only caused an unprecedented global health crisis but also triggered profound shifts in various aspects of society, including the financial landscape (Boubaker *et al.*, 2023; Pandey & Kumari, 2021; Verma & Gustafsson, 2020; Zhang & Mao, 2022). As nations grappled with the challenges posed by the pandemic, the digital finance sector emerged as a critical player in navigating the economic repercussions and ensuring financial resilience. The convergence of digital technologies and finance has become more pronounced, reshaping how individuals, businesses and governments engage with financial systems (Bhaskar *et al.*, 2022; Bhatt *et al.*, 2022; Gupta *et al.*, 2022; Pandey *et al.*, 2024; Yuan *et al.*, 2022). This chapter aims to comprehensively explore the digital finance landscape in the context of the COVID-19 crisis. By employing bibliometric analysis, we seek to map scholarly contributions and identify key themes and emerging trends at the dynamic intersection of digitalization and finance. Bibliometric analysis, a quantitative method for analyzing scholarly literature, allows us to discern patterns, identify influential works and assess the evolution of knowledge within the field (Ahmed *et al.*, 2022; Donthu *et al.*, 2021; Goyal & Kumar, 2021; Jalal *et al.*, 2021; Kumar *et al.*, 2022; Pandey *et al.*, 2023).

The COVID-19 pandemic has accelerated the adoption of digital financial technologies, transforming traditional banking, payment systems and investment practices (Agarwal *et al.*, 2022; Gupta *et al.*, 2023; Srisathan & Naruetharadhol, 2022). Rapid shifts in consumer behavior, increased reliance on online transactions and the rise of FinTech solutions have underscored the resilience and adaptability of digital finance in the face of unprecedented challenges (Hunjra & Hanif, 2023; Liu & Zhang, 2021). Understanding the scholarly landscape of digital finance during the turbulent pandemic period is crucial for policymakers, industry stakeholders and researchers alike, as it can inform strategic decisions, policy formulations and future research directions. This chapter navigates the extensive body of literature on digital finance published during the COVID-19 pandemic through a bibliometric lens. By synthesizing and analyzing the existing knowledge base, we aim to contribute valuable insights that shed light on the current state of digital finance, identify research gaps and offer a foundation for future investigations. As we embark on this bibliometric journey, our goal is to distill the collective wisdom of the scholarly community, providing a nuanced understanding of the multifaceted challenges and opportunities that characterize the digital finance landscape in the COVID-19 era.

The chapter proceeds as follows. Section 5.2 briefly discusses the research methods, followed by the results and discussion in Section 5.3. Section 5.4 presents the results of the bibliographic coupling, discussing 12 clusters of the available literature. The final section concludes by presenting the key takeaways and the limitations of this study.

5.2. Research Methodology

In this study, we conducted a systematic literature review utilizing bibliometric analysis to comprehend the landscape of research on digital finance during the COVID-19 pandemic. A systematic literature review is akin to a comprehensive overview of existing research in a field without introducing new data (Okoli & Schabram, 2010). The application of bibliometric analysis traces its origins back to library and information science. It serves as a valuable technique to quantify bibliometric data and reveal unexplored research areas (Broadus, 1987).

For this study, we opted for review papers sourced from the Scopus database, a frequently recommended platform for bibliometric reviews. Scopus provides extensive bibliometric information on its indexed publications and is considered more robust than the Web of Science (WOS) (Donthu *et al.*, 2021; Levine-Clark & Gill, 2008). The retrieval of existing literature on digital finance research during COVID-19, spanning from 2020 to 2024, employed a comprehensive search string encompassing a broad set of keywords to capture all relevant papers. The search string included terms such as "fintech," "digital finance" or "financial technology," which were filtered with "COVID-19," "pandemic" or "ncov-19." The search query targeted the title, abstract and keywords to ensure the relevance of the identified documents to the study's theme. The validation of the search string was confirmed by its ability to identify various primary studies.

The study fields were restricted to "economics, econometrics, and finance"; "business management and accounting"; and "social sciences." Through successive application of two filters – first for the English language and then for articles only – a total of 240 articles were identified. The language criterion was set to "English" to facilitate the use of software such as VOSViewer and Biblioshiny. Consequently, book chapters, review papers and conference papers were excluded. The selection of keywords for the literature search on digital finance research during COVID-19 was validated through bibliometric cartography analysis. Figure 5.1 illustrates the study design, presenting the search query employed to retrieve pertinent papers for analysis.

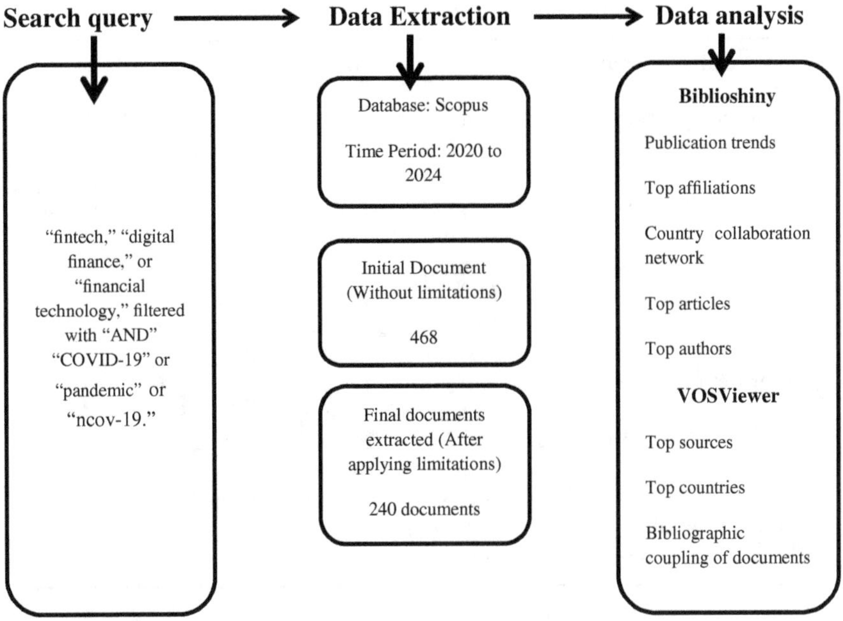

Figure 5.1. Design of the study.

5.3. Results and Discussion

Table 5.1 presents a comprehensive overview of publications on digital finance research during the COVID-19 pandemic. The data, extracted from the Scopus database, span from 2020 to 2024 and comprise 240 publications on this topic. Within these publications, 1,117 keywords are considered, encompassing both author-generated keywords and additional keywords. Notably, 702 authors actively contributed to this body of work. The research theme is disseminated across 158 sources, collectively responsible for publishing 240 papers.

5.3.1. *Annual publications and citations*

Figure 5.2 illustrates the annual growth of publications in digital finance research during the COVID-19 pandemic from 2020 to 2024. The highest number of publications occurred in 2022, reaching 92.

Table 5.1. Overview of the study.

Aspects of the study	Unit of analysis	Results
General information	Timespan	2020–2024
	Sources (journals, books, etc.)	158
	Documents	240
	Annual growth rate %	−45.09
	Document average age	0.9
	Average citations per doc	9.704
	References	14009
Keywords details	Keywords plus (ID)	289
	Author's keywords (DE)	828
Author details	Authors	702
	Authors of single-authored docs	44
Author collaboration details	Single-authored docs	45
	Co-authors per doc	3.15
	International co-authorships %	32.5
Document details	Article	225
	Review	15

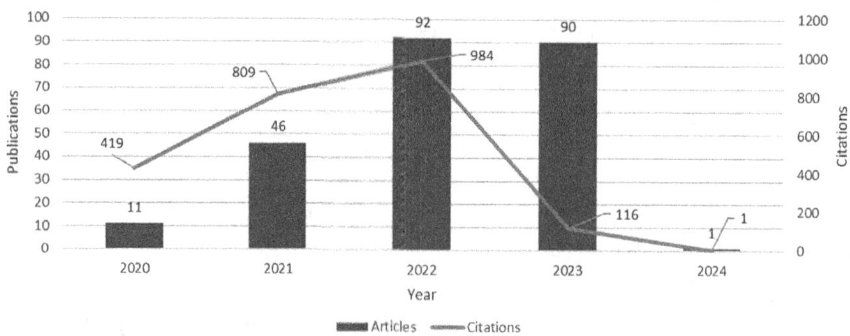

Figure 5.2. Annual trends in publications and citations.

Subsequently, in 2023 and 2021, the numbers of documents published were 90 and 46, respectively. The articles published in 2022 have received the highest number of citations (984), followed by those published in 2021 (809).

5.3.2. *Top 10 productive sources*

Table 5.2 outlines the 10 primary sources that have played a significant role in advancing research within the realm of digital finance

Table 5.2. Top 10 contributing sources.

Sources	Documents	Citations	Link strength
Journal of Open Innovation: Technology, Market, and Complexity	10	84	22
Technological Forecasting and Social Change	8	190	36
International Review of Financial Analysis	7	42	14
Sustainability	5	39	7
Journal of Financial and Quantitative Analysis	4	33	11
Research in International Business and Finance	3	59	19
International Journal of Islamic and Middle Eastern Finance and Management	3	51	22
Economic Analysis and Policy	3	47	10
Journal of Risk and Financial Management	3	41	4
Economic Research-Ekonomska Istrazivanja	2	115	4

amid the COVID-19 pandemic. The journal *Open Innovation: Technology, Market, and Complexity* stands out as the leading source, contributing the highest number of documents at 10. Following closely is *Technological Forecasting and Social Change*, which contributed eight documents. In terms of citations, *Technological Forecasting and Social Change* leads the pack, garnering 190 citations with a link strength of 36. In the second position, *Economic Research-Ekonomska Istrazivanja* achieved 115 citations with a link strength of 4.

5.3.3. *Top 10 most cited articles*

Table 5.3 presents the top 10 most cited documents in digital finance research during the COVID-19 pandemic. The research paper titled "Small Business Awareness and Adoption of State-of-the-Art Technologies in Emerging and Developing Markets, and Lessons from the COVID-19 Pandemic," authored by Akpan *et al.* (2022), holds the

Table 5.3. Top 10 cited documents.

Author	Source	Title	Total citations	Year
Akpan *et al.* (2022)	*Journal of Small Business and Entrepreneurship*	"Small business awareness and adoption of state-of-the-art technologies in emerging and developing markets, and lessons from the COVID-19 pandemic"	122	2022
Li *et al.* (2020)	*Electronic Commerce Research and Applications*	"How should we understand the digital economy in Asia? Critical assessment and research agenda"	113	2020
Murinde *et al.* (2022)	*International Review of Financial Analysis*	"The impact of the fintech revolution on the future of banking: Opportunities and risks"	87	2022
Hussan *et al.* (2020)	*Journal of Economic Cooperation and Development*	"Challenges for the Islamic finance and banking in post covid era and the role of fintech"	82	2020
Al Nawayseh (2020)	*Journal of Open Innovation: Technology, Market, and Complexity*	"Fintech in COVID-19 and beyond: What factors are affecting customers' choice of fintech applications?"	74	2020

Wójcik & Ioannou (2020)	*Tijdschrift Voor Economische en Sociale Geografie*	"COVID-19 and finance: Market developments so far and potential impacts on the financial sector and centers"	67	2020
Haider Syed *et al.* (2020)	*International Journal of Economics and Business Administration*	"An artificial intelligence and NLP based Islamic fintech model combining zakat and qardh-al-hasan for countering the adverse impact of COVID 19 on SMEs and individuals"	64	2020
Modgil *et al.* (2022)	*Technological Forecasting and Social Change*	"Has COVID-19 accelerated opportunities for digital entrepreneurship? An Indian perspective"	60	2022
Fu & Mishra (2022)	*Journal of Financial Intermediation*	"Fintech in the time of COVID-19: Technological adoption during crises"	59	2022
Raza Rabbani *et al.* (2021)	*Journal of Open Innovation: Technology, Market, and Complexity*	"The response of Islamic financial service to the COVID-19 pandemic: The open social innovation of the financial system"	58	2022

highest citation count in this field with 122 citations. It is followed by the articles "How Should We Understand the Digital Economy in Asia? Critical Assessment and Research Agenda," "The Impact of the Fintech Revolution on the Future of Banking: Opportunities and Risks" and "Challenges for Islamic Finance and Banking in the Post-COVID Era and the Role of Fintech," which have garnered 113, 87 and 82 citations, respectively.

5.3.4. *Top 10 most contributing authors*

Table 5.4 lists the top 10 contributors who have authored the highest number of research documents on digital finance during COVID-19. Rabbani leads the list with five documents, while Nathan, Setiawan and Zhang share the second spot with four documents each. Bin-Nashwan, Karim and Liu have each published three documents.

5.3.5. *Top 10 most contributing countries*

Table 5.5 presents the countries that have made the most significant contributions to digital finance research during COVID-19. China leads the list with 30 documents, closely followed by Malaysia with 28 documents. Regarding citations, the United Kingdom has 600 citations, followed by the United States of America with 517 citations.

Table 5.4. Top 10 contributing authors.

Authors	Articles	Articles fractionalized
Rabbani	5	1.09
Nathan	4	0.89
Setiawan	4	0.89
Zhang	4	1.33
Bin-Nashwan	3	1.50
Karim	3	0.64
Liu	3	0.83
Al-Okaily	2	1.25
Alam	2	0.75
Ali Mam	2	0.31

Table 5.5. Top 10 contributing countries.

Countries	Documents	Citations
China	30	292
Malaysia	28	293
United States of America	28	517
Indonesia	26	132
India	25	233
United Kingdom	22	600
United Arab Emirates	12	135
Hungary	11	108
Italy	10	173
Pakistan	8	64

Table 5.6. Top 10 most contributing affiliations.

Affiliation	Articles
Agricultural University of Athens	12
Lviv Polytechnic National University	11
North South University	10
Universiti Putra Malaysia	9
Shandong University	8
Multimedia University	7
Universitas Padjadjaran	7
Universiti Utara Malaysia	7
Hungarian University of Agriculture and Life Sciences	6
Imam Abdulrahman Bib Faisal University	6

5.3.6. *Top 10 most contributing affiliations*

Table 5.6 presents the top 10 affiliations that have made significant contributions to digital finance research during COVID-19 from 2020 to 2024. In total, these top 10 affiliations have produced 83 research documents. The Agricultural University of Athens holds the first position with 12 articles, closely followed by Lviv Polytechnic National University, which has published 11 articles.

5.3.7. *Country collaboration network*

Figure 5.3 illustrates the country collaboration network in digital finance research during COVID-19. A total of 19 countries

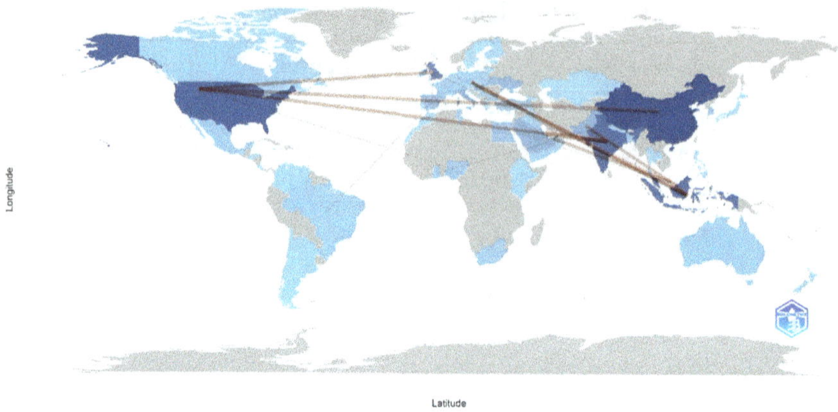

Figure 5.3. Country collaboration network.

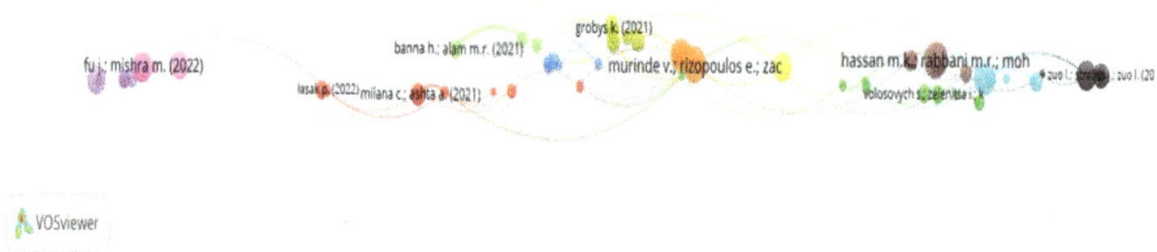

Figure 5.4. Bibliographic coupling of documents.

have engaged in collaborative efforts, including Germany, Hong Kong, Egypt, Kuwait, Oman, Tunisia, El Salvador, Serbia, Barbados, Chile, Costa Rica, Jamaica, Trinidad and Tobago, Slovakia, Honduras, Ghana, Italy, Jordan and Korea. Brazil and China emerge as the leading collaborators, each with a frequency of 7.

5.4. Bibliographic Coupling of Documents

After setting a minimum threshold of five citations per document, 12 clusters were obtained. Out of 240 documents, 89 met the citation threshold. Among these 89 documents, only 66 constitute the largest set of interconnected items through bibliographic coupling, which is used to classify and categorize the comprehensive research structure on digital finance during the COVID-19 pandemic. Figure 5.4 provides detailed information on these clusters.

5.4.1. *Cluster 1: Exploring the landscape of FinTech – insights from diverse perspectives and the impact of COVID-19*

In this cluster, 10 studies investigate various facets of financial technology (FinTech) and its repercussions, particularly in the context of the COVID-19 pandemic. Billore & Billore (2020) delve into the financial behavior of low-income customers, identifying fear, social influence, awareness and trust as key factors influencing positive FinTech adoption. Charaia *et al.* (2021) focus on digitalization trends in the Central Caucasian and Baltic States to bridge financial gaps for small- and medium-sized enterprises (SMEs) in Georgia, Azerbaijan and Armenia. Cumming *et al.* (2022) explore the interconnected dynamics of aggregate equity crowdfunding (ECF), peer-to-peer (P2P) lending and consumer bank loans. The research delves into the varied effects of COVID-19 on each funding category, simultaneously examining the influence of the U.S. CARES Act. Lanfranchi & Grassi (2022) argue for the importance of insurance companies in shaping future innovation, emphasizing the importance of a clear market role. Macchiavello & Siri (2022) initiate a discourse on "Green FinTech" to bridge the gap between finance and environmental sustainability, touching upon the European Single Access Point proposal. Milana & Ashta (2021) review the literature on the evolving applications of artificial intelligence (AI) and computing power in finance, exploring potential benefits and addressing questions about their negative impacts on sustainable growth. Nigmonov & Shams (2021) analyze the lending dynamics during the COVID-19 pandemic, finding increased default probabilities and a higher risk for borrowers with lower credit ratings. Purba *et al.* (2021) present a framework for assessing digital FinTech adoption during the pandemic in Indonesia, highlighting its positive effects on consumer choices. Tut (2023) investigates the impact of the COVID-19 pandemic on financial institutions and consumer FinTech adoption, revealing a partial alleviation of negative effects and an acceleration of FinTech adoption during specific quarters of 2022. Łasak (2022) pursues a threefold objective: exploring the role of FinTech in financing SMEs, examining entities based on financial technology in developing countries and considering the contribution of non-banking aspects to the financial improvement of SMEs.

5.4.2. *Cluster 2: Green horizons — navigating the FinTech landscape (insights into innovation, mediation and transformation)*

This cluster presents a comprehensive exploration of the impact of FinTech. Elsaid (2023) undertakes a comprehensive review of existing literature to uncover potential impacts exerted by FinTech operators on the global financial services market. The analysis meticulously outlines the advantages and obstacles faced by the traditional banking system. Furthermore, Lontchi *et al.* (2023) investigate the mediating function of financial literacy in the context of the interrelation between FinTech and SMEs during the post-COVID-19 recovery period in Cameroon. Their focus is on elucidating the pivotal mechanism through which FinTech services contribute to SMEs' operational and financial performance. Metawa *et al.* (2022) also employ an innovative methodology to scrutinize the ever-changing causal relationships between FinTech, clean technology (CleanTech) and the green economy. Patashkova *et al.* (2021) examine modern technologies in FinTech used by manufacturing companies, identifying sensors and automatic identification as the leading technologies. Sakas *et al.* (2022) employ web analytics, statistical analysis and fuzzy cognitive mapping to simulate and forecast the impact of crises on centralized payment networks (CPNs) and FinTech companies, highlighting their ability to convert new visitors into customers during challenging times. Shahzad *et al.* (2022) propose an enhanced technology acceptance model (TAM) to understand the consumer adoption of FinTech services, emphasizing trust, perceived ease of use and customer innovativeness as critical factors. Starr *et al.* (2021) introduce the concept of "Real Estate 4.0" – an integration of FinTech and PropTech within the framework of Industry 4.0 – showcasing how technology disrupts and transforms the commercial real estate sector. Volosovych *et al.* (2021) focus on the transformations of the institutional environment in the InsurTech ecosystem during the COVID-19 pandemic, identifying prospects for post-pandemic development. Vovk *et al.* (2021) examine the features of banks' lending activities and advocate for strengthened cooperation with financial companies, systematizing both internal and external innovations in the digitalization of banking.

5.4.3. *Cluster 3: Exploring dynamics in financial services and technology adoption*

This cluster encompasses seven papers that delve into diverse aspects of financial services and technology adoption. Alhammad *et al.* (2022) conduct a systematic literature review (SLR) to identify factors influencing backers' behavior in crowdfunding campaigns, contributing theoretically and empirically to understanding backer behavior. Bankuoru Egala *et al.* (2021) explore the repercussions of digital banking services amid the COVID-19 pandemic on customer satisfaction and retention. The study focuses on dimensions such as ease of use and reliability. In a separate investigation, Bin-Nashwan (2022) employs the Unified Model of Acceptance and Use of Technology (UTAUT) to scrutinize the adoption patterns of ZAKATY e-services. The findings underscore the model's significant predictive capability, with a remarkable 72% accuracy in forecasting user intentions. Furthermore, Jiang *et al.* (2022) analyze the spatial impact of digital finance on the effectiveness of monetary policy in China, offering valuable insights applicable to emerging market countries. Kumar *et al.* (2023) examine the mediating effects of digital financial literacy, financial autonomy and impulsivity on financial decision-making and well-being. Mohd Nor *et al.* (2021) explore the perceptions of blockchain technology in *zakah* management, offering a positive outlook for its adoption while acknowledging concerns. Singh & Sharma (2023) investigate the factors influencing Gen X and millennials in India to use FinTech payment services during the COVID-19 pandemic, highlighting the significance of perceived risks, norms and ease of use.

5.4.4. *Cluster 4: Navigating the financial landscape amid COVID-19 challenges*

This cluster comprises seven papers addressing the multifaceted impacts of the COVID-19 pandemic on financial dynamics. Ascarya (2022) advocates for utilizing Islamic social finance (ISF) instruments, such as *zakat*, *infaq* and *waqf*, as viable solutions to address health and economic crises. The proposal highlights their capacity to contribute significantly to government efforts and economic recovery. On a different note, Bao & Huang (2021) scrutinize lending trends among traditional and FinTech lenders in the context of the

COVID-19 pandemic. Grobys (2021) explores the dynamic correlation between Bitcoin and US stocks during the pandemic, revealing Bitcoin's limited effectiveness in hedging tail risks. Guo *et al.* (2022) provide insights into the vulnerable informal economy in China post-COVID-19, using machine learning to analyze transaction-level business data of micro-business owners. Kamran *et al.* (2022) investigate Bitcoin's safe-haven properties during the pandemic in Australia, finding weak benefits when combined with specific stock indices. Li & Xu (2022) conduct in-depth research, incorporating burst detection and co-occurrence analyses, to explore the challenges and future trends in the financial environment amid COVID-19. Zhang *et al.* (2023) examine the impact of FinTech and traditional finance on SMEs during COVID-19, revealing that well-developed financial environments and increased utilization of FinTech instruments mitigated the pandemic's impact on cash shortages for SMEs in China.

5.4.5. *Cluster 5: Unraveling FinTech dynamics — exploring interconnections, collisions and determinants*

This cluster encompasses studies that analyze the intricate relationships between FinTech and various economic facets. Cevik *et al.* (2022) study the interplay between decentralized finance and assets tied to natural resources, examining the spillover effects of returns and volatility. Karim *et al.* (2022) focus on FinTech's impact on SMEs in selected Association of Southeast Asian Nations (ASEAN) countries, revealing that the conflicting interests of new FinTech initiatives and SMEs during the COVID-19 pandemic played a crucial role in fostering FinTech growth and strengthening SMEs. Le *et al.* (2021) scrutinize the spillover effects between FinTech stocks and other financial assets amid the COVID-19 crisis, emphasizing the predominant influence of the US dollar and gold. Shifting focus to the Middle East and North African region during the pandemic, Naz *et al.* (2022) investigate the growth of FinTech, pinpointing privacy concerns, cybercrimes, financial disruption and regulatory challenges as significant obstacles that FinTech start-ups face. Additionally, Trinugroho *et al.* (2022) contribute to the field by empirically modeling the factors influencing the adoption of technology-based innovations by SMEs in Indonesia, with a specific emphasis on digital finance technologies and online sales.

5.4.6. *Cluster 6: Exploring FinTech dynamics — insights from selected studies on adoption, loyalty and resilience*

This cluster consists of studies discussing the various facets of FinTech adoption and its consequences. Al Nawayseh (2020) conducts empirical research on Jordanian citizens' inclination to use FinTech applications, revealing that perceived benefits and social norms significantly influence this intention. Alkhwaldi *et al.* (2022) investigate the determinants of users' intentions and e-loyalty toward FinTech adoption in Jordan post-COVID-19, highlighting the moderating effect of user attitude (UA) and the impact of perceived innovation (PI) on perceived enjoyment (PE) and ease of use (EE). Marcelin *et al.* (2022) explore the global landscape, indicating that increased information-sharing and financial inclusion across 84 countries from 1996 to 2020 has contributed to reduced bank risk levels, emphasizing the social returns of transparency and reaching out to financially excluded segments. Nugraha *et al.* (2022) explore the adoption of FinTech by SMEs in Indonesia amid the COVID-19 outbreak. Their findings reveal that SMEs' intention to adopt FinTech is directly influenced by perceived usefulness, ease of use, government support, trust and user innovativeness. Moreover, they identify an indirect correlation between financial literacy and FinTech adoption, mediated by user innovativeness. In a separate study, Xia *et al.* (2022) investigate the role of digital finance in enhancing corporate resilience to the challenges posed by the COVID-19 pandemic. They observe that Chinese firms in regions with higher levels of digital finance exhibit reduced losses and quicker recovery, which the authors attribute to digital finance's facilitation of access to external financing and reduction of financing costs.

5.4.7. *Cluster 7: Unveiling FinTech dynamics — insights from inclusion, risks and pandemic impacts*

This cluster encompasses a series of studies that shed light on various dimensions of FinTech. Khera *et al.* (2022) develop a pioneering digital financial inclusion index for 52 emerging markets and developing economies, revealing the pivotal role of digital financial services in advancing financial inclusion, particularly in Africa and Asia. Murinde *et al.* (2022) thoroughly review the expanding literature on FinTech and FinTech-enabled services, focusing on the opportunities and risks posed to banks. Investigating the impact of the COVID-19 pandemic on the determinants of FinTech peer-to-peer (P2P) lending, Najaf *et al.* (2022) underscore the significance of P2P platforms for borrowers with limited access to traditional credit facilities during the pandemic. Providing an interdisciplinary examination, Wójcik (2021) reviews both current and potential outcomes of FinTech, with an emphasis on geographical perspectives. The analysis delves into controversies within three key domains: the financial sector and centers, financial regulation and stability, and financial inclusion and governance. Concluding this exploration, Wójcik & Ioannou (2020) offer insightful commentary on the real and potential impacts of the pandemic on financial markets, sectors and centers, grounding their insights in the literature on financial centers, the state–finance nexus and trends that have shaped the financial landscape since the global financial crisis.

5.4.8. *Cluster 8: Navigating FinTech realms — insights from experiences and pandemic responses*

This cluster revolves around studies that explore the multifaceted aspects of FinTech adoption, experiences and responses to the COVID-19 pandemic. Abdul-Rahim *et al.* (2022) conducted a comprehensive investigation with three main objectives: examining the impact of perceived benefits and risks on FinTech services adoption, testing the role of fear of COVID-19 in FinTech adoption and investigating the potential contribution of FinTech adoption to sustainability. Hasan *et al.* (2021) focused on Dutch customers' adoption and experience of mobile payments, particularly in the context of the COVID-19 outbreak and social distancing measures. Mansour (2022) evaluates the repercussions of the COVID-19 pandemic on governmental initiatives aimed at promoting digital modes of payments and financial transactions. Haider Syed *et al.* (2020) put forth an innovative proposal – the integrated AI and natural language processing-based Islamic FinTech model. This model integrates *zakat* (Islamic tax) and *qardh-al-hasan* (benevolent loan) to counteract the adverse effects of COVID-19 on individuals and SMEs.

5.4.9. *Cluster 9: Exploring FinTech dynamics — insights from adoption and resilience*

This thematic cluster is dedicated to the comprehensive exploration of diverse dimensions related to the impact and adoption of FinTech. Chen *et al.* (2021) examine how FinTech products (FTPs) influence the performance of commercial banks in China. Their findings highlight that FTPs' perceived usefulness positively and significantly influences customer satisfaction, expectations of bank employee assistance, service quality and work efficiency. Shifting focus, Daragmeh *et al.* (2021) concentrate on evaluating the factors shaping the behavioral intentions of Hungarian Generation X toward mobile payment services during the pandemic. Their research uncovers that perceived COVID-19 risk, perceived usefulness and subjective norms significantly impact the intentions of this demographic. Meanwhile, Fu & Mishra (2022) provide documentation on the effects of the COVID-19 pandemic on digital finance and the adoption of FinTech. Leveraging mobile application data, they report a substantial surge in the rate of finance app downloads during the COVID-19 spread and associated lockdowns. Addressing a notable gap in research, Gao (2022) focuses on the insufficient investigations into the pandemic's effects on small businesses, particularly exploring the role of FinTech. The study uses firm-level data and various identification methods to reveal the interactive effect of lockdown policies and FinTech on establishing small businesses.

5.4.10. *Cluster 10: Navigating financial landscapes — insights from studies on Islamic FinTech, pandemic resilience and Chinese banking transformation*

This cluster encompasses studies on various aspects of Islamic FinTech, financial resilience during the pandemic and the digital transformation of the Chinese banking industry. Glavina *et al.* (2021) focus on designing a composite indicator to assess the competitiveness of Islamic FinTech adoption across different countries, thereby providing a comprehensive evaluation of the competitive advantages exploited in this domain. Rabbani *et al.* (2021) propose that Islamic finance could serve as a potential tool to navigate economic crises caused by the pandemic, presenting a four-stage COVID-19 model and 10 innovative Islamic financial services tailored for each stage. Additionally, a study by Rabbani *et al.* (2021) investigates the role of the Islamic financial system in post-COVID-19 recovery and explores how FinTech can be leveraged to address the economic repercussions of the pandemic. Zuo *et al.* (2021) contribute to examining the digital transformation of the Chinese banking industry by employing the DEA–Malmquist index method and conducting an empirical study to analyze improvements in efficiency and dynamic changes in productivity within the sector.

5.4.11. *Cluster 11 (light green): Navigating financial stability — insights from digital financial inclusion and resilience*

This cluster is dedicated to investigating the role of digital financial inclusion (DFI) in maintaining banking stability and stabilizing the Islamic banking sector amid the COVID-19 pandemic. Banna & Alam (2021) concentrate on investigating the potential contributions of DFI to banking stability in countries belonging to the ASEAN, with considerations for potential implications in the post-COVID-19 era. Expanding on this line of inquiry, Banna *et al.* (2022) specifically discuss the role of DFI in fostering stability within the Islamic banking sector amid the ongoing pandemic. Additionally, Ling *et al.* (2021) make a significant contribution by scrutinizing the repercussions of COVID-19 on financial constraints within Chinese listed companies, with a specific emphasis on the moderating influence of financial technology.

5.4.12. *Cluster 12 (light yellow): Exploring digital frontiers — insights from emerging areas and technologies for digital entrepreneurship*

This thematic cluster is dedicated to comprehending emerging areas and technologies in digital entrepreneurship. In their study, Modgil *et al.* (2022) aim to unravel the landscape of digital entrepreneurship opportunities, uncovering nascent areas in technology, healthcare, entertainment and e-commerce. In a complementary exploration,

Wu & Kao (2022) delve into the opportunities and challenges inherent in the FinTech business model within Southeast Asia's banking and enterprise sector, specifically in the post-COVID-19 era. The study further investigates strategies for achieving sustainable development by examining the interactions of this new operating model with existing ones, particularly in the context of the evolving "new normal" working conditions.

5.5. Conclusions

5.5.1. *Key takeaways*

By examining the literature of digital finance during COVID-19, this bibliometric study provides several key takeaways for stakeholders. First, the publication trend reveals that in 2020, 11 articles were published on digital finance research, followed by 46, 92 and 90 articles in the years 2021, 2022 and 2023, respectively. Second, this review highlights the top-contributing sources and reveals that the *Journal of Open Innovation: Technology, Market, and Complexity* is ranked first, with 10 documents, 84 citations and a total link strength of 22. In terms of citations, *Technological Forecasting and Social Change* takes the first position with 190 citations, followed by *Economic Research-Ekonomska Istrazivanja*, which has 115 citations. Third, this review identifies the most-cited documents, with Akpan *et al.* (2022) securing the first rank with 122 citations. Following closely, Li *et al.* (2020) attained the second rank with 113 citations, and Murinde *et al.* (2022) share the third rank with 87 citations. Fourth, upon further examination of the top contributing authors, it is revealed that Rabbani leads the list with five documents. Following closely, Nathan, Setiawan and Zhang share the second rank, each with four articles.

Fifth, this review explores the top contributing countries and reveals that China leads the list with 30 documents and 292 citations. Following closely, Malaysia and the United States of America share the second rank, each with 28 documents. In terms of citations, the United Kingdom tops the list with 600 citations, followed by the United States of America with 517 citations. Sixth, this review uncovers the most influential affiliations, with the Agricultural University of Athens securing the first rank with 12 documents.

Following closely, Lviv Polytechnic National University, North South University and Universiti Putra Malaysia hold the second, third and fourth ranks with 11, 10 and 9 documents, respectively. Seventh, the country collaboration network reveals that Brazil has the highest collaboration with seven countries, resulting in seven documents. While China collaborated with five countries and produced seven documents, Bahrain and Chile collaborated with four countries, producing four documents each. Eighth, bibliographic coupling reveals 12 significant themes that portray the body of knowledge in digital finance research during COVID-19. We summarized the key articles in each cluster.

5.5.2. *Limitations and future research agendas*

While this chapter provides valuable insights into the subject matter considered, it is essential to acknowledge its inherent limitations. First, the study exclusively relied on the Scopus database, omitting other reputable databases such as WOS and Dimensions. This approach may have resulted in an incomplete representation of the available literature on digital finance. Future research endeavors should consider a more comprehensive database search to ensure a thorough exploration of relevant studies. Second, the temporal focus of this chapter on the COVID-19 period may limit the broader applicability of the findings. The omission of papers from years outside the specified period might have overlooked essential trends or variations over time. To achieve a more holistic understanding, future research should encompass all relevant years when papers were published, providing a more comprehensive perspective on the evolution of the subject. Furthermore, the study's scope is not exhaustive, and its exclusion criteria – which are based on subjects, source type, document type and language (English) – may have resulted in the inadvertent omission of pertinent studies. To enhance the inclusivity of future investigations, researchers should carefully consider and justify their exclusion criteria while attempting to capture a more diverse range of contributions to the field. Lastly, it is essential to note that the current review adopts an exploratory design, limiting its capacity for confirmatory investigations. Subsequent research could benefit from incorporating meta-analytical approaches to validate and strengthen the observed patterns, thereby providing a more robust foundation for the conclusions drawn in this study. In light of these limitations, future research should address these constraints and contribute to a more nuanced and comprehensive understanding of digital finance.

References

Abdul-Rahim, R., Bohari, S. A., Aman, A., & Awang, Z. (2022). Benefit–risk perceptions of fintech adoption for sustainability from bank consumers' perspective: The moderating role of fear of covid-19. *Sustainability*, 14(14), 8357. https://doi.org/10.3390/su14148357.

Agarwal, P., Swami, S., & Malhotra, S. K. (2022). Artificial Intelligence Adoption in the Post COVID-19 New-Normal and Role of Smart Technologies in Transforming Business: A review. *Journal of Science and Technology Policy Management*. https://doi.org/10.1108/JSTPM-08-2021-0122.

Ahmed, M. E., Zafar, A. M., Hamouda, M. A., Aly Hassan, A., & Arimbrathodi, S. (2022). Biodesalination research trends: A bibliometric analysis and recent developments. *Sustainability*, 15(1), 16. https://doi.org/10.3390/su15010016.

Akpan, I. J., Udoh, E. A. P., & Adebisi, B. (2022). Small business awareness and adoption of state-of-the-art technologies in emerging and developing markets, and lessons from the COVID-19 pandemic. *Journal of Small Business & Entrepreneurship*, 34(2), 123–140. https://doi.org/10.1080/08276331.2020.1820185.

Al Nawayseh, M. K. (2020). Fintech in COVID-19 and beyond: What factors are affecting customers' choice of fintech applications? *Journal of Open Innovation: Technology, Market, and Complexity*, 6(4), 153. https://doi.org/10.3390/joitmc6040153.

Alhammad, M. M., Tan, C., Alsarhani, N., Bank Albilad, & Zolkepli, I. A. (2022). What impacts backers' behavior to fund reward-based crowdfunding projects? A systematic review study. *Pacific Asia Journal of the Association for Information Systems*, 14, 90–110. https://doi.org/10.17705/1pais.14207.

Alhammadi, S. (2023). Expanding financial inclusion in Indonesia through Takaful: Opportunities, challenges and sustainability. *Journal of Financial Reporting and Accounting*. https://doi.org/10.1108/JFRA-05-2023-0256.

Alkhwaldi, A. F., Alharasis, E. E., Shehadeh, M., Abu-AlSondos, I. A., Oudat, M. S., & Bani Atta, A. A. (2022). Towards an understanding of fintech users' adoption: Intention and e-loyalty post-covid-19 from a developing country perspective. *Sustainability*, 14(19), 12616. https://doi.org/10.3390/su141912616.

Arner, D. W., Buckley, R. P., Zetzsche, D. A., & Veidt, R. (2020). Sustainability, fintech and financial inclusion. *European Business Organization Law Review*, 21(1), 7–35. https://doi.org/10.1007/s40804-020-00183-y.

Ascarya, A. (2022). The role of Islamic social finance during Covid-19 pandemic in Indonesia's economic recovery. *International Journal of Islamic and Middle Eastern Finance and Management*, 15(2), 386–405. https://doi.org/10.1108/IMEFM-07-2020-0351.

Bankuoru Egala, S., Boateng, D., & Aboagye Mensah, S. (2021). To leave or retain? An interplay between quality digital banking services and customer satisfaction. *International Journal of Bank Marketing*, 39(7), 1420–1445. https://doi.org/10.1108/IJBM-02-2021-0072.

Banna, H. & Alam, M. R. (2021). Impact of digital financial inclusion on ASEAN banking stability: Implications for the post-Covid-19 era. *Studies in Economics and Finance*, 38(2), 504–523. https://doi.org/10.1108/SEF-09-2020-0388.

Banna, H., Hassan, M. K., Ahmad, R., & Alam, M. R. (2022). Islamic banking stability amidst the COVID-19 pandemic: The role of digital financial inclusion. *International Journal of Islamic and Middle Eastern Finance and Management*, 15(2), 310–330. https://doi.org/10.1108/IMEFM-08-2020-0389.

Bao, Z. & Huang, D. (2021). Shadow banking in a crisis: Evidence from fintech during covid-19. *Journal of Financial and Quantitative Analysis*, 56(7), 2320–2355. https://doi.org/10.1017/S0022109021000430.

Bhaskar, R., Hunjra, A. I., Bansal, S., & Pandey, D. K. (2022). Central bank digital currencies: Agendas for future research. Research in *International Business and Finance*, 62, 101737. https://doi.org/10.1016/j.ribaf.2022.101737.

Bhatt, A., Joshipura, M., & Joshipura, N. (2022). Decoding the trinity of Fintech, digitalization and financial services: An integrated bibliometric analysis and thematic literature review approach. *Cogent Economics & Finance*, 10(1). https://doi.org/10.1080/23322039.2022.2114160.

Billore, S. & Billore, G. (2020). Consumption switch at haste: Insights from Indian low-income customers for adopting Fintech services due to the pandemic. *Transnational Marketing Journal*, 8(2), 197–218. https://doi.org/10.33182/tmj.v8i2.1064.

Bin-Nashwan, S. A. (2022). Toward diffusion of e-Zakat initiatives amid the COVID-19 crisis and beyond. *Foresight*, 24(2), 141–158. https://doi.org/10.1108/FS-08-2020-0082.

Boubaker, S., Goodell, J. W., Kumar, S., & Sureka, R. (2023). COVID-19 and finance scholarship: A systematic and bibliometric analysis. *International Review of Financial Analysis*, 85, 102458. https://doi.org/10.1016/j.irfa.2022.102458.

Broadus, R. N. (1987). Toward a definition of "bibliometrics." *Scientometrics*, 12(5–6), 373–379. https://doi.org/10.1007/BF02016680.

Cevik, E. I., Gunay, S., Zafar, M. W., Destek, M. A., Bugan, M. F., & Tuna, F. (2022). The impact of digital finance on the natural resource market: Evidence from DeFi, oil, and gold. *Resources Policy*, 79, 103081. https://doi.org/10.1016/j.resourpol.2022.103081.

Charaia, V., Chochia, A., & Lashkhi, M. (2021). Promoting fintech financing for SME in S. Caucasian and Baltic states, during the covid-19 global pandemic. *Business, Management and Economics Engineering*, 19(02), 358–372. https://doi.org/10.3846/bmee.2021.14755.

Chen, X., You, X., & Chang, V. (2021). FinTech and commercial banks' performance in China: A leap forward or survival of the fittest? *Technological Forecasting and Social Change*, 166, 120645. https://doi.org/10.1016/j.techfore.2021.120645.

Cumming, D. J., Martinez-Salgueiro, A., Reardon, R. S., & Sewaid, A. (2022). COVID-19 bust, policy response, and rebound: Equity crowdfunding and P2P versus banks. *The Journal of Technology Transfer*, 47(6), 1825–1846. https://doi.org/10.1007/s10961-021-09899-6.

Daragmeh, A., Lentner, C., & Sági, J. (2021). FinTech payments in the era of COVID-19: Factors influencing behavioral intentions of "Generation X" in Hungary to use mobile payment. *Journal of Behavioral and Experimental Finance*, 32, 100574. https://doi.org/10.1016/j.jbef.2021.100574.

Donthu, N., Kumar, S., Mukherjee, D., Pandey, N., & Lim, W. M. (2021). How to conduct a bibliometric analysis: An overview and guidelines. *Journal of Business Research*, 133, 285–296. https://doi.org/10.1016/j.jbusres.2021.04.070.

Elsaid, H. M. (2023). A review of literature directions regarding the impact of fintech firms on the banking industry. *Qualitative Research in Financial Markets*, 15(5), 693–711. https://doi.org/10.1108/QRFM-10-2020-0197.

Feng, S., Zhang, R., & Li, G. (2022). Environmental decentralization, digital finance and green technology innovation. *Structural Change and Economic Dynamics*, 61, 70–83. https://doi.org/10.1016/j.strueco.2022.02.008.

Fu, J. & Mishra, M. (2022). Fintech in the time of COVID-19: Technological adoption during crises. *Journal of Financial Intermediation*, 50, 100945. https://doi.org/10.1016/j.jfi.2021.100945.

Gabor, D. & Brooks, S. (2020). The digital revolution in financial inclusion: international development in the fintech era. *In Material Cultures of Financialisation* (pp. 69–82). Routledge. https://doi.org/10.4324/9781351002103-6.

Gao, J. (2022). Has COVID-19 hindered small business activities? The role of fintech. *Economic Analysis and Policy*, 74, 297–308. https://doi.org/10.1016/j.eap.2022.02.008.

Ghosh, C. & Hom Chaudhury, R. (2022). Determinants of digital finance in India. *Innovation and Development*, 12(3), 343–362. https://doi.org/10.1080/2157930X.2020.1850012.

Glavina, S., Aidrus, I., & Trusova, A. (2021). Assessment of the competitiveness of Islamic fintech implementation: A composite indicator for cross-country analysis. *Journal of Risk and Financial Management*, 14(12), 602. https://doi.org/10.3390/jrfm14120602.

Gomber, P., Koch, J.-A., & Siering, M. (2017). Digital finance and FinTech: Current research and future research directions. *Journal of Business Economics*, 87(5), 537–580. https://doi.org/10.1007/s11573-017-0852-x.

Goyal, K. & Kumar, S. (2021). Financial literacy: A systematic review and bibliometric analysis. *International Journal of Consumer Studies*, 45(1), 80–105. https://doi.org/10.1111/ijcs.12605.

Grobys, K. (2021). When bitcoin has the flu: On bitcoin's performance to hedge equity risk in the early wake of the COVID-19 outbreak. *Applied Economics Letters*, 28(10), 860–865. https://doi.org/10.1080/13504851.2020.1784380.

Guo, F., Huang, Y., Wang, J., & Wang, X. (2022). The informal economy at times of COVID-19 pandemic. *China Economic Review*, 71, 101722. https://doi.org/10.1016/j.chieco.2021.101722.

Gupta, S., Ghardallou, W., Pandey, D. K., & Sahu, G. P. (2022). Artificial intelligence adoption in the insurance industry: Evidence using the technology-organization-environment framework. *Research in International Business and Finance*, 63, 101757. https://doi.org/10.1016/j.ribaf.2022.101757.

Gupta, S. & Kanungo, R. P. (2022). Financial inclusion through digitalisation: Economic viability for the bottom of the pyramid (Bop) segment. *Journal of Business Research*, 148, 262–276. https://doi.org/10.1016/j.jbusres.2022.04.070.

Gupta, S., Pandey, D. K., El Ammari, A., & Sahu, G. P. (2023). Do perceived risks and benefits impact trust and willingness to adopt

CBDCs? *Research in International Business and Finance*, 66, 101993. https://doi.org/10.1016/j.ribaf.2023.101993.

Haider Syed, M., Khan, S., Rabbani, M. R., & Thalassinos, Y. E. (2020). An artificial intelligence and NLP based Islamic fintech model combining zakat and qardh-al-hasan for countering the adverse impact of COVID 19 on SMEs and individuals. *International Journal of Economics and Business Administration*, VIII(Issue 2), 351–364. https://doi.org/10.35808/ijeba/466.

Hasan, R., Ashfaq, M., & Shao, L. (2021). Evaluating drivers of fintech adoption in the Netherlands. *Global Business Review*, 097215092110274. https://doi.org/10.1177/09721509211027402.

Hunjra, A. I. & Hanif, M. (2023). Central banking issues and challenges. In Hunjra, A. I. & Hanif, M. (Eds.), *Reference Module in Social Sciences*. Pakistan: Elsevier. https://doi.org/10.1016/B978-0-44-313776-1.00113-6.

Hussan, K. N., Rabbani, M. R., & Ali, M. A. (2020). Challenges for the Islamic finance and banking in post covid era and the role of fintech. *Journal of Economic Cooperation and Development*, 41(3), 93–116.

Jalal, R. N.-U.-D., Alon, I., & Paltrinieri, A. (2021). A bibliometric review of cryptocurrencies as a financial asset. *Technology Analysis & Strategic Management*, 1–16. https://doi.org/10.1080/09537325.2021.1939001.

Jiang, S., Qiu, S., & Zhou, H. (2022). Will digital financial development affect the effectiveness of monetary policy in emerging market countries? *Economic Research-Ekonomska Istraživanja*, 35(1), 3437–3472. https://doi.org/10.1080/1331677X.2021.1997619.

Kamran, M., Butt, P., Abdel-Razzaq, A., & Djajadikerta, H. G. (2022). Is bitcoin a safe haven? Application of FinTech to safeguard Australian stock markets. *Studies in Economics and Finance*, 39(3), 386–402. https://doi.org/10.1108/SEF-05-2021-0201.

Karim, S., Naz, F., Naeem, M. A., & Vigne, S. A. (2022). Is fintech providing effective solutions to small and medium enterprises (SMEs) in ASEAN countries? *Economic Analysis and Policy*, 75, 335–344. https://doi.org/10.1016/j.eap.2022.05.019.

Khando, K., Islam, M. S., & Gao, S. (2022). The emerging technologies of digital payments and associated challenges: A systematic literature review. *Future Internet*, 15(1), 21. https://doi.org/10.3390/fi15010021.

Khera, P., Ng, S., Ogawa, S., & Sahay, R. (2022). Measuring digital financial inclusion in emerging market and developing economies: A new index. *Asian Economic Policy Review*, 17(2), 213–230. https://doi.org/10.1111/aepr.12377.

Kumar, P., Pillai, R., Kumar, N., & Tabash, M. I. (2023). The interplay of skills, digital financial literacy, capability, and autonomy in financial decision making and well-being. *Borsa Istanbul Review*, 23(1), 169–183. https://doi.org/10.1016/j.bir.2022.09.012.

Kumar, S., Pandey, N., & Mukherjee, D. (2022). Cross cultural and strategic management: A retrospective overview using bibliometric analysis. *Cross Cultural & Strategic Management*, 29(1), 171–194. https://doi.org/10.1108/CCSM-08-2021-0147.

Lanfranchi, D. & Grassi, L. (2022). Examining insurance companies' use of technology for innovation. *The Geneva Papers on Risk and Insurance - Issues and Practice*, 47(3), 520–537. https://doi.org/10.1057/s41288-021-00258-y.

Łasak, P. (2022). The role of financial technology and entrepreneurial finance practices in funding small and medium-sized enterprises. *Journal of Entrepreneurship, Management and Innovation*, 18(1), 7–34. https://doi.org/10.7341/20221811.

Le, L.-T., Yarovaya, L., & Nasir, M. A. (2021). Did COVID-19 change spillover patterns between Fintech and other asset classes? *Research in International Business and Finance*, 58, 101441. https://doi.org/10.1016/j.ribaf.2021.101441.

Levine-Clark, M. & Gil, E. L. (2008). A comparative citation analysis of web of science, scopus, and google scholar. *Journal of Business & Finance Librarianship*, 14(1), 32–46. https://doi.org/10.1080/08963560802176348.

Li, B. & Xu, Z. (2022). A comprehensive bibliometric analysis of financial innovation. *Economic Research-Ekonomska Istraživanja*, 35(1), 367–390. https://doi.org/10.1080/1331677X.2021.1893203.

Li, K., Kim, D. J., Lang, K. R., Kauffman, R. J., & Naldi, M. (2020). How should we understand the digital economy in Asia? Critical assessment and research agenda. *Electronic Commerce Research and Applications*, 44, 101004. https://doi.org/10.1016/j.elerap.2020.101004.

Ling, S., Pei, T., Li, Z., & Zhang, Z. (2021). Impact of covid-19 on financial constraints and the moderating effect of financial technology. *Emerging Markets Finance and Trade*, 57(6), 1675–1688. https://doi.org/10.1080/1540496X.2021.1904883.

Liu, L. & Zhang, H. (2021). Financial literacy, self-efficacy and risky credit behavior among college students: Evidence from online consumer credit. *Journal of Behavioral and Experimental Finance*, 32, 100569. https://doi.org/10.1016/j.jbef.2021.100569.

Lontchi, C. B., Yang, B., & Shuaib, K. M. (2023). Effect of financial technology on SMEs performance in Cameroon amid covid-19 recovery:

The mediating effect of financial literacy. *Sustainability*, 15(3), 2171. https://doi.org/10.3390/su15032171.

Macchiavello, E. & Siri, M. (2022). Sustainable finance and fintech: Can technology contribute to achieving environmental goals? A preliminary assessment of 'green fintech' and 'sustainable digital finance.' *European Company and Financial Law Review*, 19(1), 128–174. https://doi.org/10.1515/ecfr-2022-0005.

Mansour, H. (2022). How successful countries are in promoting digital transactions during COVID-19. *Journal of Economic Studies*, 49(3), 435–452. https://doi.org/10.1108/JES-10-2020-0489.

Marcelin, I., Sun, W., Teclezion, M., & Junarsin, E. (2022). Financial inclusion and bank risk-taking: The effect of information sharing. *Finance Research Letters*, 50, 103182. https://doi.org/10.1016/j.frl.2022.103182.

Metawa, N., Dogan, E., & Taskin, D. (2022). Analyzing the nexus of green economy, clean and financial technology. *Economic Analysis and Policy*, 76, 385–396. https://doi.org/10.1016/j.eap.2022.08.023.

Mhlanga, D. (2020). Industry 4. 0 in finance: The impact of artificial intelligence (AI) on digital financial inclusion. *International Journal of Financial Studies*, 8(3), 45. https://doi.org/10.3390/ijfs8030045.

Milana, C. & Ashta, A. (2021). Artificial intelligence techniques in finance and financial markets: A survey of the literature. *Strategic Change*, 30(3), 189–209. https://doi.org/10.1002/jsc.2403.

Modgil, S., Dwivedi, Y. K., Rana, N. P., Gupta, S., & Kamble, S. (2022). Has Covid-19 accelerated opportunities for digital entrepreneurship? An Indian perspective. *Technological Forecasting and Social Change*, 175, 121415. https://doi.org/10.1016/j.techfore.2021.121415.

Mohd Nor, S., Abdul-Majid, M., & Esrati, S. N. (2021). The role of blockchain technology in enhancing Islamic social finance: The case of Zakah management in Malaysia. *Foresight*, 23(5), 509–527. https://doi.org/10.1108/FS-06-2020-0058.

Murinde, V., Rizopoulos, E., & Zachariadis, M. (2022). The impact of the FinTech revolution on the future of banking: Opportunities and risks. *International Review of Financial Analysis*, 81, 102103. https://doi.org/10.1016/j.irfa.2022.102103.

Najaf, K., Subramaniam, R. K., & Atayah, O. F. (2022). Understanding the implications of FinTech peer-to-peer (P2p) lending during the COVID-19 pandemic. *Journal of Sustainable Finance & Investment*, 12(1), 87–102. https://doi.org/10.1080/20430795.2021.1917225.

Naz, F., Karim, S., Houcine, A., & Naeem, M. A. (2022). Fintech growth during COVID-19 in Mena region: Current challenges and future prospects. *Electronic Commerce Research*. https://doi.org/10.1007/s10660-022-09583-3.

Nigmonov, A. & Shams, S. (2021). COVID-19 pandemic risk and probability of loan default: Evidence from marketplace lending market. *Financial Innovation*, 7(1), 83. https://doi.org/10.1186/s40854-021-00300-x.

Nugraha, D. P., Setiawan, B., Nathan, R. J., & Fekete-Farkas, M. (2022). Fintech adoption drivers for innovation for SMEs in Indonesia. *Journal of Open Innovation: Technology, Market, and Complexity*, 8(4), 208. https://doi.org/10.3390/joitmc8040208.

Okoli, C. & Schabram, K. (2010). A guide to conducting a systematic literature review of information systems research. *SSRN Electronic Journal*. https://doi.org/10.2139/ssrn.1954824.

Ozili, P. K. (2018). Impact of digital finance on financial inclusion and stability. *Borsa Istanbul Review*, 18(4), 329–340. https://doi.org/10.1016/j.bir.2017.12.003.

Pandey, D. K., Hassan, M. K., Kumari, V., Zaied, Y. Ben, & Rai, V. K. (2024). Mapping the landscape of FinTech in banking and finance: A bibliometric review. *Research in International Business and Finance*, 67, 102116. https://doi.org/10.1016/j.ribaf.2023.102116.

Pandey, D. K., Hunjra, A. I., Hassan, M. K., & Rai, V. K. (2023). Venture capital financing during crises: A bibliometric review. *Research in International Business and Finance*, 64, 101856. https://doi.org/10.1016/J.RIBAF.2022.101856.

Pandey, D. K. & Kumar, R. (2023). Russia-Ukraine War and the global tourism sector: A 13-day tale. *Current Issues in Tourism*, 26(5), 692–700. https://doi.org/10.1080/13683500.2022.2081789.

Pandey, D. K. & Kumari, V. (2021). Event study on the reaction of the developed and emerging stock markets to the 2019-nCoV outbreak. *International Review of Economics and Finance*, 71, 467–483. https://doi.org/10.1016/j.iref.2020.09.014.

Patashkova, Y., Niyazbekova, S., Kerimkhulle, S., Serikova, M., & Troyanskaya, M. (2021). Dynamics of bitcoin trading on the binance cryptocurrency exchange. *Economic Annals-XXI*, 187(1–2), 177–188. https://doi.org/10.21003/ea.V187-17.

Pazarbasioglu, C., Mora, A. G., Uttamchandani, M., Natarajan, H., Feyen, E., & Saal, M. (2020). Digital financial Services. *World Bank*, 54.

Purba, J. T., Samuel, S., & Budiono, S. (2021). Collaboration of digital payment usage decision in COVID-19 pandemic situation: Evidence from Indonesia. *International Journal of Data and Network Science*, 5(4), 557–568. https://doi.org/10.5267/j.ijdns.2021.8.012.

Rabbani, M. R., Asad Mohd. Ali, M., Rahiman, H. U., Atif, Mohd., Zulfikar, Z., & Naseem, Y. (2021). The response of Islamic financial service to the covid-19 pandemic: The open social innovation of the financial system. *Journal of Open Innovation: Technology, Market, and Complexity*, 7(1), 85. https://doi.org/10.3390/joitmc7010085.

Rabbani, M. R., Bashar, A., Nawaz, N., Karim, S., Ali, M. A. Mohd., Rahiman, H. U., & Alam, M. S. (2021). Exploring the role of Islamic fintech in combating the aftershocks of covid-19: The open social innovation of the Islamic financial system. *Journal of Open Innovation: Technology, Market, and Complexity*, 7(2), 136. https://doi.org/10.3390/joitmc7020136.

Sakas, D. P., Kamperos, I. D. G., Reklitis, D. P., Giannakopoulos, N. T., Nasiopoulos, D. K., Terzi, M. C., & Kanellos, N. (2022). The effectiveness of centralized payment network advertisements on digital branding during the covid-19 crisis. *Sustainability*, 14(6), 3616. https://doi.org/10.3390/su14063616.

Shahrokhi, M. (2008). E-finance: Status, innovations, resources and future challenges. *Managerial Finance*, 34(6), 365–398. https://doi.org/10.1108/03074350810872787.

Shahzad, A., Zahrullail, N., Akbar, A., Mohelska, H., & Hussain, A. (2022). Covid-19's impact on fintech adoption: Behavioral intention to use the financial portal. *Journal of Risk and Financial Management*, 15(10), 428. https://doi.org/10.3390/jrfm15100428.

Singh, A. K. & Sharma, P. (2023). A study of Indian Gen X and Millennials consumers' intention to use FinTech payment services during COVID-19 pandemic. *Journal of Modelling in Management*, 18(4), 1177–1203. https://doi.org/10.1108/JM2-02-2022-0059.

Srisathan, W. A., & Naruetharadhol, P. (2022). A COVID-19 disruption: The great acceleration of digitally planned and transformed behaviors in Thailand. *Technology in Society*, 68, 101912. https://doi.org/10.1016/j.techsoc.2022.101912.

Starr, C. W., Saginor, J., & Worzala, E. (2021). The rise of PropTech: Emerging industrial technologies and their impact on real estate. *Journal of Property Investment & Finance*, 39(2), 157–169. https://doi.org/10.1108/JPIF-08-2020-0090.

Thomas, H., & Hedrick-Wong, Y. (2019). How digital finance and fintech can improve financial inclusion. In Thomas, H. & Hedrick-Wong, Y. (Eds.), *Inclusive Growth* (pp. 27–41). Leeds, UK: Emerald Publishing Limited. https://doi.org/10.1108/978-1-78973-779-020191004.

Trinugroho, I., Pamungkas, P., Wiwoho, J., Damayanti, S. M., & Pramono, T. (2022). Adoption of digital technologies for micro and small business in Indonesia. *Finance Research Letters*, 45, 102156. https://doi.org/10.1016/j.frl.2021.102156.

Turi, A. N. (Ed.). (2023). *Financial Technologies and Defi: A Revisit to the Digital Finance Revolution.* New York: Springer International Publishing. https://doi.org/10.1007/978-3-031-17998-3.

Tut, D. (2023). FinTech and the COVID-19 pandemic: Evidence from electronic payment systems. *Emerging Markets Review*, 54, 100999. https://doi.org/10.1016/j.ememar.2023.100999.

Verma, S. & Gustafsson, A. (2020). Investigating the emerging COVID-19 research trends in the field of business and management: A bibliometric analysis approach. *Journal of Business Research*, 118, 253–261. h ttps://doi.org/10.1016/j.jbusres.2020.06.057.

Volosovych, S., Zelenitsa, I., Kondratenko, D., Szymla, W., & Mamchur, R. (2021). Transformation of insurance technologies in the context of a pandemic. *Insurance Markets and Companies*, 12(1), 1–13. https://doi.org/10.21511/ins.12(1).2021.01.

Vovk, V., Denysova, A., Rudoi, K., & Kyrychenko, T. (2021). Management and legal aspects of the symbiosis of banking institutions and fintech companies in the credit services market in the context of digitization. *Studies of Applied Economics*, 39(7). https://doi.org/10.25115/eea.v39i7.5013.

Wójcik, D. (2021). Financial geography II: The impacts of FinTech – Financial sector and centres, regulation and stability, inclusion and governance. *Progress in Human Geography*, 45(4), 878–889. https://doi.org/10.1177/0309132520959825.

Wójcik, D. & Ioannou, S. (2020). Covid-19 and finance: Market developments so far and potential impacts on the financial sector and centres. *Tijdschrift Voor Economische En Sociale Geografie*, 111(3), 387–400. https://doi.org/10.1111/tesg.12434.

Wu, A.-C. & Kao, D.-D. (2022). Mapping the sustainable human-resource challenges in southeast Asia's fintech sector. *Journal of Risk and Financial Management*, 15(7), 307. https://doi.org/10.3390/jrfm15070307.

Xia, Y., Qiao, Z., & Xie, G. (2022). Corporate resilience to the COVID-19 pandemic: The role of digital finance. *Pacific-Basin Finance Journal*, 74, 101791. https://doi.org/10.1016/j.pacfin.2022.101791.

Yuan, Y.-P., Tan, G. W.-H., & Ooi, K.-B. (2022). Does COVID-19 pandemic motivate privacy self-disclosure in mobile fintech transactions? A privacy-calculus-based dual-stage SEM-ANN analysis. *IEEE Transactions on Engineering Management*, 1–15. https://doi.org/10.1109/TEM.2022.3204285.

Zhang, Y. & Mao, J. (2022). COVID-19?s impact on the spillover effect across the Chinese and U.S. stock markets. *Finance Research Letters*, 47, 102684. https://doi.org/10.1016/j.frl.2022.102684.

Zhang, Y., Xing, C., & Guo, X. (2023). The shielding effect of access to finance on small and medium-sized enterprises during the covid-19 crisis: Comparing fintech and traditional finance. *Emerging Markets Finance and Trade*, 59(8), 2383–2397. https://doi.org/10.1080/1540496X.2022.2072201.

Zuo, L., Strauss, J., & Zuo, L. (2021). The digitalization transformation of commercial banks and its impact on sustainable efficiency improvements through investment in science and technology. *Sustainability*, 13(19), 11028. https://doi.org/10.3390/su131911028.

https://doi.org/10.1142/9781800616257_0006

Chapter 6

A Review on the Digital Finance Revolution, Trends and Global Impacts

Mahnoor Hanif[*,§], **Bushra Zulfiqar**[*,¶], **Rashid Mehmood**[†,‖], **and Bushra Bibi**[‡,**]

[*]*University Institute of Management Sciences, PMAS-Arid Agriculture University Rawalpindi, Rawalpindi, Pakistan*

[†]*UE Business School, Division of Management and Administrative Science, University of Education, Lahore, Pakistan*

[‡]*Department of Business Administration, Ghazi University Dera Ghazi Khan, Dera Ghazi Khan, Pakistan*

[§]*mahnoorhanif289@gmail.com*

[¶]*bushra.zulfiqar@uaar.edu.pk*

[‖]*rashidm1005@gmail.com*

[**]*bushrahashim666@gmail.com*

Abstract

This chapter summarizes the current state of digital finance (DF) research and draws attention to some of the most important worldwide trends in this area. The study highlights the crucial significance of DF within contemporary financial systems, primarily observed in various applications such as FinTech, integrated finance, open banking, decentralized finance and digital currencies issued by central banks. Additionally, it examines the global factors that influence DF, including the need for effective and streamlined financial services, the utilization of digital technologies to achieve the United Nations Sustainable Development Goals, the promotion of financial inclusion through digital methods and the improvement of payment and settlement efficiency. Further, this chapter focuses on analyzing global advancements in DF, highlighting the significant impact of investments in the FinTech and mobile money sectors. Moreover, this chapter envisions a forthcoming era in the realm of DF characterized by a conducive setting enabling the delivery of a wide range of financial offerings and solutions customized to meet the specific requirements of individuals, all within a unified digital framework. The current study proposes potential directions for future research, highlighting the importance of investigating regulatory approaches that can adapt to the changing landscape of DF.

Keywords: Digital finance, financial inclusion, FinTech, artificial intelligence, financial stability, blockchain, cryptocurrency.

6.1. Introduction

Digital finance (DF) refers to the application of digital gadgets and technology to obtain, utilize and disseminate financial resources among various economic groups, including individuals, households, corporations and government bodies (Mhlanga, 2020; Siddik & Kabiraj, 2020). The incorporation of digital technology (DT) into the financial sector commenced in the early 2000s, coinciding with the dot-com bubble. Its significance grew notably following the global financial crisis of 2007–2009 as a strategic reaction to facilitate cross-border payment processing, enhance client account management, minimize expenses and optimize financial gains (Wales, 2015; Murinde *et al.*, 2022).

The utilization of DT in the realm of finance has played a pivotal role in fostering the expeditious growth of the financial sector across multiple developed nations. According to Shabsigh *et al.* (2020), technology usage has resulted in faster dissemination of financial market information to various stakeholders such as investors, shareholders and other players in the market. Additionally, it has facilitated the expeditious execution of financial transactions, payments and the finalization of settlements (Phan *et al.*, 2020). Therefore, the integration of DT in the financial sector has been essential for enhancing remittance inflows and promoting financial inclusion, particularly in developing nations (Veloso *et al.*, 2021).

DF has garnered significant attention and has been the subject of extensive scholarly discourse (Ozili, 2021; Jünger & Mietzner, 2020; Kofman & Payne, 2021; Hui *et al.*, 2023). This discourse revolves around five key themes, namely the examination of the overall welfare benefits associated with DF, the analysis of transaction costs in terms of their structure and magnitude, the identification of specific aspects of finance that can be digitized, the exploration of the voluntary or involuntary nature of using digital financial services and the examination of the management and security of "big data" derived from digital financial operations (Ozili, 2018; Schiff & McCaffrey, 2017). These issues have elicited demands for enhanced regulation aimed at preserving the integrity of the digital financial ecosystem and enacting legislation to preserve users' digital data. Such conversations emphasize the complexities associated with DF (Michaels & Homer, 2018).

This chapter focuses on the significant features of worldwide advancements in DF observed in different geographical regions. Gaining a comprehensive understanding of these advancements is crucial for grasping the factors that influence DF and its possible implications for globalization, as well as evaluating the pace of its progression. This body of knowledge has the potential to enhance prognostications regarding the trajectory of DF in the future while simultaneously illuminating the inherent hazards linked to global digital financial systems. To conduct a comprehensive analysis of this crucial component, the current study engages in an extensive literature review on the subject of DF while also incorporating empirical observations to provide insightful viewpoints on the existing state of research and development in this field. This research holds great significance as it is one of the foremost studies investigating the worldwide progress of digital banking.

This research presents three notable contributions to the current corpus of scholarly writing. This chapter is a valuable contribution to the extant literature examining the effects of the internet and digital technologies on the finance industry. Moreover, this research study adds to the current corpus of literature on financial innovation by emphasizing the widespread use of DT in the development and implementation of diverse financial innovations. Furthermore, this study enhances the existing corpus of knowledge in the domain of DF by providing a thorough examination of the present state of research and development. Additionally, it provides significant perspectives on the future direction of DF, encompassing forecasts for the forthcoming decade or two.

This chapter comprises several sections that provide a comprehensive analysis of the importance of DF, its current applications, global factors that impact its adoption, a concise summary of post-2010 DF research conducted, global advancements in this domain, projections for the future, suggestions for further research and, finally, the conclusions of this study.

6.2. Importance of DF

The multifarious prominence of DF in contemporary financial environments has been substantiated by a range of compelling factors, underscoring its significance. The significance of DF is paramount within the framework of global financial markets, as it enables the exchange of diverse financial instruments through digital platforms, technological advances and infrastructures (Michaels & Homer, 2018). Moreover, the importance of digital business is further emphasized by its role in enabling revolutionary breakthroughs in the realm of finance. The aforementioned developments encompass a variety of transformative innovations, including private electronic currencies, cryptocurrencies, integrated financing, blockchain technology (BCT) finance, artificial neural network financing and digital currencies issued by centralized banks (Gallego-Losada *et al.*, 2023).

Moreover, the convenience offered by digital banking is a crucial aspect since it eliminates the necessity for individuals to physically visit financial institutions to carry out basic financial operations. This not only saves time but also reduces transportation expenses (Taherdoost, 2023; Nagle *et al.*, 2020). In addition, the implementation of this approach enables finance providers to prioritize improving the effectiveness of their financial products and services, thereby shifting their focus away from addressing user-related concerns (Mugume & Bulime, 2022; Wang *et al.*, 2020). Furthermore, the emergence of DF is identified as a significant catalyst for promoting financial inclusion by enabling unbanked people to have access to formal financial sectors (Bollaert *et al.*, 2021). The impact of DF on economic growth is significant, as evidenced by its ability to drive greater consumption spending and investment (Guo *et al.*, 2022). The combined effects of these elements establish DF as a catalyst for significant change in contemporary financial systems.

6.3. Contemporary Advancements in the Realm of DF

In recent times, the domain of DF has experienced significant changes, resulting in diverse forms that have influenced the contemporary financial environment. Currently, DF spans various domains such as FinTech, integrated finance, AI, BCT, decentralized finance and other related areas. Internet finance pertains to the provision of financial services through the utilization of either analog or digital networks over the internet. According to Hou *et al.* (2016), online platforms in the realm of internet finance enable various financial activities such as financing, payment, investing and information intermediary services. However, FinTech finance pertains to the provision of financial services by enterprises operating in the field of financial technology (Ndung'u, 2018). According to Ketterer (2017), these organizations utilize technology to optimize and streamline financial services and procedures by providing them to customers via user applications that serve as frontend interfaces. In contrast, open banking is a DT application that is utilized within the banking and financial sector (Creehan, 2019; Guo *et al.*, 2022).

Another recent domain of DF is embedded finance, which refers to the incorporation of financial services into the offerings or products of entities that are not primarily engaged in the financial sector (An *et al.*, 2021). This entails facilitating the provision of financial services to customers by integrating financial services into the operational frameworks of non-financial service organizations. Financial services can be accessed by customers in places not traditionally associated with them, such as grocery stores, car dealerships, hospitals or non-financial applications. In embedded finance, non-financial service organizations incorporate banking services into their operations through the utilization of banking-as-a-service (BaaS) and application programming interface (API) driven banking and payment operations (Bernier & Plouffe, 2019).

Decentralized Finance (DeFi) refers to a form of DF that leverages blockchain technology to fundamentally transform traditional financial products. This is accomplished by removing intermediaries and utilizing smart contracts deployed on a blockchain (Razzaq & Yang, 2023). DeFi encompasses the provision of financial services through a public blockchain network, thereby circumventing the need for centralized financial intermediaries. The system primarily utilizes the Ethereum blockchain platform to leverage smart contracts. DeFi is commonly regarded as a means of democratizing the financial sector, which is constructed upon decentralized and trustless networks (Gomber *et al.*, 2017).

Blockchain finance pertains to the provision of financial services through the utilization of blockchain technology; in particular, it uses a decentralized public ledger that operates inside a network (Ozili, 2019). The field of AI finance encompasses the utilization of sophisticated robotic systems to augment the process of making financial decisions, expedite various financial tasks and optimize certain financial processes (Veloso *et al.*, 2021). The integration of AI in the field of finance has been shown to augment the predictive capabilities of financial models, resulting in improved risk management strategies and more informed decision-making processes (Li *et al.*, 2023). The concept of electronic money (e-money) centers around the transformation of conventional physical currency into its digital counterpart to enhance the effectiveness of transactions. According to Wullweber (2020), digital currency refers to a form of money that exists in an electronic format or serves as a virtual representation of physical currency. Private digital currencies, commonly referred to as cryptocurrencies, including but not limited to Bitcoin, Ethereum, Litecoin and Dogecoin, are generated and distributed by entities that are not affiliated with governmental bodies or state actors. Fiat digital currency, or central bank digital currency (CBDC), refers to electronic money that is issued by state actors or central banks (Li, 2023).

6.4. Global Factors Influencing the Development and Adoption of DF

Several critical elements emerge when considering the global factors driving the growing demand for DT in financial services. The primary factor pertains to the necessity of improving efficiency in the provision of financial services. In the present context, efficiency is attained through the strategic utilization of DT to automate repetitive tasks performed by individuals within the financial sector, resulting in the reduction of labor expenses. The implementation of automation in financial institutions yields significant cost savings, hence reducing the cost-to-income ratio and enhancing long-term profit margins (Hui *et al.*, 2023; Feyen *et al.*, 2021).

Another factor that highlights the motivation to attain the United Nations (UN) Sustainable Development Goals (SDGs) is the exploitation of pre-existing digital technologies. The utilization of DT in the field of finance is suggested as a feasible approach to meet, and possibly even fully accomplish, the 17 SDGs established by the UN (Aloulou *et al.*, 2023). DF can enhance financial inclusion by providing broader access to financial resources for many groups, such as individuals living in poverty, small-scale enterprises and large corporations (Kajol *et al.*, 2022). Prominent illustrations include digital financial services, such as online rapid loans and instant stock purchases, that enable marginalized communities to access and employ existing financial products. This, in turn, contributes to the amelioration of extreme poverty, hunger and income inequality. In addition, the utilization of DF provides opportunities for utilizing credit as a means to finance educational pursuits, bolster productive economic endeavors and foster broader economic expansion (Wullweber, 2020; Ozili, 2019).

The third determinant revolves around the necessity to enhance financial inclusion using digital methods. Governments worldwide aim for greater levels of financial inclusion, envisioning advantages such as increased tax income and a reduction in the informal economy (Bernier & Plouffe, 2019). Digital financial inclusion, as per Razzaq & Yang (2023), refers to the provision of a formal digital identity credential to individuals which allows them to remotely access a wide range of digital financial services within the formal financial sector. The utilization of this digital credential not only provides users with the convenience of avoiding physical visits to financial institutions but also results in cost savings. Governments can gain advantages from the increase in digital financial transactions, as this presents a taxable channel through which significant revenue can be generated (Bollaert *et al.*, 2021).

The fourth determinant underscores the imperative of employing DT to ensure efficient payments (Taherdoost, 2023; Nagle *et al.*,

2020). The efficiency of payments can be enhanced by the utilization of DT, provided that a reliable payment system is in place. This is achieved by enabling rapid and safe value transfers between individuals or entities acting as senders and recipients (Guo *et al.*, 2022). Furthermore, the integration of DT within the payments system enhances the level of payment settlement finality, specifically in the context of both domestic and international transactions (Gallego-Losada *et al.*, 2023). DT plays a crucial role in enabling settlement finality, which is defined as the irreversible and absolute transfer of assets or financial instruments. By leveraging DT, parties involved in a transaction can effectively fulfill their contractual settlement obligations and receive timely notifications regarding any potential breaches (Ratajczak, 2022).

6.5. A Concise Overview of the Research on DF After 2010

This section presents a succinct overview of DF research conducted after 2010, based on studies obtained from Google Scholar. The literature is categorized into six main research themes. The primary topic under examination delves into the benefits of digital financial services, emphasizing their role in enhancing financial inclusion and extending their reach to sectors beyond the realm of finance (Ozili, 2018). Furthermore, DF has been acknowledged for its contributions to the gross domestic product (GDP) of different economies. It has also been found to enhance the long-term performance of banks (Phan *et al.*, 2020), stimulate aggregate expenditure, generate increased tax revenue, mitigate the circulation of counterfeit money, empower users with greater control over their finances (An *et al.*, 2021), facilitate prompt financial decision-making and mitigate money laundering linked to cash transactions (Oxford Analytica, 2021).

The second theme explores the ramifications of digital money for several sectors of the economy. According to Siddik & Kabiraj (2020), there is evidence suggesting that financial inclusion has a favorable impact on financial stability. Additionally, Kajol *et al.* (2022) argue that it leads to expanded access to financing, while Wang *et al.* (2020) contend that it improves the efficiency of the financial system.

Furthermore, financial inclusion has been found to contribute to the improved functioning of capital markets. The utilization of DF has been recognized for its role in facilitating economic recovery in times of crises and contributing to climate change mitigation (Tao *et al.*, 2022). Moreover, there is substantial evidence indicating that the use of DF has facilitated expansion across multiple industries, such as equity crowd funding, energy, agriculture, manufacturing, banking, the circular economy, tourism and foreign commerce (Chen & Zhang, 2021; Ozili, 2021; Jünger & Mietzner, 2020).

The third thematic area centers on the influence of DF on the advancement of human development and well-being. Research findings indicate that there are several favorable consequences associated with the aforementioned phenomenon. These include augmented levels of household consumption, advancements in gender equality, heightened involvement of women in economic activities, decreased financial burdens on households, mitigated gender disparities, diminished prevalence of extreme poverty and reduced levels of income inequality (Li *et al.*, 2023; Kofman & Payne, 2021; Chen & Zhao, 2021). The fourth theme examines the application of DF innovations in specific countries, such as the widespread adoption of point-of-sale (POS) devices and USSD technology in countries like Bangladesh, Nigeria and South Africa (Markose *et al.*, 2020; Peter *et al.*, 2018).

The fifth theme explores various challenges encountered in the realm of DF. These challenges encompass potential risks to national security, regulatory concerns, inadequate digital connectivity, merchant hesitancy in accepting digital payments for small transactions, elevated transaction costs impacting low-income households and limited financial literacy among impoverished and rural communities (Reshetnikova *et al.*, 2021; Ozili, 2020). The sixth theme is the regulation of the digital banking environment. The arguments put forth in the literature span a spectrum of viewpoints, with some scholars advocating for regulation as a response to emerging risks (Michaels & Homer, 2018), while others argue for establishing an environment conducive to innovation. The safeguarding of new entrants can be accomplished by implementing regulatory sandboxes, together with the pursuit of effective regulations that do not hinder innovation (Alam *et al.*, 2019; Pavlidis, 2021). The authors Zetzsche *et al.* (2020) emphasize the importance of continuous improvements in the regulatory framework.

6.6. Regional Advancements in DF

The present condition of global DF is marked by a substantial lack of accessibility to conventional banking services, with more than two billion adults facing financial exclusions. The potential implications of digital financial services for developing and emerging economies are considerable, as evidenced by projections indicating a possible rise of US$3.7 trillion in GDP and the generation of 95 million job opportunities across various industries (Luo *et al.*, 2022). The FinTech industry holds a prominent position on a global scale, with a significant increase in revenues from €92 billion in 2018 to an estimated €188 billion by 2024. In 2020, there was a significant rise of 20% in the transaction value of global mobile money services. This growth was particularly remarkable in the regions of East Asia and the Pacific, Latin America and the Caribbean, and Europe and Central Asia. However, considerably slower growth was observed in Sub-Saharan Africa, the Middle East and North Africa (Li *et al.*, 2022).

Asia is widely recognized as a prominent force in the widespread adoption of DF, with a notable achievement of having more than 700 million individuals regularly use digital banking services. Countries such as Pakistan employ digital financial services as a means to improve accessibility for excluded populations, specifically targeting the impoverished and women. The region of East Asia and the Pacific is home to a substantial population of potential female users of mobile money, estimated to exceed 775 million individuals (Hasan *et al.*, 2022). China and India exhibit the highest rates of FinTech use globally, at 87%. Subsequently, Singapore followed suit in terms of FinTech adoption. The implementation of digital financial services has the potential to enhance the GDP of Asian nations by approximately 14%. In smaller markets such as Cambodia, this increase could be even more significant, with the potential to reach up to 32%. Enabling factors encompass several elements that facilitate certain processes or activities. In the context provided, these variables consist of a supportive payment framework, widespread e-money adoption and regulations permitting both banks and non-bank organizations to employ agents in their operations. The challenges encompass regulatory arbitrage, ambiguity, inadequate client protection mechanisms and limited financial and technical literacy (Aloulou *et al.*, 2023).

The primary focus of DF investment in Europe is largely centered on the FinTech sector. The European FinTech ecosystem encompasses a total of 3,482 companies, with notable presence in countries such as the United Kingdom, Germany, Spain, France, Switzerland and the Netherlands. In Europe, the FinTech sector received a majority share of 65% in terms of total funding worldwide. In 2018, European FinTech firms secured a total funding of €3.52 billion, which experienced a significant surge to an estimated €10 billion by 2020. In 2019, the financial allocations toward AI investments surpassed €750 million but experienced a decline to approximately €400 million in 2020 as a result of the global pandemic. In 2019, funding for open banking systems exceeded €400 million; subsequently, in 2020, it reached approximately €500 million (Gallego-Losada *et al.*, 2023).

The emergence of DF in Africa can be traced back to around 2005, and it has since experienced significant growth. As of 2021, the continent is home to a substantial number of FinTech businesses, with over 514 functioning in various countries. It is worth noting that a significant portion, specifically 70%, of investments amounting to a substantial sum of US$823 million are primarily focused on payment solutions, with a particular emphasis on mobile money (Chen & Zhang, 2021; Ozili, 2021). In 2020, the African continent boasted 171 mobile money services, with a staggering 562 million registered users and 161 million active accounts. The total transaction volume amounted to 27.4 billion, accompanied by a transaction value of US$490 billion. The regions of West Africa and East Africa exhibited the most significant advancements in the adoption of mobile money. Nonetheless, African DF players encounter many challenges, including limited access to funding, regulatory obstacles, inadequate comprehension of local markets and difficulties in acquiring skilled personnel (Mugume & Bulime, 2022).

6.7. Future Prospects for DF

The evolution of DF indicates a trend toward the development of a digital ecosystem capable of offering a diverse range of tailored financial goods and services within a unified platform. This scenario envisions a situation in which customers can access a variety of services, such as insurance, banking, credit, investing and savings, without the need for human intervention. In the forthcoming era, the integration of digital identities, robots, data analytics, machine learning and AI will enable the effortless personalization of financial services (Alam *et al.*, 2019; Pavlidis, 2021). Furthermore, it is anticipated that the utilization of AI and machine learning in the domain of financial risk management will continue to develop. This advancement will involve the rapid detection of anomalies in transactions and the provision of assistance in forecasting, hence facilitating effective decision-making.

There is an urgent need for scholarly investigation into the strategies that regulators can employ to effectively adapt to the swift and profound changes occurring in the realm of DF. The bureaucratic frameworks inherent in regulatory organizations can result in delayed responses to emerging advances. The research shall aim to investigate strategies for enhancing the agility, dynamism and proactivity of DF regulation (Taherdoost, 2023; Nagle *et al.*, 2020). Recommendations encompass the implementation of regulatory frameworks grounded in principles, regulations that are impartial toward specific technologies and the promotion of enhanced cooperation between financial institutions and regulatory bodies to expedite timely revisions.

In light of potential advancements in digital banking, it is imperative for research to focus on augmenting user data security measures and ensuring compliance with data privacy regulations, given the possibility of increased vulnerability of sensitive user information. The task of reconciling the requirement for thorough user identification with the imperative to safeguard sensitive data stored in digital databases or the cloud poses a notable problem that merits meticulous examination (Chen & Zhang, 2021; Ozili, 2021). The significance of machine learning and AI in shaping the future of DF underscores the need for scholarly investigation into strategies aimed at mitigating biases arising from flawed data. The unintentional incorporation of biased material has the potential to perpetuate and reinforce social, gender or racial biases. Future research should prioritize the exploration of novel methodologies for the reconfiguration of AI-driven data gathering and processing systems to identify and mitigate instances of skewed financial and non-financial data. This emphasis on justice and equality is crucial for ensuring the integrity and impartiality of these systems. In addition to the aforementioned point, it is imperative to conduct comprehensive research on the issue of algorithmic bias in decision-making processes driven by AI and prioritize the prevention of biased outcomes in algorithms to mitigate the occurrence of unjust financial practices, such as the imposition of discriminatory interest rates or the limitation of access to financial services.

Future research endeavors should aim to develop effective methods for eliminating or reducing erroneous assumptions that contribute to algorithmic bias. The prevailing risk-averse mentality within financial institutions frequently impedes their ability to undertake more substantial risks in the realm of digital transformation. The exploration of how financial institutions may effectively negotiate the conflict between embracing a larger risk appetite in digital transformation while adhering to existing risk boundaries warrants more research. One potential area of inquiry involves adapting risk management methods to effectively address the uncertainties and experimental characteristics associated with digital transformation. These research domains provide essential perspectives for guiding the trajectory of DF toward increased innovation, security and equity.

6.8. Conclusion

The chapter highlights the growing field of DF research, which encompasses a wide range of studies exploring current topics that are significant for both policymaking and practical application. The FinTech and mobile money sectors have emerged as the key recipients of investments in the field of DF. Significantly, the cumulative number of global customers utilizing mobile money services has exceeded $US1 billion. The prospective trajectory of DF centers on the establishment of a digital ecosystem that enables the provision of a wide range of financial products and services. The anticipated characteristics of this environment include a high degree of customization and personalization, catering to the distinct requirements of users within a cohesive digital framework devoid of the need for human intermediaries. The areas that require further investigation include the examination of regulatory adaptability in response to emerging DF transformations, the enhancement of user information security, the reduction of bias in data and algorithms and the reconciliation of a risk-conscious culture with an increased risk appetite for DF transformation.

The manifestation of DF transformation is expected to vary across different regions of the world due to variations in technological progress, receptiveness to change, support from policies and regulations and the understanding of associated dangers. Diverse methodologies are anticipated, from cautious tactics in certain areas to ambitious, pioneering endeavors in others. Decisions regarding this matter should be guided by a thorough comprehension of both hazards and regulatory authorizations. Banks are increasingly under pressure to engage in innovation or face the possibility of obsolescence within the dynamic realm of DF transformation. The ambiguous role of banks highlights the importance of a cautious yet forward-looking approach to digital DF transformation.

References

Alam, N., Gupta, L., & Zameni, A. (2019). Fintech regulation. In Alam, N., Gupta, L., & Zameni. A. (Eds.), *Fintech and Islamic Finance* (pp. 137–158). Cham: Palgrave Macmillan. https://doi.org/10.1007/978-3-030-24666-2_8.

Aloulou, M., Grati, R., Al-Qudah, A. A., & Al-Okaily, M. (2023). Does FinTech adoption increase the diffusion rate of digital financial inclusion? A study of the banking industry sector. *Journal of Financial Reporting and Accounting*. https://doi.org/10.1108/JFRA-05-2023-0224.

An, Y. J., Choi, P. M. S., & Huang, S. H. (2021). Blockchain, cryptocurrency, and artificial intelligence in finance. In Choi, P. M. S. & Huang, S. H. (Eds.), *Fintech with Artificial Intelligence, Big Data, and Blockchain* (pp. 1–34). Singapore: Springer Singapore. https://doi.org/10.1007/978-981-33-6137-9_1.

Bernier, M. & Plouffe, M. (2019). Financial innovation, economic growth, and the consequences of macroprudential policies. *Research in Economics*, 73(2), 162–173. https://doi.org/10.1016/j.rie.2019.04.003.

Bollaert, H., de Silanes, F. L., & Schwienbacher, A. (2021). Fintech and access to finance. *Journal of Corporate Finance*, 68, 101941. https://doi.org/10.1016/j.jcorpfin.2021.101941.

Chen, B. & Zhao, C. (2021). Poverty reduction in rural China: Does the digital finance matter? *Plos One*, 16(12), e0261214. https://doi.org/10.1371/journal.pone.0261214.

Chen, S. & Zhang, H. (2021). Does digital finance promote manufacturing servitization: Micro evidence from China. *International Review of Economics & Finance*, 76, 856–869. https://doi.org/10.1016/j.iref.2021.07.018.

Creehan, S. (2019). How digital innovation can increase small business access to finance in Asia. Fintech for Asian SMEs. Tokyo, Japan: Asian Development Bank Institute. https://ideas.repec.org/a/fip/fedfaf/0017.html.

Feyen, E., Frost, J., Gambacorta, L., Natarajan, H., & Saal, M. (2021). Fintech and the digital transformation of financial services: implications for market structure and public policy. *Bank for International Settlements Working Paper*, No. 117, April. https://ideas.repec.org/b/bis/bisbps/117.html.

Gallego-Losada, M. J., Montero-Navarro, A., García-Abajo, E., & Gallego-Losada, R. (2023). Digital financial inclusion. Visualizing the academic literature. *Research in International Business and Finance*, 64, 101862. https://doi.org/10.1016/j.ribaf.2022.101862.

Gomber, P., Koch, J. A., & Siering, M. (2017). Digital finance and FinTech: Current research and future research directions. *Journal of Business Economics*, 87, 537–580. https://doi.org/10.1007/s11573-017-0852-x.

Guo, C., Wang, X., & Yuan, G. (2022). Digital finance and the efficiency of household investment portfolios. *Emerging Markets Finance and Trade*, 58(10), 2895–2909. https://doi.org/10.1080/1540496X.2021.2013197.

Hasan, M. M., Yajuan, L., & Khan, S. (2022). Promoting China's inclusive finance through digital financial services. *Global Business Review*, 23(4), 984–1006. https://doi.org/10.1177/0972150919895348.

Hou, X., Gao, Z., & Wang, Q. (2016). Internet finance development and banking market discipline: Evidence from China. *Journal of Financial Stability*, 22, 88–100. https://doi.org/10.1016/j.jfs.2016.01.001.

Hui, P., Zhao, H., Liu, D., & Li, Y. (2023). How does digital finance affect regional innovation capacity? A spatial econometric analysis. *Economic Modelling*, 122, 106250. https://doi.org/10.1016/j.econmod.2023.106250.

Jünger, M. & Mietzner, M. (2020). Banking goes digital: The adoption of FinTech services by German households. *Finance Research Letters*, 34, 101260. https://doi.org/10.1016/j.frl.2019.08.008.

Kajol, K., Singh, R., & Paul, J. (2022). Adoption of digital financial transactions: A review of literature and future research agenda. *Technological*

Forecasting and Social Change, 184, 121991. https://doi.org/10.1016/j.techfore.2022.121991.

Ketterer, J. A. (2017). Digital finance: New times, new challenges, new opportunities. A IDB-Inter American Development Bank Report. https://webimages.iadb.org/publications/english/document/Digital-Finance-New-Times-New-Challenges-New-Opportunities.pdf.

Kofman, P. & Payne, C. (2021). Digital financial inclusion of women: An ethical appraisal. *Handbook on Ethics in Finance* (pp. 133–157). https://doi.org/10.1007/978-3-030-29371-0_34.

Li, G., Zhang, R., Feng, S., & Wang, Y. (2022). Digital finance and sustainable development: Evidence from environmental inequality in China. *Business Strategy and the Environment*, 31(7), 3574–3594. https://doi.org/10.1002/bse.3105.

Li, J. (2023). Predicting the demand for central bank digital currency: A structural analysis with survey data. *Journal of Monetary Economics*, 134, 73–85. https://doi.org/10.1016/j.jmoneco.2022.11.007.

Li, Z., Chen, H., & Mo, B. (2023). Can digital finance promote urban innovation? Evidence from China. *Borsa Istanbul Review*, 23(2), 285–296. https://doi.org/10.1016/j.bir.2022.10.006.

Luo, D., Luo, M., & Lv, J. (2022). Can digital finance contribute to the promotion of financial sustainability? A financial efficiency perspective. *Sustainability*, 14(7), 3979. https://doi.org/10.3390/su14073979.

Markose, S., Arun, T., & Ozili, P. (2020). Financial inclusion, at what cost? Quantification of economic viability of a supply side roll out. *The European Journal of Finance*, 1–27. https://doi.org/10.1080/1351847X.2020.1821740.

Mhlanga, D. (2020). Industry 4.0 in finance: The impact of artificial intelligence (AI) on digital financial inclusion. *International Journal of Financial Studies*, 8(3), 45. https://doi.org/10.3390/ijfs8030045.

Michaels, L. & Homer, M. (2018). Regulation and supervision in a digital and inclusive world. In Chuen, D. L. K. & Deng, R. (Eds.), *Handbook of Blockchain, Digital Finance, and Inclusion, Volume 1* (pp. 329–346). Amsterdam, Netherlands: Academic Press. https://doi.org/10.1016/B978-0-12-810441-5.00014-2.

Mugume, R. & Bulime, E. W. (2022). Post-COVID-19 recovery for African economies: Lessons for digital financial inclusion from Kenya and Uganda. *African Development Review*, 34, S161–S176. https://doi.org/10.1111/1467-8268.12652.

Murinde, V., Rizopoulos, E., & Zachariadis, M. (2022). The impact of the FinTech revolution on the future of banking: Opportunities and risks. *International Review of Financial Analysis*, 81, 102103. https://doi.org/10.1016/j.irfa.2022.102103.

Nagle, F., Seamans, R., & Tadelis, S. (2020). Transaction cost economics in the digital economy: A research agenda. *Harvard Business School Strategy Unit Working Paper*, 21-009. https://papers.ssrn.com/sol3/papers.cfm?abstract_id=3661856.

Ndung'u, N. (2018). The M-Pesa technological revolution for financial services in Kenya: A platform for financial inclusion. In Chuen, D. L. K. & Deng, R. (Eds.), *Handbook of Blockchain, Digital Finance, and Inclusion, Volume 1* (pp. 37–56). Amsterdam, Netherlands: Academic Press. https://doi.org/10.1016/B978-0-12-810441-5.00003-8.

Oxford Analytica. (2021). Digital finance erodes anti-money laundering regime. *Emerald Expert Briefings.* https://doi.org/10.1108/OXAN-DB263766.

Ozili, P. K. (2018). Impact of digital finance on financial inclusion and stability. *Borsa Istanbul Review*, 18(4), 329–340. https://doi.org/10.1016/j.bir.2017.12.003.

Ozili, P. K. (2019). Blockchain finance: Questions regulators ask. In Jay Choi, J. & Ozkan, B. (Eds.), *Disruptive Innovation in Business and Finance in the Digital World.* Bingley, UK: Emerald Publishing Limited. https://doi.org/10.1108/S1569-376720190000020014.

Ozili, P. K. (2020). Contesting digital finance for the poor. *Digital Policy, Regulation and Governance*, 22(2), 135–151. https://doi.org/10.1108/DPRG-12-2019-0104.

Ozili, P. K. (2021). Financial inclusion: A strong critique. In Özen, E., Grima, S., & Dalli, R. Gonzi (Eds.), *New Challenges for Future Sustainability and Wellbeing.* Bingley, UK: Emerald Publishing Limited. https://doi.org/10.1108/978-1-80043-968-920211002.

Pavlidis, G. (2021). Europe in the digital age: Regulating digital finance without suffocating innovation. *Law, Innovation and Technology*, 13(2), 464–477. https://doi.org/10.1080/17579961.2021.1977222.

Peter, J., Benjamin, P., LeFevre, A. E., Barron, P., & Pillay, Y. (2018). Taking digital health innovation to scale in South Africa: Ten lessons from MomConnect. *BMJ Global Health*, 3(2), 1–4. http://dx.doi.org/10.1136/bmjgh-2017-000592.

Phan, D. H. B., Narayan, P. K., Rahman, R. E., & Hutabarat, A. R. (2020). Do financial technology firms influence bank performance? *Pacific-Basin Finance Journal*, 62, 101210. https://doi.org/10.1016/j.pacfin.2019.101210.

Ratajczak, M. (2022). The state in the era of digital revolution and digital finance. *Digital Finance and the Future of the Global Financial System: Disruption and Innovation in Financial Services*, Washington, DC.

Razzaq, A. & Yang, X. (2023). Digital finance and green growth in China: Appraising inclusive digital finance using web crawler technology and big data. *Technological Forecasting and Social Change*, 188, 122262. https://doi.org/10.1016/j.techfore.2022.122262.

Reshetnikova, N., Magomedov, M., & Buklanov, D. (2021). Digital finance technologies: Threats and challenges to the global and national financial security. In *IOP Conference Series: Earth and Environmental Science* (Vol. 666, No. 6). Russia: IOP Publishing. https://iopscience.iop.org/article/10.1088/1755-1315/666/6/062139/pdf.

Schiff, A. & McCaffrey, M. (2017). Redesigning digital finance for big data. *SSRN 2967122*. https://dx.doi.org/10.2139/ssrn.2967122.

Shabsigh, M. G., Khiaonarong, M. T., & Leinonen, M. H. (2020). *Distributed Ledger Technology Experiments in Payments and Settlements.* Washington, DC: International Monetary Fund.

Siddik, M. N. A. & Kabiraj, S. (2020). Digital finance for financial inclusion and inclusive growth. In Georgea, B. & Paul, J. (Eds.), *Digital Transformation in Business and Society* (pp. 155–168). Cham: Palgrave Macmillan. https://doi.org/10.1007/978-3-030-08277-2_10.

Taherdoost, H. (2023). Fintech: Emerging trends and the future of finance. In Turi, A. N. (Ed.), *Financial Technologies and DeFi: A Revisit to the Digital Finance Revolution* (pp. 29–39). Cham, Switzerland: Springer. https://doi.org/10.1007/978-3-031-17998-3_2.

Tao, R., Su, C. W., Naqvi, B., & Rizvi, S. K. A. (2022). Can Fintech development pave the way for a transition towards low-carbon economy: A global perspective. *Technological Forecasting and Social Change*, 174, 121278. https://doi.org/10.1016/j.techfore.2021.121278.

Veloso, M., Balch, T., Borrajo, D., Reddy, P., & Shah, S. (2021). Artificial intelligence research in finance: Discussion and examples. *Oxford Review of Economic Policy*, 37(3), 564–584. https://doi.org/10.1093/oxrep/grab019.

Wales, K. (2015). Internet finance: Digital currencies and alternative finance liberating the capital markets. *Journal of Governance and Regulation*, 4(4), 10–22495. http://www.virtusinterpress.org/IMG/pdf/10-22495_jgr_v4_i4_c1_p6.pdf.

Wang, Q., Yang, J., Chiu, Y. H., & Lin, T. Y. (2020). The impact of digital finance on financial efficiency. *Managerial and Decision Economics*, 41(7), 1225–1236. https://doi.org/10.1002/mde.3168.

Wullweber, J. (2020). Embedded finance: The shadow banking system, sovereign power, and a new state–market hybridity. *Journal of Cultural Economy*, 13(5), 592–609. https://doi.org/10.1080/17530350.2020.1741015.

Zetzsche, D. A., Arner, D. W., & Buckley, R. P. (2020). Decentralized finance. *Journal of Financial Regulation*, 6(2), 172–203. https://dx.doi.org/10.2139/ssrn.3539194.

https://doi.org/10.1142/9781800616257_0007

Chapter 7

Digital Innovation in Insurance

Jamaltul Nizam Bin Shamsuddin[*,‡], Christopher Gan[*,§], and Dao Le Trang Anh[†,||]

[*]*Department of Financial and Business Systems, Lincoln University, Christchurch, New Zealand*

[†]*The Business School, RMIT University, Ho Chi Minh City, Vietnam*

[‡]*j.jamaltulnizambinshamsuddin@lincolnuni.ac.nz*

[§]*christopher.gan@lincoln.ac.nz*

[||]*anh.dao28@rmit.edu.vn*

Abstract

In the past decade, the insurance business has experienced remarkable growth, as evidenced by the introduction of numerous novel products such as chatbots, digital claims, telemetric insurance and robo-advisors. The insurance industry is also experiencing a significant transformation resulting from the digital transformation. The use of digital technology opens the door for inventive architectures and the development of innovative products in the future that will benefit both insurance companies and their clients. By integrating Internet of Things devices, digital innovation revolutionizes how insurance companies collaborate with industries, ultimately benefiting all parties. This chapter reviews the history of digital innovation in insurance, also known as insurance technology (InsurTech), as well as how technology has underpinned the expansion of InsurTech in recent years. The chapter also examines previous and current studies on the use of technology in insurance transactions and how the implementation of digitalization affects the industry's long-term viability. The research identified three key InsurTech concepts that have revolutionized the insurance sector. New entrants could disrupt the entire insurance distribution process and introduce new consumer value propositions to attract and retain clients, challenging current business models. InsurTech improves incumbent insurers' value chain by providing innovative technologies and solutions that boost efficiency and reduce costs.

Keywords: Insurance, InsurTech, digital, transformation, technology, insurance industry.

7.1. Introduction

In recent years, it has been difficult for the financial industry to adapt to new technologies (also known as financial technologies, or FinTechs), such as big data, artificial intelligence and cloud computing. This is because the industry is highly sensitive, technical and regulated (Yan *et al.*, 2018). Additionally, factors such as changing economic circumstances, privacy regulations, customer rights and the requirement to access information contribute to this difficulty (Moodley, 2019). FinTech, digital payments and alternative lending have all fueled the industry's growth, and emerging sectors such as InsurTech have also contributed to this trend. The digital payment landscape is currently experiencing a remarkable level of innovation, with the rise of alternative payment channels, the establishment of payment hubs and the tokenization of payments to ensure payment security. Similarly, alternative lenders are transforming the lending process by utilizing advanced technologies and innovative business models. This transformation encompasses various aspects, including client acquisition, credit scoring, loan servicing and recovery. The insurance industry is characterized by a significantly low level of insurance penetration, along with technology-driven innovations occurring across products, pricing and distribution spectrums, creating an ideal environment for digital disruption (PwC, 2019). The aforementioned areas encompass insurance marketing and underwriting, health management and expedited claims resolution. Despite the disruptive impact of innovations in science and technology on the financial sector, it is anticipated that the insurance industry will face the most pronounced consequences in the foreseeable future. The insurance industry must undergo a transformation from a "detect and repair" approach to a "predict and prevent" strategy, resulting in comprehensive changes across all sectors of the industry. The rate of change is expected to accelerate as stakeholders, including brokers, clients, financial intermediaries, insurers and suppliers, become more adept at utilizing advanced technology to enhance decision-making processes, increase productivity, lower expenses and improve the overall customer experience (Mckinsey, 2018). InsurTech is a new type of technology that changes how the insurance industry develops and operates (McWaters, 2015).

InsurTech has exerted a substantial impact on the complete value chain of the insurance industry, encompassing asset management, capital investment, product development, underwriting, actuarial procedures and the evaluation, resolution, assessment and settlement of claims. Illustrative instances of technological advancements within the insurance sector encompass the following: usage-based insurance (wherein pricing is established via the Internet of Vehicles and mileage and driving behavior), peer-to-peer insurance selling, automated customer service (often integrated with artificial intelligence), cloud-based customer policy management and automated loss adjustment enabled by image recognition technology (Xu & Zweifel, 2020). As a result, InsurTech incorporates new insurance products, such as usage-based insurance, as well as innovative service delivery systems, such as robo-advisors. Additionally, it includes management tools such as IBM Watson and Ant Claims Adjuster, along with comprehensive corporate planning (from the "detect and repair" model to a "predict and prevent" approach) (Mckinsey, 2018). While InsurTech was created to increase the efficiency of the insurance sector, its rapid growth has resulted in a number of challenges. First, quality varies significantly among insurance companies, indicating either a high or low level of investment in innovation. Second, many InsurTech products are essentially the same. The main focus of robo-advisors is on identifying and assessing risks that require insurance and calculating premiums. As a result, greater product differentiation and innovation could be observed. In addition, a significant number of individuals or companies that describe themselves as InsurTech are free riders who do not offer any real innovation. A significant number of InsurTech companies describe themselves as being primarily engaged in the online sale of insurance or platforms that enable mutual assistance in the event of a claim. Ultimately, certain technologies merely incorporate basic existing concepts with no prospect of future development (Xu & Zweifel, 2020). Artificial intelligence, for example in simple knowledge mapping, often has limitations in its use when compared to more advanced applications such as neural networks and deep learning. The presence of these vulnerabilities in the InsurTech industry poses challenges for various stakeholders, such as insurance management, consumers, investors and regulators, in assessing the overall stability and viability of the industry. As a result, this acts as a barrier to the industry's potential to expand further. Regulators, such as those who are responsible for setting policies to promote the growth of InsurTech, typically require an assessment framework to identify competitive start-ups within the InsurTech business (Xu & Zweifel, 2020).

Consumers are opting for a robust service provider that offers exceptional InsurTech solutions, including customization of insurance cover, while investors are interested in finding viable InsurTech start-ups (Xu & Zweifel, 2020). Overall, this chapter elaborates on the literature on InsurTech. Section 7.2 defines InsurTech. Section 7.3 highlights the history of InsurTech from its early stages of development in the 2000s. Section 7.4 describes the underpinning theories that contribute to the growth of innovation in the insurance industry. Section 7.5 provides an overview of previous research on the introduction of technology in the insurance industry. Section 7.6 looks at upcoming developments and the future of InsurTech. The chapter concludes in Section 7.7.

7.2. Definition of InsurTech

Prior research and industry practices have used very broad definitions of InsurTech and FinTech, which are often difficult to interpret. For example, Arner *et al.* (2015) defined FinTech as the utilization of technology to offer financial solutions, while InsurTech is a segment within FinTech that focuses specifically on insurance (PwC, 2018). Upon analyzing these given definitions, Stoeckli *et al.* (2018) restrict their focus to inventive and information technology (IT)-driven approaches and provide a definition of InsurTech as a phenomenon characterized by the introduction of innovative approaches by either traditional or non-traditional market participants who leverage IT to offer industry-specific solutions within the insurance sector. The term in question possesses a broad scope, leading to a lack of clarity in differentiating between conventional business IT infrastructures, such as office automation systems and insurance technology. Consequently, it is important to highlight that the solutions offered by InsurTech firms can be categorized as either customer-centric or data-centric in nature. The emphasis observed can be attributed to the convergence of the two elements. The academic community and industry have focused their efforts on various technological advancements, which can be classified into eight distinct areas: artificial intelligence, big data, cloud computing, blockchain, genetic technology, internet and mobile technology, the Internet of Things (IoT) and virtual reality (Martin Eling & Lehmann, 2018). These categories serve as a foundation for the research and development of cutting-edge innovations.

Yan *et al.* (2018), argue that disruptive information technologies possess a shared characteristic of being data-driven, which sets them apart from the wider IT infrastructure. The transformative capabilities inherent to InsurTech include a data-driven infrastructure, in conjunction with three additional themes that prioritize customer needs: digital service delivery, insurance service development and customer network promotion (Stoeckli *et al.*, 2018). It is also necessary to consider the benefits identified in earlier studies, such as higher efficiency, cost reduction, increased convenience and increased customer satisfaction (Ba *et al.*, 2010; Barrett *et al.*, 2015; Bitner *et al.*, 2000). According to Xu & Zweifel (2020), InsurTech can be described as a phenomenon in which both traditional and non-traditional market participants utilize IT to provide insurance-related solutions that are data-driven or focused on enhancing the customer experience. These solutions consist of various aspects of the insurance industry, such as marketing, distribution, risk assessment and underwriting, claims handling, value-added services and the development of innovative insurance products or services.

Technology has changed the insurance industry's value chain. First, traditional insurers optimize their insurance business processes by transforming themselves or working with IT firms. Second, the rise of technology empowerment has resulted in significant developments in insurance products and services, operational processes and business models (IAIS, 2019). Insurance distribution through digital means comprises more than simply collecting quotations online; it also entails creating innovative tools that provide a smooth and customer-oriented procedure (Stoeckli *et al.*, 2018). Numerous traditional insurance companies and InsurTech start-ups, such as Trov, place significant focus on enhancing the overall user experience by offering mobile app services. In addition, the widespread use of IT in today's society allows for innovative marketing campaigns. For example, Amodo uses driving behavior data, together with other digital data sources, to design tailored marketing and sales activities, among other things (Stoeckli *et al.*, 2018).

The insurance industry has sought partnerships with prominent online companies such as Alibaba and Tencent, as well as businesses in the supply chain, to incorporate insurance offerings into internet-based business ventures. This collaboration has led to the emergence of specialized insurance products, such as return and freight insurance, tailored to specific situations (Hao, 2019). InsurTech has also made possible changes to pricing mechanisms and insurability. McCrea & Farrell (2018) explored the potential of utilizing wearable technology data to improve the prediction of general health outcomes and mortality. The ultimate goal of the study was to use the predictive score to improve the accuracy of health and life insurance pricing variations. By utilizing blockchain technology, InsurTech guarantees that risks will become easier to insure. Another study aimed to identify the barriers that hinder the widespread adoption and advancement of InsurTech (Faure & Li, 2020).

InsurTech was defined by Ricciardi (2018) as an insurance company, intermediary or segment expert operating within the insurance value chain and utilizing technological advancements to offer value-added services or compete in the insurance industry. In addition to embracing a user-centric approach, InsurTech start-ups are cultivating strong connections with insurance clients and delivering services that safeguard clients at all times while mitigating potential losses for the insurance providers via guidance services, warning systems and risk prevention mechanisms. Furthermore, Ricciardi (2018) defined InsurTech as state-of-the-art insurance technologies, including chatbots that facilitate human-to-customer (H2C) distribution, advanced analytics that identify appropriate cases within the data-driven insurance industry and artificial intelligence.

InsurTech is a term that refers to companies that employ technology to disrupt the insurance sector (Cruse & Singh, 2019). Most life and health InsurTech companies do not sell insurance policies; they provide technology solutions. They provide hardware, software and analytics to insurance carriers, other InsurTech firms and brokers to assist with underwriting, marketing, distribution, pricing and claims processing. These technology companies have begun to develop competence in areas such as underwriting and claims processing through the use of artificial intelligence and sophisticated analytics. While none of these start-ups are likely to upset the sector on their own, collectively, they constitute a significant competitive challenge to traditional insurers. In addition, by providing solutions to InsurTech carriers, they can help these businesses grow and scale more quickly than would be possible otherwise. Carrie & Kiki (2021) reported that InsurTech is developing technologies, software and user interfaces for the insurance value chain to address inefficiencies or opportunities. It requires the frequent application of technology, data and analytics aimed at analyzing the evolution or disruption of insurer–client interactions, the modification or development of new insurance products and process automation. Table 7.1 summarizes the definitions of InsurTech from previous studies.

7.3. InsurTech at a Glance

In order to gain a comprehensive understanding of the historical development of InsurTech, it is necessary to first examine the origins and evolution of FinTech. Following their original classification as a subset of FinTech, operations within the insurance industry have gained prominence and distinct characteristics, warranting their classification as a separate category independent of FinTech over time.

FinTech emerged as an early and prominent constituent within the broader category of "EverythingTech," an acronym associated with technology that originated online and has subsequently gained global recognition. A Google Trends report shows the rise in popularity of the term "FinTech," a combination of the words "financial" and "technology," in recent years (see Figure 7.1; Carrie & Kiki, 2021). It exemplifies the surge in technological progress within the financial services sector that commenced in the early 2000s and gained significant momentum around 2014. When it comes to the emergence of InsurTech, the progress is similar, except that it occurred two years later.

Table 7.1. Summary of InsurTech definitions.

Author(s)	Definition
Arner *et al.* (2015)	The use of technology to provide financial solutions in insurance industry.
PwC (2018)	The insurance-specific branch of FinTech.
Stoeckli *et al.* (2018)	The development of insurance-specific solutions through the application of information technology by one or more traditional or non-traditional market participants.
Yan *et al.* (2018)	The new disruptive information technologies that share a common data-driven trait that distinguishes them from the broader information technology infrastructure.
Xu & Zweifel (2020)	A widespread occurrence wherein traditional and non-traditional market participants employ information technology to deliver customer-focused or data-driven solutions with the intention of improving diverse facets of the insurance sector. These improvements may encompass distribution, risk assessment and underwriting, marketing, claims management, value-added services and innovation in insurance coverage products or services.
IAIS (2019)	Technology that has changed the insurance industry's value chain.
Faure & Li (2020)	The utilization of InsurTech, with a specific focus on blockchain technology, to enhance the accessibility of insurance and detect the barriers that hinder the advancement of InsurTech.
Ricciardi (2018)	All modern insurance technologies, including chatbots that facilitate H2C distribution, advanced analytics that identify viable use cases in the data-driven insurance industry and artificial intelligence.
Cruse & Singh (2019)	The leveraging of technology to disrupt the insurance industry.
Carrie & Kiki (2021)	The development of technologies, software and user interfaces for the insurance value chain to address inefficiencies or opportunities.

Organizations such as Progressive and Esurance began offering insurance online during Web 1.0 (approximately, 1991–2004), the first stage of the World Wide Web's revolutionary transformation (Lewis, 2021). At the same time, corporations began to use analytics

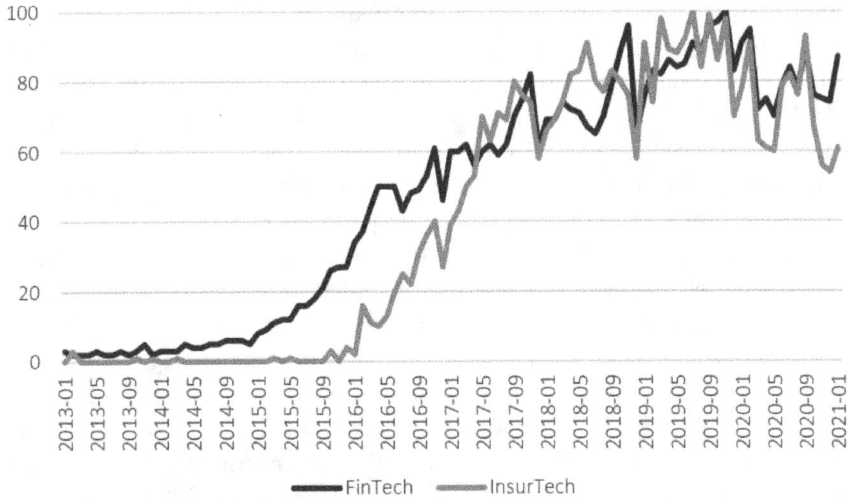

Figure 7.1. Global Google trend: interest over time (2013–2021).
Note: The numbers represent global search interest in a given period. A rating of 100 represents the term's highest popularity. A score of 50 indicates that the term is just half as popular. A score of 0 indicates that there is insufficient interest in this term.
Source: "Bibliometric Analysis of InsurTech" (Shamsuddin *et al.*, 2023).

to analyze massive insurance datasets for various applications, which frequently involved members of the actuarial community. In the early 2000s, property and casualty (P&C) insurers began to use predictive modeling to their advantage (Batty *et al.*, 2010). Soon after, life and health insurance companies jumped on the bandwagon. In 2012, the Committee on Life Insurance Mortality and Underwriting Surveys of the Society of Actuaries (SOA) surveyed approximately half of the respondents who were considering implementing predictive modeling for at least one application. FinTech emerged as an early and prominent constituent within the broader category of "EverythingTech" (Society of Actuaries, 2012).

The National Association of Insurance Commissioners (NAIC) data published in 2013 showed that the life insurance sector has "a long and illustrious history of adopting and innovating using information technology" (Carrie & Kiki, 2021, p. 7). It was one of the first organizations to extensively adopt computer technology and digital systems for data and document management (Willis Towers Watson,

2020). In addition to implementing advanced financial and risk modeling technologies and integrating modern enterprise systems, the industry has demonstrated a leading role in driving innovation. The survey also found a deficiency, stating that life insurers lagged behind their counterparts in the financial services industry when it comes to utilizing the internet and social media as direct marketing channels to reach clients (Carrie & Kiki, 2021, p. 7).

The term "InsurTech" was first used in the early 2010s and became widely accepted by the end of that year (Carrie & Kiki, 2021). There are several indicators available for examining and analyzing the rapid expansion of InsurTech. These include studying historical trends in InsurTech investments, observing the establishment of various incubators and accelerators focused on InsurTech and examining the relationships between InsurTech start-ups and established industry players. According to the fourth-quarter 2020 Quarterly InsurTech Briefing by Willis Towers Watson, there has been a significant increase in global funding for InsurTech start-ups, with the amount jumping from US$348 million in 2012 to US$7.1 billion in 2020. Based on the same report, there has been a significant surge in the number of transactions, exhibiting a growth rate of over 700%, from 46 in the year 2012 to 377 in the year 2020 (see Figure 7.2).

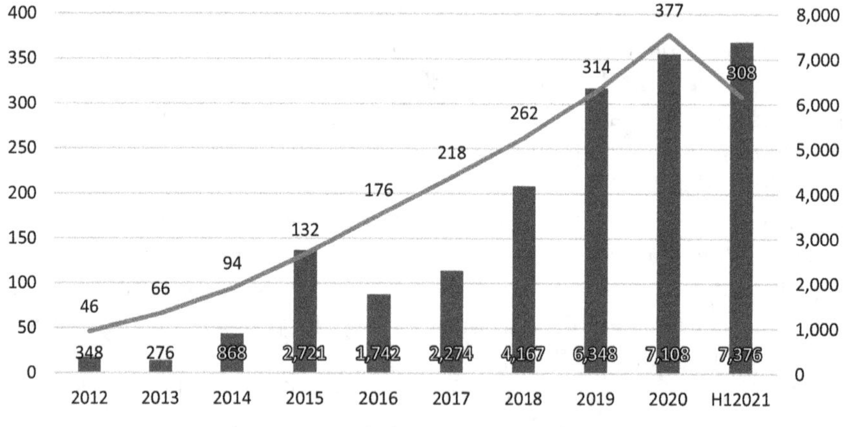

Figure 7.2. Annual InsurTech funding (US$ million) against the number of InsurTech deals from 2012 to H1 2021.

Source: Quarterly InsurTech Briefing Q12021, Willis Tower Watson, April 2021.

Historically, the insurance industry has been commonly described as "traditional" and "slow-moving," perhaps due to its extensive historical background. Its origins can be traced back to 1759, with the establishment of the Presbyterian Ministers' Fund in Pennsylvania, marking a history spanning over 260 years. Throughout this extensive chronology, the industry has demonstrated an inclination for both innovation and technological progress (Presbyterian Ministers' Fund, 2008). Several other elements contribute to the fundamental conservatism of the insurance sector, which has historically dampened or constrained innovation.

7.4. Underpinning Theories in InsurTech

7.4.1. *Diffusion of innovation theory*

It has been pointed out by Rogers (1995) that organizations and industries each have a specific rate at which they embrace and apply new technologies with growing maturity. New technology is embraced first by innovators, then by early adopters, followed by the early majority, then by the late majority and, finally, by the laggards. According to the findings of Hubert *et al.* (2018), the diffusion of innovation theory (DOI) developed by Rogers *et al.* (2003) is frequently used to explain the further progression of technology usage acceptance and the relationships in new technology diffusion. In addition, the DOI contributes to existing knowledge by including antecedents that have been overlooked in the technology acceptance model (TAM). In the DOI theory, Rogers *et al.* (2003) define innovation as a new idea that a person perceives as a new item, with the perceived newness of an object being highly dependent on the users' reaction to it. The authors emphasize that newness is not limited to new knowledge but may also refer to the newness of innovation adoption. The DOI theory provides increased comprehension of relevant aspects of the informal system, leading to a more vivid transformation in the general landscape of grassroots innovators. This theory also provides insights into their perceived IoT usage behavior.

The DOI theory considers only technology-related determinants (Blut *et al.*, 2016). DOI explains the complete diffusion of the innovation process, from the invention of the innovation through the formation of users' attitudes and the final decision on whether to adopt or reject the innovation (Moore & Benbasat, 1991; Rogers, 2003). Rogers (2003) defines the DOI as a systematic process in which an invention is transmitted through specific channels among members of a social system. The rate of adoption, which pertains to the relative speed at which individuals within the social system embrace new technology, determines the pace of dissemination. The rate of adoption, in turn, is controlled by a variety of characteristics of the innovation. Rogers (2003) identifies five key attributes that are pertinent to a potential user's viewpoint: relative advantage, complexity, compatibility (CO), trialability (TRI) and observability. According to Moore & Benbasat (1991), observability consists of two distinct characteristics, namely the perceived visibility of the invention and its perceived result demonstrability. This assertion is supported both theoretically and experimentally. The significance of visibility and outcome demonstrability in the diffusion process has been extensively explored by various scholars, establishing it as a recurring theme in the literature (Holak & Lehmann, 1990; Shih, 2013).

Because of the theoretical knowledge gained from acceptance and diffusion research, it is possible to have a better understanding of the mechanisms that underpin the adoption of technology in the insurance sector. However, the line between acceptance, adoption and diffusion in the field of information systems (IS) is frequently confused in the scientific literature (De Vries *et al.*, 2018). Following Van Offenbeek *et al.* (2013), the prevailing ideas on the adoption of information systems primarily focus on acceptance as a fundamental concept for explaining individual-level behavior toward innovation. A meta-analysis conducted by De Vries *et al.* (2018) revealed that 70% of the scientific articles on innovation diffusion and adoption included in their assessment failed to distinguish between the concepts of adoption and diffusion of innovations. In order to resolve this issue, Bui (2015) explains that adoption and diffusion refer to the execution of innovation from distinct perspectives or levels of analysis, respectively. According to this classification, the term "adoption" pertains to the execution of innovation at the micro or individual level (i.e. from the user's perspective).

In contrast, the term "diffusion" pertains to the widespread adoption of innovation on a large scale, specifically within a social system, market or industry. Technological acceptance research, also referred to as acceptance research in a broader sense, is a field of academic investigation that centers around the examination of individual conduct in relation to emerging technologies (Van Offenbeek *et al.*, 2013). According to Burton-Jones & Straub (2006), acceptance can be described as the utilization of a user's system to carry out a specific task. Van Offenbeek *et al.* (2013) state that the decision of a user to utilize technology is influenced by three distinct elements: the user's motivation, the system's capabilities and the system's usability. The three components that influence user behavior are knowledge factors, affective factors and behavioral factors. The aforementioned factors, in succession, affect individuals' perceptions, attitudes and beliefs, which subsequently influence their decision-making process regarding the adoption of new technologies (Khan, 2018).

The InsurTech industry structure indicates a high level of competitiveness and technological advancement. Additionally, it is apparent that there exists a robust network among stakeholders who possess knowledge of established processes. The network's strength is crucial in ensuring the appropriate utilization of technologies such as blockchain (O'Dair & Beaven, 2017). The level of maturity of the process plays a crucial role in ensuring the effective diffusion of that technology. Consequently, the utilization of this technology leads to a departure from centralized information management among stakeholders. This necessitates a crucial reliance on confidence and the establishment of operational norms among the relevant parties, even in the presence of modest variations in outcomes (Adams *et al.*, 2017; Grover *et al.*, 2020).

7.4.2. *Disruptive innovation theory*

The paradigm of disruptive innovation contains some intriguing discrepancies worth exploring (Christensen *et al.*, 2018). The original concept has garnered widespread recognition among professionals, and the term "disruption" has become integrated into the prevailing corporate vernacular (Christensen *et al.*, 2015). However, the fundamental notions of the theory continue to be largely misunderstood (Christensen, 2006; Raynor, 2011). The theory of disruption is expected to hold a prominent position in any evaluation of managerial significance, given its practical applications within the profession (Gulati, 2007; Hambrick, 2013; Tushman & O'Reilly, 2007). As such, it is likely to occupy a prominent position in any assessment of relevance in management. Although the foundational work has been extensively cited in a variety of disciplines, including marketing and economics (Di Stefano *et al.*, 2012) and a substantial amount of scholarly discourse about the fundamental theoretical concepts exists (Christensen, 2006; Danneels, 2004; Gans, 2016; Henderson, 2006; Slater & Narver, 1998; Sood & Tellis, 2005; Utterback & Acee, 2005), there has been a notable lack of management research focused on directing corporate behavior.

The term "disruption" is commonly employed to characterize the phenomenon in which a relatively small company, possessing limited resources, effectively challenges larger, well-established incumbent companies (Christensen *et al.*, 2015). Specifically, as established companies focus their resources on developing their products and services to satisfy their demanding (and, hence, the most lucrative) clients, they meet the requirements of certain industries while falling short of responding to the needs of other market segments. Successful market disruptors achieve their goals by focusing on untapped market segments and gaining a competitive advantage by offering more appropriate features, sometimes at a lower cost than their rivals. Companies that have already been established and are seeking greater profitability in increasingly challenging markets are less inclined to adopt an aggressive approach. Subsequently, new participants in the market use a more sophisticated approach, catering to the needs of established clients of existing companies by delivering comparable performance. Simultaneously, businesses manage to preserve the competitive advantages that initially accelerated their achievements in the sector. The acceptance of entrants' offerings by a significant proportion of mainstream customers is regarded as a disruptive phenomenon.

There were two phases of technological advancement in the modern era, according to the majority of modern historians: the steam/mechanical industry revolution at the late 18th century and the electric power/motor automobile revolution of the late 19th century (Naylor, 2017). Both of these had a profound impact on society, resulting in significantly higher average incomes and considerably improved living conditions for the general public. Conversely, both initiated significant disruptions to established social institutions and employment prospects. The initial industrial revolution, for instance, resulted in a transformation of a predominantly rural and agricultural society into one that was predominantly industrial and urban (Naylor, 2017). The general public at the time lacked comprehension of numerous benefits that are now considered indispensable and commonplace. This was evident from the extensive resistance encountered during the introduction of both the water wheel and the automobile. In each and every case, however, society as a whole benefited. Beginning around 1970, the current IT revolution ought to be perceived as a third wave capable of profoundly transforming our society, much like how the previous two industrial revolutions did over the past two centuries.

As Schmidt (2018) notes, the insurance industry is currently experiencing a substantial transformation as a result of the integration of diverse technologies linked to the fourth industrial revolution. Mobile phones, cloud computing, telematics, the IoT, artificial intelligence or cognitive computing, blockchain technology and predictive modeling are among these technologies. They are significantly contributing to the transformation of the insurance industry by facilitating innovative communication methods, information exchange and insurance practices. In this context, InsurTech is commonly recognized by scholars and practitioners as a distinct subdivision within the broader field of FinTech (Schueffel, 2018), which pertains to the utilization of digital technology within the insurance industry (Nicoletti & Nicoletti, 2017; Chishti & Barberis, 2016; Schena *et al.*, 2018; OECD, 2017). The authors used the term "InsurTech" to incorporate technological advancements in the insurance sector, including applications, software, products and services (Baumann, 2018; Chester *et al.*, 2018; Swiss Re, 2017). Despite being one of the industries slowest to embrace digital transformation, the ongoing process of digitization is exerting a substantial influence on insurance companies. This influence necessitates fundamental alterations in corporate culture, products, processes, customer relations and relationships with competitors within the sector (Albrecher *et al.*, 2019; IAIS, 2019). In conjunction with Eling & Lehmann (2018), Cappiello (2020b) introduces a conceptual framework outlining three primary domains of transformation within the insurance business. There are several ways in which new technologies impact the interaction between insurers and customers. First, the emergence of technologies such as social media, chatbots and robo-advisors has brought about significant changes in this interaction. Second, these new technologies have the potential to automate, standardize and enhance the effectiveness and efficiency of various business processes. Examples of such processes include online sales and digital claims settlements. Lastly, new technologies also facilitate the modification and advancement of existing insurance products. For instance, telemetric insurance and cyber insurance are products that have been developed and improved as a result of technological advancements (see Figure 7.3).

Digitalization is anticipated to have a profound and far-reaching impact on the financial and insurance sectors, influencing every aspect of the insurance value chain: asset and risk management, product development, pricing and underwriting, sales and distribution and policy and claims management (Martin Eling & Lehmann,

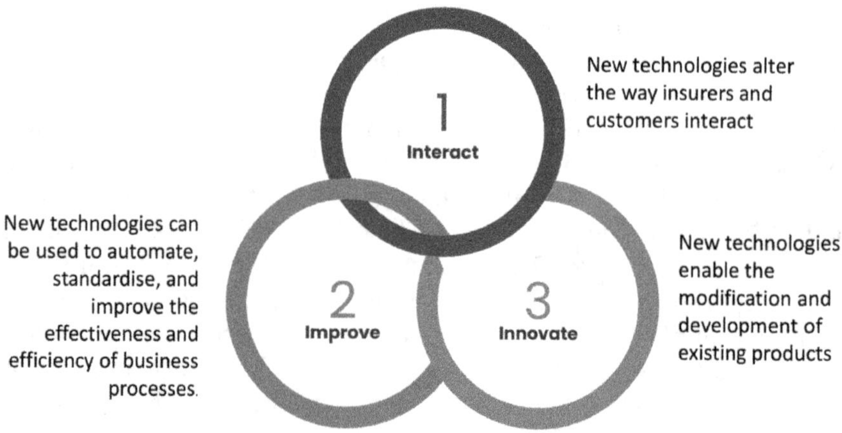

Figure 7.3. Three main areas of the insurance industry change.
Source: ©2020 Antonella Cappiello in "The digital (R)evolution of insurance business models." *American Journal of Economics and Business Administration*, 12(1), 1–13. This is an open-access article distributed under the terms of the Creative Commons Attribution License (CC BY 4.0), which permits unrestricted use, distribution, and reproduction in any medium, provided the original author and source are credited.

2018). Moreover, participants in the insurance market are presently confronted with a new insurance scenario known as "4.0," which requires them to assimilate into an ecosystem shaped by the expansion of interconnections between previously distinct industries and the emergence of new competitors. Moreover, it is imperative for all participants in the insurance industry to adapt to and operate in a macroeconomic environment marked by the exponential expansion of InsurTech start-ups, which are nascent businesses adopting technology-centric business models. As a result, the emphasis of these new market entrants has shifted from offering purely software solutions and engaging in activities that directly compete with insurance firms and brokers (Braun & Schreiber, 2017).

Insurance has traditionally demonstrated a willingness to adapt to technological developments. Nevertheless, amid the IT revolution of the past decade, the insurance sector has maintained its conventional operations while striving to endure the challenging circumstances of the Great Recession and the subsequent regulatory adjustments within the United States. As IBM (2006) explains, insurers tend to lag technologically, focusing on optimizing products and processes, accepting incremental change as if it were innovation rather than the other way around. Insurers who maintain a passive attitude toward technology in the face of future disruptions, on the other hand, are unlikely to survive because the cost advantages held by technological leaders or external disruptors will erode the cost base of laggards. Christensen (1997) asserted that adding new resources to an organization with outdated procedures and beliefs does not create a change-ready company.

7.4.3. *Theory of operational capabilities*

Insurance companies are currently experiencing extreme volatility in their existing competitive environment as a result of changes in market structure and the development of new products. In response to these changes, businesses have begun to prioritize marketing creativity and innovation by introducing new products and service delivery methods, promoting those services and providing timely customer service in an effort to establish a strong competitive position (Kogo & Kimencu, 2018). Although this transition poses certain challenges, it also offers insurers a tremendous opportunity to distinguish themselves and establish a position of authority among an emerging cohort of consumers. After identifying their position on the continuum connecting traditional insurance and digital maturity, insurers must strategize their transition to align with their overarching approach. Caillet & Gasc (2013) identified four capabilities for genuine digital mastery.

To create distinct consumer experiences through digital offerings, insurance companies must modernize their infrastructure and processes (Caillet & Gasc, 2013). Each of these skills has consequences for various components of the insurance value chain, demonstrating that digital transformation is not merely about selling products or providing customer service online, but rather about reimagining the entire business. Economic growth is contingent upon innovation and novel operational strategies aimed at improving products, services and processes (Peng *et al.*, 2008; Prieger, 2007). Academics, industry leaders and politicians pay close attention to innovation and product development as critical determinants of economic growth (Mazzucato, 2013; Piening & Salge, 2015). The significance of operational capabilities in boosting innovation performance and productivity is a particular focus (Mazzucato, 2013; Mina *et al.*, 2013)

In the discourse surrounding the pivotal significance of operational capabilities in attaining a competitive edge, certain terms are employed synonymously, including resources (Tu *et al.*, 2006), capabilities (Eisenhardt & Martin, 2000; Lee & Kelley, 2008) and best practices (Maire *et al.*, 2005; Ulusoy & İkiz, 2001), notwithstanding the fact that they denote inherently distinct notions (Flynn *et al.*, 2010). According to Wu *et al.* (2010), there exists an ambiguity regarding the conceptualization of operational capabilities and their distinction from resources and practices, as these elements are inherently interconnected. The effects of operational capabilities can primarily be attributed to resources and operational practices, which are widely regarded as crucial factors contributing to capabilities (Peng *et al.*, 2008).

The process-focused approach demonstrates that operational capabilities ought to be regarded as a means to an end, rather than as ends in themselves (Morgan & Hegarty, 1998). In a similar vein, operational capabilities are described by Flynn *et al.* (2010, p. 248) as "sets of firm-specific skills, processes and routines developed within the operations management system that are routinely utilized to resolve issues encountered by a unit and ultimately empower that unit – and the firm – to tailor the resources of the operations management system to suit its distinct requirements and challenges."

Operational capabilities are suggested as a means to establish cohesion, integration and guidance for resources and operational practices. They encompass both explicit and tacit elements, such as resources and practices, which enable organizations to effectively address diverse challenges and uncertainties (Flynn *et al.*, 2010; Wu *et al.*, 2010). Resources may be categorized into three main types: tangible, intangible and human. Tangible resources refer to assets that have a physical form, such as financial and physical assets. Intangible resources, on the other hand, are those that lack a physical presence and include elements such as technology, reputation and culture. Lastly, humans encompass the particular skills and knowledge possessed by individuals, as well as their ability to communicate and be motivated (Wu *et al.*, 2010). Operational capabilities leverage resources and operational methods to provide results that align with desired outcomes (Flynn *et al.*, 2010; Wu *et al.*, 2010). According to Teece *et al.* (1997), firms possess two distinct sets of capabilities. The first set of capabilities is concerned with converting inputs to outputs, while the second set of capabilities is concerned with modifying the capabilities of other firms. The initial grouping of capabilities is commonly known as operational capabilities, which possess a static characteristic, implying that they cannot undergo spontaneous changes until influenced by additional capabilities (Dangol & Kos, 2014). Given the inherent immutability of operational capabilities and their inherent incapability to autonomously adapt, it becomes imperative to identify complementary forms of capabilities that can facilitate the integration, reconfiguration and enhancement of existing operational capabilities. This is essential for the purpose of accommodating and responding to alterations in the surrounding environment (Dangol & Kos, 2014).

Protogerou *et al.* (2012) define operational capabilities as a firm's ability to undertake functional operations with consciously defined sets of resources. Effective operational capabilities are required to achieve and maintain competitive advantages. According to Wu *et al.* (2010), operational capabilities are extensively investigated from an outcomes viewpoint, including cost, quality, dependability, speed and adaptability (Ferdows & De Meyer, 1990; Flynn & Flynn,

2004). Using a process-oriented approach, Wu *et al.* (2010) classify six emerging operational capabilities into a taxonomy: operational reconfiguration, operational innovation, operational customization, operational cooperation and operational responsiveness. Furthermore, operational capabilities may be regarded as the process of resource reconfiguration, which entails the allocation of resources or their divestment in response to evolving environmental circumstances (Teece *et al.*, 1997; Wu *et al.*, 2010).

There are two types of innovation conceptualizations: those that focus on innovation as a process and those that focus on innovation as a consequence (Crossan & Apaydin, 2010; Jiménez-Jiménez & Sanz-Valle, 2011; Saunila & Mäkimattila, 2018). Innovation, in general, necessitates the invention and application of novel ideas to goods, processes, services and organizational structures (Schumpeter, 1934). The term "innovation performance" refers to an output whose success is decided by a variety of factors or inputs related to the process of innovation development. The inputs can be either physical (people, money, time and equipment) or intangible (motivation, knowledge and corporate culture) (Davila *et al.*, 2007). Saunila & Ukko (2014) describe findings that are consistent with those of Davila *et al.* (2007) on management structures, staff roles and attitudes and the capacity to renew or adapt to changing operating circumstances. Thus, innovation performance relates to the successful adoption of employee ideas, external data and new technologies, as well as the capacity to renew and improve internal operations.

The ability of a company to simplify its main technologies, resources and pivotal processes and respond to customers' requests efficiently and cost-effectively is referred to as operational capability (Wright *et al.*, 2001). Operational capabilities evolve over time, assimilating into the firm's particular characteristics that distinguish them and create a barrier to replication, thereby generating a competitive advantage (Takahashi *et al.*, 2017). Operational capabilities are not only a source of unity and integration but also serve as a guide for the use of current resources and the implementation of other operational procedures (Ferasso *et al.*, 2017). Process management and performance management are two characteristics of operational competence that can be thought of as a continuum. Process management includes the alignment, redefinition and execution of critical processes (Golann, 2006). The ability to provide a competitive edge by providing reliable products and services at lower costs, faster turnaround times and with the least possible use of essential resources, especially in unpredictable business contexts (Hervas-Oliver *et al.*, 2016), is a crucial component of effective process management. Agile and resilient organizations devote the maximum attention to their essential processes, which allows them to adapt more quickly to the constantly changing business environment (Ferasso *et al.*, 2017). In order to achieve and maintain efficient performance, performance management must be an ongoing, consistent exercise involving the creation, setting and readjustment of targets and goals that are strategically aligned with the organization's overall aims (Länsiluoto *et al.*, 2018). Performance objectives, also known as key performance indicators (KPIs), serve as the core of performance management since they may be used to translate company strategies into practical terms (Garengo & Sharma, 2014). KPIs should be regularly updated to ensure they meet the necessary levels of performance, clarity and relevance. The updated and amended KPIs should be communicated across the organization.

According to KPMG (2019), the insurance industry is continuing to adapt to various internet environments, and insurance products for the internet ecosystem are continuing to innovate iteratively, starting with simpler products such as return shipping insurance and progressing to more diverse and complex products over time. Products particularly demanding of insurance businesses' operational capabilities include those with greater scenario fragmentation, increased client involvement, tougher time limitations and higher volatility in sales between peaks and valleys in business. Assisted by emerging technologies such as cloud computing and big data, insurance companies' operational skills have been significantly enhanced in the following five areas:

- **More flexible resource allocation:** In the past, the primary business systems of insurance companies were equipped with fixed computing resources that fluctuated rapidly. Expanding resources for internet services is a time-consuming and inflexible process, which renders the current systems incapable of accommodating such fluctuations. Faced with fragmented, fluctuating and time-sensitive computer resource requirements, insurance companies can rapidly deploy resources to optimize business processes (KPMG, 2019).

- **Faster response:** Internet services and operations are often more time-sensitive. Insurance businesses can ensure prompt and efficient data processing while also fulfilling real-time computing needs in many complicated environments by combining cloud computing and big data technology (KPMG, 2019).
- **Increased business capacity:** The fragmented, low-value and high-frequency nature of internet insurance places a significant strain on the business support capabilities of insurance companies. From an e-commerce perspective, for example, Tmall alone received more than 800 million orders on 11 November 2017 (also known as "Double 11 Day"), with volume peaking at an astounding 325,000 transactions per second. Consequently, the provider of return shipment insurance that supports Tmall must possess advanced technological capabilities. Insurance companies now have the capability to perform real-time underwriting procedures and provide customized pricing for particular insured entities (buyers and sellers) as well as individuals by leveraging big data, artificial intelligence and cloud computing. Utilizing cutting-edge technology, insurers have amassed the capabilities required to execute the operational processes that underpin these innovative internet products (KPMG, 2019).
- **More comprehensive product range:** Online insurance products have undergone a substantial transformation over the past decade or so. Initially offering straightforward return shipping insurance, they have since expanded to encompass a vast array of consumption-related matters, such as health, credit, catastrophes, account security and transaction protection. For insurance companies, the development of centralized business operations capable of supporting the demands of numerous circumstances, timeframes, resources and product operations has been a significant obstacle. By leveraging technological advancements including blockchain, cloud computing, big data, artificial intelligence and the IoT, insurers can enhance the functionality of their product support systems, acquire numerous technological benefits and effectively respond to diverse operational demands (KPMG, 2019).

- **Smoother workflow:** Diverse product types, diverse environmental requirements, multi-level product operations and multidimensional risk monitoring have all contributed to an increase in the operational demands of insurance companies. By integrating the robust computational resources of the cloud with the sophisticated processing and analysis capabilities of big data, insurance companies can amass a more extensive dataset pertaining to business operations and construct a more comprehensive monitoring system; thus, they can consistently enhance their operational procedures and accommodate the heightened operational demands of the internet (KPMG, 2019).

7.5. Technology in the Insurance Industry

The highly developed digital technology in the insurance industry primarily concerns new online distribution channels (Dumm & Hoyt, 2002; Garven, 2002), particularly their implications for insurance agents (Eastman *et al.*, 2002), customer orientation (see Kaiser, 2002) and regulation (Kaiser, 2002). While older generations of digital technology were primarily used to increase efficiency, new generations are expected to increase market dynamics and competition as a result of increased transparency and comparability, lower transaction costs and a broader reach of online platforms (Schulte-Noelle, 2001; Taylor, 2001). Hence, the possibility of financial services convergence is considered (Beltratti & Corvino, 2008), as are the consequences of formal insurance business models (Seog, 2009).

Barkur *et al.* (2007) emphasize the insurance industry's need for organizational transformation to address the aforementioned issues. The pervasive presence of mobile, networked devices further bolsters this argument by enabling insurance companies to experiment with novel business models (Desyllas & Sako, 2013) and expand the types of risks that may be insured against (Gehrke, 2014). Big data analytics enables personalized and adaptive premium computation based on knowledge about the insurance holder's behavior (McAfee & Brynjolfsson, 2012), and previously incalculable hazards can now be calculated in ways that enable new types of insurance to address them (Eling & Schnell, 2016). Additionally, platform-based interactions can be used to supplement centralized insurance solutions for certain interest groups (see, e.g., Cole, 2015; Salman, 2014).

Eling & Lehmann (2018) provide an overview of the current body of knowledge about digital transactions in the insurance business. Big data, artificial intelligence, the IoT, cloud computing, blockchain, mobile devices and a variety of online applications are all covered as subtopics. They demonstrate that the consequences of digital technology cannot be studied in isolation (Nicoletti, 2016; ACORD, 2017). Digital innovation opportunities span multiple value chain stages and simultaneously alter the structure and reference points of insurance solutions. It is no longer possible to maintain a distinction between technological solutions designed to support corporate operations internally and those intended to assist with client contact externally. In order to maximize the transformative capabilities of digital technology, insurance companies must adopt a comprehensive strategy that considers their internal and external activities.

Although the usefulness of digital transformation as a term in systems engineering may be debatable, industry and academic experts appear to broadly agree on its orientational value in strategic decision-making (Legner *et al.*, 2017; Riedl *et al.*, 2017). This conversation takes a strategic approach by bringing together business- and technology-related issues (Hess *et al.*, 2016; Matt *et al.*, 2015). However, digitization issues are not always handled with the same level of detail. For example, Mertens & Wiener (2018) detect typical hype cycle structures in public discourse on digitization, indicating that the term is being overused (Steininger *et al.*, 2009).

Werth *et al.* (2020) compiled a list of factors influencing the digital transformation of financial services. These can be political, social, economic or technological in nature. Revathi (2020) conducted an assessment of the application of information technologies in the insurance industry, including artificial intelligence, big data, the IoT, blockchain and cloud computing, and developed specifications for an insurer's information system. Eling & Lehmann (2018) examined insurers' value creation processes through the lens of IT solutions. Table 7.2 summarizes the impact of digitization and various digital technologies on the insurance sector. Different research areas and their relevance to the insurance sector are evaluated to analyze and document the impact of digital transformation on an

Table 7.2. Summary of research on digital insurance technology.

Area of study	Title	Innovation	References
Products, processes, organizations, business models	Digital Insurance: Business Innovation in the Post-Crisis Era	Technological	Nicoletti (2016)
Life insurance industry	Spread of Marketing Innovations in the Service Industry	Innovations methodology technological guaranteed purchase option	Peterson *et al.* (1972)
Automobile insurance	Profiting from Business Model Innovation: Evidence From Pay-As-You-Drive Auto Insurance	Pay-As-You-Drive – insurance	Desyllas & Sako (2013)
The relationship between economic innovation models and innovation cycles in the British insurance business	Towards an Historical Model of Services Innovation: The Case of the Insurance Industry, 1700–1914	Different types of insurance	Pearson (1997)
Innovation degree and innovation performance	Examining the Relationship between Market Orientation and Innovation in Europe and the United States of America's Insurance Markets	New insurance products	Lado & Maydeu-Olivares (2001)

(*Continued*)

Table 7.2. (*Continued*)

Area of Study	Title	Innovation	References
Impact of digitalization advances	The Impact of Digitalization on the Insurance Value Chain and the Insurability of Risks	Customer experience, business processes and new products	Eling & Lehmann (2018)
Advances in intelligent systems and computing	Digital Technology in Insurance	Online insurance products	Mustafina *et al.* (2020)
Digital insurers	The Making of a Digital Insurer: The **Path to Enhanced Profitability, Lower Costs and Stronger Customer** Loyalty	**Technology**	Cathin *et al.* (2015)
Digital-related comprehensive approaches	Digital Agendas in the Insurance Industry: The Importance of Comprehensive Approaches	Digital business	Bohnert *et al.* (2019)
Technology and innovation in insurance	Technology and Innovation in Insurance – Present and Future Technology in Indian Insurance Industry	Technology investment	Revathi (2020)
Machine learning and blockchain	Machine Learning Applications in Nonlife Insurance	Household insurance and motor insurance	Grize *et al.* (2020)
Blockchain and contract theory	Blockchain and Contract Theory: Modeling Smart Contracts Using Insurance Markets	Smart contracts	Sheth & Subramanian (2020)

insurance company's operational efficiencies, service delivery and customer experience (Desikan & Jayanthila Devi, 2021).

According to Catlin *et al.* (2014), a thoughtful digitization program can result in cost savings of up to 65%, a 90% reduction in turnaround time for critical insurance operations and a more than 20% increase in conversion rates. The study by Desyllas & Sako (2013) validates the advantages of implementing a "pay as you drive" (PAYD) system in auto insurance, as it enables an efficient and equitable distribution of premiums and insurance reimbursements by segmenting policyholders based on their risk profile. An additional positive consequence of implementing PAYD is that policyholders' road-driving vigilance improves, leading to a reduction in insured incidents. Husnjak *et al.* (2015) demonstrate how telematics in transportation insurance may address the issue of fair insurance rates and provide clients with sufficient, favorable costs for insurance services. When analyzing innovation in the property insurance market, Bednarczyk & Jańska (2015) assess the complete chain of property insurance services, from distribution to loss reduction and retrospective replenishment of insurance risks in insurance coverage (i.e. historical change). As Nicoletti (2016) acknowledges, disruptive technologies may benefit insurance firms if they do not lose a significant geographic area or product segment.

7.6. Future of InsurTech

Digital transformation is not restricted to the sectors of risk management and insurance. In fact, the majority of, if not all, industries are undergoing a transformation, with some sectors progressing more rapidly than others. The experiences of these other sectors enable us to assess prevalent patterns in digital transformation and formulate prospective scenarios for the insurance industry, taking into account their own unique contexts. A viewpoint is presented through the lens of the theory of disruptive innovation (Christensen *et al.*, 2015).

According to Christensen *et al.* (2015), disruptive innovation often serves as the catalyst for industry transformation, with a particular emphasis on the manufacturing sector (compare Netflix and Blockbuster or Amazon and Barnes & Noble). The fundamental idea posits that niche enterprises commence by catering to customer segments with unmet needs. Over time, these enterprises iteratively enhance their offerings and eventually surpass the mainstream market, establishing themselves as the prevailing participant. Potential disruptive forces in the digital realm may consist of technology entrepreneurs or "digital giants" with sufficient financial and human resources to thrive, such as Google, Facebook and Apple. According to Venkatraman (2017), the process begins with disruptors experimenting at the market's periphery; however, they may eventually extend their reach into the mainstream market, colliding with the heart of the industry and, potentially, reshaping it from the ground up.

Possibly the most significant determinants of the insurance industry's current standing are the involved industry and target market. Nevertheless, despite persistent rumors regarding the tech titans' efforts to enter the insurance industry, their current level of engagement seems to be limited. Similarly, although certain emerging firms have attempted to transform the insurance sector, there is no evidence of their ability to achieve profitable growth at a rapid pace. One plausible rationale is the scarcity of revolutionary digital product or service advancements that disrupt the fundamental principles of the industry. In the future, however, novel concepts such as usage-based insurance, on-demand insurance and insurer-provided risk prevention services may be able to accomplish this. In fact, product innovation is indicated by the auto insurance strategy described by Guillen *et al.* (2021), which penalizes near-miss incidents.

Digital innovations include a wide range of categories, with new services and products serving as one of many examples. According to Westerman *et al.* (2014), other digital innovation efforts increase the power of core operations or improve the consumer experience. These decisions are strongly tied to the core economics of the insurance industry. Increasing the quality of insurance products and services while simultaneously enhancing fundamental operations addresses the insurance industry's demand and supply sides, respectively. Increasing client satisfaction by lowering excess risks, such as better alignment between exposure and coverage, or by cutting expenses, such as automating internal operations, will benefit the bottom line of insurance companies. The principles of behavioral economics of insurance support enhancing customers' experiences, as it is clear that customers value a reduction in the hassle and uncertainty they are experiencing – particularly that leading to unpleasant surprises – as well as a reduction in the amount of money they spend. To be clear, improving the customization of coverage options or enhancing consumer involvement does not, by itself, result in value creation.

Businesses operating within the insurance sector are proactively seeking methods to capitalize on digital opportunities, with the dual objectives of cost reduction and enhanced client satisfaction. Among the many methods that can be utilized to increase efficiency and decrease expense ratios is the automation of claims processing, underwriting decisions and subrogation judgments. The approaches provided by Gomes *et al.* (2021) for fraud detection and those proposed by Li *et al.* (2021) for detecting misrepresentations in insurance applications come within this classification. Besides, many businesses make investments to improve their digital connections with clients. Several of the benefits associated with doing so are evident. For instance, enhancing customers' experiences through the implementation of a streamlined, intuitive digital platform that enables them to easily perform tasks such as submitting claims has evident advantages. Furthermore, these platforms enable data-driven decision-making through experimentation, the collection of customer experience data and the simple integration of automated systems, among other things. As a result, it should come as no surprise that digitalization is related to an increase in insurers' market valuation. According to Fritzsch *et al.* (2021), investors appear to recognize and reward efforts to digitalize businesses.

Large incumbent insurers may find it difficult to exploit these opportunities because of legacy systems and processes, which may be one of the reasons why some believe that the insurance business is ripe for disruption (Bauer *et al.*, 2021). Significant advantages exist, at least on the surface level of the digital landscape's complexity, for tech entrepreneurs due to their systematic exploitation of digital opportunities, ideological emphasis on innovation and workforces equipped with up-to-date skills. Conversely, established players possess two notable benefits: access to historical data and personnel with extensive expertise regarding the complexities and subtleties of the insurance sector. Undoubtedly, in a contemporary society where forecasting is progressively becoming mechanized, the "most esteemed proficiencies of labor force comprise judgment," and this judgment is critically reliant on previous experience and intimate knowledge of the surroundings, as Agrawal *et al.* (2017) point out. The future will reveal whether disruptors can overcome these challenges or whether traditional insurers can reposition their businesses. Undoubtedly, the future of insurance will be more digital, and research in this field should similarly transition to digital formats.

7.7. Summary

Technological advancements are causing a paradigm shift in the traditional value chain and reconfiguring the competitive environment within the insurance sector. Although initially progressing at a snail's pace, insurers are starting to experience the consequences of digital transformation. As a result, the majority of businesses are reorienting their approaches to conducting operations, which includes investing in technology-driven start-ups that specialize in distribution. This chapter presented a comprehensive examination of the literature pertaining to the insurance industry and identified the foundations for novel ideas.

We examined the definition of InsurTech based on past research, which began with Arner *et al.* (2015) and progressed to more complex definitions given by Xu & Zweifel (2020) and Carrie & Kiki (2021). Based on our findings, it can be inferred that InsurTech, being a customer-centric or data-driven solution, aims to enhance the entire value chain of the insurance sector. This includes value-added services, marketing and sales, risk assessment and underwriting, claims management and the provision of insurance products or services.

We discovered three fundamental ideas related to InsurTech that have resulted in significant innovation in the insurance industry. First, the introduction of new entrants into the business has been identified as a disruption that has the potential to affect the whole distribution channel in the insurance industry. As InsurTech companies, they challenge the traditional business models of incumbents by generating novel consumer value propositions that attract and retain customers. Third, InsurTech enhances incumbent insurers' value chain by providing innovative technologies and solutions that increase operational efficiency and reduce costs. However, with the new millennial generation and the IoT, insurance companies must adapt to the new technologies and boost the trustworthiness of their clients. In addition, technological innovation has the potential to lower operating costs while increasing the industry's ability to work collaboratively with others in the financial sector.

As the significance of digital technology's capacity for innovation has become more widely recognized by the insurance industry, digital agendas have increasingly been integrated into business operations. The insurance industry is ripe with innovation potential as a result of the development of digital technology (Martin Eling & Lehmann, 2018). The development of new business models and value creation processes (Desyllas & Sako, 2013; Schmidt *et al.*, 2017) and the overall transformation of insurance companies into more agile organizations are examples of transformational change (Barkur *et al.*, 2007). Insurance businesses have a range of options when it comes to incorporating digital technology as a result of this variety. However, the insurance industry may reap the most benefits from the integration of digital technology into a complete strategy for innovation. Overall, a thorough assessment of insurance companies will aid in the survival of the fittest and encourage the growth of the InsurTech industry. However, a broad quantifiable foundation for this assessment is lacking in the existing literature.

There are no exhaustive analyses of the impact of InsurTech on the financial performance of insurance companies, insurance brokers, loss adjusters and insurance agents, which were excluded from our study. However, InsurTech contributes to the advancement of novel insurance agreements. For instance, InsurTech can be utilized to generate contracts that are more conducive to consumer satisfaction or that provide enhanced adaptability. The integration of InsurTech and other FinTech sub-clusters has the potential to enhance insurers' ability to efficiently handle their insurance contracts. Furthermore, the prospective research issue of examining the theoretical connection between InsurTech and various sectors has been identified.

References

ACORD. (2017, March). Insurance digital maturity study.

Adams, R., Parry, G., Godsiff, P., & Ward, P. (2017). The future of money and further applications of the blockchain. *Strategic Change*, 26(5), 417–422. https://doi.org/10.1002/jsc.2141.

Agrawal, A., Gans, J. S., & Goldfarb, A. (2017). What to expect from artificial intelligence. *MIT Sloan Management Review*, 58(3), 23–26.

Albrecher, H., Bommier, A., Filipovic, D., Koch-Medina, P., Loisel, S., & Schmeiser, H. (2019). Insurance: Models, digitalization, and data science. *SSRN Electronic Journal* (June). https://doi.org/10.2139/ssrn.3382125.

Arner, D. W., Barberis, J. N., & Buckley, R. P. (2015). The evolution of fintech: A new post-crisis paradigm? *SSRN Electronic Journal* (January). https://doi.org/10.2139/ssrn.2676553.

Ba, S., Stallaert, J., & Zhang, Z. (2010). Balancing IT with the human touch: Optimal investment in IT-based customer service. *Information Systems Research*, 21(3), 423–442. https://doi.org/10.1287/isre.1100.0282.

Barkur, G., Varambally, K. V. M., & Rodrigues, L. L. R. (2007). Insurance sector dynamics: Towards transformation into learning organization. *Learning Organization*, 14(6), 510–523. https://doi.org/10.1108/09696470710825123.

Barrett, M., Davidson, E., Prabhu, J., & Vargo, S. L. (2015). Service innovation in the digital age: Key contributions and future directions. *MIS Quarterly: Management Information Systems*, 39(1), 135–154. https://doi.org/10.25300/MISQ/2015/39:1.03.

Batty, M., Arun Tripathi, C., Kroll, A., Wu, C. P., Moore, D., Stehno, C., Lau, L., Guszcza, J., & Katcher, M. (2010). Predictive modeling for life insurance. Deloitte Consulting LLP (Issue April). https://www.soa.org/files/pdf/research-pred-mod-life-batty.pdf.

Bauer, D., Tyler Leverty, J., Schmit, J., & Sydnor, J. (2021). Symposium on insure-tech, digitalization, and big-data techniques in risk management and insurance. *Journal of Risk and Insurance*, 88(3), 525–528. https://doi.org/10.1111/jori.12360.

Baumann, N. (2018). A catalyst for change: How fintech has sparked a revolution in insurance. Deloitte Touche Tohmatsu Limited.

Bednarczyk, T. H. & Jańska, A. (2015). Product and process innovations in property insurance for individuals. *Annales Universitatis Mariae Curie-Skłodowska, Sectio H, Oeconomia*, 49(4), 45. https://doi.org/10.17951/h.2015.49.4.45.

Beltratti, A. & Corvino, G. (2008). Why are insurance companies different? The limits of convergence among financial institutions. *Geneva Papers on Risk and Insurance: Issues and Practice*, 33(3), 363–388. https://doi.org/10.1057/gpp.2008.13.

Bitner, M. J., Brown, S. W., & Meuter, M. L. (2000). Technology infusion in service encounters. *Journal of the Academy of Marketing Science*, 28(1), 138–149. https://doi.org/10.1177/0092070300281013.

Blut, M., Wang, C., & Schoefer, K. (2016). Factors influencing the acceptance of self-service technologies: A meta-analysis. *Journal of Service Research*, 19(4), 396–416. https://doi.org/10.1177/1094670516662352.

Bohnert, A., Fritzsche, A., & Gregor, S. (2019). Digital agendas in the insurance industry. *Geneva Papers on Risk and Insurance-Issues and Practice*, 44(1), 1–19.

Braun, A. & Schreiber, F. (2017). The current InsurTech landscape: Business models and disruptive potential. Institute of Insurance Economics I. VW-HSG, University of St. Gallen, 194.

Bui, Q. (2015). A review of innovation diffusion theories and mechanisms. *DIGIT 2015 Proceedings*, 11. http://aisel.aisnet.org/digit2015/11.

Burton-Jones, A. & Straub, D. W. (2006). Reconceptualizing system usage: An approach and empirical test. *Information Systems Research*, 17(3), 228–246. https://doi.org/10.1287/isre.1060.0096.

Caillet, R. & Gasc, J.-F. (2013). The digital insurer: What does it take to be a digital insurer? Four capabilities insurers need on the journey to digital mastery and high performance. http://i.accenture.com/F0nW310sv0E0X3nF000HLu4.

Cappiello, A. (2020a). The digital (R)evolution of insurance business models. *American Journal of Economics and Business Administration*, 12(1), 1–13. https://doi.org/10.3844/ajebasp.2020.1.13.

Cappiello, A. (2020b). The technological disruption of insurance industry: A review. *International Journal of Business and Social Science*, 11(1), 1–11. https://doi.org/10.30845/ijbss.v11n1a1.

Carrie, K. & Kiki, W. (2021). InsurTech: A guide for the actuarial community. Willis Tower Watson (Issue April).

Cathin, T., Hartman, R., Segev, I., & Tentis, R. (2015). The making of a digital insurer. Financial Service Practice, McKinsey Global Insurance Practice.

Catlin, T., Patiath, P., & Segev, I. (2014). Insurance companies untapped digital opportunity. *Harvard Business Review*.

Chester, A., Ham, S., Johansson, S., & Olesen, P. B. (2018). Commercial lines insurtech: A pathway to digital. *McKinsey & Company* (October).

Chishti, S. & Barberis, J. (2016). *The Fintech Book: The Financial Technology Handbook for Investors, Entrepreneurs and Visionaries.* West Sussex, UK: John Wiley & Sons Ltd. https://doi.org/10.22146/jieb.23554.

Christensen, C. M. (1997). *The Innovator's Dilemma: When New Technologies Cause Great Firms to Fail.* Management of Innovation and Change (pp. 1–14). Boston, MA: Harvard Business School Press.

Christensen, C. M. (2006). The ongoing process of building a theory of disruption. *Journal of Product Innovation Management*, 23(1), 39–55. https://doi.org/10.1111/j.1540-5885.2005.00180.x.

Christensen, C. M., McDonald, R., Altman, E. J., & Palmer, J. E. (2018). Disruptive innovation: An intellectual history and directions for future research. *Journal of Management Studies*, 55(7), 1043–1078. https://doi.org/10.1111/joms.12349.

Christensen, C. M., Raynor, M., & McDonald, R. (2015). What is disruptive innovation? *Harvard Business Review* (December).

Cole, S. (2015). Overcoming barriers to microinsurance adoption: Even from the field. *The Geneva Papers on Risk and Insurance – Issues and Practice*, 40(4), 720–740. https://doi.org/10.1057/gpp.2005.22.

Crossan, M. M. & Apaydin, M. (2010). A multi-dimensional framework of organizational innovation: A systematic review of the literature. *Journal of Management Studies*, 47(6), 1154–1191. https://doi.org/10.1111/j.1467-6486.2009.00880.x.

Cruse, B. W. & Singh, H. (2019). Insurtechs on the rise. *Brain & Company.*

Dangol, R. & Kos, A. (2014). Knightian uncertainty and risk: A basis for untangling dynamic capabilities from operational capabilities. *Journal of Strategy and Management*, 7(4), 337–353. https://doi.org/10.1108/JSMA-02-2014-0010.

Danneels, Ã. E. (2004). Disruptive technology reconsidered: A critique and research agenda. *Journal of Product Innovation Management*, 21(1), 246–258.

Davila, T., Epstein, M. J., & Shelton, R. (2007). *Stay on Top of Best in Business Knowledge* (Vol. 25, Issue 25). Ipswich, MA: Pearson Education, Inc.

De Vries, H., Tummers, L., & Bekkers, V. (2018). The diffusion and adoption of public sector innovations: A meta-synthesis of the literature. *Perspectives on Public Management and Governance*, 1(3), 159–176. https://doi.org/10.1093/ppmgov/gvy001.

Desikan, J. & Jayanthila Devi, A. (2021). Digital transformation in Indian insurance industry – A case study. *International Journal of Case Studies in Business, IT, and Education*, 5(2), 184–196. https://doi.org/10.47992/ijcsbe.2581.6942.0128.

Desyllas, P. & Sako, M. (2013). Profiting from business model innovation: Evidence from Pay-As-You-Drive auto insurance. *Research Policy*, 42(1), 101–116. https://doi.org/10.1016/j.respol.2012.05.008.

Di Stefano, G., Gambardella, A., & Verona, G. (2012). Technology push and demand pull perspectives in innovation studies: Current findings and future research directions. *Research Policy*, 41(8), 1283–1295. https://doi.org/10.1016/j.respol.2012.03.021.

Dumm, R. E. & Hoyt, R. E. (2002). Insurance distribution channels: Markets in transition. In *38th Annual Seminar of the International Insurance Society*, June (pp. 1–12).

Eastman, J. K., Eastman, A. D. A., & Eastman, K. L. (2002). Insurance sales agents and the internet: The relationship between opinion leadership, subjective knowledge, and internet attitudes. *Journal of Marketing Management*, 18(3–4), 259–285. https://doi.org/10.1362/0267257022872460.

Eisenhardt, K. M. & Martin, J. A. (2000). Dynamic capabilities. *Strategic Management Journal*, 21, 1105–1121. https://doi.org/10.1108/ebr-03-2018-0060.

Eling, M. & Lehmann, M. (2018). The impact of digitalization on the insurance value chain and the insurability of risks. *Geneva Papers on Risk and Insurance: Issues and Practice*, 43(3), 359–396. https://doi.org/10.1057/s41288-017-0073-0.

Eling, M. & Schnell, W. (2016). What do we knoiw about cyber risk and cyber risk insurance? *Journal of Risk and Insurance*, 17(5), 474–491. https://doi.org/10.1145/3132847.3132886.

Faure, M. & Li, S. (2020). Risk shifting in the context of 3D printing: An insurability perspective. *Geneva Papers on Risk and Insurance: Issues and Practice*, 45(3), 482–507. https://doi.org/10.1057/s41288-020-00164-9.

Ferasso, M., Takahashi, A. R. W., & May, M. R. (2017). Dynamic capabilities, operational capabilities and SMEs performance: A synthesis of researches. In *26th International Association for Management of Technology Conference, IAMOT 2017*, May.

Ferdows, K. & De Meyer, A. (1990). Lasting improvements in manufacturing performance: In search of a new theory. *Journal of Operations Management*, 9(2), 168–184. https://doi.org/10.1016/0272-6963(90)90094-T.

Flynn, B. B. & Flynn, E. J. (2004). An exploratory study of the nature of cumulative capabilities. *Journal of Operations Management*, 22(5), 439–457. https://doi.org/10.1016/j.jom.2004.03.002.

Flynn, B. B., Wu, S. J., & Melnyk, S. (2010). Operational capabilities: Hidden in plain view. *Business Horizons*, 53(3), 247–256. https://doi.org/10.1016/j.bushor.2010.01.001.

Fritzsch, S., Scharner, P., & Weiß, G. (2021). Estimating the relation between digitalization and the market value of insurers. *Journal of Risk and Insurance*, 88(3), 529–567. https://doi.org/10.1111/jori.12346.

Gans, J. (2016). The distruption dilemma. *Journal of Innovation & Knowledge*. https://doi.org/10.1016/j.jik.2017.06.001.

Garengo, P. & Sharma, M. K. (2014). Performance measurement system contingency factors: A cross analysis of Italian and Indian SMEs. *Production Planning and Control*, 25(3), 220–240. https://doi.org/10.1080/09537287.2012.663104.

Garven, J. R. (2002). On the implications of the internet for insurance markets and institutions. *Risk Management Insurance Review*, 5(2), 105–116. https://doi.org/10.1111/1098-1616.00014.

Gehrke, E. (2014). The insurability framework applied to agricultural microinsurance: What do we know, what can we learn. *Geneva Papers on Risk and Insurance: Issues and Practice*, 39(2), 264–279. https://doi.org/10.1057/gpp.2014.2.

Golann, B. (2006). Achieving growth and responsiveness: Process management and market orientation in small firms. *Journal of Small Business Management*, 44(3), 369–385. https://doi.org/10.1111/j.1540-627X.2006.00177.x.

Gomes, C., Jin, Z., & Yang, H. (2021). Insurance fraud detection with unsupervised deep learning. *Journal of Risk and Insurance*, 88(3), 591–624. https://doi.org/10.1111/jori.12359.

Grize, Y. L., Fischer, W., & Lützelschwab, C. (2020). Machine learning applications in nonlife insurance. *Applied Stochastic Models in Business and Industry* (October 2019), 1–15. https://doi.org/10.1002/asmb.2543.

Grover, P., Kar, A. K., & Dwivedi, Y. K. (2020). Understanding artificial intelligence adoption in operations management: Insights from the review of academic literature and social media discussions. *Annals of Operations Research*. https://doi.org/10.1007/s10479-020-03683-9.

Guillen, M., Nielsen, J. P., & Pérez-Marín, A. M. (2021). Near-miss telematics in motor insurance. *Journal of Risk and Insurance*, 88(3), 569–589. https://doi.org/10.1111/jori.12340.

Gulati, R. (2007). Tent poles, tribalism, and boundary spanning: The rigor-relevance debate in management research. *Academy of Management Journal*, 50(4), 775–782. https://doi.org/10.5465/AMJ.2007.26279170.

Hambrick, D. C. (2013). Mattered ? What if the academy actually. *Academy of Management Review*, 19(1), 11–16.

Henderson, R. (2006). The innovator's dilemma as a problem of organizational competence. *Journal of Product Innovation Management*, 23(1), 5–11. https://doi.org/10.1111/j.1540-5885.2005.00175.x.

Hervas-Oliver, J. L., Boronat-Moll, C., & Sempere-Ripoll, F. (2016). On process innovation capabilities in SMEs: A taxonomy of process-oriented innovative SMEs. *Journal of Small Business Management*, 54(December 2017), 113–134. https://doi.org/10.1111/jsbm.12293.

Hess, T., Benlian, A., Matt, C., & Wiesböck, F. (2016). How German media companies defined their digital transformation strategies. *MIS Quarterly Executive*, 15(2), 103–119.

Holak, S. L. & Lehmann, D. R. (1990). Purchase intentions and the dimensions of innovation: An exploratory model. *Journal Production Innovation Management*, 7, 59–73.

Hubert, M., Blut, M., Brock, C., Zhang, R. W., Koch, V., & Riedl, R. (2018). The influence of acceptance and adoption drivers on smart home usage. *European Journal of Marketing*, 53(6), 1073–1098. https://doi.org/10.1108/EJM-12-2016-0794.

Husnjak, S., Peraković, D., Forenbacher, I., & Mumdziev, M. (2015). Telematics system in usage based motor insurance. *Procedia Engineering*, 100(January), 816–825. https://doi.org/10.1016/j.proeng.2015.01.436.

IAIS. (2019). Issues Paper on Use of Big Data Analytics in Insurance. International Association of Insurance Super (September). https://www.iaisweb.org/page/supervisory-material/issues-papers//file/89244/issues-paper-on-use-of-big-data-analytics-in-insurance

IBM. (2006). Insurance 2020: Innovating Beyond Old Models. IBM Institute for Business Value. https://www-935.ibm.com/services/us/gbs/bus/pdf/g510-6291-01-insurance-2020.pdf.

Jiménez-Jiménez, D. & Sanz-Valle, R. (2011). Innovation, organizational learning, and performance. *Journal of Business Research*, 64(4), 408–417. https://doi.org/10.1016/j.jbusres.2010.09.010.

Kaiser, T. (2002). The customer shall lead: E-business solutions for the new insurance industry. *Geneva Papers on Risk and Insurance: Issues and Practice*, 27(1), 134–145. https://doi.org/10.1111/1468-0440.00160.

Khan, C. B. A. (2018). Estimating diffusion of technology using user perceptual values: A conceptual model. In *2018 5th International Conference on Industrial Engineering and Applications, ICIEA 2018* (pp. 401–405). https://doi.org/10.1109/IEA.2018.8387133.

Kogo, P. K. & Kimencu, L. (2018). Organizational capabilities and performance of insurance companies in Nairobi city county, Kenya. *International Academic Journal of Human Resource and Business Administration*, 3(1), 126–149.

KPMG. (2019). InsurTech: Infrastructure for New Insurance. KPMG International Cooperative.

Lado, N. & Maydeu-Olivares, A. (2001). Exploring the link between market orientation and innovation in the European and US insurance markets. *International Marketing Review*, 18(2), 130–144. https://doi.org/10.1108/02651330110389972.

Länsiluoto, A., Joensuu-Salo, S., Varamäki, E., Viljamaa, A., & Sorama, K. (2018). Market orientation and performance measurement system adoption impact on performance in SMEs. *Journal of Small Business Management*. https://doi.org/10.1111/jsbm.12393.

Lee, H. & Kelley, D. (2008). Building dynamic capabilities for innovation: An exploratory study of key management practices. *R & D Management*, 38(2), 155–168. https://doi.org/10.1111/j.1467-9310.2008.00506.x.

Legner, C., Eymann, T., Hess, T., Matt, C., Böhmann, T., Drews, P., Mädche, A., Urbach, N., & Ahlemann, F. (2017). Digitalization: Opportunity and challenge for the business and information systems engineering community. *Business and Information Systems Engineering*, 59(4), 301–308. https://doi.org/10.1007/s12599-017-0484-2.

Lewis, P. B. (2021). 1990 Annual Report Letter to Shareholders. https://www.progressive.com/about/history/.

Li, H., Song, Q., & Su, J. (2021). Robust estimates of insurance misrepresentation through kernel quantile regression mixtures. *Journal of Risk and Insurance*, 88(3), 625–663. https://doi.org/10.1111/jori.12358.

Maire, J. L., Bronet, V., & Pillet, M. (2005). A typology of "best practices" for a benchmarking process. *Benchmarking*, 12(1), 45–60. https://doi.org/10.1108/14635770510582907.

Matt, C., Hess, T., & Benlian, A. (2015). Digital transformation strategies. *Business and Information Systems Engineering*, 57(5), 339–343. https://doi.org/10.1007/s12599-015-0401-5.

Mazzucato, M. (2013). Financing innovation: Creative destruction vs. destructive creation. *Industrial and Corporate Change*, 22(4), 851–867. https://doi.org/10.1093/icc/dtt025.

McAfee, A. & Brynjolfsson, E. (2012). Big data: The management revolution. *Harvard Business Review*, 90(10), 4.

McCrea, M. & Farrell, M. (2018). A conceptual model for pricing health and life insurance using wearable technology. *Risk Management and Insurance Review*, 21(3), 389–411. https://doi.org/10.1111/rmir.12112.

Mckinsey. (2018). Digital Insurance in 2018: December (72 p.).

McWaters, R. J. (2015). The future of financial services. World Economic Forum (Issue June). https://doi.org/10.1002/9781119218906.ch59.

Mertens, P. & Wiener, M. (2018). Riding the digitalization wave: Toward a sustainable nomenclature in wirtschaftsinformatik: A comment on Riedl *et al.* (2017). *Business and Information Systems Engineering*, 60(4), 367–372. https://doi.org/10.1007/s12599-018-0545-1.

Mina, A., Lahr, H., & Hughesy, A. (2013). The demand and supply of external finance for innovative firms. *Industrial and Corporate Change*, 22(4), 869–901. https://doi.org/10.1093/icc/dtt020.

Moodley, A. (2019). Digital transformation in South Africa's short-term insurance sector: Traditional insurers' responses to the internet of things (IoT) and Insurtech. *The African Journal of Information and Communication*. https://doi.org/10.23962/10539/28657.

Moore, G. C. & Benbasat, I. (1991). Development of an instrument to measure the perceptions of adopting an information technology innovation. *Information Systems Research*, 2(3), 192–222. https://doi.org/10.1287/isre.2.3.192.

Morgan, S. & Hegarty, W. H. (1998). Product differentiation core manufacturing product differentiation. *International Journal of Operations & Production Management*, 18(4), 374–396.

Mustafina, A. A., Kaigorodova, G. N., Alyakina, P. D., Velichko, N. Y., & Zainullina, M. R. (2020). Digital technology in insurance. *Advances in Intelligent Systems and Computing*, 908, 678–685.https://doi.org/10.1007/978-3-030-11367-4_65.

Naylor, M. (2017). *Insurance Transformed: Technological Distruption*. Palgrave Studies in Financial Service Technology. London, UK: Palgrave Macmillan. https://doi.org/10.1007/978-3-319-63835-5.

Nicoletti, B. (2016). *Digital Insurance Business Innovation in the Post-crisis Era*. London, UK: Palgrave Macmillan. https://doi.org/10.1057/9781137553270.

Nicoletti, B. & Nicoletti, B. (2017). A business model for Insurtech initiatives. In Nicoletti, B. (Ed.), *The Future of FinTech* (pp. 211–249). London, UK: Palgrave Macmillian. https://doi.org/10.1007/978-3-319-51415-4_8.

O'Dair, M. & Beaven, Z. (2017). The networked record industry: How blockchain technology could transform the record industry. *Strategic Change*, 26(5), 471–480. https://doi.org/10.1002/jsc.2147.

OECD. (2017). Technology and innovation in the insurance sector.

Pearson, R. (1997). Towards an historical model of services innovation: The case of the insurance industry, 1700-1914. *Economic History Review*, 50(2), 235–256. https://doi.org/10.1111/1468-0289.00053.

Peng, D. X., Schroeder, R. G., & Shah, R. (2008). Linking routines to operations capabilities: A new perspective. *Journal of Operations Management*, 26(6), 730–748. https://doi.org/10.1016/j.jom.2007.11.001.

Peterson, R. A., Rudeliust, W., & Wood, G. L. (1972). Spread of marketing innovations in a service industry. *The Journal of Business*, 45(4), 485–496.

Piening, E. P. & Salge, T. O. (2015). Understanding the antecedents, contingencies, and performance implications of process innovation: A dynamic capabilities perspective. *Journal of Product Innovation Management*, 32(1), 80–97. https://doi.org/10.1111/jpim.12225.

Presbyterian Ministers' Fund. (2008). The Historical Society of Pennsylvania.

Prieger, J. E. (2007). Regulatory delay and the timing of product innovation. *International Journal of Industrial Organization*, 25(2), 219–236. https://doi.org/10.1016/j.ijindorg.2006.05.001.

Protogerou, A., Caloghirou, Y., & Lioukas, S. (2012). Dynamic capabilities and their indirect impact on firm performance. *Industrial and Corporate Change*, 21(3), 615–647. https://doi.org/10.1093/icc/dtr049.

PwC. (2018). Driving innovation with InsurTech. PwC Global InsurTech Report.

PwC. (2019). Emerging technologies disrupting the financial sector. *Background Paper* (May).

Raynor, M. E. (2011). *The Innovator's Manifesto: Deliberate Disruption for Transformational Growth* (1st edn). New York: Crown Business.

Revathi, D. P. (2020). Technology and innovation in insurance – Present and future technology in indian insurance industry. *International Journal of Engineering and Management Research*, 10(01), 21–25. https://doi.org/10.31033/ijemr.10.1.4.

Ricciardi, V. (2018). InsurTech definition as its own manifesto (pp. 6–8). McKinsey & Company (June), 2017. https://doi.org/10.1002/9781119444565.ch1.

Riedl, R., Benlian, A., Hess, T., Stelzer, D., & Sikora, H. (2017). On the relationship between information management and digitalization. *Business and Information Systems Engineering*, 59(6), 475–482. https://doi.org/10.1007/s12599-017-0498-9.

Rogers, E. M. (1995). *Diffusion of Innovations* (4th edn.). New York: Free Press. http://www.cs.nyu.edu/courses/fall10/V22.0480-002/Rogers1985.pdf.

Rogers, E. M. (2003). *Diffusion of Innovations* (5th edn.). New York: Free Press. https://doi.org/10.1016/j.jmig.2007.05.018.

Rogers, E. M., Singhal, A., & Quinlan, M. M. (2003). Diffusion of innovations. In Stacks, D. W. & Salwen, M. B. (Eds.), *An Integrated Approach to Communication Theory and Research* (3rd edn., pp. 415–433). New York: Routledge. https://doi.org/10.4324/9780203710753-35.

Salman, S.A. (2014). Contemporary issues in takaful (Islamic insurance). *Asian Social Science*, 10(22), 210–2165. https://doi.org/10.5539/ass.vnn22p210.

Saunila, M. & Mäkimattila, M. (2018). A dynamic learning perspective on innovation control: Balancing freedom and constraint. Palgrave Studies (pp. 273–291). Cham, London, UK: Palgrave Macmillan. https://doi.org/10.1007/978-3-319-90945-5_14.

Saunila, M. & Ukko, J. (2014). Intangible aspects of innovation capability in SMEs: Impacts of size and industry. *Journal of Engineering and Technology Management - JET-M*, 33(October 2017), 32–46. https://doi.org/10.1016/j.jengtecman.2014.02.002.

Schena, C., Tanda, A., Arlotta, C., & Potenza, G. (2018). The development of FinTech: Opportunities and risks for the financial industry in the digital age. In *CONSOB Series* (Issue March).

Schmidt, C. (2018). Insurance in the Digital Age. The Geneva Association (Issue September). https://www.genevaassociation.org/research-topics/new-technologies-and-data/insurance-digital-age-research-report.

Schmidt, R., Möhring, M., Bär, F., & Zimmermann, A. (2017). The impact of digitization on information system design – An explorative case study of digitization in the insurance business. Lecture Notes in Business Information Processing (Vol. 303, pp. 137–149). https://doi.org/10.1007/978-3-319-69023-0_13.

Schueffel, P. (2018). Taming the beast: A scientific definition of Fintech. *SSRN Electronic Journal* (December 2016). https://doi.org/10.2139/ssrn.3097312.

Schulte-Noelle, H. (2001). Technological changes in IT and their influence on insurance: The change ahead (I). *Geneva Papers on Risk and Insurance: Issues and Practice*, 26(1), 83–88. https://doi.org/10.1111/1468-0440.00096.

Schumpeter, J. A. (1934). The theory of economic development – An inquiry into profits, capital, credit, interest, and the business cycle. Cambridge, MA: Havard University Press. https://doi.org/10.1080/00343404.2017.1278975.

Seog, S. H. (2009). Insurance markets with differential information. *The Journal of Risk and Insurance*, 76(2), 279–294.

Shamsuddin, J. N., Gan, C., & Anh, D. L. T. (2023). Bibliometric analysis of InsurTech. *Journal of Advanced Research in Applied Sciences and Engineering Technology*, 2(2), 103–132.

Sheth, A. & Subramanian, H. (2020). Blockchain and contract theory: Modeling smart contracts using insurance markets. *Managerial Finance*, 46(6), 803–814. https://doi.org/10.1108/MF-10-2018-0510.

Shih, T. Y. (2013). Determinates of consumer adoption attitudes: An empirical study of smart home services. *International Journal of E-Adoption*, 5(2), 40–56. https://doi.org/10.4018/jea.2013040104.

Slater, S. F. & Narver, J. C. (1998). Customer-led and market-oriented: Let's not confuse the two. *Strategic Management Journal*, 19(10), 1001–1006. https://doi.org/10.1002/(SICI)1097-0266(199810)19:10⟨1001::AID-SMJ996⟩3.0.CO;2-4.

Society of Actuaries. (2012). Report of the Society of Actuaries Predictive Modeling Survey Subcommittee.

Sood, A. & Tellis, G. J. (2005). Technological evolution and radical innovation. *Journal of Marketing*, 69(3), 152–168. https://doi.org/10.1509/jmkg.69.3.152.66361.

Steininger, K., Riedl, R., Roithmayr, F., & Mertens, P. (2009). Fads and trends in business and information systems engineering and information systems research – A comparative literature analysis. *Business & Information Systems Engineering*, 1(6), 411–428. https://doi.org/10.1007/s12599-009-0079-7.

Stoeckli, E., Dremel, C., & Uebernickel, F. (2018). Exploring characteristics and transformational capabilities of InsurTech innovations to understand insurance value creation in a digital world. *Electronic Markets*, 28(3), 287–305. https://doi.org/10.1007/s12525-018-0304-7.

Swiss Re. (2017). Technology and insurance: Themes and challenges. *Sigma Expertise* (June), 1–32. http://media.swissre.com/documents/expertise_publication_technology_and_insurance_themes_and_challenges.pdf.

Takahashi, A. R. W., Bulgacov, S., & Giacomini, M. M. (2017). Capacidades dinâmicas, capacidades operacionais (Educacional-marketing) e desempenho. *Revista Brasileira de Gestao de Negocios*, 19(65), 375–393. https://doi.org/10.7819/rbgn.v0i0.2831.

Taylor, M. (2001). Technological changes in IT and their influence on insurance: The change ahead (II). *Geneva Papers on Risk and Insurance: Issues and Practice*, 26(1), 89–104. https://doi.org/10.1111/1468-0440.00096.

Teece, D. J., Pisano, G., & Shuen, A. (1997). Dynamic capabilities and strategic management. *Strategic Management Journal*, 18(7), 509–133. https://doi.org/10.1176/appi.psychotherapy.2009.63.1.13.

Tu, Q., Vonderembse, M. A., Ragu-Nathan, T. S., & Sharkey, T. W. (2006). Absorptive capacity: Enhancing the assimilation of time-based manufacturing practices. *Journal of Operations Management*, 24(5), 692–710. https://doi.org/10.1016/j.jom.2005.05.004.

Tushman, M. & O'Reilly, C. (2007). Research and relevance: Implications of Pasteur's quadrant for doctoral programs and faculty development. *Academy of Management Journal*, 50(4), 769–774. https://doi.org/10.5465/AMJ.2007.26279169.

Ulusoy, G. & İkiz, İ. (2001). Benchmarking best manufacturing practices. *International Journal of Operations & Production Management*, 21(7), 1020–1043. https://doi.org/10.1108/01443570110393478.

Utterback, J. M. & Acee, H. J. (2005). Disruptive technologies: An expanded view. *International Journal of Innovation Management*, 09(01), 1–17. https://doi.org/10.1142/s1363919605001162.

Van Offenbeek, M., Boonstra, A., & Seo, D. B. (2013). Towards integrating acceptance and resistance research: Evidence from a Telecare case study. *European Journal of Information Systems*, 22(4), 434–454. https://doi.org/10.1057/ejis.2012.29.

Venkatraman, V. (2017). *New Rules for Business Transformation through Technology*. Vancouver, BC: LifeTree Media Book. https://doi.org/10.52292/j.eca.2017.631.

Werth, O., Schwarzbach, C., Rodríguez Cardona, D., Breitner, M. H., & Graf von der Schulenburg, J. M. (2020). Influencing factors for the digital transformation in the financial services sector. *ZVerWiss*, 109, 155–179. https://doi.org/10.1007/s12297-020-00486-6.

Westerman, G., Bonnet, D., & McAfee, A. (2014). *Leading Digital: Turning Technology into Business Transformation*. Boston, MA: Harvard Business Press. https://doi.org/10.5860/choice.188022.

Willis Towers Watson. (2020). Quarterly InsurTech Briefing Q4 2020. *CB Insights* (October), 61.

Wright, P. M., Dunford, B. B., & Snell, S. A. (2001). Human resources and the resource based view of the firm. *Journal of Management*, 27(6), 701–721. https://doi.org/10.1177/014920630102700607.

Wu, S. J., Melnyk, S. A., & Flynn, B. B. (2010). Operational capabilities: The secret ingredient. *Decision Sciences Journal*, 41(4), 721–754.

Xu, X. & Zweifel, P. (2020). A framework for the evaluation of InsurTech. *Risk Management and Insurance Review*, 23(4), 305–329. https://doi.org/10.1111/rmir.12161.

Yan, T. C., Schulte, P., & Lee Kuo Chuen, D. (2018). InsurTech and FinTech: Banking and insurance enablement. In Chuen, D. L. K. and Deng, R. (Eds.), *Handbook of Blockchain, Digital Finance, and Inclusion* (Vol. 1). Cambirdge, MA: Elsevier Inc. https://doi.org/10.1016/B978-0-12-810441-5.00011-7.

https://doi.org/10.1142/9781800616257_0008

Chapter 8

Big Data Applications in Banks: Systematic Review and Future Research Agenda

Vikesh Kumar[*,||], **Gul Afshan**[†,**], **Adnan Manzoor**[‡,††], **Mansoor Ahmed Khuhro**[§,‡‡], and **Muhammad Hussain**[¶,§§]

[*]*Texas Tech University, Lubbock, USA*
[†]*Sukkur IBA University, Sukkur, Pakistan*
[‡]*IBA Karachi, Karachi, Pakistan*
[§]*Shaheed Benazir Bhutto University, Sanghar Campus, Sanghar, Pakistan*
[¶]*University of Wollongong, Wollongong, Australia*
[||]*vikeshkumar@iba-suk.edu.pk*
[**]*gul.afshan@iba-suk.edu.pk*
[††]*adnan-manzoor@outlook.com*
[‡‡]*mehran.mann@gmail.com*
[§§]*mh634@uowmail.edu.au*

Abstract

In this chapter, we explain the application of big data in banks through a systematic review, which is done by using the PRISMA method to research articles from the big data literature with the help of a theoretical framework on big data. A few parameters have been set for inclusion, such as selecting papers published from 2010 to the present. Several themes are generated from the findings of the reviewed studies. A Google Scholar search was conducted using the keywords "big data in business" to find articles for this review. The Google Scholar search covered the years 2010–2020. We quickly captured Google Scholar results using Zotero software. The review highlighted three main trends in banks regarding big data applications. First, fraud risk analysis can help banks detect fraud in financial transactions and safeguard them to survive in a competitive environment. Second, we discovered customer analysis using big data analytics. Banks have understood the value of utilizing digital technologies for client acquisition, retention and satisfaction. Finally, there are several facets of operational analysis, such as developing new business models, offering new products and services, increasing efficiency, and reducing costs in the banking sector. To enhance big data research in the banking sector, this study also has implications for researchers and future research agendas.

Keywords: Big data, digital banking, digital finance, fraud and risk analysis, customer analysis.

8.1. Introduction

Academics highlight that the study of big data is fundamentally an empirical question. Big data provides a competitive advantage for banks and creates a winning edge for them in the digital economy (Berman *et al.*, 2018). In today's competitive digitalized world, advanced information technology has aided organizations in extracting various types of data. Particularly, banking and financial markets have advanced their activities with the help of technology in recent years. For instance, the online lending, business management operations, management of finances and assets and many more processes of banks have become easy and quick through big data technology. Organizations retrieve useful information through unstructured, semi-structured and structured big data to enhance daily operations and improve organizational performance and profitability.

The big data revolution started in the 21st century, gaining momentum in the banking industry when it began using big data for its banking operations. Customers' data were useful for banks, and big data enabled banks to utilize the data more efficiently. Big data has benefited banks and customers in many ways, such as credit risk management and knowing your customer (KYC). Big data has allowed the banking sector to make better decisions about their strategic management decisions, marketing management and customer analysis (Hassani *et al.*, 2018). With the assistance of internal and external partners, the bank of the future will be more data-driven and will safeguard consumer data in real time. Future banks based on data-driven mechanisms will fulfill consumer demands by offering required products and services and expanding the life cycle of utility delivery (Ohene-Afoakwa & Nyanhongo, 2017). The application of big data can help commercial banks improve their ability to understand customer demands and create modern information technology-based banking. Through the mining and processing of vast amounts of data and the research and analysis of target customers, commercial banks can predict customer behaviors and improve their products, services and marketing efforts (Berman *et al.*, 2018).

Bank customers, employees, CEOs and experience are the four important pillars of the future bank (Sparks, 2018). From the client's perspective, their banking experience will go beyond branch services. Instead, if the customer's experience with the banking services is not up to their expectations, they will suffer from anxiety and emotional breakdowns (Sparks, 2018). Branches with a low walk-in rate will be available as troubleshooting and solution centers. Branches will include appointment scheduling through a variety of channels. Some job titles might become obsolete, but new roles influenced by digital technology will increase the number of employees (Sparks, 2018).

Big data is more complex and challenging than it sounds. The complex data sets within big data have gained wide recognition due to their wide applications. Managers in financial institutions use big data to make decisions and design policies, which help them realize fruitful results and achieve long-term goals. Thousands of data points have been generated through different banking operations by using the big data. However, more research needs to be carried out to comprehensively present the findings of various recent studies in order to understand big data and its applications in the banking industry. This book chapter aims to thoroughly review what has been studied on big data in the banking sector, its role and applications, how it has facilitated banking operations and how these findings have implications for the banking industry. This review addresses the following research questions: What does big data mean in banking? What are the different applications of big data in banking? What are the implications of the findings of big data studies in banking? We contribute to the literature by examining big data applications in the banking sector and how they help banks contribute at the macroeconomic level. We have applied the PRISMA model to study the available literature. The following sections explain our theoretical framework, data, methodology, the trends in big data in banks, their implications, our conclusion and future research agendas.

8.2. Literature Review

Big data significantly impacts the business, politics, culture and daily lives of individuals. In finance, enormous amounts of economic and financial data can be continuously gathered and generated. The height, width, depth and precision of omnidirectional data boost banking business capacity; this is one of the most important exploratory paths in financial big data research. It allows banks to use and exchange existing financial data fully and to get support and services. FinTech, or bank financial platforms, is experiencing a data service revolution due to the quick development of big financial data. This revolution includes personalized services, big data credit investigations, intelligent investment, risk pricing, quantitative investment, tax and financial behavior profiling and more.

8.2.1. *Big data and its characteristics*

"Big data" refers to extensive, intricate data sets that are challenging to manage with conventional database management systems. As defined by Kusnetzky (2010), big data is the terminology for the tools and techniques that allow an organization to generate, utilize and store vast amounts of data. Moreover, computerized systems, including social networking sites, produce considerable amounts of data. They are transmitted through digital systems, sensor devices, cameras, handheld devices, cell phones and their applications. Big data is generated at a never-before-seen rate and originates from various sources. We need high computational power, analytical skill and expertise to extract significant value from this enormous amount of data. People are being pushed to see everything through the prism of big data by the current data eruption.

Lately, there has been rapid development in applications involving sensor, web-based, transactional and electronic medical data (Lee, 2017). Machine-generated data, demographic data, transactional data, web-based data and sensor-based data are categories into which these data can be divided. Social networking sites such as Facebook, Twitter and blogs are web-based data sources. Sensor-based gadgets and other devices are used to extract machine-generated data. Biometrics, vital signs, radiography and other medical imaging systems are sources of transactional data. Emails, prescription drugs and digitalized copies of medical reports are examples of human-generated data.

The term "big data" refers to this new idea, which has emerged due to notable advancements in data expansion. Big data refers to any complicated data set that substantially impacts the performance, analysis, storage and upkeep of typical data warehouses (Tiwari *et al.*, 2018). Big data is also explicitly defined by De Mauro *et al.* (2016): Big data is abundant information that needs technology and analytical techniques to be transformed into value. It is characterized by a large quantity, high velocity and extraordinary variety. Stated differently, the McKinsey Global Institute defines big data as sets of information bigger than those that can be gathered, stored, managed and analyzed by conventional database systems (Analytics, 2016). Information compiled from multiple sources, such as corporate databases, constitutes big data (Silahtaroğlu & Yılmaztürk, 2021).

In the following, we present some examples of common aspects of big data. Measured in terabytes, petabytes, zettabytes, etc., volume denotes the size of the data. Big data now finds various applications; therefore, many scientists and researchers have added new features in addition to the qualities mentioned above. According to Zhong *et al.* (2016), the definition of big data is one example of something that is constantly changing due to technology improvements, data transfer and storage rates and other system capabilities. More specifically, these dimensions are growing over time as big data continues to evolve.

8.2.2. *Customer relationship management*

According to Anshari *et al.* (2019), there is evidence in the literature that how customers use smart mobile devices and engage in online activities impacts the banking sector. Customer relationship management has evolved beyond the traditional organization-to-customer, or single-channel, relationship. The emergence of information and communication technology, particularly in smart mobile devices, has given rise to multi-channel relationships (customer–machine–organization). Srivastava & Gopalkrishnan (2015) also found that big data can help find patterns such as customer spending patterns in the segmentation of consumers to capture the market more efficiently, as well as in fraud detection. Big data may support data governance, data literacy and the development of a data-driven culture (Maja *et al.*, 2022). Biases in data-driven industries like banking can be reduced in this way. Delgosha *et al.* (2020) found that credit risk analysis and fraud detection through the Delphi technique are the two main uses of big data in banks. These results advance our knowledge of the main challenges presented by big data in a dynamic business environment by providing more useful suggestions for scholars and decision-makers.

The entire world is reliant on the banking system. Banks possess enormous amounts of client information, acquired through points of sale, ATMs, know-your-customer (KYC) processes and compliance checks. Banks invest in big data to swiftly process and interpret the data and enhance internal processes, including operations and compliance, and augment scalability, where data and data analytics are being employed increasingly. They are also being used to understand more about customers. Because big data analytics (BDA) can track customer transactions, it offers useful insights into customer behavior. Big data is needed to integrate a bank's operations into a centralized, practical platform. Corporate banking institutions can use big data technologies to assess staff performance measures and distribute them in real time across branches. The banking industry will better understand customer wants and provide these services when needed if it keeps up with big data and other current global trends.

8.2.3. *Market data analytics*

Marketing is an impactful factor that enhances the visibility and credibility of big data. With market data analytics, banks can easily understand consumer transaction trends. Banks can even track consumer behavior in real time using customer data. Big data can also help marketing managers forecast customer demand more accurately and help decision-makers make decisions more strategically based on the available information (Jeble *et al.*, 2018). Big data can also help the Securities Exchange Commission (SEC) track illegal buying and selling transactions (Goyal *et al.*, 2017). It can also be helpful in online marketing, such as on digital platforms, on banks' websites and through email. Competition is intensifying in the banking industry, with customers increasingly using online tools; that's why, nowadays, banks offer their products online through mobile banking and ATMs. Big data can be crucial in connecting with that client base (Zhong *et al.*, 2016; Breed & Verster, 2019; Rana, 2019). Wamba *et al.* (2017) discovered that big data is beneficial for risk management, fraud detection and marketing analytics.

It is also observed from the literature that many studies have identified different aspects in the relationship between big data and banks. It is important to understand the specific trends of big data in banks that are critical for banks to function better in a competitive environment. In the following section, we explain the methodology through which we identified more relevant articles.

8.2.4. *Theoretical considerations*

The association between financial development and economic growth is well established in the theoretical and empirical literature (Bagehot, 1873). A few decades ago, after an extended break, the topic regained interest when Gurley & Shaw (1955) and Goldsmith (1969) re-examined the connection. In modern economics literature, it has become commonplace to state that a healthy financial system mobilizes and distributes funds to the most efficient user (McKinnon, 2010; Shaw, 1973). Levine (2005) discusses the positive correlation between financial market expansion and economic growth, highlighting that the interaction between savers and investors is the fundamental basis for economic growth in a free market (Kim *et al.*, 2018).

Stable financial intermediaries are also necessary for a developed financial system to promote growth, draw in foreign direct investment and support domestic investment (Haini, 2020; Kim *et al.*, 2018). In addition to maintaining competitiveness, foreign direct investment crosses national borders and transmits advanced technology and managerial skills (Sultana & Turkina, 2020). According to Aghion *et al.* (2018), financial development promotes economic activity, lowers borrowing rates, makes it easier to obtain funding, creates new job opportunities, enhances labor participation and opens new markets. It also drives demand for new infrastructure. Asteriou & Spanos (2019) point out that a robust financial sector promotes macroeconomic efficiency by shielding an economy from shocks coming from both the inside and the outside (Prochniak & Wasiak, 2017). The above mechanism has two distinct ways in which it functions. First, reduced loan costs encourage entrepreneurship, advance industrial expansion and improve well-being in general (Dutta & Meierrieks, 2021). Credit availability promotes human capital development, which is necessary for economic growth, innovation and technological improvement (Qamruzzaman *et al.*, 2021). Levine (2005) notes that the availability of information reduces transaction costs, facilitates decision-making and ultimately promotes growth, all of which are benefits of financial development.

Big data has been used at different levels in banking sectors, such as retail, commercial and capital markets as well as asset management (Mohanty *et al.*, 2015). Also, big data can play an important role in handling banking risk. Cerchiello & Giudici (2016) developed a Bayesian framework to explain financial institutions' interrelationships. A few studies have also demonstrated that big data helps in detecting fraud in financial institutions (Ngai *et al.*, 2017; Ravishankar & Clarke, 2018; Hu *et al.*, 2014). To further understand the trends in big data for banks, we delve into the literature and elaborate on a few trends in the following sections, beginning with the data and methodology used.

8.3. Data and Methodology

Although systematic reviews originated in the health sciences, they have gained popularity recently in the social sciences as a tool for examining specific topics and publications. Systematic reviews reduce biases by identifying relevant articles (Uman, 2011). It is important to do a meta-analysis first before doing reviews. A meta-analysis helps one collect data from different articles and then analyze them using quantitative techniques. Systematic reviews provide a more efficient summary of the available research on a given subject (Chang *et al.*, 2020; Li *et al.*, 2018). Numerous studies have conducted big data reviews to comprehend the applications of big data, including BDA (Elgendy & Elragal, 2014; Frizzo-Barker *et al.*, 2016; Ghasemaghaei, 2020; Gillespie, 2020; Torabi Asr & Taboada, 2019), e-commerce (Dekimpe, 2020; Felt, 2016), healthcare (Chen *et al.*, 2020; Mehta & Pandit, 2018), supply chain management (He *et al.*, 2020; Wang *et al.*, 2016) and organizational performance (Upadhyay & Kumar, 2020; Wamba *et al.*, 2015). Particularly in scientific and medical domains, where practitioners cannot always stay up to date with the latest advancements reported in the literature, systematic reviews help save time (Milan, 2020; Uman, 2011; Zhou *et al.*, 2020). Bhasker *et al.* (2022) likewise employed a content and bibliographic analysis of 174 papers that were obtained from Scopus in order to determine the trends in digital currency use by central banks. We have utilized their methods to improve our own analysis.

In this study, a systematic review has been done by using the PRISMA method to review articles from the big data literature. A few parameters have been set for inclusion, such as selecting papers published from 2010 to 2020. Several themes are generated from the findings of the reviewed studies. A Google Scholar search was performed using the keywords "big data in business" to locate the articles used for this review. The Google Scholar search covered the years 2010–2020. Using the Zotero program, we were able to capture results from Google Scholar swiftly. We used Google Scholar because it can access both the Web of Science and Scopus databases. Martín-Martín *et al.* (2019) reported that the search engine located 89% of the citations in Scopus and 93% on Web of Science. Google Scholar was the sole source that contributed more than half of the citations to social science papers. One of the reasons for selecting this particular time frame was because 2010 was a year of advances in big data tools. Moreover, relatively few studies discussing commercial applications in the big data literature were published before 2010, with the majority appearing after that year.

After eliminating duplicate records, book chapters, book reviews and citations, 60 articles were gathered by the search. Twenty articles were eliminated because they contained drafts, opinions, Microsoft Word documents, PowerPoint presentations, editorials, lecture notes and viewpoints. After all of this, 40 articles were manually reviewed to ensure that their primary focus was on banks' use of big data. Consequently, 20 articles out of 40 were discarded because they

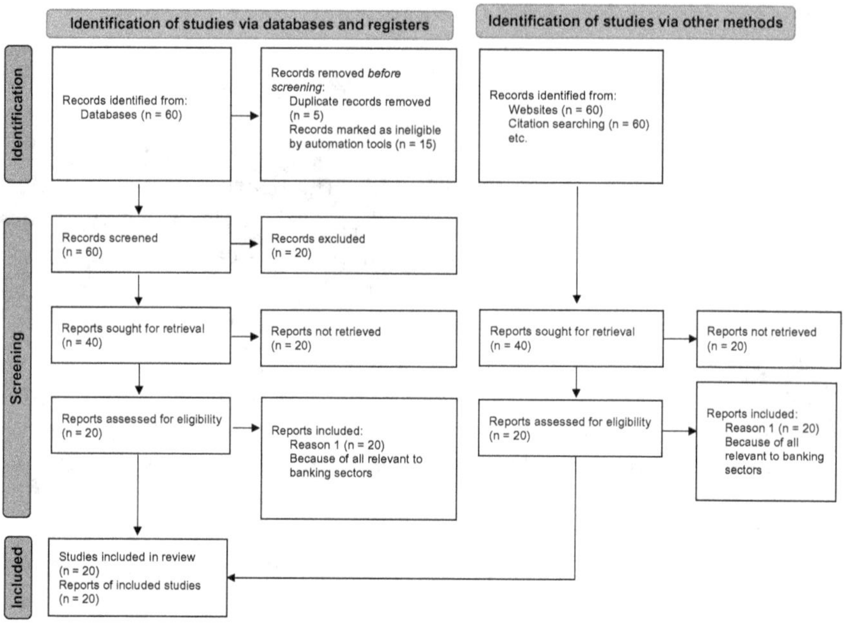

Figure 8.1. PRISMA 2020 flow diagram for new systematic reviews.

veered too far from the business angle we sought and dealt with subjects such as science, education, politics or data. They were also too deeply entrenched in the scientific nature of big data, including algorithms and clouds. In the end, 20 publications were retained for the PRISMA[1] meta-analysis. Figure 8.1 shows the PRISMA 2020 flow diagram for new systematic reviews, which included searches of databases, registers and other sources.

8.3.1. *Trends in banks for big data*

Three primary big data applications are highlighted in the literature: fraud and risk analysis, customer analysis and operation analysis. Also, it has applications in retail, commerce, capital markets and asset management for banks.

---

[1]Page *et al.* (2021). For more information, visit: http://www.prisma-statement.org/.

8.3.2. *Fraud and risk analysis*

Fraud and risk analysis are important to banks. Detecting fraud is critical to the survival of banks in a competitive environment, enabling them to sustain themselves in the financial markets. Otherwise, they risk being penalized by the SEC (Cordella *et al.*, 2018). Due to the potential loss of billions of dollars in yearly bank revenue, fraud and risk analysis are vital for banks (Bhattacharyya *et al.*, 2011). Banks are also bound by the Basel III requirements to use advanced frameworks such as BDA to manage credit, the market and operational risk (Baesens *et al.*, 2016). BDA has enabled banks to analyze large amounts of data to minimize operational risk. Earlier, banks were only evaluating one part of the transaction for fraud detection, and chances were high of not detecting suspicious transactions. However, with the help of BDA, it is possible to track all unusual transactions (West & Bhattacharya, 2016).

8.3.3. *Customer analysis*

The second trend we found is customer analysis or segmentation of customers through BDA. Banks have realized the use of digital technologies to acquire customers as well as for their retention and satisfaction. Although structured data are primarily used by banks, unstructured data can also be a good source of information that is useful for understanding customer behaviors. Customer segmentation, customer 360, customer recommender systems, customer sentiment analysis and methods for increasing or decreasing customer attrition are just a few techniques used in customer analysis (Sun *et al.*, 2014). Additionally, banks generate information and insights to enhance the customer experience through internal and unstructured data (Vieira & Sehgal, 2018). A few studies have found that 50% of banks required unstructured external data of customers to understand their behaviors. Such unstructured external data include social media activities and online buying behaviors (Coumaros *et al.*, 2014). With intense competition in the banking industry, banks have begun to realize that the point of their operations should be the customers, and banks should be more customer-centric than product-oriented (Michael *et al.*, 2017).

The literature clarifies that big data has brought new ideas to marketing analytics to give marketers a stronger competitive edge. It has made service invitations possible in the banking sector, giving banks a strategic advantage (Abbasi *et al.*, 2016; Watson, 2019; Wedel & Kannan, 2016). Big data provides benefits to both banks and customers. Leveraging business intelligence while simultaneously protecting customer privacy helps banks build relationships through marketing. Bank managers can use data from websites and online banking platforms to help customers find the best available products. They can compare these products for customers when they search for suitable options on the bank's website (Palmatier & Martin, 2019).

Studies show why banks are constantly vulnerable to losing client information. Banks have developed customer analytics through which they can segment their customers effectively so that they will not lose the data. As a result, banks will be better able to determine the ideal marketing mix, customer approach and marketing strategy (Pramanick, 2013). Morabito (2015), in support of this, added that marketing automation would help increase a bank's return on investment (ROI) because automation will reduce the bank's overall cost and enhance the customer experience, which will impact the ROI positively. Jarvinen & Karjaluoto (2015) also found that marketing analytics would increase the bank's profitability and lead to higher ROIs. A few studies have also explained the creditworthiness of clients in line with the ROI. Pérez-Martín *et al.* (2018) explained that big data technologies can help identify which customers can make their payments on time; this will improve the predictability of banks. Moreover, banks' default rates on loans will be lower, and their ROIs will be higher.

8.3.4. *Operational analysis*

Creating new business models, providing new products and services, boosting productivity and cutting expenses are all considered aspects of operational analysis in the banking industry. Banks can enhance their operations with BDA in two ways. First, implementing new technologies to swiftly evaluate large amounts of data can improve the effectiveness of current procedures (Ghoshal *et al.*, 2014). Another way banks can improve their business models with the help of BDA is by acquiring new segments and entering new markets while improving the quality of their products and services (Woerner & Wixom, 2015). It is also evident from the literature that, although banks use BDA, they don't operate like big data firms. They only incorporate BDA for some parts of their business models, such as identifying the customer base, but not as a whole, to improve the banks' efficiency (Loebbecke & Picot, 2015). Banks can use BDA to operationalize their business models to interact with customers innovatively (Günther *et al.*, 2017).

Consequently, the banking industry can benefit from deploying BDA in several ways. The first benefit is that it can give banks the resources and methods to obtain data quickly and easily and conduct analyses. By enabling banks to create suitable strategies through BDA, their effectiveness can be improved (Manyika *et al.*, 2011). Second, using customer data in big data can improve forecasting accuracy for banks. Third, banks can comprehend consumer behavior and create appropriate products and services by using BDA (Manyika *et al.*, 2011). In addition, banks can also track customer transactions to reduce the risk of defaults on loans and detect any suspicious transactions (Fang & Zhang, 2016). Finally, BDA can enhance customer data security by eliminating the risk of theft losses and helping banks save a significant portion of the cost of monitoring customer information (Kshetri, 2016). However, along with these advantages, big data also gives rise to challenges, which are important to mention here. First, it is challenging to choose the correct data sources; second, storing large data is not easy, and more importantly, managing such extensive data requires specialized skills (Bagchi, 2014).

8.4. Implications

Previous research shows that companies use BDA from an IT perspective only. However, our examination has shown that BDA goes beyond the technical side. It improves how businesses make decisions. BDA can help banks make better business decisions and have a long-term effect on their sustainability, so banks should invest in it (Sharma *et al.*, 2014). Developing new products and services and establishing strong connections with consumers is a major benefit of BDA for banks (Fernandez *et al.*, 2018). Banks must align their business objectives with analytical priorities when making decisions. They should also use BDA to achieve their objectives, including fraud detection, risk management, designing new models and operational analytics. BDA can also help managers understand customer segmentation and sentiments to alter their products and services accordingly.

However, there are a few limitations as well. BDA in the banking sector needs more skilled experts – an obstacle to deploying it in banks. Furthermore, implementing data privacy and quality solutions in the banking sector can be costly. Additionally, the BDA journey should be initiated with top management's awareness, support and commitment.

8.5. Conclusion and Future Research Agenda

In this study, we used the PRISMA method to review articles from the big data literature, and papers were selected from 2010 to 2020. Several themes were generated from the findings of the reviewed studies. A Google Scholar search was conducted using the keywords "big data in business" to find the articles used for this review. We quickly captured Google Scholar results using Zotero software. An upward trend in research interest is evident from the increase in the number of publications since 2010. The research focuses mostly on big data applications, their significance and their systematic framework. We also performed thematic analysis and found the following three trends in the application of big data in banks: fraud and risk analysis, customer analysis and operational analysis. After this trend analysis, we found that big data previously revolved around healthcare and supply chain systems; however, later on, in 2010, it evolved around the financial industry, including banks, to secure customer data, avoid any theft losses and provide more financial security to the banks through their operations.

This study offers valuable insights for big data applications within banks. Big data has the potential to become the key determinant of bank performance. Banks should further intensify the utilization of big data by researching BDA and its applications. BDA helps banks deliver better services, as mentioned above. It is observed that banks, with the help of sentiment analysis, acquire data from social media and websites and use them for the customers' benefit, for example by offering them better products. It is also essential to implement a sophisticated system so that it can handle suspicious transactions with sentiment analysis. Putting a BDA system in place is imperative for the banking industry. Additionally covered in this work are the different data mining strategies banks can employ to raise the quality of their analyses. Further work is needed on theoretical development and methodological contributions concerning the use of big data in banks.

References

Abbasi, A., Sarker, S., & Chiang, R. H. (2016). Big data research in information systems: Toward an inclusive research agenda. *Journal of the Association for Information Systems*, 17(2), 3. DOI: 10.17705/1jais.00423.

Allen, F., Gu, X., & Kowalewski, O. (2018). Financial structure, economic growth and development. In Beck, T. & Levine, R. (Eds.), *Handbook of Finance and Development* (pp. 31–62). Northampton, MA: Edward Elgar Publishing.

Analytics, M. (2016). The age of analytics: competing in a data-driven world. McKinsey Global Institute Research. https://www.alvaroriascos.com/mineriadatos/The-age-of-analytics-Executive-summary.pdf.

Anshari, M., Almunawar, M. N., Lim, S. A., & Al-Mudimigh, A. (2019). Customer relationship management and big data enabled: Personalization & customization of services. *Applied Computing and Informatics*, 15(2), 94–101. https://doi.org/10.1016/j.aci.2018.05.004.

Asteriou, D. & Spanos, K. (2019). The relationship between financial development and economic growth during the recent crisis: Evidence from the EU. *Finance Research Letters*, 28, 238–245. https://doi.org/10.1016/j.frl.2018.05.011.

Baesens, B., Roesch, D., & Scheule, H. (2016). *Credit Risk Analytics: Measurement Techniques, Applications, and Examples in SAS.* John Wiley & Sons.

Bagchi, S. (2014). Data analytics play a key role in banks' growth. Springer International Publishing, 4(6), 361–390.

Bagehot, W. (1873). *Lombard Street: A Description of the Money Market Scribner*. New York: Armstong & Co.

Berman, E., Felter, J. H., & Shapiro, J. (2018). *Small Wars, Big Data: The Information Revolution in Modern Conflict.* Princeton University Press. https://doi.org/10.23943/9781400890118.

Bhattacharyya, S., Jha, S., Tharakunnel, K., & Westland, J. C. (2011). Data mining for credit card fraud: A comparative study. *Decision Support Systems*, 50(3), 602–613. https://doi.org/10.1016/j.dss.2010.08.008.

Breed, D. G. & Verster, T. (2019). An empirical investigation of alternative semi-supervised segmentation methodologies. *South African Journal of Science*, 115(3–4), 1–7. http://dx.doi.org/10.17159/sajs.2019/5359.

Cerchiello, P. & Giudici, P. (2016). Big data analysis for financial risk management. *Journal of Big Data*, 3(1), 1–12. https://doi.org/10.1186/s40537-016-0053-4.

Chang, Y. C., Ku, C. H., & Chen, C. H. (2020). Using deep learning and visual analytics to explore hotel reviews and responses. *Tourism Management*, 80, 104129. https://doi.org/10.1016/j.tourman.2020.104129.

Chen, P. T., Lin, C. L., & Wu, W. N. (2020). Big data management in healthcare: Adoption challenges and implications. *International Journal of Information Management*, 53, 102078. https://doi.org/10.1016/j.ijinfomgt.2020.102078.

Cordella, T., Dell'Ariccia, G., & Marquez, R. (2018). Government guarantees, transparency, and bank risk taking. *IMF Economic Review*, 66(1), 116–143. https://doi.org/10.1057/s41308-018-0049-5.

Coumaros, J., Roys, S. D., Chretien, L., Buvat, J., Kvj, S., Clerk, V., & Auliard, O. (2014). Big data alchemy: How can banks maximize the value of their customer data? *Capgemini Consulting*.

De Mauro, A., Greco, M., & Grimaldi, M. (2016). A formal definition of big data based on its essential features. *Library Review*, 65(3), 122–135. https://doi.org/10.1108/LR-06-2015-0061.

Dekimpe, M. G. (2020). Retailing and retailing research in the age of big data analytics. *International Journal of Research in Marketing*, 37(1), 3–14. https://doi.org/10.1016/j.ijresmar.2019.09.001.

Delgosha, M. S., Hajiheydari, N., & Fahimi, S. M. (2020). Elucidation of big data analytics in banking: A four-stage Delphi study. *Journal of Enterprise Information Management*, 34(6), 1577–1596. https://doi.org/10.1108/JEIM-03-2019-0097.

Dutta, N. & Meierrieks, D. (2021). Financial development and entrepreneurship. *International Review of Economics & Finance*, 73, 114–126. https://doi.org/10.1016/j.iref.2021.01.002.

Elgendy, N. & Elragal, A. (2014). Big data analytics: A literature review paper. In Perner, P. (Ed.), *Advances in Data Mining. Applications and Theoretical Aspects. ICDM 2014*. Lecture Notes in Computer Science (Vol. 8557, pp. 214–227). Cham, Germany: Springer. https://doi.org/10.1007/978-3-319-08976-8_16.

Fang, B. & Zhang, P. (2016). Big data in finance. In Yu, S. & Guo, S. (Eds.), *Big Data Concepts, Theories, and Applications* (pp. 391–412). Cham: Springer. https://doi.org/10.1007/978-3-319-27763-9_11.

Felt, M. (2016). Social media and the social sciences: How researchers employ big data analytics. *Big Data and Society*, 3(1). https://doi.org/10.1177/2053951716645828.

Fernandez Naveria, C., Jacob, I., Rifai, K., Simon, P., & Windhagen, E. (2018). Smarter analytics for banks. https://www.mckinsey.com/industries/financial-services/our-insights/smarter-analytics-for-banks (Accessed 30 October 2018).

Frizzo-Barker, J., Chow-White, P. A., Mozafari, M., & Ha, D. (2016). An empirical study of the rise of big data in business scholarship. *International Journal of Information Management*, 36(3), 403–413. https://doi.org/10.1016/j.ijinfomgt.2016.01.006.

Ghasemaghaei, M. (2020). The role of positive and negative valence factors on the impact of the bigness of data on big data analytics usage. *International Journal of Information Management*, 50, 395–404. https://doi.org/10.1016/j.ijinfomgt.2018.12.011.

Ghoshal, A., Larson, E., Subramanyam, R., & Shaw, M. (2014). The impact of business analytics strategy on social, mobile, and cloud computing adoption. https://doi.org/10.5465/ambpp.2015.17096abstract.

Gillespie, T. (2020). Content moderation, AI, and the question of scale. *Big Data and Society*. https://doi.org/10.1177/2053951720943234.

Goldsmith, R. W. (1969). Financial structure and growth.

Goyal, Y., Monga, Y., & Mittal, M. (2017). Study and analytical perspective on big data. *International Journal of Computational Systems Engineering*, 3(4), 193–202. https://doi.org/10.1504/IJCSYSE.2017.089190.

Günther, W. A., RezazadeMehrizi, M. H., Huysman, M., & Feldberg, F. (2017). Debating big data: A literature review on realizing value from big data. *The Journal of Strategic Information Systems*, 26, 191–209. https://doi.org/10.1016/j.jsis.2017.07.003.

Gurley, J. G. & Shaw, E. S. (1955). Financial aspects of economic development. *The American Economic Review*, 45(4), 515–538. https://www.jstor.org/stable/1811632.

Haini, H. (2020). Examining the relationship between finance, institutions and economic growth: Evidence from the ASEAN economies. *Economic Change and Restructuring*, 53, 519–542. https://doi.org/10.1007/s10644-019-09257-5.

Hassani, H., Huang, X., & Silva, E. (2018). Digitalization and big data mining in banking. *Big Data and Cognitive Computing*, 2(3), 18. https://doi.org/10.3390/bdcc2030018.

He, L., Xue, M., & Gu, B. (2020). Internet-of-things enabled supply chain planning and coordination with big data services: Certain theoretic implications. *Journal of Management Science and Engineering*, 5(1), 1–22. https://doi.org/10.1016/j.jmse.2020.03.002.

Hu, R., Dou, W., & Liu, J. (2014). ClubCF: A clustering-based collaborative filtering approach for big data application. *IEEE Transactions on Emerging Topics in Computing*, 2(3), 302–313. https://doi.org/10.1109/TETC.2014.2310485.

Jarvinen, J. & Karjaluoto, H. (2015). The use of web analytics for digital marketing performance measurement. *Industrial Marketing Management*, 50, 117–127. https://doi.org/10.1016/j.indmarman.2015.04.009.

Jeble, S., Dubey, R., Childe, S. J., Papadopoulos, T., Roubaud, D., & Prakash, A. (2018). Impact of big data and predictive analytics capability on supply chain sustainability. *The International Journal of Logistics Management*, 29(2), 513–538. https://doi.org/10.1108/IJLM-05-2017-0134.

Kim, D. W., Yu, J. S., & Hassan, M. K. (2018). Financial inclusion and economic growth in OIC countries. *Research in International Business and Finance*, 43, 1–14. https://doi.org/10.1016/j.ribaf.2017.07.178.

Kshetri, N. (2016). Big data's role in expanding access to financial services in China. *International Journal of Information Management*, 36(3), 297–308. https://doi.org/10.1016/j.ijinfomgt.2015.11.014.

Kusnetzky (2010), What is "big data?" Look out, big data is coming your way. https://www.zdnet.com/article/what-is-big-data/.

Lee, I. (2017). Big data: Dimensions, evolution, impacts, and challenges. *Business Horizons*, 60(3), 293–303. https://doi.org/10.1016/j.bushor.2017.01.004.

Levine, R. (2005). Finance and growth: Theory and evidence. *Handbook of Economic Growth*, 1, 865–934. https://doi.org/10.1016/S1574-0684(05)01012-9.

Levine, R., Loayza, N., & Beck, T. (2000). Financial intermediation and growth: Causality and causes. *Journal of Monetary Economics*, 46(1), 31–77. https://doi.org/10.1016/S0304-3932(00)00017-9.

Li, J., Xu, L., Tang, L., Wang, S., & Li, L. (2018). Big data in tourism research: A literature review. *Tourism Management*, 68, 301–323. https://doi.org/10.1016/j.tourman.2018.03.009.

Loebbecke, C. & Picot, A. (2015). Reflections on societal and business model transformation arising from digitization and big data analytics: A research agenda. *The Journal of Strategic Information Systems*, 24(3), 149–157. https://doi.org/10.1016/j.jsis.2015.08.002.

Maja, M. M. & Letaba, P. (2022). Towards a data-driven technology roadmap for the bank of the future: Exploring big data analytics to support technology roadmapping. *Social Sciences & Humanities Open*, 6(1), 100270. https://doi.org/10.1016/j.ssaho.2022.100270.

Manyika, J., Chiu, M., Brown, B., Bughin, J., Dobbs, R., & Roxburgh, C. (2011). *Big Data: The Next Frontier for Innovation, Competition, and Productivity*. New York: McKinsey Global Institute.

Martín-Martín, A., Orduna-Malea, E., Thelwall, M., & Delgado-López-Cózar, E. (2019). Google Scholar, Web of Science, and Scopus: Which is best for me? *Impact of Social Sciences Blog*. https://blogs.lse.ac.uk/impactofsocialsciences/.

McKinnon, R. I. (2010). *Money and Capital in Economic Development*. Washington, DC: Brookings Institution Press.

Mehta, N. & Pandit, A. (2018). Concurrence of big data analytics and healthcare: A systematic review. *International Journal of Medical Informatics*, 114, 57–65. https://doi.org/10.1016/j.ijmedinf.2018.03.013.

Michael, J., Maxwell, M., & Taraporevala, Z. (2017). A consumer-centric approach to retail banking sales. *Mckinsey & Company*.

Milan, S. (2020). Techno-solutionism and the standard human in the making of the COVID-19 pandemic. *Big Data and Society*, 7(2). https://doi.org/10.1177/2053951720966781.

Mohanty, H., Bhuyan, P., & Chenthati, D. (Eds.). (2015). *Big Data: A Primer* (Vol. 11, p. 183). Berlin: Springer.

Morabito, V. (2015). *Big Data and Analytics*. Heidelberg: Springer International Publishing.

Ngai, E. W., Gunasekaran, A., Wamba, S. F., Akter, S., & Dubey, R. (2017). Big data analytics in electronic markets. *Electronic Markets*, 27(3), 243–245. https://doi.org/10.1007/s12525-017-0261-6.

Ohene-Afoakwa, E. & Nyanhongo, S. (2017). Banking in Africa: Strategies and systems for the banking industry to win in the fourth industrial revolution. *Bank Seta: Africa Expansion Project 2017*.

Page, M. J., McKenzie, J. E., Bossuyt, P. M., Boutron, I., Hoffmann, T. C., Mulrow, C. D., *et al.* (2021). The PRISMA 2020 statement: An updated guideline for reporting systematic reviews. *BMJ*, 372(71). DOI: 10.1136/bmj.n71.

Pérez-Martín, A., Pérez-Torregrosa, A., & Vaca, M. (2018). Big data techniques to measure credit banking risk in home equity loans. *Journal of Business Research*, 89, 448–454. https://doi.org/10.1016/j.jbusres.2018.02.008.

Prochniak, M. & Wasiak, K. (2017). The impact of the financial system on economic growth in the context of the global crisis: Empirical evidence for the EU and OECD countries. *Empirica*, 44, 295. https://doi.org/10.1007/s10663-016-9323-9.

Qamruzzaman, M., Jianguo, W., Jahan, S., & Yingjun, Z. (2021). Financial innovation, human capital development, and economic growth of selected South Asian countries: An application of ARDL approach. *International Journal of Finance & Economics,* 26, 4032–4053. https://doi.org/10.1002/ijfe.2003.

Rana, S. (2019). Moving in the realm of big data: Using analytics in management research and practices. *FIIB Business Review*, 8(1), 7–8. https://doi.org/10.1177/2319714519839802.

Ravishankar Rao, A. & Clarke, D. (2018). Facilitating the exploration of open health-care data through BOAT: A big data open source analytics tool. In *Emerging Challenges in Business, Optimization, Technology, and Industry* (pp. 93–115). Cham: Springer. https://doi.org/10.1007/978-3-319-58589-5_7.

Sharma, R., Mithas, S., & Kankanhalli, A. (2014). Transforming decision-making processes: A research agenda for understanding the impact of business analytics on organisations. *European Journal of Information Systems*, 23, 433–441. https://doi.org/10.1057/ejis.2014.17.

Shaw, E. S. (1973). *Financial Deepening in Economic Development.* New York: Oxford University Press.

Silahtaroğlu, G. & Yılmaztürk, N. (2021). Data analysis in health and big data: A machine learning medical diagnosis model based on patients' complaints. *Communications in Statistics-Theory and Methods*, 50(7), 1547–1556. https://doi.org/10.1080/03610926.2019.1622728.

Sparks, E. (2018). The bank of the future. *ABA Banking Journal* (American Bankers Association), 110(3), 20–28.

Srivastava, U. & Gopalkrishnan, S. (2015). Impact of big data analytics on banking sector: Learning for Indian banks. *Procedia Computer Science*, 50, 643–652. https://doi.org/10.1016/j.procs.2015.04.098.

Sultana, N. & Turkina, E. (2020). Foreign direct investment, technological advancement, and absorptive capacity: A network analysis. *International Business Review*, 29, 101668. https://doi.org/10.1016/j.ibusrev.2020.101668.

Sun, N., Morris, J. G., Xu, J., Zhu, X., & Xie, M. (2014). iCARE: A framework for big data-based banking customer analytics. *IBM Journal of Research and Development*, 58(5/6), 4:1–4:9.

Tiwari, S., Wee, H. M., & Daryanto, Y. (2018). Big data analytics in supply chain management between 2010 and 2016: Insights to industries. *Computers & Industrial Engineering*, 115, 319–330. https://doi.org/10.1016/j.cie.2017.11.017.

Torabi Asr, F. & Taboada, M. (2019). Big Data and quality data for fake news and misinformation detection. *Big Data & Society*, 6(1), 2053951719843310. https://doi.org/10.1177/2053951719843310.

Uman, L. S. (2011). Systematic reviews and metaanalyses. *Journal of the Canadian Academy of Child and Adolescent Psychiatry*, 20(1), 57.

Upadhyay, P. & Kumar, A. (2020). The intermediating role of organizational culture and internal analytical knowledge between the capability of big data analytics and a firm's performance. *International Journal of Information Management*, 52, 102100. https://doi.org/10.1016/j.ijinfomgt.2020.102100.

Vieira, A. & Sehgal, A. (2018). How banks can better serve their customers through artificial techniques. In Linnhoff-Popien, C., Schneider, R., & Zaddach, M. (Eds.), *Digital Marketplaces Unleashed* (pp. 311–326). Berlin, Germany: Springer. https://doi.org/10.1007/978-3-662-49275-8_31.

Wamba, S. F., Akter, S., Edwards, A., Chopin, G., & Gnanzou, D. (2015). How 'big data' can make big impact: Findings from a systematic review and a longitudinal case study. *International Journal of Production Economics*, 165, 234–246. https://doi.org/10.1016/j.ijpe.2014.12.031.

Wamba, S. F., Gunasekaran, A., Akter, S., Ren, S. J. F., Dubey, R., & Childe, S. J. (2017). Big data analytics and firm performance: Effects of dynamic capabilities. *Journal of Business Research,* 70, 356–365. https://doi.org/10.1016/j.jbusres.2016.08.009.

Wang, G., Gunasekaran, A., Ngai, E. W. T., & Papadopoulos, T. (2016). Big data analytics in logistics and supply chain management: Certain investigations for research and applications. *International Journal of Production Economics*, 176, 98–110. https://doi.org/10.1016/j.ijpe.2016.03.014.

Watson, H. J. (2019). Update tutorial: Big data analytics: Concepts, technology and applications. *Communications of the Association for Information Systems*, 44(1), 364–379. https://doi.org/10.17705/1CAIS.04421.

Wedel, M. & Kannan, P.K. (2016). Marketing analytics for data-rich environments. *Journal of Marketing* (Forthcoming), 80(6). https://doi.org/10.1509/jm.15.0413.

West, J. & Bhattacharya, M. (2016). Intelligent financial fraud detection: A comprehensive review. *Computers and Security*, 57, 47–66. https://doi.org/10.1016/j.cose.2015.09.005.

Woerner, S. L. & Wixom, B. H. (2015). Big data: Extending the business strategy toolbox. *Journal of Information Technology*, 30(1), 60–62. https://doi.org/10.1057/jit.2014.31.

Zhong, R., Newman, S., Huang, G., & Lan, S. (2016). Big data for supply chain management in the service and manufacturing sectors: Challenges, opportunities and future perspectives. *Computers and Industrial Engineering*, 101. https://doi.org/10.1016/j.cie.2016.07.013.

Zhou, X., Liang, W., Wang, K. I., & Yang, L. T. (2020). Deep correlation mining based on hierarchical hybrid networks for heterogeneous big data recommendations. *IEEE Transactions on Computational Social Systems*, 8(1), 171–178. https://doi.org/10.1109/TCSS.2020.2987846.

https://doi.org/10.1142/9781800616257_0009

Chapter 9

Digital Assets in Disarray: Unraveling Herd Behavior Amid COVID-19 and the Russia–Ukraine War

Tanveer Bagh[*,†,§], **Mirza Muhammad Naseer**[‡,||], **and Kainat Iftikhar**[*,¶]

[*]*School of Finance, Central University of Finance and Economics, Beijing, China*

[†]*Business Administration Department, Faculty of Management Sciences, ILMA University, Karachi, Pakistan*

[‡]*International Business School, Teesside University, Middlesbrough, UK*

[§]*baghtanveer@gmail.com*

[||]*m.naseer@tees.ac.uk*

[¶]*kainatiftikhar0298@gmail.com*

Abstract

The cryptocurrency market has experienced remarkable growth since the global financial crisis, attracting widespread attention and concern due to its departure from traditional financial systems. The evolving dynamics of this market, influenced by factors such as a loss of confidence in conventional systems, underscore the need for a deeper understanding of herd behavior. Within the context of global crises, this exploration holds significance for gaining insights into investor behavior, risk management strategies and market efficiency. The study sets out to uncover patterns of herd behavior during distinct temporal segments, including the full sample, and during periods of geopolitical tension and global crises, namely the Russia–Ukraine War and the post-COVID-19 era, respectively. The dataset spans from 1 January 2018 to 31 July 2022, segmented into three periods. We employ the static method, Markov regime-switching and the GARCH method. Empirical findings indicate herd behavior in the selected cryptocurrency market considering the full sample during periods of geopolitical tension and global crises, including the Russia–Ukraine War and the COVID-19 pandemic. The chapter contributes to the literature by bringing fresh empirical perspectives into the dynamics of herd behavior during crises, emphasizing distinct patterns observed during geopolitical conflicts and global pandemics. These significant findings offer valuable insights for portfolio management, trading strategies and risk management. Understanding the determinants of herd behavior can assist investors in navigating and avoiding such patterns, particularly during crisis periods.

Keywords: Herd behavior, digital assets, cryptocurrency market, COVID-19, Russia–Ukraine conflict.

9.1. Introduction

The landscape of digital assets, particularly cryptocurrencies, has undergone tumultuous shifts, marked by unprecedented volatility and uncertainty against the backdrop of two major geopolitical events – the global COVID-19 pandemic and the ongoing Russia–Ukraine conflict. Within this context, the realm of digital assets finds itself in a state of disarray, presenting a unique and dynamic environment for exploration. The outbreak of the global COVID-19 pandemic has not only posed severe threats to global public health but also significantly impacted financial markets, triggering a cascade of economic repercussions. The cryptocurrency market, known for its inherent volatility, has become a focal point of attention during this period of heightened uncertainty. The rapid spread of COVID-19, coupled with the deluge of information and news flow, has given rise to potential herd behavior among investors in the digital asset space. As investors grapple with the multifaceted impacts of the pandemic, ranging from economic downturns to shifts in investor sentiment, understanding the dynamics of herding behavior becomes imperative.

Simultaneously, geopolitical tensions arising from the Russian invasion of Ukraine have added an additional layer of complexity to the digital asset landscape. The unique characteristics of cryptocurrencies, together with their decentralized nature and global accessibility, position them as intriguing instruments during periods of geopolitical disorder. The ongoing war between Russia and Ukraine, with its distinctive geopolitical dynamics, serves as a compelling backdrop for investigating how herd behavior manifests in the digital asset market during times of heightened global political unrest. The cryptocurrency market has witnessed unprecedented growth since the global financial crisis, drawing considerable attention and scrutiny due to its divergence from traditional financial systems (Ha *et al.*, 2021; Paule-Vianez *et al.*, 2020). Amid the evolving dynamics of this market, characterized by diminishing confidence in conventional financial systems, there is a pressing need for a comprehensive understanding of herd behavior (Urquhart & Zhang, 2019). This exploration gains added significance in the context of global crises, such as the COVID-19 pandemic and the ongoing war between Russia and Ukraine, offering valuable insights into investor behavior, risk management strategies and market efficiency.

Recent discourse has positioned cryptocurrencies as a distinctive financial instrument, captivating the interest of regulators, the public and investors due to their hedging opportunities and substantial investment potential (Mokni, 2021; Mokni *et al.*, 2020; Urquhart & Zhang, 2019). Discussions have primarily centered around significant price fluctuations in the cryptocurrency market, prompting questions about its fundamental value and regulatory concerns (Agosto *et al.*, 2022; Bhaskar *et al.*, 2022; Hunjra & Hanif, 2023; Mnif *et al.*, 2022). Notably, the global COVID-19 pandemic has brought the crypto markets under intense scrutiny, with researchers exploring their substantial impact on global financial markets (Haroon & Rizvi, 2020). Classical finance theory (CFT), rooted in the efficient market hypothesis (EMH), posits that behavioral factors do not influence asset prices, assuming that investors behave rationally (Fama, 1970). In contrast, behavioral finance theory challenges this notion, suggesting that contemporary behavioral factors play a crucial role in shaping asset prices (Aslam *et al.*, 2022; Kijkasiwat *et al.*, 2022). This theoretical dichotomy has given rise to studies that contradict EMH, revealing systematic deviations driven by behavioral biases, leading to market anomalies and fragility. The cryptocurrency market, with its unique characteristics, has garnered growing interest from serious investors, hinting at a potential trend toward increased efficiency (Fernandes *et al.*, 2022). Herd behavior, a phenomenon where investors deviate from individual rational assessments to exhibit irrational conduct (Christie & Huang, 1995), has been studied in crypto markets during both bullish and bearish periods (Ballis & Drakos, 2020; Vidal-Tomás *et al.*, 2019) and on days with varying trading volumes (Haryanto *et al.*, 2020). However, the backdrop of significant global events, including the Russia–Ukraine conflict and the COVID-19 pandemic, presents an exclusive prospect for exploration in the cryptocurrency market. There is a need for additional research into the Bitcoin market since herd behavior could potentially be influenced by increased uncertainty and the rapid influx of information in such situations.

Despite the surge in interest in cryptocurrencies, a research gap in understanding herd behavior in the crypto market remains, particularly during significant global events. This study aims to address this gap by focusing on the cryptocurrency market during the Russia–Ukraine conflict and the COVID-19 pandemic – periods marked by increased geopolitical tensions and global crises. By employing a dataset spanning from 1 January 2017 to 31 July 2022, segmented into three periods, and utilizing a temporal segmentation approach, the study features a greater temporal scope than prior research (Vidal-Tomás *et al.*, 2019; Zhang *et al.*, 2020).

Moreover, unlike many previous studies that predominantly focused on small samples, this study considers the top 30 cryptocurrencies, providing a more comprehensive view of market dynamics and uncovering potential variations in herd behavior across different digital assets (Bouri *et al.*, 2019). Methodologically, the study introduces a temporal segmentation analysis incorporating a static cross-sectional absolute deviation (CSAD) model as well as a generalized autoregressive conditional heteroskedasticity (GARCH) model, GARCH (1,1), offering a refined understanding of herd behavior dynamics (Katsiampa, 2017). By delving into the dynamics of herd behavior within this context, the study contributes novel insights into market anomalies, fragility and the behavioral patterns of participants during crises, enriching the landscape of behavioral finance.

The study sets out to uncover patterns of herd behavior during distinct temporal segments, including the full sample period and during periods of geopolitical tension and global crises, namely the

Russia–Ukraine War and post-COVID-19 periods. Understanding these processes is essential for grasping market stability, volatility and the actions of participants in times of crisis.

Next, we make use of the static approach, the Markov regime-switching method and the GARCH model. In addition to two crisis periods, the empirical data show that herd behavior occurs in the cryptocurrency market throughout the model period. The chapter contributes to the literature by adding fresh insights into the dynamics of herd behavior during crises, emphasizing distinct patterns observed during geopolitical conflicts and global pandemics.

The study's innovative approach, incorporating CSAD with the GARCH model, enhances granularity. Practical implications extend to portfolio management and risk mitigation, offering valuable guidance for investors and policymakers in navigating global crisis situations. In essence, this research enriches our understanding of cryptocurrency market dynamics amid unique challenges, contributing key insights in the field of behavioral finance.

The chapter unfolds through key sections: Introduction, Literature Review and Hypothesis Development (Section 9.2), Data and Methodology (Section 9.3), Results and Discussion (Section 9.4) and Conclusions and Implications (Section 9.5). This structure guides a comprehensive exploration of the research topic.

9.2. A Review of Key Literature

The exploration of herd behavior traces back to the roots of behavioral finance, challenging the assumptions of classical financial theories. Traditional finance, epitomized by the EMH, posits that market participants act rationally based on available information. However, pioneers in behavioral finance, such as Daniel Kahneman and Amos Tversky in the late 20th century, began unraveling the role of psychological biases in decision-making, laying the groundwork for the study of herd behavior. This concept gained prominence in the 1990s as researchers sought to explain the observed phenomenon of investors following the crowd rather than making independent decisions. Notable works by scholars such as Terrance Odean and Brad Barber have explored this phenomenon in the context of stock markets, revealing how individuals tend to mimic others' actions, often leading to suboptimal outcomes. The study of herd behavior began in the 1990s, when researchers explored how investors tend to follow crowds, especially in stock markets. Initially focused on stocks, studies later expanded to include other markets such as commodities and foreign exchange, each showing unique herding patterns. The 2008 financial crisis highlighted how herd behavior can worsen market volatility during extreme situations. With the rise of cryptocurrencies in 2010, researchers found a new area to study this behavior, considering the decentralized and volatile nature of crypto markets. Today, studies continue to adapt methods to explore herd behavior in cryptocurrency markets during global events, representing a field that has evolved from challenging traditional financial ideas to understanding collective decision-making in various markets.

According to Blasco *et al.* (2022), herd behavior refers to the phenomenon where individuals, often influenced by the actions of others, tend to follow the prevailing trend or decision in financial markets. In traditional financial markets, this has been extensively examined as investors, driven by the fear of missing out or uncertainty, mimic the actions of their peers. Historically, researchers have examined herd behavior across diverse financial markets. Recently, blockchain technology, initially developed for payments, has gained traction among investors seeking alternatives in times of market turbulence (Bouri *et al.*, 2017).

Classical theorists, such as Fama (1970), posit that there is no connection between behavioral factors and asset prices. In contrast, proponents of behavioral finance argue for the opposite viewpoint. Bagh *et al.* (2023) assert that the EMH suggests investors behave rationally within an informationally efficient market. In contrast, behavioral finance theory disputes this perspective, contending that market participants are not entirely rational, resulting in systematic errors and inefficient pricing. According to Ballis & Drakos (2020), the EMH asserts that asset prices reflect all available information, while behavioral finance highlights deviations from rational decision-making, resulting in anomalies. The cryptocurrency market, acknowledged as an emerging asset class, has drawn investors because of its limited correlation with conventional assets (Corbet *et al.*, 2019). However, debates persist on its status as merely a bubble, given extreme price variations and regulatory concerns. The impact of global events, such as the COVID-19 pandemic and the ongoing Russia–Ukraine War, on herd behavior is an emerging area of research. The cryptocurrency market has become a focal point during the two global events mentioned above. These events, characterized by heightened uncertainty, shape herding behavior. The geopolitical dynamics of the Ukraine-Russia conflict contribute to the market's overall dynamics, with nation-states engaging in cryptocurrency-related financial activities.

9.2.1. *Empirical literature review*

Many researchers have investigated how COVID-19 has impacted the stock market. Ashraf (2020) shows that the rise in confirmed cases of COVID-19 has a detrimental bearing on the stock market. Similarly, Albulescu (2021) argues that the pandemic increased market volatility in the US. Shehzad *et al.* (2022) conducted a comparative analysis of the effects on financial stock returns in the US, Germany, Italy, Japan and China, and they concluded that the COVID-19 emergency had a larger influence on American and European markets than the GFC did on Asian markets. In addition, Demirer *et al.* (2015), examining commodity markets, find that herd behavior occurs in the grains industry during periods of high volatility.

Past studies attempting to demonstrate the herd behavior in the cryptocurrency market during bullish and bearish periods yield mixed results (Ballis & Drakos, 2020; Bouri *et al.*, 2019; Haryanto *et al.*, 2020). Research indicates that COVID-19 has heightened market volatility, impacting investor sentiment and behavior (Zhang *et al.*, 2022). Understanding the interplay of global events in the cryptocurrency market is crucial for comprehending resilience, volatility and participant behavior during crises.

In addition, herd behavior was also studied in 50 cryptocurrencies from 2015 to 2018 by da Gama Silva *et al.* (2019), who relied on the beta-herding model developed by Hwang & Salmon (2004) and the CSAD and CSSD models. While the CSSD model revealed herding during bear markets, the beta-herding model showed both herding and unfavorable herding were present. However, Vidal-Tomás *et al.* (2019) observed the opposite, suggesting that herd behavior was only present during bear markets for 65 digital currencies. The intricacy of herding dynamics, for instance, was reflected in the wide range of results from the various models. Ballis & Drakos (2020) explored herd behavior in six big cryptocurrencies from 2015 to 2018. They found evidence of this behavior, especially when the market was going up in the top sector. The herd mentality, as documented by Kallinterakis & Wang (2019), is more pronounced during periods of bull markets, low volatility and high volume. In contrast, Bouri *et al.* (2019) discovered contradictory evidence in 14 cryptocurrencies between 2013 and 2018, utilizing the rolling windows approach and the CSAD static model.

Prior investigations employed diverse models, encompassing, for example, static models, which provide a broad overview of trends and behaviors in the cryptocurrency market. These models offer a snapshot of the overall herd dynamics without accounting for temporal variations. They serve as an initial foundation for understanding the general patterns of investor behavior (Bagh *et al.*, 2023; Bouri *et al.*, 2019). Some studies employed Markov regime-switching, a dynamic approach that allows for a detailed examination of herd behavior as it evolves over time. This method considers shifts in market conditions and investor sentiment, providing a more nuanced understanding of how herd dynamics change during different temporal segments (Youssef & Waked, 2022). Some studies have employed the GARCH model to analyze the conditional volatility patterns within the cryptocurrency market. By focusing on how volatility changes in response to new information, the GARCH model contributes to the identification of distinct temporal segments. During times of geopolitical conflict, such as the Russia–Ukraine War, and worldwide disasters, such as the time after the COVID-19 pandemic, this helps reveal patterns of herd behavior. Threshold models increases the study's ability to capture the complex dynamics of the market and investor behavior under different conditions by using the GARCH model (Glaser *et al.*, 2014), Threshold "GARCH" and "TGARCH" (Dyhrberg, 2016) GARCH (EGARCH) (Bouoiyour & Selmi, 2015).

The literature review underscores the evolving nature of herd behavior in cryptocurrency markets, emphasizing the need for further research during critical global events. Understanding the dynamics of investor behavior in these markets is crucial for both individual and institutional investors as the cryptocurrency market continues to grow.

The CSAD model supports herd behavior, notably in the up-market; however, Vidal-Tomás *et al.* (2019) determined that this behavior was observed exclusively when the market is down, exhibiting contradicting conclusions. The empirical findings from previous research on herd behavior in cryptocurrency markets amid global crises such as COVID-19 and the Russia–Ukraine conflict are inconclusive, as shown by the work of Corbet *et al.* (2019). Some studies suggest that herding occurs during certain market conditions, while others find no conclusive evidence (Manahov, 2022; Senarathne & Jianguo, 2020). While in financial markets, herd behavior has been extensively studied, the cryptocurrency market, especially during critical global events, remains relatively unexplored. Past research has primarily focused on traditional markets, with a recent surge in interest in cryptocurrencies due to turbulence in conventional financial markets. The conflicting theories of classical and behavioral finance further shape the discourse (Evrim Mandaci & Cagli, 2022; Rubbaniy *et al.*, 2021).

This study aims to reveal herd behavior patterns over diverse temporal segments, focusing on the Russia–Ukraine War and post-COVID-19 periods. Unlike previous research, it focuses specifically on the cryptocurrency market, including the full sample period and key geopolitical and crisis phases. The Russia–Ukraine conflict's involvement of major nation-states in cryptocurrency-related activities adds a unique dimension to market dynamics. Furthermore, the study addresses the underexplored effect of the global COVID-19 pandemic on market volatility and investor sentiment. Using innovative methodologies such as static Markov regime-switching and GARCH (1,1) for temporal segmentation, along with the CSAD and GARCH models, the research provides nuanced insights into herd behavior during critical periods. The practical implications extend to portfolio management and risk mitigation, offering valuable guidance for stakeholders navigating global crisis situations. In summary, this study enhances our understanding of cryptocurrency market dynamics amid unique challenges, contributing valuable insights to behavioral finance.

9.2.2. *Theoretical framework and hypothesis formulation*

The study employs a combination of EMH and behavioral finance theory to deliver an inclusive framework for gaining a detailed understanding of herd behavior in the cryptocurrency market. EMH posits that in an informationally efficient market, investors act rationally, making decisions based on all available information. This theory serves as the foundation for understanding market efficiency and the role of information in shaping investor behavior. In contrast to EMH, behavioral finance theory contends that investors are not fully rational and may exhibit cognitive biases, leading to deviations from rational decision-making. This theory accommodates the study of herd behavior, emphasizing the psychological factors influencing market participants. By integrating these theories, the framework acknowledges the coexistence of rational and behavioral elements in the cryptocurrency market. It recognizes that while market efficiency plays a role, behavioral biases can lead to herd behavior, especially during distinct temporal segments and geopolitical and global crises. Understanding the intricacies of the cryptocurrency market and the reasons influencing herd behavior requires an appreciation of the interplay between these theories.

Though previous research has shed some light on herd behavior in the Bitcoin market, using different samples and temporal development have been mostly unexplored. As markets mature, new technologies emerge and new regulations are implemented, investors' habits may shift over time.

H_1: *There are distinct patterns of herd behavior observed during different temporal segments of the cryptocurrency market. Specifically, we anticipate variations in the intensity and nature of herding across different time periods within the full sample.*

Geopolitical events have a profound impact on financial markets, influencing investor sentiment and decision-making. The Russia–Ukraine War represents a unique geopolitical tension that can significantly shape the behavior of cryptocurrency market participants.

H_2: *During the Russia–Ukraine War, there will be a discernible increase in herd behavior in the cryptocurrency market. The heightened uncertainty and geopolitical risk associated with the conflict are expected to amplify the tendency of investors to follow the crowd.*

The post-COVID-19 period has been marked by a mix of recovery and ongoing uncertainties. Understanding how herd behavior manifests in the aftermath of a global crisis is crucial for comprehending the resilience and adaptability of the cryptocurrency market.

H_3: *In the post-COVID-19 period, there will be identifiable patterns of herd behavior in the cryptocurrency market distinct from those observed during the full sample period. The market's response to the aftermath of a global crisis is expected to influence investor herding tendencies.*

In essence, the cryptocurrency market has been dynamically shaped by geopolitical events, such as the Russia–Ukraine conflict, and global crises, such as the COVID-19 pandemic, impacting herd behavior and how investors respond to unfolding information. Grasping these dynamics is essential for gaining insights into the market's resilience, volatility and behavioral tendencies of participants during crisis situations. By analyzing daily observations of the market value of the top 30 cryptocurrencies, this study uncovers the impact of herd behavior throughout the full sample period, the COVID-19 outbreak and the Russian invasion of Ukraine.

9.3. Data and Methodology

9.3.1. *Data and sample construction*

This study aims to identify herd behavior in the cryptocurrency market across three periods: the entire sample duration, the entire COVID-19 pandemic and the ongoing war between Russia and Ukraine, considering market capitalization. Employing a quantitative research design, the study conducts diagnostic tests before performing regression analysis using the daily closing prices of the top 30 cryptocurrencies. The dataset is sourced from the website of CoinMarketCap (https://coinmarketcap.com/), aligning with exchange processes. The ranges of the three periods considered for temporal analysis are as follows: full sample — 1 January 2018 to 31 July 2022, post-war period — 24 February 2022 to 31 July 2022 and post-COVID-19 period — 31 December 2019 to 24 February 2022.

9.3.2. *Variable descriptions*

The term "cryptocurrency market return" refers to the overall performance or change in value of the entire cryptocurrency market over a specific period. It is often expressed as a percentage and represents the average movement of various cryptocurrencies within that market during the chosen timeframe. Changes in the market value of individual cryptocurrencies are used to determine the market return.

Depending on the analytical or reporting needs, it might be measured on a daily, weekly, monthly or annual basis.

We calculate the average daily market return for a selected cryptocurrency as given by Ballis & Drakos (2020), Dasman (2021) and King & Koutmos (2021). We use Equation (9.1) to compute the cryptocurrency market return:

$$\text{CR}_{i,t} = \frac{\sum_{i=1}^{n} \left(\frac{\text{Current Price}_t - \text{Previous Price}_t}{\text{Previous Price}_t} \right)}{\text{Previous Price}_{t-1}} * 100. \tag{9.1}$$

The current closing price is the closing price of the cryptocurrency on day i, previous price is the closing price of the cryptocurrency on the previous day and n is the total number of days for which data are available.

Herd behavior refers to the phenomenon where individuals mimic the actions of a larger group, leading to a lack of diversity in decision-making and potential market inefficiencies. Investors often follow the crowd, driven by fear of missing out (FOMO) or the belief that others possess superior information. In behavioral economics, herd behavior is viewed as a cognitive bias influenced by social factors. Individuals tend to conform to the actions of a majority, even if their own information or analysis suggests a different course of action. This behavior can be influenced by emotions, cognitive shortcuts and the desire for social validation. In order to study herd behavior, various models and methods are employed (Bouri *et al.*, 2019). Some include CSAD, which measures the dispersion of individual asset returns; return dispersion models, which assess return variability across assets (Youssef & Waked, 2022); information cascade models, which study decision-making sequences; and agent-based models, which simulate market interactions (Bagh *et al.*, 2023). The computation is delineated as follows:

$$\text{CSSD}_t = \frac{\sqrt{\sum_{i=1}^{N} (Ri,t - Rm,t)^2}}{N-1}. \tag{9.2}$$

When investor returns are highly correlated with market returns, the strategy aims to learn whether investors sometimes set aside independent thinking to go along with the herd. Rm,t is the CSAD of N price returns in the portfolio at time t, and CSAD is the cross-sectional absolute deviation of returns at time t. Statistically significant negative characteristics, an indication of herd behavior, for the cryptocurrency market, which is illustrative of realized crypto values (Youssef & Waked, 2022). Using CSAD static regression models is the first stage in a generally accepted methodology (Chang *et al.*, 2000) to identify herd behavior.

9.3.3. *Econometric models and empirical strategy*

Building on recent literature, we employ both static and Markov regime-switching models in our methodology to capture time-series behavior by identifying recurring "regimes," or "states." This approach, distinct from traditional models, allows for the adaptation of characteristics such as mean, variance and parameters across these regimes (Balcılar *et al.*, 2017; Demirer *et al.*, 2015; Youssef & Waked, 2022). Unlike conventional models, this method assumes a probability of transitioning between states, rendering it particularly effective for modeling data that exhibit fluctuations between recurring states. This flexibility provides a more accurate picture of real-world dynamics. As a robustness check, we use a GARCH model, in particular GARCH (1,1), for temporal segmentation estimation using our primary equations. This complements our analysis by capturing the evolving volatility within different temporal segments.

To these ends, we first conduct a comprehensive sample analysis using Equation (9.1) to see if there is any evidence of herd behavior in the cryptocurrency market. Following this, we perform subsample analyses considering the periods of the Russia–Ukraine conflict and the COVID-19 crisis by adjusting Equation (9.3) with dummy variables representing these extraordinary events. Equations (9.4) and (9.5) further explore the dynamics affected by the above events. These equations form the basis of our empirical study, allowing us to examine in depth the dynamics of herd behavior in the cryptocurrency market:

$$\text{CSSD}_t = \alpha + \beta_1|R_{m,t}| + \beta_2 R^2_{m,t} + \varepsilon_t, \tag{9.3}$$

$$\text{CSSD}_t = \alpha + \beta_1|R_{m,t}| + \beta_2 R^2_{m,t} + \Upsilon_1 D\_\text{War}_{m,t} + \varepsilon_t, \tag{9.4}$$

$$\text{CSSD}_t = \alpha + \beta_1|R_{m,t}| + \beta_2 R^2_{m,t} + \Upsilon_1 D\_C_{m,t} + \varepsilon_t. \tag{9.5}$$

In the above equations, $R_{m,t}$ denotes the market return and t represents the daily return for each cryptocurrency, the dummy variable "Pre-War 0" refers to observations recorded from 1 January 2018 to 24 February 2022. Similarly, "Post-War 1" designates observations from 24 February 2022 to 31 July 2022. The dummy variable "pre-Covid 0" encompasses observations from 1 January 2018 to 31 December 2019, while "post-Covid1" comprises observations from 31 December 2019 to 31 July 2022. Chang *et al.* (2000) proposed a model which is valid only for static structures when its parameters are kept constant over time. Thus, this model has been critiqued for taking a one-dimensional view of herd behavior. To address this issue, researchers of the stock and commodities markets, such as Balcılar *et al.* (2017) and Demirer *et al.* (2015), have developed studies that extend the static model to a regime-switching framework, for example. This modification is implemented to accommodate structural breaks, a crucial consideration during periods of elevated volatility that might suggest a higher likelihood of investors engaging in herd behavior. Our analysis employs a regime-switching model that distinguishes between low- and high-volatility states, as follows:

$$\begin{aligned}\mathrm{CSSD}_t = \alpha_0, S_t + \alpha_1, S_t|\mathrm{R}_{m,t}| + \alpha_{2,} S_t \mathrm{R}^2_{m,t} + \varepsilon_t S_t,\\ + \varepsilon_t, S_t N(0, \sigma^2 S_t). \end{aligned} \tag{9.6}$$

In this setting, s can take on values in the range $S_t \in \{1, 2\}$, which corresponds to a two-state Markov process signaling either crises (high-volatility) or typical (low-volatility) circumstances. A negative and statistically significant value of t during state $\alpha_{2,} S_t$ indicates the presence of herd behavior in the crypto market at that time. We modify Equation (9.5) by including a dummy variable in order to specify the timeframe of the COVID-19 and war periods to evaluate the existence of herd behavior throughout these periods in the cryptocurrency market. We use the GARCH (1, 1) specification of the GARCH model to ensure the consistency of our results. The fundamental equations are used in this model to estimate temporal segmentation.

9.4. Empirical Results and Discussion

9.4.1. *Summary statistics*

Table 9.1 offers a concise overview of key variables covering the period from 1 January 2017 to 31 July 2022, incorporating essential

Table 9.1. Summary statistics.

	Full sample period		War period		COVID-19 period	
Parameters	**CSAD**	*rm*, *t*	**CSAD**	*rm*, *t*	**CSAD**	*rm*, *t*
N	30	30	30	30	30	30
Mean	0.047	0.023	0.032	0.028	0.039	0.021
Std. Dev.	0.009	0.057	0.008	0.027	0.007	0.039
Min	0.002	−0.240	0.037	−0.213	0.017	−0.211
Max	0.174	0.173	0.168	0.112	0.171	0.169
ADF	−22.323*	−14.315*	−21.991*	−12.401*	−31.219*	−4.109*
Jarque–Bera	0.2492	0.2829	0.3125	0.2914	0.2311	0.3123
P value (Jarque–Bera)	0.1145	0.1129	0.434	0.401	0.401	0.211

Notes: This table provides key statistics on CSAD and average daily returns (rm) for the top 30 cryptocurrencies across three time periods: the full sample (1 January 2018 – 31 July 2022), pre-COVID-19 (1 January 2018 – 31 December 2022) and post-COVID-19/Russia–Ukraine War. Jarque–Bera and augmented Dickey–Fuller (ADF) values are included. Notably, values during the full sample period exceed those in specific event periods. Figures 9.1 and 9.2 illustrate market capitalization and trading volume, highlighting UNUS SED LED for high trading volume and Bitcoin for market capitalization. * represents 10% level of significance.

metrics, such as average market returns (mr_t), and CSAD. The dataset encompasses a total of 2,038 observations, presenting statistical summaries (Mean, Std. Dev., Min and Max) for 12 selected cryptocurrencies, average daily market returns (rm) and both CSSD and CSAD herding measures. Analyzing the dataset over various timeframes reveals distinctive trends in the statistical measures of market returns and CSAD. Over the entire sample period, the (ADMR) average daily market return stands at 0.0791%, with a standard deviation of 0.0493%. Simultaneously, the average CSAD registers at 0.0929%, indicating higher variability compared to the market return standard deviation. For the period before the Russia–Ukraine War, the mean rm is 0.0361%, with a standard deviation of 0.0533%, while the mean CSAD is 0.0551%, demonstrating lower variability than the rm standard deviation. Conversely, the post-Russia–Ukraine War period witnessed a decrease in dispersion, as indicated by a significantly lower CSAD of 0.0349% compared to the market return standard deviation of 0.1271%, while in the face

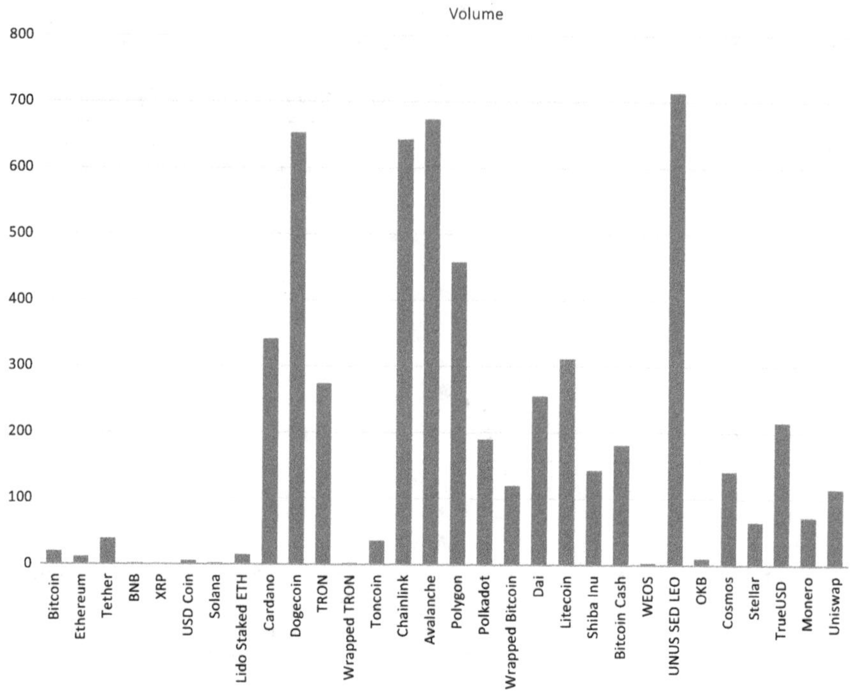

Figure 9.1. Top 30 cryptocurrencies markets: Volume.

of the global COVID-19 pandemic, rm is 0.0691%, with a standard deviation of 0.0495%, and CSAD averages 0.0418%, once again showcasing lower variability than the rm standard deviation. However, for the post-COVID-19 period, both the market return and CSAD exhibit diminished values of 0.0129% and 0.0515%, respectively. Notably, CSAD surpasses the market return standard deviation, signaling an increase in dispersion for the period marked by the COVID-19 pandemic. In summary, the analysis uncovers fluctuations in dispersion, with notable reductions observed after the Russia–Ukraine War and heightened dispersion in the post-COVID-19 period. As we progress with time-series regression models, the focus shifts toward evaluating the stationarity and distribution of the data.

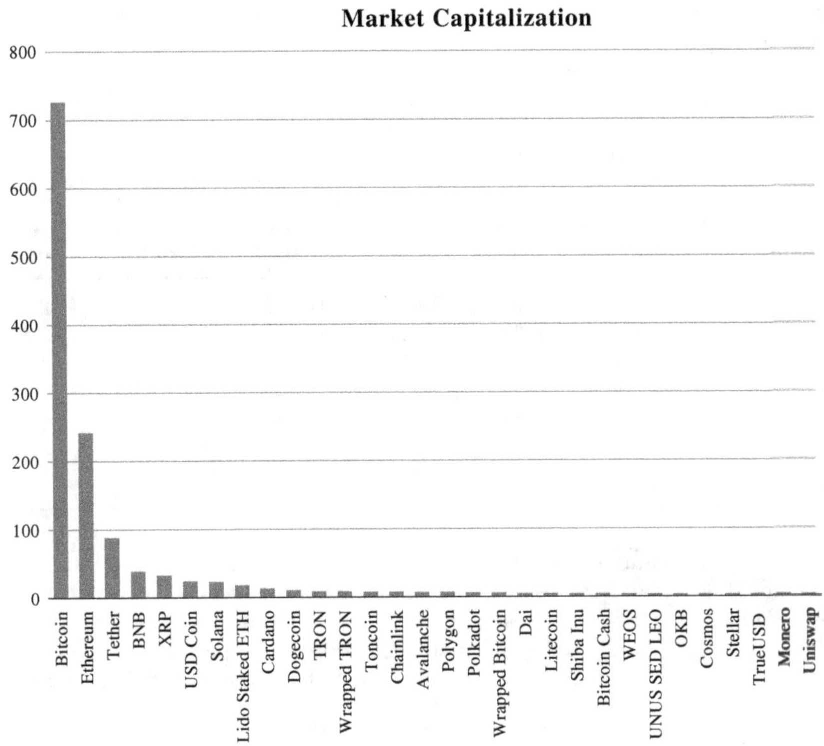

Figure 9.2. Top 30 cryptocurrencies markets: Market capitalization.

9.4.2. *Regression analysis*

Table 9.2 presents the findings of the estimation employing both the static (1) and regime-switching models (2 and 3, consisting of low volatility state, or LVS: Regime 1, and high volatility state, or HVS: Regime 2, respectively, for the CSAD model). No evidence of herd behavior can be seen in the static regression findings, as demonstrated by the positive but negligible parameter $\alpha 2$. Our results are consistent with those of the studies by Bouri *et al.* (2019) and Youssef & Waked (2022), both of which take a static approach and find no evidence of herd behavior in the Bitcoin market. The results shown in Table 9.2 highlight the differences in the variance $\sigma^2\varepsilon$ across states within the conceptual framework of the regime-switching model, demonstrating the superiority of the regime-switching method over

Table 9.2. Regression results for static and regime-switching models for the full sample period.

	Static model		**Low-volatility state = LVS: Regime 1**		**High-volatility state = HVS: Regime 2**	
	(1)		**(2)**		**(3)**	
Parameters	**Coef.**	***t*-test**	**Coef.**	***t*-test**	**Coef.**	***t*-test**
abs rm	0.044***	(8.231)	0.017***	(5.231)	0.057***	(7.201)
r^2m	0.005	(0.331)	−0.013	(0.391)	−0.024***	(2.391)
cons_	1.077***	(11.271)	2.077***	(21.041)	3.071***	(18.041)
N	50		50	50		
σ_t^2		3.129		4.213		6.011
LL	−7311.44		−6222.111			
AIC	−4.9781		−4.1201			

Notes: This table displays estimates for both static and Markov regime-switching models, encompassing two regimes throughout the entire dataset from 1 January 2018 to 31 July 2022, across a set of 30 currency markets. The variable $\sigma^2 t$ represents the variance of the residual term. LL and AIC denote the log-likelihood value at the optimum and Akaike information criteria, respectively. Significance levels are indicated as follows: *** for $p < 0.01$, ** for $p < 0.05$ and * for $p < 0.1$.

the static model. This nuanced analysis allows for a more comprehensive understanding of the underlying dynamics, as it accommodates shifts in the statistical properties of the data. Furthermore, in this study, we observed a higher $\sigma^2\varepsilon$ value for Regime 2 compared to Regime 1, which provides additional insights into herd behavior (Susana *et al.*, 2020). This discrepancy suggests that Regime 2 is characterized by a heightened level of volatility, indicating a distinct and potentially more turbulent market environment during periods associated with Regime 2. In addition, comparing the AIC values of the static (model 1) and regime-switching (2 and 3)[1] models, the

[1]AIC $= -2 \times$ LL $+ 2\times$ number of parameters.

For Model 1: AIC $= -2 \times (-7311.44) + 2 \times 5 = 14624.88 + 10 = 14634.88$.

For Model 2: AIC $= -2\times(-6222.111)+2\times 7$ AIC $=$ Model 2 $= 12444.222+14 = 12458.222$ AIC. Comparatively, the regime-switching model (2 and 3) has a lower AIC value of 12458.222 and is considered preferable to Model 1 (static model) with an AIC of 14634.88. (The existence of herd behavior in the cryptocurrency market is indicated by a negative parameter which is significant statistically.)

latter has a lower AIC value of 12458.222 and is therefore considered preferable to the former, which has an AIC value of 14634.88.

Table 9.3 lists the results of the static model, pointing to the absence of signals indicating herd behavior in the cryptocurrency market. However, upon incorporating dummy variables reflecting the COVID-19 pandemic and the Russia–Ukraine War, the results reveal noteworthy insights. In particular, the coefficients for both variables are significantly negative. Herd dynamics in the crypto market appear to have been intensified by the pandemic and war. Our results indicate the presence of herd behavior in both of these periods.

The findings of our study align with existing theories and underscore the economic connectivity inherent in cryptocurrency markets. Specifically, our results resonate with the theoretical frameworks proposed by researchers such as Bouri *et al.* (2019), Coskun *et al.* (2020), Kumar (2022) and Youssef & Waked (2022). The theory of herd behavior, as supported by traditional stock markets during crises, contrasts with our observations during the Russia–Ukraine crisis in the cryptocurrency market. This deviation highlights the distinctive nature of cryptocurrency markets and their response to geopolitical events. The economic connectivity in this context can be understood through the lens of market participants' characteristics and their decision-making processes. Specifically, the insights into the demographic profile of cryptocurrency market participants provide a plausible explanation for the observed herding behavior. The tendency of younger and less experienced individuals to be guided by market sentiment suggests that economic pronouncements in the cryptocurrency market are influenced by issues beyond traditional economic indicators. This underscores the importance of considering psychological and behavioral aspects in understanding economic connectivity within the cryptocurrency space.

The identification of herd behavior in our study across the full sample, COVID-19 pandemic and Russia–Ukraine War periods is substantiated by existing literature. Previous research has acknowledged the phenomenon of herd behavior, especially during times of crisis (Chiang & Zheng, 2010). The justification lies in the consistent patterns observed in the behavior of market participants across different temporal segments. Economic theories, such as behavioral finance theory, provide a conceptual framework to understand why individuals may collectively adjust their investment strategies, contributing

Table 9.3. Subsample (temporal segmentation): Static model and Markov regime-switching model.

	War period		COVID-19 period		War_LVS		War_HVS		Covid_LVS		Covid_HVS	
	(1)		(2)		(3)		(4)		(5)		(6)	
Parameters	**Coef.**	***t*-test**	**Coef.**	***t*-test**	**Coef.**	***t*-test**	**Coef.**	***t*-test**	**Coef.**	***t*-test**	**Coef.**	***t*-test**
abs r_m	0.215***	(12.331)	0.014***	(3.331)	0.343***	(3.331)	0.237***	(6.231)	0.277***	(3.391)	0.341***	(9.131)
r_m^2	**0.013*** **	**(2.231)**	**0.193*** **	**(2.201)**	**−0.011**	**(0.271)**	**−0.007*** **	**(2.091)**	**−0.008**	**(0.009)**	**−0.006*** **	**(11.271)**
*D*_War	**−0.024*** **	**(8.201)**			**0.003**	**(0.203)**	**−0.027*** **	**(5.331)**				
*D*_*C*			**−0.041*** **	**(3.121)**					**−0.071**	**(0.231)**	**−0.101*** **	**(3.331)**
cons_	1.077***	(9.123)	2.077***	(7.321)	5.077***	(7.111)	1.071***	(7.271)	4.141***	(2.271)	2.101***	(5.211)
N	50		50		50		50		50		50	
σ^2		3.434		4.321		1.075		1.135		5.176		8.032
LL	4.8779		4.3451			4.1201				4.0031		
AIC	−7311.11		−71.11.44			−6911.87				−6841.55		

Notes: This table presents estimates for both static and Markov regime-switching models: it includes two regimes covering the entire dataset from 1 January 2019 to 31 July 2022, across a selection of 50 currency markets. We enhance our full-sample regression equation by introducing dummy variables that specifically highlight periods corresponding to the COVID-19 pandemic and the Russia–Ukraine conflict. The variable σ^2t represents the variance of the residual term. LL and AIC refer to the log-likelihood value at the optimum and Akaike information criteria, respectively. Significance levels are denoted as follows: *** for $p < 0.01$, ** for $p < 0.05$ and * for $p < 0.1$.

to observable evidence of heard behavior in the cryptocurrency market during both crisis and non-crisis periods. The alignment of our findings with the established literature strengthens the validity and significance of our findings of herd behavior across diverse market conditions.

On possible explanations, Youssef & Waked (2022) discuss a few potential causes. People who trade cryptocurrencies tend to be young, inexperienced and guided by market sentiment, all of which contribute to this result. As a result, herd behavior is common as a coping mechanism for dealing with high levels of stress. The results of our research are consistent with those reported in prior investigations (Bouri *et al.*, 2019; Coskun *et al.*, 2020; Kumar, 2022; Youssef & Waked, 2022). In summary, our work contributes to the current body of knowledge by providing empirical evidence for theories of herd behavior, thereby highlighting the unique economic interconnection and participant dynamics within the financial ecosystem of the cryptocurrency market.

9.4.3. *Robustness check*

To assess the robustness of the results presented in this chapter, a comprehensive analysis was conducted using the CSAD model supplemented with the GARCH model. Table 9.4 showcases the outcomes of the CSAD model incorporating the GARCH model for the full sample, COVID-19, and war periods. This involved integrating the Russia–Ukraine War and the COVID-19 crisis conditions into an augmented model, which revealed insightful findings. A statistically significant and negative correlation exists between the two variables, showing that events such as the two mentioned above exacerbated the herd dynamics in the Bitcoin market. In summary, our results demonstrate the prevalence of herd behavior during the war and the pandemic as well as throughout the sample period. Furthermore, the robustness of our results is underscored by the GARCH model outcomes, affirming the pivotal and statistically significant role of the lagged term Lag 1 in explaining and predicting volatility. This is supported by the high significance level of the coefficient and t-statistic associated with Lag 1.

These striking results have important implications for asset allocation, trading methods and risk management. Gaining an

Table 9.4. GARCH model for the full sample, COVID-19 and war periods.

	Full-sample		**War_Period**		**COVID-19_Period**	
Parameters	**Coef.**	***t*-test**	**Coef.**	***t*-test**	**Coef.**	***t*-test**
abs r_m	0.117***	(9.001)	0.235***	(7.341)	0.123**	(1.960)
r_m^2	−0.050***	(3.006)	−0.052***	(5.381)	−0.034***	(7.271)
*D*_War			0.063	(4.245)		
*D*_*C*					−0.078***	(6.351)
cons_	−0.929***	(2.396)	5.077***	(7.111)	0.971***	(7.271)
N	50		50		50	
ARCH [Lag 1]	0.41001***		0.4511***		0.4356***	
t-stat	(10.218)		(14.008)		(17.008)	
GARCH [Lag 1]	0.6211***		0.6932***		0.7004***	
t-stat	(19.234)		(8.201)			(32.201)

Notes: This table presents the robustness check and the results of the CSAD model utilizing the GARCH model for the full sample, COVID-19 and war periods. The GARCH model outcomes strongly affirm that the lagged term Lag 1 plays a pivotal and statistically significant role in elucidating and forecasting volatility. This assertion is substantiated by the high significance level of the coefficient and *t*-statistic associated with Lag 1. *** represents 1% level of significance, ** represents 5% level of significance, * represents 10% level of significance.

understanding of the factors influencing herd behavior can aid investors in navigating away from such patterns, particularly in times of crisis. The study's findings confirm the irrational tendencies observed in the conduct of cryptocurrency market investors. Particularly, decision-making processes among cryptocurrency market participants are significantly swayed by their enthusiasm and responses to market dynamics. During situations with significant price fluctuations, herd behavior manifests itself, indicating the inefficiency of crypto markets. This runs counter to the rationality postulated by the Capital Asset Pricing Model (CAPM). These findings are consistent with those obtained using the method based on CSAD, lending credence to the presence of herd behavior in highly volatile markets, as observed in previous studies (Ballis & Drakos, 2020; Dasman, 2021; King & Koutmos, 2021; Raja Nabeel-Ud-Din *et al.*, 2021). Notable among the study's outcomes are valuable insights into portfolio management, market inefficiencies, trading strategies and risk management.

9.5. Conclusion

In the volatile landscape of digital assets, the cryptocurrency market is vulnerable to shocks in the dynamic digital asset ecosystem, especially amid global crises such as the COVID-19 pandemic and the Russia–Ukraine conflict. In periods of high uncertainty, herd behavior, in which investors follow one another in responding to market developments, is more common. In the context of global tensions and crises, this research investigated herd behavior in the cryptocurrency market. Focusing on the periods of the global COVID-19 pandemic and the war between Russia and Ukraine, the research addresses a crucial gap by analyzing market capitalization using daily data from the top 30 cryptocurrencies. The objective was to unravel herd behavior dynamics to obtain insights for improved risk management and investment strategies in digital asset markets.

To fulfill our research objectives, we employed CSAD static, regime-switching and GARCH-based CSAD models for temporal segmentation analysis considering the full sample and subsamples of the COVID-19 pandemic and Russia–Ukraine conflict. The empirical results indicate a prevalence of herd behavior throughout the sample and in the subsamples. Our research confirms what others have found when using a static methodology: there are no instances of herd behavior in the cryptocurrency market. Because it can account for changes in the statistical features of the data, the regime-switching model gives us a more complete picture of the underlying dynamics than static models. These significant results have important implications for asset allocation, trading methods and risk evaluation and management.

During times of geopolitical stress and crises, comprehending the widespread nature of herd behavior in the cryptocurrency market has important policy implications. Policymakers may need to consider measures to address market stability and low investor confidence during such turbulent periods. Additionally, regulatory frameworks could be adapted to account for the unique dynamics of digital asset markets, providing a more resilient environment in the face of global disruptions.

The study contributes theoretically by employing various analytical models (CSAD static model, regime-switching model and

CSAD with GARCH model) to explore herd behavior dynamics. The regime-switching model, in particular, offers a nuanced understanding by accommodating shifts in statistical properties, surpassing the limitations of static models. These theoretical insights expand our understanding of investor behavior in cryptocurrency markets and add to the growing body of knowledge on behavioral finance and market dynamics.

For practitioners in the cryptocurrency market, the study offers practical insights for portfolio management, trading strategies and risk management. Recognizing the prevalence of herd behavior can guide investors in making more informed decisions, especially during crises. This understanding can inform the development of risk mitigation strategies and investment approaches that consider the behavioral aspects of market participants. Despite the useful information obtained, there are caveats to this study. Since this study only covers a subset of cryptocurrencies, its conclusions may not be applicable to the entire digital asset market. Additionally, the study relies on historical data, and market conditions can evolve. The chosen analytical models, while robust, may have inherent limitations in capturing the full complexity of market behavior.

Further investigations could build upon this study by expanding the scope to encompass a broader array of cryptocurrencies and extending the analysis to include more recent data. An exploration into the impact of regulatory changes on herd behavior and market dynamics holds the potential to offer valuable insights for policymakers. Additionally, delving into the role of sentiment analysis and social media in shaping investor behavior during cryptocurrency market crises could open avenues for a more thorough comprehension of market dynamics. This extended research effort could contribute significantly to the evolving understanding of how various factors influence investor actions in the cryptocurrency landscape.

References

Agosto, A., Cerchiello, P., & Pagnottoni, P. (2022). Sentiment, Google queries and explosivity in the cryptocurrency market. *Physica A: Statistical Mechanics and Its Applications*, 605, 128016. https://doi.org/10.1016/j.physa.2022.128016.

Albulescu, C. T. (2021). COVID-19 and the United States financial markets' volatility. *Finance Research Letters*, 38, 101699. https://doi.org/10.1016/j.frl.2020.101699.

Ashraf, B. N. (2020). Stock markets' reaction to COVID-19: Cases or fatalities? *Research in International Business and Finance*, 54, 101249. https://doi.org/10.1016/j.ribaf.2020.101249.

Aslam, F., Hunjra, A. I., Ftiti, Z., Louhichi, W., & Shams, T. (2022). Insurance fraud detection: Evidence from artificial intelligence and machine learning. *Research in International Business and Finance*, 62, 101744. https://doi.org/10.1016/j.ribaf.2022.101744.

Bagh, T., Khan, M. A., Fenyves, V., & Olah, J. (2023). Asymmetric effect of investors sentiments on herding behavior and stock returns: Pre and post Covid-19 analysis. *Montenegrin Journal of Economics*, 19(1), 43–55. https://doi.org/10.14254/1800-5845/2023.19-1.4.

Balcılar, M., Demirer, R., & Ulussever, T. (2017). Does speculation in the oil market drive investor herding in emerging stock markets? *Energy Economics*, 65, 50–63. https://doi.org/10.1016/j.eneco.2017.04.031.

Ballis, A. & Drakos, K. (2020). Testing for herding in the cryptocurrency market. *Finance Research Letters*, 33, 101210. https://doi.org/10.1016/j.frl.2019.06.008.

Bhaskar, R., Hunjra, A. I., Bansal, S., & Pandey, D. K. (2022). Central bank digital currencies: Agendas for future research. *Research in International Business and Finance*, 62, 101737. https://doi.org/10.1016/j.ribaf.2022.101737.

Blasco, N., Corredor, P., & Satrústegui, N. (2022). The witching week of herding on bitcoin exchanges. *Financial Innovation*, 8(1), 26. https://doi.org/10.1186/s40854-021-00323-4.

Bouoiyour, J. & Selmi, R. (2015). Exchange volatility and export performance in Egypt: New insights from wavelet decomposition and optimal GARCH model. *The Journal of International Trade & Economic Development*, 24(2), 201–227. https://doi.org/10.1080/09638199.2014.889740.

Bouri, E., Gupta, R., & Roubaud, D. (2019). Herding behaviour in cryptocurrencies. *Finance Research Letters*, 29, 216–221. https://doi.org/10.1016/j.frl.2018.07.008.

Bouri, E., Molnár, P., Azzi, G., Roubaud, D., & Hagfors, L. I. (2017). On the hedge and safe haven properties of Bitcoin: Is it really more than a diversifier? *Finance Research Letters*, 20, 192–198. https://doi.org/10.1016/j.frl.2016.09.025.

Chang, E. C., Cheng, J. W., & Khorana, A. (2000). An examination of herd behavior in equity markets: An international perspective. *Journal of Banking & Finance*, 24(10), 1651–1679. https://doi.org/10.1016/S0378-4266(99)00096-5.

Chiang, T. C. & Zheng, D. (2010). An empirical analysis of herd behavior in global stock markets. *Journal of Banking & Finance*, 34(8), 1911–1921. https://doi.org/10.1016/j.jbankfin.2009.12.014.

Christie, W. G. & Huang, R. D. (1995). Following the pied piper: Do individual returns herd around the market? *Financial Analysts Journal*, 51(4), 31–37. https://doi.org/10.2469/faj.v51.n4.1918.

Corbet, S., Lucey, B., Urquhart, A., & Yarovaya, L. (2019). Cryptocurrencies as a financial asset: A systematic analysis. *International Review of Financial Analysis*, 62, 182–199. https://doi.org/10.1016/j.irfa.2018.09.003.

Coskun, E. A., Lau, C. K. M., & Kahyaoglu, H. (2020). Uncertainty and herding behavior: Evidence from cryptocurrencies. *Research in International Business and Finance*, 54, 101284. https://doi.org/10.1016/j.ribaf.2020.101284.

da Gama Silva, P. V. J., Klotzle, M. C., Pinto, A. C. F., & Gomes, L. L. (2019). Herding behavior and contagion in the cryptocurrency market. *Journal of Behavioral and Experimental Finance*, 22, 41–50. https://doi.org/10.1016/j.jbef.2019.01.006.

Dasman, S. (2021). Analysis of return and risk of cryptocurrency bitcoin asset as investment instrument. *Accounting and Finance Innovations* (p. 51). USA: IntechOpen.

Demirer, R., Lee, H.-T., & Lien, D. (2015). Does the stock market drive herd behavior in commodity futures markets? *International Review of Financial Analysis*, 39, 32–44. https://doi.org/10.1016/j.irfa.2015.02.006.

Dyhrberg, A. H. (2016). Bitcoin, gold and the dollar – A GARCH volatility analysis. *Finance Research Letters*, 16, 85–92. https://doi.org/10.1016/j.frl.2015.10.008.

Evrim Mandaci, P. & Cagli, E. C. (2022). Herding intensity and volatility in cryptocurrency markets during the COVID-19. *Finance Research Letters*, 46, 102382. https://doi.org/10.1016/j.frl.2021.102382.

Fama, E. F. (1970). Efficient capital markets: A review of theory and empirical work. *The Journal of Finance*, 25(2), 383–417. https://doi.org/10.2307/2325486.

Fernandes, L. H. S., Bouri, E., Silva, J. W. L., Bejan, L., & de Araujo, F. H. A. (2022). The resilience of cryptocurrency market efficiency to COVID-19 shock. *Physica A: Statistical Mechanics and Its Applications*, 607, 128218. https://doi.org/10.1016/j.physa.2022.128218.

Glaser, F., Zimmermann, K., Haferkorn, M., Weber, M. C., & Siering, M. (2014). Bitcoin-asset or currency? Revealing users' hidden intentions (April 15, 2014). *ECIS*. https://ssrn.com/abstract=2425247.

Ha, M., Gan, C., Nguyen, C., & Anthony, P. (2021). Self-organising (Kohonen) maps for the Vietnam banking industry. *Journal of Risk and Financial Management*, 14(10). https://doi.org/10.3390/jrfm14100485.

Haroon, O. & Rizvi, S. A. R. (2020). COVID-19: Media coverage and financial markets behavior – A sectoral inquiry. *Journal of Behavioral and Experimental Finance*, 27, 100343. https://doi.org/10.1016/j.jbef.2020.100343.

Haryanto, S., Subroto, A., & Ulpah, M. (2020). Disposition effect and herding behavior in the cryptocurrency market. *Journal of Industrial and Business Economics*, 47, 115–132. https://doi.org/10.1007/s40812-019-00130-0.

Hunjra, A. I. & Hanif, M. (2023). Central banking issues and challenges. In Hunjra, A. I. & Hanif, M. (Eds.), *Reference Module in Social Sciences.* Pakistan: Elsevier. https://doi.org/10.1016/B978-0-44-313776-1.00113-6.

Hwang, S. & Salmon, M. (2004). Market stress and herding. *Journal of Empirical Finance*, 11(4), 585–616. https://doi.org/10.1016/j.jempfin.2004.04.003.

Kallinterakis, V. & Wang, Y. (2019). Do investors herd in cryptocurrencies – and why? *Research in International Business and Finance*, 50, 240–245. https://doi.org/10.1016/j.ribaf.2019.05.005.

Katsiampa, P. (2017). Volatility estimation for Bitcoin: A comparison of GARCH models. *Economics Letters*, 158, 3–6. https://doi.org/10.1016/j.econlet.2017.06.023.

Kijkasiwat, P., Shahid, A. U., Hassan, M. K., & Hunjra, A. I. (2022). Access to finance, social capital and the improvement of corporate performance: Evidence from Southeast Asia. *Managerial Finance*, 48(7), 1047–1068. https://doi.org/10.1108/MF-10-2021-0519.

King, T. & Koutmos, D. (2021). Herding and feedback trading in cryptocurrency markets. *Annals of Operations Research*, 300(1), 79–96. https://doi.org/10.1007/s10479-020-03874-4.

Kumar, A. (2022). Asymmetrical herding in cryptocurrency: Impact of COVID-19. *Quantitative Finance and Economics*, 6(2), 326–341. https://doi.org/10.3934/QFE.2022014.

Manahov, V. (2022). Cryptocurrency liquidity during extreme price movements: Is there a problem with virtual money? In *Commodities* (pp. 731–762). UK: Taylor & Francis.

Mnif, E., Salhi, B., Mouakha, K., & Jarboui, A. (2022). Investor behavior and cryptocurrency market bubbles during the COVID-19 pandemic. *Review of Behavioral Finance*, 14(4), 491–507. https://doi.org/10.1108/RBF-09-2021-0190.

Mokni, K. (2021). When, where, and how economic policy uncertainty predicts Bitcoin returns and volatility? A quantiles-based analysis. *The Quarterly Review of Economics and Finance*, 80, 65–73. https://doi.org/10.1016/j.qref.2021.01.017.

Mokni, K., Ajmi, A. N., Bouri, E., & Vo, X. V. (2020). Economic policy uncertainty and the Bitcoin-US stock nexus. *Journal of Multinational Financial Management*, 57, 100656. https://doi.org/10.1016/j.mulfin.2020.100656.

Paule-Vianez, J., Prado-Román, C., & Gómez-Martínez, R. (2020). Economic policy uncertainty and Bitcoin. Is Bitcoin a safe-haven asset? *European Journal of Management and Business Economics*, 29(3), 347–363. https://doi.org/10.1108/EJMBE-07-2019-0116/full/html.

Raja Nabeel-Ud-Din, J., Di Pietro, F., & Leonelli, S. (2021). The influence of investors' risk attitude and market information on cryptocurrency investment: Evidence from an experimental study.

Rubbaniy, G., Polyzos, S., Rizvi, S. K. A., & Tessema, A. (2021). COVID-19, lockdowns and herding towards a cryptocurrency market-specific implied volatility index. *Economics Letters*, 207, 110017. https://doi.org/10.1016/j.econlet.2021.110017.

Senarathne, C. W. & Jianguo, W. (2020). Herd behaviour in the cryptocurrency market: Fundamental vs. spurious herding. *The European Journal of Applied Economics*, 17(1), 20–36. https://doi.org/10.5937/ejae17-22053.

Shehzad, K., Xiaoxing, L., Kazouz, H., Balsalobre-Lorente, D., Zeraibi, A., & Rauf, A. (2022). An asymmetric spillover between China and Pakistan'stock markets: A comparative analysis before and during COVID-19 crisis. *Journal of Sustainable Finance & Investment*, 12(4), 1265–1284. https://doi.org/10.1080/20430795.2020.1870203.

Susana, D., Kavisanmathi, J., & Sreejith, S. (2020). Does herding behaviour among traders increase during COVID 19 pandemic? Evidence from the cryptocurrency market. In *Re-imagining Diffusion and Adoption of Information Technology and Systems: A Continuing Conversation: IFIP WG 8.6 International Conference on Transfer and Diffusion of IT, TDIT 2020*, Tiruchirappalli, India, December 18–19, 2020, Proceedings, Part I. https://doi.org/10.1007/978-3-030-64849-7_17.

Urquhart, A. & Zhang, H. (2019). Is Bitcoin a hedge or safe haven for currencies? An intraday analysis. *International Review of Financial Analysis*, 63, 49–57. https://doi.org/10.1016/j.irfa.2019.02.009.

Vidal-Tomás, D., Ibáñez, A. M., & Farinós, J. E. (2019). Herding in the cryptocurrency market: CSSD and CSAD approaches. *Finance Research Letters*, 30, 181–186. https://doi.org/10.1016/j.frl.2018.09.008.

Youssef, M. & Waked, S. S. (2022). Herding behavior in the cryptocurrency market during COVID-19 pandemic: The role of media coverage. *The North American Journal of Economics and Finance*, 62, 101752. https://doi.org/10.1016/j.najef.2022.101752.

Zhang, D., Hu, M., & Ji, Q. (2020). Financial markets under the global pandemic of COVID-19. *Finance Research Letters*, 36, 101528. https://doi.org/10.1016/j.frl.2020.101528.

Zhang, H., Hong, H., Guo, Y., & Yang, C. (2022). Information spillover effects from media coverage to the crude oil, gold, and Bitcoin markets during the COVID-19 pandemic: Evidence from the time and frequency domains. *International Review of Economics & Finance*, 78, 267–285. https://doi.org/10.1016/j.iref.2021.12.005.

https://doi.org/10.1142/9781800616257_0010

Chapter 10

Forecasting Bitcoin: A Comparative Analysis of Traditional versus Machine Learning Approach

Muhammad Arslan[*,¶], **Akmal Shahzad**[†,‖], **Anum Shafique**[‡,**], **and Wajid Shakeel Ahmed**[§,††]

[*]*Sir Syed CASE Institute of Technology, Islamabad, Pakistan*
[†]*Preston University, Islamabad, Pakistan*
[‡]*CUST, Islamabad, Pakistan*
[§]*COMSATS University Islamabad, Islamabad, Pakistan*
[¶]*arslanbutt18@gmail.com*
[‖]*as.butt76@gmail.com*
[**]*an_shafique@yahoo.com*
[††]*wajid_shakeel@comsats.edu.pk*

Abstract

This study attempts to forecast Bitcoin using both traditional and machine learning approaches to determine which methods are more robust. For the traditional method, the GARCH method is used to forecast Bitcoin returns. For the machine learning method, LSTM is used. A hybrid approach of GARCH–LSTM is also applied to the data to compare the results. Hourly data for Bitcoin are obtained from CoinMarketCap for three years, from 2019 to 2022. The findings of the study reveal that machine learning methods outperform traditional methods. The study has useful implications for researchers.

Keywords: Bitcoin, GARCH, machine learning, LSTM.

10.1. Introduction

Financial markets are considered a barometer of the financial system. One of the popular markets that has emerged in recent times is the crypto market, also known as the digital currency market. Bhasker *et al.* (2022), in a research study, highlight the importance of central bank digital currencies in contemporary times. These researchers are of the view that, although technological advancements and the creation of digital currencies appear to disrupt traditional platforms, certain factors still restrict and potentially impact their implementation.

Literature on cryptocurrencies, especially Bitcoin, suggests that they behave as an asset, seemingly independent of the various uncertainties that exist in the traditional financial system. In scenarios where the behavior of the crypto market differs from that of traditional markets, it is worthwhile to explore this market in terms of forecasting returns. It would be in the interest of investors to consider the crypto market as an opportunity when creating portfolios for their investments.

Some studies show how the crypto market reacts and the level of volatility under different scenarios. Kristoufek (2013) shows that cryptocurrencies tend to exhibit outstanding price growth. A few studies focus on the volatility element in the crypto market (Chu *et al.*, 2017; Urquhart, 2017; Gkillas & Katsiampa, 2018). Therefore, it is of great importance for investors to explore the crypto market by comparing it with traditional stock, currency and fixed income markets.

The current study contributes to the literature by focusing on the crypto market. Moreover, the use of advanced forecasting methods such as machine learning is considered in conjunction with traditional methods of forecasting for comparison purposes and to check the robustness of these methods. There are research studies that emphasize using advanced forecasting methods for forecasting returns as compared to traditional methods. For instance, a study conducted by Khairalla & Al-Jallad (2017) compared traditional models with machine learning methods such as artificial neural networks (ANNs) and found that machine learning methods outperformed traditional models. In addition to this, research studies have also highlighted modeling errors resulting from both high-frequency and traditional low-frequency data. Generally, the same modeling techniques are traditionally used for both low- and high-frequency data, which leads to modeling errors. According to the studies conducted by Jobson & Korkie (1981), high-frequency data are non-linear and non-normal. Under these conditions, the high-frequency data often do not conform to traditional forecasting models, resulting in forecasting errors.

Research studies such as the ones above showcase the necessity of using hybrid techniques for forecasting. There are several studies in the literature that have applied these hybrid forecasting techniques to traditional markets, but only very few have considered other market types. Therefore, the current study attempts to fill the gap by considering the crypto market for hybrid forecasting.

The focus of the study is on finding answers to the following research questions:

- Are traditional models effective at forecasting the price behavior of Bitcoin returns?
- Are machine-learning-based models effective at forecasting the price behavior of Bitcoin returns?
- Do machine-learning-based models outperform classical models in forecasting?

The objectives of the research study are as follows:

- to compare traditional and machine-learning-based forecasting models for Bitcoin returns;
- to determine which method is better at forecasting price trends.

The remainder of the chapter is organized as follows. Section 10.2 gives a brief overview of the theoretical and empirical literature. Sections 10.3 and 10.4 explain the data and methodologies used in the study. Section 10.5 highlights the application of the results, followed by Sections 10.6 and 10.7, in which a discussion of the results and conclusions are presented.

10.2. Literature Review

10.2.1. *Theoretical literature*

As suggested by Fama (1970) in his market efficiency theory, efficient markets are those that fully reflect all available information; it can be inferred clearly that when asset prices contain all the available information, it is favorable for investors to make more informed investments and financing decisions (Boehmer & Kelley, 2009). To make such decisions, forecasting plays a pivotal role (Wan *et al.*, 2014). In this regard, Goldman (1999) has made a key contribution with his computational learning theory. The theory argues that advanced learning methods can improve forecasting, which leads to better decision-making in environments where market efficiency prevails in different forms.

10.2.2. *Empirical literature*

Goodell & Shen (2021) assert that the role of digital finance is crucial for a country's prosperity, as it can increase the efficiency and accessibility of financial services for its population under any economic conditions. It may also attract foreign investment due to its ease of use and could lead to an increase in the demand for domestic currency. More specifically, central bank digital currencies have greater potential to play a positive role as compared to traditional currencies. Therefore, there is an increased probability that the demand for domestic physical currency may be impacted by the introduction of digital currency. However, the size of the economy is a key factor in accelerating this impact because only a strong, growing and robust economy can attract investors. On the other hand, if the country is facing economic challenges, the situation can be reversed.

Further, Howell & Potgieter (2021) state that digital finance offers several opportunities for economies to prosper. It is important to note that these opportunities are made possible due to globalization. However, several contextual factors limit globalization and also influence a central bank's digital currencies. These factors include economic, social, political, ethical and environmental aspects. For instance, the overall economic stability of the country, the readiness of the population to adopt digital currencies, political and regulatory issues, state sovereignty, geopolitical considerations and the energy consumption of blockchain networks are some of the challenges highlighted that hinder the growth of digital currencies. All of this necessitates a reassessment of the financial systems.

The world in recent times has witnessed a shift in response towards digital currencies. Ashraf (2020) and Famiglietti & Leibovici

(2022) state that the success of economic policies hinges on an effective monetary and payment system. In that connection, cryptocurrency has added a new dimension to this traditional system. It is evident from the pandemic period that cryptocurrency has become relevant to the existing system. Further, cryptocurrencies are based on decentralized blockchain technology, in contrast to traditional banking systems. This provides greater resilience to the system during uncertain times and offers alternative means of payment that are less vulnerable than those offered by traditional systems in times of crisis. They contribute to financial inclusion by not only offering contactless transactions but also cross-border transactions without the need for intermediaries such as banks.

10.2.3. *Forecasting models and financial markets*

Cryptocurrencies are decentralized currencies because they operate on decentralized blockchain technology. In contrast to traditional payment and currency systems, these currencies are not controlled by governments or central banks; rather, they are based on distributed ledgers that keep a record of the transactions. It is pertinent to note that cryptocurrencies only exist in digital form and are limited in their supply. This limit on their supply creates scarcity and is intended to match the demand, as in the case of commodities such as gold, ultimately serving the purpose of controlling inflation.

Further, it is important to note that the market capitalization reached US$221 billion in 2019, with Bitcoin making the highest contribution. However, due to the huge volatility in the market, the price of Bitcoin has ranged from $US0.0008 in January 2009 to $US10,168 in 2020. Due to this high level of volatility, it is difficult to forecast the prices of cryptocurrency as limited information is available about digital assets, unlike with physical currencies. Therefore, different models are tested to improve forecasting. It is the only way for users to minimize the risk of losses. It can also help investors make informed decisions regarding their buying and selling decisions for these currencies.

Investors seek effective forecasting approaches to mitigate risks and increase profits in cryptocurrency markets amid their volatility and dynamic nature. It is important for investors to predict price fluctuations in advance in order to make good investment decisions.

Therefore, volatility forecasts are pertinent to estimating potential price swings. Such forecasting and information are also useful for devising quantitative financial trading strategies. However, it must be noted that the situation in crypto markets differs from that encountered in traditional markets. Crypto markets are high in volatility and complexity and forecasting prices is one of the most formidable tasks in these markets (Murray *et al.*, 2023). The literature suggests that one of the most common approaches followed by researchers to address this problem is to frame it as a time-series forecasting problem. Different models have been applied to ascertain the accuracy of price predictions (Wirawan & Widiyaningtyas, 2019).

Derbentsev *et al.* (2021) employed machine learning models for the purpose of forecasting. The researchers used stochastic gradient boosting machines, random forests, support vector machines (SVM), etc. These techniques help focus on identifying the most influential features in order to improve prediction accuracy.

In addition to machine learning models, a strand of research focuses on deep learning models to predict prices. Khedr *et al.* (2021) showed how deep learning models can enhance forecasting accuracy in cryptocurrency price predictions. They further delved into the widespread success of these models in the area of quantitative finance. Deep learning models are proficient at recognizing patterns, particularly neural networks. These models have the ability to identify intricate relationships in historical data, which can be challenging for traditional methods.

Pabuçcu & Ongan (2023) forecasted Bitcoin price movements. The researchers adopted four different methods of machine learning, ANN, naïve Bayes (NB), SVM and random forest, and one traditional method, logistic regression, as a benchmark. The researchers tested the algorithm and found that ANN is the most robust method, whereas NB is the worst performing model on the dataset.

A study conducted by Zhang *et al.* (1998) found that the application of ANN is more useful for predicting time series. The technique invalidates the findings of linear statistical method ARIMA. Racine (2001) further confirms this result in his study, in which the researcher argues that ARIMA, as a linear method of forecasting, could not capture the non-linear patterns of complex problems. A research study conducted by Kim (2003) found that stock market predictions could be made more accurate by using machine learning methods. Moreover, a study by Chen *et al.* (2015) found that LSTM, a deep-learning-based model, works best for forecasting stock returns. The researchers used this method to forecast Chinese stock market returns. Sagheer & Kotb (2019) used the same technique for past production forecasting. The study further examined the performance of models based on long- and short-term memory. The findings of the study reveal the failure of classical methods in forecasting due to the complexity of data and models.

Siami-Namini & Namin (2018) conducted an empirical study using the machine-learning-based technique LSTM and traditional forecasting methods such as ARIMA. The findings of the study reveal that LSTM outperforms the ARIMA method. The study used monthly data from different indices, such as NIKKIE, S&P 500, DJI and HIS.

Further, a study conducted by Lie *et al.* (2020) used hybrid methods, such as ARIMA–LSTM, to investigate the forecasting power of those models. The findings reveal that the hybrid method has exceptional forecasting power. Livieris *et al.* (2020) tested a similar technique on gold prices to accurately predict profitable opportunities from fluctuations in the prices.

Bhasker *et al.* (2022), in their research study, provided a bibliometric analysis and highlighted the significance of digital currencies. The researchers emphasized that the advancements in technology and the increase in the level of globalization have empowered digital currencies. In addition to this, the study also asserts that the digital currencies of major economies have the potential to challenge the supremacy of the dollar. In this context, it is essential not only to study digital currencies but also to apply robust methods for developing and analyzing models that enable better forecasting.

Aslam *et al.* (2022) used predictive models to propose a framework for fraud detection models. The study employed AI methods to develop an effective fraud detection mechanism. The focus of the study was on the insurance industry. The findings of the study reveal that SVM outperform other machine learning methods, including ANN (artificial neural networks, NB (Naive Bayes, and Random Forests, in terms of accuracy and efficiency in detecting fraud. The study did not limit itself to empirical testing; it also provided functions for real-time problem-solving.

Moreover, Aggarwal *et al.* (2023) forecasted Bitcoin prices through machine learning and AI-based models. The study highlighted the highly volatile nature of the digital currency Bitcoin, labeling it "explosive behavior." The researchers used different models, such as ARIMA, decision trees, random forest, SVM and LSTM, to forecast the series. The focus of the study was to analyze the behavior of Bitcoin returns during the period of COVID-19 and the Russia–Ukraine War. The findings of the study reveal that among all the models, the AI–LSTM model performs best.

Murray *et al.* (2023) also studied cryptocurrency forecasting by performing a comparative analysis of machine learning and deep learning methods. The study considered five popular currencies and proposed a temporal fusion transformer. The study concluded that deep learning models, such as LSTM, are the best predictors.

10.3. Hypotheses

H_1: Traditional forecasting methods forecast Bitcoin price behavior better than machine learning methods.

H_2: Machine learning forecasting methods predict Bitcoin price behavior better than classical methods.

H_3: Hybrid GARCH–LSTM outperforms classical forecasting methods in predicting Bitcoin price behavior.

10.4. Methodology

This study considers the hourly data of Bitcoin price to achieve the set objectives. Hourly data were obtained for three years, from April 2019 to April 2022, from the CoinMarketCap website. We extracted the tables and figures using the Python programming language. Figure 10.1 shows the distribution of closing prices for the Bitcoin series from April 2019 to April 2022. The figure clearly shows that the data are not normally distributed and depicts an asymmetrical double-peak trend.

The period was selected based on the availability of hourly data. The classical methods considered are the ARIMA, ARFIMA and GARCH techniques, whereas for the machine learning methods, LSTM, ARIMA–LSTM and GARCH–LSTM are considered. The study follows the method used by Li *et al.* (2020) and Arslan (2021) for hybrid modeling.

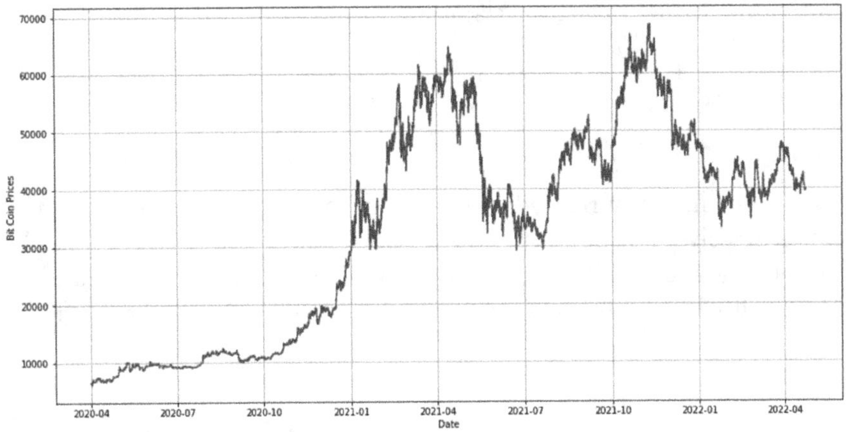

Figure 10.1. Plot of Bitcoin prices.
Source: Data provided by CoinMarketCap.

10.4.1. *ARIMA model*

To analyze the time-series data, the ARIMA (p, d and q) model is an important method. It is the combination of the autoregressive (AR) and moving average (MA) models. The structure of the ARMA model is as follows:

$$\begin{aligned} z_t = \delta_0 + \delta_1 z_{t-1} + \delta_2 z_{t-2} + \cdots + \delta_p z_{t-p} \\ + \epsilon_0 - \gamma_1 \epsilon_{t-1} + \gamma_2 \epsilon_{t-2} + \cdots + \gamma_q \epsilon_{t-q}, \end{aligned} \tag{10.1}$$

where

$$\begin{gathered} \delta_i = 0, \gamma_q \neq 0, \\ E(\epsilon_t) = 0, \mathrm{Var}(\epsilon_t) = {\sigma_u}^2, \\ E(\epsilon_t \epsilon_s) = 0, s \neq t, \\ E(\gamma_s \epsilon_t) = 0, \forall s < t. \end{gathered}$$

z_t is an independent variable, and z_{t-1} is the lag sequence. δ_1 is the self-regressive parameter, and ϵ_0 is the error term.

Equation (10.1) is used to implement the ARMA model, which models stationary data. However, when the sequence is non-stationary, there is a need to make it stationary by taking differentials, for which the ARIMA model is appropriate. This converted stationary model is written as follows:

$$Z_t^* + (1 - B)^d Z_t. \tag{10.2}$$

10.4.2. *ARFIMA model*

Long-term memory-related issues in the data are handled using the autoregressive fractionally integrated moving average (ARFIMA) model. The parameters established under this model are also used to deal with the long-term correlations:

$$\theta(B)Y_t = \theta(B)(1 - B)^{-d}\epsilon_t,$$

where $(1 - B)^{-d}$ is a fractional term and $\theta(B) = 1\theta(B)\ldots\ldots\theta_p$ and $\theta(B) = 1 + \theta(B) + \cdots\theta_q B^q$ are the AR and MA operators, respectively.

10.4.2.1. *GARCH model*

This model belongs to the ARCH family and is used to measure volatility in time-series data:

$$Z_t = \alpha_0 + \alpha_t Z_{t-1} + \mu_t,\ \mu_t \sim \mathbb{N}\{0\sigma_u^2\},$$
$$\sigma_u^2 = \alpha_0 + \alpha_1\mu_{t-1}^2 + \beta_1\sigma_{u-1}^2,$$

where Z_t are the returns calculated from the series, σ_u^2 is the conditional variance and μ_{t-1}^2 is the unexpected return squared.

10.4.3. *Machine learning methods*

The study used LSTM, ARIMA–LSTM and GARCH–LSTM to investigate the forecasting ability of machine learning methods.

10.4.3.1. *LSTM*

This machine learning algorithm uses LSTM networks to forecast time series. The usefulness of the information is measured by adding an LSTM processor. This processor is based on RNN. The model uses three important gates to process information: forget gate, input gate and output gate.

The LSTM method follows a sequence where each LSTM unit's output from one step serves as the input for the subsequent step.

Each step in this process yields an output. Further, for each current step, an LSTM unit generates a state vector that contains very important information. The model also uses three important gates in the process, as described above. The following depicts the cell state formula, a model with forget, input and output gates, representing the information carried by each gate:

$$x_t = W_t x_{t-1} + j_t \tanh(Z_{xc} Y_t + Z_{hc} h_{t-1} + b_c),$$

where x_t is the cell state, W_t is the current forget state, j_t is the current input layer, Y_t represents the token of the current input sentence and h_{t-1} represents the hidden layer output.

The forget gate l_t (eq,), input gate (m_t) and, finally, output gate n_t implement the following information:

$$l_t = \sigma(\emptyset_{xf} x_t + \delta_{hf} h_{t-1} + \vartheta_{cf} c_{t-1} + b_f),$$

$$m_t = \sigma(\emptyset_{xi} x_t + \delta_{hi} h_{t-1} + \vartheta_{ci} c_{t-1} + b_i),$$

$$n_t = \sigma(\emptyset_{xo} x_t + \delta_{ho} h_{t-1} + \vartheta_{co} c_{t-1} + b_o).$$

The model for the hidden layer output is as follows:

$$H_t = n_t \tanh(c_i).$$

10.4.3.2. *ARIMA LSTM*

This modified ARIMA model can be obtained through the following steps, which are used in the current study for analyzing high-frequency financial time-series data.

The steps include first observing the pulse of the data using their descriptive statistics and preparing the data according to the model requirements. Second, the ARIMA model is constructed after executing the ADF test for any lag values. The third step involves obtaining the optimal values, calculating the residuals of the ARIMA model using optimal parameters and modeling the residuals through LSTM.

Evaluation Criteria

For evaluation, the following parameters are used. Here, R_i is the forecasted value and P_i is the actual value.

Mean Squared Error (MSE):

$$\mathrm{MSE} = \frac{1}{n}\Sigma(X_1 - Y_1)\hat{}2.$$

Mean Absolute Error (MAE):

$$\mathrm{MAE} = \frac{1}{n}\Sigma|X_i - Y_i|.$$

Root Mean Squared Error (RMSE):

$$\mathrm{RMSE} = \sqrt{\mathrm{MSE}}.$$

Mean Absolute Percentage Error (MAPE):

$$\mathrm{MAPE} = \frac{100}{n}\Sigma|X_i - Y_i|/Z_i.$$

Monte Carlo Simulations

It is pertinent to note that the generation of relevant data is critical for applying ARIMA to financial time-series data.

The stochastic differential equation based on the Black–Scholes model is as follows:

$$dY_t = rY_t dt + \sigma Y_t dB_t,$$

where Y_t is the targeted level of asset price at time t; σ is the volatility at the targeted level, which is fixed; r denotes the risk-free, fixed and short-term rate of interest and Brownian motion is represented by B.

To measure the high-frequency financial time series, the following model is used, which is expressed as a stochastic differential equation (SDE):

$$Y_t = Y_{t-\Delta t}\exp\left\{\left(r - \frac{1}{2}\sigma^2\right)\Delta t + \sigma\sqrt{\Delta t B_t}\right\}.$$

Figure 10.2 presents the Monte Carlo simulation pathways for the Bitcoin series selected for this study. The simulation comprehensively exhibits the actual situation and trends. It serves as a reliable source of data for ARIMA applications.

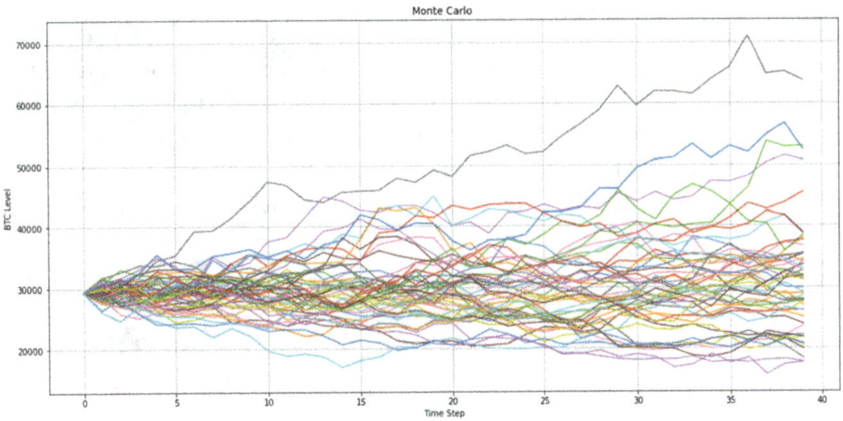

Figure 10.2. Monte Carlo simulations.
Source: Data provided by CoinMarketCap.

10.4.3.3. *Model estimation for machine learning*

The study used a 70:30 data set split for training and testing the machine learning models, respectively. Numerous parameters were used to optimize the learning ability of the machine.

For LSTM, this study used the closing prices of Bitcoin as the only input to predict the output. Two layers of neurons were utilized. The first layer contained 64 neurons and 20 dense neurons. The second layer comprised 50 neurons and 1 dense neuron to generate output. A drop out rate of 20% has been applied to the nodes to prevent overfitting. (Li *et al.*, 2020).

As for the activation function, which is the most pivotal part of the optimization of neural networks, the number and types of activation functions available in the Keras library can be found. The current study used the tanh activation function as it performs better than other functions. Lie *et al.* (2020) also used the same activation function for stock market prediction in their study. Further, RMSProp was used as an optimizer function for the study, and MSE was used to define the loss. The batch size was set at 256, while the buffer size of 1,700 was set based on sample data. The study maintained an evaluation interval of 300 in each epoch, and the number of epochs (iterations) was set as 100.

10.4.4. *Model comparison*

Figures 10.3 and 10.4 demonstrate that the ARIMA model captures the overall trend only and does not depict the large deviations within the data. On the contrary, the ARIMA–LSTM model, after forecasting the overall trend, can correct the error term through deep learning. Consequently, the curve predicted by the ARIMA–LSTM

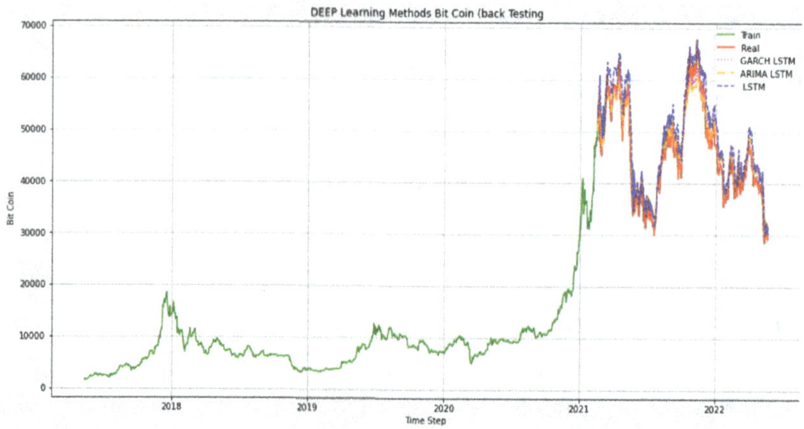

Figure 10.3. Deep learning methods (Bitcoin back-testing plot).
Source: Data provided by CoinMarketCap.

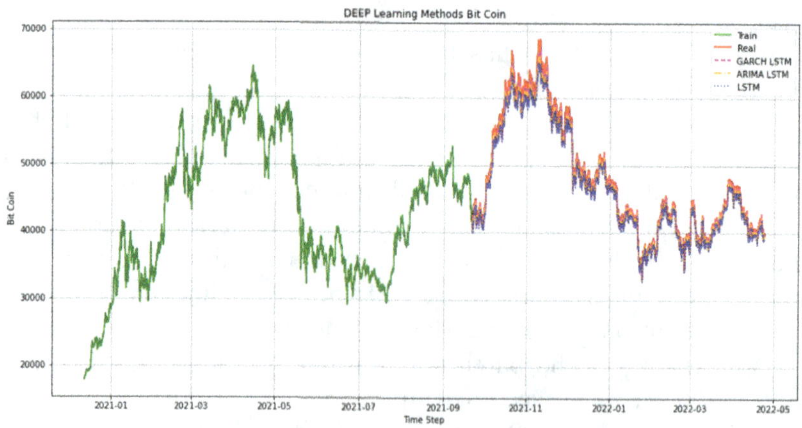

Figure 10.4. Machine learning forecasting method for Bitcoin.
Source: Data provided by CoinMarketCap.

model is more consistent with the curve plotted using the original data.

10.5. Analysis

Table 10.1 presents a summary of the data set that has been used for this study. The value of the mean represents the average point of the considered data series. The dispersion of data from its mean values is described by the standard deviation. Skewness and kurtosis generally measure the location of the data; the negative value of skewness shows that the data are left-skewed, while the kurtosis value being less than 3 shows the platykurtic behavior of the series.

10.5.1. *Data preprocessing*

To check for stationarity and seasonality in the data, the ADF test is applied. The p-value of ADF for the Bitcoin return series used in the analysis is shown in Table 10.2. It indicates a lag correlation result with one lag.

Table 10.1. Descriptive statistics.

	Prices ($)
Mean	34934.8
Median	38795
Maximum	68577
Minimum	6134
Std. Dev.	17613.06
Skewness	−0.24043
Kurtosis	1.755039
Jarque-Bera	1264.029
Probability	0

Table 10.2. ADF and ARCH tests.

	***t*-statistic**	**Prob.**	**ARCH**
Level	−1.719981	0.4211	0
1st Diff.	−130.5767	0.0001	

Table 10.3. Classical model computation.

	Model	AR	MA	AIC	d	ARCH(−4)	GARCH(−3)
ARIMA	(4, 4)	−0.7708	0.7857	−6.6652	–	–	–
		(0.000)	(0.000)	–	–	–	–
ARFIMA	(2, 2)	0.3457	−0.3753	−6.6629	−0.0121	–	–
		(0.0189)	(0.0101)	–	(0.0089)	–	–
GARCH	(4, 3)	–	–	−7.0544	–	0.0893	−0.6351
		–	–	–	–	(0.000)	(0.000)

Table 10.3 shows that for the Bitcoin series, the ARIMA order (4, 4) is the best-fitting model. The AIC value is −6.6652. The AR term has a coefficient value of −0.7708, with a significant p-value. This means that the pattern exists in the Bitcoin market. The results of the MA term show an adjustment in delayed information. Further, for the ARFIMA model specification for the Bitcoin stock returns, Table 10.3 shows that the model uses orders (2, 2) for p and q. The AIC value is −6.6629. The d parameter value is estimated at −0.0121 for the Bitcoin market. As the p-value of the d parameter is significant, it shows that the market follows an intermediate memory pattern. This means the ARFIMA model is a good fit for this market. Finally, as the ARCH term is present in the series, the GARCH (4, 3) model was computed for the Bitcoin data. The results show that $\alpha 1$, i.e. ARCH (−4), has a coefficient value of 0.0893 and $\beta 1$, i.e. GARCH (−3), has a coefficient value of −6.351. Both coefficients have significant p-values, which show the existence of the ARCH effect and its persistence. This implies that the current price behavior is due to past price behavior.

Table 10.4 shows the MSE, MAE, RMSE and MAPE values for all the models, both classical and machine learning. It is evident that all indicator values are higher for ARIMA, ARFIMA and GARCH. On the other hand, R^2, which indicates goodness of fit, is significantly smaller – ARIMA: 0.004729, ARFIMA: 0.001661 and GARCH: 0.000103. This situation is reversed in the machine learning models, and their results show improved forecasting of the high-frequency financial data. The machine learning technique improves the accuracy of models.

Table 10.4. Comparative model computation.

	MSE	MAE	RMSE	MAPE	R^2
ARIMA	2.66E+08	10818.08	16317.07	27.59012	0.004729
ARFIMA	2.62E+08	10652.82	16172.06	27.07349	0.001661
GARCH	4.52E+08	15940.31	21271.23	42.27892	0.000103
LSTM	1805038	1192.591	1343.517	2.401418	0.974879
ARIMA–LSTM	720187.1	723.1542	848.6384	2.401418	0.989976
GARCH–LSTM	402232.9	489.2288	634.2183	0.96566	0.994402

Table 10.5. *P*-statistics of the KS test.

	ARIMA	ARFIMA	GARCH	LSTM	ARIMA–LSTM	GARCH–LSTM
ARIMA	1					
ARFIMA	0	1				
GARCH	0	0	1			
LSTM	0	0	0	1		
ARIMA–LSTM	0	0	0	0	1	
GARCH–LSTM	0	0	0	0	0	1

Moreover, it is pertinent to note that the classical ARIMA model only predicts the overall trend in the original data (and may not predict/identify large fluctuations), whereas the LSTM–ARIMA model can address this limitation by using a deep learning algorithm.

The purpose of the KS (Kolmogorov–Smirnov) test is to perform a pairwise test on the residual series of the model. The null hypothesis of the KS test is that two sequences have the same distribution. If the p-value at a 5% level of significance is less than 0.05, then this null hypothesis is rejected, and it is considered that the series likely have different distribution characteristics in different models. The results of the KS test (Table 10.5) for the data series used in the current study for different models show that the two models do not follow the same distribution and the difference between them prevails.

Forecasting indicators in Table 10.6 show MSE (2.76E+08), MAE (10729.09), RMSE (16602.02) and MAPE (42.24232). For the ARFIMA model, the estimated results are MSE: 2.74E+08, MAE: 10709.91, RMSE: 16561.31 and MAPE: 42.21824. For the

Table 10.6. Back-testing (daily data).

	MSE	MAE	RMSE	MAPE	R2
ARIMA	2.76E+08	10729.09	16602.02	42.24232	0.016664
ARFIMA	2.74E+08	10709.91	16561.31	42.21824	0.017638
GARCH	5.04E+08	15459.86	22450.42	61.51013	0.000877
LSTM	13265744	3114.246	3642.217	6.927074	0.842231
ARIMA–LSTM	7239982	2257.02	2690.721	4.812663	0.913895
GARCH–LSTM	6626202	2092.534	2574.141	4.1341	0.921287

GARCH model, 100 observations are used to train the model and 20 observations-ahead forecasting windows are used. The forecasting accuracy indicators are MSE: 5.04E+08, MAE: 15459.86, RMSE: 22450.42 and MAPE: 61.51013.

For the Bitcoin market LSTM, the values of the parameters are MSE: 13265744, MAE: 3114.246, RMSE: 3642.217 and MAPE: 6.927074. For the hybrid ARIMA–LSTM method, the values are MSE: 7239982, MAE: 2257.02, RMSE: 2690.721 and MAPE: 4.812663. Finally, for the hybrid GARCH–LSTM method, the values are MSE: 6626202, MAE: 2092.534, RMSE: 2574.141 and MAPE: 4.812663. Lower values of the indicators for the machine learning models imply their better performance as compared to the classical models. Table 10.6 shows the back-testing results on daily data; it shows similar results as obtained in the hourly data for all the classical and machine learning models.

10.6. Discussion

The current study comparing traditional forecasting methods with machine learning methods for predicting Bitcoin returns yields meaningful insights. The findings demonstrate the superiority of machine learning methods over traditional methods. The results show a clear indication of the robustness of the former. One of the reasons for this forecasting performance may be attributed to the proficiency of the machine learning models in handling high-frequency data, a characteristic prevalent in the underlying study. Given the dynamic and highly volatile nature of the Bitcoin market as well as the hourly data used for this study, these two features align with the strengths of the machine learning models. The study also provides clear evidence that, in order to capture the nuanced market dynamics in the case of Bitcoin, these models are more suitable.

This study contributes to the literature by showing the robustness of forecasting using machine learning when compared to using classical methods. A number of research studies, such as those by Murray *et al.* (2023) and Aggarwal *et al.* (2023), support and strengthen the results of this work. These studies show a consensus regarding the efficacy of machine learning models for cryptocurrency forecasting.

10.7. Conclusion

This study aimed to investigate which forecasting method is most useful for forecasting Bitcoin returns. We applied traditional forecasting models and machine learning methods to perform the forecasting. The empirical results show that machine learning methods outperform traditional methods, as the explanatory power of the models under machine learning forecasting is strong. One of the reasons for the superior forecasting performance of machine learning methods lies in their ability to effectively handle the high frequency of the data used in this study.

10.7.1. *Critical analysis in the light of previous studies*

The findings of this study affirm those of earlier studies conducted by researchers such as Siami-Nimini & Namin (2018) and Lie *et al.* (2020) in recent years. The current study also confirms the hypotheses posed at the beginning of the study and suggests that machine learning and hybrid methods are more robust than classical methods. The findings of Murray *et al.* (2023) and Aggarwal *et al.* (2023) also support this conclusion.

10.7.2. *Limitations*

The study is not free from limitations.

First, the market under consideration for this study was Bitcoin, and not all the markets are the same. Therefore, different parameters are required to handle the dynamics of different markets.

Second, the frequency of data used for this study was hourly, and back-testing was conducted using 10-minute intervals. Therefore, computational limitations should be considered. Changing parameters and using some other functions (such as batch size and number of neurons) may add value and improve the results further. Lastly, other variants may also be used in future research; for instance, wavelet data denoising techniques and other variants of the GARCH family of models, such as EGARCH, can advance this research further.

10.7.3. *Policy implications*

Overall, the results show that investors must take into consideration the discussed factors while making investment decisions. The risk of using forecasting methods which cannot make accurate predictions can adversely affect their investments. Policymakers should consider these factors while forming their decisions. If research techniques are not wisely used, the results could be misleading, which in turn could inform policy decisions that have adverse effects instead of stabilizing the situation.

References

Aggarwal, V., Sharma, S., Kumar, P., Mohnot, J., & Yadav, M. (2023). Lessons from the Russia-Ukraine War: portfolio optimisation in cryptos and stocks for investors in Ghana. *International Journal of Diplomacy and Economy*, 9(2), 160–175.

Arslan, M. (2021). Forecasting Bettle in High Frequency Data: Classical, Machine Learning and Deep Learning Methods. (Master of Science Major in Finance), Capital University of Science and Technology Pakistan. https://thesis.cust.edu.pk/UploadedFiles/Muhammad%20Arslan-MMS191017.pdf.

Ashraf, B. N. (2020). Economic impact of government interventions during the COVID-19 pandemic: International evidence from financial markets. *Journal of Behavioral and Experimental Finance*, 27, 100371. https://doi.org/10.1016/j.jbef.2020.100371.

Aslam, F., Hunjra, A. I., Ftiti, Z., Louhichi, W., & Shams, T. (2022). Insurance fraud detection: Evidence from artificial intelligence and machine learning. *Research in International Business and Finance*, 62, 101744.

Bhaskar, R., Hunjra, A. I., Bansal, S., & Pandey, D. K. (2022). Central bank digital currencies: agendas for future research. *Research in International Business and Finance*, 62, 101737.

Boehmer, E. & Kelley, E. K. (2009). Institutional investors and the informational efficiency of prices. *The Review of Financial Studies*, 22(9), 3563–3594. https://doi.org/10.1093/rfs/hhp028.

Chen, X., Jin, S., Qin, S., & Li, L. (2015). Short-term wind speed forecasting study and its application using a hybrid model optimized by cuckoo search. *Mathematical Problems in Engineering*, 2015, 18. https://doi.org/10.1155/2015/608597.

Chu, J., Chan, S., Nadarajah, S., & Osterrieder, J. (2017). GARCH modelling of cryptocurrencies. *Journal of Risk and Financial Management*, 10(4), 17. https://doi.org/10.3390/jrfm10040017.

Derbentsev, V., Babenko, V., Khrustalev, K., Obruch, H., & Khrustalova, S. (2021). Comparative performance of machine learning ensemble algorithms for forecasting cryptocurrency prices. *International Journal of Engineering*, 34, 140–148. https://doi.org/10.5829/ije.2021.34.01a.16.

Fama, E. F. (1970). Efficient capital markets: A review of theory and empirical work. *The Journal of Finance*, 25(2), 383–417. https://doi.org/10.2307/2325486.

Famiglietti, M. & Leibovici, F. (2022). The impact of health and economic policies on the spread of COVID-19 and economic activity. *European Economic Review*, 144, 104087. https://doi.org/10.1016/j.euroecorev.2022.104087.

Gkillas, K. & Katsiampa, P. (2018). An application of extreme value theory to cryptocurrencies. *Economics Letters*, 164, 109–111. https://doi.org/10.1016/j.econlet.2018.01.020.

Goldman, S. (1999). Computational learning theory. In Goldman, S. A. (Ed.), *Algorithms and Theory of Computation Handbook: General Concepts and Techniques*. Missouri: Citeseer.

Goodell, J. W. & Shen, D. (2021). The Chinese sovereign digital currency as a catalyst for change: A new trilemma? In *Understanding Cryptocurrency Fraud* (pp. 177–186). Berlin/Boston, MA: De Gruyter. https://doi.org/10.1515/9783110718485-014.

Howell, B. E. & Potgieter, P. H. (2021). Central Bank issued digital currencies. *SSRN Electronic Journal*. https://doi.org/10.2139/ssrn.3782968.

Jobson, J.D. and Korkie, B.M. (1981) Performance hypothesis testing with the Sharpe and Treynor measures. *The Journal of Finance*, 36, 4. https://doi.org/10.1111/j.1540-6261.1981.tb04891.x

Khairalla, M. & AL-Jallad, N. T. (2017). Hybrid forecasting scheme for financial time-series data using neural network and statistical methods. *International Journal of Advanced Computer Science and Applications*, 8(9), 319–327.

Khedr, A. M., Arif, I., El-Bannany, M., Alhashmi, S. M., & Sreedharan, M. (2021). Cryptocurrency price prediction using traditional statistical and machine-learning techniques: A survey. *Intelligent Systems in Accounting, Finance and Management*, 28(1), 3–34. https://doi.org/10.1002/isaf.1488.

Kim, K.-J. (2003). Financial time series forecasting using support vector machines. *Neurocomputing*, 55(1), 307–319. https://doi.org/10.1016/S0925-2312(03)00372-2.

Kristoufek, L. (2013). BitCoin meets Google Trends and Wikipedia: Quantifying the relationship between phenomena of the Internet era. *Scientific Reports*, 3(1), 1–7. https://doi.org/10.1038/srep03415.

Li, Z., Han, J., & Song, Y. (2020). On the forecasting of high-frequency financial time series based on ARIMA model improved by deep learning. *Journal of Forecasting*, 39(7), 1081–1097. https://doi.org/10.1002/for.2677.

Livieris, I. E., Pintelas, E., & Pintelas, P. (2020). A CNN–LSTM model for gold price time-series forecasting. *Neural Computing and Applications*, 32, 17351–17360. https://doi.org/10.1007/s00521-020-04867-x.

Murray, K., Rossi, A., Carraro, D., & Visentin, A. (2023). On forecasting cryptocurrency prices: A comparison of machine learning, deep learning, and ensembles. *Forecasting*, 5(1), 196–209.

Pabuçcu, H., Ongan, S., & Ongan, A. (2023). Forecasting the movements of Bitcoin prices: An application of machine learning algorithms. *arXiv preprint* arXiv:2303.04642. https://doi.org/10.3934/QFE.2020031.

Racine, J. (2001). On the nonlinear predictability of stock returns using financial and economic variables. *Journal of Business & Economic Statistics*, 19(3), 380–382. https://doi.org/10.1198/073500101681019927.

Sagheer, A. & Kotb, M. (2019). Time series forecasting of petroleum production using deep LSTM recurrent networks. *Neurocomputing*, 323, 203–213. https://doi.org/10.1016/j.neucom.2018.09.082.

Siami-Namini, S. & Namin, A. S. (2018). Forecasting economics and financial time series: ARIMA vs. LSTM. *arXiv preprint* arXiv:1803.06386. https://doi.org/10.48550/arXiv.1803.06386.

Urquhart, A. (2017). Price clustering in Bitcoin. *Economics Letters*, 159, 145–148. https://doi.org/10.1016/j.econlet.2017.07.035.

Wan, C., Xu, Z., Wang, Y., Dong, Z. Y., & Wong, K. P. (2013). A hybrid approach for probabilistic forecasting of electricity price. *IEEE*

Transactions on Smart Grid, 5(1), 463–470. https://doi.org/10.1109/TSG.2013.2274465.

Wirawan, I. M., Widiyaningtyas, T., & Hasan, M. M. (2019, September). Short term prediction on bitcoin price using ARIMA method. In *2019 International Seminar on Application for Technology of Information and Communication* (iSemantic) (pp. 260–265). IEEE. https://doi.org/10.1109/ISEMANTIC.2019.8884257.

Zhang, G., Patuwo, B. E., & Hu, M. Y. (1998). Forecasting with artificial neural networks: The state of the art. *International Journal of Forecasting*, 14(1), 35–62. https://doi.org/10.1016/S0169-2070(97)00044-7.

https://doi.org/10.1142/9781800616257_0011

Chapter 11

Does Economic Policy Uncertainty Predict Cryptocurrency Returns?

Muhammad A. Cheema[*,§], **Kenneth R. Szulczyk**[†,¶], **and Elie Bouri**[‡,||]

[*]*Otago School of Business, University of Otago, Dunedin, New Zealand*

[†]*Al Akhawayn University School of Business, Ifrane, Morocco*

[‡]*USEK Business School, Holy Spirit University of Kaslik, Jounieh, Lebanon*

[§]*muhammad.cheema@otago.ac.nz*

[¶]*k.szulczyk@aui.ma*

[||]*eliebouri@usek.edu.lb*

Abstract

We examine whether the economic policy uncertainty (EPU) index can predict cryptocurrency returns in countries with the highest number of Bitcoin nodes, which include the US, Germany, France, the Netherlands, Singapore, Canada, the UK, China, Russia and Japan. To the extent that cryptocurrencies are a speculative asset, we hypothesize that an increase in EPU drives cryptocurrency prices below their fundamental values due to the flight-to-quality effect. Then, the prices subsequently undergo correction. Furthermore, we hypothesize that the EPU index predicts better in the long run than in the short run since mispricing takes time to correct. Consistent with our hypothesis, we find that EPU positively predicts cryptocurrency returns in the short run for subsequent 1-month returns and in the long run for subsequent 6- and 12-month returns. Thus, cryptocurrencies cannot act as a hedge or safe haven against other financial assets during uncertain times.

Keywords: Cryptocurrency, return predictability, economic policy uncertainty index, economic policy uncertainty, speculative assets.

> *It's a gambling device ⋯ there's been a lot of frauds connected with it. There's been disappearances, so there's a lot lost on it. Bitcoin hasn't produced anything.*
>
> —Warren Buffett

11.1. Introduction

Cryptocurrencies have become one of the most popular assets in financial markets in recent years because they enable online payments between parties without involving financial institutions. Their prices have also appreciated exponentially. Given this scenario, numerous studies show that investors utilize cryptocurrencies as speculative investments (e.g. Baek & Elbeck, 2015; Baur *et al.*, 2018; Bouoiyour *et al.*, 2015; Cheah & Fry, 2015; Ciaian *et al.*, 2016; Yermack, 2015). However, several studies argue that cryptocurrencies could serve as a hedge or safe haven against other financial assets during uncertain times (e.g. Dyhrberg, 2016; Fang *et al.*, 2019; Stensås *et al.*, 2019; Urquhart & Zhang, 2019). Researchers have widely debated the notion of cryptocurrencies being a safe haven, with many arguing against their effectiveness during financial turmoil or market downturns (see, e.g., Bouri *et al.*, 2017; Cheema *et al.*, 2022; Klein *et al.*, 2018; Smales, 2018). Wu *et al.* (2019) show that Bitcoin serves as a weak hedge against economic policy uncertainty (EPU) during bear and bull markets, while Gurdgiev & O'Loughlin (2020) show that investor sentiment can detect the price direction of cryptocurrencies. Then, cryptocurrencies can hedge against the stock market during times of higher uncertainty. However, Baur *et al.* (2018) find that Bitcoin and the S&P500 are positively correlated during natural disasters, which refutes the notion of cryptocurrencies being a safe haven.

The EPU index can measure uncertainty stemming from market turmoil. Government policy changes, particularly tax and regulatory policies, can trigger uncertainty and, thus, raise the EPU index. Therefore, a high level of EPU raises the risk premium and causes businesses and individuals to delay spending and investments until this uncertainty subsides (Baker *et al.*, 2016). Furthermore, a high

EPU or recession could trigger market uncertainty that affects speculative assets more than safe assets due to the flight-to-quality effect (e.g. Bekaert & Hoerova, 2016; Brogaard & Detzel, 2015; Caballero & Krishnamurthy, 2008; Li *et al.*, 2015).

Several studies examine EPU's impact on cryptocurrency returns and trading behavior. For example, Bouri *et al.* (2019) show that EPU tends to drive herd behavior in 14 leading cryptocurrencies, while Bouri *et al.* (2021) argue that EPU positively affects the integration among cryptocurrencies. However, Demir *et al.* (2018) find a negative relationship between EPU and daily Bitcoin returns and suggest that a rise in EPU causes investors to lose their confidence in the global financial system and traditional currencies while increasing Bitcoin's attractiveness. However, they find positive and significant relationships at both the lower and higher quantiles of EPU and Bitcoin returns. Meanwhile, Al-Yahyaee *et al.* (2019) report a negative relationship between EPU and daily Bitcoin returns. In contrast, Wang *et al.* (2018) find that EPU has little impact on Bitcoin returns, suggesting that investors use Bitcoin as a safe haven during EPU shocks. Finally, Cheng & Yen (2019) find a positive relationship between China's EPU index and monthly Bitcoin returns, while they observe insignificant relationships between monthly Bitcoin returns and the EPU indices of the US, Japan and South Korea.

The research literature on EPU's impact on cryptocurrencies is limited and contradictory for four reasons. First, existing studies use daily data (e.g. Demir *et al.*, 2018). Although the literature is well documented, mispricing could take a long time to correct (e.g. Daniel *et al.*, 1998; Diether *et al.*, 2002; Lamont & Thaler, 2003; Shleifer & Vishny, 1990). Therefore, researchers should examine long time horizons to identify economic indicators' impact on cryptocurrency returns. In fact, several studies use monthly and yearly sentiment data to examine the returns predictability of investor sentiment on the cross-section of stock returns (e.g. Baker & Wurgler, 2006; Huang *et al.*, 2014; Stambaugh *et al.*, 2012).[1]

Second, most of the existing studies examine the impact of EPU on a single cryptocurrency, Bitcoin (Demir *et al.*, 2018;

---

[1]Barrero *et al.* (2017) argue that EPU is crucial for predicting long-term uncertainty.

Al-Yahyaee *et al.*, 2019; Wang *et al.*, 2018). The exception is Bouri *et al.* (2019), who use 14 cryptocurrencies to show that EPU predicts cryptocurrency returns. Therefore, it is imperative to investigate the impact of EPU on the aggregate returns of a large set of cryptocurrencies to obtain conclusive evidence on the return predictability of EPU.

Third, existing studies are inconclusive as to whether EPU can predict cryptocurrency returns. For example, Demir *et al.* (2018) find a negative relationship between EPU and daily Bitcoin returns using a contemporaneous and one-day lagged daily US EPU index. However, they find a positive but insignificant relationship between EPU and daily Bitcoin returns when using 2- to 24-day lagged EPU values. Furthermore, the existing studies, except the one by Cheng & Yen (2019), examine the impact of the US EPU index on Bitcoin returns, although investors outside the US are also able to own Bitcoin. For example, the US, Germany, France and the Netherlands possess almost 50% of the Bitcoin nodes. Thus, a study must include global EPU indices. Refer to Table 11.1 for the countries with the largest number of Bitcoin nodes.

Finally, Cheng & Yen (2019) use mean-based models to study how the EPU indices of China, the US, Japan and South Korea can predict Bitcoin returns and other altcoins. However, we use quantile regression (QR), which is robust to outliers, heteroskedasticity and

Table 11.1. The top 10 countries with the largest Bitcoin nodes.

Rank	Country	Nodes	Percentage (%)
1	US	2,053	20.79
2	Germany	1,807	18.30
3	France	600	6.08
4	Netherlands	462	4.68
5	Canada	305	3.09
6	Singapore	284	2.88
7	UK	256	2.59
8	China	248	2.51
9	Russia	227	2.30
10	Japan	163	1.65

Source: Bitnodes, https://bitnodes.io/.

the skewness of the dependent variables (e.g. Koenker & Hallock, 2001; Schulze, 2004; Zhu *et al.*, 2016).

Because of the contradictory and limited studies, we examine whether a country's monthly EPU index can predict aggregate cryptocurrency returns using data from the top 10 countries with the most Bitcoin nodes. We expect that the countries with the highest number of Bitcoin nodes will also likely have the highest number of non-Bitcoin cryptocurrencies. Cryptocurrencies are considered speculative assets since we expect an EPU surge to lower their prices as uncertainty triggers a flight to quality. Subsequently, cryptocurrency prices revert to their fundamental values following a high level of EPU. Thus, we hypothesize that EPU positively predicts the aggregate returns of cryptocurrencies over 1, 6 and 12 months. Furthermore, we expect EPU to better predict subsequent returns over a longer horizon of 6- and 12-month periods than a 1-month period because mispricing takes time to correct.

We use three estimation techniques: ordinary least squares (OLS), multivariate augmented regression (mARM) by Amihud *et al.* (2009) and QR. Accordingly, we find that EPU positively influences the subsequent returns of cryptocurrencies over the next one month, with exceptions in China, the Netherlands and Russia. Furthermore, consistent with our hypothesis, we find that EPU predicts the subsequent returns better over a longer horizon because mispricing takes time to correct. For example, EPU positively affects the aggregate cryptocurrency returns over the next 6 and 12 months and is statistically significant for all countries, except China and the Netherlands. The results remain robust when using the aggregate returns of the top 30 and 144 cryptocurrencies and the three regression methods.

We make two contributions to the literature. First, we are the first to show a positive impact of EPU indices, covering 10 developed and emerging economies, on the aggregate returns of cryptocurrencies over longer horizons of 6 and 12 months. Second, based on various models, including a quantile-based one, we provide empirical evidence that cryptocurrencies are speculative assets and are not safe havens during periods of high uncertainty.

This chapter has the following structure. Section 11.2 explains the data sources and methodology. Section 11.3 analyzes results from the OLS, mARM and QR estimators, while Section 11.4 discusses the results. Section 11.5 concludes the chapter.

11.2. Data and Methods

Following the academic literature (e.g. Grobys & Sapkota, 2019), the sample includes all cryptocurrencies that use the proof-of-work mechanism and are available before 31 December 2014. The cryptocurrency data come from CoinMarketCap.com, which provides cryptocurrency data after 28 April 2013. The data period ranges from 1 May 2013 to 30 April 2019, yielding 72 monthly observations. In total, 144 cryptocurrencies meet the criteria. The data include Bitcoin and other leading cryptocurrencies, such as Paycoin, Litecoin, Stellar and Dogecoin, representing about 90% of the cryptocurrency market capitalization.

To estimate aggregate cryptocurrency returns, we use all 144 cryptocurrencies. Furthermore, to address concerns about how small cryptocurrencies may skew our results due to their high volatility, we also estimate aggregate returns utilizing the top 30 cryptocurrencies by market capitalization.

The EPU indices come from the top 10 countries with the most Bitcoin nodes: the US, Germany, France, Netherlands, Singapore, Canada, the UK, China, Russia and Japan. The EPU Index (2019), which Baker *et al.* (2016) developed, is based on policy uncertainty derived by analyzing newspaper articles.

To examine the EPU's predictability for subsequent aggregate cryptocurrency returns, we estimate the following regression:

$$\mathrm{RC}_{t+k} = \alpha + \beta \cdot \mathrm{EPU}_t + \mu_{t+k}, \qquad (11.1)$$

where RC is the equal-weighted (EW) aggregate cryptocurrency returns in month $t+k$ ($k = 1, 6 \text{ or } 12$) based on either the log-returns of the 144 or top 30 cryptocurrencies.[2] The slope, β, represents the sensitivity of aggregate cryptocurrency returns over the k months to the EPU index in month t. A positive slope indicates that the EPU positively affects cryptocurrency returns.

We use OLS, mARM proposed by Amihud *et al.* (2009) and QR developed by Koenker & Bassett (1978) to estimate Equation (11.1). Even though OLS can estimate the slope, it is susceptible to the well-known Stambaugh (1999) small-sample bias. Therefore, we utilize

[2]The results remain similar when we use value-weighted aggregate returns of cryptocurrencies. For the sake of brevity, we do not report those results.

mARM to minimize this bias. An incorrect magnitude or sign of $\hat{\beta}$ could lead to erroneous conclusions. Furthermore, we estimate the QR for the 0.05, 0.10, 0.25, 0.50, 0.75, 0.90 and 0.95 quantiles. The 0.75, 0.90 and 0.95 quantiles contain positive cryptocurrency returns during bull markets, while the 0.05, 0.10 and 0.25 quantiles contain negative cryptocurrency returns during bear markets. The 0.95 and 0.05 quantiles capture the largest gains or losses in cryptocurrency returns (Rejeb & Arfaoui, 2016). The 0.50 quantile corresponds to the central tendency, while OLS estimates the mean.

QR offers several benefits:

1. QR is not sensitive to outliers.
2. Each quantile models different investor behavior.
3. QR preserves the heteroscedasticity of the error terms, μ_{t+k}, by using a wild bootstrap (e.g. Koenker & Hallock, 2001; Schulze, 2004; Zhu *et al.*, 2016). The standard error of the slope, $\hat{\beta}$, is estimated using a wild bootstrap with 2,000 replications.

11.3. Empirical Findings

We discuss the results in three sections. The first section examines the descriptive statistics of EPU and cryptocurrency returns. The second section estimates the regression with one lag to assess whether the EPU can predict the next month's cryptocurrency return. The third section tests EPU's predictability over 6 and 12 months.

11.3.1. *Descriptive statistics*

Table 11.2 summarizes the descriptive statistics of each country's EPU and aggregate cryptocurrency returns. Panel A shows that the mean aggregate return based on all 144 (top 30) cryptocurrencies is −2.80% (−1.00%) per month. The returns drop to a minimum of −111.00% (−89.80%) and rise to a maximum of 90% (171.1%) per month, indicating that aggregate cryptocurrency returns experience wide swings.

Panel B shows the correlations between EPU indices and aggregate cryptocurrency returns. Each country's EPU strongly and positively correlates with other countries' EPUs, except for the

Table 11.2. Descriptive statistics.

Panel A: Descriptive statistics

Variable	Obs.	Mean	Median	Minimum	Maximum
US EPU	72	132	119	64	284
Germany EPU	72	170	161	65	454
France EPU	72	256	239	132	575
Netherlands EPU	72	86	85	28	203
Singapore EPU	72	160	144	77	351
Canada EPU	72	225	217	111	450
UK EPU	72	164	136	62	558
China EPU	72	163	130	59	438
Russia EPU	72	203	199	55	400
Japan EPU	72	105	101	63	208
RC all	72	−0.028	−0.058	−1.110	0.904
RC top30	72	−0.010	−0.053	−0.898	1.711

Panel B: Correlation matrix

	1	2	3	4	5	6	7	8	9	10	11	12
(1) USA	1.00											
(2) Germany	0.55	1.00										
(3) France	0.58	0.66	1.0									
(4) Netherlands	−0.08	—	0.0	1.00								
(5) Singapore	0.70	0.69	0.6	—	1.0							
(6) Canada	0.57	0.40	0.3	—	0.6	1.00						
(7) UK	0.47	0.72	0.5	—	0.6	0.32	1.0					
(8) China	0.43	0.27	0.2	—	0.6	0.58	0.2	1.0				
(9) Russia	0.13	0.14	0.0	0.04	0.1	0.06	0.0	0.1	1.00			
(10) Japan	0.40	0.66	0.5	0.08	0.5	0.12	0.6	0.0	0.03	1.00		
(11) RC all	0.05	0.18	0.2	—	0.1	—	0.2	0.0	0.03	0.03	1.0	
(12) RC	0.00	0.06	0.1	—	0.0	—	0.0	0.0	—	—	0.9	1.0

Notes: Panel A summarizes the descriptive statistics of each country's EPU index and the aggregate EW returns for the 144 cryptocurrencies (RC All) and the top 30 cryptocurrencies (RC top30). Panel B shows the variables' pairwise correlations.

Netherlands and Russia. For example, the correlation between the US and other countries, excluding the Netherlands and Russia, is at least 0.40, indicating that the EPU indices of these countries move in the same direction as that of the US. Finally, the correlation between the average monthly aggregate returns based on all 144 and the top 30 cryptocurrencies is 0.91, indicating that both aggregate returns should yield similar results.

11.3.2. *Short-run predictive regressions*

Tables 11.3 and 11.4 provide the OLS and mARM estimations of each country's EPU index for the following monthly aggregate returns based on all 144 cryptocurrencies (RC all) and the top 30 cryptocurrencies (RC top 30), respectively. The tables report the slope estimates, $\widehat{\beta}$, of the EPU indices. The tables also report the t-statistics adjusted using the Newey–West procedure (1987) and the empirical p-values from the wild bootstrap procedure, as described by Huang *et al.* (2014), for both the OLS and mARM. The tables also include the mARM bias correction of Amihud *et al.* (2009).

Table 11.3 shows that EPU, in general, positively predicts the aggregate returns of all cryptocurrencies. For example, the EPU indices of all countries, except the Netherlands and Russia, positively relate to the next month's aggregate returns of RC all. However, the bias-corrected slope coefficients based on the EPU indices of only the US, Germany, France, Singapore and the UK are statistically significant at the 10% significance level with two-tailed tests. Our alternative hypothesis, for which $\beta > 0$, justifies using one-tailed tests; therefore, the bias-corrected slope coefficients would be significant at the 5% significance level using one-tailed tests since the p-values would be smaller.

Table 11.4 shows that the results hold when using the aggregate returns of the RC top 30 since the EPU indices of all countries except the Netherlands and Russia positively relate to the next month's aggregate returns of RC top30.[3] However, the bias-corrected slope coefficients (AH p-value) for the EPUs of France and US are significant at the 10% confidence level with two-tailed tests.

Table 11.5 shows the QR results and confirms the OLS and mARM results from Table 11.3. China has no statistically significant slope coefficients in any quantiles, while the Netherlands and Russia have only one. Furthermore, other countries have at least two or more statistically significant positive slopes.

[3]The results remain robust when we estimate the aggregate returns of cryptocurrencies based on the top 20, top 10 and top 5 cryptocurrencies. Furthermore, our results remain consistent when we only use Bitcoin returns. We do not report those results for brevity, but they are available upon request.

Table 11.3. Short-run OLS and mARM regressions of all cryptocurrencies.

Predictive regressions over $t+1$ month returns of all cryptocurrencies						
Method	**Beta**	**NW t-stat**	**NW p-value**	**Empir. p-value**	**AH p-value**	R^2
US EPU						
OLS	0.23	2.22	(0.03)**	(0.03)**	—	0.08
mARM	0.23	2.20	(0.03)**	(0.03)**	(0.02)**	0.08
Germany EPU						
OLS	0.12	1.74	(0.09)*	(0.08)*	—	0.04
mARM	0.12	1.78	(0.08)*	(0.08)*	(0.08)*	0.05
France EPU						
OLS	0.14	2.63	(0.01)***	(0.01)***	—	0.12
mARM	0.14	2.74	(0.01)***	(0.01)***	(0.00)***	0.13
Netherlands EPU						
OLS	−0.13	−1.00	(0.32)	(0.32)	–	0.01
mARM	−0.14	−1.06	(0.29)	(0.28)	(0.32)	0.04
Singapore EPU						
OLS	0.11	1.60	(0.11)	(0.11)	—	0.04
mARM	0.11	1.57	(0.12)	(0.12)	(0.09)*	0.05
Canada EPU						
OLS	0.07	1.33	(0.19)	(0.18)	—	0.02
mARM	0.06	1.20	(0.23)	(0.22)	(0.26)	0.06
UK EPU						
OLS	0.08	1.70	(0.09)*	(0.09)*	—	0.04
mARM	0.08	1.72	(0.09)*	(0.09)*	(0.10)*	0.05
China EPU						
OLS	0.04	0.69	(0.49)	(0.51)	—	0.01
mARM	0.04	0.67	(0.50)	(0.52)	(0.42)	0.01
Russia EPU						
OLS	−0.01	−0.24	(0.81)	(0.83)	—	0.00
mARM	−0.01	−0.23	(0.82)	(0.82)	(0.87)	0.00
Japan EPU						
OLS	0.18	1.54	(0.13)	(0.11)	—	0.02
mARM	0.17	1.41	(0.16)	(0.15)	(0.29)	0.03

Notes: Table 11.3 reports the estimation results for the predictive regression based on the EW monthly log-returns of all cryptocurrencies:

$$\mathrm{RC}_{t+1} = \alpha + \beta \cdot \mathrm{EPU}_t + \mu_{t+1},$$

where RC is the EW aggregate returns of all cryptocurrencies in $t+1$ month. EPU is the EPU index in month t for each country. The table shows the slopes obtained from both OLS and mARM methods, the Newey–West adjusted t-statistics (NW t-stat) and p-values (NW p-value) and empirical p-values (Empir p-value) using the wild bootstrap, as given by Huang *et al.* (2014). The table also includes the p-values (AH p-value) based on the bias-correction procedure by Amihud *et al.* (2009). *, ** and *** indicate the 10%, 5% and 1% significance levels, respectively.

Table 11.4. Short-run OLS and mARM regressions of the top 30 cryptocurrencies.

Predictive regressions over t + 1 month returns of the top 30 cryptocurrencies						
Method	**Beta**	**NW t-stat**	**NW p-value**	**Empir. p-value**	**AH p-value**	R^2
US EPU						
OLS	0.25	1.68	(0.10)*	(0.09)*	—	0.07
mARM	0.25	1.69	(0.10)*	(0.09)*	(0.03)**	0.08
Germany EPU						
OLS	0.07	0.95	(0.35)	(0.35)	—	0.01
mARM	0.07	0.96	(0.34)	(0.33)	(0.37)	0.01
France EPU						
OLS	0.12	1.98	(0.05)**	(0.05)**	—	0.07
mARM	0.13	1.99	(0.05)**	(0.04)**	(0.02)**	0.07
Netherlands EPU						
OLS	−0.12	−0.88	(0.38)	(0.39)	—	0.01
mARM	−0.12	−0.88	(0.38)	(0.36)	(0.43)	0.01
Singapore EPU						
OLS	0.07	1.11	(0.27)	(0.26)	—	0.01
mARM	0.07	1.04	(0.30)	(0.30)	(0.36)	0.02
Canada EPU						
OLS	0.05	0.98	(0.33)	(0.32)	—	0.01
mARM	0.04	0.83	(0.41)	(0.41)	(0.50)	0.07
UK EPU						
OLS	0.03	0.70	(0.49)	(0.48)	—	0.00
mARM	0.03	0.74	(0.46)	(0.46)	(0.58)	0.01
China EPU						
OLS	0.03	0.48	(0.63)	(0.63)	—	0.00
mARM	0.02	0.47	(0.64)	(0.65)	(0.66)	0.00
Russia EPU						
OLS	−0.03	−0.82	(0.42)	(0.44)	—	0.00
mARM	−0.03	−0.83	(0.41)	(0.41)	(0.60)	0.01
Japan EPU						
OLS	0.12	1.07	(0.29)	(0.29)	—	0.01
mARM	0.10	0.93	(0.36)	(0.34)	(0.57)	0.03

Notes: Table 11.4 reports the estimation results for the following predictive regression based on the EW monthly log-returns of the top 30 cryptocurrencies:

$$\mathrm{RC}_{t+1} = \alpha + \beta \cdot \mathrm{EPU}_t + \mu_{t+1},$$

where RC is the EW aggregate cryptocurrency returns of the top 30 in $t+1$ month. EPU is the EPU index in month t for each country. The table shows the slopes from both OLS and mARM methods with the Newey–West adjusted t-statistics (NW t-stat) and p-values (NW p-value) and empirical p-values (Empir p-value) using the wild bootstrap, as given by Huang *et al.* (2014). The table also includes the p-values (AH p-value) of the bias-correction procedure by Amihud *et al.* (2009). *, ** and *** indicate the 10%, 5% and 1% significance levels, respectively.

Table 11.5. Short-run quantile regressions of all cryptocurrency returns.

	Quantiles						
Country	**0.05**	**0.1**	**0.25**	**0.5**	**0.75**	**0.9**	**0.95**
US EPU	0.378**	0.252**	0.171**	0.107*	0.468*	0.413*	0.459**
	(0)	(0.026)	(0.008)	(0.04)	(0.054)	(0.079)	(0.028)
Germany EPU	0.165**	0.144**	0.113**	0.046	−0.053	0.264	0.417**
	(0.027)	(0.023)	(0.05)	(0.238)	(0.562)	(0.338)	(0.003)
France EPU	0.271**	0.198**	0.104**	0.062	0.204***	0.121*	0.241
	(0)	(0)	(0.029)	(0.106)	(0.001)	(0.082)	(0.132)
Netherlands EPU	0.025	0.017	−0.132	−0.142	—	−0.14	−0.364
	(0.722)	(0.922)	(0.4)	(0.473)	(0.003)	(0.705)	(0.504)
Singapore EPU	0.155**	0.173**	0.120**	0.075**	−0.026	0.068	0.220**
	(0)	(0.044)	(0.035)	(0.033)	(0.776)	(0.71)	(0.016)
Canada EPU	0.005	0.164**	0.048	0.053*	0.106	0.156	0.275*
	(0.898)	(0.001)	(0.364)	(0.087)	(0.14)	(0.35)	(0.055)
UK EPU	0.111**	0.101**	0.074*	0.054*	0.108	0.153	0.394*
	(0.02)	(0)	(0.055)	(0.098)	(0.239)	(0.426)	(0.092)
China EPU	0.018	0.074	0.019	0.02	−0.03	0.117	0.318
	(0.819)	(0.281)	(0.716)	(0.554)	(0.583)	(0.39)	(0.197)
Russia EPU	−0.033	0.125**	0.032	0.008	−0.069	−0.008	−0.096
	(0.723)	(0.03)	(0.517)	(0.812)	(0.302)	(0.943)	(0.622)
Japan EPU	0.06	0.377**	0.235**	0.243	0.201	−0.113	−0.502
	(0.877)	(0.022)	(0.049)	(0.139)	(0.235)	(0.676)	(0.312)

Notes: The table reports the estimation results for the following QR based on the EW monthly log-returns of all cryptocurrencies:

$$\mathrm{RC}_{t+1} = \alpha + \beta \cdot \mathrm{EPU}_t + \mu_{t+1},$$

where RC is the EW aggregate returns of all cryptocurrencies in $t+1$ month. EPU is the EPU index in month t for each country. The table shows the slopes with p-values below them in parentheses from QR based on the 0.05, 0.10, 0.25, 0.50, 0.75, 0.90 and 0.95 quantiles. The modified Barrodale and Roberts algorithm estimates the parameters (Koenker & d'Orey, 1987, 1994), while a wild bootstrap with 2,000 replications estimates the standard errors, t-statistics and p-values. *, ** and *** indicate the 10%, 5% and 1% significance levels, respectively.

Table 11.6 presents the QR results and confirms the OLS and mARM results in Table 11.4 for the top 30 cryptocurrency returns. Canada and the Netherlands do not exhibit any statistically significant slopes for any quantiles, while China and Russia have one. The other countries have at least two or more statistically significant positive slopes. The exception is Germany, with a significant but negative slope.

Table 11.6. Short-run quantile regressions of the top 30 cryptocurrency returns.

	Quantiles						
Country	**0.05**	**0.1**	**0.25**	**0.5**	**0.75**	**0.9**	**0.95**
US EPU	0.336**	0.257*	0.133*	0.098	−0.028	0.538	0.948*
	(0.001)	(0.054)	(0.068)	(0.201)	(0.839)	(0.151)	(0.012)
Germany EPU	0.113**	0.093	0.122*	0	−0.108*	0.17	0.452*
	(0)	(0.446)	(0.018)	(0.998)	(0.025)	(0.623)	(0.089)
France EPU	0.065	0.120**	0.070*	0.005	0.187**	0.162	0.126
	(0.384)	(0.039)	(0.077)	(0.86)	(0.036)	(0.142)	(0.274)
Netherlands EPU	0.055	−0.038	0.035	0.024	−0.163	−0.236	−0.389
	(0.729)	(0.829)	(0.844)	(0.9)	(0.463)	(0.656)	(0.118)
Singapore EPU	0.038	0.150**	0.105*	0.058	−0.034	0.169	0.087
	(0.829)	(0.001)	(0.024)	(0.349)	(0.666)	(0.292)	(0.615)
Canada EPU	−0.063	−0.048	0.024	0.013	−0.034	0.225	0.115
	(0.312)	(0.601)	(0.629)	(0.683)	(0.589)	(0.203)	(0.636)
UK EPU	0	0.072**	0.036	−0.007	−0.026	0.22	0.27
	(0.999)	(0.022)	(0.211)	(0.726)	(0.661)	(0.312)	(0.313)
China EPU	−0.056**	−0.056	0.017	0.011	−0.026	0.091	0.145
	(0.026)	(0.518)	(0.726)	(0.754)	(0.612)	(0.487)	(0.522)
Russia EPU	0.065	0.022	−0.006	−0.01	−0.073**	−0.028	−0.228
	(0.183)	(0.797)	(0.904)	(0.759)	(0.044)	(0.854)	(0.33)
Japan EPU	0.321**	0.281	0.266*	0.108	−0.159	—	−0.624
	(0.015)	(0.156)	(0.025)	(0.425)	(0.361)	(0.04)	(0.194)

Notes: The table reports the estimation results for the following QR based on the EW monthly log-returns of all cryptocurrencies:

$$\mathrm{RC}_{t+1} = \alpha + \beta \cdot \mathrm{EPU}_t + \mu_{t+1},$$

where RC is the EW aggregate cryptocurrency returns of the top 30 in $t+1$ month. EPU is the EPU index in month t of the respective country. The table shows the slopes with p-values below them in parentheses from QR based on the 0.05, 0.10, 0.25, 0.50, 0.75, 0.90 and 0.95 quantiles. The modified Barrodale and Roberts algorithm estimates the parameters (Koenker & d'Orey, 1987, 1994), while a wild bootstrap with 2,000 replications estimates the standard errors, t-statistics and p-values. *, ** and *** indicate the 10%, 5% and 1% significance levels, respectively.

11.3.3. *Long-run predictive regressions*

Tables 11.7 and 11.8 provide the OLS and mARM estimation results for the 6- and 12-month time horizons of the EPU considering all 144 (RC all) and the top 30 (RC top30) cryptocurrency returns.[4]

[4]We find similar results over the horizons of 3- and 9-month aggregate returns. We do not report those results for brevity, but they are available upon request.

Table 11.7. Long-run OLS and mARM regressions for all cryptocurrencies.

Method	Beta	NW t-stat	NW p-value	Empir. p-value	AH p-value	R^2
Panel A: Predictive regressions over t + 6 month returns of all cryptocurrencies						
US EPU						
OLS	1.75	1.60	(0.11)	(0.10)*	—	0.15
mARM	1.78	1.65	(0.10)*	(0.09)*	(0.00)***	0.19
Germany EPU						
OLS	1.00	1.49	(0.14)	(0.11)	—	0.15
mARM	1.03	1.48	(0.14)	(0.10)*	(0.00)***	0.21
France EPU						
OLS	1.07	2.52	(0.01)***	(0.02)**	—	0.32
mARM	1.11	3.24	(0.00)***	(0.01)***	(0.00)**	0.48
Netherlands EPU						
OLS	−0.36	−1.08	(0.28)	(0.29)	—	0.00
mARM	−0.37	−1.08	(0.29)	(0.28)	(0.57)	0.01
Singapore EPU						
OLS	1.68	2.11	(0.04)**	(0.03)**	—	0.36
mARM	1.71	2.07	(0.04)**	(0.04)**	(0.00)***	0.37
Canada EPU						
OLS	0.61	1.12	(0.27)	(0.25)	—	0.08
mARM	0.62	1.10	(0.27)	(0.26)	(0.02)**	0.09
UK EPU						
OLS	0.62	1.40	(0.17)	(0.15)	—	0.11
mARM	0.63	1.37	(0.17)	(0.13)	(0.00)***	0.12
China EPU						
OLS	0.24	0.70	(0.49)	(0.49)	—	0.01
mARM	0.27	0.65	(0.52)	(0.50)	(0.30)	0.07
Russia EPU						
OLS	0.50	1.27	(0.21)	(0.20)	—	0.06
mARM	0.51	1.31	(0.19)	(0.20)	(0.04)**	0.11
Japan EPU						
OLS	1.89	1.25	(0.21)	(0.19)	—	0.10
mARM	1.92	1.25	(0.22)	(0.18)	(0.01)***	0.11
Panel B: Predictive regressions over t + 12 month returns of all cryptocurrencies						
US EPU						
OLS	4.07	2.07	(0.04)**	(0.04)**	—	0.19
mARM	4.17	2.18	(0.03)**	(0.03)**	(0.00)***	0.26
Germany EPU						
OLS	3.42	3.15	(0.00)***	(0.01)***	—	0.39
mARM	3.50	3.13	(0.00)***	(0.01)***	(0.00)***	0.51
France EPU						
OLS	2.34	2.91	(0.01)***	(0.01)***	—	0.35
mARM	2.43	3.58	(0.00)***	(0.01)***	(0.00)***	0.52

Table 11.7. (*Continued*)

Panel B: Predictive regressions over t + 12 month returns of all cryptocurrencies

Method	Beta	NW t-stat	NW p-value	Empir. p-value	AH p-value	R^2
Netherlands EPU						
OLS	−1.17	−1.43	(0.16)	(0.15)	—	0.01
mARM	−1.18	−1.43	(0.16)	(0.16)	(0.42)	0.01
Singapore EPU						
OLS	4.98	4.45	(0.00)***	(0.00)***	—	0.61
mARM	5.13	5.00	(0.00)***	(0.00)***	(0.00)***	0.69
Canada EPU						
OLS	1.94	1.43	(0.16)	(0.14)	—	0.15
mARM	1.97	1.40	(0.17)	(0.13)	(0.00)***	0.16
UK EPU						
OLS	2.14	3.61	(0.00)***	(0.00)***	—	0.31
mARM	2.20	3.45	(0.00)***	(0.01)***	(0.00)***	0.34
China EPU						
OLS	1.31	1.15	(0.25)	(0.24)	—	0.05
mARM	1.41	1.07	(0.29)	(0.29)	(0.08)*	0.15
Russia EPU						
OLS	1.24	1.26	(0.21)	(0.20)	—	0.08
mARM	1.27	1.30	(0.20)	(0.20)	(0.02)**	0.14
Japan EPU						
OLS	6.55	2.78	(0.01)***	(0.01)***	—	0.27
mARM	6.70	2.70	(0.01)***	(0.02)***	(0.00)***	0.30

Notes: Panels A and B report the estimation results for the following predictive regression for the 6- and 12-month EW monthly log-returns of all cryptocurrencies:

$$\mathrm{RC}_{t+k} = \alpha + \beta \cdot \mathrm{EPU}_t + \mu_{t+k},$$

where RC is the EW aggregate returns of cryptocurrencies in $t+k$ ($k = 6$ and 12) months based on the individual monthly log-returns of all cryptocurrencies. EPU is the news-based EPU index in month t. The slopes are estimated with OLS and mARM methods employing the Newey–West adjusted t-statistics (NW t-stat) and p-values (NW p-value) and empirical p-values (Empir p-value) using the wild bootstrap, as given by Huang *et al.* (2014). The mARM regression includes the p-values (AH p-value) using the bias-correction procedure by Amihud *et al.* (2009). *, ** and *** indicate significance levels at 10%, 5% and 1%, respectively.

The tables report the parameter estimates of the slope, β, where standard errors and t-statistics are adjusted using Newey–West, and the empirical p-values from the wild bootstrap procedure, as described by Huang *et al.* (2014). The tables also include p-values of the bias-correction procedure by Amihud *et al.* (2009).

Table 11.8. Long-run OLS and mARM regressions of the top 30 cryptocurrency returns.

Method	Beta	NW t-stat	NW p-value	Empir. p-value	AH p-value	R^2
Panel A: Predictive regressions over t + 6 month returns of top 30 cryptocurrencies						
US EPU						
OLS	1.16	1.44	(0.15)	(0.14)	—	0.11
mARM	1.18	1.48	(0.14)	(0.13)	(0.01)***	0.15
Germany EPU						
OLS	0.59	1.15	(0.25)	(0.23)	—	0.08
mARM	0.61	1.16	(0.25)	(0.24)	(0.02)**	0.16
France EPU						
OLS	0.67	1.92	(0.06)*	(0.05)**	—	0.20
mARM	0.69	2.31	(0.02)**	(0.03)**	(0.00)***	0.33
Netherlands EPU						
OLS	0.24	0.85	(0.40)	(0.41)	—	0.00
mARM	0.26	0.95	(0.35)	(0.33)	(0.61)	0.02
Singapore EPU						
OLS	1.10	1.75	(0.08)*	(0.08)*	—	0.25
mARM	1.13	1.72	(0.09)**	(0.08)*	(0.00)***	0.27
Canada EPU						
OLS	0.40	0.98	(0.33)	(0.32)	—	0.06
mARM	0.40	0.96	(0.34)	(0.32)	(0.05)**	0.06
UK EPU						
OLS	0.31	1.05	(0.30)	(0.28)	—	0.05
mARM	0.32	1.03	(0.31)	(0.25)	(0.07)*	0.05
China EPU						
OLS	0.00	0.00	(1.00)	(1.00)	—	0.00
mARM	0.02	0.11	(0.91)	(0.91)	(0.90)	0.06
Russia EPU						
OLS	0.35	1.19	(0.24)	(0.22)	—	0.05
mARM	0.36	1.24	(0.22)	(0.23)	(0.06)*	0.12
Japan EPU						
OLS	1.37	1.17	(0.25)	(0.23)	—	0.08
mARM	1.41	1.17	(0.25)	(0.22)	(0.01)***	0.10
Panel B: Predictive regressions over t + 12 month returns of top 30 cryptocurrencies						
US EPU						
OLS	1.45	2.29	(0.03)**	(0.02)**	—	0.17
mARM	1.48	2.40	(0.02)**	(0.02)**	(0.00)***	0.23
Germany EPU						
OLS	1.35	5.62	(0.00)***	(0.00)***	—	0.44
mARM	1.39	5.65	(0.00)***	(0.00)***	(0.00)***	0.60

Table 11.8. (*Continued*)

Panel B: Predictive regressions over t + 12 month returns of top 30 cryptocurrencies

Method	Beta	NW t-stat	NW p-value	Empir. p-value	AH p-value	R^2
France EPU						
OLS	0.81	3.18	(0.00)***	(0.01)***	—	0.31
mARM	0.85	3.75	(0.00)***	(0.00)***	(0.00)***	0.47
Netherlands EPU						
OLS	−0.56	−1.67	(0.10)*	(0.09)*	—	0.02
mARM	−0.56	−1.65	(0.10)*	(0.10)*	(0.30)	0.02
Singapore EPU						
OLS	1.75	5.94	(0.00)***	(0.00)***	—	0.55
mARM	1.81	6.57	(0.00)***	(0.00)***	(0.00)***	0.64
Canada EPU						
OLS	0.61	1.37	(0.17)	(0.16)	—	0.11
mARM	0.61	1.34	(0.18)	(0.17)	(0.01)***	0.11
UK EPU						
OLS	0.90	6.25	(0.00)***	(0.00)***	—	0.40
mARM	0.93	6.57	(0.00)***	(0.00)***	(0.00)***	0.47
China EPU						
OLS	0.34	0.80	(0.42)	(0.41)	—	0.02
mARM	0.37	0.78	(0.44)	(0.46)	(0.21)	0.09
Russia EPU						
OLS	0.41	1.26	(0.21)	(0.21)	—	0.07
mARM	0.42	1.30	(0.20)	(0.19)	(0.04)**	0.10
Japan EPU						
OLS	2.82	4.16	(0.00)***	(0.00)***	—	0.37
mARM	2.89	4.00	(0.00)***	(0.00)***	(0.00)***	0.41

Notes: Panels A and B in Table 11.8 report the estimation results for the following predictive regression over 6- and 12-month EW monthly log-returns of the top 30 cryptocurrencies:

$$\mathrm{RC}_{t+k} = \alpha + \beta \cdot \mathrm{EPU}_t + \mu_{t+k},$$

where RC is the EW aggregate returns of cryptocurrencies in $t + k$ (k = 6 and 12) months based on the individual monthly log-returns of the top 30 cryptocurrencies. EPU is the news-based EPU index in month t. The tables also include the slopes from both OLS and mARM methods with the Newey–West adjusted t-statistics (NW t-stat) and p-values (NW p-value), and empirical p-values (Empir p-value) using the wild bootstrap, as given by Huang *et al.* (2014). The table also includes the bias-correction p-values (AH p-value) from Amihud *et al.* (2009). *, ** and *** indicate the 10%, 5% and 1% significant levels, respectively.

EPU is expected to strongly predict cryptocurrency returns for long time horizons, as opposed to a one-month horizon, because mispricing takes time to correct. Therefore, EPU would have a long-term effect on cryptocurrency returns. Consistent with expectations, Panels A and B in Table 11.7 show that all country EPU indices, except for the Netherlands, positively predict aggregate cryptocurrency returns for the following 6 and 12 months. Most importantly, the bias-corrected slope coefficients (AH) based on the EPU indices are also statistically significant at the 10% level with two-tailed tests for all countries, except the Netherlands and China.[5]

In Table 11.8, Panels A and B show that the results hold for the top 30 cryptocurrency returns (RC top30)[6] since the EPU indices of

Table 11.9. Long-run quantile regressions of all cryptocurrency returns.

Panel A. Predictive regressions over the $t + 6$ month returns of all cryptocurrencies

	Quantiles						
Country	**0.05**	**0.1**	**0.25**	**0.5**	**0.75**	**0.9**	**0.95**
US EPU	−0.033	−0.13	0.062	0.587	1.924*	4.063***	6.988***
	(0.91)	(0.554)	(0.839)	(0.303)	(0.052)	(0.001)	(0.003)
Germany EPU	0.216	0.218	0.1949*	0.392	1.497**	1.975***	2.380***
	(0.141)	(0.189)	(0.089)	(0.273)	(0.043)	(0)	(0)
France EPU	0.167	0.148	0.279**	0.516*	0.879**	1.664***	2.990***
	(0.175)	(0.413)	(0.04)	(0.053)	(0.002)	(0)	(0)
Netherlands EPU	−0.294*	−0.267	−0.029	—	−0.583	−0.543	−3.422
	(0.083)	(0.314)	(0.892)	(0.036)	(0.333)	(0.625)	(0.495)
Singapore EPU	0.158	0.191	0.408**	1.078**	2.099**	2.981***	3.783***
	(0.358)	(0.32)	(0.03)	(0.024)	(0)	(0.001)	(0)
Canada EPU	0.077	0.084	0.048	−0.103	0.553	2.223***	2.319***
	(0.241)	(0.386)	(0.501)	(0.614)	(0.302)	(0.001)	(0)
UK EPU	0.211**	0.205*	0.184*	0.513*	1.117	1.789***	2.675***
	(0.005)	(0.044)	(0.069)	(0.071)	(0.102)	(0)	(0.001)
China EPU	0.07	0.056	0.025	−0.198	0.459	0.941***	1.69
	(0.315)	(0.68)	(0.792)	(0.113)	(0.339)	(0)	(0.13)
Russia EPU	0.021	0.058	0.019	0.181	0.2	1.5014**	2.5472**
	(0.822)	(0.559)	(0.837)	(0.277)	(0.161)	(0.002)	(0.011)
Japan EPU	0.022	0.533*	0.612**	0.598*	1.357	7.511***	12.021**
	(0.957)	(0.079)	(0.006)	(0.061)	(0.18)	(0)	(0)

[5]The bias-corrected slope coefficient based on the EPU index from China is significant over the following 12 months.

[6]The results remain robust when we estimate the aggregate returns of cryptocurrencies based on the top 20, top 10 and top 5 cryptocurrencies. Furthermore, the results are similar for Bitcoin returns. We do not report those results for brevity, but they are available upon request.

Table 11.9. (*Continued*)

Panel B. Predictive regressions over the t + 12 month returns of all cryptocurrencies

	Quantiles						
Country	**0.05**	**0.1**	**0.25**	**0.5**	**0.75**	**0.9**	**0.95**
US EPU	0.004	0	0.078	1.13	4.793**	10.482**	8.4801**
	(0.988)	(1)	(0.854)	(0.253)	(0)	(0.002)	(0.017)
Germany EPU	0.022	0.291	1.061	2.298**	2.793**	5.556**	8.160**
	(0.926)	(0.523)	(0.102)	(0)	(0)	(0)	(0.02)
France EPU	−0.002	0	0.605*	0.981**	2.598**	5.016***	4.830***
	(0.99)	(0.999)	(0.026)	(0.003)	(0.002)	(0)	(0)
Netherlands EPU	−0.103	−0.083	−0.124	−0.681**	−1.258	−5.305	−7.466
	(0.441)	(0.394)	(0.314)	(0.04)	(0.197)	(0.177)	(0.312)
Singapore EPU	0.278	0.386	1.307	2.868**	4.987**	7.505***	7.553***
	(0.44)	(0.48)	(0.112)	(0.003)	(0)	(0)	(0)
Canada EPU	0.035	0.024	0.027	0.617	2.935**	6.557***	7.041***
	(0.819)	(0.881)	(0.804)	(0.245)	(0.013)	(0)	(0.001)
UK EPU	0.114	0.215	0.683	1.841**	3.092**	3.753***	7.542***
	(0.557)	(0.357)	(0.101)	(0)	(0)	(0)	(0)
China EPU	0.033	0.028	0.065	−0.071	0.935	4.800*	7.220*
	(0.835)	(0.851)	(0.63)	(0.783)	(0.181)	(0.086)	(0.054)
Russia EPU	0.017	0.019	0.022	0.056	0.386	3.196	5.087**
	(0.884)	(0.804)	(0.791)	(0.779)	(0.409)	(0.108)	(0.013)
Japan EPU	−0.009	−0.005	1.163	4.120**	5.977**	16.584**	21.240**
	(0.98)	(0.993)	(0.256)	(0.001)	(0)	(0.001)	(0)

Notes: In Table 11.9, Panels A and B report the estimation results for the following QR based on the EW monthly log-returns of all cryptocurrencies:

$$\mathrm{RC}_{t+k} = \alpha + \beta \cdot \mathrm{EPU}_t + \mu_{t+k},$$

where RC is the EW aggregate returns of cryptocurrencies over $t+k$ ($k = 6$ and 12) months based on the individual monthly log-returns of all cryptocurrencies. The EPU index is in month t for each respective country. The table shows the slopes with p-values in parentheses below from QR based on the 0.05, 0.10, 0.25, 0.50, 0.75, 0.90 and 0.95 quantiles. The modified Barrodale and Roberts algorithm estimates the parameters (Koenker & d'Orey, 1987, 1994), while a wild bootstrap with 2,000 replications estimates the standard errors, t-statistics and p-values. *, ** and *** indicate the 10%, 5% and 1% significance levels, respectively.

all countries are positive and significant for the subsequent 6- and 12-month aggregate returns, except for the Netherlands and China. In sum, the results of the predictive regressions support our hypothesis that the EPU positively predicts the aggregate returns of cryptocurrencies over the long horizon.

In Table 11.9, Panels A and B confirm the results of Tables 11.7 and 11.8, where the EPU positively predicts the aggregate cryptocurrency returns using QR. China has only one statistically significant QR in Panel A, while Russia has only one in Panel B. Furthermore, the Netherlands exhibits unusual behavior since it has two significant but negative slopes in Panel A and one in Panel B. In addition, Panels A and B in Table 11.10 corroborate the results in Table 11.9. The QR estimates give weak results for China, the Netherlands and Russia. The scatter plots of the countries with the plotted quantile regressions are omitted for the sake of brevity but are available upon request. However, the plotted QRs explain the high EPU values for all countries except China, the Netherlands and Russia. Thus, the QR establishes that a country's EPU, except for China, the Netherlands and Russia, can predict the aggregate cryptocurrency returns for the following 6 and 12 months.

Table 11.10. Long-run quantile regressions of the top 30 cryptocurrency returns.

Panel A. Predictive regressions over the t + 6 month returns of top 30 cryptocurrencies

	Quantile						
Country	**0.05**	**0.1**	**0.25**	**0.5**	**0.75**	**0.9**	**0.95**
US EPU	0.039	−0.1	−0.058	0.326	1.093**	2.579***	4.135***
	(0.716)	(0.466)	(0.794)	(0.441)	(0.042)	(0.001)	(0.002)
Germany EPU	0.154**	0.159	0.093	0.245	0.41	1.497***	0.953
	(0.041)	(0.132)	(0.428)	(0.321)	(0.374)	(0.002)	(0.201)
France EPU	0.138	0.129	0.146**	0.244*	1.077**	1.314***	1.963***
	(0.192)	(0.329)	(0.011)	(0.089)	(0.011)	(0)	(0)
Netherlands EPU	−0.252	−0.124	0.135	−0.008	0.404	0.730*	−1.21
	(0.11)	(0.618)	(0.446)	(0.978)	(0.579)	(0.082)	(0.745)
Singapore EPU	0.135	0.16	0.244	0.513*	1.333**	1.752***	3.449***
	(0.278)	(0.281)	(0.125)	(0.018)	(0.012)	(0.002)	(0)
Canada EPU	0.064	0.095	−0.013	−0.062	0.365	0.982***	2.935*
	(0.173)	(0.142)	(0.824)	(0.633)	(0.413)	(0.007)	(0.062)
UK EPU	0.133***	0.13	0.089*	0.156	0.474	1.118**	0.803***
	(0.006)	(0.311)	(0.087)	(0.237)	(0.207)	(0.021)	(0.001)
China EPU	0.056	0.042	−0.017	−0.095	0.032	−0.22	0.624
	(0.615)	(0.712)	(0.835)	(0.323)	(0.871)	(0.453)	(0.394)
Russia EPU	0.033	0.094	0.015	0.013	0.240*	0.711	1.959
	(0.733)	(0.201)	(0.834)	(0.898)	(0.099)	(0.295)	(0.101)
Japan EPU	0.167	0.357	0.323*	0.211	1.602*	5.635***	8.643**
	(0.646)	(0.165)	(0.06)	(0.371)	(0.076)	(0)	(0.012)

Table 11.10. (*Continued*)

Panel B. Predictive regressions over the t + 12 month returns of top 30 cryptocurrencies

	Quantile						
Country	**0.05**	**0.1**	**0.25**	**0.5**	**0.75**	**0.9**	**0.95**
US EPU	0.011	0.008	0.105	0.651	1.256**	3.856**	2.102*
	(0.924)	(0.973)	(0.709)	(0.274)	(0.046)	(0)	(0.096)
Germany EPU	0.023	0.132	0.79	1.204**	1.344**	1.866**	2.603**
	(0.873)	(0.562)	(0.02)	(0)	(0)	(0.001)	(0.001)
France EPU	0.036	0.073	0.295**	0.401**	1.035**	1.776**	1.848**
	(0.735)	(0.597)	(0.017)	(0.01)	(0.002)	(0)	(0)
Netherlands EPU	−0.101	−0.041	−0.122	−0.355	−0.904**	−2.176**	1.461
	(0.42)	(0.573)	(0.303)	(0.155)	(0.019)	(0.028)	(0.787)
Singapore EPU	0.2799	0.262	0.905**	1.347**	2.171**	2.437**	2.049**
	(0.068)	(0.283)	(0.004)	(0)	(0)	(0)	(0)
Canada EPU	0.022	0.026	0.036	0.22	0.643	2.573**	2.591**
	(0.732)	(0.75)	(0.595)	(0.295)	(0.11)	(0)	(0)
UK EPU	0.072	0.075	0.427**	0.875**	1.106**	1.523**	2.613**
	(0.351)	(0.512)	(0.013)	(0)	(0)	(0)	(0.001)
China EPU	0.028	0.017	0.04	−0.041	0.141	1.54	1.641
	(0.673)	(0.858)	(0.617)	(0.857)	(0.697)	(0.137)	(0.14)
Russia EPU	0.006	0.019	0.029	0.038	0.31	1.292**	0.992
	(0.921)	(0.737)	(0.622)	(0.804)	(0.279)	(0.007)	(0.138)
Japan EPU	0.076	0.086	0.631	1.868**	3.466**	6.655**	7.215**
	(0.768)	(0.804)	(0.259)	(0.001)	(0)	(0)	(0)

Notes: Table 11.10 reports the estimation results for the following QR based on the EW monthly log-returns of all cryptocurrencies:

$$\mathrm{RC}_{t+k} = \alpha + \beta \cdot \mathrm{EPU}_t + \mu_{t+k},$$

where RC is the EW aggregate cryptocurrency returns in $t + (k = 6 \text{ and } 12)$ months based on the individual monthly log-returns of all cryptocurrencies. The EPU index is in month t for the respective country. The table shows the slopes with p-values in parentheses from the QR based on the 0.05, 0.10, 0.25, 0.50, 0.75, 0.90 and 0.95 quantiles. The modified Barrodale and Roberts algorithm estimates the parameters (Koenker & d'Orey, 1987, 1994), while a wild bootstrap with 2,000 replications estimates the standard errors, t-statistics and p-values. *, ** and *** indicate the 10%, 5% and 1% significance levels, respectively.

11.4. Discussion

The descriptive statistics show that aggregate cryptocurrency returns can vary by over 100% per month, which signifies a lucrative but risky investment. Furthermore, a country's EPU highly correlates to other countries' EPUs, indicating that they move together, except for China, the Netherlands and Russia.

OLS, mARM and QR indicate that the EPU can predict the next month's returns, except for the cases of China, the Netherlands and Russia. Figures 11.1 and 11.2 illustrate this relationship because the scatter diagrams of aggregate cryptocurrency returns show that most of the positively sloped lines of QR intersect at the points where the EPU index is high. The exceptions, again, are the same three countries. Thus, the high uncertainty associated with a high EPU positively affects the next month's cryptocurrency returns.

The results show that a country's EPU can influence cryptocurrency returns over the next 6 and 12 months because the market takes time to correct. The notable exceptions are China, the Netherlands and Russia. Thus, a high EPU triggers a flight to quality and safety, which persists in cryptocurrency markets over the long term.

The overall results showing that the EPU positively predicts cryptocurrency returns agree with those of Bouri *et al.* (2019), who show that the EPU drives herd behavior in the 14 leading cryptocurrencies. The results also align with those of Demir *et al.* (2018), who indicate that a rising EPU causes investors to lose confidence in the global financial system and traditional currencies while raising Bitcoin's attractiveness. In addition, our analyses provide new insights into how the EPU indices from various countries positively predict aggregate cryptocurrency returns over long time horizons. Our findings suggest a long-term association between economic uncertainty and cryptocurrency returns, adding more fuel to the heated debate over whether cryptocurrencies serve as a safe haven in the global financial system (Bouri *et al.*, 2017).

The next research phase should investigate methods to derive trading rules to incorporate the long-term effects of EPU on cryptocurrency returns (refer to Bhaskar *et al.*, 2022; Hunjra & Hanif, 2023).

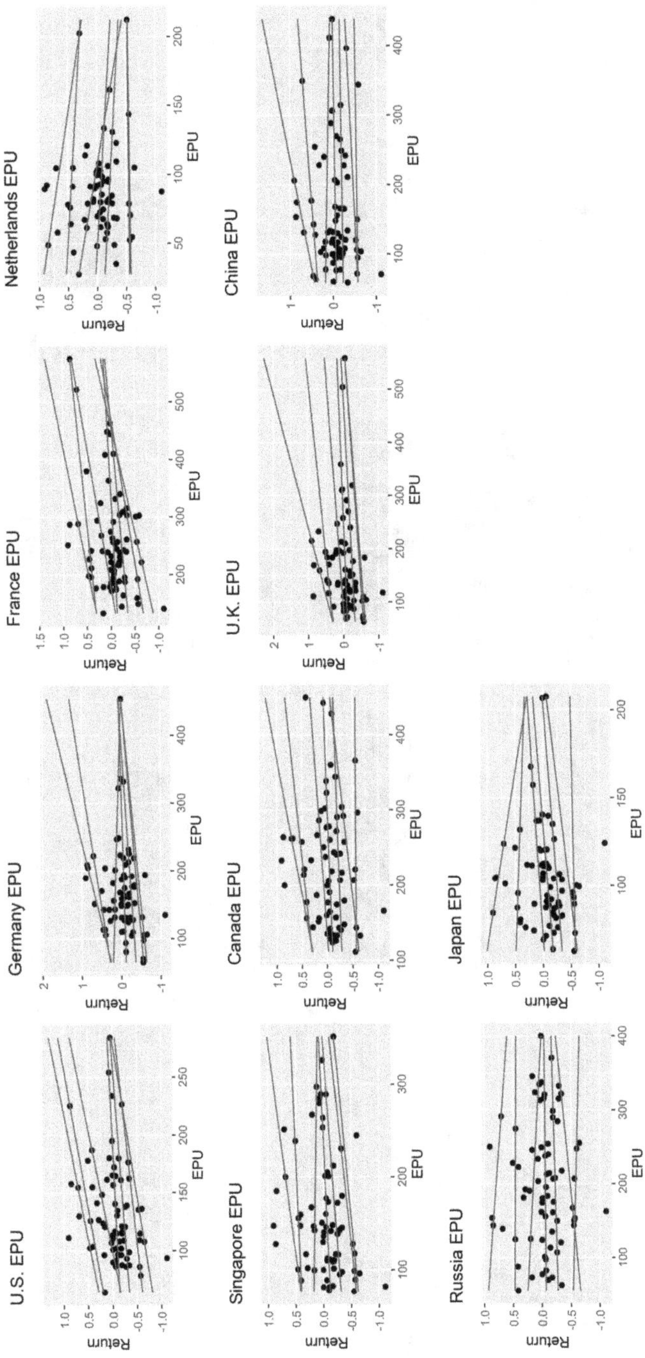

Figure 11.1. Quantile regression for all cryptocurrency returns.

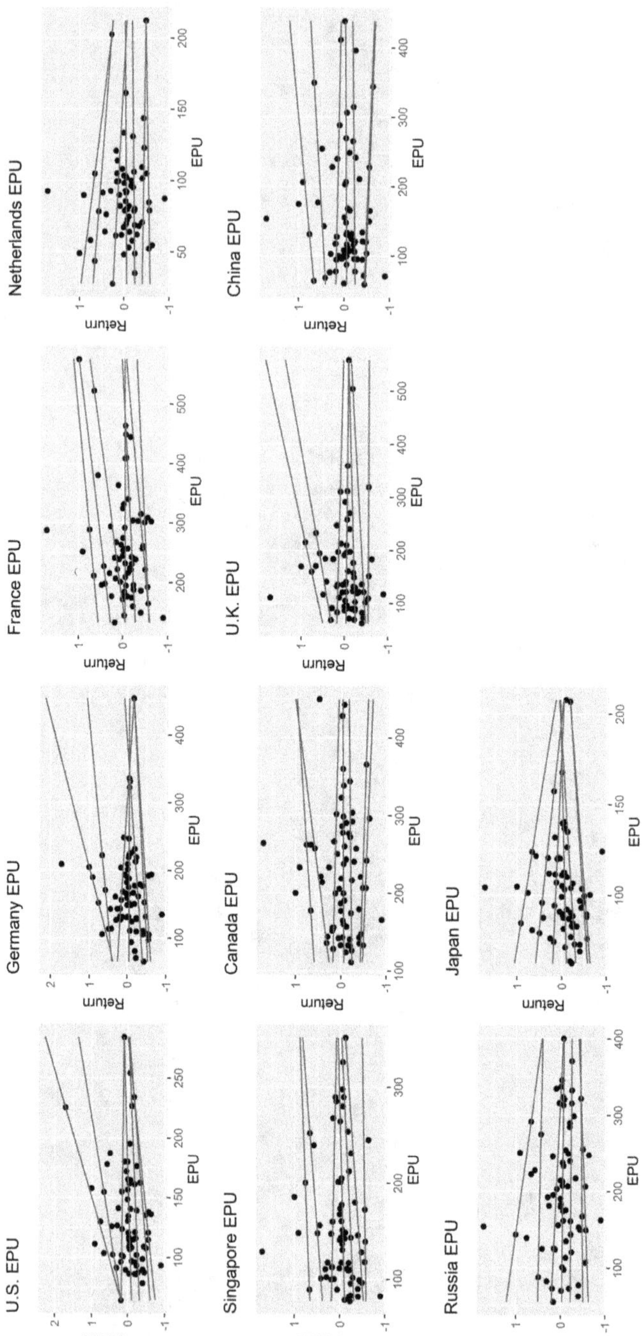

Figure 11.2. Quantile regressions for the top 30 cryptocurrency returns.

11.5. Conclusion

This chapter examines whether the EPU index can predict aggregate cryptocurrency returns using EPU indices from the 10 countries with the highest concentration of Bitcoin nodes. The countries are the US, Germany, France, the Netherlands, Singapore, Canada, the UK, China, Russia and Japan. We hypothesized that EPU drives the prices of cryptocurrencies below their fundamental values due to the flight-to-quality effect and that they subsequently undergo correction.

For a robustness check, we used OLS, mARM and QR to estimate the predictive regressions. Consistent with our hypothesis, we showed that the EPU index predicts the subsequent 2-month returns for the short run and the 6- and 12-month returns for the long run, except for China, the Netherlands and Russia. The statistical significance of the results is stronger for mARM with bias correction and the QR. The bias-correction procedure corrects the bias in the estimated slope parameter and standard error. In contrast, QR can estimate different behaviors for each quantile, thus providing a richer response than OLS and mARM.

Our results have two important implications for investors, fund managers, policymakers and regulatory authorities:

1. Since EPU positively predicts the aggregate returns of cryptocurrencies in the long run, investors and fund managers should avoid using them as a safe haven during financial turmoil or uncertainty. Future research could consider whether gold or other precious metals may serve as superior investment vehicles during periods of heightened EPU.
2. Our results indicate that cryptocurrencies are a speculative asset; therefore, regulatory authorities should institute consumer protection policies to protect individuals from the speculative nature of cryptocurrencies. Policymakers and regulatory authorities should exercise caution when classifying cryptocurrencies as commodities or as an alternative to traditional currencies.

Future research could compare the response of the prices of cryptocurrencies, commodities and traditional currencies to EPU and, in addition, look at how investors can use the long-term effects of EPU on cryptocurrency returns by devising trading rules and investment strategies.

References

Al-Yahyaee, K. H., Rehman, M. U., Mensi, W., & Al-Jarrah, I. M. W. (2019). Can uncertainty indices predict bitcoin prices? A revisited analysis using partial and multivariate wavelet approaches. *The North American Journal of Economics and Finance*, 49, 47–56. https://doi.org/10.1016/j.najef.2019.03.019.

Amihud, Y., Hurvich, C., & Wang, Y. (2009). Multiple-predictor regressions: Hypothesis testing. *Review of Financial Studies*, 22(1), 413–434. https://doi.org/10.1093/rfs/hhn056.

Baek, C. & Elbeck, M. (2015). Bitcoins as an investment or speculative vehicle? A first look. *Applied Economics Letters*, 22(1), 30–34. https://doi.org/10.1080/13504851.2014.916379.

Baker, M. & Wurgler, J. (2006). Investor sentiment and the cross-section of stock returns. *The Journal of Finance*, 61(4), 1645–1680. https://doi.org/10.1111/j.1540-6261.2006.00885.x.

Baker, S. R., Bloom, N., & Davis, S. J. (2016). Measuring economic policy uncertainty. *The Quarterly Journal of Economics*, 131(4), 1593–1636. https://doi.org/10.1093/qje/qjw024.

Barrero, J. M., Bloom, N., & Wright, I. (2017). Short and long run uncertainty (No. w23676). National Bureau of Economic Research.

Baur, D. G., Hong, K., & Lee, A. D. (2018). Bitcoin: Medium of exchange or speculative assets? *Journal of International Financial Markets, Institutions and Money*, 54, 177–189. https://doi.org/10.1016/j.intfin.2017.12.004.

Bekaert, G. & Hoerova, M. (2016). What do asset prices have to say about risk appetite and uncertainty? *Journal of Banking & Finance*, 67, 103–118. https://doi.org/10.1016/j.jbankfin.2015.06.015.

Bhaskar, R., Hunjra, A. I., Bansal, S., & Pandey, D. K. (2022). Central bank digital currencies: Agendas for future research. *Research in International Business and Finance*, 62, 101737. https://doi.org/10.1016/j.ribaf.2022.101737.

Bouoiyour, J., Selmi, R., & Tiwari, A. K. (2015). Is Bitcoin business income or speculative foolery? New ideas through an improved frequency domain analysis. *Annals of Financial Economics*, 10(01), 1550002. https://doi.org/10.1142/S2010495215500025.

Bouri, E., Gupta, R., & Roubaud, D. (2019). Herding behaviour in cryptocurrencies. *Finance Research Letters*, 29, 216–221. https://doi.org/10.1016/j.frl.2018.07.008.

Bouri, E., Molnár, P., Azzi, G., Roubaud, D., & Hagfors, L. I. (2017). On the hedge and safe haven properties of bitcoin: Is it really more than a diversifier? *Finance Research Letters*, 20, 192–198. https://doi.org/10.1016/j.frl.2016.09.025.

Bouri, E., Vo, X. V., & Saeed, T. (2021). Return equicorrelation in the cryptocurrency market: Analysis and determinants. *Finance Research Letters*, 38, 101497. https://doi.org/10.1016/j.frl.2020.101497.

Brogaard, J. & Detzel, A. (2015). The asset-pricing implications of government economic policy uncertainty. *Management Science*, 61(1), 3–18. https://doi.org/10.1287/mnsc.2014.2044.

Caballero, R. J. & Krishnamurthy, A. (2008). Collective risk management in a flight to quality episode. *The Journal of Finance*, 63(5), 2195–2230. https://doi.org/10.1111/j.1540-6261.2008.01394.x.

Cheah, E.-T. & Fry, J. (2015). Speculative bubbles in bitcoin markets? An empirical investigation into the fundamental value of bitcoin. *Economics Letters*, 130, 32–36. https://doi.org/10.1016/j.econlet.2015.02.029.

Cheema, M. A., Faff, R., & Szulczyk, K. R. (2022). The 2008 global financial crisis and COVID-19 pandemic: How safe are the safe haven assets? *International Review of Financial Analysis*, 83, 102316. https://doi.org/10.1016/j.irfa.2022.102316.

Cheng, H.-P. & Yen, K.-C. (2019). The relationship between the economic policy uncertainty and the cryptocurrency market. *Finance Research Letters*, 101308. https://doi.org/10.1016/j.frl.2019.101308.

Ciaian, P., Rajcaniova, M., & Kancs, D. A. (2016). The economics of BitCoin price formation. *Applied Economics*, 48(19), 1799–1815. https://doi.org/10.1080/00036846.2015.1109038.

Daniel, K. D., Hirshleifer, D., & Subrahmanyam, A. (1998). Investor psychology and security market under-and overreactions. *The Journal of Finance*, 53(6), 1839–1885. https://doi.org/10.1111/0022-1082.00077.

Demir, E., Gozgor, G., Lau, C. K. M., & Vigne, S. A. (2018). Does economic policy uncertainty predict the bitcoin returns? An empirical investigation. *Finance Research Letters*, 26, 145–149. https://doi.org/10.1016/j.frl.2018.01.005.

Diether, K. B., Malloy, C. J., & Scherbina, A. (2002). Differences of opinion and the cross section of stock returns. *The Journal of Finance*, 57(5), 2113–2141. https://doi.org/10.1111/0022-1082.00490.

Dyhrberg, A. H. (2016). Hedging capabilities of bitcoin. Is it the virtual gold? *Finance Research Letters*, 16, 139–144. https://doi.org/10.1016/j.frl.2015.10.025.

Economic Policy Uncertainty. (2019). Monthly EPU Indices for 22 Countries. http://www.policyuncertainty.com/all_country_data.html.

Fang, L., Bouri, E., Gupta, R., & Roubaud, D. (2019). Does global economic uncertainty matter for the volatility and hedging effectiveness of bitcoin? *International Review of Financial Analysis*, 61, 29–36. https://doi.org/10.1016/j.irfa.2018.12.010.

Grobys, K. & Sapkota, N. (2019). Cryptocurrencies and momentum. *Economics Letters*, 180, 6-10. https://doi.org/10.1016/j.econlet.2019.03.028.

Gurdgiev, C. & O'Loughlin, D. (2020). Herding and anchoring in cryptocurrency markets: Investor reaction to fear and uncertainty. *Journal of Behavioral and Experimental Finance*, 25, 100271. https://doi.org/10.1016/j.jbef.2020.100271.

Huang, D., Jiang, F., Tu, J., & Zhou, G. (2014). Investor sentiment aligned: A powerful predictor of stock returns. *The Review of Financial Studies*, 28(3), 791–837. https://doi.org/10.1093/rfs/hhu080.

Hunjra, A. I. & Hanif, M. (2023). Central banking issues and challenges. https://doi.org/10.1016/B978-0-44-313776-1.00113-6.

Klein, T., Thu, H. P., & Walther, T. (2018). Bitcoin is not the new gold–a comparison of volatility, correlation, and portfolio performance. *International Review of Financial Analysis*, 59, 105–116. https://doi.org/10.1016/j.irfa.2018.07.010.

Koenker, R. & Bassett, G. (1978). Regression quantiles. *Econometrica*, 46, 33–50. https://doi.org/10.2307/1913643.

Koenker, R. W. & d'Orey. (1987). Computing regression quantiles. *Applied Statistics*, 36, 383–393. https://doi.org/10.2307/2347802.

Koenker, R. W. & d'Orey. (1994). Computing regression quantiles. *Applied Statistics*, 43, 410–414. https://doi.org/10.2307/2986030.

Koenker, R. & Hallock, K. F. (2001). Quantile regression. *Journal of Economic Perspectives*, 15(4), 143–156. https://doi.org/10.1257/jep.15.4.143.

Lamont, O. A. & Thaler, R. H. (2003). Can the market add and subtract? Mispricing in tech stock carve-outs. *Journal of Political Economy*, 111(2), 227–268. https://doi.org/10.1086/367683.

Li, X.-M., Zhang, B., & Gao, R. (2015). Economic policy uncertainty shocks and stock–bond correlations: Evidence from the US market. *Economics Letters*, 132, 91–96. https://doi.org/10.1016/j.econlet.2015.04.013.

Newey, W. K. & West, K. D. (1987). A simple, positive semi-definite, heteroskedasticity and autocorrelation consistent covariance matrix. *Econometrica*, 703–708.

Rejeb, A. B. & Arfaoui, M. (2016). Financial market interdependencies: A quantile regression analysis of volatility spillover. *Research in International Business and Finance*, 36, 140–157. https://doi.org/10.1016/j.ribaf.2015.09.022.

Schulze, N. (2004). *Applied Quantile Regression: Microeconometric, Financial, and Environmental Analyses.* Eberhard-Karls-Universität Tübingen.

Shleifer, A. & Vishny, R. W. (1990). Equilibrium short horizons of investors and firms. *The American Economic Review*, 80(2), 148–153. https://www.jstor.org/stable/2006560.

Smales, L. A. (2018). Bitcoin as a safe haven: Is it even worth considering? *Finance Research Letters.* https://doi.org/10.1016/j.frl.2018.11.002.

Stambaugh, R. F. (1999). Predictive regressions. *Journal of Financial Economics*, 54(3), 375–421. https://doi.org/10.1016/S0304-405X(99)00041-0.

Stambaugh, R. F., Yu, J., & Yuan, Y. (2012). The short of it: Investor sentiment and anomalies. *Journal of Financial Economics*, 104(2), 288–302. https://doi.org/10.1016/j.jfineco.2011.12.001.

Stenslås, A., Nygaard, M. F., Kyaw, K., & Treepongkaruna, S. (2019). Can bitcoin be a diversifier, hedge or safe haven tool? *Cogent Economics & Finance* (just-accepted), 1593072. https://doi.org/10.1080/23322039.2019.1593072.

Urquhart, A. & Zhang, H. (2019). Is bitcoin a hedge or safe haven for currencies? An intraday analysis. *International Review of Financial Analysis*, 63, 49–57. https://doi.org/10.1016/j.irfa.2019.02.009.

Wang, G.-J., Xie, C., Wen, D., & Zhao, L. (2018). When bitcoin meets economic policy uncertainty (EPU): Measuring risk spillover effect from EPU to bitcoin. *Finance Research Letters.* https://doi.org/10.1016/j.frl.2018.12.028.

Wu, S., Tong, M., Yang, Z., & Derbali, A. (2019). Does gold or bitcoin hedge economic policy uncertainty? *Finance Research Letters*, 31, 171–178. https://doi.org/10.1016/j.frl.2019.04.001.

Yermack, D. (2015). Is bitcoin a real currency? An economic appraisal. In Chuen, D. L. K. (Ed.), *Handbook of Digital Currency* (pp. 31–43). Singapore: Elsevier. https://doi.org/10.1016/B978-0-12-802117-0.00002-3.

Zhu, H., Guo, Y., You, W., & Xu, Y. (2016). The heterogeneity dependence between crude oil price changes and industry stock market returns in China: Evidence from a quantile regression approach. *Energy Economics*, 55, 30–41. https://doi.org/10.1016/j.eneco.2015.12.027.

https://doi.org/10.1142/9781800616257_0012

Chapter 12

Valuation of Bank Shares in the Digital Age: A Case Study of a South African Bank

Vusani Moyo[*,‡] **and Ayodeji Michael Obadire**[†,§]

[*]Faculty of Management, Commerce and Law, University of Venda, Thohoyandou, South Africa

[†]School of Finance and Professional Studies, Botswana Accountancy College, Gaborone, Botswana

[‡]*vusani.moyo@univen.ac.za*

[§]*ayodejio@bac.ac.bw*

Abstract

The valuation of bank equity assets is a complex exercise since the operations of banking firms are highly segmented, regulated and digitally inclined. They trade in financial securities whose prices are significantly correlated with wider macroeconomic variables, employ different accounting policies and possess highly leveraged capital structures. This complexity partly explains why the literature on bank valuation is very limited. This study evaluated the suitability and equivalency of the variants of the dividend discount, market multiples, residual income and abnormal earnings growth equity asset valuation models for valuing bank shares in the digital age. The study discusses the variants of these models using FirstRand Limited's financial data. The multiples valuation models used in the study only require the target firm's data as input, which makes them more relevant to firm valuation. The equity asset valuation models used in this study yielded similar intrinsic values for FirstRand Limited's shares, with the 2019 intrinsic values being closer to the bank's realized share prices. The equity pricing error of the models is also very low. These results confirm the equivalency and suitability of these valuation models for valuing bank shares. Given the rapid pace of technological advancements, the study recommends that analysts integrate scenario analysis to account for potential technological disruptions in valuations. Other practical implications include adaptability, dynamic metrics and incorporating digital assets, enhancing the relevance and reliability of valuation models for digital banking and providing valuable insights to analysts and investors.

Keywords: Abnormal earnings growth, digital banking, dividend discount model, market multiples, residual income, valuation.

12.1. Introduction

The advent of digitalization has revolutionized the financial landscape, introducing a paradigm shift in how we perceive, assess and value bank shares (Hunjra & Hanif, 2023). As traditional banking models embrace digital transformation, the valuation of bank shares is intricately tied to the innovations and disruptions that digitalization brings (Dermine, 2016). The integration of cutting-edge technologies, such as artificial intelligence, blockchain and data analytics, has not only reshaped the operational landscape of financial institutions but also introduced new dimensions to the criteria for evaluating the worth of bank shares (Murinde *et al.*, 2022). This transformative impact extends beyond traditional valuation methodologies, challenging stakeholders to navigate a dynamic landscape where the value of digital assets, cybersecurity resilience and regulatory compliance play pivotal roles in determining the market perception and intrinsic value of bank shares (Dermine, 2016). According to Ericson & Koller (2020), the principles of valuation remain consistent in the digital age. They argue that, whether tech-enabled or old-school, proposed projects should be assessed based on the cash flows they generate, emphasizing the importance of developing an honest base case and exploring a full range of cash-flow scenarios for meaningful comparisons (Bailey & Koller, 2017). Consequently, the process of valuing bank shares established before digitalization still holds true in the digital era, underlining the significance of understanding the intricate effects of technological advancements for investors, analysts and financial institutions in navigating the complexities of a rapidly evolving financial ecosystem.

Despite the groundbreaking potential inherent in digitalization, corporate finance literature has consistently overlooked the financial policies and valuations of banking and other financial services firms. Dermine (2010) and Gounder & Venkateshwaralu (2014) note that only a limited number of finance papers and textbooks discuss the valuation of banks and other financial service firms. Operational complexity, as highlighted by Koller *et al.* (2010), is cited as the main reason for considering the valuation of a bank to be very difficult. Damodaran (2013) asserts that this complexity arises from the special nature of a banking firm's operations, which differentiates it from a non-banking one in several respects. First, their capital structures are heavily regulated in most, if not all, regimes across the globe. In South Africa, for example, the South African Reserve Bank, which regulates banks in the country, has set the minimum capital adequacy ratios for all local banks at 6.5% for Common Equity Tier 1 (CET1), 8.0% for Tier 1 and 10.0% for total capital (FirstRand Group, 2015:20). These ratios are much stricter than the current Basel III codes of 4.5% for CET 1, 6.0% for Tier 1 and 8.0% for total capital (Basel Committee on Banking Supervision, 2011:14; Obadire *et al.*, 2023). Second, banks tend to rely more on debt for financing their operations, making them more highly leveraged than non-banking firms. Furthermore, the definition of debt capital is not always clear in banking firms, as it may also include interest-bearing customer deposits.

Third, banks trade in financial securities whose prices are highly volatile. The prices of these securities, which banks trade in, are significantly correlated with macroeconomic fundamentals such as interest rates, exchange rates, inflation and economic growth rates. Slight changes in any or all of these macroeconomic variables can cause large swings in the prices of these securities and bank share prices. This volatility in the prices of financial securities which banks trade in explains why banks use the mark–market accounting policy for determining the fair value of their assets and liabilities. It also explains why banking firms place a strong emphasis on the creation of provisions to cover possible future loses.

Lastly, banking firms are normally highly segmented, with most of them having several businesses as well as geographical segments (Koller *et al.*, 2010:765). For example, as of 30 June 2015, 52% of FirstRand Limited's normalized earnings came from retail banking,

29% from corporate and investment banking and 19% from commercial banking. Geographically, 90.75% of the bank's profit came from the South African market, with only 9.25% coming from the African market (FirstRand Group, 2015:28). This segmentation turns a bank into a multi-business enterprise, further complicating the valuation process. In summary, these distinct characteristics of banks clearly differentiate them from non-banking firms and make their valuation a complex but special exercise.

The aim of this study is to evaluate the suitability and equivalency of the variants of the dividend discount, market multiples, residual income and abnormal earnings growth valuation models in valuing bank shares. The study first discusses the theoretical foundations of the variants of these valuation models. The suitability and equivalency of the variants of these valuation approaches are then illustrated using FirstRand Limited's financial data. The share statistics of FirstRand Limited used in this study are contained in Annexure 12A, and the annual financial statement extracts that were used to compile the share statistics are contained in Annexure 12B. The variants were used to estimate the trailing, leading and target share prices for FirstRand Limited as of 17 March 2020. In all variants of the models, the estimated intrinsic values for the trailing, leading and target share prices were 6,659.04, 7,225.06 and 7,839.19 cents (in South African Rand), respectively. The trailing share price was within the 12-month period up to 30 June 2019, with the price ranging from an average high of 6,693.42 cents per share to an average low of 6,512.92 cents per share. These results confirm the equivalency and suitability of these variants for valuing bank shares under specific assumptions. FirstRand Limited was selected as the case study for this research due to its early adoption of digitalization in its operations and its representative capacity for the majority of Southern African banks.

The study contributes significantly to existing bank valuation literature in three ways. First, it illustrates the practical applications of the variants of the dividend discount, market multiples, residual income and abnormal earnings growth valuation models for valuing bank shares. Second, it adds to the number of models available for analysts to use in the valuation of bank shares. The alternative valuation models provide analysts with a robustness check for the calculated share prices. Lastly, the direct target share price estimation models developed in this study will be invaluable to investors and analysts, as the bank valuation process also involves the determination of future target share prices as they navigate the complexities of a rapidly evolving financial ecosystem. The remainder of the chapter proceeds as follows. Section 12.2 discusses the general approach to the valuation of bank equity. The bank valuation methods are discussed and illustrated in Section 12.3. Section 12.4 concludes the study.

12.2. The General Approach to the Valuation of Bank Equity

The fundamental assumption underlying the valuation of a target firm's share is that the firm is a going concern. This means that the firm will continue or eventually commence generating cash flows or earnings in the foreseeable future. This assumption implies that by investing in the firm, an investor is effectively purchasing the future earnings and cash flows that the firm is expected to generate. Past earnings are irrelevant in this case, as they have already been consumed and any residuals incorporated into today's share prices. The historical earnings only serve as a guide to the firm's historic performance, which may or may not reflect the expected future earnings trends. The valuation process therefore seeks to establish the price of future net cash flows. Using the time value of money, the future price is therefore the present value of all expected future cash flows. This is the fundamental principle of valuation. The value of an asset is equal to the net present value of cash flows expected to be generated by the asset over its useful economic life. The risk-adjusted cash flows are discounted at the investors' expected rate of return to arrive at their net present value. The net present value is the asset's current price.

12.2.1. *A brief overview of the valuation process*

The valuation process normally begins with a statement of the purpose of valuation. Is the valuation intended to evaluate the correctness of the existing price or calculate the target price for an investor seeking a short-term investment? The valuation statement is then followed by a detailed review of the target bank's operations and business portfolio, which constitutes bank and banking industry analysis. The aim of the review is to identify the target bank's historical performance trends, current and future value drivers, future performance trends and its sources of short- and long-term growth. The target bank's historical, current and expected performance is evaluated against the performance of its local and international peers. The review process further provides a sensitivity analysis of the impact of predicted changes in the regulatory framework, macroeconomic and microeconomic variables and international capital markets on the bank's expected future earnings. The bank and banking industry analysis seeks to answer the following questions: What are the main drivers of the bank's earnings? What is the bank's expected future earnings and what will be the main drivers of these earnings? Where will growth originate? How is the bank performing compared to its local and international peers? Which business and geographic segments significantly contribute to the bank's earnings? How have the bank's earnings grown over the past five or ten years, and what is the firm's current sustainable growth rate? What is the impact of predicted macroeconomic changes on the bank's earnings? The most frequently used earnings measures are the return on equity (ROE), headline earnings per share (HEPS), basic earnings per share (EPS) and dividend per share. The growth in dividends is normally estimated by calculating the geometric mean of the past five-year dividend payouts, while the growth in earnings is estimated using the bank's historic or normalized sustainable growth rate.

The output of the review process is a detailed three- to five-year forecast of the bank's financial statements. These statements are used to calculate the appropriate share statistics such as dividend per share (DPS), HEPS, EPS, ROE and book value per share (BVPS). Finally, the valuation expert must estimate the appropriate discount rate, which, in the case of equity valuation, is the cost of equity. The capital asset pricing model (CAPM), developed by William Sharpe (1964), John Lintner (1975), Jack Treynor (1962) and Jan Mossin (1966), is the most widely used model to estimate a firm's cost of equity. A recent survey by Bancel & Mittoo (2014:109) found that 80% of European valuation experts use the CAPM to estimate the cost of equity. The valuation process ends with an estimation of the firm's trailing, leading or target price of its shares. The estimated values are then compared with those of peers to rationalize them.

12.2.2. *Estimating dividend growth rate from historical dividends*

In the case of the dividend valuation model, the growth in dividends can be estimated using the bank's historic dividends. If past dividends grew at a constant rate, g, then future dividends can be estimated from past dividends using the model

$$D_n = D_{-n}(1+g)^n,$$

where D_0 is the current dividend and D_{-n} is the dividend in year $-n$. If n periods are considered, this model can be expressed as follows:

$$\begin{aligned}(1+g) &= \left(\frac{D_0}{D_{-n}}\right)^{1/n} \Rightarrow g \\ &= \left(\frac{D_0}{D_{-n}}\right)^{1/n} - 1. \end{aligned} \tag{12.1}$$

This model, which estimates the dividend geometric growth rate, can generally be stated as

$$g = \left[\left(\frac{\text{Last dividend}}{\text{Starting period dividend}}\right)^{1/\text{no. of years}} - 1\right]. \tag{12.2}$$

Using FirstRand Limited's data, the bank's gross dividend growth rate between 2015 and 2019 is calculated as

$$g = \left(\frac{291.00}{210.00}\right)^{1/4} - 1 = 8.50\%.$$

The dividend growth rate of 8.50% per annum is the same as the firm's EPS growth rate estimated by Infront Analytics (2020). The geometric mean model can also be used to estimate growth rates in basic EPS, ROE and BVPS. FirstRand Limited's growth rates in EPS, ROE and BVPS between 2015 and 2019 are calculated as follows:

$$g_{\text{EPS}} = \left(\frac{566.17}{412.25}\right)^{1/4} - 1 = 8.25\%,$$

Table 12.1. FirstRand Limited's year-to-year changes in DPS, EPS, ROE and BVPS between the years 2015 and 2019.

	2015	**2016**	**2017**	**2018**	**2019**	**Std. dev.**
DPS (cents [in South African Rand])	—	7.62%	12.83%	7.84%	5.82%	3.01%
EPS (cents)	—	4.11%	8.57%	7.66%	12.85%	3.59%
ROE (%)	—	−5.00%	0.12%	−3.54%	2.08%	3.26%
BVPS (cents)	—	9.59%	8.44%	11.61%	10.55%	1.35%

$$g_{\text{ROE}} = \left(\frac{21.96\%}{23.45\%}\right)^{1/4} - 1 = -1.62\%,$$

$$g_{\text{BVPS}} = \left(\frac{2{,}577.65}{1{,}757.91}\right)^{1/4} - 1 = 10.04\%.$$

The main problem with these growth rates is that they assume a constant historic growth rate over the past five years (Moyo & Mache, 2018). This is clearly not the case for FirstRand Limited. Table 12.1 shows the bank's historic year-to-year growth rates in DPS, EPS, ROE and BVPS for the years 2015–2019. Clearly, all the year-to-year growth rates are non-constant. The bank's BVPS has the lowest standard deviation of 1.35%. The DPS, EPS and ROE metrics are however stable, as demonstrated by their low standard deviations of 3.01%, 3.59% and 3.26%, respectively.

The DPS, EPS and BVPS growth rates are positive during the period under review, and they have low volatilities as well. These growth rates can be used as proxies for the firm's dividend and earnings long-term growth rates, and hence they are very useful in equity valuation. The ROE growth rate is, however, inconsistent, with negative growth in some years. This makes it less useful for valuation, as valuation is concerned with steady or constant growth in perpetuity. The other proxy for the growth rates in the firm's EPS and DPS that is widely used by valuation specialists is the firm's sustainable growth rate.

12.2.3. *The sustainable growth rate model*

Pinto *et al.* (2015) define the sustainable growth rate as the growth in dividends and earnings that can be sustained for a given level of

ROE if the firm's capital structure remains unchanged. This means that the sustainable growth rate can be a proxy of long-term growth in both dividends and earnings for a given level of ROE if the capital structure of the firm remains unchanged. The bank's sustainable growth rate is estimated using the following model:

$$g = b \times \text{ROE}, \tag{12.3}$$

where b is the earnings retention rate and ROE is the firm's return on equity. The retention rate is calculated as $b = 1 - \text{payout ratio}$ or

$$b = \frac{\text{Profit after tax} - \text{dividends}}{\text{Profit after tax}} \times 100.$$

The ROE is calculated from

$$\text{ROE} = \frac{\text{Total earnings attributable to equity holders}}{\text{Total shareholders' interest}} \times 100.$$

Once calculated, the sustainable growth rate is then normalized by comparing it to the bank's local and international peers. The normalized growth rate is then used as a proxy for the long-term growth rate in DPS, EPS and BVPS in equity asset valuation models. FirstRand Limited's 2019 sustainable growth rate is

$$g = 48.60\% \times 21.96\% = 10.68\%.$$

FirstRand Limited's year-to-year growth in SGR is shown in Table 12.2.

As with the ROE, the bank's year-to-year SGR is also non-constant, exhibits negative changes in most years and also has a high standard deviation of 6.83%. The SGR is also higher than the calculated growth rates in DPS (8.50%) and EPS (8.25%). The magnitude and volatility of the bank's SGR make it a less suitable proxy for long-term growth rate in the bank's DPS and EPS. The DPS and EPS growth rates are both closer to the firm's future earnings growth

Table 12.2. FirstRand Limited: Year-to-year changes in the SGR between 2011 and 2015.

	2015	2016	2017	2018	2019	Std. dev.
SGR (%)	—	−8.32%	−4.24%	−3.73%	9.79%	6.83%

rate of 8.50% per annum provided by Infront Analytics (2020). As the bank's dividend growth is less volatile than the EPS growth, it can be used as a proxy for the long-term growth rate in both DPS and EPS. The study thus used the long-term growth rate of 8.50% per annum as the bank's SGR. If the firm's 2019 dividend pay-out ratio of 51.80% is maintained in the long term, the 8.50% per annum long-term growth rate implies that the bank's long-term ROE will be

$$\text{ROE} = \frac{g}{b} = \frac{8.50\%}{48.60} = 17.49\%.$$

The bank's long-term ROE is therefore forecasted to remain unchanged at 17.49%. The firm's ROE is related to its EPS and BVPS as follows (Pinto *et al.*, 2015):

$$\text{ROE} = \frac{\text{EPS}}{\text{BVPS}}. \tag{12.4}$$

From model (12.4), the firm's long-term BVPS is then estimated as follows:

$$\text{BVPS} = \frac{\text{EPS}}{\text{ROE}} = \frac{566.17}{17.49\%} = 3{,}237.30 \text{ cents.}$$

If EPS grows at 8.50% and ROE remains unchanged at 17.49%, then FirstRand Limited's BVPS will remain unchanged at 3,237.30 cents per share. After determining the long-term growth rate in DPS and EPS and the long-term values of the BVPS and ROE, the next step is to estimate the firm's suitable discount rate. This is the rate that will be used to discount the future cash flows to arrive at the value of the bank. In the case of bank equity valuation, the relevant discount rate is the cost of equity.

12.2.4. *The cost of equity*

The cost of equity is the investor's opportunity cost of investing in the equity asset. The capital asset pricing model developed by William Sharpe (1964), John Lintner (1975), Jack Treynor (1962) and Jan Mossin (1966) is the most popular model used in estimating the cost of equity (Bancel & Mittoo, 2014; Moyo & Mache, 2018). The model is formally stated as

$$E(r_i) = k_e = r_f + \beta_i \times [E(r_m) - r_f], \tag{12.5}$$

where $E(r_i)$ is the expected return from stock$_i$, k_e is the firm's cost of equity which is equal to $E(r_i)$, r_f is the risk-free rate whose proxy is normally the yield of either a 1-year or 10-year government debt instrument (Treasury Bill or bond), β_i measures the systematic (non-diversifiable) risk of stock$_i$ relative to the market portfolio and $E(r_m)$ is the expected return from the market portfolio. The Bancel & Mitoo (2014, p. 109) survey of top European CFOs revealed that 78% of the CFOs use the yield of the 10-year maturity government bond as a proxy for the risk-free rate. For the 12 months up to 17 March 2019, the listed long-term RSA government bonds were the R186 (which matures on 21 December 2026) and the R213 (which matures on 28 February 2031). Thus, the study used the R186 bond, whose average yield over the past 12 months is 8.60% as on 17 March 2019. FirstRand Limited's share beta average for the past 12 months was 0.58. Damodaran's (2014) estimate for the South African equity market risk premium is 7.37%. The bank's cost of equity is therefore

$$k_e = 8.60\% + 0.58 \times 7.37\% = 12.87\%.$$

This is the final input data required for the valuation process. It is the appropriate discount rate that is used to estimate the bank's equity.

12.3. Valuing Bank Shares

The last stage of the valuation process is to calculate the expected value of the bank's shares, rationalize the calculated values and then recommend a fair price. The variants of the valuation methods described and illustrated in this study are the constant growth dividend valuation, the multiples methods, the residual income and abnormal earnings growth.

12.3.1. *The constant or single-phase growth dividend discount model*

Digitalization often leads to shifts in business models, with banks increasingly relying on technology-driven services. Assessing the constant or single-phase growth of dividends requires a nuanced understanding of how digital strategies influence revenue streams and payout policies (Ericson & Koller, 2020). For instance, if digitalization accelerates customer acquisition and engagement, leading to sustained revenue growth, it could positively impact the constant growth rate used in this valuation method. However, uncertainties related to technological disruptions and the rapid evolution of digital services may introduce complexities in projecting stable dividend growth over the long term. In mature firms, investors receive steady dividends, which, in most cases, grow at a predictable constant rate. The dividend constitutes a direct cash flow return to the investor and hence the value of the share can be linked to anticipated future dividends plus any realized capital gains or losses. If future dividends grow at a constant rate, g, and an investor holds a share for a finite period, then the value of the share can be estimated using the following discount model estimating the dividend and any realized capital gains or losses:

$$P_0 = \frac{D_0(1+g)}{(1+k_e)^1} + \frac{D_0(1+g)^2}{(1+k_e)^2} + \cdots + \frac{D_0(1+g)^n}{(1+k_e)^n} + \frac{P_n}{(1+k_e)^n}. \tag{12.6}$$

If the cost of equity is expected to change over the holding period, then model (12.5) is restated as

$$P_0 = \frac{D_0(1+g)}{(1+k_{e1})^1} + \frac{D_0(1+g)^2}{(1+k_{e2})^2} + \cdots + \frac{D_0(1+g)^n}{(1+k_{en})^n} + \frac{P_n}{(1+k_{en})^n}. \tag{12.7}$$

The challenge in using models (12.6) and (12.7) to estimate the current fair price of the share is that both models require an estimation of P_n, which can be problematic. Assuming that P_0 reflects the fair current share price, models (12.6) and (12.7) can be used to directly estimate the target share price, P_n. This makes these two models very useful in bank valuation, as analysts often require a one- to five-year target price.

In some cases, investors hold the shares for an indefinite period. In such cases, the constant growth dividend valuation model can be stated as

$$P_0 = \frac{D_0(1+g)}{(1+k_{e1})^1} + \frac{D_0(1+g)^2}{(1+k_{e2})^2} + \cdots + \frac{D_0(1+g)^\infty}{(1+k_{en})^\infty} + \frac{P_\infty}{(1+k_{en})^\infty}. \tag{12.8}$$

As $\frac{P_\infty}{(1+k_{en})^\infty} \to 0$, model (12.8) can be restated as

$$P_0 = \sum_{t=1}^{\infty} \frac{D_0(1+g)^t}{(k_e-g)^t} \equiv D_0 \sum_{t=1}^{\infty} \frac{(1+g)^t}{(k_e-g)^t}. \tag{12.9}$$

This is a growing perpetuity, and thus model (12.9) reduces to

$$P_0 = \frac{D_0(1+g)}{(k_e-g)} \equiv \frac{D_1}{(k_e-g)}, \quad \text{noting that}$$
$$\sum_{t=1}^{\infty} \frac{(1+g)^t}{(k_e-g)^t} = \frac{1+g}{k_e-g}, \tag{12.10}$$

where $D_1 = D_0(1+g)$. This constant growth dividend discount model is also called the *Gordon Dividend Valuation*, or the *Gordon–Shapiro Dividend Valuation* model after Gordon & Shapiro (1956) and Gordon (1962). As the dividend growth rate is highly volatile, the bank's sustainable growth rate, which is less volatile, is used as a proxy for dividend growth rate in this model. The model is formally stated as

$$P_0 = \frac{D_0(1+g)}{(k_e-g)} \equiv \frac{D_1}{(k_e-g)}. \tag{12.11}$$

In the FirstRand Limited case, the 2020 target share price (NTM from 1 July 2019 to 30 June 2020) is calculated as

$$P_0 = \frac{291.00 \times (1+8.50\%)}{(12.87\% - 8.50\%)} = 7{,}225.06\,\text{cents}.$$

As model (12.11) uses D_1 to calculate P_0, it is essentially a leading price-to-dividends multiple model. This analysis is helpful when comparing it to the other multiples valuation models. The only multiples models that naturally match with this model are the leading multiples, as opposed to the trailing ones.

The trailing constant growth dividend discount model uses the past year's dividend and sustainable growth rate, and it is stated as

$$P_0 = \frac{D_{-1}(1+g_{-1})}{(k_e - g_{-1})} \equiv \frac{D_0}{(k_e - g_{-1})}. \quad (12.12)$$

$D_{-1}(1+g_{-1})$ and g_{-1} are the past year's estimates of the current dividend and sustainable growth rates, respectively. These have since been realized as D_0, and hence the more relevant dividend and sustainable growth rate will be D_0 and g_0, respectively. The trailing dividend discount model is therefore stated as

$$P_0 = \frac{D_0}{(k_e - g_0)}. \quad (12.13)$$

FirstRand Limited's trailing share price is calculated as

$$P_0 = \frac{291.00}{(12.87\% - 8.50\%)} = 6{,}659.04 \text{ cents}.$$

This should have been the target share price during the 12 months up to 30 June 2019. It is the bank's leading share price as of 30 June 2018.

The main problem with model (12.11) is that it cannot be used directly to estimate the share's leading target price beyond a year's time. Analysts and investors normally require a target price to appraise the investment in a particular share. To estimate the leading target price beyond next year, P_T, the bank's leading target dividend, D_T, must first be estimated using

$$D_T = D_0 \times (1+g)^T. \quad (12.14)$$

Substituting for D_0 and D_1 in model (12.11) yields the leading target price estimation dividend discount model:

$$P_T = \frac{D_0 \times (1+g)^T \times (1+g)}{(k_e - g)} \equiv \frac{D_0 \times (1+g)^{T+1}}{(k_e - g)} \equiv \frac{D_{T+1}}{(k_e - g)}. \quad (12.15)$$

Model (12.15) allows for a direct estimation of the firm's target price beyond next year. This model differs from model (12.11) in that is does not require the current price in estimating the target price. Assume that an analyst wants to estimate FirstRand Limited's share target price by the end of 2021 (two years from 2019). The leading target price is

$$P_{2021} = \frac{291.00 \times (1 + 8.50\%)^2}{(12.87\% - 8.50\%)} = 7{,}839.19 \text{ cents.}$$

This is the target price that the potential investors will expect to pay or receive in 2021.

The constant growth dividend valuation model can be modified to use EPS instead of DPS. Parrino (2005:23) presents a modified dividend discount model that uses EPS and the bank's payout ratio. The firm's current dividend, D_0, is given by

$$D_0 = \text{EPS}_0 \times b, \tag{12.16}$$

where EPS_0 is current EPS and b is the dividend payout ratio ($b = \frac{D_0}{\text{EPS}_0}$). Substituting for D_0 in model (12.11), the constant growth dividend discount model yields

$$P_1 = \frac{\text{EPS}_0(1+g) \times b}{(k_e - g)} \equiv \frac{\text{EPS}_1 \times b)}{(k_e - g)}. \tag{12.17}$$

This model is equivalent to model (12.11), except that it is the leading price-to-earnings multiple instead of the leading price-to-dividend multiple. FirstRand's 2020 leading share price is estimated as

$$P_1 = \frac{566.17 \times (1 + 8.50\%) \times 51.40\%}{(12.87\% - 8.50\%)} = 7{,}225.06 \text{ cents.}$$

As with model (12.13), the trailing dividend discount model is given by

$$P_0 = \frac{\text{EPS}_{-1}(1+g_{-1}) \times b}{(k_e - g_{-1})} \equiv \frac{\text{EPS}_0 \times b}{(k_e - g_0)}. \tag{12.18}$$

The trailing price of FirstRand's share is calculated as

$$P_0 = \frac{566.17 \times 51.40\%}{(12.87\% - 8.50\%)} = 6{,}659.04 \text{ cents.}$$

As is the case with model (12.11), model (12.17) cannot be used directly to estimate the leading target price beyond next year. The leading target price can be estimated by first estimating the target EPS beyond next year, EPS_T, which is given by

$$\text{EPS}_T = \text{EPS}_0 \times (1+g)^T. \tag{12.19}$$

Substituting for EPS_0 and EPS_1 in model (12.17) yields

$$P_T = \frac{\text{EPS}_0 \times (1+g)^T \times (1+g) \times b}{(k_e - g)}. \tag{12.20}$$

This can also be written as

$$P_T = \frac{\text{EPS}_0 \times (1+g)^{T+1} \times b}{(k_e - g)} \equiv \frac{\text{EPS}_{T+1} \times b}{(k_e - g)}. \tag{12.21}$$

The 2021 leading target share price is calculated as

$$P_{2021} = \frac{566.17 \times (1+8.50\%)^2 \times 51.40\%}{(12.87\% - 8.50\%)} = 7{,}839.19 \text{ cents.}$$

The following section discusses the multiples valuation method.

12.3.2. *Bank equity valuation using multiples*

The multiples, market-based, or relative valuation models are based on the law of one price, which states that, in equilibrium, similar assets will have a similar price. The models involve using a comparable firm's multiple to value the target firm. Equity or firm value is determined as the value of the comparable firm multiplied by a specific denominator of the firm or share being valued. In equity valuation, the share value is calculated using

$$V_0 = \text{Comparable firm multiple} \times \text{Equity} - \text{Specific denominator}. \tag{12.22}$$

The target firm will be considered overvalued (undervalued) if the calculated price (or multiple) is greater (less) than the current market price (comparable firm multiple).

The multiple is equal to the share price per equity-specific denominator. Common denominators used in bank equity valuation are EPS, BVPS and price–earnings growth (PEG). The market multiples valuation models assume that comparable firms, on average, are fairly valued and share similar fundamental characteristics with the firm being valued. The difficulty always lies in finding a firm that matches the exact profile of the target firm. Firms differ in financial performance, risk profiles, operational efficiencies and size. This makes it extremely difficult to find a firm that exactly matches the target in all aspects. To resolve this dilemma, modified multiples can be used instead of traditional ones. The modified multiples make use of the firm's earnings measures, such as EPS, BVPS and ROE. Depending on the price to be determined, the multiple can either be a trailing, leading or target multiple. The trailing multiples make use of the target firm's historical data, while leading and target multiples use forecasted data. This chapter discusses the use of the price-to-earnings (P/E) ratio, PEG and the price-to-book value (P/BVPS) multiples to value bank shares.

12.3.2.1. *Price-to-earnings ratio*

The P/E ratio is simply the firm's price scaled up by its EPS. As discussed above, this ratio can be leading, trailing or a target depending on the EPS used. In digital finance, the P/E ratio could be impacted by the perceived growth potential of digital initiatives, reflecting investor confidence in the bank's ability to capitalize on digital opportunities. A trailing P/E ratio is obtained by dividing the current share price by the past year's EPS or the current EPS, (EPS_0). According to Moyo & Mache (2018), the standard textbook method of obtaining a firm's trailing P/E valuation model is by dividing the trailing dividend discount model (12.12) by the current year's EPS, (EPS_0):

$$\frac{P_0}{\mathrm{EPS}_0} = \frac{D_0/\mathrm{EPS}_0}{(k_e - g)},$$
$$\frac{P_0}{\mathrm{EPS}_0} = PE_0 = \frac{\frac{D_0}{\mathrm{EPS}_0}}{(k_e - g)}. \tag{12.23}$$

The ratio $\frac{D_0}{\mathrm{EPS}_0}$ gives the firm's payout ratio, $(1 - b)$, where b is the firm's retention rate. The equation can then be simplified to

$$\frac{P_0}{\mathrm{EPS}_0} = \mathrm{PE}_0 = \frac{(1 - b)}{(k_e - g)}. \tag{12.23.1}$$

As $(1-b)$ is the firm's payout ratio, this model can also be written as

$$\frac{P_0}{\text{EPS}_0} = \text{PE}_0 = \frac{\text{Payout ratio}}{(k_e - g)}. \tag{12.23.2}$$

The trailing share price is then given by

$$P_0 = \frac{\text{Payout ratio}}{(k_e - g)} \times \text{EPS}_0 \equiv \frac{(1-b)}{(k_e - g)} \times \text{EPS}_0. \tag{12.24}$$

This model assumes that the firm's current payout ratio will remain unchanged in the long-term. It is equivalent to model (12.13), the alternative dividend valuation model. FirstRand's trailing share price is calculated as

$$P_0 = \left(\frac{51.40\%}{12.87\% - 8.50\%}\right) \times 566.17 = 6{,}659.04 \text{ cents}.$$

This share price implies a trailing P/E multiple of

$$\frac{P_0}{\text{EPS}_0} = \frac{6{,}659.04}{566.17} = 11.76x.$$

The standard textbook leading P/E valuation model is obtained by dividing the basic dividend discount model (12.11) by the firm's leading EPS, (EPS_1):

$$\frac{P_1}{\text{EPS}_1} = PE_1 = \frac{\frac{D_0(1+g)}{\text{EPS}_1}}{(k_e - g)} \equiv \frac{\frac{D_1}{\text{EPS}_1}}{(k_e - g)}. \tag{12.25}$$

The ratio $\frac{D_1}{\text{EPS}_1}$ gives the firm's leading payout ratio, $(1-b)$, where b is the firm's retention rate. The equation can then be simplified to

$$\frac{P_1}{\text{EPS}_1} = \text{PE}_1 = \frac{(1-b)}{(k_e - g)}. \tag{12.25.1}$$

As $(1-b)$ is the firm's leading payout ratio, this model can also be written as

$$\frac{P_1}{\text{EPS}_1} = PE_1 = \frac{\text{Payout ratio}}{(k_e - g)}. \tag{12.25.2}$$

Parrino (2005:23) obtained the same leading P/E model by dividing the basic dividend discount model (12.11) by the past year's EPS, EPS_0:

$$\frac{P_1}{\text{EPS}_1} = \text{PE}_0 = \frac{\frac{D_0(1+g)}{\text{EPS}_1}}{(k_e - g)}. \tag{12.26}$$

The ratio $\frac{D_1}{\text{EPS}_1}$ gives the firm's leading payout ratio, $(1 - b)$, where b is the firm's retention rate (Pinto *et al.*, 2015). The equation can then be simplified to

$$\frac{P_1}{\text{EPS}_1} = \text{PE}_1 = \frac{(1-b)}{(k_e - g)}. \tag{12.26.1}$$

The leading share price is then calculated by

$$P_1 = \frac{(1-b)}{(k_e - g)} \times \text{EPS}_0 \times (1+g). \tag{12.27.1}$$

As $\text{EPS}_0 \times (1+g) = \text{EPS}_1$, the model can also be written as

$$P_1 = \frac{(1-b)}{(k_e - g)} \times \text{EPS}_1. \tag{12.27.2}$$

This model is the same as model (12.25.2). The leading price per share, P_1, is therefore given by

$$P_1 = \frac{\text{Payout ratio} \times \text{EPS}_1}{(k_e - g)} \equiv \frac{(1-b) \times \text{EPS}_1}{(k_e - g)}. \tag{12.27.3}$$

This model is equivalent to model (12.11) of the alternative dividend valuation model. Using FirstRand's share statistics, the 2020 leading share price is

$$P_0 = \left(\frac{51.40\%}{12.87\% - 8.50\%}\right) \times 566.17 \times (1 + 8.50\%) = 7{,}225.06 \text{ cents.}$$

This intrinsic share value implies a leading P/E multiple of

$$\frac{P_1}{\text{EPS}_1} = \frac{7{,}225.06}{566.17} = 12.76x.$$

Models (12.25.2) and (12.26.1) are equivalent, and they are also equivalent to the alternative constant growth dividend discount model (12.11), as they use the leading EPS, EPS_1. Similar to the alternative constant growth dividend valuation model, these models can be modified to give a model that can be used directly to estimate the leading target price. As $\text{EPS}_1 = \text{EPS}_0 \times (1+g)$, the target price is calculated as

$$P_T = \frac{(1-b)}{(k_e - g)} \times \text{EPS}_{T+1} \equiv \frac{(1-b)}{(k_e - g)} \times \text{EPS}_0 \times (1+g)^{T+1}. \quad (12.28)$$

This can also be expressed as

$$P_{T+1} = \frac{\text{Payout ratio}}{(k_e - g)} \times \text{EPS}_0 \times (1+g)^{T+1}. \quad (12.29)$$

This model is the same as model (12.15) of the alternative dividend valuation model. FirstRand's 2021 leading target price is

$$\begin{aligned} P_{2021} &= \left(\frac{51.40\%}{12.87\% - 8.50\%}\right) \times 566.17 \times (1 + 8.50\%)^2 \\ &= 7{,}839.19 \text{ cents.} \end{aligned}$$

FirstRand's 2021 leading target P/E multiple is

$$\frac{P_{2021}}{\text{EPS}_{T+1}} = \frac{7{,}839.19}{566.17 \times (1 + 8.50\%)^2} = 11.76x.$$

Suozzo *et al.* (2001) derived an alternative P/E multiple model that uses the firm's long-term ROE, ROE_L. The firm's retention rate can be obtained from the sustainable growth model as

$$g = b \times \text{ROE}_L \Rightarrow b = \frac{g}{\text{ROE}_L}. \quad (12.30)$$

Substituting for b in model (12.23.1) gives the firm's trailing P/E ratio as

$$\frac{P_0}{\text{EPS}_0} = \frac{(1 - \frac{g}{\text{ROE}_L})}{(k_e - g)}. \quad (12.31)$$

This simplifies to

$$\frac{P_0}{\text{EPS}_0} = \frac{ROE_L - g}{\text{ROE}_L \times (k_e - g)}. \quad (12.32)$$

The trailing share price is therefore given by

$$P_0 = \frac{\text{ROE}_L - g}{\text{ROE}_L \times (k_e - g)} \times \text{EPS}_0. \quad (12.33)$$

This model uses the firm's long-term ROE, ROE_L, and the sustainable growth rate for the firm's EPS. Using this model, FirstRand's 2019 trailing price is calculated as

$$P_0 = \left(\frac{17.49\% - 8.50\%}{17.49\% \times (12.87\% - 8.50\%)}\right) \times 566.17 = 6{,}659.04 \text{ cents.}$$

The implied trailing P/E multiple is calculated as

$$\frac{P_0}{\text{EPS}_0} = \frac{6{,}659.04}{566.17} = 11.76x.$$

Substituting for b with $b = \frac{g}{\text{ROE}_L}$ into model (12.25.1) yields the leading P/E model:

$$\frac{P_1}{\text{EPS}_1} = \frac{(1 - \frac{g}{\text{ROE}_L})}{(k_e - g)}. \tag{12.34}$$

This simplifies to

$$\frac{P_1}{\text{EPS}_1} = \frac{\text{ROE}_L - g}{\text{ROE}_L \times (k_e - g)}. \tag{12.35}$$

The leading share price is calculated using

$$P_1 = \frac{\text{ROE}_L - g}{\text{ROE}_L \times (k_e - g)} \times \text{EPS}_1. \tag{12.36}$$

FirstRand's 2020 leading share price is calculated as

$$P_1 = \left(\frac{(17.49\% - 8.50\%)}{17.49\% \times (12.87\% - 8.50\%)}\right) \times 566.17 \times (1 + 8.50\%)$$
$$= 7{,}225.06 \text{ cents.}$$

The leading P/E multiple is calculated as

$$\frac{P_1}{\text{EPS}_1} = \frac{7{,}225.06}{566.17 \times (1 + 8.50\%)} = 12.76x.$$

Model (12.36) can be modified to allow for the determination of the leading target price. This model also uses the long-term ROE,

ROE_L. It is only the EPS that requires forecasting using $\text{EPS}_{T+1} = \text{EPS}_0 \times (1+g)^{T+1}$. The leading target price is then calculated from

$$P_T = \frac{\text{ROE}_L - g}{\text{ROE}_L \times (k_e - g)} \times \text{EPS}_0 \times (1+g)^{T+1}. \tag{12.37}$$

This model can also be written as

$$P_T = \frac{\text{ROE}_L - g}{\text{ROE}_L \times (k_e - g)} \times \text{EPS}_{T+1}. \tag{12.38}$$

FirstRand's 2021 leading target share price is

$$\begin{aligned} P_{2021} &= \left(\frac{(17.49\% - 8.50\%)}{17.49\% \times (12.87\% - 8.50\%)}\right) \times 566.176 \times (1 + 8.50\%)^2 \\ &= 7{,}839.19 \text{ cents.} \end{aligned}$$

The implied leading target P/E multiple is calculated as

$$\frac{P_{2021}}{\text{EPS}_{T+1}} = \frac{7{,}839.19}{566.17 \times (1 + 8.50\%)^2} = 11.76x.$$

The other price multiple that can also be used to value bank shares is the PEG ratio.

12.3.2.2. *Price earnings to earnings growth*

Damodaran (2006:261) defines a firm's PEG ratio as

$$\text{PEG ratio} = \frac{\text{P/E}}{\text{Expected growth rate}}. \tag{12.39}$$

From Suozzo *et al.* (2001), a firm's P/E leading ratio is defined as

$$\frac{P_1}{\text{EPS}_1} = \frac{\text{ROE}_L - g}{\text{ROE}_L \times (k_e - g)}.$$

Substituting this into the PEG model (12.39) yields the following model:

$$\text{PEG ratio} = \frac{\frac{\text{ROE}_L - g}{\text{ROE}_L \times (k_e - g)}}{g}.$$

This model simplifies to

$$\text{PEG ratio} = \frac{\text{ROE}_L - g}{g \times \text{ROE}_L \times (k_e - g)}. \tag{12.40}$$

This model gives the PEG ratio in cents as the share price is also expressed in cents. The PEG ratio for FirstRand's share price is obtained by dividing the right-hand side of the equation by 100, that is,

$$\text{PEG ratio} = \frac{\text{ROE}_L - g}{100 \times g \times \text{ROE}_L \times (k_e - g)}. \tag{12.41}$$

Both models (12.40) and (12.41) use the firm's long-term ROE, ROE_L. FirstRand Limited's PEG ratio in cents is calculated as

$$\text{PEG ratio} = \frac{17.49\% - 8.50\%}{8.50\% \times 17.49\% \times (12.87\% - 8.50\%)} = 138.37.$$

The bank's trailing share price in cents is calculated from the trailing PEG ratio:

$$\text{PEG ratio} = \frac{\frac{P_0}{\text{EPS}_0}}{g} \Rightarrow \frac{P_0}{\text{EPS}_0} = \text{PEG ratio} \times g. \tag{12.42}$$

The trailing share price is then calculated from

$$P_0 = \text{PEG ratio} \times g \times \text{EPS}_0. \tag{12.43}$$

Using FirstRand Limited's data, the trailing share price is calculated as

$$P_0 = 138.37 \times 8.50\% \times 566.17 = 6{,}659.04 \text{ cents}.$$

This share price gives a trailing P/E multiple of

$$\frac{P_0}{\text{EPS}_0} = \frac{6{,}659.04}{566.17} = 11.76x.$$

On the other hand, the leading share price, in cents, is therefore calculated from the leading PEG ratio:

$$\text{PEG ratio} = \frac{\frac{P_1}{\text{EPS}_1}}{g} \Rightarrow \frac{P_1}{\text{EPS}_1} = \text{PEG ratio} \times g. \tag{12.44}$$

This simplifies to

$$P_1 = \text{PEG ratio} \times g \times \text{EPS}_1 \equiv \text{PEG ratio} \times g \times \text{EPS}_0 \times (1+g). \tag{12.45}$$

FirstRand's 2020 leading share price is

$$P_1 = 138.37 \times 8.50\% \times 566.17 \times (1 + 8.50\%) = 7{,}225.06\,\text{cents}.$$

The leading P/E multiple implied by this share price is

$$\frac{P_1}{\text{EPS}_1} = \frac{7{,}225.06}{566.17 \times (1 + 8.50\%)} = 12.76x.$$

As with other equity asset valuation models, the PEG ratio model can also be extended to allow for a direct calculation of the bank's target share price. The modified PEG ratio model is expressed as

$$P_T = \text{PEG ratio} \times g \times \text{EPS}_0 \times (1 + g)^T. \tag{12.46}$$

FirstRand's 2021 leading target price is

$$P_{2021} = 138.37 \times 8.50\% \times 566.17 \times (1 + 8.50\%)^2 = 7{,}839.19 \text{ cents}.$$

The leading target P/E multiple is

$$\frac{P_{2021}}{\text{EPS}_T} = \frac{7{,}839.19}{566.17 \times (1 + 8.50\%)^2} = 11.76x.$$

Valuation multiples are not only limited to the bank's earnings. Other price multiples valuation models are based on the book value or net assets of the company. These models are referred to as the price to book value per share (P/BVPS), price to net asset value per share (P/NAV) or price to tangible net asset value per share (P/tNAV).

12.3.2.3. *The price-to-book (P/BV) value of equity ratio*

The P/BVPS multiple is based on the firm's market capitalization and its book value of equity, and it is calculated by dividing the firm's market capitalization by its total book value of equity. The variants of this multiple are P/NAV (calculated by scaling the firm's market capitalization by its total net assets) and P/tNAV (calculated by scaling the firm's market capitalization by its tangible net assets). Several bank stock analysts rely on either the P/NAV (which is equivalent to the P/BVPS) or the P/tNAV in valuing target bank equity. In P/BV, the book value of equity may be influenced by the bank's digital assets and technology infrastructure.

The standard textbook trailing P/BVPS valuation model is obtained by dividing both sides of model (12.24) by the firm's current book value per share, $BVPS_0$:

$$\frac{P_0}{\text{BVPS}_0} = \frac{P}{\text{BVPS}_0} = \frac{\frac{\text{EPS}_0 \times (1-b)}{\text{BVPS}_0}}{(k_e - g)}. \qquad (12.47)$$

From model (12.4), the ratio $\text{EPS}_0/\text{BVPS}_0$ defines the firm's ROE_0, and thus this model can be written as

$$\frac{P_0}{\text{BVPS}_0} = P/\text{BVPS}_0 = \frac{\text{ROE}_0 \times (1-b)}{(k_e - g)}. \qquad (12.47.1)$$

The trailing share price is given by

$$P_0 = \frac{\text{ROE}_0 \times (1-b)}{(k_e - g)} \times \text{BVPS}_0. \qquad (12.47.2)$$

This model uses the firm's current ROE, BVPS and payout ratio. It assumes that the BVPS grows at the same rate as the firm's EPS and DPS. FirstRand's trailing share price is therefore calculated as

$$P_0 = \left(\frac{21.96\% \times 51.40\%}{12.87\% - 8.50\%}\right) \times 2{,}577.65 = 6{,}659.04 \,\text{cents}.$$

This share price implies a trailing P/BVPS of

$$\frac{P_0}{\text{BVPS}_0} = \frac{6{,}659.04}{2{,}577.65} = 2.58x.$$

The firm's leading P/BVPS ratio is obtained by dividing model (12.27.2) by the firm's leading book value per share, BVPS_1:

$$\frac{P_1}{\text{BVPS}_1} = \frac{P}{\text{BVPS}_1} = \frac{\frac{\text{EPS}_1 \times (1-b)}{\text{BVPS}_1}}{(k_e - g)}. \qquad (12.48)$$

Since growth in EPS_0 is equal to growth in BVS_0, it follows that

$$\frac{\text{EPS}_0 \times (1+g)}{\text{BVPS}_0 \times (1+g)} = \frac{\text{EPS}_1}{\text{BVPS}_1}. \qquad (12.48.1)$$

Thus,

$$\frac{\text{EPS}_0}{\text{BVPS}_0} = \frac{\text{EPS}_1}{\text{BVPS}_1} = \text{ROE}_1 = \text{ROE}_0. \qquad (12.48.2)$$

This therefore implies that the leading P/BVPS ratio, $\frac{P_1}{\text{BVPS}_1}$, is given by

$$\frac{P_1}{\text{BVPS}_1} = \frac{P}{\text{BVPS}_1} = \frac{\text{ROE}_0 \times (1-b)}{(k_e - g)}. \tag{12.48.3}$$

The leading share price is estimated from

$$\begin{aligned} P_1 &= \frac{\text{ROE}_0 \times (1-b)}{(k_e - g)} \times \text{BVPS}_1 \\ &\equiv \frac{\text{ROE}_0 \times (1-b)}{(k_e - g)} \times \text{BVPS}_0 \times (1+g). \end{aligned} \tag{12.48.4}$$

The 2020 leading share price for FirstRand's shares is

$$\begin{aligned} P_0 &= \left(\frac{21.96\% \times 51.40\%}{12.87\% - 8.50\%}\right) \times 2{,}577.65 \times (1 + 8.50\%) \\ &= 7{,}225.06 \text{ cents}. \end{aligned}$$

The 2020 leading P/BVPS multiple implied by this price is

$$\frac{P_1}{\text{BVPS}_1} = \frac{7{,}225.06}{2{,}577.65 \times (1 + 8.50\%)} = 2.80x.$$

The firm's leading target price model uses the current ROE, ROE_0, and the leading BVPS, $BVPS_{T+1}$. It is estimated from

$$\begin{aligned} P_T &= \frac{\text{ROE}_0 \times (1-b)}{(k_e - g)} \times \text{BVPS}_T \\ &\equiv \frac{\text{ROE}_0 \times (1-b)}{(k_e - g)} \times \text{BVPS}_0 \times (1+g)^T. \end{aligned} \tag{12.49}$$

FirstRand's 2021 target share price is

$$\begin{aligned} P_{2021} &= \left(\frac{21.96\% \times 51.40\%}{12.87\% - 8.50\%}\right) \times 2{,}577.65 \times (1 + 8.50\%)^2 \\ &= 7{,}839.19 \text{ cents}. \end{aligned}$$

This share price implies a leading target P/BVPS of

$$\frac{P_T}{\text{BVPS}_{T+1}} = \frac{7{,}839.19}{2{,}577.65 \times (1 + 8.50\%)^2} = 2.58x.$$

The other variant of the P/BVPS multiples model was derived by Suozzo *et al.* (2001). The difference between this model and the standard textbook model is that it uses the firm's long-term ROE, ROE_L, and BVPS, BVPS_L, which are both assumed to remain constant. The firm's sustainable growth rate is given by $g = b \times \text{ROE} \Rightarrow b = g/\text{ROE}$. Substituting for b in model (12.47.2) gives the firm's trailing P/BVPS ratio, P_0/BVPS_L

$$\frac{P_0}{\text{BVPS}_L} = \frac{P}{\text{BVPS}_L} = \frac{\text{ROE}_L \times \left(1 - \frac{g}{\text{ROE}_0}\right)}{(k_e - g)}. \qquad (12.50)$$

This can also be expressed as

$$\frac{P_0}{\text{BVPS}_L} = P/\text{BVPS}_L = \frac{\text{ROE}_L - g}{\text{ROE}_L \times (k_e - g)} \times \text{ROE}_L \equiv \frac{\text{ROE}_L - g}{(k_e - g)}. \qquad (12.50.1)$$

The trailing share price is therefore given by

$$P_0 = \left(\frac{\text{ROE}_L - g}{(k_e - g)}\right) \times \text{BVPS}_L. \qquad (12.50.2)$$

Using this model, FirstRand's trailing price is calculated as

$$P_0 = \left(\frac{17.49\% - 8.50\%}{12.87\% - 8.50\%}\right) \times 3{,}237.30 = 6{,}659.04 \text{ cents.}$$

This share price gives a trailing P/BVPS multiple of

$$\frac{P_0}{\text{BVPS}_0} = \frac{6{,}659.04}{3{,}237.30} = 2.06x.$$

The leading P/BVPS uses the leading book value per share, BVPS_{L1}, instead of the trailing book value per share, BVPS_L. It is obtained by substituting for b in model (12.48.4), which gives

$$\frac{P_1}{\text{BVPS}_{L1}} = \frac{P}{\text{BVPS}_{L1}} = \frac{\text{ROE}_L \times \left(1 - \frac{g}{\text{ROE}_L}\right)}{(k_e - g)}. \qquad (12.51)$$

This simplifies to

$$\frac{P_1}{\text{BVPS}_{L1}} = \text{BVPS}_{L1} = \frac{\text{ROE}_L - g}{(k_e - g)}. \qquad (12.51.1)$$

The share price is then calculated from

$$P_1 = \left(\frac{\text{ROE}_L - g}{(k_e - g)}\right) \times \text{BVPS}_{L1}. \qquad (12.51.2)$$

FirstRand's 2020 leading share price is therefore calculated as

$$P_1 = \left(\frac{17.49\% - 8.50\%}{12.87\% - 8.50\%}\right) \times 3{,}237.30 \times (1 + 8.50\%)$$
$$= 7{,}225.06 \text{ cents.}$$

The implied leading P/BVPS multiple is

$$\frac{P_1}{\text{BVPS}_{L1}} = \frac{7{,}225.06}{3{,}237.30 \times (1 + 8.50\%)} = 2.23x.$$

In this version of the P/BVPS multiples, the target price model uses the long-term ROE, ROE_L, and long-term BVPS, BVPS_L. The 2021 leading target price can be estimated from the following model:

$$P_T = \left(\frac{\text{ROE}_L - g}{(k_e - g)}\right) \times \text{BVPS}_L \times (1 + g)^{T+1}$$
$$\equiv \left(\frac{\text{ROE}_L - g}{(k_e - g)}\right) \times \text{BVPS}_{LT}, \tag{12.52}$$

$$P_{2021} = \left(\frac{17.49\% - 8.50\%}{12.87\% - 8.50\%}\right) \times 3{,}237.30 \times (1 + 8.50\%)^2$$
$$= 7{,}839.19 \text{ cents.}$$

The leading target P/BVPS multiple is

$$\frac{P_T}{\text{BVPS}_{LT}} = \frac{7{,}839.19}{3{,}237.30 \times (1 + 8.50\%)^2} = 2.06x.$$

The residual income valuation model is discussed next.

12.3.3. *Equity valuation using the residual income valuation model*

The residual income valuation model, which is derived from the dividend discount model, was first introduced by Edwards *et al.* (1961) in their paper, "The theory and measurement of business income". The model was further developed by Peasnell (1982), Ohlson (1995) and Feltham & Ohlson (1995). Residual income is simply defined as net income less the capital charge for generating the income. The model uses accounting variables instead of free cash flows to estimate income for the firm as well as for equity holders. Evaluating the impact of digital strategies on residual income and abnormal earnings growth is integral to capturing the true value of bank shares in the digital age. To arrive at the residual income valuation model, the following zero-sum expression is added to the dividend valuation model:

$$0 = Y_t + \sum_{i=1}^{\infty} \frac{Y_{t+i} + D_{t+i} - (1 + k_e)Y_{t+i-1}}{(1 - k_e)^i}, \tag{12.53}$$

where $(Y_{t+i})(1 - k_e)^{-i} \to 0$ as $s \to \infty$, or Y could be a finite series that is expected to terminate at time $t+T$, where $(Y_{t+T}) = 0$. Adding the zero-sum expression to the dividend valuation model yields the model

$$V_t = Y_t + \sum_{i=1}^{\infty} \frac{Y_{t+i} + D_{t+i} - (1 + k_e)Y_{t+i-1}}{(1 - k_e)^i}. \tag{12.54}$$

Defining Y to be the book value of equity (BVE) yields the model

$$V_t = \text{BVE}_t + \sum_{i=1}^{\infty} \frac{\text{BVE}_{t+i} + D_{t+i} - (1 + k_e)\text{BVE}_{t+i-1}}{(1 - k_e)^i}. \tag{12.55}$$

In terms of clean surplus accounting, net income, NI_{t+i}, is expressed as

$$\text{NI}_{t+i} = \text{BVE}_{t+i} + D_{t+i} - \text{BVE}_{t+i-1}. \tag{12.56}$$

In equity valuation, the residual income (RI) is defined as net income less equity capital charge. Under the clean surplus accounting, residual income is therefore expressed as (Elliott *et al.*, 2007:116)

$$\text{RI}_{t+i} = \text{NI}_{t+i} - k_e\text{BVE}_{t+i-1}. \tag{12.57}$$

Substituting for NI_{t+i} gives

$$\text{RI}_{t+i} = \text{BVE}_{t+i} + D_{t+i} - \text{BVE}_{t+i-1} - k_e\text{BVE}_{t+i-1}. \tag{12.58}$$

This simplifies to

$$\text{RI}_{t+i} = \text{BVE}_{t+i} + D_{t+i} - (1 + k_e)\text{BVE}_{t+i-1}. \tag{12.59}$$

Substituting equation (12.59) into (12.55) gives the general equity residual income valuation model:

$$V_0 = \mathrm{BVE}_0 + \frac{\mathrm{NI}_1 - k_e \times \mathrm{BVE}_0}{(1+k_e)} + \frac{\mathrm{NI}_2 - k_e \times \mathrm{BVE}_1}{(1+k_e)^2} + \frac{\mathrm{NI}_3 - k_e \times \mathrm{BVE}_2}{(1+k_e)^3} + \cdots. \tag{12.60}$$

This can be simplified to

$$V_0 = \mathrm{BVE}_0 + \sum_{\tau=1}^{\infty} \frac{E_t \mathrm{RI}_{t+i}}{(1+k_e)^t} \equiv \mathrm{BV}_0 + \sum_{t=1}^{\infty} \frac{E_t\left(\mathrm{NI}_{t+i} - k_e \mathrm{BVE}_{t+i-1}\right)}{(1+k_e)^t}. \tag{12.61}$$

The intrinsic value of common stock can therefore be expressed as

$$P_0 = \mathrm{BVS}_0 + \sum_{t=1}^{\infty} \frac{\mathrm{RIS}_t}{(1+k_e)^t} \equiv \mathrm{BVE}_0 + \sum_{t=1}^{\infty} \frac{\mathrm{NIS}_t - k_e \mathrm{BVS}_{t-1}}{(1+k_e)^t}, \tag{12.62}$$

where P_0 is the intrinsic value of ordinary shares today ($t = 0$); BVE_0 is the current book value per share; BVS_{t-1} is the past year's book value per share; k_e is the cost of equity; NIS_t is the expected net income (net profit) per share for period t; and RIS_t is the expected residual income per share, equal to $\mathrm{NIS}_t - k_e \mathrm{BVS}_{t-1}$. The residual income valuation model therefore assumes that the value of a share is equal to the present value of the expected residual income per share. The model is termed the Ohlson (1995) and Feltham & Ohlson (1995) residual income model. According to Frankel & Lee (1998), Gebhardt *et al.* (2001) and Hirst & Hopkins (2012), the second fundamental relationship after the surplus income is expressed as follows:

$$\mathrm{NIS}_t = \mathrm{ROE}_t \times \mathrm{BVS}_{t-1}. \tag{12.63}$$

Substituting for NI_t in the Ohlson (1995) and Feltham & Ohlson (1995) residual income model yields the finite period residual income model expressed in terms of ROE_t:

$$P_0 = \mathrm{BVPS}_t + \sum_{t=1}^{\infty} \frac{\mathrm{ROE}_{t+1} \times \mathrm{BVPS}_{t-1} - k_e \mathrm{BVS}_{t-1}}{(1+k_e)^t}.$$

This can also be written as

$$P_0 = \text{BVPS}_t + \sum_{t=1}^{\infty} \frac{(\text{ROE}_{t+1} - k_e) \times \text{BVPS}_{t-1}}{(1 + k_e)^t}.$$

This simplifies to

$$P_0 = \text{BVPS}_t + \sum_{t=1}^{\infty} \frac{(\text{ROE}_t \times (1 + g) - k_e) \times \text{BVPS}_{t-1}}{(1 + k_e)^t}. \quad (12.64)$$

As with the dividend discount model, if both long-term ROE, ROE_L, and BVPS, BVPS_L, remain unchanged, the model reduces to

$$P_0 = \text{BVPS}_L + \left(\frac{\text{ROE}_L - k_e}{k_e - g}\right) \times \text{BVPS}_L. \quad (12.65)$$

This model, which is also called *the excess earnings model*, states that value-creating firms will have an *ROE* that is higher than the firm's cost of equity (k_e); otherwise, the firm will be destroying value. It assumes that both long-term ROE, ROE_L, and BVPS, BVS_L, will remain unchanged. Pinto *et al.* (2015:477) derived an equivalent model starting with the trailing P/BVPS model:

$$\frac{P_0}{\text{BVPS}_L} = \left(\frac{\text{ROE}_L - g}{k_e - g}\right). \quad (12.66)$$

Rearranging the equation yields

$$\frac{P_0}{\text{BVPS}_L} = 1 + \left(\frac{\text{ROE}_L - k_e}{k_e - g}\right). \quad (12.67)$$

The trailing share price given by this single-stage constant growth residual income model is

$$P_0 = \text{BVPS}_L + \left(\frac{\text{ROE}_L - k_e}{k_e - g}\right) \times \text{BVPS}_L. \quad (12.68)$$

To apply this model, we need to first establish the firm's long-term ROE, ROE_L, and the book value per share, BVS_L, denoted by ROE_L. This was done using models (12.3) and (12.4) earlier. Using the residual income model, the trailing share price of FirstRand is

$$P_0 = 2{,}577.65 + \left(\frac{17.49\% - 12.87\%}{12.87\% - 8.50\%}\right) \times 3{,}237.30$$

$$= 6{,}693.42 \text{ cents.}$$

Equally, the leading P/BVPS value is given by

$$\frac{P_1}{\text{BVPS}_{L1}} = 1 + \left(\frac{\text{ROE}_L - k_e}{k_e - g}\right). \tag{12.69}$$

This means that the leading share price is given by

$$P_1 = \text{BVPS}_{L1} + \left(\frac{\text{ROE}_L - k_e}{k_e - g}\right) \times \text{BVPS}_{L1}. \tag{12.70}$$

This can also be written as

$$P_1 = \text{BVPS}_L \times (1+g) + \left(\frac{\text{ROE}_L - k_e}{k_e - g}\right) \times \text{BVPS}_L \times (1+g). \tag{12.71}$$

FirstRand's 2020 leading share price is therefore calculated as

$$P_1 = 3{,}237.30 \times (1 + 8.50) + \left(\frac{17.49\% - 12.87\%}{12.87\% - 8.50\%}\right) \times 3{,}237.30 \times (1 + 8.50\%) = 7{,}225.06 \text{ cents.}$$

The residual income model can be extended to calculate the leading target share price. The only adjustment required is in the target book value per share:

$$P_T = \text{BVPS}_L \times (1+g)^T + \left(\frac{\text{ROE}_L - k_e}{k_e - g}\right) \times \text{BVPS}_L \times (1+g)^T. \tag{12.72}$$

This can also be written as

$$P_T = \text{BVPS}_{L,T} + \left(\frac{\text{ROE}_L - k_e}{k_e - g}\right) \times \text{BVPS}_{L,T}. \tag{12.73}$$

Using the extended residual income valuation model, FirstRand's 2021 leading target share price is calculated as

$$P_{2021} = 3{,}237.30 \times (1 + 8.50\%)^2 + \left(\frac{17.49\% - 12.87\%}{12.87\% - 8.50\%}\right) \times 3{,}237.30 \times (1 + 8.50\%)^2 = 7{,}839.19 \text{ cents.}$$

The last valuation model that is discussed in this chapter is the Ohlson & Juettner-Nauroth (2005) abnormal earnings growth valuation model.

12.3.4. *The Ohlson & Juettner-Nauroth (2005) abnormal earnings growth valuation model*

According to the Ohlson & Juettner-Nauroth (2005) (OJ) abnormal earnings growth (ARG) model, equity value consists of two components: first, the capitalized next-period earnings and, second, the present values of all future abnormal earnings growth.

The model allows for the relaxation of the clean surplus assumptions. It assumes economy-wide growth rates after the two-year forecast period. The model is derived from the following assumptions (Gode & Mohanram, 2003:403):

Assumption 1: $P_0 = \sum_{t=1}^{\infty} \frac{E_0(\text{DPS}_t)}{(1+k_e)^t}$, where E_0 is the equity value at time t, DPS_t is the dividend per share at time t and $k_e > 0$ is the cost of equity.

Assumption 2: The sequence $\{z_t\}_{t=1}^{\infty}$ satisfies $z_{t+1} = \gamma \times z_t$, $t = 1, 2, \ldots,$ where $1 \leq \gamma < 1 + k_e$, $z_t = \frac{E_0[\text{EPS}_{t+1} + k_e \times \text{DPS}_t - (1+k_e) \times \text{EPS}_t]}{k_e} > 0$, and EPS_t is the EPS during time t.

From these two assumptions, the two-period Ohlson & Juettner-Nauroth (2005) AEG model can be stated as

$$\text{P}_1 = \frac{\text{EPS}_1}{k_e} + \frac{(\text{EPS}_2 - \text{EPS}_1 - k_e(\text{EPS}_1 - \text{DPS}_1))}{k_e(k_e - g_p)}. \tag{12.74}$$

This model is an equivalent of the constant growth dividend discount model. It gives the leading share price. Penman (2006: 53) expresses it differently as

$$P_1 = \frac{\text{EPS}_1}{k_e} \times \frac{1}{k_e}\left[\frac{G_2 - g}{k_e - g}\right], \tag{12.75}$$

where

$$\text{G}_2 = \frac{\text{EPS}_2 + k_e \times \text{DPS}_1}{\text{EPS}_1} - 1. \tag{12.76}$$

Substituting for G_2 in the first equation yields the Ohlson & Juettner-Nauroth (2005) AEG leading share price model shown in equation (12.74). The 2020 leading share price of FirstRand is calculated as

$$\begin{aligned}
\text{EPS}_1 &= 566.17 \times (1 + 8.50\%) = 614.29,\\
\text{EPS}_2 &= 566.17 \times (1 + 8.50\%)^2 = 666.51,\\
\text{DPS}_1 &= 291.00 \times (1 + 8.50\%) = 315.74,\\
P_1 &= \frac{614.29}{12.87\%} + \frac{(666.51 - 614.29 - 12.87\% \times (614.29 - 315.74)}{12.87\% \times (12.87\% - 8.50\%)}\\
&= 7{,}225.06 \text{ cents.}
\end{aligned}$$

The trailing share price is given by

$$P_0 = \frac{\text{EPS}_0}{k_e} + \frac{(\text{EPS}_1 - \text{EPS}_0 - k_e(\text{EPS}_0 - \text{DPS}_0))}{k_e(k_e - g_p)}. \tag{12.77}$$

The trailing share price of the bank is calculated as

$$\begin{aligned}
\text{EPS}_0 &= 566.17,\\
\text{EPS}_1 &= 566.17 \times (1 + 8.05\%) = 614.29,\\
\text{DPS}_0 &= 291.00,\\
P_0 &= \frac{566.17}{12.87\%} + \frac{(614.29 - 566.17 - 12.87\% \times (566.17 - 291.00)}{12.87\% \times (112.87\% - 8.50\%)}\\
&= 6\,659.04 \text{ cents.}
\end{aligned}$$

The leading Ohlson & Juettner-Nauroth (2005) AEG model can also be modified to estimate the leading target price. As $\text{EPS}_{T+1} = \text{EPS}_0 \times (1+g)^{T+1}$, $\text{EPS}_{T+2} = \text{EPS}_0 \times (1+g)^{T+2}$ and $\text{DPS}_{T+1} = \text{DPS}_0 \times (1+g)^{T+1}$, the leading target price is given by

$$P_T = \frac{\text{EPS}_T}{k_e} + \frac{(\text{EPS}_{T+1} - \text{EPS}_T - k_e(\text{EPS}_T - \text{DPS}_T))}{k_e(k_e - g_p)}. \tag{12.78}$$

Using this model, FirstRand's 2021 target share price is calculated as

$$\begin{aligned}
\text{EPS}_T &= 566.17 \times (1 + 8.50\%)^2 = 666.51,\\
\text{EPS}_{T+1} &= 566.17 \times (1 + 8.50\%)^3 = 723.16,\\
\text{DPS}_T &= 291.00 \times (1 + 8.50\%)^2 = 342.57,
\end{aligned}$$

$$P_{2021} = \frac{666.51}{12.87\%} + \frac{(723.16 - 666.51 - 12.87\% \times (666.51 - 342.57)}{12.87\% \times (12.87\% - 8.50\%)}$$
$$= 7{,}839.19 \text{ cents.}$$

Table 12.3 shows a summary of FirstRand Limited's 2019 trailing, 2020 target and 2021 target share prices that were estimated using the Gordon–Shapiro constant growth, the Parrino (2005) alternative Gordon–Shapiro constant growth, the standard P/E multiple, the standard P/BVPS multiple, the Suozzo *et al.* (2001) P/E multiple, the Suozzo *et al.* (2001) PEG multiple, the Suozzo *et al.* (2001) P/BVPS multiple, the residual income and the Ohlson & Juettner-Nauroth (2005) AEG equity asset valuation models. All the prices are expressed in cents per share.

All the equity asset valuation models used in this study yielded similar estimates for FirstRand Limited's 2019 trailing, 2020 target and 2021 target share prices. These results confirm that under certain assumptions, the models, although based on different inputs, yield

Table 12.3. Summary of the estimated share prices of FirstRand Limited.

	Share prices (cents per share [in South African Rand])		
Model	**Target, 2020**	**Target, 2021**	**Trailing, 2019**
Gordon–Shapiro CG-DDM	7,225.06	7,839.19	6,659.04
Parrino (2005) alternative CG-DDM	7,225.06	7,839.19	6,659.04
Standard P/E	7,225.06	7,839.19	6,659.04
Standard P/BVPS	7,225.06	7,839.19	6,659.04
Suozzo *et al.* (2001) P/E	7,225.06	7,839.19	6,659.04
Suozzo *et al.* (2001) PEG	7,225.06	7,839.19	6,659.04
Suozzo *et al.* (2001) P/BVPS	7,225.06	7,839.19	6,659.04
Residual income	7,225.06	9,349.66	6,659.04
Ohlson & Juettner-Nauroth (2005) AEG	7,225.06	7,839.19	6,659.04

similar estimates of intrinsic share values. The equivalence of the models was achieved by making the following assumptions:

- The long-term growth rate of the firm's DPS is equal to that of its EPS.
- The firm's current dividend payout ratio and retention rate will remain constant in the long term.
- The Suozzo *et al.* (2001) P/E and PEG multiples models are based on the firm's long-term ROE, which was obtained by dividing its EPS and DPS growth rate by its long-term earnings retention rate.
- The Suozzo *et al.* (2001) P/BV multiple and the residual income equity asset valuation models are based on the firm's long-term ROE and BVPS. The long-term BVPS per share is calculated by dividing its current EPS by its long-term ROE.
- The standard textbook P/E multiple model uses the firm's current BVPS, which is assumed to grow at the same rates as its EPS and DPS. The model further assumes that the firm's current ROE is a proxy for its long-term ROE.
- The standard textbook P/BVPS multiple model uses the firm's current EPS and its long-term growth rate.

As the 2019 trailing share price was FirstRand Limited's leading or target share price for the 12 months up to 30 June 2019, the actual prices of the shares are now available. The bank's share prices during the 12 months up to 29 June 2019 are shown in Figure 12.1.

This figure shows the actual daily share prices of FirstRand Limited in the period 30 June 2018–29 June 2019. The volume traded together with the volatility of the share's price are also shown in Figure 12.1.

During this period, the bank's highest share price of 7,140 cents per share was achieved on the 29 June 2019. The specific dates and prices where the bank's share price traded over the 7,000 cents per share mark are shown in Table 12.4.

The table shows FirstRand Limited's highest share prices achieved during the period 30 June 2018–29 June 2019. The dates when these prices were achieved are also shown in the table.

As shown in Figure 12.1, there were also several periods during the year when the bank's shares traded over the 6,500 cents per share mark. These specific periods were 29 June 2018–10 August 2018, 21 August 2018–02 October 2018, 01 November 2018–17 December

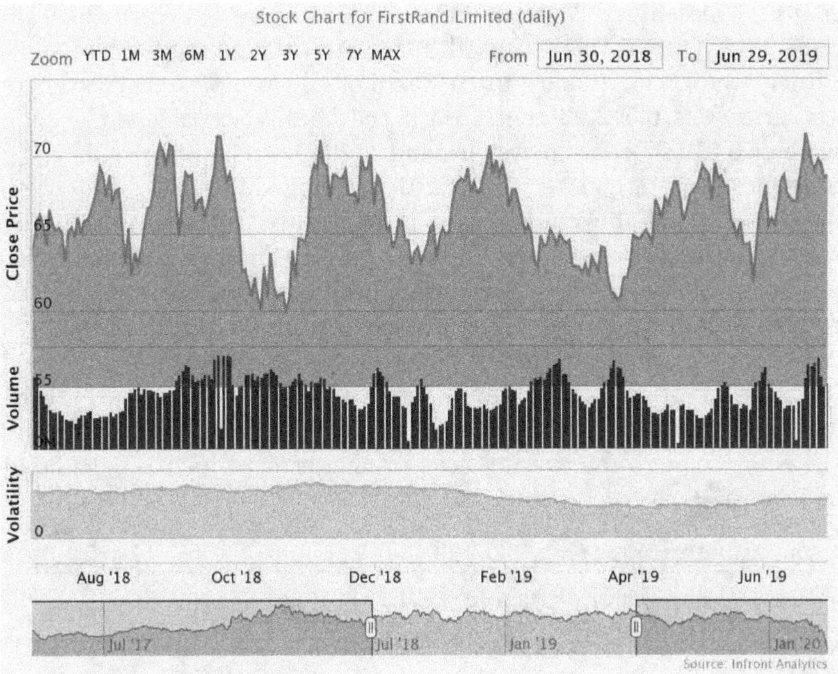

Figure 12.1. FirstRand Limited's daily share prices during the 12 months up to 29 June 2019.
Source: Infront Analytics (2023). FirstRand Limited's daily share prices. https://www.infrontanalytics.com/fe-EN/30425KS/FirstRandLimited/share%20price (Accessed 26 November 2023).

Table 12.4. Highest prices achieved by FirstRand Limited's shares during the 12 months up to 29 June 2019.

Date	Price (cents)
28/08/2018	7,078
03/09/2018	7,058
24/09/2018	7,123
7/11/2018	7,100
25/01/2019	7,061
29/06/2019	7,140

2018, 28 December 2018–13 February 2019 and 01 April 2019–30 June 2019. During the period 01 July 2018–30 June 2019, the bank's actual average high share price was 6,693.42 cents, and its average low price was 6,512.92 cents. Both the bank's actual average high price of 6,512.92 cents per share and its highest share price of 7,140 cents per share are closer to the 2019 trailing share prices that were predicted by all the models used in the study. These results imply that these equity asset valuation models do provide realistic price estimates of the bank's share prices. The pricing accuracy of the equity valuation models can be evaluated using FirstRand Limited's 2019 target and actual prices. Following Forte, Gianfrate and Rossi (in press), Dittmann and Mang (2008), Cooper and Cordeiro (2008) and Rossi and Forte (2016), the pricing accuracy can be measured by the equity asset valuation model's pricing error, which is calculated as follows:

$$\text{Valuation error}\,(x;t) = \frac{\text{Predicted share price}\,(x;t) - \text{Actual share price}\,(x;t)}{\text{Actual share price}\,(x;t)} \times 100.$$

The bank's actual average high share price of 6,693.42 cents per share was used to calculate each model's valuation error, and the results are contained in Table 12.5.

Table 12.5. Pricing errors of the equity asset valuation models.

Model	Trailing, 2019	Mean, actual, high, 2019	% Pricing error
Gordon–Shapiro CG-DDM	6,659.04	6,693.42	−0.51%
Parrino (2005) alternative CG-DDM	6,659.04	6,693.42	−0.51%
Standard P/E	6,659.04	6,693.42	−0.51%
Standard P/BVPS	6,659.04	6,693.42	−0.51%
Suozzo *et al.* (2001) P/E	6,659.04	6,693.42	−0.51%
Suozzo *et al.* (2001) PEG	6,659.04	6,693.42	−0.51%
Suozzo *et al.* (2001) P/BVPS	6,659.04	6,693.42	−0.51%
Residual income	6,659.04	6,693.42	−0.51%
Ohlson & Juettner-Nauroth (2005) AEG	6,659.04	6,693.42	−0.51%

The table shows the pricing errors of the Gordon–Shapiro constant growth, the Parrino (2005) alternative Gordon–Shapiro constant growth, the standard P/E multiple, the standard P/BVPS multiple, the Suozzo *et al.* (2001) P/E multiple, the Suozzo *et al.* (2001) PEG multiple, the Suozzo *et al.* (2001) P/BVPS multiple, the residual income and the Ohlson & Juettner-Nauroth (2005) AEG equity asset valuation models that were used to predict FirstRand Limited's 2019 trailing share price. These pricing errors are based on the share's 2019 estimated trailing price and the actual mean for the 2019 high prices. The pricing error is calculated as

$$\text{Valuation error }(x;t) = \frac{\text{Predicted share price }(x;t) - \text{actual share price }(x;t)}{\text{Actual share price }(x;t)} \times 100.$$

All the equity asset valuation models used in the study are accurate in pricing bank shares as they have a very low pricing error of −0.15%. Based on these results, the Gordon–Shapiro constant growth, the Parrino (2005) alternative Gordon–Shapiro constant growth, the standard P/E multiple, the standard P/BVPS multiple, the Suozzo *et al.* (2001) P/E multiple, the Suozzo *et al.* (2001) PEG multiple, the Suozzo *et al.* (2001) P/BVPS multiple, the residual income and the Ohlson & Juettner-Nauroth (2005) AEG equity asset valuation models provide an accurate estimate of the bank's share price, and hence they are suitable for valuing bank shares.

In summary, the constant growth dividend discount model is most applicable to mature, profitable firms with a history of stable dividend payments. The dividend history provides the analyst with a base from which to forecast future dividends. The model assumes that there is a consistent relationship between dividends and the firm's earnings. Dividends should be related to firm earnings if they are to be a good indicator of future firm and shareholder wealth. The main weakness of this model is that it assumes constant growth in dividends. This may not be the case in practice, as firms may face multiple growth rates over a finite period.

12.3.4.1. *A special note on the residual income valuation model*

According to Pinto *et al.* (2015:469), the residual income valuation model is most appropriate for firms with unpredictable dividend patterns and cash flows, firms with consistent negative cash flows and firms that have high-quality accounting disclosures. The model is, however, unsuitable for valuing firms whose EPS, NI and ROE cannot be accurately forecasted. The residual income valuation is also inappropriate when the clean surplus accounting assumption is violated (Ohlson, 2005:324; Penman, 2005:372). This is normally the case where there are pension adjustments, gains or losses from foreign currency translations, employee stock options are widely used and gains on marketable securities are accounted for in shareholders' equity as comprehensive income instead of income on the income statement.

12.4. Conclusion and Practical Insights

This study used FirstRand Limited's financial data to evaluate the suitability and equivalency of several variants of the dividend discount, market multiples, residual income and abnormal earnings growth valuation models in valuing bank shares. The models yielded similar estimates for the trailing, leading and target share price values. The trailing intrinsic values were closer to the share's past 12-month price range. The results confirm that, under specific assumptions, these models are equivalent and are suitable for the valuation of bank shares.

Furthermore, the study recommends relevant practical insights. In the digital era, constant growth dividend valuation should adapt its projections to account for the evolving nature of revenue streams in digital banking. Analysts need to carefully consider how digital initiatives impact dividend stability. Hence, banks need to include continuous monitoring of digital revenue growth, potential shifts in customer behavior and the adaptability of digital strategies. This ensures that dividend growth projections align with the dynamic landscape of digital banking, enhancing the accuracy of valuations. Also, the multiples methods, being sensitive to market perceptions, require dynamic metrics in the digital era. As such, the incorporation of digital-specific metrics in P/E and P/BV ratios is recommended. Investors and analysts should consider factors such as digital customer acquisition costs, the value of digital assets and the impact of technological advancements on future earnings. By incorporating these dynamic metrics, the multiples methods can provide a more nuanced and reflective valuation of bank shares in the digital age. Lastly, residual income models and abnormal earnings growth models should consider the unique aspects of digital assets in the valuation process. Consequently, this entails a thorough understanding of how digital assets, such as technology platforms and customer data, contribute to residual income and abnormal earnings growth. Analysts should develop methodologies to quantify the value derived from digital assets and their impact on sustained earnings growth. This ensures a more comprehensive and accurate assessment of a bank's value in the context of its digital investments.

Given the rapid pace of technological advancements, practical implications for all valuation methods in the digital era involve incorporating scenario analysis for potential technological disruptions. Analysts should assess how various digital scenarios, such as the introduction of innovative FinTech solutions or changes in regulatory landscapes, could impact valuations. Scenario analysis enables a more robust understanding of the range of potential outcomes, assisting stakeholders in making informed decisions in an environment characterized by digital uncertainties.

The models, however, suffer two limitations. The first limitation of these models is that they assume constant growth in DVS, EPS, ROE and BVPS. In practice, firms may face multi-stage growth rates over a finite period, especially in a fast-paced digital age. In such cases, it is appropriate to use the multi-stage variants of the valuation models. The second limitation of the models is that they rely on accounting information. This may be manipulated by management to meet certain objectives. Future research may focus on developing and testing the pricing accuracy of the multi-stage variants of the market multiples and the Ohlson & Juettner-Nauroth (2005) AEG valuation models. Furthermore, future studies can test the validity of the assumptions made in this study as well as the pricing accuracy of these models using a larger data sample.

References

Bailey, J. & Koller, T. (2017). Sustainability and rewriting the book on valuation: An interview with Tim Koller. *Journal of Applied Corporate Finance*, 29(2), 16–20. https://doi.org/10.1111/jacf.12229.

Bancel, F. & Mittoo, U. R. (2014). The gap between the theory and practice of corporate valuation: Survey of European experts. *Journal of Applied Corporate Finance*, 26(4), 106–117. https://doi.org/10.1111/jacf.12095.

Basel Committee on Banking Supervision. (2011). Basel III: A global regulatory framework for more resilient banks and banking systems. *Bank for International Settlements*, 1–77. http://www.bis.org/publ/bcbs189.pdf (Accessed 30 November 2022).

Damodaran, A. (2006). *Damodaran on Valuation: Security Analysis for Investment and Corporate finance* (2nd edn.). Hoboken: John Wiley & Sons.

Damodaran, A. (2013). Valuing financial services firms. *Journal of Financial Perspectives*, 1(1), 1–16. https://ssrn.com/abstract=3075980.

Damodaran, A. (2014). Emerging markets data: January 2014. http://people.stern.nyu.edu/adamodar/ (Accessed 10 November 2022).

Dermine, J. (2010). Bank valuation with an application to the implicit duration of non-maturing deposits. *International Journal of Banking, Accounting and Finance*, 2(1), 1–30. https://doi.org/10.1504/IJBAAF.2010.031573.

Dermine, J. (2016). Digital banking and market disruption: A sense of déjàvu. *Financial Stability Review*, 20, 17–23.

Edwards, E. O., Edwards, E. O., & Bell, P. W. (1961). *The Theory and Measurement of Business Income*. University of California Press, California.

Elliott, W. B., Koëter-Kant, J., & Warr, R. S. (2007). A valuation-based test of market timing. *Journal of Corporate Finance*, 13(1), 112–128. https://doi.org/10.1016/j.jcorpfin.2006.12.001.

Ericson, L. & Koller, T. (2020). Why 'digital' is no different when it comes to valuation. https://www.mckinsey.com/businessfunctions/strategy-and-corporate-finance/our-insights/why-digital-is-no-differentwhen-it-comes-to-valuation (Accessed 26 November 2023).

Feltham, G. A. & Ohlson, J. A. (1995). Valuation and clean surplus accounting for operating and financial activities. *Contemporary Accounting Research*, 11(2), 689–731. https://doi.org/10.1111/j.1911-3846.1995.tb00462.x.

FirstRand Group Limited. (2015). Annual Integrated Report (pp. 1–456). https://www.firstrand.co.za/investors/integrated-reporting-hub/financial-reporting/ (Accessed 26 November 2023).

Frankel, R. & Lee, C. M. (1998). Accounting valuation, market expectation, and cross-sectional stock returns. *Journal of Accounting and Economics*, 25(3), 283–319. https://doi.org/10.1016/S0165-4101(98)00026-3.

Gebhardt, W. R., Lee, C. M., & Swaminathan, B. (2001). Toward an implied cost of capital. *Journal of Accounting Research*, 39(1), 135–176. https://doi.org/10.1111/1475-679X.00007.

Gode, D. & Mohanram, P. (2003). Inferring the cost of capital using the Ohlson–Juettner model. *Review of Accounting Studies*, 8, 399–431. https://doi.org/10.1023/A:1027378728141.

Gordon, M. J. (1962). *The Investment, Financing, and Valuation of the Corporation*. Homewood: Richard D. Irwin.

Gordon, M. J. & Shapiro, E. (1956). Capital equipment analysis: The required rate of profit. *Management Science*, 3(1), 102–110. https://doi.org/10.1287/mnsc.3.1.102.

Gounder, C. & Venkateshwaralu, M. (2014). Review on bank valuation approaches with reference to developing economy. *Asian Journal of Research in Banking and Finance*, 4(3), 84–104.

Hirst, D. E. & Hopkins, P. E. (2012). Earnings: Measurement, disclosure, and the impact on equity valuation. In *Valuation Techniques: Discounted Cash Flow, Earnings Quality, Measures of Value Added, and Real Options* (Vol. 5, p. 293). Hoboken, NJ: John Wiley & Sons.

Hunjra, A. I. & Hanif, M. (2023). Central banking issues and challenges. *Reference Module in Social Sciences*. https://doi.org/10.1016/B978-0-44-313776-1.00113-6.

Koller, T., Goedhart, M., & Wessels, D. (2010). *Valuation: Measuring and Managing the Value of Companies* (5th edn.). Hoboken, NJ: John Willey and Sons.

Lintner, J. (1975). The valuation of risk assets and the selection of risky investments in stock portfolios and capital budgets. In *Stochastic Optimization Models in Finance* (pp. 131–155). Cambridge, MA: Academic Press. https://doi.org/10.1016/B978-0-12-780850-5.50018-6.

Mossin, J. (1966). Equilibrium in a capital asset market. *Econometrica: Journal of the Econometric Society*, 768–783. https://doi.org/10.2307/1910098.

Moyo, V. & Mache, F. (2018). Inferring the cost of equity: Does the CAPM consistently outperform the income and multiples valuation models? *Journal of Applied Business Research (JABR)*, 34(3), 519–532. https://doi.org/10.19030/jabr.v34i3.10174.

Murinde, V., Rizopoulos, E., & Zachariadis, M. (2022). The impact of the FinTech revolution on the future of banking: Opportunities and risks. *International Review of Financial Analysis*, 81, 102103. https://doi.org/10.1016/j.irfa.2022.102103.

Obadire, A. M., Moyo, V., & Munzhelele, N. F. (2023). An empirical analysis of the dynamics influencing bank capital structure in Africa.

International Journal of Financial Studies, 11(4), 127. https://doi.org/10.3390/ijfs11040127.

Ohlson, J. A. (1995). Earnings, book values, and dividends in equity valuation. *Contemporary Accounting Research*, 11(2), 661–687. https://doi.org/10.1111/j.1911-3846.1995.tb00461.x.

Ohlson, J. A. (2005). On accounting-based valuation formulae. *Review of Accounting Studies*, 10, 323–347. https://doi.org/10.1007/s11142-005-1534-4.

Ohlson, J. A. & Juettner-Nauroth, B. E. (2005). Expected EPS and EPS growth as determinants of value. *Review of Accounting Studies*, 10, 349–365. https://doi.org/10.1007/s11142-005-1535-3.

Parrino, R. (2005). Choosing the right valuation approach. In *CFA Institute Conference Proceedings* (pp. 15–28).

Peasnell, K. V. (1982). Some formal connections between economic values and yields and accounting numbers. *Journal of Business Finance and Accounting*, 9(3), 361–381.

Penman, S. H. (2005). Discussion of "On Accounting-Based Valuation Formulae" and "Expected EPS and EPS Growth as Determinants of Value". *Review of Accounting Studies*, 10, 367–378.

Penman, S. H. (2006). Handling valuation models. *Journal of Applied Corporate Finance*, 18(2), 48–55. https://doi.org/10.1111/j.1745-6622.2006.00087.x.

Pinto, J. E. Henry, E., Robinson, T. R., & Stowe, J. D. (2015). *Equity Asset Valuation* (2nd edn.). Hoboken: John Wiley and Sons, Inc.

Sharpe, W. F. (1964). Capital asset prices: A theory of market equilibrium under conditions of risk. *The Journal of Finance*, 19(3), 425–442. https://doi.org/10.1111/j.1540-6261.1964.tb02865.x.

Suozzo, P., Cooper, S., Sutherland, G., & Deng, Z. (2001). Valuation Multiples: A Primer. UBS Warburg Global Equity Research. Valuation Primer Series (Issue 1, pp. 1–46).

Treynor, J. L. (1962). Toward a theory of market value of risky assets. Unpublished Manuscript.

Annexure 12A

Table 12A.1. FirstRand Limited: Summary share statistics.

	2015	2016	2017	2018	2019	Growth rate (%)
Dividend per share (cents [in South African Rand])	210.00	226.00	255.00	275.00	291.00	8.50%
Earnings per share (EPS) (cents)	412.25	429.20	466.00	501.71	566.17	8.25%
Return on equity (ROE) (%)	23.45%	22.28%	22.31%	21.52%	21.96%	−1.62%
Book value per share (BVPS) (cents)	1 757.91	1 926.58	2 089.15	2 331.72	2 577.65	10.04%
Dividend pay-out ratio (%)	50.94%	52.66%	54.72%	54.81%	51.40%	−0.22%
Earnings retention rate	49.06%	47.34%	45.28%	45.19%	48.60%	−0.23%

The statistics are calculated from the extracts of the annual financial statement in Annexure 12B using the following formulas:

$$\text{Dividend per share} = \frac{\text{Total dividend paid to ordinary shareholders}}{\text{Total number of shares in issue at end of year}},$$

$$\text{Earnings per share} = \frac{\text{Profit attributable to ordinary shareholders}}{\text{Total number of shares in issue at end of year}},$$

$$\text{Return on equity} = \frac{\text{Profit attributable to ordinary shareholders}}{\text{Total ordinary shareholders'equity}} \times 100,$$

Book value per share

$$= \frac{\text{Total ordinary shareholders' equity}}{\text{Total number of shares in issue at end of year}},$$

Dividend pay-out ratio

$$= \frac{\text{Total dividend paid to ordinary shareholders}}{\text{Total profit attributable to ordinary shareholders}},$$

Earnings retention

$$= 1 - \text{pay-out ratio}.$$

The growth rate is calculated using the geometric mean. For example, the dividend growth rate is calculated as $g = \left(\frac{D_0}{D_{-n}}\right)^{1/n} - 1 = \left(\frac{291}{210}\right)^{1/4} - 1 = 8.50\%$.

Annexure 12B

Table 12B.1. FirstRand Limited: Extracts from the annual financial statements from 2015 to 2019.

	2015	2016	2017	2018	2019
Total profit attributable to equity holders (R000)	23,123,690	24,074,658	26,138,644	28,143,534	31,759,333
Total dividend paid (R)	11,779,269,600	12,676,737,760	14,303,398,800	15,426,125,000	16,323,645,000
Total equity (R000)	98,604,000	108,065,000	117,184,000	130,798,000	144,593,000
Shares in issue at year-end (000)	5,609,176	5,609,176	5,609,176	5,609,500	5,609,500

https://doi.org/10.1142/9781800616257_0013

Chapter 13

Exploring the Intersection of Corporate Governance and Digital Finance: Risks, Rewards and Policy Ramifications

Muhammad Azam*, Imran Lohdi†, Muhammad Haroon‡, and Hammad Ali§

Department of Economics, Ghazi University, Dera Ghazi Khan, Pakistan

*muazam@gudgk.edu.pk
†milodhi@gudgk.edu.pk
‡haroonbaloch007.hb@gmail.com
§redbm73@gmail.com

Abstract

This book chapter delves into the complex dynamics between corporate governance and digital finance, thoroughly examining this intersection's risks, rewards and policy ramifications. The story begins with a look back at the development of corporate governance and then traces the revolutionary effects of digital money on established institutions. We examine how the two worlds are converging, focusing on how technological advancements influence new approaches to money management. This section helps readers understand the difficulties policymakers confront in keeping up with the ever-shifting digital world as they attempt to modify existing regulatory frameworks. Regulatory flexibility, cybersecurity risks, openness and data governance are emerging as essential policy issues. Case studies shed light on practical implementations, offering assistance for businesses only beginning to incorporate digital finance into their management systems. As the digital finance era unfolds, the chapter explores future directions, anticipating trends that include decentralized governance models, enhanced cybersecurity measures, the integration of artificial intelligence (AI) and global standardization. Ethical considerations, sustainability and social responsibility are integral to governance. Insights gained from real-world experiences underscore the importance of adaptability, collaboration and ethical decision-making. The narrative concludes with a forward-looking perspective, positioning organizations to navigate the evolving landscape with resilience and innovation. The abstract encapsulates a holistic view of the chapter, offering readers a glimpse into the complexities and opportunities at the intersection of corporate governance and digital finance.

Keywords: Corporate governance, digital finance, technological advancements.

13.1. Introduction

Corporate governance and digital finance, two formerly distinct aspects of the business environment, are now intertwined through evolutionary and revolutionary developments. This book chapter explores the dynamic connection between these two cornerstones of modern business. As we begin our inquiry, we must fully understand the essential concepts. Digital finance has been a game-changer for businesses' financial management. It increasingly crosses corporate governance, which traditionally focuses on the framework of decision-making processes and guaranteeing responsibility. The progressive replacement of traditional organizational structures with those that include digital finance symbolizes the exciting development of corporate governance. The early stages of corporate governance focused on creating designs that bolstered ethical norms and ensured a healthy equilibrium among the many stakeholders. However, things have returned to being as they were before the advent of computerized banking systems. Traditional, linear procedures are directly embedded in technology, calling for a rethink of the regulatory framework (Huo *et al.*, 2022).

A new landscape is emerging at the convergence of corporate governance and digital finance. This environment is one in which technology plays an essential role in determining how choices are made, as traditional discussions in the boardroom are increasingly supplemented by algorithms and data analytics. Previously dependent on human intuition, the process of making financial decisions is now heavily affected by the speed and precision of digital instruments. For businesses aiming to successfully navigate the intricacies of the digital era, an understanding of this nexus is a prerequisite.

Nevertheless, the further we venture into this dynamic connection, the more obstacles and opportunities we encounter. The smooth incorporation of digital financial systems into governance institutions faces fierce opposition due to regulatory roadblocks. Cybersecurity concerns are growing, and they pose a danger to the basic foundation of the financial system. However, if you can overcome these obstacles, you will open up a world of opportunities for yourself. Organizations that are prepared to include digital money in their governance frameworks have the opportunity to improve transparency, reduce risks and ensure ethical financial practices (Zhang, 2023).

This chapter investigates best practices by examining how organizations might modify their governance structures to suit the digital age. It is of the utmost importance to establish efficient governance structures, placing primary emphasis on developing risk management techniques compatible with the fundamentals of digital finance. Real-world case studies provide valuable insights into successful implementations and serve as a guide for others to follow as they traverse the challenges of this transformational journey. As we look into the future, we will focus on the emerging themes that will significantly impact corporate governance and the digital finance environment. Emerging technologies such as blockchain and AI are more than just buzzwords; they are drivers of change. Recognizing and capitalizing on these trends will be essential for businesses that want to maintain a competitive advantage in a digital world that is constantly shifting. During our investigation, we uncovered the central importance of collaboration and cooperation. Because organizations will need to cooperate to understand the complexities of digital finance, industry cooperation will become an essential component of good governance. In addition, the actions taken by the government play a critical part in fostering an environment favorable to the implementation of responsible financial practices (Ren *et al.*, 2023).

Ethical questions have taken center stage in this digital banking era. Organizations must preserve ethical standards even as they welcome technical improvements because of the challenges presented by emerging moral dilemmas in this environment. As individuals working in governance are required to regularly upgrade their skills to meet the needs of the digital era, education emerges as a valuable instrument that may help achieve these objectives. Perspectives from other parts of the world provide insight into how various areas approach corporate governance. It is essential for businesses that operate on a global scale in the digital banking ecosystem to have a thorough understanding of these variances. In addition, the chapter investigates recent developments such as blockchain and smart contracts, offering a window into how new technologies are changing traditional forms of governance. The capacity for adaptation becomes an increasingly important aspect of determining success in a world that is in a state of perpetual flux. This chapter emphasizes the significance of maintaining flexibility in governance structures, gaining knowledge from past mistakes and iteratively refining procedures to remain relevant in the face of rapid developments in technical capabilities (Zhang & Liu, 2022).

As we work through the complexities of the link between corporate governance and digital finance, one essential facet that is often disregarded is the need to balance the influence of technology with the human element. While technological advances have increased productivity and speed, more is needed to replace the value of personal interaction. Maintaining this equilibrium guarantees that businesses may take advantage of technological advancements without losing sight of their core principles or the effects their actions will have on society. In sum, the purpose of this chapter is to act as a guide through the ever-changing environment at the intersection of corporate governance and digital finance. It provides a road map for organizations seeking to comprehend this connection and flourish amid change (Ji *et al.*, 2021).

By providing a detailed and comprehensive analysis of the relationship between corporate governance and digital finance, this chapter substantially adds to the ongoing conversation about these topics. It significantly contributes to our theoretical and practical grasp of this interdependent system in several crucial ways.

The chapter begins with a thorough review of the development of corporate governance over time, laying the groundwork for a discussion of the radical effects of digital finance on existing governance models. Understanding the intricacies and issues organizations confront in the digital finance age requires this historical backdrop as a foundation.

Second, case studies provide real-world examples that complement the theoretical foundation. This chapter provides helpful insights and a roadmap for businesses wishing to integrate digital finance into corporate governance by analyzing existing examples of practical implementation. These case studies offer real-world illustrations of successful strategies and joint problems.

In addition, the chapter discusses the critical ramifications for policymaking brought about by merging corporate governance and digital finance. To adapt regulatory frameworks, mitigate cybersecurity risks and ensure ethical decision-making in a technology-driven financial sector, policymakers and regulatory bodies may find helpful ideas here.

The forward-looking viewpoint adds to the academic literature by forecasting future trends and directions. This chapter lays the groundwork for prospective study and strategic planning by examining possible advancements such as decentralized governance models, improved cybersecurity measures and the incorporation of AI.

13.2. Literature and Theoretical Background

Both academics and businesspeople are increasingly interested in how corporate governance and digital money overlap. Exploring the theoretical frameworks and scholarly works that explain the interplay between different fields is essential for understanding their complex connections.

13.2.1. *Corporate governance: A historical perspective*

The origins of "corporate governance" may be in the early 20th century. The guiding principles were developed to guarantee that businesses act ethically and responsibly toward their stakeholders. The pioneering work of Razzaq *et al.* (2023) emphasized the separation of ownership and control in significant organizations, setting the framework for future governance ideas.

Many schools of thought have developed, each adding to our knowledge of corporate governance. Lee & Wang (2022) utilized the agency theory (Jensen & Meckling, 1976), which analyzes the connection between principals (shareholders) and agents (managers). This theory underlines the potential for shareholder conflicts of interest when agents prioritize their own interests over those of the company.

In contrast, the stewardship theory stresses the need for management and shareholders to have congruent goals. It proposes that good managers should assume the role of stewards, carefully overseeing the capital entrusted to them by their shareholders.

13.2.2. *Digital finance: From FinTech to blockchain*

Recent technological developments have been directly linked to the emergence of digital finance. Fintech, an acronym for "financial technology," arose in the late 20th century and has revolutionized the financial services industry by applying cutting-edge computer science and engineering to it. Among the first developments in digital finance were mobile banking, internet payments and robo-advisors.

Bitcoin's introduction of blockchain technology in 2009 shook up the global financial system. Its decentralized and public character completely changed the verification and recording of financial transactions. Blockchain's theoretical underpinnings in cryptography and distributed systems provide a new standard for trustless monetary exchanges (Xu *et al.*, 2023).

13.2.3. *The intersection: Corporate governance meets digital finance*

The combination of corporate governance and digital finance represents a fundamental change in how organizations function and make financial decisions. The rapid changes in digital finance put pressure on traditional governance systems developed in an analog age.

The resource dependence theory provides a valuable framework for investigating this crossroad. This hypothesis, first proposed by Liu *et al.* (2021), highlights the importance of outside resources for businesses. Organizations rely heavily on digital technology, which shifts power relations and impacts decision-making in corporate governance and digital finance.

In addition, institutional theory sheds light on how businesses adapt to society's standards and external forces. As digital finance becomes increasingly integrated into company operations, organizations confront institutional pressures to embrace these technologies in their governance structures to remain legal and competitive.

13.2.4. *Challenges and opportunities in the literature*

The literature also highlights the challenges and opportunities of integrating digital finance into corporate governance. Regulatory challenges are a recurring theme as existing regulatory frameworks struggle to keep up with the rapid evolution of digital financial instruments. Scholars argue for adaptive regulatory approaches that foster innovation while ensuring consumer protection and financial stability (Macchiavello & Siri, 2022).

Cybersecurity concerns constitute another significant challenge. The immutable nature of blockchain technology, while enhancing security, also poses unique challenges related to the privacy and confidentiality of sensitive financial information (Lee *et al.*, 2022).

On the flip side, the literature emphasizes digital finance's opportunities for enhancing transparency, accountability and efficiency in corporate governance. Smart contracts, enabled by blockchain, automate and enforce contractual agreements, reducing the need for intermediaries and minimizing the risk of fraud (Chen *et al.*, 2021).

13.2.5. *Best practices and case studies*

Exploring best practices in the literature provides a practical understanding of how organizations navigate the complexities of integrating digital finance into their governance frameworks. Governance frameworks that leverage the advantages of digital finance focus on real-time data analytics, AI-driven decision-making and blockchain-based transparency (Yu *et al.*, 2020).

Case studies offer valuable insights into successful implementations. The case of Estonia, often cited in the literature, exemplifies a nation that has embraced digital governance, including blockchain-based e-governance solutions (Xu *et al.*, 2023). Organizations such as Overstock, which implemented blockchain for transparent supply chain management, serve as practical examples of successful integration (Li *et al.*, 2023).

13.2.6. *Global perspectives and adaptation to change*

Global perspectives highlighted in the literature emphasize the need for organizations to adapt their governance structures to diverse regulatory environments. The varying approaches to digital finance governance in countries such as China, the United States and the members of the European Union underscore the importance of contextualized strategies (Ma *et al.*, 2023).

The literature also highlights the adaptability of governing institutions. To remain relevant in the rapidly evolving technological landscape, businesses must maintain flexibility by incorporating lessons learned from past mistakes and iterating on current strategies (Chen *et al.*, 2021).

Finally, the literature investigates the tension between automation and people in authority. The literature cautions against the dehumanization of decision-making that may result from the increased efficiency and automation of digital banking. Organizations may reap the benefits of technology while maintaining respect for human values and ethical norms if they can identify a balance between the two (Wang *et al.*, 2023).

Our investigation of the connection between corporate governance and digital finance is grounded in the literature and the theoretical framework. Understanding this dynamic interaction requires combining theoretical frameworks, case studies and future developments.

In this work, we investigate how AI and machine learning can be utilized to detect fraudulent activity in the insurance industry. The investigation by Aslam and his colleagues into the efficiency of modern technology in detecting fraudulent activities within the insurance industry is discussed here. The research, which was published in *Research in International Business and Finance*, makes a significant contribution to the ongoing efforts aimed at improving security measures within the insurance business. Central bank digital currencies (CBDCs) are the primary focus of Aslam *et al.*, who also offer a comprehensive roadmap for future study in this field. In this work, the authors explore the changing landscape of CBDCs and outline critical research goals. Specifically, the article contributes to the continuing discussion over the function of digital currencies and their implications for the financial system. Next, Ha *et al.*, in their investigation of the banking business in Vietnam, used self-organizing maps, also known as Kohonen maps, to examine patterns and structures. This study, published in the *Journal of Risk and Financial Management*, demonstrates the usefulness of this analytical technique in generating insights into the dynamics of the banking industry in Vietnam. The disciplines of risk management and financial analysis may benefit significantly from this research's contribution. Hunjra & Hanif, in their paper, discuss the problems and difficulties associated with central banking. The study contributes to the understanding of the modern issues that central banks are confronted with. Academics and professionals in the field who are interested in gaining a better understanding of the complexity of central banking in the current period will find this study to be an invaluable resource.

13.3. The Effect of New Technology on Corporate Governance and Digital Finance

There has been a dramatic transformation in the business world as innovative technologies become embedded in corporate governance and digital finance. Beyond simple digitization, the far-reaching implications of modern technologies are explored in this section. The current effects include fundamental changes to decision-making processes and a redefinition of financial strategies.

13.3.1. *The technological revolution: Shaping corporate governance*

The introduction of cutting-edge technologies has ushered in a new age of progressive boardroom practices. Digital technologies are reshaping traditional governance systems that are predicated on hierarchies and laborious procedures. AI, machine learning and data analytics are not merely buzzwords but vital components impacting decision-making processes in the boardroom. There has been a dramatic shift in board meetings, deliberations and strategic decision-making dynamics (Sun *et al.*, 2023).

Speeding up decision-making processes is a significant way in which new technologies have impacted corporate governance. In today's age of rapid digital finance, data-driven insights provide a more complete picture of business success. Boards armed with real-time data can quickly adapt to market shifts, offering a degree of agility that was previously impossible.

However, along with this increased velocity, a new set of difficulties arises. When new technologies emerge rapidly, it may take time for regulatory structures to catch up. The use of cutting-edge technology by businesses increases the need for well-established governance mechanisms. Boards must master the art of balancing the rapid adoption of new technologies with the need for compliance and ethical considerations (Tang *et al.*, 2022).

13.3.2. *Technological advancements in decision-making processes*

In the epoch of AI and machine learning, decision-making within corporate governance structures has undergone a metamorphosis. Algorithms, endowed with the ability to analyze vast datasets at unprecedented speeds, have become the linchpin of a new decision-making paradigm. This section delves into the profound impact of these technological strides, elucidating how organizations recalibrate their decision-making frameworks in the crucible of advanced analytics.

The traditional reliance on historical data and subjective human judgment gives way to a more dynamic and data-centric approach. AI-driven tools sift through intricate patterns, predict outcomes with remarkable precision and substantively contribute to the strategic tapestry. The result is not merely an efficiency improvement but a paradigm shift in which decisions, informed by data-driven insights, are made with unparalleled acuity (Mo *et al.*, 2023).

13.3.3. *Blockchain and transparent financial transactions*

Blockchain, synonymous with the evolution of cryptocurrencies, extends its tendrils beyond digital coins and fundamentally alters corporate finance's landscape. This section discusses the transformative impact of blockchain, where transparency and accountability become watchwords, mitigating the lurking risks of fraud and errors.

The decentralized blockchain architecture offers an immutable ledger, an indelible record that drastically reduces the possibility of financial discrepancies. Smart contracts, digital sentinels of agreements, execute themselves with unwavering fidelity to pre-programmed code, ushering in an era of automated processes that elevate transparency and circumvent the need for intermediaries (Skare *et al.*, 2023).

13.3.4. *Enhanced cybersecurity measures*

In an era where digital finance permeates every facet of corporate transactions, the specter of cyber threats looms ominously. This section discusses how advanced cybersecurity measures are crucial for fortifying corporate governance structures and securing financial transactions against the relentless onslaught of cyber adversaries.

Technological strides in cybersecurity comprise an extensive digital arsenal, encompassing advanced encryption algorithms, biometric authentication protocols and threat detection systems steeped in the power of machine learning. These measures function as impregnable shields guarding sensitive financial data and serve as custodians of the trust placed in digital economic systems (Maria *et al.*, 2023).

13.3.5. *Data analytics and strategic financial planning*

At the nexus of data analytics and strategic financial planning lies a transformative force reshaping how organizations navigate the complex terrain of finance. This section touches upon the profound impact of big data analytics, which organizations have harnessed to process colossal datasets with the aim of gaining insights into market trends, consumer behavior and financial risks.

Predictive analytics, an avant-garde tool in the data analytics arsenal, empowers organizations to peer into the future, facilitating proactive decision-making. The infusion of data-driven insights into financial planning fortifies risk management strategies and endows organizations with the agility to navigate uncertainties with wisdom anchored in empirical evidence (Ding *et al.*, 2023).

13.4. The Principles of Corporate Governance and Digital Finance

The principles of corporate governance and digital finance, as explored in this chapter, represent a dynamic interplay between traditional governance structures and the transformative forces of technology. At its core, corporate governance, steeped in tradition, seeks to establish frameworks that guide ethical decision-making, ensure accountability and maintain equilibrium among stakeholders. On the other hand, digital finance introduces a paradigm shift by infusing technology into financial processes and altering decision-making processes within organizations. The principles governing this intersection necessitate a delicate balance between established governance norms and the disruptive potential of digital finance. Central to these principles is the understanding that the evolution of corporate governance is not linear but iterative, adapting to the changing landscape sculpted by technological advancements. In embracing digital finance, organizations must navigate regulatory challenges, acknowledging that seamless technological integration requires a reassessment of governance structures to align with the principles of transparency and accountability. Risk management is increasingly recognized as a cornerstone principle, with organizations being urged to adopt strategies that effectively navigate the complexities of the digital landscape (Cao *et al.*, 2021).

The chapter underscores the significance of real-world case studies, illustrating how successful implementations of digital finance in governance provide practical insights into best practices. Looking forward, the principles delve into the trends shaping the future of corporate governance and digital finance, emphasizing the need for organizations to stay attuned to emerging technologies such as blockchain and AI. Collaboration and partnerships are essential, recognizing that industry cooperation and government initiatives are pivotal in fostering an environment conducive to responsible financial practices. Ethical considerations loom large as organizations grapple with the ethical dilemmas posed by digital finance, necessitating the upholding of moral standards alongside technological advancements. Education is a transformative principle, as individuals involved in governance must continually enhance their skills to navigate the intricacies of the digital age. Global perspectives highlight that corporate governance and digital finance principles are not uniform but vary across regions, emphasizing the importance of understanding these differences for organizations operating on an international scale. Innovations such as blockchain and smart contracts represent principles that are reshaping governance structures, demanding adaptability from organizations (Yu *et al.*, 2022).

As a guiding principle, flexibility underscores the need for organizations to embrace change, learn from failures and iteratively improve their governance structures. Intertwined with technology, the human element emerges as a foundational principle, urging organizations to strike a balance between leveraging technology for efficiency while maintaining the human touch in decision-making processes. In summary, the principles of corporate governance and digital finance articulated in this chapter serve as a compass for organizations navigating the intricate dance between tradition and innovation and between ethics and technology, providing a holistic framework for the governance of organizations in the digital era (Chen & Zhang, 2021).

13.4.1. *Encouragement of the use of corporate governance and digital finance by government incentives and policies*

In fostering a conducive environment for the harmonious integration of corporate governance and digital finance, governments worldwide are increasingly recognizing the need for strategic incentives and policies. This profound shift in approach signifies a departure from traditional regulatory frameworks toward a proactive stance aimed at catalyzing innovation and responsible financial practices. Governments, conscious of the transformative potential of digital finance, are strategically deploying a multifaceted arsenal of incentives and policies to encourage businesses to embrace modern corporate governance paradigms. At the heart of this endeavor lies the understanding that a dynamic and responsive regulatory landscape facilitates the seamless adoption of digital finance and acts as a catalyst for the evolution of corporate governance structures (Wu & Huang, 2022).

Monetary bonuses are only one example of an incentive. Governments increasingly employ tax incentives, grants and subsidies to persuade corporations to invest in digital financial infrastructure and technology that enhance corporate governance. These financial rewards aim to ease the financial strain of early implementation and promote a culture of continuous improvement in management practices. As a method of rewarding and showcasing enterprises that have implemented digital finance into their governance structures, governments are also exploring non-monetary incentives, such as recognition programs and certifications.

Policies that create the regulatory environment may offer the necessary structure for corporate governance and digital finance. Governments are working on comprehensive rules to address the nuances of this integration, including the new opportunities and challenges that the digital age ushers in. To guarantee that the widespread use of digital currency is consistent with broader societal norms and goals, regulations covering data privacy, cybersecurity and ethics have been developed. To ensure that rules remain practical and flexible enough to keep up with the evolving digital financial ecosystem, governments are also actively engaging in collaborative initiatives with industry actors, adopting a consultative approach that allows for the co-creation of regulations.

The government places a high priority on the development of regulatory sandboxes. Companies may test innovative digital financial products under close supervision in a regulatory system encouraging innovation. By allowing controlled testing, the government may promote innovation and learn more about the risks and benefits of integrating digital finance into corporate governance. By iteratively updating policies, we can ensure that they will continue to be flexible and responsive to the ever-changing nature of technology (Li *et al.*, 2022).

Governments are actively tackling the educational component of this transformative journey. To ensure the success of digital financial integration, governments are investing in education to ensure that corporate governance professionals possess the necessary skills and expertise. Training programs, seminars and partnerships with educational institutions are all helping to equip professionals to handle the complexities of digital money. This preventive approach ensures that organizations have access to a pool of experts who can install digital finance solutions and assess their influence on current governance procedures.

Governments are also actively supporting P3s (Public-Private Partnerships) as part of the overall policy framework. Partnerships between the public and commercial sectors are showing significant potential for accelerating growth in the disciplines of corporate governance and digital finance. By collaborating with the private sector, governments want to create an ecosystem that can withstand the challenges of the digital era and make the most of the knowledge gained from working together. Governments are looking into international alliances to standardize laws and pave the way for global digital banking initiatives, expanding this approach beyond their borders.

For the reasons above, government incentives and rules supporting corporate governance and digital finance have ushered in a new era of regulatory approaches. Governments are not only watchdogs but also promoters since they see the need for good corporate governance to ensure the ethical growth of digital currency. As the digital world evolves, the capacity of governments to provide innovative incentives, establish adaptable policies and promote collaboration is becoming increasingly crucial. In their positions as regulators, governments are shaping a future in which ethical business practices and digital currencies can coexist to greater benefit. It is more important than ever for governments to drive businesses toward a future of sustainable prosperity and social well being at the intersection of innovation, responsibility and governance (Lee *et al.*, 2023).

The participation of stakeholders in the realms of corporate governance and digital finance is a multifaceted aspect that significantly shapes the dynamics of modern business. Stakeholders, representing a spectrum ranging from shareholders and employees to customers and the wider community, play a pivotal role in influencing governance structures and digital finance practices. Their involvement extends beyond mere financial interest; it encompasses a shared responsibility for organizations' ethical conduct, transparency and long-term sustainability. In corporate governance, stakeholders often engage in dialogue with boards and management to ensure that decision-making processes consider diverse perspectives. Shareholders, driven by their financial interests, seek governance practices that optimize returns, while employees advocate for fair labor practices and an inclusive corporate culture. On the other hand, customers are increasingly demanding transparency and ethical behavior, pushing organizations to align their values with those of the broader society. The participation of stakeholders is not only a reflection of the evolving expectations placed on corporations but also a catalyst for positive change, encouraging governance structures that go beyond profit maximization to embrace broader societal goals (Razzaq *et al.*, 2023).

However, there are difficulties in this participative world as well. Corporations face complex and multidimensional challenges in corporate governance and digital finance. The advancement of technology outpacing the creation of legal frameworks is a major obstacle. This loophole may be exploited, potentially leading to significant governance difficulties and financial hazards. Organizations are left vulnerable to cybersecurity attacks with far-reaching implications due to the interconnected structure of the digital ecosystem. Another challenge, particularly when stakeholders want greater openness, is balancing the requirement for transparency with the preservation of sensitive information. In addition, there is always the issue of how to act morally while using digital tools. Concerns about the ethical basis of business decisions in the digital age have been raised due to the potential for abuse. In addition, the complexity of the environment makes harmonizing standards difficult due to the wide range of opinions on governance practices and digital finance worldwide. To solve these issues, businesses and other groups need to work together proactively to find solutions, encourage new ideas and provide a solid groundwork for the future of corporate governance and digital finance (Yu *et al.*, 2020).

13.4.2. *Barriers to effective corporate governance in the era of digital finance*

The merger of corporate governance with digital finance has created new possibilities and threats in today's ever-changing business environment. As businesses transition into the digital era, they face many challenges that call for creative responses. This research looks deeply into the complicated issues that arise when companies adopt digital finance and overhaul their corporate governance.

13.4.2.1. *Regulatory challenges in the digital era*

Corporate governance and digital finance provide a complex regulatory landscape that must be explored and understood. Traditional regulatory systems built for a pre-digital period need help keeping up with today's technological developments. As digital banking offers innovative ideas such as blockchain, smart contracts and decentralized finance, regulators are struggling to update and adapt current frameworks.

The international character of digital banking compounds the difficulty of regulatory oversight. It is a considerable challenge to harmonize legislation in a globalized environment where financial transactions cross borders. Companies with international operations face higher compliance expenses and significant legal concerns due to the complexities involved in interpreting and adhering to legislation from various countries.

13.4.2.2. *Cybersecurity concerns: Safeguarding financial integrity*

The dangers facing businesses grow tremendously as more departments use digital money. Cyberattacks' potential to compromise the stability of financial systems makes cybersecurity a top priority. The interconnected nature of digital systems implies that a breach in one section of the network can lead to cascading repercussions, resulting in financial losses, reputational harm and erosion of confidence.

Preventing cyber assaults is difficult, but so is creating effective defenses against them. A complete cybersecurity plan must include rapid detection and mitigation of threats. To remain ahead of cyber threats, businesses must invest in cutting-edge technology, perform frequent cybersecurity assessments and encourage a culture of alertness among staff (Yu *et al.*, 2020).

13.4.2.3. *Enhancing transparency and accountability*

While digital finance promises increased efficiency and streamlined processes, it also introduces challenges related to transparency and accountability. Traditional governance structures relied on manual processes that, while time-consuming, provided a tangible audit trail. In the digital realm, where transactions occur almost instantaneously, maintaining the same level of transparency becomes a challenge.

Blockchain technology, touted for its transparency benefits, introduces its own set of challenges. Balancing the inherent transparency of blockchain with the need for data privacy poses a delicate dilemma. Organizations must find the right balance to ensure that stakeholders have access to necessary information without compromising sensitive data (Xu *et al.*, 2023).

13.4.3. *Ensuring ethical considerations in digital governance*

Ethical considerations gain prominence as organizations navigate the ethical dilemmas inherent in digital finance. The use of algorithms in decision-making processes raises questions of bias and fairness. The responsible use of data, the protection of customer privacy and the ethical implications of emerging technologies such as AI have become focal points of concern.

Addressing these ethical considerations involves complying with regulatory standards and adhering to a higher moral compass. Organizations must establish ethical frameworks to guide decision-making in the digital realm, ensuring that technological advancements align with societal values and norms.

13.5. Policy Implications of Corporate Governance and Digital Finance

The convergence of corporate governance and digital finance creates a disruptive force that alters the economic environment, prompting governments to reevaluate their current approaches. This junction has far-reaching policy ramifications, including questions of regulation, security and the moral elements of financial decision-making. This paper examines the potential and problems for policymakers in establishing a sound regulatory framework brought about by the convergence of corporate governance and digital finance.

13.5.1. *Regulatory challenges in the digital age*

Revised and flexible rules are among the most pressing policy concerns in corporate governance and digital finance. In many cases, authorities need assistance to keep up with the rapid development of financial technology. Traditional regulatory frameworks designed for brick-and-mortar financial institutions may not capture the intricacies of digital transactions, smart contracts and blockchain technologies.

Policymakers must grapple with striking a balance between fostering innovation and ensuring consumer protection. The agility required to keep pace with the rapid advancements in digital finance requires a fundamental shift in regulatory approaches. Policymakers must be proactive in understanding emerging technologies, engaging with industry stakeholders and regularly revisiting and revising regulations to maintain relevance.

13.5.2. *Cybersecurity concerns and regulatory responses*

Integrating digital finance into corporate governance heightens the risk of cybersecurity threats. The interconnected nature of digital financial systems creates vulnerabilities that malicious actors may exploit. Policymakers must address these concerns by developing robust cybersecurity regulations that mandate stringent security measures for financial institutions.

Moreover, the policy response should extend to creating incident reporting and response frameworks. Timely and transparent reporting of cybersecurity incidents is crucial for mitigating their impact and preventing future occurrences. Policymakers should incentivize organizations to invest in state-of-the-art cybersecurity measures while establishing penalties for non-compliance to ensure a strong deterrent against potential threats.

13.5.3. *Enhancing transparency and accountability*

Digital finance introduces novel challenges to traditional notions of transparency and accountability. Smart contracts, decentralized finance (DeFi) platforms and blockchain technologies operate based on principles that may deviate from those of conventional financial structures. Policymakers must navigate the complexities of these innovations to ensure that transparency and accountability remain at the forefront of corporate governance.

Creating policies that mandate transparent reporting mechanisms for blockchain-based transactions and decentralized governance structures becomes imperative. Additionally, policymakers need to explore how traditional auditing practices can adapt to verify the integrity of digital financial processes. Striking the right balance between embracing innovation and upholding transparency is a nuanced policy challenge that requires thoughtful consideration.

13.5.4. *Data governance and privacy considerations*

The digital finance landscape thrives on data, and the policy implications surrounding data governance and privacy are paramount. Policymakers grapple with who owns the data generated in digital financial transactions and how it can be responsibly utilized. Striking a balance between fostering innovation and protecting individuals' privacy rights is a delicate policy challenge.

Comprehensive data protection regulations and ethical guidelines for data usage in the financial sector are essential. Policymakers must collaborate with industry experts, privacy advocates and technologists to craft policies that safeguard individual privacy and encourage responsible data management practices within the digital finance ecosystem.

13.5.5. *Cross-border implications and global coordination*

The digital nature of finance knows no borders, which challenges policymakers in ensuring regulatory coherence across jurisdictions. Cross-border transactions, global digital financial platforms and decentralized governance structures require a coordinated international effort. Policymakers must engage in dialogue with their counterparts globally to establish common standards and principles that facilitate seamless cross-border transactions.

It takes work to find common ground on regulatory measures between countries, especially given their widely varying legal and cultural norms. The value of international organizations and alliances in supporting such cooperation cannot be overstated. Politicians should participate in these discussions to advance a global regulatory framework that encourages innovation, safeguards consumers and maintains the security of the international monetary system.

13.5.6. *Incentivizing ethical corporate governance*

Incorporating digital money into corporate governance frameworks presents a problem for regulators in rewarding moral decision-making. Given the growing influence of algorithms and other forms of automated processing on modern decision-making, established codes of ethics need to be revised. Governments should investigate how they may better include moral principles in developing and managing digital financial infrastructures.

Creating incentives for companies prioritizing ethical corporate governance, such as tax advantages or favorable regulatory treatment, may develop a culture of responsibility. Legislators should consider enacting frameworks that hold organizations responsible for the ethical consequences of their digital financial actions to ensure that societal values are not compromised in the name of technical progress.

13.5.7. *Education and capacity building*

Policymakers will need training and instruction for corporate governance and digital money to be adequately regulated. If policymakers are to successfully guide the development of blockchain, smart contracts and other digital financial technologies, they must first understand their complexities. To better comprehend emerging technologies, policymakers should invest in training programs and collaborate with professionals in the area.

Furthermore, politicians play a critical role in fostering community-wide education and awareness. Educating firms, customers and other stakeholders about the implications of digital finance on corporate governance may build a culture of informed decision-making and ethical practices.

Cross-Border Coordination: Because digital finance is a global phenomenon, governments must prioritize cross-border coordination to unify corporate governance requirements. This makes it easier to adopt a uniform approach to risk management and corporate monitoring, which in turn helps reduce regulatory arbitrage and raise awareness of best practices worldwide.

Standardization and Development of Ethical Guidelines: Policymakers can define and implement ethical guidelines and standards for the digital financial industry. These recommendations ensure that corporate governance processes align with public values and expectations and address possible ethical difficulties that may arise due to technology improvements.

Increasing the number of consumer protection measures is something that policymakers need to do, given the dangers associated with digital banking. Among these measures is the implementation of rules that protect users' interests in digital financial services. These regulations include transparent dispute resolution systems and safeguards against fraudulent activities.

Adaptive Governance Frameworks: Because digital finance is inherently dynamic, governments need to push for the implementation of adaptive governance frameworks. These frameworks must be able to accommodate iterative modifications in response to technology improvements. This will guarantee that regulations remain practical and relevant in the quickly changing digital ecosystem.

Monitoring and Evaluation Systems: Policymakers should create rigorous monitoring and evaluation systems to examine the performance of corporate governance measures in the digital finance sphere. Conducting regular assessments may assist in identifying new hazards, evaluating the effects of policies and directing the refinement of rules to handle growing difficulties.

Collaborations Between the Public and Private Sectors: Policymakers can encourage public–private partnerships to collaboratively solve difficulties faced by the intersection of corporate governance and digital finance. Through the participation of industry stakeholders in the policymaking process, it is possible to build a regulatory environment that is both more comprehensive and more responsive to the sector's needs.

13.6. Conclusions

After delving into the complicated convergence of corporate governance and digital finance, we reach a turning point where we may take stock and draw conclusions. To close this chapter, it is necessary to highlight the most important learnings, consequences and next steps.

Our study began with a brief overview of how corporate governance and digital finance interact. We traveled through time to see how corporate governance has developed, from its early days of purely hierarchical systems to its present-day embrace of digital finance. The junction of these two spheres became a focal point, emphasizing technology's vital role in transforming decision-making processes and the financial landscape. We looked at the advantages and disadvantages of this integration in detail. Emerging regulatory difficulties have prompted calls for a radical departure from established regulatory methods. Cybersecurity fears palliated the online financial industry, prompting authorities to shore up protections. Decentralized economic systems forced a reevaluation of long-held beliefs, as the need to increase transparency and accountability came to the forefront.

Corporate governance best practices in the digital finance age were investigated, focusing on the significance of flexible frameworks and effective risk management techniques. Successful implementations were shown via real-world case studies, which provided valuable insights and lessons for businesses beginning their digital financial journey. The future of corporate governance and digital finance was revealed, focusing on how new technologies such as blockchain and AI will shape the industry. The emphasis placed on collaboration and partnerships highlighted the necessity of teamwork in handling the challenges of the digital era.

Our research was saturated with ethical questions, highlighting the need to maintain ethical practices despite technical progress. The importance of educational efforts grew as people realized the need for lifelong learning to meet the ever-changing requirements of digital governance. Global views emphasize diverse approaches to corporate governance, reminding us of the necessity for a comprehensive understanding in an international setting. The revolutionary potential of innovations such as blockchain and smart contracts was explored by examining their application to corporate governance. It became clear that one of the keys to success in today's rapidly evolving digital environment is the ability to quickly adapt to new circumstances.

Stressed the importance of maintaining a personal touch in governance while using technological advancements to increase productivity. In the modern era of technology, this equilibrium has become essential to good corporate governance. A few overarching themes emerge as we reflect on the multitude of insights garnered throughout this chapter. The digital finance era is not merely a technological shift but a redefinition of how organizations operate, make decisions and interact with stakeholders. Integrating digital finance into corporate governance is not a linear progression but a multidimensional transformation that demands a holistic and adaptive approach. Regulation stands at the forefront of this transformation. Traditional regulatory frameworks, which function effectively in a non-digital context, must evolve to keep pace with rapid technological advancements. Policymakers face the intricate challenge of striking a delicate balance between fostering innovation and safeguarding consumers and between enabling progress and mitigating risks.

Cybersecurity requires meticulous attention as an integral part of this regulatory landscape. The interconnected nature of digital finance creates vulnerabilities that demand robust defenses. Policymakers must adopt proactive measures, incentivize cybersecurity investments and establish precise incident response mechanisms to protect the integrity of financial systems.

Transparency and accountability, pillars of effective governance, are reevaluated in the digital era. As smart contracts and decentralized structures become more prevalent, policymakers must craft policies that ensure transparency without stifling innovation. The challenge lies in adapting traditional auditing practices to the intricacies of digital financial processes.

Data governance and privacy considerations represent another critical dimension. Policymakers must navigate the fine line between encouraging innovation that relies on data and protecting individuals' privacy rights. Comprehensive data protection regulations and ethical guidelines are essential to this delicate balance.

The global nature of digital finance necessitates international collaboration. Policymakers must engage in dialogue, harmonize regulatory approaches and establish common standards to facilitate cross-border transactions. Ethical concerns have guided every step of this evolution. Policymakers must incentivize organizations to prioritize ethical corporate governance, ensuring that society's values are not surrendered in the quest for technical development. Educating policymakers and stakeholders is crucial because it promotes a norm of making well-informed choices and acting ethically.

13.6.1. *Looking ahead: The path forward*

At this juncture between corporate governance and digital finance, the lessons learned and the obstacles encountered shed light on the way ahead. To succeed in today's ever-changing digital environment, businesses and government agencies must accept that the path is never-ending and flexibility is essential.

Including digital financial management in corporate governance is more than a one-size-fits-all task. The rate at which various sectors, regions and institutions adopt this approach will be determined by their respective settings and obstacles. Policymakers should welcome this variety by developing flexible, scalable regulatory frameworks that accommodate regional and sectoral differences.

The importance of working together becomes apparent. For businesses to succeed, internal technology and governance teams must work together. The business community must collaborate and form partnerships to effectively confront external concerns. To be informed and proactive, policymakers must also create cooperation by actively interacting with industry experts, foreign peers and technological innovators.

Innovation remains a critical factor in our success. Companies that are open to new technologies and use them to their advantage will lead in digital governance. Governments should foster a climate conducive to innovation by providing financial incentives to businesses that engage in R&D and monitoring their progress to ensure that ethical concerns are never overlooked.

Learning now represents an ongoing process. Policymakers must invest in programs that expand their awareness of new technologies, cybersecurity and the subtleties of digital money. Companies should invest heavily in their workers' continual education to ensure that they always have the necessary tools to succeed in a dynamic industry.

Maintaining an optimum balance between technology and human interaction is also essential. Organizations must build a culture that appreciates both the efficiency of technology and the wisdom of human judgment. Policymakers should include this nuance in their regulatory frameworks to inspire businesses to innovate without sacrificing their ideals.

In conclusion, the merger of corporate governance and digital finance is more than just technological innovation; it also represents a fundamental change in how businesses are run and governed. The road ahead is challenging, yet opportunities for creativity, teamwork and sound are hidden in its obstacles. Let us move forward with the promise of a technologically advanced and ethically grounded corporate governance environment, mindful of the lessons of the past and the wisdom of the present.

13.6.2. *Practical insights*

Real-world experience shows that flexible and adaptable governance frameworks are essential for the smooth introduction of digital finance. To reap the advantages of digital finance, businesses must quickly adapt their governance structures to suit new technologies.

The practical application of digital finance emphasizes the importance of data in decision-making processes. Organizations harness the power of analytics and data insights to make informed strategic decisions, optimize financial performance and enhance governance efficiency.

Real-world examples also demonstrate that collaboration between different stakeholders is critical. The integration of digital finance often involves various departments, from finance to IT and legal. Effective collaboration ensures a holistic approach to governance, mitigating challenges and maximizing opportunities.

Organizations prioritizing continuous learning and training for their workforce are more successful in navigating the complexities of digital finance. Practical insights underscore the need for ongoing education to keep employees abreast of technological advancements and changes in governance practices.

Practical experiences highlight the importance of placing ethical considerations at the forefront of digital finance integration. Organizations that prioritize ethical decision-making foster trust and navigate regulatory landscapes more effectively.

13.6.3. *Future directions*

The future of corporate governance in the digital age may witness the rise of decentralized governance models. Blockchain technology and smart contracts have the potential to enable decentralized decision-making, reducing reliance on traditional hierarchical structures.

Future directions in digital finance governance point toward enhanced cybersecurity measures. As cyber threats evolve, organizations must invest in cutting-edge technologies and protocols to safeguard their financial processes and maintain the integrity of governance frameworks.

AI is poised to play a significant role in the future of corporate governance. AI-driven decision support systems can enhance management by providing real-time insights, automating routine tasks and predicting potential risks.

The future promises regulatory evolution that will keep pace with digital finance advancements. Policymakers are likely to refine and expand regulatory frameworks, balancing the promotion of innovation with consumer protection.

Anticipated future directions suggest a move toward global standardization in digital finance governance. Efforts to harmonize regulations across borders will facilitate international transactions and collaborations while addressing the challenges of diverse regulatory environments.

The future of corporate governance in the digital finance era may witness a heightened focus on sustainability and social responsibility. Organizations are expected to integrate environmental, social and governance considerations into their governance frameworks, aligning with broader societal expectations.

In conclusion, practical insights gained from current experiences underscore the importance of adaptability, collaboration and ethical considerations in integrating corporate governance and digital finance. Looking ahead, future directions point toward decentralized models, advanced cybersecurity measures, the integration of AI, regulatory evolution, global standardization and an emphasis on sustainable and socially responsible governance. Organizations that embrace these insights and navigate future directions will be well-positioned to thrive in the evolving landscape of corporate governance and digital finance.

References

Cao, S., Nie, L., Sun, H., Sun, W., & Taghizadeh-Hesary, F. (2021). Digital finance, green technological innovation and energy-environmental performance: Evidence from China's regional economies. *Journal of Cleaner Production*, 327. https://doi.org/10.1016/J.JCLEPRO.2021.129458.

Chen, S. & Zhang, H. (2021). Does digital finance promote manufacturing servitization: Micro evidence from China. *International Review of Economics and Finance*, 76, 856–869. https://doi.org/10.1016/J.IREF.2021.07.018.

Chen, Y., Kumara, E. K., & Sivakumar, V. (2021). Investigation of finance industry on risk awareness model and digital economic growth. *Annals of Operations Research*. https://doi.org/10.1007/s10479-021-04287-7.

Ding, Q., Huang, J., & Chen, J. (2023). Does digital finance matter for corporate green investment? Evidence from heavily polluting industries in China. *Energy Economics*, 117. https://doi.org/10.1016/j.eneco.2022.106476.

Huo, D., Zhang, X., Meng, S., Wu, G., Li, J., & Di, R. (2022). Green finance and energy efficiency: Dynamic study of the spatial externality of institutional support in a digital economy by using hidden Markov chain. *Energy Economics*, 116. https://doi.org/10.1016/j.eneco.2022.106431.

Jensen, M. C., & Meckling, W. H. (2019). Theory of the firm: Managerial behavior, agency costs and ownership structure. In Corporate governance (pp. 77–132). Gower. https://doi.org/10.1016/0304-405X(76)90026-X.

Ji, X., Wang, K., Xu, H., & Li, M. (2021). Has digital financial inclusion narrowed the urban-rural income gap: The role of entrepreneurship in China. *Sustainability* (Switzerland), 13(15). https://doi.org/10.3390/SU13158292.

Lee, C. C., Tang, M., & Lee, C. C. (2023). Reaping digital dividends: Digital inclusive finance and high-quality development of enterprises in China. *Telecommunications Policy*, 47(2). https://doi.org/10.1016/J.TELPOL.2022.102484.

Lee, C. C. & Wang, F. (2022). How does digital inclusive finance affect carbon intensity? *Economic Analysis and Policy*, 75, 174–190. https://doi.org/10.1016/J.EAP.2022.05.010.

Lee, C. C., Wang, F., & Lou, R. (2022). Digital financial inclusion and carbon neutrality: Evidence from non-linear analysis. *Resources Policy*, 79. https://doi.org/10.1016/J.RESOURPOL.2022.102974.

Li, X., Wang, H., & Yang, C. (2023). Driving mechanism of digital economy based on regulation algorithm for development of low-carbon industries. *Sustainable Energy Technologies and Assessments*, 55. https://doi.org/10.1016/J.SETA.2022.102909.

Li, Z., Yang, C., & Huang, Z. (2022). How does the fintech sector react to signals from central bank digital currencies? *Finance Research Letters*, 50. https://doi.org/10.1016/j.frl.2022.103308.

Liu, Y., Lei, J., Zhang, Y., Liu, Y., Lei, J., & Zhang, Y. A. (2021). A study on the sustainable relationship among the green finance, environment regulation and green-total-factor productivity in China. *Sustainability*, 13(21), 11926. https://doi.org/10.3390/SU132111926.

Ma, M., Zhu, X., Liu, M., & Huang, X. (2023). Combining the role of green finance and environmental sustainability on green economic growth: Evidence from G-20 economies. *Renewable Energy*, 207, 128–136. https://doi.org/10.1016/j.renene.2023.02.046.

Macchiavello, E.& Siri, M. (2022). Sustainable finance and fintech: Can technology contribute to achieving environmental goals? A preliminary assessment of "Green Fintech" and "Sustainable Digital Finance." *European Company and Financial Law Review*, 19(1), 128–174. https://doi.org/10.1515/ECFR-2022-0005.

Maria, M. R., Ballini, R., & Souza, R. F. (2023). Evolution of green finance: A bibliometric analysis through complex networks and machine learning. *Sustainability*, 15(2), 967. https://doi.org/10.3390/SU15020967.

Mo, Y., Sun, D., & Zhang, Y. (2023). Green finance assists agricultural sustainable development: Evidence from China. *Sustainability*, 15(3), 2056. https://doi.org/10.3390/SU15032056.

Razzaq, A., Sharif, A., Ozturk, I., & Skare, M. (2023). Asymmetric influence of digital finance, and renewable energy technology innovation on green growth in China. *Renewable Energy*, 202, 310–319. https://doi.org/10.1016/j.renene.2022.11.082.

Ren, X., Zeng, G., & Gozgor, G. (2023). How does digital finance affect industrial structure upgrading? Evidence from Chinese prefecture-level cities. *Journal of Environmental Management*, 330. https://doi.org/10.1016/j.jenvman.2022.117125.

Skare, M., de las Mercedes de Obesso, M., & Ribeiro-Navarrete, S. (2023). Digital transformation and European small and medium enterprises (SMEs): A comparative study using digital economy and society index data. *International Journal of Information Management*, 68. https://doi.org/10.1016/j.ijinfomgt.2022.102594.

Sun, G., Li, T., Ai, Y., & Li, Q. (2023). Digital finance and corporate financial fraud. *International Review of Financial Analysis*, 87. https://doi.org/10.1016/j.irfa.2023.102566.

Tang, X., Ding, S., Gao, X., & Zhao, T. (2022). Can digital finance help increase the value of strategic emerging enterprises? *Sustainable Cities and Society*, 81. https://doi.org/10.1016/J.SCS.2022.103829.

Wang, W., Gao, P., & Wang, J. (2023). Nexus among digital inclusive finance and carbon neutrality: Evidence from company-level panel data analysis. *Resources Policy*, 80. https://doi.org/10.1016/j.resourpol.2022.103201.

Wu, Y. & Huang, S. (2022). The effects of digital finance and financial constraint on financial performance: Firm-level evidence from China's new energy enterprises. *Energy Economics*, 112. https://doi.org/10.1016/J.ENECO.2022.106158.

Xu, J., She, S., Gao, P., & Sun, Y. (2023). Role of green finance in resource efficiency and green economic growth. *Resources Policy*, 81. https://doi.org/10.1016/j.resourpol.2023.103349.

Yu, L., Zhao, D., Xue, Z., & Gao, Y. (2020). Research on the use of digital finance and the adoption of green control techniques by family farms in China. *Technology in Society*, 62. https://doi.org/10.1016/J.TECHSOC.2020.101323.

Yu, M., Tsai, F. S., Jin, H., & Zhang, H. (2022). Digital finance and renewable energy consumption: Evidence from China. *Financial Innovation*, 8(1). https://doi.org/10.1186/S40854-022-00362-5.

Zhang, M. & Liu, Y. (2022). Influence of digital finance and green technology innovation on China's carbon emission efficiency: Empirical analysis based on spatial metrology. *Science of the Total Environment*, 838. https://doi.org/10.1016/J.SCITOTENV.2022.156463.

Zhang, Y. Q. (2023). Impact of green finance and environmental protection on green economic recovery in South Asian economies: Mediating role of FinTech. *Economic Change and Restructuring*. https://doi.org/10.1007/S10644-023-09500-0.

https://doi.org/10.1142/9781800616257_0014

Chapter 14

Assets Tokenization: Prospects and Challenges

Asad Abbas*, **Ghulam Hussain Khan Zaigham**†, **and Arslan Ali Raza**‡

COMSATS University Islamabad, Islamabad, Pakistan
**asad.abbas@comsats.edu.pk*
†zaigham.khan@comsats.edu.pk
‡arslanraza@cuivehari.edu.pk

Abstract

Asset tokenization is about to reshape the world of investment and finance due to its enormous potential for providing customized solutions to those aspiring to be part of a financial ecosystem. Tokenization is the process of transferring large assets into a large number of small tokens of ownership, provided with a unique digital identity and presence in a blockchain with its immutability and interoperability. It is incredibly secure, remarkably liquid, significantly cost-effective, reasonably transparent, easily accessible and very broad in spectrum and scope. It encompasses all financial and real assets, ranging from commodities to securities, real estate, artworks, sports, the corporate sector and even collectibles. It can provide convenient, customized and cost-effective access to anyone in the digital world of blockchain technology. It also removes the role of any intermediary, avoids delays in transferring ownership of assets and subsequently eliminates transaction costs. Due to its immense potential of distributed ledger technology (DLT), it can manage transactions involving huge sums in a transparent and speedy manner. Despite its massive potential, there are some challenges that potential entrants must face, hindering the unleashing of this potential. This chapter attempts to unfold some of the prospects and challenges of asset tokenization which the decentralized financial world of tokenization and its players face, including the complexities associated with the codification and creation of digital tokens, regulatory challenges, fear of entering the universe of virtual reality, a lack of tangible holding of assets, the rapid evolution and development of digital markets, overcoming trust deficits among counterparties, finding appropriate assets and the discovery and integration of demand–supply mechanisms.

Keywords: Tokenization, block chain, ownership, distributed ledger technology.

14.1. Introduction to Asset Tokenization and Some Insights

This chapter investigates asset tokenization, a rising field in digital finance. The process of representing an asset's ownership rights as digital tokens and storing them on a blockchain can be referred to as digital asset tokenization. Tokenization, according to the Financial Stability Board, is the representation of conventional assets on distributed ledger technology (DLT), such as financial instruments, collections of collateral or actual assets (FSB, 2019). Tokens can serve as virtual certificates of ownership in these situations, representing nearly any kind of asset, including digital, physical, fungible and non-fungible ones. As a store of value, tokens issued through asset tokenization exist on the chain and possess the rights to the assets they represent. To guarantee that the tokens are consistently backed by real assets, physical real-world assets would normally need to be held in custody.

However, the real assets on which the tokens are issued remain in the "off-chain" world. This suggests that asset custodianship will play a larger role in tokenization transactions. Owners can retain custody of their assets because they are kept on a blockchain (or in a secure cryptocurrency wallet). The tremendous long-term potential of this use case is matched by the ongoing adoption efforts. Major corporations, including Black Rock, Deloitte, BNY Mellon, EY, the Boston Consulting Group and ADDX, have examined asset tokenization and determined that it has the potential to upend a number of industries, including the global securities market. Additionally, projects to tokenize securities and industrial assets have been launched by Vanguard and Microsoft, respectively, and they have gone live.

Based on these indicators, asset tokenization is already one of the most popular blockchain use cases and is widely adopted by many enterprises.

In order to support crowdsourcing- and crowdfunding-based initiatives for the large-scale application of digital resources, researchers have devised multiple protocols and solutions to support and optimize these efforts. Blockchain-based distributed ledgers have facilitated this by enabling secure and comprehensive solutions such as the Trust and Transition Chain (TTC) protocol, which ensures correctness and consensus among crowd sources and provides further resilience against cyberattacks (Afzaal *et al.*, 2023; Li *et al.*, 2022).

Tokenization makes possible a simplified and effective financial system powered by blockchain technology by combining origination, distribution, trading, clearing, settlement and safekeeping into a single layer. Determining the type of token (fungible or non-fungible), choosing the blockchain to issue the tokens on, choosing an external auditor to confirm off-chain assets, issuing the assets and other procedures are all part of the process of establishing tokenized assets. Figure 14.1 elaborates the working of asset tokenization.

To gain some insights into asset tokenization, let's review the proliferation of Web3 technology. Smart contracts are digital agreements made with computer code that are cryptographically secure and kept on a blockchain; they are a form of extremely secure database. To issue tokens, a developer creates a smart contract on a blockchain with functions that allow users with control over those addresses to

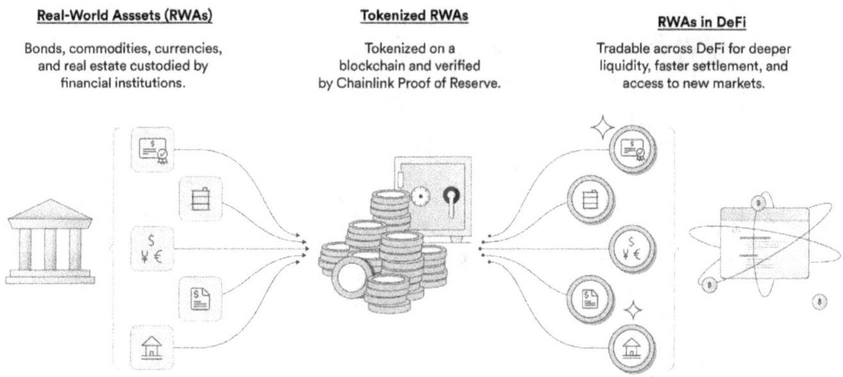

Figure 14.1. Working of asset tokenization.

add or remove balances, mapping positive balances to a series of wallet or smart contract addresses. Similarly, for assets not on the chain, communication between the "off-chain" (conventional financial market infrastructure) and "on-chain" environments is essential. Any asset can theoretically be tokenized, and the rights to do so can be shown on a distributed ledger. One type of "stable coin," a type of token backed by fiat money, has surged quickly as a result of the issuance of numerous new stablecoins and their increasing market capitalization. Real assets include commodities such as gold, art and real estate. The tokenization of intangible assets, including intellectual property, has the potential to generate novel digital assets and markets. Figure 14.2 illustrates the on-chain and off-chain worlds.

Blockchain networks could gain trillions of dollars' worth of real value through asset tokenization. Compared to traditional assets, tokenized assets offer lower liquidity, open access, on-chain transparency and lower transactional friction. Moreover, researchers are focusing on the need to digitalize various assets, including securities and currencies, in order to cope with challenges, such as pandemics and wars, as well as the ramifications of a new world order and to

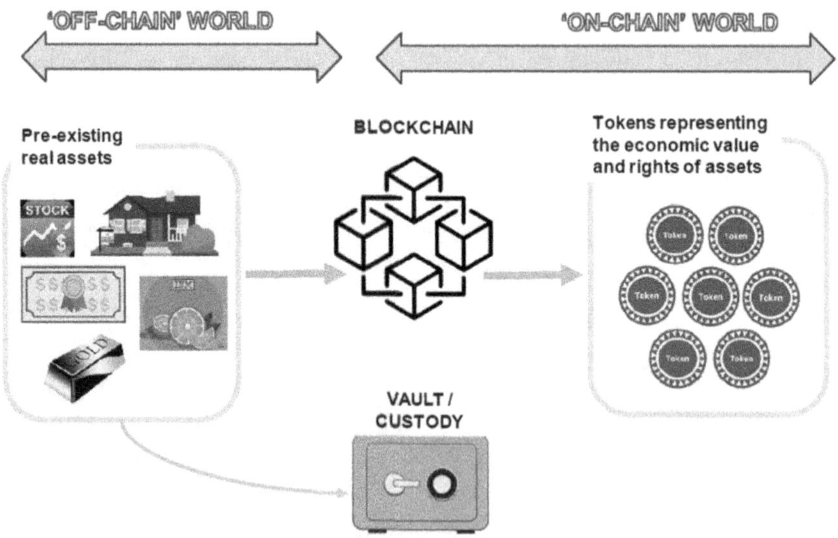

Figure 14.2. Tokenization of real assets.

reduce the dominance of traditional systems which may have many flaws (Bhaskar *et al.*, 2022; Goodell, 2020; Jia *et al.*, 2021). The objective of such a transformation is to avoid intermediation and value loss and, in turn, enable the full transfer of benefits to end users (Famiglietti & Leibovici, 2022).

14.2. Native Tokens and Blockchain

It is crucial to distinguish between tokens that are native to the blockchain and tokenized assets that exist off-chain. Native tokens are only present on the distributed ledger and are created directly on the blockchain. Native tokens include Bitcoin and other cryptocurrencies, as well as payment tokens. Native tokens are defined by their presence on the blockchain and possess intrinsic value. Another kind of native token is that distributed through initial coin offerings (ICOs). In an ICO, start-up businesses create digital tokens and offer them to investors in exchange for money in order to raise funding (OECD, 2019). In an ICO, tokens are created on the blockchain and are not backed by any off-chain assets or securities. Figure 14.3 depicts the tokenization of assets which are native to the blockchain. Considering that tokens created in ICOs are separate from the traditional, off-chain portion of the market, this has significant implications for market structure and governance.

Let's assume a scenario in which we are tokenizing the equity of a non-listed company. In this scenario, the company's free float is

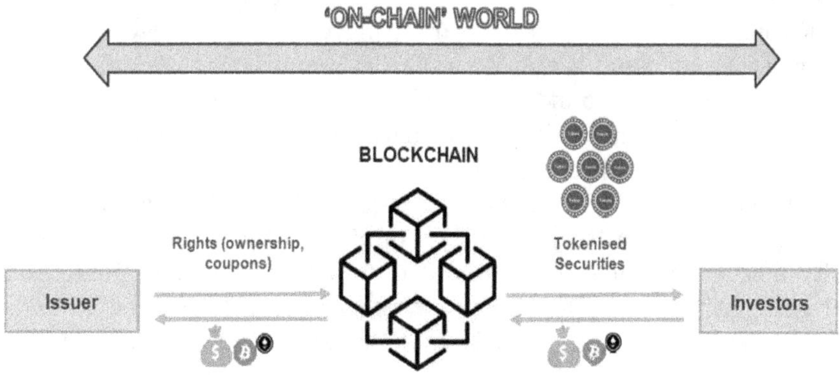

Figure 14.3. Native tokens and the on-chain world.

represented digitally by tokens and made available to investors on the blockchain. An analogous transaction to this would be the digitalized on-chain private placement of securities. A comparable framework would be applicable to private debt placements. Given the almost complete lack of participation and liquidity in investment funds and alternatives, such as private equity and venture capital funds, as well as real estate investment vehicles, these all would be available on chain in tokenized form. Similarly, consider the repercussions of a possible breakdown of the underlying blockchain technology to show how tokenization of dematerialized real-world goods, which also exist in the real world, differs from that of assets native to the blockchain. Unlike native token holders, who have no relationship to the real world whatsoever, shareholders whose shares exist off the chain and were recorded on the blockchain would remain stockholders in the event of an operational failure of the blockchain.

14.3. Tokenization of Financing Assets

The market believes that the financial asset segment with the most immediate growth potential is the tokenization of securities, which includes debt and/or equity. The current hype surrounding tokens issued mostly through unregulated ICOs and "security token offerings," or STOs, which are currently popular and have been positioned as a more "regulatory-compliant" alternative to ICOs for capital raising, as well as "security tokens" that represent existing securities in secondary DLT markets, are the main drivers of this trend. The classifications are self-defined by market players, and the determination of whether an issue satisfies regulatory requirements is contingent upon the specific issuance in question.

In order to comply with the security regulatory framework in both the jurisdiction of issuance and the jurisdictions where the offering is marketed to investors, STOs involve the issue of DLT-based tokens. On the blockchain, regulations pertaining to the offering and security lifecycle are digitally reflected by programmable ownership and trading restriction enforcement ("programmable securities," bonds issued by EU investment banks and GS DAP, BENJI tokens). Since there is no official classification for these kinds of token offers, STOs are self-described. Self-defined security tokens are tokenized versions of securities that were formerly issued through traditional means (current share certificates), with the intention of bringing these assets onto the digital, secondary on-chain market. The market and institutions, including central banks, are now facing many challenges in continuing with their traditional products and services due to digital transformation; therefore, they must transition toward digitalization accordingly (Hunjra & Hanif, 2023). Their researchers are also extensively utilizing the models and frameworks of machine learning and artificial intelligence to innovate traditional methodologies for identifying issues in the corporate sector (Aslam *et al.*, 2022).

14.4. Prospects of Asset Tokenization

Asset tokenization offers numerous advantages beyond simply providing a decentralized and trust-minimized substitute for a physical good, investment vehicle or service. To be more precise, the tokenization of physical assets via blockchain technology offers a direct route to increasing the value, utility and accessibility of many assets. It also establishes a channel through which off-chain data can increase their utility within the decentralized finance (DeFi) ecosystem. The enormous array of benefits and added value that tokenized assets offer over non-tokenized assets constitutes the core of asset tokenization's current success as well as its future possibilities. Increased liquidity of traditionally illiquid assets, improved accessibility and ease of access to otherwise closed investment opportunities, increased transparency regarding ownership and ownership history and a decrease in trading-related administrative costs, such as management, issuance and transactional intermediaries are all made possible by tokenization. Finally, through asset-backed composability, tokenization opens up a whole new world of opportunities for assets that were previously unable to enter the DeFi ecosystem.

14.4.1. *Liquidity*

Financial events are typically recorded across compartmentalized ledgers in traditional markets, which leads to substantial market inefficiencies such as higher costs and longer settlement times. Because of these disparities in system interoperability, asset tokenization holds significant potential for addressing fractionalized liquidity by creating interoperable tokenized assets.

Small and medium enterprises, as well as private equity and venture capital funds, limited liability companies and private placements, can also benefit from such on-chain tokenization and in turn unlock illiquid assets through these on-chain mechanisms, thereby increasing trade activity. Hence, tokenization can promote price discovery and capital formation by utilizing such illiquid assets.

Assets that previously lacked liquidity may also benefit from tokenization. Tokenization allows for the representation of an asset as millions or even billions of tokens, resulting in fractional ownership that can then be listed on numerous exchanges, which are easily accessible and widely available. This keeps the tokens linked to a specific asset, expands the pool of possible buyers and eliminates the need for pricey transactional middlemen. Tokenization thus encourages an all-inclusive approach, which can increase the potential for marketability and accessibility of assets and the subsequent return on assets.

14.4.2. *Accessibility*

Due to regulatory or budgetary restrictions, many of the assets with the largest potential are unavailable to regular investors. For example, let's say you want to finance a big-budget film. The upfront expenditures and the possibility of a production crew exceeding their budget can easily drive away all but the wealthiest investors. On the other hand, a profitable movie can pay for itself several times over in a comparatively short amount of time. Investing in distressed foreign assets, collecting sports vehicles or buying and renting multifamily real estate are some more low-access, high-return examples.

In this scenario, tokenization's advantages resemble crowdsourcing in theory, but in a way where investors who fund or buy an asset also profit monetarily from their involvement. This provides smaller investors with a way to use comparatively small capital to invest in riskier yet more lucrative assets.

14.4.3. *Transparency*

A common problem with high-value assets is the lack of easily accessible and trustworthy data on returns, ownership, sales and other important criteria essential for investors in order to make wise financial decisions. When assessing foreign assets or in situations where a buyer is unable to physically inspect an asset before purchase, this knowledge gap is particularly severe. Because many blockchains are inherently public, tokenization offers the advantage of enabling open tracking and auditing of all this information. Depending on the asset's smart contract logic, tokenization allows users to view an ownership history in addition to receiving rewards in the form of dividends or interest. The blockchain's provenance tracking feature ensures that data are unchangeable, thus reducing the risks associated with investment security.

14.4.4. *Composability*

Linking the value of physical assets to the defensibility of the DeFi ecosystem is one of the most exciting yet under explored benefits of asset tokenization. Users can earn an equity percentage of the income generated from off-chain collateral by participating in decentralized money markets centered around tokenized real-world assets. Retail investors now have easier access to an otherwise difficult-to-access investment class while also increasing the liquidity of the broader DeFi industry. By combining tokens linked to different assets, it is simple to create entirely new kinds of synthetic assets, indexes and token baskets. Additionally, the ability to convert actual revenue streams into such assets adds yet another innovative spark to the rapidly growing DeFi industry.

14.4.5. *Instantaneous repo activity*

A repo activity is an overnight activity in which a party borrows money from another to meet its short-term liquidity requirement, with an agreement to repurchase the government security as soon as the requirement is satisfied. With the help of on-chain transactions, repo activities became faster and cheaper, making the transfer and trading of securities almost instantaneous, convenient and globally accessible. The collateral can thus be quickly transferred across different accounts, and the associated liquidity is improved significantly, allowing more trading activity and driving more investment. The recording of transactions on a DLT enables greater traceability of assets and collateral since their movements are transparent and seamless. However, netting of collateral and assets is not possible in such scenarios, and assets must be mobilized on a gross basis.

14.4.6. *Disintermediation*

An important aspect of off-chain conventional financial transaction is the involvement of intermediaries between two parties. This involvement entails costs in terms of both money and time lag. DLT-based transactions of tokenized assets do not require the involvement of intermediaries for clearing and settlement. They are also very fast and hence save a substantial amount of cost and time.

14.5. Challenges of Asset Tokenization

Several technological obstacles would need to be overcome before asset tokenization could be widely implemented.

14.5.1. *Scalability*

Scalability refers to the ability to perform hundreds and thousands of transactions at superfast speeds, often within seconds. In order to make blockchain-based technologies valuable, uncapped scalability is a prerequisite. Though researchers are working to devise solutions to support multimillion transactions (Buldas *et al.*, 2022a), it is still a challenge to devise a coordinated, integrated and systematic platform that can support such fast-paced levels of transactions in a trusted and adaptive manner.

Regarding asset tokenization, scalability remains a technological obstacle for DLT-enabled networks because of the large throughput needed to accommodate the vast scales of the global financial markets. For certain blockchains, settlement finality, that is, the final and irreversible settlement of payment instructions with deterministic finality, may still present a challenge. For connectivity between markets to be permitted, interoperability across various networks must be protected. Additional operational risks include those related to network reliability, cyber-risk exposure, hacking and 51% attacks, as well as business risks associated with transitioning to a DLT-enabled environment.

14.5.2. *Governance concerns*

Governance concerns, which are especially pertinent to completely decentralized ledgers, relate to the difficulties involved in identifying a single node or owner responsible for the entire network. Another issue with regulating DLT networks, or needing to assign blame for a network failure, is the lack of a single point of accountability. If the majority of the network decides to implement changes that are contrary to the original plan, participants can launch "51% attacks" against the network. Alternatively, they can "fork" the network if they disagree with the original protocol and choose to diverge from it, creating a new network by changing the basic code (for permissionless DLTs).

14.5.3. *Legal and regulatory concerns*

The swift progress of digital technology raises prospective concerns regarding the technological resilience of DLT-based market infrastructure against quantum threats to symmetric and asymmetric encryption. For example, the latter is helpful when signing transactions on open blockchains. For asymmetric post-quantum cryptography to be used safely in tokenized marketplaces, more research is needed. Market players may be at risk from certain tokenized assets that have an ambiguous legal and regulatory status. This can be reduced by financial regulatory and supervisory agencies providing clear interpretations of the existing law and regulations.

Since most jurisdictions still do not view smart contracts as legitimate contracts, the legal standing of these agreements remains a topic of ongoing debate. Enforceability and financial protection concerns will remain unresolved until it becomes clear whether contract law governs smart contracts. Market participants who want to verify the foundations upon which such smart contracts are implemented will need to provide more resources in order for the code of such contracts to be auditable.

14.5.4. *Privacy and data concerns*

Concerns about privacy and data protection also surface, along with issues related to data storage and the laws governing the use, sharing and storage of data. This is especially important in areas where there are data privacy laws, such as the GDPR in Europe, which demand the establishment of strict consent management procedures and efficient data rights management systems. Permissioned blockchains may be able to help meet these requirements. However, data erasure clauses grant customers the "right to be forgotten," which runs counter to the blockchain's immutability and will be more difficult to implement. However, it has been demonstrated that transaction privacy is possible in tokenized environments, where access to transaction details is restricted to pertinent parties (e.g., EY's zero-knowledge proof (ZKP) private transaction protocol of Project Nightfall, the Monetary Authority of Singapore and Project Ubin – Phase 2; EY, 2019). It will also be necessary to handle more general identity-related concerns and the large-scale management of digital identities.

14.5.5. *Identity concerns or anonymity*

Currently, there are no well-defined procedures in place to stop practices such as "wash trading" and other forms of market manipulation. Through such methods, parties can manipulate the price of a digital asset in the absence of a consistent approach to digital identity. This risk increases when trading moves beyond an exchange and into other exchanges and jurisdictions. AML/CFT risks are common in DLT-based systems, and they are especially significant in tokenized markets built on public permission-less networks, more so if the protocol permits user anonymity. Important guidelines regarding the responsibilities of virtual asset activities and service providers have been released by the Financial Action Task Force in 2019 (FATF, 2019).

14.5.6. *Digital financial literacy*

Participants in the market are not equally motivated to move to a blockchain-enabled market because private incentives created through the securities lifecycle are anticipated to change, wane or vanish in a tokenized setting. Tokenized assets must benefit investors as well as the issuer in terms of cost and prospective returns in order to reach sufficient depth to be traded exclusively on-chain.

To that end, if tokenized markets were to reach regular investors, public investment in financial education would be required.

14.5.7. *Resistance to change*

It takes substantial financial commitment from market players to transition from legacy infrastructure to DLT-based networks; however, efficiency improvements must first be demonstrated and made quantifiable for every kind of security asset and at every stage of the securities lifecycle before results are realized. The adoption of DLT-enabled tokenized markets may still face obstacles due to the vested interests of some market participants.

It is not guaranteed that the industry will be willing or able to reach an agreement on concerted efforts to develop global or interoperable infrastructure solutions. Some have suggested that, for the system as a whole to move to an on-chain environment, it would require unambiguous incentives to switch to a financial market infrastructure enabled by blockchain technology. The potential for inflated expectations from certain industry players could encourage them to switch to DLT-based solutions before they have a solid reason to do so. Only in situations where there is: a strong business case for the application of DLTs. The application of DLT-enabled in financial markets. Are there safety or trust gaps, is there enough space for disintermediation and are there quantifiable efficiency gains to be realized? What differences exist between the traditional case and the DLT-based? A technical feasibility assessment proving that the application of DLTs provides significant advantages while addressing major technical challenges.

Researchers are now proposing return-based tokens and devising mechanisms for the distribution of returns from such tokenized assets by suggesting improvements in the traditional return distribution model and following a regulatory compliant approach (Zhitomirskiy *et al.*, 2023).

14.5.8. *Market depth*

In order to realize the benefits of asset tokenization and subsequent liquidity, the existence of a parallel demand side is inevitable.

Without a sufficient number of demanders of tokenized assets, trading activity would not be possible; as a result, sufficient market depth and, in turn, economies of scale would not be created. A substantial number of demanders would not be available in the market unless all the associated confusion, obstacles and complications were removed. Similarly, smooth functioning of the market would not be possible unless a holistic change in the mindset of investors and the removal of reluctance toward a DeFi ecosystem were ensured.

14.6. Further Prospects of Tokenization

Tokenization has the potential to offer a number of advantages, such as opening up markets to investors that would otherwise be closed off or extremely expensive to participate in. In contrast to real estate investment trusts (REITs), where investors own shares of a portfolio of real estate investments, real estate tokenization, for instance, may permit investment in a portion of the underlying asset, allowing buyers to purchase shares in particular commercial buildings or residential investments. In general, the capacity to program crypto tokens and use smart contracts makes it possible to incorporate additional features into the tokenized asset, which may help the markets for the underlying reference assets. For instance, even if they cannot be applied to their real-world equivalents, liquidity-saving techniques may still be used in the settlement of tokenized assets (Martin & McAndrews, 2008). These characteristics could make markets more liquid and competitive, leading to improved price discovery by lowering entry barriers for a larger group of investors.

In situations where lending secured by the reference asset can be more difficult or expensive, tokenization may also make lending easier by allowing the use of tokens as collateral, as in the case of the above-discussed tokenized grain. Furthermore, compared to transactions involving financial reference assets and their related real-world counterparts, transactions in tokenized assets can be settled faster. Conventional securities settlement organizations, such as the Depository Trust and Clearing Corporation (DTCC) and Fedwire Securities Services, settle trades throughout the settlement cycle, which usually starts on the business day after the trade, on a gross or net basis (Madhavan & Sobczyk, 2016).

The process by which tokenization may also increase market liquidity for reference assets may be suggested by the empirical data now available on exchange-traded funds (ETFs), which are financial instruments that most closely resemble tokenization in terms of reflecting other assets. Scholarly research on ETFs reveals a robust positive relationship between the ETF's liquidity and the underlying securities. It also indicates that greater trading activity in ETFs leads to improved information efficiency for the underlying assets in the ETF (Madhavan & Sobczyk, 2016). A similar trend for tokens would suggest that increased token liquidity in cryptocurrency markets could be linked to higher market accuracy concerning the token's reference assets.

14.6.1. *Implications of tokenization in terms of financial stability*

In comparison to traditional financial systems and crypto-asset markets, the total value of tokenized markets, currently in the low single-digit billion range, is still small and does not pose a serious threat to the stability of existing financial systems. On the other hand, tokenization can weaken their financial stability and create vulnerabilities in the cryptocurrency asset markets if its quantity and scope continue to increase. The main long-term effects of tokenization on financial stability are related to its connections with the ecosystem of digital assets and the established financial system through tokenization redemption mechanisms. A fire sale of tokenized assets, for instance, might have an impact on traditional financial markets if it were large enough. This is because price movements in cryptocurrency markets encourage buyers to purchase tokens, exchange them for reference assets and then sell the latter. As a result, tokenization might offer a way to transfer shocks from the cryptocurrency markets to the market for token reference assets.

For tokenization, whose reference assets are not liquid, a stress transmission vulnerability might be a bigger worry. Real estate and other less liquid reference assets could be examples. A related issue is covered in the academic literature on ETFs, where price discovery, liquidity and volatility of the underlying assets are strongly correlated with each other (Ben-David *et al.*, 2018). Similar to ETFs, there is a chance that increased market liquidity for crypto assets could boost not only market liquidity for the underlying reference assets but also transfer market volatility from cryptocurrency to the underlying reference asset markets. Runs on the issuer of tokenized assets are another issue with financial stability. Redeemable tokenized assets may face problems akin to those encountered by collateralized stablecoins such as Tether. Investors may be more inclined to redeem the reference assets in the event of any confusion regarding the tokens' collateralization levels, particularly if this uncertainty is coupled with a lack of disclosures and correct information about the issuers. This might lead to a fire sale of tokenized reference assets.

Nuances applicable to crypto asset trading venues but not to those dealing with reference assets (or vice versa) might also exacerbate the transmission of volatility. While the majority of reference asset markets are only available during work hours, cryptocurrency exchanges enable continuous, round-the-clock trading of crypto assets. Upon the occurrence of a stress event, investors or institutions may experience unforeseen consequences due to the mismatch in trading hours. For instance, a fire sale over the weekend might be faced by the issuer of a tokenized asset with a redemption option.

Redeemers cannot immediately acquire reference assets, as regular marketplaces would be closed because the reference asset is held off-chain. Any institution holding a sizable portion of a tokenized asset on its balance sheet may find its solvency threatened if redemptions cannot be fulfilled, which might prolong the fire sale and lower the asset's value. Furthermore, such an institution would not be able to secure funding on a weekend if it were to benefit from infusions of liquidity from traditional money markets. Therefore, a sizable fire sale can swiftly lower the market value of the assets owned by the issuer and the affected institutions, jeopardizing their ability to borrow money and, consequently, their solvency. Another illustration would be the automated margin call systems in DeFi exchanges, which necessitate the liquidation or redemption of cryptocurrency tokens and may have unforeseen effects on the markets for reference assets (particularly during a stress event).

Tokenized assets may eventually become reference assets for specific deals in both traditional financial markets and cryptocurrency as tokenization technology and tokenized asset markets continue to grow. This tokenization may transfer volatility to traditional financial markets to the extent that the prices of crypto assets become more erratic than those of their real-world counterparts. Traditional financial institutions may become more exposed to cryptocurrency asset markets as tokenization increases in size and scope, either through direct ownership of tokenized assets or by the use of tokens as collateral for other financial instruments (Chang & Chuan, 2023). Examples of this may include Santander's use of tokenized grain as collateral for loans to farmers, which we have explained above, and ongoing projects to tokenize different money market assets, such as Ondo Finance's tokenization of US government money market funds (MMFs).

Furthermore, even though J.P. Morgan's original use of tokenized ownership interests in MMF shares as collateral for repo and securities lending transactions was similar in spirit, Ondo Finance's initiative may have a greater range of applications and result in more connections with traditional financial markets. Instead of being placed on a permissioned blockchain within an organization, Ondo Finance's tokens are deployed on the public blockchain Ethereum, suggesting that it has no influence over how users and DeFi protocols decide to use these tokens (J.P. Morgan, 2022). According to DeFi Llama, the largest project in this category as of May 2023 is Ondo Finance's tokenized ETFs, which account for 32% of the market value of assets issued by decentralized protocols linked to real-world assets. Additionally, OUSG can be used as collateral for Flux Finance, the 19th-largest lending protocol, which is accessible to the public (Keely, 2022). Lastly, tokenization has the ability to create secure and easily tradeable reference assets that are riskier or less liquid, similar to the role played by securitization during the Great Financial Crisis. This could encourage higher leverage and risk-taking. Systemic events could potentially be triggered by an abrupt reversal of these attitudes.

14.7. Conclusion

It is an undeniable fact that the blockchain-based DLT has immense potential to commercialize a multitude of real-world assets through its extremely vast platform, capable of supporting the economic activities of asset tokenization and subsequent trading and investment with due transparency, liquidity, accessibility and security. It also features the ability to make transactions without intermediation possible, thereby saving enormous amounts of cost and time. It can also commercialize a substantial number of illiquid and costly assets, such as real estate and artwork, and hence increase the market base. In addition, it has the capacity to synthesize new assets, indices and portfolios, thus promoting investment and the exchange of value. On-chain presence enables fast-tracking of repo activities.

There are, however, certain challenges that tokenization of real-world assets faces. The scalability of a vast range of transactions over the blockchain is an important concern, as it is a prerequisite for realizing the on-chain need to facilitate thousands of transactions in a matter of seconds and accommodate their associated stack. The coexistence of assets on-chain and off-chain could lead to a bifurcation of liquidity, with one of them potentially becoming illiquid. Since the concept of tokenization is quite novel, there is a lack of legal and regulatory standing for the transactions associated with it. The regulations either do not exist or, if they do, there are complications in complying with them, especially to ensure disintermediation. Due to the existence of identity challenges, there are governance ramifications as well, which complicate the smooth functioning and control of such transactions. This, in turn, increases the likelihood of cyber theft and fraud due to a lack of control mechanisms.

Moreover, the anonymity of market participants and subsequent identity concerns complicate the process further, raising doubts and trust deficit issues. To introduce a vast level of tokenization, the same level of awareness and digital financial literacy is indispensable in order to realize the vision of tokenizing real-world assets. People would only participate in on-chain transactions if they were familiar with the system and their doubts and concerns were addressed. Moreover, for the sake of increasing the magnitude of transactions, a significant level of market depth is required. To accommodate a great number of suppliers, there should simultaneously be an equal number of demanders as well. The majority of people are still fearful or skeptical about on-chain tokenization activities due to uncertainty and ambiguity, so there is still a great deal of progress to be made. The size of the market remains limited, and the trust deficit needs to be addressed. Further research is required in this area to identify ways to overcome the systematic deficiencies and attract investors to participate in this field.

References

Afzaal, H., Imran, M., & Janjua, M. U. (2023). Formal verification of fraud-resilience in a crowdsourcing consensus protocol. *Computers & Security*. https://doi.org/10.1016/j.cose.2023.103290.

Aslam, F., Hunjra, A. I., Ftiti, Z., Louhichi, W., & Shams, T. (2022). Insurance fraud detection: Evidence from artificial intelligence and machine learning. *Research in International Business and Finance*, 62, 101744. https://doi.org/10.1016/j.ribaf.2022.101744.

Ben-David, I., Franzoni, F., & Moussawi, R. (2018). Do ETFs increase volatility? *The Journal of Finance*, 73(6), 2471–2535. https://doi.org/10.1111/jofi.12727.

Bhaskar, R., Hunjra, A. I., Bansal, S., & Pandey, D. K. (2022). Central bank digital currencies: Agendas for future research. *Research in International Business and Finance*, 62, 101737. https://doi.org/10.1016/j.ribaf.2022.101737.

Buldas, A., Draheim, D., Gault, M., Laanoja, R., Nagumo, T., Saarepera, M., & Truu, A. (2022a). An ultra-scalable blockchain platform for universal asset tokenization: Design and implementation. *IEEE Access*, 10, 77284–77322. DOI: 10.1109/ACCESS.2022.3192837.

Buldas, A., Saarepera, M., Steiner, J., & Draheim, D. (2022b). A unifying theory of electronic money and payment systems. *TechRxiv*, 1–45. DOI: 10.36227/techrxiv.14994558.v1.

Chang, J. W. & Chuan, G. (2023). Contagion in debt and collateral markets. https://dx.doi.org/10.17016/FEDS.2023.016.

Famiglietti, M. & Leibovici, F. (2022). The impact of health and economic policies on the spread of COVID-19 and economic activity. *European Economic Review*, 144, 104087. https://doi.org/10.1016/j.euroecorev.2022.104087.

Financial Action Task Force (FATF). (2019). Public Statement on Virtual Assets and Related Providers. https://www.fatf-gafi.org/publications/fatfrecommendations/documents/public-statement-virtualassets.Html.

Financial Stability Board (FSB). (2019). Decentralised Financial Technologies: Report on Financial Stability, Regulatory and Governance Implications. https://www.fsb.org/2019/06/decentralised-financialtechnologies-report-on-financial-stability-regulatory-and-governance-implications/.

Goodell, J. W. (2020). COVID-19 and finance: Agendas for future research. *Finance Research Letters*. https://doi.org/10.1016/j.frl.2020.101512.

Hunjra, A. I. & Hanif, M. (2023). Central banking issues and challenges. In Hunjra, A. I. & Hanif, M. (Eds.), *Reference Module in Social Sciences*. Pakistan: Elsevier. https://doi.org/10.1016/B978-0-44-313776-1.00113-6.

Jia, B., Goodell, J. W., & Shen, D. (2021). US partisan conflict and high-yield exchange rates. *Finance Research Letters*, 40, 101785. https://doi.org/10.1016/j.frl.2020.101785.

Keely, A. (2022). Overstock converts preferred stock token to common stock. *The Block*.

Li, S., Bai, X., & Wei, S. (2022). Blockchain-based crowdsourcing framework with distributed task assignment and solution verification. *Security and Communication Networks*, 2022. https://doi.org/10.1155/2022/9464308.

Madhavan, A. & Sobczyk, A. (2016). Price dynamics and liquidity of exchange-traded funds. *Journal of Investment Management*, 14(2), 1–17.

Martin, A. & McAndrews, J. (2008). An economic analysis of liquidity-saving mechanisms. *Federal Reserve Bank of New York Research Paper Series-Economic Policy Review*. https://dx.doi.org/10.2139/ssrn.1141361.

Morgan, J. P. (2022). Blockchain brings collateral mobility to traditional assets. Technical Report.

OECD. (2019). Initial Coin Offerings for SME Financing. http://www.oecd.org/finance/ICOs-for-SMEFinancing.Pdf.

Zhitomirskiy, E., Schmid, S., & Walther, M. (2023). Tokenizing assets with dividend payouts—a legally compliant and flexible design. *Digital Finance*, 5(3), 563–580.

https://doi.org/10.1142/9781800616257_0015

Chapter 15

The Future of Money: A Review on Central Bank Digital Currencies

Bushra Zulfiqar[*,‡], **Faten Moussa**[†,§], **and Mahnoor Hanif**[*,¶]

[*]*University Institute of Management Sciences, PMAS-Arid Agriculture University Rawalpindi, Pakistan*

[†]*Mediterranean School of Business MSB, South Mediterranean University, Tunisia*

[‡]*bushra.zulfiqar@uaar.edu.pk*

[§]*moussafaten@gmail.com, faten.moussa@msb.tn*

[¶]*mahnoorhanif289@gmail.com*

Abstract

This chapter explores the intricate aspects and consequences associated with central bank digital currencies (CBDCs), which are an emerging subject of interest in both scholarly research and policy deliberations. The chapter presents the rationale for the introduction of CBDCs, which includes the goals of enhancing financial inclusion, improving the implementation of monetary policy and accelerating the development of digital payment systems. Furthermore, the chapter examines scholarly viewpoints on the possible consequences of CBDCs for monetary policy composition and economic stability. The chapter also highlights important areas that require future research, such as exploring an optimal CBDC design that effectively resolves competing objectives as well as conducting empirical analyses of the effects of CBDCs on financing costs and financial stability. Moreover, the chapter emphasizes the importance of conducting country- and region-specific case studies to fully comprehend the complex ramifications of CBDC layout in various social and economic circumstances.

Keywords: CBDCs, future of money, digital finance, cryptocurrency, financial inclusion, monetary policy, financial stability.

15.1. Introduction

The swift transition in emphasis from "FinTech" to "cryptocurrency" and finally to "CBDC," a more recent development, demonstrates the exponential transformation of the digital finance domain. Private cryptocurrencies, including Bitcoin, Dogecoin, Ethereum and Litecoin, proliferated during the cryptocurrency surge that lasted from 2017 to 2021, with the greatest influx occurring between 2019 and 2021. Cryptocurrencies are held by individuals either as a means of trading or as a potential asset class, despite their limited supply (Minesso *et al.*, 2022). The substantial surge in the value of digital currencies (DCs) and assets secured by cryptocurrencies was caused by their limited supply and the high demand for them (Lee *et al.*, 2021). As a consequence, cryptocurrency evolved from an unstable means of exchange to a lucrative asset. Despite the extreme volatility of cryptocurrencies, a growing number of individuals in many economies have started trading in them at the risk of incurring enormous personal losses. In response, several central banks (CBs), including those in Egypt, China, Bolivia and Indonesia, outright prohibited cryptocurrencies. Others, including the United Kingdom, Singapore, Ireland and Nigeria, have issued statements cautioning citizens against using cryptocurrencies in light of their hazards. As soon as possible, CBs declared publicly their intention to issue CBDCs as a counteraction to privately controlled digital assets and as an alternative form of currency (Kim & Kwon, 2023).

In contemporary times, there has been a notable escalation in competition among financial entities, coinciding with significant worldwide disruptions such as the global financial crisis, the COVID-19 pandemic and geopolitical confrontations like the Russian–Ukrainian conflict. They have contributed to an increased need for flexible monetary and fiscal policies (Salampasis *et al.*, 2023). The challenges encompass a range of factors, including the growing prevalence of digitization, declining reliance on cash, ineffective monetary policies and the deepening social inequalities that coexist with private financial solutions such as FinTech and cryptocurrencies

(Ozili, 2023a). These challenges pose a significant threat to the economic sovereignty of nations. With the increasing dependence of the digital economy on privately held platforms characterized by opaque rules, central banks are making preparations for substantial action. CBDCs are a new type of DC issued by central banks, designed to facilitate the transition to a digital economy (Barrdear & Kumhof, 2022). The objective is to provide appealing financial instruments for both wholesale and retail purposes, thereby strengthening the central banks' authority over the economy by utilizing novel policy tools and programmable functionalities. The deployment of this technology has the potential to substantially impact the banking sector, as it may lead to the disintermediation of commercial banks and certain private money suppliers.

Even though a significant majority of CBs, around 86%, are actively involved in researching CBDCs, with 60% now engaged in experimental activities and 14% in the process of piloting them (Kulasekhar & Reddy, 2023), the availability of comprehensive and independent academic research on this subject remains relatively scarce. Conducting a comprehensive critical evaluation is of utmost importance to thoroughly assess the available literature, not merely organize it. This process serves as a fundamental basis for ongoing debates around CBDCs, allowing for the identification of pertinent features and the flagging of outdated views (Ozili, 2023b). Additionally, a critical review can identify nascent research directions and potential future trajectories within this field.

This review adopts an interdisciplinary framework, incorporating the fields of finance and economics. The analysis takes both macroeconomic and regulatory factors into account, establishing a connection between the developments of CBDCs and the dynamics observed within the cryptocurrency industry. Many literature evaluations in current scholarship exhibit a deficiency in critical assessment and neglect the incorporation of many disciplinary viewpoints, resulting in a limited understanding of the overall context (Ekong & Ekong, 2022). This study provides a thorough and interdisciplinary analysis which critically evaluates various aspects of the topic. It aims to establish a strong basis for the discussion on CBDCs and identify new areas of emerging research.

This chapter is structured into five distinct sections. The structure of the remainder of the chapter is as follows. In Section 15.2, the conceptualization of CBDCs is expounded. In Section 15.3, the principal themes of CBDC research are outlined. Several potential avenues for future research are proposed in Section 15.4, and Section 15.5 concludes the chapter.

15.2. Conceptualization of CBDCs

A CBDC is a DC issued by a CB which carries the obligation of the issuing CB. A CBDC can be perceived by a non-expert as a digital representation of the corresponding paper currency issued by a central bank. Additional refined interpretations of CBDCs can be found in scholarly publications. Kulasekhar & Reddy (2023) define a CBDC as a digital representation of a CB's money that distinguishes itself from funds held in conventional reserves or settling accounts. In Huber's (2023) definition, a CBDC is described as a form of a CB's liability that is available to the public at large. It is a digitized, account-based system that may bear interest and is issued by CBs.

Bibi & Canelli (2023) define a CBDC as electronic money issued by a CB that can be accessed by a wider range of users than just banks, has more advanced features for retail transactions than physical cash and operates independently from other forms of currency issued by the CB, potentially serving a distinct primary function. Maryaningsih *et al.* (2022) provide a definition of a CBDC as a digital form of an economy's currency that is created and guaranteed by its CB or another monetary authority in that jurisdiction. Salampasis *et al.* (2023) define a CBDC as a form of electronic storage that symbolizes a financial obligation of the central bank and can be utilized for conducting transactions. Ozili (2023a) provides a definition of a digital currency as a form of fiat digital money that is granted by a CB. These criteria jointly demonstrate that a CBDC is a financial obligation of the CB and possesses physical characteristics distinct from the actual currency. Despite this, a CBDC serves the same purpose as cash, namely facilitating payments.

CBDC is a form of digital finance that explores innovative ways to provide financial solutions and services through internet-based technologies (Minesso *et al.*, 2022). CBDC is a significant development in the field of digital finance. CBDC is classified within monetary economics, a field that examines the characteristics, functions and incorporation of money into the economic system. CBDC is an innovative form of currency in the realm of monetary economics, representing a new aspect of money in the financial sector. The literature's discussion on the issuance of a CBDC is driven by a range of motivations. These include endorsing non-traditional monetary policies, maintaining financial stability, promoting financial inclusion (Van Roosebeke & Defina, 2023), increasing competition in payment systems, preventing illegal financial activities and addressing private cryptocurrencies such as Bitcoins by introducing a government-supported alternative (Keister & Sanches, 2023). Moreover, the literature outlines certain advantages linked to the issuance of CBDC. It emphasizes the potential of CBDCs as a highly effective means of transaction, a secure method of storing money and an alternative measure of value. Furthermore, CBDC is proposed to diminish dependence on tangible currency and exhibit characteristics similar to cash and rival paper money while also minimizing the overall expenses related to manufacturing and handling physical cash in the economy. Furthermore, the implementation of CBDCs is expected to improve the efficacy of monetary policy. However, a token-based CBDC not linked to an identity system associates a CBDC with an access technology that relies on digital tokens. When using a token-based CBDC, an individual must confirm the legitimacy of the token for each payment transaction. A CBDC token is a digital entity that represents a specific value denominated in the national currency and serves as a representation of a claim on the CB. Typically, the CBDC token is stored at a remote location rather than on local devices.

15.3. Themes in CBDC Research

15.3.1. *Adoption and advancement of CBDCs*

In their study, Ekong & Ekong (2022) surveyed the adoption of CBDCs. They discovered that a significant majority of CBs, specifically 86%, were actively engaged in exploring the feasibility of issuing a CBDC. In addition, 60% of central banks were engaging in experimentation with technological advancements related to CBDCs, while 14% were in the development and pilot stages for the deployment of CBDCs. In a recent study conducted by Hoang *et al.* (2023), it was discovered that only seven African nations have formally expressed their intentions to use CBDCs. Just four African nations have advanced to the pilot testing phase of CBDC implementation. Out of all African countries, only three possess a highly developed payment system architecture capable of accommodating CBDCs. Among these countries, Nigeria stands as the sole African nation to have officially implemented a CBDC. Notably, 78% of African nations have displayed little inclination toward CBDCs. The West African region exhibits the highest prevalence of countries with no inclination toward CBDCs.

Empirical studies conducted alongside real-world implementations indicate that blockchains may not be an optimal replacement for traditional databases due to the supplementary expenses associated with consensus processes (Minesso *et al.*, 2022). Moreover, discussions on tokens versus accounts as means of access were considered insignificant because of the need for reporting and the intrinsic characteristics of digital transactions, which create distinctive "fingerprints." However, Van Roosebeke & Defina (2023) proposed that CBDCs have the potential to generate significant efficiency improvements by circumventing charges for cash withdrawals and transaction processing.

15.3.2. *Financial inclusion and CBDCs*

Many studies in the literature on CBDCs have forecasted a correlation between CBDCs and the promotion of financial inclusion. Banerjee & Sinha (2023) demonstrate that the implementation of CBDC can advance financial inclusion through the digitization of economic value chains. This would enhance accessibility to digital financial services, expand the digital economy, improve the efficiency of digital payments and decrease transaction costs. As noted by Ekong & Ekong (2022), a CBDC can enhance financial inclusion for underprivileged individuals by granting them access to CB currency through a wallet system enabled by FinTech agents. This would enable people who are in extreme financial distress to circumvent the exorbitant fees imposed by mobile banking providers and organizations. Ozili (2023a) suggests that implementing a CBDC with an interest-bearing feature could decrease dependence on physical money and enhance financial inclusivity. Moreover, Salampasis *et al.* (2023) present evidence that a well-designed CBDC can enhance financial inclusion by allowing individuals to hold CBDC without requiring a traditional bank account. Further, Bibi & Canelli (2023) highlight the significant influence of a CBDC on promoting financial inclusion, which serves as a strong incentive for its adoption in developing nations.

Without a CBDC, individuals who choose not to use cash transactions rely solely on money issued by the private sector. Furthermore, should the availability of physical currency continue to decline, it will have significant consequences for the promotion of financial inclusivity (Auer *et al.*, 2022). Deposits and e-money, which are provided by commercial banks and other financial intermediaries, are profit-oriented entities that serve as primary alternatives to cash. Hence, they may restrict their offerings based on profitability, possibly exposing marginalized communities to risks, particularly in areas with weak financial institutions and restricted accessibility, where commercial banks encounter financial limitations. The aforementioned references highlight the significance of a CBDC in addressing financial exclusion by serving as both a medium of trade and a store of wealth (Rehman *et al.*, 2023). Moreover, CBDCs can assist CBs in regaining the seigniorage revenue lost as a result of a decrease in cash usage.

Additionally, Kulasekhar & Reddy (2023) contend that a CBDC can promote financial inclusion solely if it is seen as a viable substitute for traditional currency. Moreover, they contend that the need for CBDCs will be limited to situations where there is less reluctance to utilize formal financial systems, particularly in countries with a significant informal sector. Van Roosebeke & Defina (2023) demonstrate in their study on a CBDC survey that CBs are issuing CBDCs intending to expand financial inclusion objectives. They contend that while numerous CBs remain unconvinced about the superiority of the advantages of a CBDC over its drawbacks, developing nations seem to be intrigued by the financial inclusion benefits of a retail CBDC. Ekong & Ekong (2022) assert that a meticulously crafted CBDC can provide a practical remedy to the issues of financial exclusion in the Pacific region. However, they strongly recommend that regulators in this region allocate additional time to thoroughly research CBDC to develop the specialized knowledge and experience necessary for the implementation of a meticulously constructed CBDC.

15.3.3. *CBDC design*

Concerning the configuration of CBDCs, Allen *et al.* (2020) argue that the choice of ledger is determined by CBs implementing CBDCs. Their responsibility is to determine whether the CBDC should utilize Distributed Ledger Technology (DLT) or the traditional infrastructure of a central bank. Furthermore, Allen *et al.* (2020) provide evidence that countries with a comprehensive understanding of DLT will have a competitive advantage when it comes to creating a CBDC. They illustrate that, to uphold the CBDC, it will be imperative to consistently evaluate existing regulations after their implementation. In addition, it might be necessary to modify the CBDC in light of developments in the global environment. Barrdear & Kumhof (2022) investigate the feasibility of a CBDC attaining official recognition as a payment method. Account-and token-based CBDCs are two distinct financial forms, with their regulatory dispositions depending on the particular attributes of their designs. They provide evidence that a CBDC is a CB's liability that is transferred to consumers via its integration into a digital token. Auer *et al.* (2022) present evidence indicating that an increasing number of central banks are implementing retail CBDC structures, in which the CBDC serves as an immediate claim on the CB, comparable to cash. According to Kumhof & Noone (2021), the issuance of CBDC to raise competition in retail transactions may not be adequately justifiable, given that a CBDC's efficacy is contingent on its particular characteristics.

15.3.4. *Central banks' functions and CBDCs*

CBs should establish their own DCs, according to Huber (2023), to preserve the effectiveness of monetary policy in a market saturated with commercial DCs. The potential for a CBDC to increase the openness of monetary policies is investigated by Bindseil (2019). It is emphasized that for a CBDC to operate as a cost-free medium of exchange, ensure secure value storage and function as a reliable unit of evaluation, it must be founded upon unique accounts and accumulate interest. The significance of collaboration among CBs in understanding the impact of private digital assets on CBDC payments is underscored by Bhaskar *et al.* (2022), even though each CB is independently making preparations to issue its own CBDC. Minesso *et al.* (2022) propose the notion of the CBDC trilemma, which posits that CBs face an unconquerable predicament when attempting to implement a CBDC. This trilemma requires them to prioritize efficiency, financial stability or price stability, as it is impossible to achieve all three goals simultaneously. In his work, Davoodalhosseini (2022) argues that it is unattainable to achieve complete convertibility and parity between CBDC and bank money while upholding CB sovereignty in a monetary system where both the CB and commercial banks have the power to generate cash. Lee *et al.* (2021) observe that while many CBs are studying CBDCs, only a select few have advanced to conducting trial programs for CBDCs, and even fewer are considering issuing them in the near or medium-term future.

15.3.5. *CBDC implications for macroeconomic and financial stability*

The current research on the possible consequences of CBDCs on the financial system suggests that the impact depends on the infrastructure of the CBDC, its ability to replace different types of money, the limitations set to prevent substitution and its effect on the market power of banks. Rehman *et al.* (2023) primarily contemplate a hybrid CBDC approach, which is logical as it enables each party to focus on their respective areas of expertise: the central bank on facilitating secure monetary access and the private sector on handling client connections. Existing research has predominantly examined the probable impact of various CBDC designs on factors such as bank funding, deposits, lending and the vulnerability of the financial system in situations involving bank runs (Keister & Sanches, 2023). If a CBDC can effectively replace cash and deposits while also offering higher interest rates and advanced technological features, customers may opt for it over other assets, resulting in significant disruptions to the financial system. On the other hand, a CBDC with less utility than existing financial instruments could result in less disturbance but also the possibility of becoming unnecessary (Ekong & Ekong, 2022). In general, a CBDC has the potential to improve the allocation of resources, especially if accompanied by a fair interest rate. Nevertheless, there is a lack of research in the literature about other aspects such as safety, privacy and innovative characteristics like programmability.

Kim & Kwon (2023) contend that the implementation of a CBDC in China would enhance macroeconomic and financial stability. This would be achieved by ensuring that money maintains a consistent and reliable value while also providing effective instruments for macroeconomic regulation. Chen & Siklos (2022) developed a comprehensive model to examine the impact of CBDC on various payment methods. They demonstrate that CBDC effectively reduces criminal activity linked to physical currency while also enabling the payment of interest on a significant liability of the CB. Agur *et al.* (2023) analyze the consequences of CBDCs on financial stability by employing a monetary general equilibrium model. They demonstrate that the implementation of deposits in CBDC accounts reduces the availability of private credit from commercial banks, resulting in an increase in the nominal interest rate and a fall in the reserve-to-deposit ratio of commercial banks. This can adversely impact financial stability by increasing the probability of a bank panic, wherein commercial banks experience a shortage of cash reserves to fulfill depositor withdrawals. Ozili (2023b) investigates the potential dangers and effects of CBDC in an open economy. They demonstrate that the existence of a CBDC can greatly enhance the transmission of shocks across the global economy. However, the extent of these impacts will rely on the precise configuration of the CBDC and can be considerably reduced if the CBDC incorporates risk-mitigation characteristics.

15.3.6. *Challenges associated with CBDCs*

Cheng (2023) delineates the policy options associated with formulating a CBDC and their implications for privacy. They contend that CBs have several objectives that may ultimately compromise privacy, including the prevention of illicit use of the banking system, geopolitical considerations and advancements in the private sector. They additionally contend that existing CBDC models pose privacy risks that could result in many losses, including the loss of anonymity, loss of personal freedom, loss of individual autonomy and loss of regulatory oversight. Rehman *et al.* (2023) contend that a privacy-preserving CBDC must guarantee adherence to legal requirements as well as compliance with anti-money-laundering and counter-terrorism financing frameworks. They contend that the transaction privacy characteristic of physical currency can only be achieved by CBDCs when they are implemented on systems that utilize tokens.

Keister & Sanches (2023) and Minesso *et al.* (2022) conduct comprehensive analyses of prospective technological developments that may bolster privacy safeguards within a CBDC system. The primary emphasis is on ascertaining whether specific information requires confidentiality and identifying the parties from whom it ought to be withheld. However, divergent viewpoints persist among individuals concerning the notion of privacy. The researchers investigated the safety implications linked to the construction and operation of a CBDC in a study authored by Elsayed & Nasir (2022). CBs are authorized to utilize operational configurations and cryptographic methods that include a privacy framework in light of these findings. Moreover, Chen & Siklos (2022) note that while it is possible to integrate anonymity into the structure of a CBDC system, doing so increases the risk and complications associated with the increased need for user data. Furthermore, it is important to incorporate security mechanisms into the initial design of a CBDC (Hoang *et al.*, 2023). This involves the enforcement of operational safeguards, including the implementation of safety protocols for authorization, regular external evaluations of critical system components and continuous assessment.

15.4. Future Research Avenues

The establishment of a CBDC with a particular objective may hinder its ability to accomplish other critical objectives. Difficulties may arise when attempting to design a CBDC to promote financial inclusion in the face of digital currency deception. The pursuit of creating a CBDC with the simultaneous aims of achieving affordability and financial stability could present difficulties, potentially impeding the achievement of CBDC efficiency. It is necessary to identify the most efficient CBDC configuration that satisfies the many conflicting objectives of a CBDC. Further research should investigate the most effective configuration of a CBDC that fulfills several goals related to the stability of the financial system and the overall macroeconomy.

The CBDC literature lacks empirical information about the impact of CBDCs on the cost of credit and financial stability. It is also necessary to investigate the impact of CBDCs on the cost of borrowing and the stability of the financial system. When CBDCs are implemented as replacements for physical currency, it is anticipated that widespread acceptance of CBDCs could result in a decrease in the amount of money kept in bank accounts. The decline in the quantity of bank deposits can lead to an escalation in the cost of credit since banks will have fewer reserves to lend from. Financial instability can be caused by the consequent exorbitant cost of loans. However, this expectation must be validated or disproven using the currently accessible CBDC data. Subsequent research should examine the probable influence of CBDC adoption on the cost of borrowing and the stability of the financial system.

Imposing a cap on CBDC deposits diminishes its appeal in comparison to physical currency. Ultimately, this can result in a greater inclination toward cash, given that there are no restrictions on the quantity of cash an individual can own and no limitations on the magnitude of bank deposits in a depositor's account. Implementing a restriction on CBDC holdings is primarily motivated by regulatory considerations, although it restricts the user's ability to possess the maximum number of CBDC units. This may lead to a greater inclination toward cash payments and subsequent abandonment of CBDCs by a larger number of individuals. Hence, it is imperative to find a middle ground between limiting CBDC possession and respecting user preferences. Future research should strive to achieve a harmonious equilibrium between imposing limitations on the storage capacity of CBDCs for users and satisfying users' desire to possess unconstrained quantities of CBDCs. It is imperative to prevent consumers from being discouraged and to ensure their complete utilization of CBDC.

The research has not yet conducted a comparative examination of the design of CBDCs in individual countries and regions. There exist prospects for further investigation in this domain. By examining a regional case study, researchers and policymakers may acquire knowledge about the shared design characteristics of CBDCs, while analyzing individual country examples can provide information about the specific adaptations made to the local CBDC to cater to the requirements of the local economy. It would be intriguing to ascertain the characteristics of a regional CBDC and the characteristics of a country-specific CBDC. Subsequent research endeavors can also include a comparative analysis of the characteristics of CBDCs in different regions and countries.

15.5. Conclusion

This research examined the definitions of CBDC as presented in the existing literature. The literature indicates a widespread agreement that a CBDC is an obligation of the CB and possesses characteristics similar to physical cash. The analysis additionally outlined the rationale and advantages of implementing a CBDC, including the imperative to enhance financial inclusivity, optimize monetary policy implementation and facilitate streamlined digital transactions. The assessment also indicated that a majority of CBs are researching the feasibility of issuing a CBDC owing to its numerous advantages. Nevertheless, several studies advise against excessive excitement regarding the possible advantages of CBDCs due to the constraining characteristics of their designs and their incapability to fulfill various conflicting objectives. The chapter proposed several areas for future research, including the identification of the most effective CBDC design that satisfies all competing objectives, the acquisition of empirical evidence regarding the impact of CBDC on credit costs and financial stability, the establishment of a balance between restricting CBDC holdings and the preferences of users and the exploration of country-specific and regional case studies on CBDC design.

The outcomes of this chapter suggest that CBs should prioritize the design of their CBDCs. Before implementing a CBDC, they must initially determine their desired objectives and then tailor the architecture of the CBDC to incorporate those specific characteristics. Whenever feasible, it is important to create possibilities for redesigning and reinventing the CBDC to align with the objectives of CBs. A crucial aspect is that CBs must consistently prioritize the security and privacy of CBDCs. Despite the significant expense, CBs are convinced that the issuance of a national CBDC is worth the cost. Ultimately, it is currently premature to determine the precise advantages and drawbacks of CBDCs, as well as whether they will deliver the anticipated results as described in the literature and whether they can fulfill their intended potential (Morales-Resendiz *et al.*, 2021; Ozili, 2022).

References

Agur, I., Ari, A., & Dell'Ariccia, G. (2022). Designing central bank digital currencies. *Journal of Monetary Economics*, 125, 62–79. https://doi.org/10.1016/j.jmoneco.2021.05.002.

Allen, F., Gu, X., & Jagtiani, J. (2022). Fintech, cryptocurrencies, and CBDC: Financial structural transformation in China. *Journal of International Money and Finance*, 124, 102625. https://doi.org/10.1016/j.jimonfin.2022.102625.

Allen, S., *et al.* (2020). Design choices for central bank digital currency: Policy and technical considerations (No. w27634). National Bureau of Economic Research. https://www.nber.org/system/files/working_papers/w27634/w27634.pdf.

Auer, R., Frost, J., Gambacorta, L., Monnet, C., Rice, T., & Shin, H. S. (2022). Central bank digital currencies: Motives, economic implications, and the research frontier. *Annual Review of Economics*, 14, 697–721. https://doi.org/10.1146/annurev-economics-051420-020324.

Banerjee, S. & Sinha, M. (2023). Promoting financial inclusion through central bank digital currency: An evaluation of payment system viability in India. *Australasian Accounting, Business and Finance Journal*, 17(1), 176–204. http://dx.doi.org/10.14453/aabfj.v17i1.14.

Barrdear, J. & Kumhof, M. (2022). The macroeconomics of central bank digital currencies. *Journal of Economic Dynamics and Control*, 142, 104148. https://doi.org/10.1016/j.jedc.2021.104148.

Bhaskar, R., Hunjra, A. I., Bansal, S., & Pandey, D. K. (2022). Central bank digital currencies: Agendas for future research. *Research in International Business and Finance*, 62, 101737. https://doi.org/10.1016/j.ribaf.2022.101737.

Bibi, S. & Canelli, R. (2023). The interpretation of CBDC within an endogenous money framework. *Research in International Business and Finance*, 65, 101970. https://doi.org/10.1016/j.ribaf.2023.101970.

Bindseil, U. (2019). Central bank digital currency: Financial system implications and control. *International Journal of Political Economy*, 48(4), 303–335. https://doi.org/10.1080/08911916.2019.1693160.

Chen, H. & Siklos, P. L. (2022). Central bank digital currency: A review and some macro-financial implications. *Journal of Financial Stability*, 60, 100985. https://doi.org/10.1016/j.jfs.2022.100985.

Cheng, P. (2023). Decoding the rise of Central bank digital currency in China: Designs, problems, and prospects. *Journal of Banking Regulation*, 24(2), 156–170. https://doi.org/10.1057/s41261-022-00193-5.

Davoodalhosseini, S. M. (2022). Central bank digital currency and monetary policy. *Journal of Economic Dynamics and Control*, 142, 104150. https://doi.org/10.1016/j.jedc.2021.104150.

Ekong, U. M. & Ekong, C. N. (2022). Digital currency and financial inclusion in Nigeria: Lessons for development. *Journal of Internet and Digital Economics*, 2(1), 46–67. https://doi.org/10.1108/JIDE-11-2021-0018.

Elsayed, A. H. & Nasir, M. A. (2022). Central bank digital currencies: An agenda for future research. *Research in International Business and Finance*, 62, 101736. https://doi.org/10.1016/j.ribaf.2022.101736.

Hoang, Y. H., Ngo, V. M., & Vu, N. B. (2023). Central bank digital currency: A systematic literature review using text mining approach. *Research in International Business and Finance*, 101889. https://doi.org/10.1016/j.ribaf.2023.101889.

Huber, J. (2023). Central banks and monetary policy under conditions of CBDC. In *The Monetary Turning Point: From Bank Money to Central Bank Digital Currency (CBDC)* (pp. 151–188). Cham: Springer Nature Switzerland. https://doi.org/10.1007/978-3-031-23957-1_8.

Keister, T. & Sanches, D. (2023). Should central banks issue digital currency? *The Review of Economic Studies*, 90(1), 404–431. https://doi.org/10.1093/restud/rdac017.

Kim, Y. S. & Kwon, O. (2023). Central bank digital currency, credit supply, and financial stability. *Journal of Money, Credit and Banking*, 55(1), 297–321. https://doi.org/10.1111/jmcb.12913.

Kulasekhar, M. & Reddy, K. S. (2023). The role of central bank digital currencies (CBDCS) in reshaping monetary policy: A global analysis of economic implications and implementation challenges. *European Economic Letters (EEL)*, 13(5), 362–371. https://doi.org/10.52783/eel.v13i5.763.

Kumhof, M. & Noone, C. (2021). Central bank digital currencies – Design principles for financial stability. *Economic Analysis and Policy*, 71, 553–572. https://doi.org/10.1016/j.eap.2021.06.012.

Lee, D. K. C., Yan, L., & Wang, Y. (2021). A global perspective on central bank digital currency. *China Economic Journal*, 14(1), 52–66. https://doi.org/10.1080/17538963.2020.1870279.

Maryaningsih, N., Nazara, S., Kacaribu, F. N., & Juhro, S. M. (2022). Central bank digital currency: What factors determine its adoption? *Bulletin of Monetary Economics and Banking*, 25(1), 1–24. https://doi.org/10.21098/bemp.v25i1.1979.

Minesso, M. F., Mehl, A., & Stracca, L. (2022). Central bank digital currency in an open economy. *Journal of Monetary Economics*, 127, 54–68. https://doi.org/10.1016/j.jmoneco.2022.02.001.

Morales-Resendiz, R., *et al.* (2021). Implementing a retail CBDC: Lessons learned and key insights. *Latin American Journal of Central Banking*, 2(1), 100022. https://doi.org/10.1016/j.latcb.2021.100022.

Ozili, P. K. (2022). CBDC, Fintech and cryptocurrency for financial inclusion and financial stability. *Digital Policy, Regulation and Governance*, 25(1), 40–57. https://doi.org/10.1108/DPRG-04-2022-0033.

Ozili, P. K. (2023a). Central bank digital currency research around the world: A review of literature. *Journal of Money Laundering Control*, 26(2), 215–226. https://doi.org/10.1108/JMLC-11-2021-0126.

Ozili, P. K. (2023b). eNaira central bank digital currency (CBDC) for financial inclusion in Nigeria. In *Digital Economy, Energy and Sustainability: Opportunities and Challenges* (pp. 41–54). Cham: Springer International Publishing. https://doi.org/10.1007/978-3-031-22382-2_3.

Rehman, M. A., Irfan, M., Naeem, M. A., Lucey, B. M., & Karim, S. (2023). Macro-financial implications of central bank digital currencies. *Research in International Business and Finance*, 64, 101892. https://doi.org/10.1016/j.ribaf.2023.101892.

Salampasis, D., Schueffel, P., Dominic, R., & Cameron, D. (2023). Central bank digital currencies: Opening pandora's box or paving the future of money? In Baker, H.K., Benedetti, H., Nikbakht, E. & Smith, S.S. (Eds.), *The Emerald Handbook on Cryptoassets: Investment Opportunities and Challenges* (pp. 283–306). Bingley, UK: Emerald Publishing Limited. https://doi.org/10.1108/978-1-80455-320-620221019.

Van Roosebeke, B. & Defina, R. (2023). Central bank digital currencies: The motivation. In Kim, S.-J. (Ed.), *Fintech, Pandemic, and the Financial System: Challenges and Opportunities* (Vol. 22, pp. 185–200). Bingley, UK: Emerald Publishing Limited. https://doi.org/10.1108/S1569-376720220000022009.

https://doi.org/10.1142/9781800616257_0016

Chapter 16

How Does Digital Financial Inclusion Influence Bank Innovation Capability in China? Evidence from a Risk-Taking Perspective

Yi Zhou

Internal Audit Department, Bank of Jiangsu, Nanjing, Jiangsu, China
z1audit@hotmail.com

Abstract

This study investigates the influence of digital financial inclusion (DFI) on the innovation capability of commercial banks in China from a risk-taking perspective. Utilizing a robust econometric model and data from 40 banks over a period from 2011 to 2019, the research identifies a positive and significant relationship between DFI and banks' innovation capability. It also highlights the mediating role of risk-taking levels in this relationship. The heterogeneity analysis further reveals that the impact of DFI varies across different types of banks. The findings reveal that while all bank categories benefit from DFI, the intensity of its impact varies, with state-owned and joint-stock banks showing a stronger association than their urban and rural counterparts. The robustness tests, using alternative proxies for DFI and innovation capability, confirm the stability of the results. This study contributes to the literature by providing empirical evidence on the critical role of DFI in enhancing the innovative activities of banks and underscores the importance of risk management in the digital era.

Keywords: Digital financial inclusion, innovation capability, risk-taking level, bank risk management.

16.1. Introduction

Digital technologies are now integral to diverse sectors, including education, business and government operations, marking a crucial phase in humanity's digital evolution (Yusheng & Ibrahim, 2020; Stefanelli & Manta, 2022; Li *et al.*, 2022a). This digital wave has notably transformed commercial banking, which is evident in the rapid integration of technological advancements and intelligence into services such as financial payment systems and the modernization of insurance, lending and investment processes. As a result, traditional financial services find themselves increasingly overshadowed by the burgeoning concept of "digital finance."

Figure 16.1, as presented by Khera *et al.* (2022), showcases the significant potential for enhanced financial inclusion across 52 emerging and developing economies, with notable strides in Asian nations such as China and Malaysia. This graph reveals a dual enhancement in both digital and conventional financial inclusion, predominantly fueled by innovations in technology-centered financial services.

In the realm of emerging markets, China stands out for its substantial shift from traditional financial practices to digital inclusion.

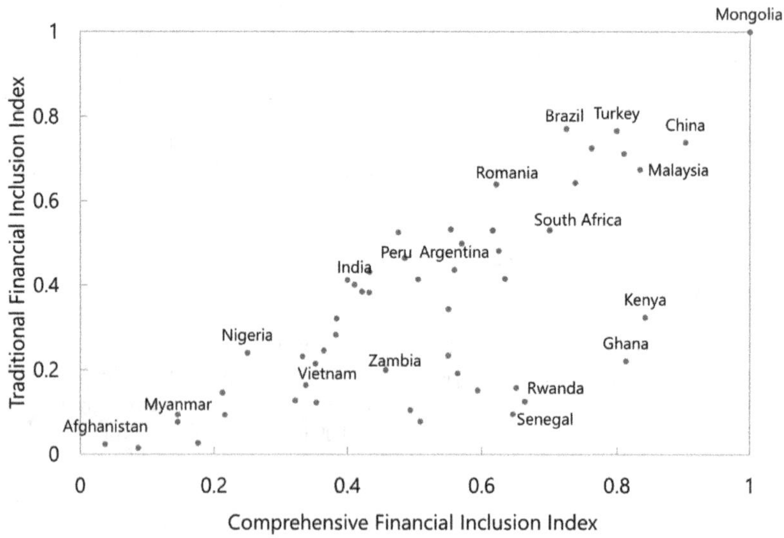

Figure 16.1. Comprehensive versus traditional financial inclusion index.

Source: Khera *et al.* (2022).

This transition has been marked by the integration of financial technology (FinTech) across various financial services and products. This evolution has not only injected new energy into China's financial market but also escalated competition, particularly among commercial banks. These banks, which are central to China's economic framework and crucial supporters of the real economy, play a vital role in the nation's societal advancement and progress. As digital finance gains wider acceptance, intertwining finance and technology, commercial banks in China have adapted by modifying their operational strategies, innovation approaches and asset management to meet the challenges of the digital finance era.

Figure 16.2 illustrates the progressive trajectory of FinTech innovation across all of China's commercial banks, including four distinct bank types, showing a general upward trend. These banks have embraced FinTech comprehensively, leveraging it to drive innovation and transformation. They are assimilating fresh ideas and new technologies in digital finance to bolster their FinTech capabilities, thereby advancing their overall innovative strength. Figure 16.2 also highlights notable disparities in the degree of financial innovation among different bank types. Notably, the FinTech innovation levels in state-owned and joint-stock commercial banks markedly surpass those in rural commercial and urban banks.

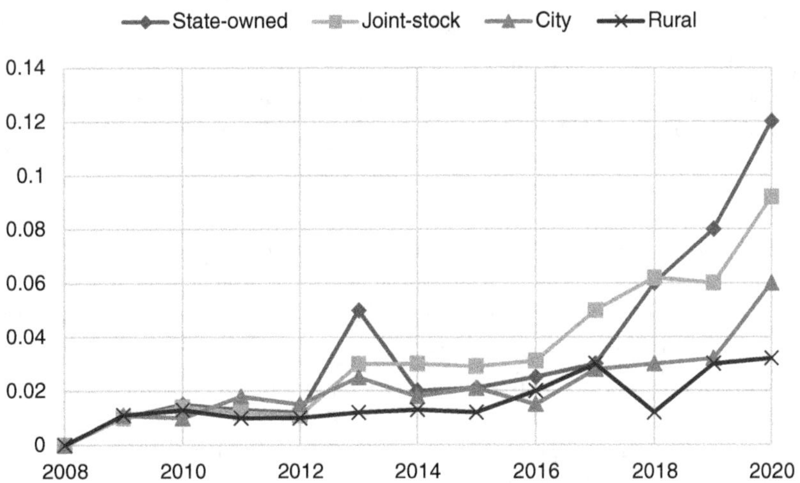

Figure 16.2. FinTech innovation level of China's commercial banks.

Source: Li *et al.* (2022b).

Digital finance has profoundly influenced the primary operations of China's commercial banks, propelling them to expedite the development and deployment of FinTech products. This race to innovate involves introducing diverse new financial services and products with the aim of swiftly adapting to the digital finance landscape while securing a lasting competitive edge. While numerous studies have examined how FinTech and digital finance affect the financial performance and innovation capabilities of commercial banks, there remains a gap in understanding how digital financial inclusion (DFI) impacts various types of commercial banks. This study, therefore, seeks to address the following research questions:

1. Does DFI positively influence the innovation capability of banks in China?
2. Does the relationship between DFI and innovation capability differ among various types of commercial banks?
3. Can risk-taking act as a mediating factor in the relationship between DFI and innovation capability?

Building on this discussion, the structure of this chapter is laid out as follows: Section 16.2 delves into related literature and formulates the hypotheses of this research. This is followed by Section 16.3, which details the data and methodology used. Section 16.4 presents the empirical findings and describes a robustness test conducted for the study. Finally, Section 16.5 draws conclusions and discusses potential policy implications.

16.2. Literature Review and Research Hypotheses

This section explores the intricate dynamics between DFI and the innovative capabilities of banks, a topic that has garnered considerable attention in recent academic discourse. The existing body of research, with its multifaceted approach encompassing both internal and external factors (as categorized by Rajapathirana & Hui, 2018), provides a foundational understanding for this study's focus on the impacts of DFI on banking innovation.

16.2.1. *DFI and bank innovation capability*

The advent of digital technology in financial services, known as DFI, has been identified as a pivotal influence on innovation within the banking sector. Research, including seminal works by Li *et al.* (2023) and Yang *et al.* (2021), illustrates how DFI addresses issues such as capital misallocation and financing constraints, thereby fostering a more innovative banking environment. This effect is pronounced in developing economies, where digital solutions offer a leapfrogging opportunity over traditional banking limitations (Banna & Alam, 2021a).

Additionally, the ripple effect of DFI extends beyond mere financial access, spurring advancements in areas such as green innovation, as demonstrated by Xue & Zhang. Yet, the relationship is not devoid of complexities. Gabor & Brooks (2017) highlight potential adverse effects, such as heightened financial exclusion for marginalized groups, calling for a nuanced application of digital financial strategies.

Hypothesis 1 (H1): DFI is posited to significantly enhance the innovation capabilities of commercial banks, with variations expected across different bank types.

16.2.2. *Risk-taking level and bank innovation capability*

The interplay between DFI and risk-taking in banks is pivotal for innovation. Wang contends that digital inclusion lowers enterprise financial risk, which is crucial for innovation-friendly environments. Kraus *et al.* (2022) emphasize the need for a balanced approach to innovation and risk management within digital financial systems. Additionally, the post-COVID-19 era has underscored the importance of banking stability, to which DFI contributes by mitigating default risks and boosting financial mobility (Banna & Alam, 2021b; Yang *et al.*, 2021).

Saputro *et al.* (2022) and Yang *et al.* (2022) further expand this perspective by illustrating how DFI propels the growth of SMEs and influences various facets of innovation. However, as Gu (2021) notes, this does not negate the inherent risks in the financial sector, necessitating prudent risk management strategies.

Moreover, the evolution of FinTech, as explored by Deng *et al.* (2021), suggests a reduction in risk-taking behaviors among banks, which is integral to fostering an environment conducive to innovation.

Hypothesis 2 (H2): This study hypothesizes that the level of risk-taking within banks positively mediates the relationship between DFI and innovation capability.

16.3. Data and Methodology

16.3.1. *Econometric model*

The following econometric model is constructed to explore the effect of DFI on the innovation capability of commercial banks. The explained variable "innovation capability of commercial banks" is represented by IC and is a function of DFI, control variables (CVs) and fixed effects. The model is specified as

$$IC_{it} = \alpha_0 + \beta_1 DFI_{it} + X'_{it}\gamma + u_i + \lambda_t + \varepsilon_{it}, \tag{16.1}$$

where IC_{it} represents the innovation capability of commercial bank i at time t, DFI_{it} represents the level of DFI for bank i at time t, and $\beta 1$ measures the marginal effect of DFI on the innovation capability. The null hypothesis is that $\beta 1$ is equal to 0. If $\beta 1$ is significant at the 10% level, we reject the null hypothesis, indicating that DFI affects the innovation capability. The CVs are the capital adequacy ratio, non-performing loans ratio, loan-to-deposit ratio and GDP growth rate. X denotes a CV, u_i denotes the individual fixed effect and λ_t denotes the time fixed effect. ε_{it} is the random error term.

To investigate the potential indirect influence of DFI on innovation capability through risk-taking level, the following mediating effect model is established:

$$RTL_{it} = \alpha_0 + \beta_2 DFI_{it} + X_{it}\gamma + u_i + \lambda_t + \varepsilon_{it}, \tag{16.2}$$

$$IC_{it} = \alpha_0 + \beta_3 DFI_{it} + \beta_4 RTL_{it} + X'_{it}\gamma + u_i + \lambda_t + \varepsilon_{it}, \tag{16.3}$$

where RTL_{it} represents the risk-taking level of bank i at time t, and $\beta 2$ measures the effect of DFI on risk-taking level. The null hypothesis of model (16.2) is that $\beta 2$ equals 0. In model (16.3), $\beta 3$ and $\beta 4$ measure the direct and indirect effects (through risk-taking level) of DFI on innovation capability, respectively. If $\beta3$ and $\beta4$ are both significant at the 10% level, there is a partial mediation effect. If $\beta4$ is statistically significant but $\beta3$ is not, it suggests a complete mediation by risk-taking level.

16.3.2. *Variable definition and data source*

16.3.2.1. *Explained variable: Innovation capability in commercial banks*

Innovation capability within commercial banks is defined as their proficiency in creating new financial products, services or processes. This involves, but is not limited to, rolling out digital banking platforms, mobile banking innovations or pioneering financial instruments. Common metrics for assessing innovation capability include the quantity of newly introduced products or services, investment levels in research and development and the number of FinTech-related patents filed. Some researchers further segment innovation capability into categories such as business, technological, human resources and risk control capability innovation. Nevertheless, these measures may not fully encapsulate banks' core business strategies and services.

As an alternative, several scholars suggest using the ratio of non-interest income to total operating income as a more comprehensive indicator of innovation capability. This choice is grounded in the rationale that the growth of intermediary business represents a significant facet of financial innovation in commercial banks. Given that intermediary business largely contributes to non-interest income, this single metric offers a more comprehensive and reliable measure of banking innovation. The data for this analysis are sourced from the annual reports of 40 banks over the period from 2011 to 2019, deliberately selected to minimize distortions caused by the COVID-19 pandemic's impact on financial markets.

16.3.2.2. *Explanatory variable: DFI*

DFI in China is gauged by the extent to which individuals and enterprises can access affordable financial services via digital channels. This encompasses a spectrum of services, including online banking, mobile money solutions and digital payment systems. Key metrics here include the proliferation of digital account holders, the volume and value of digital transactions and the penetration of digital financial services, especially in rural regions. This study also takes into account the breadth and depth of DFI by utilizing the DFI index formulated by Peking University for data.

16.3.2.3. *Mediating variable: Risk-taking level*

The risk-taking level of Chinese commercial banks is evaluated through indicators such as the non-performing loan ratio, the loan-to-deposit ratio and the capital adequacy ratio. These metrics reflect various risk dimensions, including credit, liquidity and the overall financial stability of the institutions. For instance, a higher non-performing loan ratio or a lower capital adequacy ratio may suggest increased risk-taking. This information is primarily derived from the banks' financial statements and annual reports.

Based on the above discussion, the explained variables and explanatory variables are described in Table 16.1.

16.3.3. *Sample selection*

This study discusses the impact of DFI on the innovation capabilities of Chinese commercial banks, especially the heterogeneous impact on four different types of commercial banks. Therefore, the selection of the sample should not only reflect the development of digital financial services and products but also consider the diversity of types. After comprehensive consideration and sorting of the data, a total of 40 commercial banks were selected. Among them, there are 5 state-owned banks, 15 joint-stock banks, 17 urban commercial banks and 8 rural commercial banks. The specific distribution of banks is shown in Figure 16.3.

16.3.4. *Summary statistics*

Table 16.2 reports the statistical description. In the empirical analysis, a panel dataset comprising 360 observations was utilized to ascertain the determinants of innovation capability within the banking sector. Descriptive statistics offer a synopsis of the data employed in the econometric estimations.

Table 16.1. Data and variable description.

Type	Name	Symbol	Definition	Source	Reference
Explained variable	Innovation capability	*IC*	Non-interest income/operating income	Wind; annual reports (2011–2019)	Li *et al.* (2022b) and Edeh *et al.* (2022)
Explanatory variable	Digital financial inclusion	*DFI*	Digital financial inclusion index	Institute of Digital Finance Peking University	Niu *et al.* (2022) and Huang *et al.* (2022)
	Digital financial inclusion depth	*DFI depth*	Use depth of DFI		
	Digital financial inclusion breadth	*DFI breadth*	Coverage breadth of DFI		
Mediator	Risk-taking	*RTL*	Asset liability ratio	Wind; CSMAR; annual reports (2011–2019)	Li *et al.* (2022b)
Control variable	Capital adequacy ratio	*CAR*	Capital/weighted risk assets		Li *et al.* (2022c)
	Non-performing loans ratio	*NPLR*	Non-performing loans/total loan balance		Li *et al.* (2022b)
	Loan-to-deposit ratio	*LDR*	Total loans/total deposits		
	GDP growth rate	*RGDP*	GDP annual growth rate		

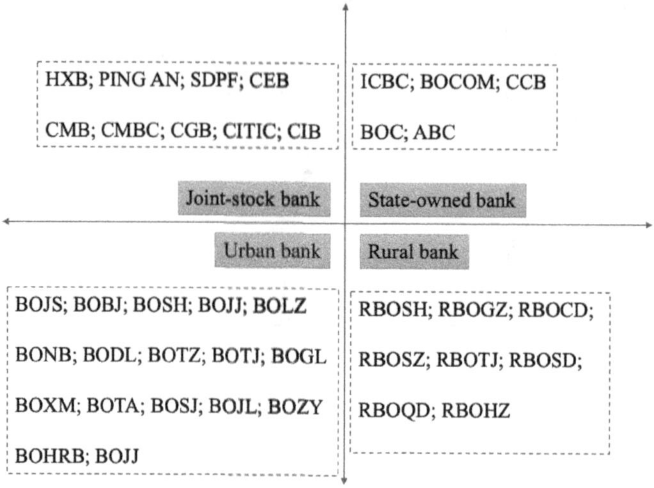

Figure 16.3. Distribution of selected banks.

Table 16.2. Summary statistics.

Variable symbol	Obs.	Mean	SD	Min.	Max.
IC	360	21.11	11.02	0.65	49.21
DFI	360	220.31	81.02	50.88	350.32
DFI depth	360	221.45	81.23	48.90	345.21
DFI breadth	360	218.20	80.78	49.12	361.25
RSL	360	89.20	1.03	90.21	96.43
CAR	360	14.41	1.29	11.22	20.31
NPLR	360	1.08	0.53	0.21	8.90
LDR	360	54.87	30.21	0.62	115.32
RGDP	360	7.62	1.32	6.01	14.54

16.4. Results and Discussion

16.4.1. *Benchmark model estimation results*

The estimations presented in Table 16.3 reveal the impact of DFI on banks' innovation capability (IC). Columns (1)–(3) of the table detail the results excluding additional CVs, while columns (4)–(6) list the firm-level control variables. Across all specifications, year and

Table 16.3. Estimated results of the benchmark model.

	(1) *IC*	*(2)* *IC*	*(3)* *IC*	*(4)* *IC*	*(5)* *IC*	*(6)* *IC*
DFI	1.2821***					
	(0.1421)					
DFI depth		1.0219***				
		(0.0120)				
DFI breadth			0.9824***			
			(0.0115)			
CAR				0.2567***	0.2431***	0.2245***
				(0.0214)	(0.0189)	(0.0117)
NPLR				−0.0421***	−0.0521***	−0.0389***
				(0.0121)	(0.0189)	(0.0118)
LDR				−0.0231**	−0.0421**	−0.0210**
				(0.0190)	(0.0178)	(0.0120)
RGDP				0.0429	0.0562	0.0391
				(0.0319)	(0.0325)	(0.0289)
RSL	0.6210**	0.5890	0.2342	31.2055***	31.0210***	30.0620***
	(0.3820)	(0.0316)	(0.2101)	(0.7204)	(0.7136)	(0.7189)
Year fixed effects	Yes	Yes	Yes	Yes	Yes	Yes
Bank fixed effects	Yes	Yes	Yes	Yes	Yes	Yes
N	2136	2136	2136	2004	2004	2004
R^2	0.4150	0.1320	0.4150	0.5230	0.5230	0.5230

Note: ***,** and * denote significance at the 1% , 5% and 10% levels, respectively (hereinafter inclusive).

bank fixed effects are controlled to account for time- and institution-specific heterogeneity.

The coefficient for DFI in column (1) is reported at 1.2821 (standard error: 0.1421), indicating a strong positive relationship with innovation capability when CVs are excluded. This suggests that DFI is a robust predictor of innovation within the banking sector. The components of DFI, namely depth and breadth, are analyzed separately in columns (2) and (3), each demonstrating significant positive effects with coefficients of 1.0219 (standard error: 0.0120) and 0.9824 (standard error: 0.0115), respectively, reinforcing the multifaceted influence of digital finance on innovation.

Upon the inclusion of firm-level CVs in columns (4)–(6), the capital adequacy ratio (CAR) consistently displays a positive and significant effect on innovation capability, with coefficients ranging from 0.2245 to 0.2567, suggesting that a well-capitalized bank is more inclined to engage in innovative activities. The non-performing loans ratio (NPLR) retains a negative relationship with innovation capability across all models, with coefficients varying slightly but remaining statistically significant, highlighting the adverse impact of non-performing assets on the capacity for innovation. The loan-to-deposit ratio (LDR) also maintains its negative association with innovation capability in models that include additional CVs, indicating a consistent theme where higher liquidity reserves correlate with reduced innovation propensity. The real GDP growth rate (RGDP) remains non-significant in all models, suggesting that the influence of macroeconomic conditions on the innovation capability of individual banks may be indirect or obscured by other factors.

Additionally, risk-taking level (RSL) is notably associated with a significant negative impact on innovation capability in the model presented in column (4), with a coefficient of −31.2055 (standard error: 0.7204). This implies that within the dataset, higher risk-taking may be inversely related to the ability of banks to innovate effectively. The regression analyses demonstrate robustness, controlling for year and bank fixed effects, and show that the inclusion of firm-level CVs adds depth to our understanding of the determinants of innovation within banks. The R-squared values across models indicate substantive explanatory power, confirming the relevance of the selected variables in elucidating the innovation dynamics in the banking sector.

16.4.2. *Endogeneity discussion*

In addressing endogeneity within the econometric model that estimates the impact of DFI on the IC of banks while considering the RSL, the study employs a comprehensive approach. The use of the first-order lagged term of DFI as a core explanatory variable in model (1) addresses potential reverse causality, with a significant coefficient of 0.1623 (standard error: 0.0620) suggesting that past levels of DFI positively affect current innovation capability (see Table 16.4). This method aligns with established research practices, adding robustness to the findings. In models (2) and (3), the analysis continues to demonstrate a positive and significant relationship between current DFI and IC, with coefficients of 0.3821 (standard error: 0.0231) and 0.1923 (standard error: 0.0412), respectively. This consistency in

Table 16.4. Endogeneity test results.

	(1) *IC*	*(2)* *IC*	*(3)* *IC*
L.DFI	0.1623*** (0.0620)		
DFI		0.3821*** (0.0231)	0.1923*** (0.0412)
RSL	0.9123** (0.5421)	1.1224** (0.3210)	0.5138** (0.1820)
Control variables	Yes	Yes	Yes
Year fixed effects	Yes	Yes	Yes
Bank fixed effects	Yes	Yes	Yes
N	2004	2004	2004
R^2	0.4421	0.3110	0.4050

results across different model specifications, even after controlling for reverse causality, reinforces the role of DFI as a key driver of banking innovation.

The impact of RSL on IC is explored through varying coefficients across the models, reflecting the multifaceted nature of risk-taking in the banking sector. With coefficients of 0.9123 in model (1), 1.1224 in model (2) and 0.7812 in model (3), these variations highlight the complex interplay between risk-taking and innovation capability, necessitating further investigation. The inclusion of CVs, year and bank fixed effects in all models meticulously addresses unobserved heterogeneity, enhancing the credibility of the study's results. With consistent observations across all models (N = 2004) and varying R-squared values, the analysis provides a comprehensive and robust framework for understanding the dynamics of DFI and its influence on innovation in the banking sector.

16.4.3. *Heterogeneity analysis*

The heterogeneity analysis presented in the study explores the distinct impacts of various dimensions of DFI on the IC of banks. The analysis disaggregates DFI into its overall level, depth and breadth, offering a nuanced understanding of how different aspects of digital finance contribute to fostering innovation.

Table 16.5. The estimated results of different dimensions of DFI.

	(1) *IC*	*(2)* *IC*	*(3)* *IC*
DFI	0.2110***		
	(0.0678)		
DFI depth		0.1765***	
		(0.0182)	
DFI breadth			0.1244***
			(0.0120)
RSL	0.5231	1.2445**	0.235
	(0.4230)	(0.7821)	(0.2910)
Control variables	Yes	Yes	Yes
Year fixed effects	Yes	Yes	Yes
Bank fixed effects	Yes	Yes	Yes
N	2136	2136	2136
R^2	0.3677	0.3521	0.2870

As presented in Table 16.5, in model (1), the overall DFI shows a significant positive effect on IC, with a coefficient of 0.2110 (standard error: 0.0678), indicating that a higher level of DFI broadly enhances the innovative capacity of banks. This is complemented by the findings in model (2), where DFI depth, representing the intensity of digital finance usage, has a coefficient of 0.1765 (standard error: 0.0182), significant at the 1% level. This suggests that deep engagement with digital financial services is key to promoting innovation. In model (3), the breadth of DFI, reflecting its coverage and accessibility, also demonstrates a positive impact on innovation capability, with a coefficient of 0.1244 (standard error: 0.0120), reinforcing the importance of widespread digital financial access in enhancing innovation.

The RSL exhibits varying influences across models. In model (1), the effect of RSL on IC is not significant, whereas in model (2), RSL shows a significant positive effect (coefficient: 1.2445, standard error: 0.7821), suggesting that the relationship between risk-taking and innovation capability might be context-dependent, particularly influenced by the depth of digital financial usage.

All models control for relevant variables, year and city fixed effects, addressing potential confounders and ensuring the robustness of the results. With consistent observations across all models ($N = 2136$) and R-squared values indicating a good model fit, the analysis underscores the multifaceted nature of DFI and its differential impact on innovation in the banking sector. The findings highlight that not only the presence of digital finance but also its deep and widespread use are instrumental in fostering innovation within banks. Therefore, the aforementioned H1 is verified.

The heterogeneity analysis in Table 16.6 explores the differential impacts of DFI on the IC across various types of banks, revealing significant variances based on bank classification. The analysis includes state-owned banks (1), joint-stock banks (2), urban banks (3) and rural banks (4), with each bank type demonstrating a unique relationship between DFI and IC.

For state-owned banks, DFI has a significant positive impact on IC with a coefficient of 0.3241 (standard error: 0.0745), suggesting a strong association between the two within this group. This relationship is even more pronounced in joint-stock banks, which exhibit the highest coefficient of 0.4160 (standard error: 0.0328), indicating that DFI plays a pivotal role in driving innovation in these banks.

Urban banks show a positive but weaker relationship, with a coefficient of 0.1276 (standard error: 0.0132), implying that while DFI contributes to IC, its effect is less pronounced compared to that in state-owned and joint-stock banks. Rural banks present the smallest positive effect of DFI on IC, with a coefficient of 0.0434 (standard error: 0.0023), reflecting the possibility that rural banks may have

Table 16.6. The heterogeneity analysis in banks with different types.

	(1) *IC*	*(2)* *IC*	*(3)* *IC*	*(4)* *IC*
DFI	0.3241***	0.4160***	0.1276**	0.0434**
	(0.0745)	(0.0328)	(0.0132)	(0.0023)
RSL	0.3451	0.4361	0.5489*	0.4890**
	(0.0431)	(0.5420)	(0.6033)	(0.1432)
Control variables	Yes	Yes	Yes	Yes
Bank fixed effects	Yes	Yes	Yes	Yes
Year fixed effects	Yes	Yes	Yes	Yes
N	267	534	908	427
R^2	0.5105	0.4820	0.3561	0.3125

Table 16.7. Analysis of influencing mechanisms.

	(1) RSL	(2) IC	(3) IC
DFI	0.8931***	0.2345*	0.2190***
	(0.0122)	(0.0042)	(0.0035)
RSL		5.2882***	5.1120***
		(1.6170)	(1.4231)
Control variables	Yes	Yes	Yes
Year fixed effects	Yes	Yes	Yes
Bank fixed effects	Yes	Yes	Yes
N	2136	2136	2136
R^2	0.6234	0.5021	0.4890

different mechanisms or face different challenges when leveraging DFI for innovation.

The RSL varies across the bank types without showing a consistent pattern of significance, suggesting that the propensity for risk-taking may have heterogeneous effects on IC, potentially influenced by the specific operational and regulatory environments of the different bank types.

All models consistently control for relevant variables, year and bank fixed effects to ensure a robust analysis, accounting for potential confounders and idiosyncratic traits of each bank category. The number of observations (N) and R-squared values indicate a good model fit, with state-owned and joint-stock banks having higher R-squared values, which suggests a better explanatory power of the model for these bank types.

The significance levels, denoted by asterisks, indicate that the results are statistically significant at conventional levels, reinforcing the reliability of the findings. This heterogeneity analysis underscores the importance of considering bank types when assessing the impact of DFI on IC, thereby providing strong evidence to support H1.

16.4.4. *Influence mechanism analysis*

Table 16.7 provides insights into the mechanisms through which DFI influences the RSL and IC of banks. In model (1), DFI has a substantial and highly significant positive effect on RSL, with a coefficient of 0.8931 (standard error: 0.0122), suggesting that increased DFI is associated with higher levels of risk-taking within banks.

Models (2) and (3) shift focus to the impact on IC, with DFI showing a positive effect, though the significance levels vary. In model (2), the coefficient is 0.2345 (standard error: 0.0042), marked with an asterisk, indicating significance at a lower confidence level compared to model (1). Model (3) presents a coefficient of 0.2190 (standard error: 0.0035), with a higher level of statistical significance, denoted by three asterisks.

RSL is introduced as an additional independent variable in models (2) and (3), and it has a significant positive effect on IC, with coefficients of 5.2882 (standard error: 1.6170) and 5.1120 (standard error: 1.4231), respectively. This indicates that the level of risk-taking within banks significantly contributes to their IC and may act as a mediating variable between DFI and IC, thereby providing empirical evidence to support H2.

The models control for relevant variables, year and bank fixed effects to ensure a comprehensive and robust analysis. The inclusion of these controls is critical for isolating the specific effects of DFI and RSL on IC. With a consistent number of observations across all models ($N = 2136$) and R-squared values indicating substantial explanatory power, the findings provide strong evidence of the positive influence of DFI on both risk-taking behavior and innovation within banks.

This influence mechanism analysis contributes to the understanding of how DFI may indirectly enhance innovation through its effect on risk-taking attitudes in the banking sector. The results emphasize the multifaceted role of digital finance in shaping the strategic behaviors that drive innovation.

16.4.5. *Further robust analysis*

A further robustness analysis provided in the study explores the stability of the results by modifying core variables. This two-part analysis includes a robustness test of both the dependent variable and the explanatory variables.

For the explanatory variables, the study transitions from using the city-level DFI index to the provincial digital inclusive finance index (SDFI) as an alternative explanatory variable, which may provide a broader context for DFI. As shown in Table 16.8, in models (1) and (5), SDFI is positively associated with the RSL, with a highly significant coefficient of 0.7321 (standard error: 0.0210). In models (2) and (3), SDFI demonstrates a positive effect on IC, with coefficients of 0.1156 (standard error: 0.0012) and 0.1670 (standard error: 0.0011), respectively, indicating the robustness of the relationship between DFI at the provincial level and bank innovation.

The study also re-examines the dependent variable by replacing non-interest income as an indicator of bank innovation capability with the bank's R&D investment (SIC), allowing for a more direct measure of innovation activities. In models (6) and (7), SDFI continues to exhibit a positive and significant effect on SIC, with coefficients of 0.7621 (standard error: 0.0421) and 0.2783 (standard error: 0.0110), respectively, reaffirming the positive link between provincial DFI and the bank's commitment to innovation through R&D investment.

Additionally, RSL is included as an independent variable in models (2) and (3), showing a substantial positive impact on IC, with coefficients of 5.2882 (standard error: 1.6170) and 4.3210 (standard error: 0.7934), further emphasizing its significant role in driving innovation capability.

CVs, along with year and bank fixed effects, are consistently applied across all models to address potential confounders and ensure

Table 16.8. Robustness test results.

	(1) *RSL*	*(2)* *IC*	*(3)* *IC*	*(5)* *RSL*	*(6)* *SIC*	*(7)* *SIC*
SDFI	0.7321***	0.1156*	0.1670***			
	(0.0210)	(0.0012)	(0.0011)			
RSL		5.2882***	4.3210***			
		(1.6170)	(0.7934)			
DFI				0.8931***	0.7621***	0.2783***
				(0.0122)	(0.0421)	(0.0110)
Control variables	Yes	Yes	Yes	Yes	Yes	Yes
Year fixed effects	Yes	Yes	Yes	Yes	Yes	Yes
Bank fixed effects	Yes	Yes	Yes	Yes	Yes	Yes
N	2136	2136	2136	2136	2136	2136
R^2	0.2320	0.2234	0.2549	0.1912	0.2064	0.2091

that the results are not driven by unobserved heterogeneity. With a consistent number of observations ($N = 2136$) and R-squared values indicating significant explanatory power, the robustness analysis confirms the strength and reliability of the core relationships between DFI, risk-taking, and innovation capability within banks. The positive association between SDFI and both RSL and SIC supports the hypothesis that the digital financial environment at the broader provincial level remains a critical factor in enhancing banks' propensity for innovation.

16.5. Conclusions and Policy Implications

This research embarked on an in-depth analysis of the complex dynamics between DFI and innovation capability within commercial banks in China, scrutinizing how this interaction is influenced by risk-taking behaviors and its variability across diverse banking categories, including state-owned, joint-stock, urban and rural banks.

Our empirical findings reveal a significant, positive impact of DFI on the innovation capabilities of banks. However, this impact is not homogeneous across different bank types. Resource-rich state-owned and joint-stock banks, with their superior access to digital technologies, exhibit a more robust ability to harness DFI for innovation compared to their counterparts in urban and rural areas.

Furthermore, the study highlights the pivotal role of risk-taking as a mediator. Banks that engage in higher levels of calculated risk-taking are more adept at translating DFI opportunities into concrete innovative outcomes. This intricate interplay between DFI, risk-taking and innovation underscores the importance of strategic risk management, particularly in the realm of financial innovation.

The study's insights lay a foundation for policy and managerial strategies aimed at maximizing the benefits of DFI in fostering innovation across the banking sector. They also pave the way for further research into the long-term effects of digital finance on the banking industry and its wider economic implications:

(1) **Differentiated DFI Strategies:** Policymakers should craft customized DFI enhancement strategies that cater to the specific needs of various bank types, particularly focusing on addressing the subdued effects observed in rural and urban banks.

(2) **Encouraging Prudent Risk-Taking:** Banks should be encouraged to engage in judicious risk-taking to fully leverage DFI's innovative potential. This necessitates the development of sophisticated risk assessment frameworks that are in sync with innovation goals driven by DFI.
(3) **Facilitating Innovation in Varied Bank Types:** Given that state-owned and joint-stock banks demonstrate a higher capability to convert DFI into innovation, initiatives such as innovation labs and FinTech incubators should be more prevalently implemented within these entities.
(4) **Stimulating R&D Investments:** In light of the correlation between DFI and R&D investments, fiscal policies and incentives geared toward encouraging R&D expenditure in banks could significantly enhance their innovative capacity.
(5) **Tailored Support for Rural and Urban Banks:** To address the distinct challenges faced by rural and urban banks in adopting digital finance, customized support programs can help these institutions better capitalize on DFI for innovation.
(6) **Enhancing Provincial Digital Infrastructure:** Recognizing the influence of provincial DFI on banking innovation, investments in strengthening digital infrastructure at the provincial level are imperative to create an enabling environment for innovation across all bank types.

By adopting these policy measures, stakeholders can cultivate a banking ecosystem where DFI acts as a springboard for innovation, fostering a more dynamic and resilient financial sector.

References

Banna, H. & Alam, R. (2021a). Does digital financial inclusion matter for bank risk-taking? Evidence from the dual-banking system. *Journal of Islamic Monetary Economics and Finance,* 7, 401–430. https://doi.org/10.21098/jimf.v7i2.1320.

Banna, H. & Alam, R. (2021b). Impact of digital financial inclusion on ASEAN banking stability: Implications for the post-Covid-19 era. *Studies in Economics and Finance*, 38, 504–523. https://doi.org/10.1108/SEF-09-2020-0388.

Deng, L., Lv, Y., Liu, Y., & Zhao, Y. (2021). Impact of fintech on bank risk-taking: Evidence from China. *Risks*, 9(5), 99. https://doi.org/10.3390/risks9050099.

Du, M., Hou, Y., Zhou, Q., & Ren, S. (2022). Going green in China: How does digital finance affect environmental pollution? Mechanism discussion and empirical test. *Environmental Science and Pollution Research*, 29(60), 89996–90010. https://doi.org/10.1007/s11356-022-21909-0.

Edeh, F. O., Zayed, N. M., Nitsenko, V., Brezhnieva-Yermolenko, O., Negovska, J., & Shtan, M. (2022). Predicting innovation capability through knowledge management in the banking sector. *Journal of Risk and Financial Management*, 15(7), 312. https://doi.org/10.3390/jrfm15070312.

Farooq, U., Al-Gamrh, B., & Dai, J. (2024). Green drives greenbacks: The impact of sustainable innovation on corporate cash holdings in BRICS nations. *Journal of Cleaner Production*, 140533. https://doi.org/10.1016/j.jclepro.2023.140533.

Gabor, D. & Brooks, S. (2017). The digital revolution in financial inclusion: International development in the fintech era. *New Political Economy*, 22, 423–436. https://doi.org/10.1080/13563467.2017.1259298.

Gu, N. (2021). Digital financial inclusion risk prevention based on machine learning and neural network algorithms. *Journal of Intelligent & Fuzzy Systems* (Preprint), 1–16. http://dx.doi.org/10.3233/JIFS-219061.

Hong, C. Y., Lu, X., & Pan, J. (2022). FinTech adoption and household risk-taking: From digital payments to platform investments. *Working Paper,* Shanghai Advanced Institute of Finance, Shanghai Jiao Tong University. https://nsd.pku.edu.cn/docs/2023-03/20230327093824330381.pdf.

Huang, H., Mbanyele, W., Fan, S., & Zhao, X. (2022). Digital financial inclusion and energy-environment performance: What can learn from China. *Structural Change and Economic Dynamics*, 63, 342–366. https://doi.org/10.1016/j.strueco.2022.10.007.

Institute of Digital Finance, Peking University. http://nsd.pku.edu.cn/docs/20221017131046905230.pdf.

Khera, P., Ng, S., Ogawa, S., & Sahay, R. (2022). Measuring digital financial inclusion in emerging market and developing economies: A new index. *Asian Economic Policy Review*, 17(2), 213–230. https://doi.org/10.1111/aepr.12377.

Kraus, K., Kraus, N., & Pochenchuk, G. (2022). Institutional aspects and digitalization of financial inclusion in the national economy. *Innovation and Sustainability*, 2, 18–28. http://dx.doi.org/10.31649/ins.2022.2.18.28.

Li, C., He, S., Tian, Y., Sun, S., & Ning, L. (2022b). Does the bank's FinTech innovation reduce its risk-taking? Evidence from China's banking industry. *Journal of Innovation & Knowledge*, 7(3), 100219. https://doi.org/10.1016/j.jik.2022.100219.

Li, G., Elahi, E., & Zhao, L. (2022c). FinTech, bank risk-taking, and risk-warning for commercial banks in the era of digital technology. *Frontiers in Psychology*, 13, 934053. DOI:10.3389/fpsyg.2022.934053.

Li, X., Shao, X., Chang, T., & Albu, L. L. (2022a). Does digital finance promote the green innovation of China's listed companies? *Energy Economics*, 114, 106254. https://doi.org/10.1016/j.eneco.2022.106254.

Li, Y., Sun, G., Gao, Q., & Cheng, C.-F. (2023). Digital financial inclusion, financial efficiency and green innovation. *Sustainability*, 15(3), 1879. https://doi.org/10.3390/su15031879.

Lumsden, E. (2018). The future is mobil: Financial inclusion and technological innovation in the emerging world. *Stanford Journal of Law, Business & Finance*, 23, 1.

Luo, Y., Peng, Y., & Zeng, L. (2021). Digital financial capability and entrepreneurial performance. *International Review of Economics & Finance*, 76, 55–74. https://doi.org/10.1016/j.iref.2021.05.010.

Niu, G., Jin, X., Wang, Q., & Zhou, Y. (2022). Broadband infrastructure and digital financial inclusion in rural China. *China Economic Review*, 76, 101853. https://doi.org/10.1016/j.chieco.2022.101853.

Rajapathirana, R. J. & Hui, Y. (2018). Relationship between innovation capability, innovation type, and firm performance. *Journal of Innovation & Knowledge*, 3(1), 44–55. https://doi.org/10.1016/j.jik.2017.06.002.

Stefanelli, V. & Manta, F. (2022). Digital financial services and open banking innovation: Are banks becoming 'invisible'? *Global Business Review*, 09721509231151491. https://doi.org/10.1177/09721509231151491.

Wang, Z., Huang, Y., Ankrah, V., & Dai, J. (2023). Greening the knowledge-based economies: Harnessing natural resources and innovation in information and communication technologies for green growth. *Resources Policy*, 86, 104181. https://doi.org/10.1016/j.resourpol.2023.104181.

Yang, Y., Liu, S., & Li, Y. (2021, April). Research on the influence mechanism and regional heterogeneity of digital finance on enterprise innovation: Empirical analysis based on private enterprises on GEM. In *2021 International Conference on Computer, Blockchain and Financial Development (CBFD)* (pp. 514–518). IEEE. https://doi.org/10.1109/CBFD52659.2021.00109.

Yang, Y., Shi, S., & Wu, J. (2022). Digital financial inclusion to corporation value: The mediating effect of ambidextrous innovation. *Sustainability*, 14(24), 16621. https://doi.org/10.3390/su142416621.

YuSheng, K. & Ibrahim, M. (2020). Innovation capabilities, innovation types, and firm performance: Evidence from the banking sector of Ghana. *Sage Open*, 10(2), 2158244020920892. https://doi.org/10.1177/2158244020920892.

https://doi.org/10.1142/9781800616257_bmatter

Index

www.ingramcontent.com/pod-product-compliance
Lightning Source LLC
LaVergne TN
LVHW010326220926
848484LV00004BB/850